Arab Gulf States

Bahrain, Kuwait, Oman, Qatar, Saudi Arabia & the United Arab Emirates

Gordon Robison

Arab Gulf States

2nd edition

Published by
  Lonely Planet Publications
  Head Office: PO Box 617, Hawthorn, Vic 3122, Australia
  Branches: 155 Filbert St, Suite 251, Oakland, CA 94607, USA
              10 Barley Mow Passage, Chiswick, London W4 4PH, UK
              71 bis rue du Cardinal Lemoine, 75005 Paris, France

Printed by
  Colorcraft Ltd, Hong Kong
  Printed in China

Photographs by
  Gordon Robison (GR), Ray Chadwick (RC)

  Title page: Qasr Ibrahim, Saudi Arabia (GR)
  Chapter title pages: Qal'at Abu Mahir, Bahrain (GR); Dhow, Kuwait (GR);
  Bin Ali Tomb, Oman (GR); Umm Salal Mohammed Fort, Qatar (GR);
  Mosque of Omar, Saudi Arabia (GR); Sand Dunes, UAE (RC)

  Front cover: Beached boat, Saudi Arabia (Ronald R Johnson, The Image Bank)

First Published
  March 1993

This Edition
  October 1996

Although the authors and publisher have tried to make the information as accurate as possible, they accept no responsibility for any loss, injury or inconvenience sustained by any person using this book.

National Library of Australia Cataloguing in Publication Data

Robison, Gordon
  Arab Gulf States

    2nd ed.
    Includes index.
    ISBN 0 86442 390 X.

    1. Persian Gulf States – Guidebooks. I. Title.
    (Series: Lonely Planet travel survival kit).

915.360453

text & maps © Lonely Planet 1996
photos © photographers as indicated 1996

All rights reserved. No part of this publication may be reproduced, stored in a retrieval system or transmitted in any form by any means, electronic, mechanical, photocopying, recording or otherwise, except brief extracts for the purpose of review, without the written permission of the publisher and copyright owner.

Gordon Robison

Gordon Robison grew up in Maine and Vermont, in the north-eastern USA. He attended Westminster School in London and graduated from Pomona College in Claremont, California, with a degree in government. He later studied Arabic at Cairo's International Language Institute. After university Gordon travelled in Europe, the Middle East and Mexico and worked for a year in Saudi Arabia. From 1989 until 1994 he lived in Cairo where he worked as a freelance journalist, reporting regularly for the American ABC Radio News. His work has also been published in *The Irish Times*, the London *Sunday Times*, the *Financial Times*, the *Miami Herald* and the *Atlanta Journal-Constitution*. Gordon's other work for Lonely Planet includes writing and updating the Arab Gulf States chapters in *Middle East on a shoestring*. He now lives in Atlanta where he works for CNN International. He is married to Dona Stewart. They have one daughter, Halle.

From the Author

After a generation of breakneck development the pace of change has finally begun to slow in many of the Gulf States. It used to be commonplace that people returning to a Gulf city they once knew well could not, after an absence of five years, find their way around. By and large that is no longer the case.

When I arrived in Saudi Arabia to research this edition, friends warned that I would find almost everything changed. What I actually found was an explosion of US fast-food joints in Riyadh and Jeddah and a surprising lack of change almost everywhere else. Elsewhere it was much the same story: in a few places everything was different, but that tended to be the exception. Muscat's Mutrah Corniche looks pretty much the way it did when I first saw it in 1990 and remarkably little has changed on Manama's Government Ave since my first visit there, way back in 1987. Dubai is the only major city in Arabia that is still perpetually torn up by construction crews.

That is the big picture. Up close many of the details, as one might expect, are different. Restaurants and hotels come and go, bus schedules change and paved roads are extended far into the desert. Technology drives other changes. A decade ago fax machines were rare and expensive gadgets seen only in a handful of five-star hotels, and TV throughout the region was little more than heavily censored reruns of ancient US and British shows. Fax machines today are so common that even the smallest hotels often have them – right beside the controller for the satellite dish that brings seven or eight foreign channels into the budget traveller's room.

Then there are the administrative changes: visas have become easier to obtain in some Gulf countries and taking a laptop computer into Bahrain is no longer a problem. You can now get a beer in Doha, and an easing of regional tensions has led Oman's military to open up the wondrous scenery of the Musandem Peninsula to tourists.

And, of course, there is tourism. What was an infant industry in 1992 is growing, as things in the Gulf tend to do, *very* quickly. But if a few places are becoming rather well-trodden, much of the region remains one of the world's last great tracts of unexplored territory for visitors on any budget.

During my travels I received much help from both old and new friends. Full credit and appreciation is given to them at the back of this book.

From the Publisher

This second edition of *Arab Gulf States* was edited at Lonely Planet's Melbourne office by Michelle Glynn, with assistance from Diana Saad, Miriam Cannell, Helen Castle and Lyn McGaurr. Verity Campbell coordinated the cartography, illustration and design. Chris Klep, Indra Kilfoyle, Michael Signal and Daryl Cheney assisted with the cartography. Trudi Canavan illustrated the Silver Jewellery. Simon Bracken designed the cover with cartographic assistance from Adam McCrow. Thanks to Samantha Carew and Greg Herriman for their invaluable support and assistance. Finally, a big thanks to Ray Chadwick of Adventure Travel UK for supplying such wonderful shots of the UAE.

Thanks

A special thanks to those readers who found the time and energy to write to us from all over the world with their suggestions and comments. Their names appear at the back of this book.

Warning & Request

Things change – prices go up, schedules change, good places go bad and bad places go bankrupt – nothing stays the same. So if you find things better or worse, recently opened or long since closed, please write and tell us and help make the next edition better.

Your letters will be used to help update future editions and, where possible, important changes will also be included in an Update section in reprints.

We greatly appreciate all information that is sent to us by travellers. Back at Lonely Planet we employ a hard-working readers' letters team to sort through the many letters we receive. The best ones will be rewarded with a free copy of the next edition or another Lonely Planet guide if you prefer. We give away lots of books, but, unfortunately, not every letter/postcard receives one.

Contents

THE UNITED ARAB EMIRATES 420

Map Legend

BOUNDARIES

............International Boundary
..................Regional Boundary
.................Disputed Boundary

ROUTES

.... Freeway
.... Highway
.... Major Road
.............Unsealed Road or Track
.... City Road
.... City Street
.... Railway
.... Underground Railway
.... Walking Track
.... Walking Tour
....Ferry Route
.... Cable Car or Chairlift

AREA FEATURES

....Parks
.... Built-Up Area
.........Pedestrian Mall or Square
............................Market (Souk)
.................................Cemetery
....Reef
.... Beach or Desert
..............Rocks or Gravel Desert

HYDROGRAPHIC FEATURES

.... Coastline
.....................................River, Creek
Intermittent River or Creek (Wadi)
.... Rapids, Waterfalls
.... Lake, Intermittent Lake
.... Canal, Salt Lake
.... Swamp

SYMBOLS

✪ CAPITAL		.....................National Capital
◉ Capital		......................Regional Capital
🌀 CITY		.... Major City
● City		.... City
● Town		.... Town
● Village		.... Village

■	▼	.........Place to Stay, Place to Eat
☕	🍴	.... Cafe, Pub or Bar
✉	☎	.... Post Office, Telephone
🛈	🏦	.... Tourist Information, Bank
☎	☗	Bus Station or Terminal, Bus Stop
🏛	⌂	.............Museum, Youth Hostel
🚐	⚑	Caravan Park, Camping Ground
P	☪	......................Parking, Mosque
✝	✚	.... Church, Cathedral
卍	卐	Buddhist Temple, Hindu Temple
✚	★	.... Hospital, Police Station

☉	⛽	.............Embassy, Petrol Station
✈	✚	........................Airport, Airfield
〰	✿	...........Swimming Pool, Gardens
❖	🐘	...............Shopping Centre, Zoo
⚘	📷	...Winery or Vineyard, Picnic Site
←	A25	One Way Street, Route Number
⚐	⚑	.............Golf Course, Monument
	🏛	...............Stately Home or Palace
♜	◙	......Castle, Tomb or Mausoleum
⌒	⌂	.... Cave, Hut or Chalet
▲	☀	.... Mountain or Hill, Lookout
💡	⚓	...............Lighthouse, Shipwreck
)(	◉	.... Pass, Spring
	∴	...... Archaeological Site or Ruins
		..........Ancient or City Wall, Fort
		.... Cliff or Escarpment, Tunnel
		.... Railway Station

Note: not all symbols displayed above appear in this book

Introduction

> What moved thee, or how couldst thou take such journeys into the fanatic Arabia?
> **Doughty,** *Travels in Arabia Deserta*

In our age of space shuttles and satellite telephones, at a time when mass tourism has penetrated even such famously remote places as Siberia and the Amazon, few regions of the world have remained as mysterious as Arabia. Misconceptions about travel in Arabia and the Gulf abound. The caricature of the region as inaccessible, expensive and dull has little in common with the reality of the place.

Many people believe that travel in the Gulf is effectively impossible. Wrong. Since the 1980s Arabia has been a fairly easy place to visit. Bahrain, Oman, Qatar and the United Arab Emirates (UAE) are all working to promote tourism, and visits to Kuwait can be arranged relatively easily. Only Saudi Arabia lives up to the region's reputation for inaccessibility.

Myth number two is that any visit to the Gulf will be astronomically expensive. Wrong again. Moderately priced hotels and cheap meals can be found almost everywhere in the Gulf. If Egypt or Thailand is your sole definition of 'cheap' well, yes, the Gulf is rather expensive, but (with the exception of Kuwait) it is hardly in the same price category as London, Paris or Geneva.

Myth number three is that the first two myths don't matter because there is nothing to see or do anyway. This myth is the silliest and the most enduring of them all. For 5000 years the Gulf has lain along some of the most heavily travelled trade routes on the planet. If the region's archaeology – from 3rd millennium BC temples and tombs to Portuguese forts – is not enough for you, then what about its scenery? There is more to Arabia than the desert: Saudi Arabia has forests, the mountains of Oman are stunning and oases throughout the region offer cool greenery in the midst of the desert. The desert itself is an attraction – for years expatriates have spent their weekends camping there, and desert

The external boundaries of India on this map have not been authenticated and may not be correct

safaris are one of the main selling points of package tours to the Gulf.

Even the Gulf's somewhat sterile cities are fascinating contrasts of the old and the new. Over the last 25 or 30 years the countries of the Arabian Gulf have experienced a degree of development which the west eased itself through over a period of nearly two centuries. The resulting juxtaposition of tradition and modernity is arguably the region's single most fascinating feature.

Travelling in the Gulf is not always easy but it is invariably interesting. Go beyond the myths and aim to see and understand the Gulf on its own terms. You may be surprised at what you'll find.

Facts about the Region

HISTORY

The most surprising thing about the Gulf States is the degree to which their histories differ. While it might seem fair to assume that a group of tiny countries sharing a single, relatively small region would also share a great deal of their history, this has been the case in the Gulf in only the broadest terms. What follows is a very general summary of the region's history. Detailed histories of the six countries covered in this book appear in the relevant Facts about the Country sections.

Beginnings

Ten thousand years ago Arabia probably looked much the way east Africa does today, with huge stretches of savannah land and abundant annual rainfall. It is not known when Arabia was first settled, but excavations at Thumamah, in central Saudi Arabia, have shown that the peninsula has been inhabited at least since Neolithic times – about 8000 years ago. The earliest known settlements on or near the Gulf coast date from about 5000 BC.

In Bahrain a civilisation known as Dilmun arose during the 3rd millennium BC. Dilmun eventually became a powerful empire controlling much of the central and northern Gulf. The same period also saw significant settlements at Umm An-Nar, near modern Abu Dhabi, and in the Buraimi Oasis on what is now the border between the United Arab Emirates (UAE) and Oman.

The cities of ancient Arabia derived their sometimes considerable wealth from trade. The Gulf lay on the main trade routes linking Mesopotamia with the Indus Valley. Western Arabia flourished through its position along the frankincense route which linked the southern Arabian regions of Dhofar and Hadhramaut to the Levant and Europe.

The frankincense trade made southern Arabia one of the richest regions of the ancient world. This wealth drew the attention of Alexander the Great who was planning an expedition to the frankincense lands when he died in 323 BC. One of his admirals, Nearchus, established a colony on Failaka Island, off the coast of Kuwait, which became an important trading centre and for several centuries maintained trade links with India, Rome and Persia. During the 950 years between Alexander's death and the coming of Islam much of the Gulf came under the sway of a succession of Persian dynasties: the Seleucids, the Parthians and, from the 3rd century AD, the Sassanians. The Gulf was of only marginal political and economic importance to these empires.

Central and western Arabia, meanwhile, became a patchwork of city-states living off the frankincense trade and, in the oases, farming. A Roman legion marched down the western coast of the peninsula around 25 BC in an unsuccessful attempt to conquer the frankincense-producing regions, but the soldiers seem to have left remarkably little behind them. Between about 100 BC and 100 AD the Nabataean Empire controlled most of north-western Arabia and grew extremely rich by taxing the caravans travelling between southern Arabia and Damascus. The remains of the Nabataean civilisation can be seen today at Madain Salah in Saudi Arabia where, as at their capital Petra (in modern Jordan), the Nabataeans carved spectacular tombs into the desert cliffs.

A New Era

The destruction of the great dam at Ma'rib (in modern Yemen) in 570 AD marked the end of southern Arabia's prosperity, though the region's decline actually took place over several generations. Arabian tradition had long attached great significance to the dam, which was the symbol of Arabia's 'old order'. In the same year that the dam broke the Prophet Mohammed was born. The two events mark the end of one era and the beginning of another in the history of Arabia.

Mohammed received his first revelation in 610 and began to preach publicly three years later. It was only after he and a small band of followers fled Mecca for Medina in 622 that Islam became the established faith of an existing temporal community. From Medina the new religion spread out across the peninsula with remarkable speed between 622 and 632, and within a century Muslim armies had conquered an enormous empire stretching from Spain to India.

Arabia, however, became increasingly

The Life of the Prophet

Mohammed was born in Mecca, a prosperous centre of trade and pilgrimage, in 570 AD. He came from a less well-off branch of the Quraysh, the ruling tribe of Mecca, and his father died before he was born. When Mohammed was seven his mother died and he was subsequently raised first by his grandfather and later by an uncle. As a young man he worked as a shepherd and accompanied caravans to Syria on at least two occasions. At the age of 25 he married a wealthy, and much older, widow named Khadija by whom he had four daughters and two sons (both of the boys died in infancy).

Mohammed received his first revelation in 610 at the age of 40. He was meditating in a cave near Mecca when a voice commanded him to 'Recite'. This first revelation is preserved in the Koran as Sura 96:1-8.

Recite: In the Name of thy Lord who created,
        created Man of a blood-clot.
Recite: And thy Lord is the Most Generous,
        who taught by the Pen,
        taught Man that he knew not.
        No indeed; surely Man waxes insolent,
        for he thinks himself self-sufficient.
        Surely unto thy Lord is the returning.

After an initial period of doubt Mohammed came to believe that this, and the many later revelations he received, was the actual speech of God, conveyed to him through the archangel Gabriel. He had been commanded to preach the religion of the one true God (allah in Arabic) whose messages sent through earlier prophets had been distorted and misunderstood.

Mohammed did not begin to preach in public until 613, three years after this first revelation. When he did reveal himself as God's prophet to the Arabs, the people of Mecca did not exactly rush to embrace the new religion – after four years of preaching Mohammed is said to have had only about 70 followers. The reason for this lay partly in the fact that in attacking the paganism and corruption he saw around him, Mohammed was attacking the foundation of his native city's wealth. Much of Mecca's prosperity was built on its status as a pagan pilgrimage centre.

Eventually Mohammed's verbal assaults on the pagan pilgrim trade so angered the local establishment that they plotted to murder him. Hearing of this the Prophet, in June 622, secretly fled Mecca for Yathrib (present-day Medina), a largely Jewish city in an oasis 360 km to the north. This date marks the starting point of the Muslim calendar which also takes its name, Hejira, from the Arabic word hijrah meaning 'migration', the term given to the Prophet's journey.

Mohammed quickly established himself in Yathrib, where he already had a substantial following, and the name of the city was changed to Medinat An-Nabi – the City of the Prophet. Medina became the Prophet's model community. Over the next eight years Mohammed's following increased dramatically in Medina and in the rest of Arabia.

The Medina-based Muslims and the still-pagan Meccans fought a series of battles, both military and political, throughout the 620s. Finally, in January 630, the Muslims marched on Mecca with an army of 10,000. The city surrendered without a fight and the next day the Prophet entered the pagan temple (now the Grand Mosque), removed 365 idols from the Kaaba, the shrine at its centre, and declared it cleansed. Later that year he returned to Medina, where he continued to live. In 632 he travelled again to Mecca to perform the pilgrimage and established in their final form the rituals which are still performed by Muslim pilgrims today. After his trip to Mecca, Mohammed returned to Medina where he died later that year. ∎

marginal as this empire grew. Within 30 years of the Prophet's death (in 632) the Muslim capital had been moved from Medina to Damascus. By the early 9th century Mecca and Medina were stripped of their earlier political importance and had become the purely spiritual centres that they are today.

In world-historical terms the Gulf, during this era, was the back end of nowhere. From the 9th to the 11th centuries, during which time it was dominated first by the Umayyad and later by the Abbasid empires, the region was neither wealthy nor important. From the 11th century it became an area of petty shaikhdoms constantly at war with each other.

The Europeans Arrive

Portugal was the first European power to take an interest in the Gulf. In 1498 the explorer Vasco de Gama visited Oman's northern coast, the Strait of Hormuz (then the seat of an independent kingdom) and the shaikhdom of Julfar, in what is now the UAE. Within 20 years the Portuguese controlled much of the lower Gulf. Their power eventually extended as far north as Bahrain and lasted until the 1630s. Throughout this period the Portuguese were trying to build an empire in India, and they realised that control of the sea routes linking Lisbon to Bombay and Goa, in other words control of the Gulf, was the key to their success or failure.

The Portuguese gradually gave way to Britain's seemingly omnipresent East India Company, which had trading links with the Gulf as early as 1616. During the 17th and early 18th centuries the British concentrated on driving their French and Dutch competitors out of the region, a task they had largely accomplished by 1750. By 1770 the Royal Navy was much in evidence in the Gulf and in 1798 the British signed a treaty with the sultan of Muscat. The treaty was specifically aimed at keeping the French away from Oman and safeguarding Britain's route to India. It was around this time – the early to mid-18th century – that all of the families

which today rule the Gulf States first came to prominence.

In the Gulf States (but not in Saudi Arabia or Oman) the power of these families became entrenched during the 19th century when they signed protection treaties, known as Exclusive Agreements, with the British. Under these agreements the local rulers gave Britain control of their dealings with the outside world and agreed not to make treaties with, or cede land to, any other foreign power without first receiving Britain's permission. In exchange, the Royal Navy guaranteed their independence from Turkey, Persia and anyone else who might pose a threat.

The British administration in the Gulf fell under the jurisdiction of the British Raj in India. (Until India became independent the rupee was the common currency of all the Gulf States; after 1948 it was replaced by a 'Gulf rupee' which was in circulation until 1971.) The chief British officer in the region was the Political Resident, who was based in Bushire, on the coast of what is now Iran. The Resident supervised the Political Agents, usually junior officers, stationed in the various shaikhdoms of the Gulf. The system was designed to keep the British presence at a low key while allowing it to be felt quickly if the need arose.

In the early years of this century the British were concerned about two main threats to their interests in the Gulf. The first came from the north, where the Ottomans were working to boost their own presence in the region in cooperation with the Germans. The second threat came from within Arabia itself. In 1902 Abdul Aziz Bin Abdul Rahman Al-Saud, known as Ibn Saud, began a series of conquests which eventually led to the formation of Saudi Arabia. By 1912 the Saudis posed a serious threat to the Gulf shaikhdoms. Had it not been for British promises of protection, there is little doubt that Saudi Arabia would have today included most or all of Kuwait, Qatar and the UAE.

When WWI broke out the British encouraged and funded a revolt against Ottoman rule in the western part of the peninsula, an area traditionally known as the Hejaz. The Ottoman presence in Arabia was limited and the revolt involved little more than bottling up a Turkish garrison at Medina. The overly romantic (and rather self-serving) account of the revolt later written by TE Lawrence, who came to be known as Lawrence of Arabia, concerned events that mostly took place in Syria and what is today Jordan.

After the war the Sherif (governor) of Mecca declared himself 'King of the Arabs'. The British, however, did not honour their promise of support for the Sherif's pan-Arab dreams and forced him to confine his kingdom to the Hejaz where, less than a decade later, it was overrun by Ibn Saud, who became 'King of the Hejaz and Sultan of Najd'. In 1932 Ibn Saud combined these two crowns and renamed his country the 'Kingdom of Saudi Arabia'.

Oil

The first commercially viable oil strike in the Gulf was made at Masjid-i-Suleiman, in Persia, in May 1908. At this time, however, the Arab side of the Gulf was of little interest to the oil industry. Masjid-i-Suleiman is about 200 km north of the head of the Gulf, and even today many of Iran's major oilfields lie well inland.

The search for oil on the Arab side of the Gulf began shortly after WWI. The most famous early prospector was a New Zealander named Frank Holmes, who obtained the first oil concessions in Saudi Arabia and Bahrain in 1923 and 1925, respectively. Holmes let the Saudi concession lapse after failing to find backing for his exploration projects but he eventually secured funding for his Bahrain venture. The British and the local rulers were initially very sceptical about the prospects of finding oil in the Gulf. Their interest only picked up after oil was found in commercial quantities in Bahrain in 1932.

Among the Gulf's Arab rulers, interest in oil was spurred on by the collapse, around 1930, of the pearling industry which for centuries had been the mainstay of the Gulf's economy. The pearl trade fell victim to both

the worldwide depression that began in 1929 and to the Japanese discovery, about the same time, of a method by which pearls could be cultured artificially.

Within a few years almost every ruler in the Gulf had given out an oil concession in a desperate attempt to bolster their finances. By the time WWII broke out, a refinery was operating in Bahrain and exports of Saudi crude oil had also begun. Saudi and Kuwaiti operations had to be suspended because of the war, though by the time the fighting began the companies were well aware of how valuable their concessions were. Export operations in both countries took off as soon as the war was over.

The first enormous jump in the region's wealth came in the early '50s when Iran's prime minister Mohammed Mossadiq nationalised the Anglo-Iranian Oil Company, which was then the world's biggest producer. The oil companies stepped up production in the Arab Gulf, particularly Kuwait, to make up for the supplies they had lost in Iran. By 1960 the Middle East was producing 25% of the non-Communist world's oil.

In 1968 Britain announced that it would withdraw from the Gulf by the end of 1971, a move which came as a shock to the rulers of the small shaikhdoms of the middle and lower Gulf. (Kuwait had already become independent in 1961.) In late 1971 Bahrain and Qatar became independent states. A few months later the small shaikhdoms of the lower Gulf combined to form the UAE.

The Oil Weapon

What came to be called the 'oil weapon', ie the embargo by the Gulf States of oil supplies to the west, was first used during the 1967 Arab-Israeli War. At that time the cutoff lasted only a few days and proved ineffective, a result which may have lulled the west into a false sense of security. By the time the Arabs and Israelis went to war again in 1973 things had changed. On 17 October 1973, 11 days after the war began, Arab oil producers, led by Saudi Arabia, cut off oil supplies to the USA and Europe in protest at the west's

GORDON ROBISON

GORDON ROBISON

GORDON ROBISON

Bahrain

Top: The Al-Fatih Mosque, Bahrain's largest, holds up to 7000 worshippers.
Left: The Friday Mosque was built in 1938 with the island's first oil revenues.
Right: On Muharraq Island, Bait Seyadi and its adjacent mosque are good examples of traditional Bahraini architecture.

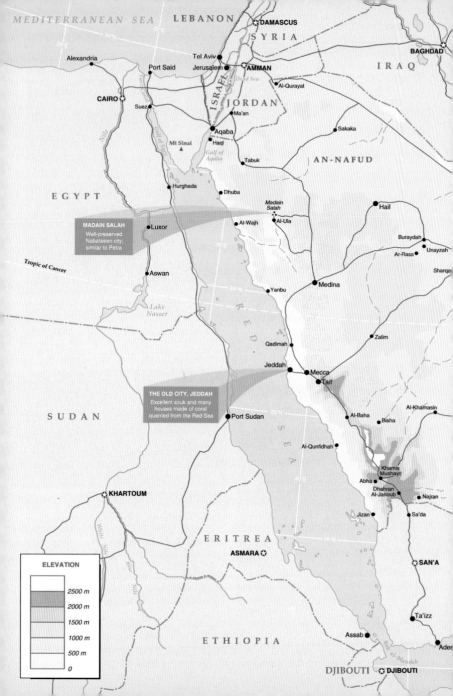

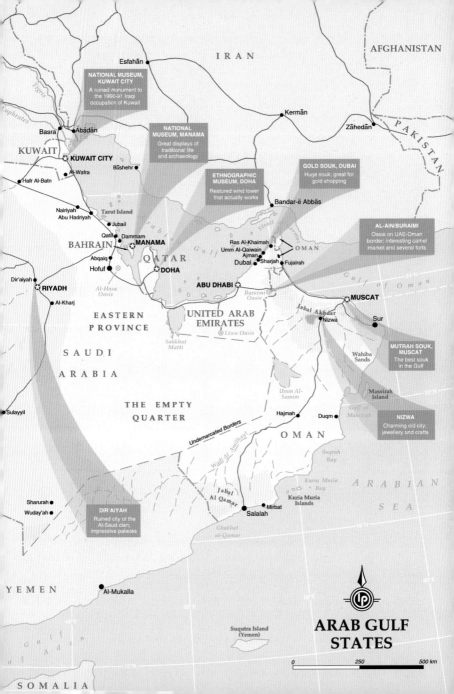

IRAN

AFGHANISTAN

Esfahān

Kermān

Zāhedan

PAKISTAN

Tigris

NATIONAL MUSEUM, KUWAIT CITY
A ruined monument to the 1990-91 Iraqi occupation of Kuwait

Basra ● Ābādān

Euphrates

KUWAIT

KUWAIT CITY

NATIONAL MUSEUM, MANAMA
Great displays of traditional life and archaeology

Al-Wafra

Hafr Al-Batn ●

Būshehr ●

ETHNOGRAPHIC MUSEUM, DOHA
Restored wind tower that actually works

GOLD SOUK, DUBAI
Huge souk; great for gold shopping

Bandar-é Abbās ●

AL-AIN/BURAIMI
Oasis on UAE-Oman border; interesting camel market and several forts

Nairiyah ●
Abu Hadriyah ●

Tarut Island

Jubail ●

Qatif ● Dammam

BAHRAIN **MANAMA**

QATAR

Abqaiq ●

Hofuf ●

Dir'aiyah ●

RIYADH

Al-Kharj ●

Al-Hasa
Oasis

EASTERN
PROVINCE

SAUDI

ARABIA

Ras Al-Khaimah ●
Umm Al-Qaiwain ●
Ajman ●
Dubai ● Sharjah ● Fujairah

OMAN

ABU DHABI

Buraimi
Oasis

DOHA

UNITED ARAB
EMIRATES

Jabal Akhdar
● Nizwa

Gulf of Oman

MUSCAT

Sur ●

Sabkhat
Matti

Liwa Oasis

Wahiba
Sands

MUTRAH SOUK, MUSCAT
The best souk in the Gulf

Massirah
Island

THE EMPTY

QUARTER

Umm Al-
Samim

Gulf of
Massirah

NIZWA
Charming old city; jewellery and crafts

Sulayyil ●

Hajmah ●

Duqm ●

OMAN

Suqrah
Bay

Undemarcated Borders

Wadi Al-Amilhat

ARABIAN

Sharurah ●
Wuday'ah ●

DIR'AIYAH
Ruined city of the Al-Saud clan; impressive palaces

Jabal
Al Qamar

Kuria Muria
Bay

Kuria Muria
Islands

SEA

Mirbat ●

Salalah ●

Ghubbat
al-Qamar

YEMEN

Al-Mukalla ●

Gulf

of

Aden

Suqutra Island
(Yemen)

SOMALIA

**ARAB GULF
STATES**

0   250   500 km

Kuwait

Top: Kuwait's distinctive water towers won the Aga Khan award for Islamic architecture in 1989.

Middle: Enjoying lunch at one of Kuwait City's popular beaches.

Bottom: The Al-Jahra gate marks the southern corner of Kuwait City's commercial centre.

support for Israel. Within a few days the embargo had been lifted on all countries except the USA and Holland. The embargo was relatively short-lived (supplies were resumed to the USA in March 1974, and to Holland in July 1974) and its effects proved to be more psychological than practical, but if the goal was to get the west's attention then it certainly worked.

Ironically the long-term result was to tie the USA and the Gulf States, particularly Saudi Arabia, more closely to one another. In the final analysis the west needs the oil and the Gulf States need the revenue that the oil generates. The embargo drove home to both sides the degree to which their economies had become interdependent.

The Oil Boom

With the surge in oil prices that followed the embargo, an enormous building boom began in the Gulf. The mid-70s to early '80s was a time when almost anything seemed possible. In 1979 the Iranian revolution shook the Gulf States, but it also made them even richer as the oil companies increased their production to fill the gap left first by the revolution and later by the outbreak of the Iran-Iraq War in 1980. This gap also caused prices once again to soar – fuelling yet another surge of building throughout the region.

Obviously this could not go on forever. In 1985 the bottom fell out of the oil market and everything changed. To varying extents all of the Gulf countries had trouble keeping up their building programmes while maintaining the generous welfare states that their people had come to expect. The Iran-Iraq War continued to drag on, scaring away potential foreign investors and becoming a constant source of concern throughout the region. This was particularly the case in Kuwait, which was only a few km from the front line.

In May 1981 Saudi Arabia, Kuwait, Bahrain, Qatar, the UAE and Oman formed the Gulf Cooperation Council (GCC) in an effort to increase economic cooperation, but also in response to the threat from Iran.

Recent History

When Iran and Iraq grudgingly agreed to a cease-fire in August 1988 the Gulf breathed a collective sigh of relief. After Ayatollah Khomeini, the spiritual leader of Iran's Islamic revolution, died in the summer of 1989, Iran began to seem a bit less frightening. The economic climate in the Gulf looked reasonably good during late 1989 and the spring and summer of 1990.

In retrospect this period appears to have been the calm before the storm. On 2 August 1990 Iraq invaded Kuwait and annexed it a few days later. Within days King Fahd of Saudi Arabia had asked the USA to send troops to defend Saudi Arabia against a possible Iraqi attack. The result was Operation Desert Shield, the formation of a US-led coalition in Saudi Arabia and the Gulf which eventually numbered over 500,000 troops. On 17 January 1991 the coalition launched Operation Desert Storm to drive Iraq out of Kuwait. This was accomplished after a six-week bombing campaign and a four-day ground offensive. Kuwaitis returned to their country to find hundreds of burning oil wells blackening the sky.

A year after the war Kuwait's oil fires had been extinguished and the government was working feverishly to erase every trace of Iraq's seven-month occupation of Kuwait City. As a result, building companies in eastern Saudi Arabia were having their best year in a decade. In the UAE bookings for package tours were up 200% on the 1989-90 travel season. Superficially, the war appeared to have changed nothing as trade, once again, dominated the lives of most of the Gulf's residents, or so everyone said.

That explanation was a bit too simple. In fact, many things have changed since, and to some extent because of, the war. The most visible change was the restoration of a limited form of democracy in Kuwait, whose freewheeling parliament stands in marked contrast to the opaque world of politics in the other Gulf States.

On the broader international stage the Gulf countries have become involved in the Arab-Israeli peace process in ways that would have been unthinkable a few years ago. The GCC sent an observer to the 1991 Arab-Israeli peace conference in Madrid. In 1993, in the wake of his country's historic peace agreement with the Palestine Liberation Organization (PLO), Israeli Prime Minister Yitzak Rabin was welcomed in Muscat by Sultan Qaboos. In late 1995 Qatar signed an agreement to supply natural gas to Israel, albeit through a third party.

But the mid-90s have also brought long-repressed tensions to the surface. Since late 1994 Bahrain has suffered periodic unrest centred on the island nation's poorer villages. In November 1995 a bomb destroyed an office in Riyadh where US soldiers trained members of Saudi Arabia's National Guard, bringing into the open the Saudi government's struggles with its own dissidents. Some old tensions never entirely went away – Iraq has made menacing gestures toward Kuwait several times since 1991.

For the visitor, all of this generally remains safely in the background. As far as most visitors and residents are concerned, the Gulf remains a trade centre of the first order and an increasingly popular holiday destination. The Gulf has always been a region of contrasts, and never more so than it is today.

GEOGRAPHY

The Gulf States (Kuwait, Bahrain, Qatar and the UAE) have relatively similar geography. They consist almost entirely of low-lying desert areas and salt flats. Bahrain, which has an abundance of underground springs, has a lot more natural greenery than the others, though the cities of all these countries have created parks and gardens over the last generation through modern irrigation and desalinated water.

The east coast of the UAE and the areas around Ras Al-Khaimah and Al-Ain provide a break from the monotonous landscape with striking mountain scenery. Equally striking, though less easily accessible, scenery is to be found in the Empty Quarter, the great sand desert occupying around a quarter of the peninsula. Saudi Arabia, Oman and the UAE

all border on the Empty Quarter. The UAE's Liwa Oasis, at the Empty Quarter's north-eastern corner, is slowly being developed as a tourist area, and is already a popular destination for 4WD travellers.

There are two principal mountain ranges in Arabia. In western Arabia, the Hejaz range runs the length of Saudi Arabia's west coast, generally getting higher as one moves further south. These mountains are part of the huge geological fault that begins along the east coast of the Mediterranean, runs south through Arabia and re-emerges in Africa as the Great Rift Valley. Arabia's other mountains are in the east of the peninsula where Oman's Jabal Akhdar range, of which the UAE's Hajar Mountains and the extraordinary wilderness of the Musandem Peninsula are both extensions, separates the communities of the Gulf of Oman from the deserts of the interior.

Deserts themselves come in several varieties. The rolling sand dunes that dominate the western imagination are easiest to find in the Empty Quarter and around the oases that line its edges. Gravel plains, sometimes bare and sometimes teeming with vegetation, make up much of the inland deserts while low humid plains and salt flats are common in coastal areas.

The Gulf itself is extremely shallow in many places.

GEOLOGY

The Arabian Peninsula is thought to have originally been part of a larger landmass that included Africa. A split in this ancient continent created both Africa's Great Rift Valley (which extends up through western Yemen and Saudi Arabia into Jordan) and the Red Sea. As Arabia moved away from Africa, part of this process involved the peninsula's 'tilting', with the western side rising and the eastern edge dropping in elevation, a process that led to the formation of the Arabian Gulf.

Geologists speak of the peninsula in terms of two distinct regions: the Arabian shield and the Arabian shelf. The shield consists of the volcanic and folded, compressed sedimentary rocks that make up the western third of today's Arabian Peninsula. The shelf is made up of the lower-lying areas that slope gently away from the shield from central Arabia to the waters of the Gulf. The rocks beneath the sands of the Arabian shelf are mostly sedimentary.

Hundreds of millions of years ago, as the shelf was being formed, the Gulf (if we can call it that) extended much further west. It was in the waters and, later, marshes of this area that plants, animals and other organic matter died, sank to the bottom and eventually were covered with rock and compressed to form oil.

CLIMATE

From April to October much of the Gulf experiences daytime highs of around 40°C almost daily. In Bahrain, Qatar, the coastal areas of Saudi Arabia and most of the UAE the humidity during summer is stifling. During high summer the central deserts of Saudi Arabia are spared this humidity while in the west of the Kingdom many people retreat to the Asir Mountains.

Winter in the Asir Mountains can be bitterly cold, and fog in some places cuts visibility to near zero. Saudi Arabia's central deserts also experience near-freezing overnight temperatures from November to early March. The climate along the Gulf coast, from Kuwait to the UAE, is milder but still chilly enough to warrant a sweater (sometimes even two) in the evenings.

Oman, separated from the rest of Arabia by the Hajar Mountains, is just as hot and humid as the Gulf during the summer but it also catches the Indian monsoon, leaving portions of the south of the country lush each September. The Indian Ocean breezes also guarantee Muscat a slightly warmer climate than Bahrain, Kuwait or Riyadh in midwinter. See the individual country chapters for more information.

ECOLOGY & ENVIRONMENT

Historically, the Gulf States – with the exception of Oman – have not been known for their enthusiasm for environmental protection, but this is changing. Oil and natural

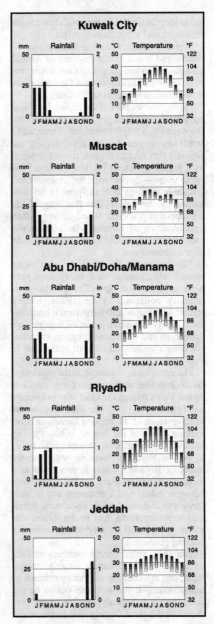

gas aside, the Gulf is an area with few natural resources and a fragile ecosystem.

Water is more valuable than oil in the desert, and it is a scarce resource in Arabia. Campaigns to get people to save water, and to be more careful about how they use it, are now common throughout the Gulf.

Governments around the region have also moved to make their people more aware that the desert is a fragile resource. There was a tendency a generation ago, during the region's first rush of wealth, to see the desert as a gigantic rubbish tip. On one level this made sense – for centuries the Bedouins had left their garbage behind them to be consumed by the desert. But that way of life presupposed a society based on very small communities of people who continually moved around and were in harmony with their surroundings.

The waters of the Gulf are also being treated with greater care today than they were a generation ago. Though the pearl industry collapsed in the 1930s, fishing remains a major industry throughout the area. Safety standards in the oil industry are fairly high and, with one exception, there has not been a significant oil spill in the Gulf in many years.

The exception, of course, is the enormous oil slick deliberately released into the Gulf by the Iraqis during the Gulf War in January and February of 1991. The slick is estimated to have reached 11 million barrels in size, making it one of the largest in history. The slick was apparently an attempt by the Iraqis to poison Riyadh's drinking water supply (most of Riyadh's water is processed at a large desalination plant on the Gulf coast between Jubail and Dammam) and to shut down the industrial facilities around Jubail that were supplying fuel to the Allied war effort (these facilities rely on sea water for cooling purposes).

The slick killed untold numbers of fish, birds and marine animals, notably cormorants, and effected the migratory patterns of many others. It did not turn out to be the environmental apocalypse that many predicted at the time, largely due to the major international cleanup that was mounted in the months after the war.

In Kuwait itself, the Iraqis torched virtually every oil well in the country, blackening the sky for months and leaving huge lakes of oil throughout the desert oilfields. In these lakes, oil saturated the sand to depths of 35 cm; the risk of the lakes, up to several metres deep, catching fire, was always high. Astonishingly, the Kuwaitis managed to get the mess cleaned up within about 18 months. The last of the famous oil-well fires was extinguished less than a year after the war ended, despite early predictions that putting out the blazes might take up to five years.

FAUNA

The average traveller to Arabia is likely to see little wildlife beyond camels and donkeys. The desert teems with other animals, of course, but many of them are nocturnal, some are endangered and all are hard to spot.

A number of species have evolved to meet the demands of desert life. Some of the better-known ones include the sand cat, the sand fox and the desert hare. All of these are typified by unusually large ears compared to other cats, foxes and rabbits, and tufts of hair on their feet. The large ears allow the animal to hear possible predators from a great distance, while the hair on their feet enables them to cross dunes and other areas of loose sand with ease.

In the Asir region of south-west Arabia hamadryas baboons can often be seen along the side of the main roads.

As any early morning visit to the fish markets around the region will show, the Gulf teems with fish life. Diners will be most familiar with the *hamour*, a species of grouper, but the Gulf is also home to an extraordinary range of tropical fish and even several species of sharks.

Several species of turtles, notably the endangered green turtle and hawksbill turtle, nest in the Gulf, though the region's best known turtle nesting grounds are on the Omani coast of the Arabian Sea. The turtles, an endangered species, can be seen at both

Qatar's National Museum and the National Aquarium in Muscat, where they are bred in captivity and later released back into the wild as part of the Omani government's extensive conservation programme.

Endangered Species

With the exception of camels and baboons, most of the species listed above are endangered. Over the last 50 years the houbara bustard, sort of a wild desert chicken that was once plentiful throughout Arabia, has been hunted nearly to extinction. Other animals, such as sand cats, have been both hunted and sought (illegally) by foreign collectors.

The Arabian oryx has long been among the most endangered of the peninsula's native species, going to the very brink of extinction in the late '70s and early '80s. The Omani government has an extensive programme to revive oryx herds, and breeding reservations also exist in Saudi Arabia and the UAE. The oryx remains endangered but is no longer in imminent danger of extinction. Oman also runs a breeding centre for Arabian tahr (a kind of wild goat) and has been instrumental in helping to protect Arabian wolves, striped hyaenas, Arabian

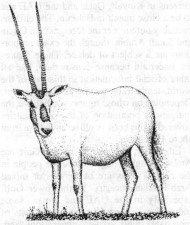

The Arabian, or white, oryx, once hunted to the brink of extinction, can be seen in many of the peninsula's native reserves such as Bahrain's Al-'Areen Wildlife Sanctuary.

leopards and the sooty falcon, a species of grey falcon which nests in Oman every year in April and May. With a few limited exceptions, such as Bahrain's Al-'Areen Wildlife Sanctuary, conservation areas and breeding centres throughout the region are not open to the public.

National Parks

Saudi Arabia's gigantic Asir National Park, in the south-west of the country, is the largest and best known in the Gulf. See the Asir section in general and the Abha entry in particular in the Saudi Arabia chapter for specific information regarding the park and its facilities.

Most of the other park areas around the Gulf are much smaller. The Al-'Areen Wildlife Sanctuary in Bahrain is open to the public, as are parts of Muscat's Qurm Nature Reserve. In late 1995, Sharjah opened its new natural history museum in the desert, west of Sharjah city. Attached to the museum is a small area that the local government hopes to develop into a safari park where endangered Arabian animals can be seen by the public.

GOVERNMENT & POLITICS

All of the Arab Gulf States are monarchies. All six of the countries covered in this book also have some formal system of outside consultation to advise the monarch on affairs of state, but only Kuwait has an elected parliament. In the other Gulf countries various types of consultative councils are appointed by the ruler but are allowed only to debate such issues as the ruler, or the Cabinet, places before them. Kuwait's parliament has extensive powers, including the right to approve the state's budget, but it has been dissolved several times over the years and continues to exist, to some extent, at the pleasure of the royal family.

Arabian culture and tradition, however, allow for – indeed, require – much more consultation by the ruler than may at first be apparent. Rulers must always retain the support of both their family and the public at large, particularly the powerful merchant families. Throughout the region, the rulers and other senior members of the ruling families are accessible to any and all of their subjects in ways that would be unthinkable almost anywhere else in the world. They regularly sit in a *majlis*, or formal meeting room, where any citizen can come and present a petition or discuss a problem.

This constant, if somewhat formalised, consultation is a far cry from western notions of democratic life, but it does mean that the Gulf's rulers are not as detached from their citizens as many in the west often imagine.

Access, however, should not be confused with activism. Outside of Kuwait politics, in the western sense of the term, is essentially nonexistent in the Gulf. TV and newspaper accounts of meetings of the Cabinet or the local consultative council never impart any of the substance of whatever discussions may have taken place, and sometimes they do not even mention what decisions, if any, were actually made.

In all the Gulf States members of the ruling family hold several key Cabinet portfolios (usually defence, foreign affairs and interior and often the labour, information and oil ministries). Non-royal ministers are usually technocrats who have little clout outside their area of specialisation. Real political authority tends to remain within a small circle of senior members of the ruling family and their advisers. See the individual country chapters for further information.

ECONOMY

Oil, natural gas and petrochemicals dominate the economies of all the Arab Gulf States either directly or indirectly. Bahrain, for example, produces only a token amount of oil, but it refines a large amount of Saudi oil that arrives via an undersea pipeline. It also has an extensive oilfield services industry that caters to the entire region. Though oil concessions were originally issued to foreign companies a generation or two ago, the production and refining work is now handled entirely by state-owned companies throughout the region.

That said, the distribution of oil wealth

across the region varies greatly. Saudi Arabia is one of the world's largest oil producers. Its size and population, however, mean that on a per capita basis it is a far less wealthy country than Kuwait or Qatar. Within the UAE, Abu Dhabi has enormous amounts of oil, Dubai and Sharjah some. The other four emirates have little or none and receive large subsidies from oil-rich Abu Dhabi. Oman has only modest oil wealth but the government there has shepherded its resources carefully.

Oil wealth has also made some of the Gulf States, particularly Kuwait, large investors. Prior to the 1990 Iraqi invasion, Kuwait actually made more money from its investments each year than it did from oil. Saudi Arabia and Abu Dhabi also have extensive overseas holdings.

Beyond oil there is a large financial services industry in Bahrain and, to a much lesser extent, Abu Dhabi. Much of Dubai's wealth has been founded on trade (which, at least in the past, often meant smuggling).

POPULATION & PEOPLE

The exact population of most of the Gulf States is difficult, if not impossible, to determine. Expatriates are thought to outnumber citizens in Kuwait, Qatar and the UAE and to be a close match in Bahrain. The citizens probably outnumber the foreigners in Oman and Saudi Arabia, though the exact proportions are a subject of debate. These figures are uncertain because census data, like all other official information in this part of the world, tends to be treated as a state secret. Depending on whose figures you believe, the indigenous population of the six countries covered in this book could be anywhere from six to 15 million.

Ethnically, the people of the Gulf are Arabs, though a large number of people in the coastal areas are of Persian or mixed Arab-Persian ancestry. In the lower Gulf, especially in the UAE and Oman, some Indian families, usually the descendants of merchants who arrived generations ago, have been assimilated into the local population. Western Saudi Arabia is a different story, particularly around Mecca and Jeddah, where 14 centuries of pilgrims coming and going from the Hejaz region has left the area with a very heterogeneous population.

Though armies of foreign workers are employed throughout the Gulf these people, be they labourers or investment bankers, are legally regarded as hired help, not immigrants. Even if you work in the Gulf for 30 or 40 years (and many people do), you will be expected to leave once you no longer have a job. It is virtually impossible for a foreigner of any nationality to acquire citizenship in one of the Gulf countries. A handful of foreigners (almost invariably from other Arab countries) may be granted citizenship now and then, but these are usually people who have rendered important services to the ruler or the state over a period of many years.

SOCIETY & CONDUCT
Traditional Dress

The majority of men in the Gulf States wear traditional dress. This consists of a floor-length shirt-dress which in Saudi Arabia, Bahrain and Qatar is called a *thobe* and in Kuwait and the UAE, a *dishdasha*. These are usually white though blue, brown and black ones are common during winter. Omanis also call their national dress dishdasha, though Omani dishdashas tend to be less tightly cut than those worn by other Gulf Arabs. Omani dishdashas also come in a wider variety of colours, white and light blue being the most common.

Omani dishdashas tend to be fairly traditional in their styling (eg there are no pockets), and aficionados can even tell where the wearer is from by examining the garment's cut and collar design. In the Gulf States, thobes and dishdashas have adopted many of the conventions of western men's shirts, particularly among wealthier people. Thobes and dishdashas sold outside of Oman now routinely have side and breast pockets. Expensive thobes in Saudi Arabia and the northern Gulf may even have western-style collars and French cuffs.

In all the Gulf countries except Oman men

wear a loose headscarf called a *gutra*. This is usually white, though (particularly in Saudi Arabia) it may also be red-and-white check. The black head ropes used to secure the gutra are called *agal* and are said to have originated from the rope which Bedouins would use to hitch up their camels at night. Men from Qatar and parts of the UAE often have two long cords hanging from the back of their agals by way of decoration. Omanis usually wear a solid-coloured turban with intricate and brightly coloured embroidery around its edges, or a small brimless cap, also intricately embroidered.

In south-western Saudi Arabia, particularly in areas near the Yemeni border, men often wear the skirts which are common in northern Yemen, and usually wrap their gutras turban-like around their heads without using an agal.

Traditional women's dress, at least in public, is little more than an enormous, all-covering black cloak. This may completely obscure the wearer's face, in which case the portion of the cloak which covers the face will be made from a thin black gauze that allows the wearer to look out but prevents the world from looking in. Alternatively, the woman's eyes may be visible between her headscarf and veil. Small masks covering the nose, cheeks and part of the mouth are most often seen in rural areas or among old women in the cities. What a woman wears beneath her cloak may be anything from a traditional caftan to the latest haute couture from Paris or Milan. The exception, again, is Oman, where traditional women's clothing is far more colourful (though no more revealing) than that found elsewhere in the region.

Arab women walking around a Gulf city with their faces, or even their heads, uncovered are almost always not from the Gulf but rather Egyptian, Palestinian, Jordanian etc. The only countries in the region where significant numbers of local women no longer wear veils or headscarves are Kuwait and, to a lesser extent, Bahrain.

Dos & Don'ts
Etiquette is very important in Arab culture

and you will find that your time in the Gulf goes much more smoothly if a few simple rules and rituals are followed.

General Etiquette Always stand when someone (other than the coffee boy) enters the room. Upon entering a room yourself

---

Traditional Architecture

Wind Towers Called *barjeel* in Arabic, wind towers are the Gulf's unique form of non-electrical air-conditioning. In most of the region's cities a handful still exist, sometimes on people's homes and sometimes carefully preserved or reconstructed at museums. In Sharjah a set of massive wind towers are used to cool the modern Central Market building.

Traditional wind towers rise five or six metres above a house. They are usually built of wood or stone but can also be made from canvas. The tower is open on all four sides and catches even small breezes. These are channelled down around a central shaft and into the room below. In the process the air speeds up and is cooled. The cooler air already in the tower shaft pulls in, and subsequently cools, the hotter air outside through simple convection.

The towers work amazingly well. Sitting beneath a wind tower on a day when it is 40°C and humid you will notice a distinct drop in temperature and a consistent breeze even when the air outside feels heavy and still.

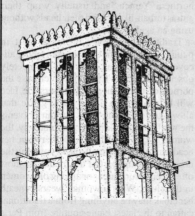

Wind Tower

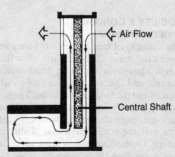

Air Flow

Central Shaft

Barasti The term *barasti* describes both the traditional Gulf method of building a palm-leaf house and the completed house itself. Barastis consist of a skeleton of wooden poles onto which palm leaves are woven to form a strong structure through which air can still circulate. They were extremely common throughout the Gulf in the centuries before the oil boom but are now almost nonexistent. The few examples which survive are fishers' shacks, storage buildings in rural areas and a few examples sitting in the courtyards of museums. For a detailed description of how a barasti is constructed see Geoffrey Bibby's book *Looking for Dilmun*.

Coral In some of the Gulf's cities, and especially in the Saudi Arabian port of Jeddah on the Red Sea, coral has been used as a building material for centuries. The coral would be quarried from offshore reefs and then cut into stone for building, sometimes in combination with gypsum.

In Jeddah, many of the grander houses in the old city are constructed entirely of coral, including the Municipality Museum and the Naseef House. Bahrain's Al-Jasra House and Shaikh Saeed's House in Dubai are examples of large buildings constructed using a mixture of coral and gypsum. ■

shake hands with everyone, touching your heart with the palm of the right hand after each handshake. This goes for both Arab men and women, though men finding themselves in the presence of Arab women should not offer to shake hands unless the woman takes the lead by extending her hand first. When two men meet it is considered polite for them to enquire after each other's families but *not* each other's wives.

Western men should not wear thobes or dishdashas because traditional dress has become an unofficial national uniform throughout the Gulf, visually setting natives of the region apart from the foreign population. Many Gulf Arabs will think that you are making fun of them if you adopt Arabian dress.

Do not sit in such a way that the soles of your feet are pointing at someone else and do not eat or offer things with your left hand.

It is also considered polite to let your host set the pace in any conversation. Many Gulf Arabs prefer to begin meetings with what, in the west, would be considered an excessive amount of small talk. In such situations you may cause offence if you try to move directly to business. Not surprisingly, this traditional propensity for chitchat becomes more pronounced as one moves away from the cities and when one is dealing with older people.

While researching this edition I visited a remote archaeological site in Saudi Arabia where the attendant served me endless coffee, tea and dates and engaged me in conversation for well over an hour before unlocking the gate. After taking me around the site he insisted on another 45 minutes of small talk before I was allowed to leave.

Dress The Gulf is a very conservative place. Even cities like Dubai which are extremely liberal by Middle Eastern standards are still very conservative in comparison with the west.

Men should never appear bare-chested in public, except when at the beach or at a swimming pool. Shorts are generally a bad idea too but if you insist on wearing them they should be relatively long – all the way down to the knee if possible.

Women should wear loose-fitting clothing that is not revealing either because of its cut or because you can see through it. Even in places where a knee-length skirt probably would not be a problem (eg Dubai) you should consider the impression you are making. People will treat you more seriously and with greater respect if you show respect for their culture. Single-piece bathing suits are a good idea at the beach (and in some places may be mandatory). Skirts above the knee should be reserved for trips to nightclubs.

All of this goes double for trips to rural areas.

Forms of Address Throughout the Arab world it is common to attach forms of address to people's given, as opposed to their family, names. Just as Arabs refer to each other as 'Mr Mohammed' or 'Mr Abdullah', they will refer to you as 'Mr John', 'Mr Stephen', 'Miss Simone' or 'Mrs Susan'.

The word 'shaikh' (or sheikh) has two quite different meanings in the Gulf. In Saudi Arabia it is a general term of respect and is commonly applied to senior businessmen, high government officials and older men to whom one is not related. It is only rarely applied to men who are not Gulf Arabs, and it is *never* applied to male members of the royal family (who are called 'princes').

By contrast, in Kuwait, Bahrain, Qatar and the UAE the term 'shaikh' applies *only* to members of the ruling family. The rulers themselves carry the formal title of 'Emir' (literally, 'Prince'), but are usually referred to as 'shaikhs', as in 'The Emir of Bahrain, Shaikh Isa Bin Salman Al-Khalifa'.

If, for example, you work for a trading company in Saudi Arabia it would be normal for employees to address the company's Saudi owner as 'Shaikh Ahmed'. In Kuwait you would only refer to the owner as Shaikh Ahmed if he also happened to be a member of the ruling Al-Sabah family.

The feminine form of shaikh is 'shaikha' (or sheikha). This word is rarely, if ever, used in Saudi Arabia. In the other Gulf States it applies to all female members of the ruling family.

Coffee & Tea It is considered very impolite to refuse an offer of coffee or tea in any social or business setting. If you are the host it is considered equally impolite to fail to make such an offer. Throughout the Gulf, but particularly in Saudi Arabia, you may be offered Arabian coffee (sometimes called Arabic or Bedouin coffee), and this involves a certain ritual all its own. Arabian coffee is served in tiny handleless cups which hold only two or three sips of coffee. The coffee is flavoured with cardamom which makes it green, or sometimes greenish-brown, in colour. The version served in the cities is fairly tame but should you ever find yourself out in the desert with Bedouins be prepared for an extremely bitter taste. After finishing your coffee hold out the cup in your right hand for more. If you have had enough, rock the cup gently back and forth to indicate that you're through. (At all other times act as though the coffee boy is invisible.) It is generally considered impolite to drink more than three cups, though if the conversation drags on for an extended period of time the coffee and tea may be passed around again.

In cities it is most likely that you will be offered Turkish coffee. This will usually be served *mazboot*, or with medium sugar, unless you specify otherwise. If you only want a little sugar ask to have the coffee *areeha*. *Khafeef* means with a lot of sugar and *saada* with no sugar at all. Those unfamiliar with Turkish coffee should be aware that it is very thick and strong. Even if you drink regular coffee black you will probably want to have at least some sugar in your Turkish coffee. Turkish coffee is served in small cups similar to those used for espresso. You will find a layer of grounds, possibly quite thick, in the bottom of the cup.

RELIGION
Islam
Life in the Gulf revolves around the Islamic religion. Muslims believe the religion preached in Arabia by the Prophet Mohammed to be God's final revelation to humanity. For them the Koran, God's words revealed through the Prophet, supplements and completes the earlier revelations around which the Christian and Jewish faiths were built, and corrects human misinterpretations of those earlier revelations. For example, Muslims believe that Jesus was a prophet second only to Mohammed in importance but that his followers later introduced into Christianity the heretical idea that Jesus was the son of God. Adam, Abraham, Moses and a number of other Christian and Jewish holy men are regarded as prophets by Muslims. Mohammed, however, was the 'Seal of the Prophets' – the last one who has, or will, come.

The Faith The essence of Islam is the belief that there is only one God and that it is the people's duty to believe in and serve Him in

Ramadan
This month, during which Muslims fast from dawn until dusk, is observed more strictly in the Gulf than in many other parts of the Muslim world. Those Gulf countries in which alcohol is legal usually ban its sale during Ramadan. Discos, where they exist, are closed throughout the month. In all Gulf countries everyone, regardless of their religion, is required to observe the fast in public. That not only means no eating and drinking but no smoking as well. The few restaurants open during the daytime will invariably be ones that passers-by cannot see into. The penalties for publicly breaking the fast vary – in Saudi Arabia you can go to jail for merely smoking a cigarette while driving in your own car.

Non-Muslims offered coffee or tea when meeting a Muslim during the daytime in Ramadan should initially refuse politely. If your host insists, and repeats the offer several times, you should accept so long as it does not look as though your doing so is going to anger anyone else in the room who may be fasting.

The month of Ramadan varies from year to year as the Islamic calendar is 11 days shorter than the Gregorian calendar. For dates see the table of holidays near Public Holidays in the Regional Facts for the Visitor chapter. ■

the manner which He has laid out in the Koran. In Arabic, *islam* means submission and a *muslim* is one who submits to God's will.

In the first instance, one does this by observing the five pillars of the faith:

1. The profession of faith *(shahadah)*. To become a Muslim one need only state the Islamic creed, 'There is no God but God, and Mohammed is the messenger of God', with conviction.

2. Prayer *(salat)*. Muslims are required to pray five times every day: at dawn, noon, mid-afternoon, sunset and 1½ hours after sunset. Prayers follow a set ritual pattern which varies slightly depending on the time of day. During prayers a Muslim must perform a series of prostrations while facing in the direction of the Kaaba, the ancient shrine at the centre of the Grand Mosque in Mecca. Before a Muslim can pray, however, he or she must perform a series of ritual ablutions, and if no water is available for this purpose sand or dirt may be substituted.

3. Charity or Alms *(zakat)*. Muslims must give a portion of their income to help those poorer than themselves. How this has operated in practice has varied over the centuries: either it was seen as an individual duty or the state collected zakat as a form of income tax to be redistributed through mosques or religious charities.

4. Fasting *(sawm)*. It was during the month of Ramadan that Mohammed received his first revelation in 610 AD. Muslims mark this event by fasting from sunrise until sunset throughout Ramadan each year. During the fast a Muslim may not take anything into his or her body. This means that not only food and drink but also smoking and sex are banned. Young children, travellers and those whose health will not permit it are exempt from the fast, though those who are able to do so are supposed to make up the days they missed at a later time.

5. Pilgrimage *(hajj)*. All Muslims who are able to do so are required to make the pilgrimage to Mecca at least once during their lifetime. However, the pilgrimage must be performed during a specific few days in the first and second weeks of the Muslim month of Dhul Hijja. Visiting Mecca and performing the prescribed rituals at any other time of the year is considered spiritually desirable, but it is not hajj. Such visits are referred to as *umrah*, or 'little pilgrimage'.

Beyond the five pillars of Islam there are many other duties incumbent on Muslims. In the west the best known and least understood of these is *jihad*. This word is usually translated into English as 'holy war', but literally means 'striving in the way of the faith'. Exactly what this means has been a subject of keen debate among Muslim scholars for the last 1400 years. Some scholars have tended to see jihad in spiritual, as opposed to martial, terms.

Muslims are forbidden to eat or drink anything containing pork, alcohol, blood or the meat of any animal which died of natural causes (as opposed to having been slaughtered in the prescribed manner). Muslim women may not marry non-Muslim men, though Muslim men are permitted to marry Christian or Jewish women (but not, for example, Hindus or Buddhists).

The Law The Arabic word *sharia* is usually translated as 'Islamic Law'. This is misleading. The sharia is not a legal code in the western sense of the term. It refers to the general body of Islamic legal thought. At the base of this lies the Koran itself, which Muslims believe to be the actual speech of God, revealed to humankind through Mohammed. Where the Koran does not provide guidance on a particular subject Muslim scholars turn to the Sunnah, a body of works recording the sayings and doings of the Prophet and, to a lesser extent, his companions as reported by a string of scholarly authorities. There are many Sunnah authorities and their reliability is determined by the school of Islamic jurisprudence to which one subscribes. There are four main Sunni and two principal Shiite schools of Islamic jurisprudence.

The orthodox Sunni schools of jurisprudence are the Shafi'i, Hanbali, Hanafi and Maliki. All but the first of these schools, or rites as they are sometimes known, are found widely in the Gulf though Hanbalis are probably the most numerous. This owes much to the fact that Wahhabism, the predominant Islamic sect in Saudi Arabia and Qatar, follows the Hanbali school. Hanbali Islam is generally regarded as the sternest of the four orthodox Sunni rites. The largest schools of

Shiite jurisprudence are the Jafari and the Akhbari. Bahrain's Shiite majority mostly subscribe to the Akhbari school. Ibadi Islam, the variety practiced in Oman, has its own separate school of jurisprudence.

The Koran and Sunnah together make up the sharia. In some instances the sharia is quite specific, such as in the areas of inheritance law and the punishments for certain offences. In many other cases it acts as a series of guidelines. Islam does not recognise a distinction between the secular and religious lives of believers. Thus, a learned scholar or judge can with enough research and if necessary, through use of analogy,

determine the proper 'Islamic' position on or approach to any problem.

Sunnis & Shiites The schism that divided the Muslim world into two broad camps took place only a few years after the death of the Prophet. When Mohammed died, in 632, he left no clear instructions either designating a successor as leader of the Muslim community or setting up a system by which subsequent leaders could be chosen. Some felt that leadership of the community should remain with the Prophet's family, and supported the claim of Ali Bin Abi Taleb, Mohammed's cousin and son-in-law and one

---

Mosque Vocabulary

The Grand Mosque in Mecca and the Prophet's Mosque in Medina, Islam's two holiest sites, can each accommodate hundreds of thousands of worshippers at a time. But along road sides throughout the Gulf you can also see small enclosed areas – impromptu mosques available to any passing traveller, open to the sky and capable of holding no more than a handful of people.

A mosque is fundamentally a simple thing, made up of a few basic elements. The most visible of these is the minaret, the tower from which the call to prayer is issued five times every day. Virtually every mosque in the world has a minaret. Many have several. Minarets can be plain or ornate. Some – such as the Giralda at Seville, in Spain – are architectural works of great beauty. The first minarets were not built until the early 8th century, some 70 years after the Prophet's death. Prior to that time the *muezzin*, or

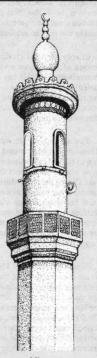

prayer caller, often stood on a rooftop or some other elevated position so as to be heard as widely as possible. The idea for minarets as we now know them may have originated with the watchtowers that Muslim armies found attached to some of the churches they converted into mosques during the early years of Islam. The watchtower at the Church of St John the Baptist in Damascus – the building now known as the Omayyad Mosque – is one such example. The minaret at the Mosque of Omar in Domat Al-Jandal in northern Saudi Arabia may be another.

A mosque must also have a *mihrib*, a niche in the wall facing Mecca and indicating the *qibla*, the direction believers must face while praying. Like minarets,

Mihrib

Minaret

of the first converts to Islam, to become the *khalif* (caliph), or leader. But the community initially chose Abu Bakr, the Prophet's closest companion, as leader, and Ali was also passed over in two subsequent leadership contests.

Those who took Ali's side in these disputes became known as the *shi'a*, or 'partisans (of Ali)'. Ali eventually became caliph, the fourth of Mohammed's successors, in 656 but was assassinated five years later by troops loyal to the Governor of Syria, Mu'awiyah Bin Abu Sufyan, a distant relative of the Prophet who subsequently set himself up as caliph.

This split the Muslim community into two competing factions. The Sunnis favoured the Umayyads, the dynasty which was established by Mu'awiyah. As it developed over the succeeding generations Sunni doctrine emphasised the position of the caliph as both the spiritual head of the Muslim community and the temporal ruler of the state in which that community existed. Sunni belief essentially holds that any Muslim who rules with justice and according to the sharia deserves the support of the Muslim community as a whole.

Shiites, on the other hand, believed that a descendant of the Prophet through Ali's line

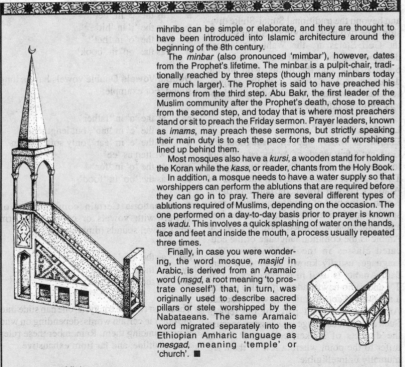

mihribs can be simple or elaborate, and they are thought to have been introduced into Islamic architecture around the beginning of the 8th century.

The *minbar* (also pronounced 'mimbar'), however, dates from the Prophet's lifetime. The minbar is a pulpit-chair, traditionally reached by three steps (though many minbars today are much larger). The Prophet is said to have preached his sermons from the third step. Abu Bakr, the first leader of the Muslim community after the Prophet's death, chose to preach from the second step, and today that is where most preachers stand or sit to preach the Friday sermon. Prayer leaders, known as *imams*, may preach these sermons, but strictly speaking their main duty is to set the pace for the mass of worshipers lined up behind them.

Most mosques also have a *kursi*, a wooden stand for holding the Koran while the *kass*, or reader, chants from the Holy Book.

In addition, a mosque needs to have a water supply so that worshippers can perform the ablutions that are required before they can go in to pray. There are several different types of ablutions required of Muslims, depending on the occasion. The one performed on a day-to-day basis prior to prayer is known as *wadu*. This involves a quick splashing of water on the hands, face and feet and inside the mouth, a process usually repeated three times.

Finally, in case you were wondering, the word mosque, *masjid* in Arabic, is derived from an Aramaic word (*msgd*, a root meaning 'to prostrate oneself') that, in turn, was originally used to describe sacred pillars or stele worshipped by the Nabataeans. The same Aramaic word migrated separately into the Ethiopian Amharic language as *mesgad*, meaning 'temple' or 'church'. ■

Minbar

Kursi

should lead the Muslims. Because Shiites have rarely held temporal power their doctrine came to emphasise the spiritual position of their leaders, the *imams*.

This split widened and became permanent when Ali's son Hussein was killed in brutal circumstances at Karbala (now in southern Iraq) in 680. Over the centuries Sunnism has developed into the 'orthodox' strain of Islam. Today, most of the world's Muslims are Sunnis. In the Gulf, Shiites are a majority only in Bahrain (though Bahrain's ruling family are Sunnis). There are significant Shiite minorities in Kuwait, the UAE and Saudi Arabia's Eastern Province.

As with any religion embracing about one billion people, Islam has produced many sects, movements and offshoots both within and beyond the traditional Sunni-Shiite division. The two most important Sunni sects in the Gulf States are the Wahhabis, whose doctrines are the official form of Islam in Saudi Arabia, and the Ibadis, who are the dominant sect in Oman. See the religion sections of the Saudi Arabia and Oman chapters for more information.

LANGUAGE

English is widely spoken throughout the Gulf, but a few words of Arabic can do a lot to ease your passage through the region. There are several different varieties of Arabic. Classical Arabic, the language of the Koran, is the root of all of today's dialects of spoken and written Arabic. A modernised and somewhat simplified form of classical Arabic is the common language of the educated classes in the Middle East. This language, usually known as Modern Standard Arabic, is used in newspapers and by TV and radio newsreaders. It is also used as a medium of conversation by well-educated Arabs from different parts of the region. Such a written language is necessary because the dialects of spoken colloquial Arabic differ to the point where a few of them are mutually unintelligible.

Mercifully, the words and phrases a traveller is most likely to use are fairly standard throughout the Gulf. The words and phrases

that follow should be understood anywhere in the region. Local variants, where applicable, have been noted.

Pronunciation

Pronunciation of Arabic can be somewhat tongue-tying for someone unfamiliar with the intonation and combination of sounds. Pronounce the transliterated words and phrases slowly and clearly.

The following guide should help, but it isn't complete because the myriad rules governing pronunciation and vowel use are too extensive to be covered here.

Vowels

a	as the 'a' in 'had'
e	as the 'e' in 'bet'
i	as the 'i' in 'hit'
o	as the 'o' in 'hot'
u	as the 'oo' in 'book'

Double Vowels Double vowels have a long sound. For example:

aa	as the 'a' in 'father'
ee	as the 'e' in 'ten', but lengthened
ii	as the 'e' in 'ear', only softer, often written as 'ee'
oo	as the 'o' in 'for'
uu	as the 'oo' in 'food'

Combinations Certain combinations of vowels with vowels or consonants form other vowel sounds (diphthongs):

aw	as the 'ow' in 'how'
ay	as the 'i' in 'high'
ei	as the 'a' in 'cake'

These last two are tricky, as one can slide into the other in certain words, depending on who is pronouncing them. Remember these rules are an outline, and far from exhaustive.

Consonants The consonants used in this section are pronounced as in English with the exception of the following:

' The glottal stop is the sound you hear between the vowels in the expression 'oh oh!'. It is actually a closing of the glottis at the back of the throat so that the passage of air is halted.

ch as in 'church'

gh (or 'rayn') is produced by tightening your throat and sort of growling with a slight 'r' sound at the beginning – it is quite a bit like the French 'r'. The best way to learn these sounds is to listen to a native speaker pronounce their written equivalents.

H a strongly whispered 'h', almost like a sigh of relief.

q strong guttural 'k' sound. Often transcribed as 'k'.

kh a slightly gurgling sound, like the 'ch' in Scottish 'loch'

r a rolled 'r', as in Spanish 'para'

s pronounced as in English 'sit', never as in 'wisdom'

sh as in 'shelf'

th as in 'these'

Double Consonants In Arabic, double consonants are both pronounced. For example the word *el-hammam*, which means 'toilet', is pronounced 'el-ham-mam'.

Basics

Yes.	*ai/aiwa/na'am*
No.	*la'*
Maybe.	*mumkin*
Please.	
(to a man)	*min fadhlik/ lau samaHt/ lau tismaH*
(to a woman)	*min fadhlich/ lau samaHti/ lau tismiHin*
(to a group)	*min fadhelkum/ lau samaHtu/ lau tismuHun*
Thank you.	*shukran*
(to a man)	*mashkur*
(to a woman)	*mashkura*
(to a group)	*mashkurin*
You're welcome.	*afwan/al-afu*

Excuse me.	
(to a man)	*lau samaHt*
(to a woman)	*lau samaHti*
(to a group)	*lau samaHtu*
After you.	*atfaddal*
OK.	*zein/kwayyis/tayib*
No problem.	*mafeesh mushkala*
Impossible.	*mish mumkin*
It doesn't matter/ I don't care.	*ma'alish*
Go/Get lost!	*imshi!*

Greetings

Hello.	*as-salaamo alaykum*
Hello.(response)	*wa alaykum e-salaam*
Goodbye.	*ma'al salaama*
Goodbye. (response)	
(to a man)	*alla ysalmak*
(to a woman)	*alla ysalmich*
(to a group)	*alla ysallimkum*
Goodbye.	
(to a man)	*Hayyaakallah*
(to a woman)	*Hayyachallah*
(to a group)	*Hayyakumallah*
Goodbye. (response)	
(to a man)	*alla yHai'eek*
(to a woman)	*alla yHai'eech*
(to a group)	*alla yHai'eekum*
Goodbye. (UAE only)	*fi aman ullah*
Good morning.	*sabaH al-kheir*
Good morning. (response)	*sabaH an-nur*
Good afternoon/ evening.	*masa' al-kheir*
Good afternoon/ evening. (response)	*masa' an-nur*
Good night.	
(to a man)	*tisbaH ala-kheir*
(to a woman)	*tisbiHin ala-kheir*
(to a group)	*tisbuHun ala-kheir*
Good night. (response)	
(to a man)	*wa inta min ahlil-kheir*
(to a woman)	*wa inti min ahlil-kheir*
(to a group)	*wa intu min ahlil-kheir*

Welcome. *ahlan wa sahlan/ marHaba*

Welcome to you.
  (to a man) *ahlan feek*
  (to a woman) *ahlan feech*
  (to a group) *ahlan feekum*

Pleased to meet you. *fursa sa'ida*
  (also said to people as they are leaving)
Pleased to meet you. (response)
  (by an individual) *wa ana as'ad*
  (by a group) *wa iHna as'ad*

Small Talk

How are you?
  (to a man) *shlonik/kef Halak*
  (to a woman) *shlonich/kef Halik*
  (to a group) *shlonkum/ kef Halkum*
Fine, thanks. *bkheir al-Ham- dulillah*
  (by a man) *zein al-Hamdulillah*
  (by a woman) *zeina al-Ham- dulillah*
  (by a group) *zeinin al-Ham- dulillah*

What is your name?
  (to a man) *shismak*
  (to a woman) *shismich*
  (to a group) *shisimkum*
My name is ... *ismi ...*
I am ... *ana ...*

I am from ... *ana min ...*
  Australia *usturalia*
  France *faransa*
  Germany *almania*
  Netherlands *holanda*
  Switzerland *swissra*
  the UK *britania*
  the USA *amrika*

Language Difficulties

I understand.
  (by a man) *ana fahim*
  (by a woman) *ana fahma*
We understand. *iHna fahmeen*
I do not understand.
  (by a man) *ana mu fahim*
  (by a woman) *ana mu fahma*

We do not understand.
  iHna mu fahmeen
Do you speak English/French/German?
  titkallam ingleezi/fransawi/almaani
I don't speak Arabic.
  ma-atkallam arabi

Getting Around

How far is ...? *cham yibe'id ...*
  the bus stop *mokaf al-bas*
  the bus station *maHattat al-bas*
  the train station *maHattat al-qatar*
  a taxi stand *maHattat tax/ maHattat ajara*
  the airport *al-mataar*

Where is the ...? *wein al ...*
  boat *markab*
  bus *bas*
  camel *jamal*
  car *sayyara*
  donkey *Hmaar*
  horse *Hsan*
  taxi *tax/ajara*
  ticket office *maktab al-tathaaker*

I want to go to ...
  abga arouH li ...
When does the ... leave?
  mata yamshi il ...
  muta yamshi il ... (in Kuwait)
When does the ... arrive?
  mata tosal il ...
  muta tosal il ... (in Kuwait)
What is the fare to ...?
  cham il tathkara li ...
Which bus/taxi goes to ...?
  ai bas/tax yrouH il ...
Does this bus/taxi go to ...?
  Hathal bas yrouH il ...
How many buses go to ...?
  cham bas yrouH li ...
Please tell me when we arrive at ...
  lau samaHtit goul li mata nosal li ...
May I sit here?
  mumkin ag'id hina
May we sit here?
  mumkin nag'id hina

Stop here, please.
'ogaf hina, law samaHt
Please wait for me.
law samaHt, intitherni

Directions

to/for	*lil*
left	*shimal/yasaar*
right	*yimeen*
straight	*ala tool*
	seeda (Kuwait only)
	doghri (UAE only)
street	*shaari'*
number	*raqam*
city	*madina*
village	*qaria*

Around Town

Can you show me the way to ...?
mumkin tdallini mukaan ...

Where is the ...?	*wein al ...*
bank	*el-bank*
barber	*el-Hallaq*
beach	*il-shatt/il-shaat'i*
embassy	*es-safara*
hotel	*el-funduq*
market	*es-souk*
mosque	*el-masjid*
museum	*el-matHaf*
old city	*el-madina il-qadima*
palace	*el-qasr*
police station	*el-makhfar*
post office	*maktab al-bareed*
restaurant	*el-mataam*
telephone	*el-telefon/el-hataf*
toilet	*el-Hammam*
university	*il-jam'a*
zoo	*Hadiqat il-Haywan*

I want to change ...	*abga asrif ...*
money	*floos*
US$	*dolarat amrikiia*
UK£	*jneihat isterlini*
A$	*dolarat usturaliia*
FF	*frankat fransi*
DM	*markat almani*
travellers' cheques	*sheikat syaHiia*

Accommodation

May I see the room?
mumkin ashuf al-ghurfah
May I see other rooms?
mumkin ashuf ghuraf thaania
How much is this room per night?
cham ujrat haathil ghurfah fil-leila
Do you have any cheaper rooms?
fih ghuraf arkhas
This is very expensive.
wai'd ghali
hatha ghali jeddan (in Saudi Arabia)
This is fine.
hatha zein.

Food

bread	*khubz*
chicken	*dajaj*
coffee	*qahwa*
fish	*samak*
meat	*laHma*
milk	*laban*
pepper	*felfel*
potatoes	*batatas*
rice	*roz*
salt	*sel/melaH*
sugar	*suker*
tea	*chai*
water	*mayya*

Shopping

I want...
abga...
abi... (Kuwait & Bahrain)
Do you have ...?
indik (to a man)
indich (to a woman)
Where can I buy ...?
wein agdar ashtiri
How much is this?
bcham hatha
How much is that?
bcham hathak
How much are those?
bcham hathol
How much ...?
qedaish (Saudi Arabia, Qatar & UAE)
It costs too much.
ghalia wai'd

Time & Dates

		11	*Hda'ash*
What time is it?		12	*thna'ash*
as-sa'a kam		13	*thalathta'ash*
It is ...	*as-sa'a ...*	14	*arba'ata'ash*
one o'clock	*waHda*	15	*khamista'ash*
1.15	*waHda wa rob'*	16	*sitta'ash*
1.20	*waHda wa tilt*	17	*sabi'ta'ash*
1.30	*waHda wa nus*	18	*thimanta'ash*
1.45	*ithneen illa rob'*	19	*tisi'ta'ash*
	(literally 'quarter	20	*'ishreen*
	to two')	21	*waHid wa 'ishreen*
		22	*ithneen wa 'ishreen*
daily	*kil yom*	23	*thalatha wa 'ishreen*
today	*al-yom*	30	*thalatheen*
yesterday	*ams*	40	*arbi'een*
tomorrow	*bukra*	50	*khamseen*
early	*mbach'ir/badri*	60	*sitteen*
late	*mit'akhir*	70	*saba'een*
		80	*thimaneen*
Monday	*yom al-ithneen*	90	*tis'een*
Tuesday	*yom al-thalath*	100	*imia*
Wednesday	*yom al-arbaa'*	101	*imia w-aHid*
Thursday	*yom al-khamis*	102	*imia wa-ithneen*
Friday	*yom al-jama'a*	103	*imia wa-thalatha*
Saturday	*yom as-sabt*	200	*imiatain*
Sunday	*yom al-Had*	300	*thalatha imia*
		1000	*alf*

Numbers

0	*sifir*		
1	*waHid*	1st	*awwal*
2	*ithneen*	2nd	*thaani*
3	*thalatha*	3rd	*thaalith*
4	*arba'a*	4th	*raabi'*
5	*khamsa*	5th	*khaamis*
6	*sitta*	6th	*saadis*
7	*sab'a*	7th	*saabi'*
8	*thimania*	8th	*thaamin*
9	*tis'a*	9th	*taasi'*
10	*ashra*	10th	*'ashir*

Regional Facts for the Visitor

PLANNING

When to Go

If possible, avoid the Gulf from April to early October, when temperatures can soar over 40°C. The tourist season, in those countries that admit tourists, is November to February.

The monsoon season in southern Oman is June to September, and this is a good time to avoid that part of the country. However, late September when everything is green in the wake of the rains is one of the best times to visit the Salalah area.

You should avoid visiting the Gulf during Ramadan (see the table of holidays near Public Holidays later in this chapter). Unfortunately, Ramadan will overlap with at least part of the November to February tourist season from now until 2006 so plan carefully. At hajj time it would also be a good idea to avoid Jeddah unless you have a pressing reason to be there.

What Kind of Trip?

The first thing to be said about any trip to the Gulf is that you should not plan to show up, hang around for a while, maybe pick up a bit of work and then move on. First, it is too expensive a place to hang around for any length of time. Second, the visa rules do not work like that and, in any case, you will not be able to find quasi-legal work teaching English, waiting tables or tending bar. If you want to work in the Gulf find a job before you go.

The visa rules for tourists require that you do some advance planning, though you may be able to avoid this by booking a package tour. Package tours, of course, have their drawbacks but they do tend to make it easy for you to cover a lot of territory in a short amount of time.

Many people make the Gulf a stopover on a longer trip from Europe to Asia or vice versa. Few cities in the Gulf are packed with things to see and do. With a couple of exceptions, such as Muscat, you don't need to spend more than three days in any major city if you want to see the sites. Even if you only have a couple of days, you should try to get out of the city: take a day trip from Dubai to Al-Ain or Ras Al-Khaimah. If you are in Muscat make a short excursion to Nizwa. Even tiny Bahrain has something to offer in the villages south-west of Manama.

If you are restricted by time you should plan to rent a car. You'll appreciate the increased mobility. Everything covered in this book can be reached using a regular car. If time is not a factor you are in luck – most of what this book covers can be reached using some form of public transport.

Because there are few cities that cannot be seen in a couple of days, and because air service around the region tends to be very good, the Gulf is ideally suited for long weekends.

If you want to see something of the desert you should consider booking a half-day, full-day or overnight 4WD trip. These are available from most of the region's major cities.

Maps

Bartholomew publishes maps of the Gulf and the Arabian Peninsula. These are both somewhat out of date, but are usually pretty adequate for navigation on the ground, especially if you use them in conjunction with a good locally available map (see the individual country chapters for details of local maps). A number of other good maps of Arabia are available, though these are often big regional maps that also include north-east Africa or areas as far east as India.

Anything along those lines is going to be of little use in the UAE and of no use whatsoever in Bahrain, Qatar or Kuwait. For any of the smaller Gulf countries you will have to pick up a local map when you arrive.

What to Bring

A good hat and sunglasses are essential even

if you do not plan to spend time travelling in the desert. Long, loose clothing is always the best idea in conservative Islamic countries and the Gulf is no exception.

Almost anything you can get in the west can easily be purchased in any of the Gulf's bigger cities, though voracious readers of anything other than spy novels should note that there are few really good bookshops in the Gulf. Also, most western works on the history and politics of the Middle East are unavailable in the Gulf States.

SUGGESTED ITINERARIES
One Week
One Country If you only have one week in which to visit one country head for the UAE. Spend a day or two each in Dubai, Al-Ain and Ras Al-Khaimah and leave a day at the end for a trip to Dubai's gold souk.

You can also cover quite a lot of Oman in one week. With a rented car you could see Muscat and most or all of northern Oman in that time; using public transport you will probably have to leave something out.

If you somehow find yourself with a week to spare in Saudi Arabia, try a few days in Jeddah and a weekend trip to Madain Salah or Abha and Najran. This will probably require taking a domestic flight, but it is worth the expense.

Two Countries Start with two days in Dubai and then make an all-day trip to either Al-Ain (if you want to see the desert) or to Ras Al-Khaimah (if you are more interested in mountains). Using Dubai as a base, spend a day in Sharjah before flying on to either Bahrain or Muscat for a brief stopover.

Another good option for two countries in one week is Kuwait and Bahrain. Two or three days in Kuwait and three or four in Bahrain will be enough time to cover most of the sites listed in this book (bear in mind

---

Highlights
Saudi Arabia is something of an acquired taste, but if you have the slightest interest in the Arab world you cannot help but be intrigued by this vast, closed kingdom. People who bad-mouth Saudi Arabia usually have never been outside the main cities. Do not make the mistake of thinking that a trip to Riyadh has shown you the real Saudi Arabia. At the very least spend some time in Jeddah. Better yet visit Najran on the Yemeni border, or the Asir National Park around Abha. My favourite town is Najran. I love the feel of the place, especially wandering through its weird little souk looking for Bedouin jewellery.

The remote northern region of Jof, centred on the towns of Sakaka and Domat Al-Jandal, is one of the Kingdom's great undiscovered treasures. The extraordinary ruins of Qasr Marid and the ancient minaret of the Mosque of Omar alone are worth the airfare to Jof. Following the line of the Hejaz Railway from Medina through Buwayr and Madain Salah to Tabuk is another good trip off the beaten path.

Kuwait is the only place in the Gulf where politics is a spectator sport. Post-liberation Kuwait has proven to be a much less uptight place than pre-invasion Kuwait and it is much easier to strike up conversations with Kuwaitis than it used to be. Wander around looking at the sights and hanging out in the coffee houses. Attend a session of the parliament (they provide simultaneous translation into English) and admire Jorn Utzon's design for the National Assembly building. Kuwait has a lot to offer.

If I have a favourite spot in the entire Gulf, however, it has to be Muscat in Oman. Both the Mina and the Corniche hotels each have a handful of rooms overlooking the Mutrah Corniche, and I would not trade that view for a room in one of the local five-star hotels. You can also get much the same view – and a beer to go with it – from the restaurant on the 2nd floor of the Mina Hotel.

Oman's remote Musandem Peninsula is another spot worth going far out of your way for. As you bump around the unpaved roads near Khasab, it is almost impossible to believe that the bright lights of Dubai are only 100 km away. Try to fly into Khasab if you can – the view from the plane is more than worth the cost of the ticket.

And then there are the little things: an *abra* (water-taxi) ride on Dubai Creek, coffee at the House of Coffee outlet in Jeddah's Al-Mahmal Centre (the one overlooking the square), a *shisha* pipe in one of Jizan's traditional coffee houses, a night on the town in Dubai, or a visit to Madain Salah. ∎

that in Kuwait a trip to Failaka Island will take most of a day).

Three Countries With a little advance planning you could easily hit Muscat, Dubai and Bahrain in one hectic week. If you can arrange to take three full days of this week in Muscat try to work in a day trip from Muscat to Nizwa, Bahla and Jabrin. Bahrain is compact enough that whirlwind two-day visits are not much of a problem and two days is also long enough to see Dubai's Creek, museum, gold souk and experience some of the nightlife.

Two Weeks

One Country Assuming that you cannot get into Saudi Arabia (and, unless you have a job there, you probably can't) your best bet for a two week trip is Oman. Two weeks gives you plenty of time to explore the north of the country, even by public transport. You should also have time for a three or four day excursion either north to the Musandem Peninsula or south to Dhofar, even if you travel by road. If you can afford to fly to both Salalah and Khasab and are willing to cut things back a bit in the north, you might even be able to do all three, though this might be pushing it a bit.

Spending two weeks in the UAE allows you to add an excursion to the Liwa Oasis, Hatta and Abu Dhabi (or a few days lying on the beach) to the one week itinerary outlined earlier.

On the wild off-chance that you do get into Saudi Arabia, start your two weeks in Jeddah. After a day or two there drive or take buses to Taif and then down through the Asir Mountains through Al-Baha to Abha and, finally, Najran. Return via the bleak-but-fast road that runs up the Red Sea coast from Jizan to Jeddah. You will want to spend a couple of days each in both Abha and Najran and at least three or four days in Jeddah. If you have time at the end, try to make a quick trip to Madain Salah, though on the itinerary outlined here the only way you can do this will probably be to join an organised tour.

Two weeks in Kuwait, Qatar or Bahrain is likely to get very boring, very fast.

Two Countries This is where the possibilities start to spin out. With two weeks and two countries you might want to see Kuwait and the UAE, or (visas willing) combine visits to Riyadh and Jeddah with a stop in either Kuwait or Bahrain.

For my money, though, a UAE-Oman trip would be the best way to spend two weeks in the Gulf. Try flying into Dubai, spending a few days there including side trips to Al-Ain, Sharjah and, possibly, Ras Al-Khaimah. Take the bus from Dubai to Muscat and then spend the remainder of your time touring Oman, including a three day side trip (by air) to the Musandem Peninsula.

The more adventurous could travel overland from Ras Al-Khaimah to Khasab, the main town in the Musandem, and fly to Muscat from there. Do *not* try this unless you either have made airline reservations from Khasab to Muscat in advance, or have a visa that will allow you to return to Dubai or Muscat by land if you have to. The Khasab airport is tiny, there are only a couple of planes a week and you could easily be stranded if you do not have a return ticket.

Three Countries It would be fairly easy to get a quick look at some combination of Kuwait, Bahrain and Qatar and then spend a week or so in the UAE or Oman in the course of two weeks, though it could get a bit expensive. You might try starting in either Kuwait or Bahrain, flying to the UAE and then taking the bus to Muscat and back. How you split the time between the UAE and Oman depends a lot on what interests you. Dubai has better shopping, Muscat has more to see.

One Month

With a month on your hands you can do a lot. Most of Saudi Arabia can easily be covered in three or four weeks. You could even whistle stop through all six of the countries covered in this book spending, say, two weeks in the Kingdom, three days in Bahrain, two days each in Kuwait and Qatar, and splitting the final week between the UAE and Oman.

A more relaxed version of the same thing might involve three weeks split between Saudi Arabia and the UAE or the UAE and Oman and a final week consisting of a few days each in Kuwait, Bahrain and/or Qatar.

The Grand Tour

With three or four months on your hands, and a lot of money at your disposal, you could have a look at everything covered in this book. If you have the time, the money, the desire – and the visas – to see absolutely everything try the following: a week to 10 days in Bahrain, another week each in Kuwait and Qatar, three weeks in the UAE, a month in Oman and two months in Saudi Arabia.

VISAS & DOCUMENTS
Passport

Your passport should be valid for at least six months beyond whenever you plan to leave the region. Make sure there is ample room in your passport, and take a dozen or so extra passport photos. In addition, there should be no Israeli stamps in your passport. Despite the peace process – and the fact that several Gulf countries have had some form of official contact with Israel – all of the Arab Gulf States except Saudi Arabia still officially bar travellers whose passports contain Israeli stamps. In Saudi Arabia the rule allowing people to enter the country with Israeli stamps in their passports seems to exist more in theory than in practice, so it would not be a good idea to show up there with Israeli stamps in your passport either. A good rule of thumb is to assume that Israeli stamps in your passport will cause problems in any Arab country that has not signed a peace treaty with Israel.

Visas

The visa situation in the Gulf ranges from fairly simple and straightforward (Bahrain) to nightmarishly complicated (Saudi Arabia). Bahrain, Qatar, the UAE and Oman all issue tourist visas. Saudi Arabia and Kuwait do not, so you have to get a transit or a business visa to visit them.

Bahrain issues visas to most native-born western nationals at the airport and on the causeway connecting Bahrain to Saudi Arabia. Oman and Qatar issue both business and tourist visas through their embassies in some countries, and it is possible in some circumstances to obtain a Qatari visa on arrival at Doha airport. Omani visas can also be arranged through four and five-star hotels for pick-up at Muscat's Seeb airport. Most UAE visas are easy to obtain through medium-sized and larger hotels. These visas (the type most visitors use) are issued for pick-up at the country's airports, but Americans and Germans can get multiple-entry visas through UAE embassies overseas.

Saudi and Kuwaiti visas, whether for a visit or for transit, must always be obtained prior to arrival. Saudi Arabia issues transit visas for people travelling overland between Jordan and Bahrain, Kuwait, Oman, Qatar, the UAE or Yemen. The transit visas are issued at Saudi Arabian embassies in these countries. For more details on each country's visa regulations see Visas in the individual country chapters.

If you do not hold a passport from an OECD country, or if you are a naturalised citizen of an OECD country and you originally came from somewhere in the developing world, obtaining a visa to visit any Gulf country can be difficult. Because most labour in the Gulf is done by expatriates from the Indian subcontinent, South-East Asia or the poorer parts of the Arab world, the authorities throughout the region are especially sensitive to people from these countries trying to slip into the Gulf to look for work. There is a tendency to assume that anyone from a poor country is a labourer in search of a job, and you may have a hard time convincing the authorities otherwise. Fear of AIDS has also led some Gulf countries to cut back on visas for anyone holding a passport from sub-Saharan Africa.

Inter-Arab political tensions also come into play when searching for a visa. If you are of Palestinian, Iraqi, Libyan, Algerian or

Lebanese origin you may have trouble getting a visa even if you hold a western passport. Obtaining a visa in such circumstances is not impossible, but it generally requires more advance planning. If Americans, Brits or Germans can get a visa through a hotel in a week, a person from any of those countries with a recognisably Palestinian name, or whose passport lists Baghdad as their place of birth, should probably allow a month to get the paperwork processed.

Israeli stamps in your passport will still keep you out of the Gulf, though South African stamps are no longer a problem.

Visa Sponsorship If you cannot obtain a visa to the Gulf States through an embassy, you can get it through a sponsor. A sponsor is a national of the country you are visiting who is willing to vouch for your good behaviour while in the country and take responsibility for your departure when you're supposed to leave. How easy it is to get a sponsor, and what you must do once you have found one, varies from country to country.

In Kuwait, Qatar, the UAE and Oman all the larger hotels can sponsor visas for travellers. The documentation required varies from one country to another and its processing can take anything from a few days to a few weeks. In Bahrain, hotels can arrange sponsorship for those unable to obtain a visa on arrival.

Collecting Visas Once approved, Kuwaiti and Saudi visas have to be picked up at a Kuwaiti or Saudi embassy before you travel. Visas for the other Gulf States are usually issued for pick-up at the destination airport or port, though there are some exceptions, as outlined earlier. If you are travelling to one of these countries and are supposed to get your visa at the airport, be sure to have some proof (a fax or telex with a visa number) that you have a visa waiting for you at your destination or you may not be allowed to board the plane.

Photocopies
Photocopies of your passport, health certificate, insurance information, plane tickets, employment documents, professional qualifications and anything else of similar importance that you plan to take with you should be left in a secure place back home where someone else can access them for you if the need arises. Leave copies of your travellers' cheques and credit card numbers in the same place. It is also a good idea to carry a second set of photocopies of all this stuff with you in some secure place so that if everything else gets stolen you will have all this information. You might also want to put US$100 or so in that secure place, just in case.

Travel Permits
Travel permits are only necessary in Saudi Arabia and Oman.

In Saudi Arabia, foreigners resident in the Kingdom need a letter from their sponsor to travel anywhere outside the province in which they reside. People visiting the country on a business visa do not need these letters. Everyone, however, needs a site permit to visit old forts and archaeological sites. These are issued at the Riyadh Museum and, for some Eastern Province sites, at the Dammam Museum. Processing a permit usually takes a couple of days. The permits are free.

Permits are also needed to visit most of Oman's sites of interest. These are issued free and in about one minute at the Ministry of Culture & National Heritage adjacent to the Natural History Museum in the Medinat Qaboos section of Muscat.

Foreigners living in Oman need a road permit to enter or leave the country by land. These must be obtained through your sponsor.

See the Saudi Arabia and Oman chapters for further details.

Travel Insurance
Travel insurance is always a good idea and is often quite affordable. In the USA, Council Travel, which has offices in many

major US cities, offers affordable policies that cover most contingencies. Similar affordable policies are available in Britain through BUPA.

Driving Licence

You can use a western driving licence in any Gulf country except Bahrain, where an International Driving Permit (IDP) is required. The length of time you can use your home licence for varies from place to place. In Saudi Arabia and the UAE it seems to be more or less open-ended. In Qatar, you have to get a local licence after seven days.

In all of the Gulf States you will have to get a local licence if you are coming to the country to live and work. These can usually be issued against your old driving licence from your home country without your having to take a test.

IDPs, while not strictly necessary outside of Bahrain, are a useful document to have. They do not cost much and are usually issued through travel agencies or the automobile association in your home country. Remember that an IDP is only valid when carried in conjunction with your licence from home.

Hostel Card

Saudi Arabia, Bahrain and the UAE all have youth hostels. These countries are HI members and HI cards are always required. Foreigners can purchase cards on the spot in all three countries.

Other Documents

Student, Youth and Seniors' cards are of little use anywhere in the Gulf.

CUSTOMS

The import of alcohol is forbidden in Saudi Arabia, Kuwait, Qatar and Sharjah (UAE). You can only bring alcohol into Oman if you arrive by air. See the relevant Facts for the Visitor sections in the individual country chapters for information on duty-free allowances for tobacco.

Video tapes are a particularly sensitive subject throughout the Gulf and customs officers in all the countries covered in this book are likely to take them from you at the airport. They will be viewed by censors from the information or interior ministry and returned to you in a few days, though you will probably have to trek back out to the airport to get them.

Video cameras are another pet peeve in many Gulf countries, though these are simply likely to be recorded in your passport.

MONEY
Costs

These vary greatly from place to place, but it is safe to say that you will find it hard to get around on much less than US$40 per day, and in some places a lot more than that will be necessary unless you have a free place to sleep.

Eating cheap is rarely a problem in the Gulf and transport costs range from very cheap to reasonable.

Carrying Money

The Gulf is a very safe place and carrying cash around is not really a problem. Indeed, changing money outside the big cities is enough of a hassle that you may wind up carrying a lot of cash just to spare yourself the bother.

Cash

At the lowest commercial levels – cheap restaurants, bus stations, youth hostels – you will need cash for most transactions. Always try to have small bills handy when you travel by taxi. If you get into an argument over the fare it helps not to have to ask for change.

Travellers' Cheques

Travellers' cheques are appealing because they are safe. The problem can be finding someone to change them. Saudi banks, in particular, seem to have decided that travellers' cheques are not worth the trouble. There are a number of moneychangers in Dubai who seem to agree with them. Carry either AMEX or Thomas Cook cheques as these are the most widely recognised brands. Make sure you have your original purchase receipt with you, since many banks and moneychangers will insist on seeing this before they will change travellers' cheques.

ATMs

Most of the larger banks in the Gulf have ATMs linked into one of the big global clearing systems: Cirrus, Plus, Global Access or Switch. Most Visa and MasterCards issued in the USA and Western Europe are now coded to operate with at least one of these systems, as are many bank-issued ATM cards. A few of the region's cash machines are also linked with AMEX's Express Cash system.

You will need a personal identification number, or PIN, to operate the machines and if you do not have one you should request one from your card issuer several weeks before travelling.

It also pays to find out what sort of commissions are charged by both your bank or card issuer and the local bank whose machine you will be using.

Credit Cards

Credit cards are very widely accepted in the Gulf, even by very small hotels and restaurants. AMEX is probably the most widely accepted card, but users of Visa and MasterCard should have few problems finding someone willing to take their plastic.

International Transfers

Unless you have an account at a local bank in the Gulf these are difficult, if not impossible, to arrange.

Currency Exchange

Moneychangers tend to offer better rates than banks, though they are less likely to take travellers' cheques. At both banks and moneychangers make sure to ask what sort of commission is being charged on the transaction.

Tipping & Bargaining

Tips are not generally expected in the Gulf. Note, however, that the service charge added to most hotel and restaurant bills is not an automatic gratuity that goes to the waiters. It usually goes into the till, and is simply the restaurant's way of making the prices on the menu look 10 to 15% cheaper than they really are. Waiters in the Gulf tend to be paid appallingly low wages, so if the service is good a small tip, while not required, is definitely in order.

As for bargaining, well, this is the Middle East. You can bargain over hotel rates, plane tickets and taxi fares. I've even bargained with moneychangers over the exchange rate. Menu prices are fixed, as are taxi rides when the taxi has a meter. So are the prices in grocery stores. Almost everything else is negotiable. The Gulf is not like Morocco where shopkeepers will routinely quote prices eight or 10 times higher than what they will settle for. I've rarely seen anything come down much below half the originally offered price, and 25 to 30% off the first quote is more or less the norm. This will vary from place to place and product to product. See the individual country sections for further details.

Taxes & Refunds

By western standards the Gulf is a very low-tax area. There is often a tax of 5% or so on hotel bills, and sometimes on restaurant bills as well, but the smallest places often simply ignore this.

POST & COMMUNICATIONS
Post

The postal systems in all the Gulf countries are very good. Even from the remoter parts of Saudi Arabia you should have no trouble sending mail home.

Incoming mail is a different story. Poste restante is not widely available in the Gulf and AMEX will hold clients' mail in only a few countries. Incoming packages, even fairly small ones, are usually sent to customs for lengthy searches, in the course of which almost any books or magazines that may have been included disappear. Anyone foolish enough to mail you videos has, essentially, thrown away the cost of the postage.

Telephone

The telephone systems throughout the Gulf are excellent. Home country direct services are available from every Gulf country except Oman, though in some cases the home country direct services only work to the USA. Bahrain has the largest system of these services.

Telephone offices are located in most towns of any size. In the UAE and Oman widespread phonecard systems make calling home relatively easy without either going to an office and booking a call or carrying around a small mountain of change.

Fax

Fax machines are now widespread in the Gulf. Even the smallest hotels often have them. Whenever possible, fax numbers for hotels (in all price categories) have been included. In most countries you can send faxes from the local telephone office. If this does not work, or the service is not available, it is usually possible to send faxes from any medium-size or larger hotel.

BOOKS

Most books are published in different editions by different publishers in different countries. As a result, a book might be a hardcover rarity in one country while it's readily available in paperback in another. Fortunately, bookshops and libraries search by title or author, so your local bookshop or library is best placed to advise you on the availability of the following recommendations.

The books listed here contain general information about the Gulf or the Middle East. Many of these books may also be listed in the country chapters.

Lonely Planet

LP's *Middle East on a shoestring* provides a condensed coverage of the Gulf, in addition to Turkey, Egypt, Syria, Jordan, Israel, Lebanon, Iraq, Iran, Yemen and Afghanistan.

Guidebooks

If you walk into a bookshop in most places

in the Gulf and ask to see the local guidebooks, the clerk is likely to show you either a shelf of glossy coffee-table books or a local commercial directory with a title like *Kuwait Business & Tourism Guide*. The former might be a nice souvenir to take home. The latter is likely to consist of little more than advertising interspersed with lists of telephone numbers.

There are few good travel guides to the Gulf and fewer still that are updated as often as they ought to be. Most of what is available could generously be described as sketchy, and far too much of it is, essentially, advertising. Most books cover only one of the Gulf countries and many, the few available regional guides included, are aimed exclusively at up-market business travellers.

If you need a guidebook that also covers things like commercial law in detail, your best bet is probably *The Economist Business Traveller's Guide to the Arabian Peninsula*. This is an excellent reference tool for those looking for a commercial licence, but it tells you precious little about what to do in your spare time, where to stay (if you can't afford a five-star hotel) or where to eat (aside from the restaurants in those same big hotels).

The London-based *Middle East Economic Digest* publishes a series of country-by-country travel guides to the Gulf, the *MEED Practical Guides*. These were originally issued in the late 1970s and a few, such as *Qatar*, have hardly been updated since then. At the time of writing the only really up-to-date titles in the series were the books on Saudi Arabia and the UAE. MEED Guides have their good points. They, too, cover commercial law in depth, and they are aimed largely at expatriate residents. However, their coverage of things like museums and archaeological sites is sketchy and the descriptions of hotels and restaurants appear to be written by the establishments themselves. They are also expensive – US$30 to US$40 a copy.

History

Most books covering the history of the Gulf tend to be either heavy academic works or propagandist in tone. Books on the broader history of the Middle East pass only fleetingly over the Gulf. An exception is Peter Mansfield's *The Arabs*, which is also one of the better books with that particular catch-all title. In addition to a broad-brush history of the Middle East, Mansfield comments on the individual countries in the region. Dilip Hiro's *Inside the Middle East* is also quite good.

If you are genuinely serious about the region's history, politics and economics (and you like books that are heavy on statistical charts), there's the *Area Handbook for the Persian Gulf States* by Richard Nyrop et al. This is a manual compiled by a team of researchers at the American University in Washington DC and published by the US Government Printing Office. It is used for training US diplomats and soldiers headed for the region. It covers Kuwait, Bahrain, Qatar, the UAE and Oman. Another book in the same series covers Saudi Arabia. You will almost certainly have to go to a specialist bookshop to find it, or order a copy directly from the USGPO. The handbooks are available only in hard cover.

Daniel Yergin's *The Prize*, a history of the oil industry, is essential reading for anyone headed to the Gulf, though its scope is worldwide rather than strictly Middle Eastern.

There have been dozens, maybe hundreds, of books written on the Gulf War. These run the gamut from breathless glorification of the military aspects of the conflict to furious polemics against one side or the other. The war also produced an extraordinary number of self-serving memoirs by everyone from the politicians and generals at the top of the chain of command to the journalists who covered the fighting. One of the few really good books on the subject is *Guardians of the Gulf* by Michael A Palmer. It is particularly useful because it traces the US and British involvement in the region's security arrangements back to the late 18th century, rather than acting as though the events of 1990-91 emerged out of nowhere (Iraq does not invade Kuwait until you are more than halfway through the book).

Among the best general histories of the Middle East is Albert Hourani's *A History of the Arab Peoples*. There's not a lot of information specifically on the Gulf in Hourani's book, but as a general introduction to the region's history and philosophy you could hardly do better. Among the old-line Orientalists, John Bagot Glubb's *A Short History of the Arab Peoples* is still worth reading today.

People & Society

Possibly the best single overview of life, business and culture in the Gulf is *The Merchants* by Michael Field. While ostensibly focusing on the rise of nine of the Gulf's prominent merchant families, it is really a book about Arabian society, how it works and how it has changed since the discovery of oil. *The New Arabians* (1981) by Peter Mansfield is an introduction to both the history and society of the Gulf, though the focus is mostly on Saudi Arabia. The general tone of the book is fairly uncontroversial, and it might also be noted that it only carries the history of the region up to about late early 1980.

Peter Theroux gives a witty, candid portrait of culture and politics in the Middle East in his book *Sandstorms – Days and Nights in Arabia*.

For travel literature try Jonathan Raban's *Arabia Through the Looking Glass*. Raban's observations on expatriate life in the region are as valid today as they were during the oil boom (he visited in early 1979) and, unlike many travel writers, he found the time to speak with a lot of Gulf Arabs in addition to the expats. Another good read is Christopher Dickey's *Expats*, which explores the interaction between the Arabs and the expats in the Middle East.

Women

Women's role in society in the Middle East is a topic often discussed, and often misunderstood, in the west. Over the last few years a number of books addressing the subject have come out, helping to take the perception of women and their role in the Muslim world beyond old stereotypes.

Fatima Mernissi, a Moroccan scholar, and Nawal El-Saadawi, an Egyptian physician and novelist, are probably the female Arab writers best known to western readers. Mernissi's *Beyond the Veil – Male/Female Dynamics in Modern Muslim Society* and El-Saadawi's *The Hidden Face of Eve* are among the best for starting your exploration of the subject of women in the Muslim world. *She Has No Place in Paradise*, a collection of El-Saadawi's short fiction, is another widely available work.

On an academic level the work of the Norwegian scholar Unni Wikan has been ground breaking. Her book *Behind the Veil in Arabia – Women in Oman* may take a bit of looking to find, but is well worth the effort. Wikan's focus is primarily on rural society. For a historical look at women in the more urban parts of the Middle East, see *Images of Women – The Portrayal of Women in Photography in the Middle East 1860-1950* by Sarah Graham-Brown.

A more recent addition to this genre of literature is *Nine Parts of Desire – The Hidden World of Islamic Women* by Geraldine Brooks.

Be warned that, aside from Wikan, few of these books have much to say about the Gulf countries per se. Also, none of them find much favour with the (all-male) powers that be in the Gulf States.

Islam

You cannot hope to understand the Gulf without some understanding of Islam and its history. If you are looking for a relatively short book on Islamic beliefs and practices which is aimed at the general reader, one of the best is *Mohammedanism – An Historical Survey* by HAR Gibb. If, on the other hand, you want to immerse yourself in the minutiae

What is Islamic Fundamentalism?

Is there a more over-used term in the Western media these days? Since the Iranian revolution of 1979, the western world has been alternately fascinated and appalled by the excesses committed in the name of 'Islamic Fundamentalism'. Yet for most scholars, the term is almost meaningless since it lumps together a wide range of groups and individual believers – some violent, but most not – with little in common save their profession of the Islamic faith.

It is instructive to note that the word is rarely used in the Arabic-speaking world. In the strict sense 'fundamentalism' (the term, by the way, originated in the USA in the 1920s and was used almost exclusively to refer to protestant Christians as recently as the late '70s) is an entirely laudable desire to return to the basics of religion, to the uncluttered essence of Islam as a faith. A handful of Muslim governments, such as Saudi Arabia and Iran, claim to have achieved this and most others say they are working hard at it.

Arab governments tend to refer to religiously-based opposition groups or parties they do not like as 'extremists' or 'terrorists', regardless of whether or not the groups in question use or advocate violence (and most do not). These Islamist parties, as western scholars usually call them, tend to refer to their governments as 'infidels', 'apostates' or 'secularists'. Each side, in effect, excommunicates the other for the crime of failing to adhere to its own vision of Muslim life.

The problem with the term 'fundamentalist' is that it is essentially undefinable. Members of Egypt's Muslim Brotherhood tell visitors their goal is to build a truly Islamic society. But both Saudi Arabia and Iran, as different as they are, claim to have such a society already, and one thing Egypt's Muslim Brothers are at pains to emphasise is that they do not want to remake their country along either Saudi or Iranian lines. That, they will tell you, is overdoing it. Yet in Saudi Arabia itself there are people who believe their society has strayed from the path of Islam and must return to a *more* conservative life style than it now has. By Saudi standards, the 'fundamentalist' members of the Kuwaiti parliament are shockingly liberal.

Social trends in a religion as widely spread as Islam cannot be encapsulated in a single word. The scholarly community has been trying to retire the term 'fundamentalist' for more than a decade. More power to them. ■

of Islamic history, culture and civilisation, the best work on the subject in English is Marshall GS Hodgson's *The Venture of Islam*. Even if you have no intention of wading through three volumes of Hodgson (totalling some 1500 pages), the first 100 pages of volume one (the 'Introduction to the Study of Islamic Civilization' and the 'General Prologue') are required reading for anyone headed for the Middle East.

Another work worth taking a look at is Richard Burton's *Personal Narrative of a Pilgrimage to Al-Madinah & Meccah*, originally published in 1855. Burton, an English soldier and explorer, joined the 1853 hajj caravan from Cairo. He remains one of the few non-Muslims to have participated in the hajj.

The Koran itself is considered to be notoriously difficult to translate. Pious Muslims insist that it cannot be translated, only rendered or interpreted, into other languages. AJ Arberry's *The Koran Interpreted* is generally accounted to be the best version available in English.

Those interested in Islamic literature should try another of Arberry's works, *Aspects of Islamic Civilization*, or James Kritzeck's *Anthology of Islamic Literature*.

Islam & The West

The idea that the west is locked in some sort of struggle with the Islamic world (for which, usually, read the Arab Middle East and Iran) has captured the imagination of many scholars, journalists and politicians in both the west and the Middle East in recent years. This struggle is usually seen as taking place on a variety of levels – security, immigration and economics to name but a few – and there is a growing cottage industry in books on the subject.

One of the best in this genre is *The Closed Circle – An Interpretation of the Arabs* by David Pryce-Jones. Other noteworthy contributions to the literature include *Islam and the West* by the respected US scholar Bernard Lewis and *The Failure of Political Islam* by Olivier Roy.

NEWSPAPERS & MAGAZINES

All of the Gulf countries have local English-language newspapers. The best are *Arab Times* in Kuwait, *Arab News* in Saudi Arabia and *Gulf News* in the UAE. These, and their erstwhile competitors, provide fairly comprehensive coverage of regional events, though they will not tell you a lot about the Gulf itself.

Foreign publications such as the *International Herald Tribune*, the *Financial Times*, *The Daily Telegraph*, *The Independent*, *Le Monde* and the major German papers are all widely available in the Gulf. These arrive between one and three days late, depending on the country.

RADIO & TV

English-language stations are on the air in eastern Saudi Arabia, Bahrain, Kuwait, Qatar, Abu Dhabi, Dubai and Muscat. In Riyadh, Jeddah and Kuwait City you can also pick up the US military's Armed Forces Radio & Television Service (AFRTS) broadcasts, which mix canned programmes and news from the USA with US military DJs.

BBC broadcasts can be received on a number of short-wave frequencies including 12.095 MHz, 11.760 MHz, 9.410 MHz and 15.070 MHz, 15.575 MHz throughout the day. You can also get the BBC 1323 MW in some places. Rental cars often come equipped with short-wave radios.

All of the Gulf countries also have English-language TV stations. These usually broadcast in the evening and carry a mix of old US, British and Australian shows and the occasional locally produced magazine programme. Most hotels, including small ones, have satellite TV.

VIDEO SYSTEMS

All of the Gulf States use the PAL video system. This has limited compatibility with the SECAM system in use in France and is not compatible with the NTSC systems in use in the USA. Videos sent out from the USA will not work on Gulf TVs unless the set and video player are both 'multi-system' units that accept the NTSC system.

PHOTOGRAPHY & VIDEO

The basic rules in the Gulf are simple – do not photograph anything even vaguely military in nature (this always includes airports); do not photograph people without their permission; and never photograph women.

Bahrain and the UAE are the most relaxed countries in the Gulf when it comes to photography, while Kuwait and Oman seem to have the broadest definitions of what constitutes a 'strategic' site. In Saudi Arabia it often seems that the authorities just don't like cameras.

Few officials in the Gulf will be pleased by photographs of tents, run-down houses or anything which resembles poverty, as the tendency is to emphasise what the country has achieved in the last few decades.

TIME

Saudi Arabia, Kuwait, Bahrain and Qatar are three hours ahead of GMT/UTC. The UAE and Oman are four hours ahead of GMT/UTC. Summer daylight saving time is not observed in any of the Gulf countries.

ELECTRICITY

Everything from 110 to 240 volts AC can be found coming out of the wall somewhere in the Gulf. Continental, British-style and US-style sockets are all in use. See the individual country chapters for details.

WEIGHTS & MEASURES

The metric system is in use throughout the Gulf, but there are some local variations – for example, petrol is sold by the imperial gallon in the UAE.

LAUNDRY

There are no laundrettes in the Gulf but most larger cities have small (usually Indian-run) laundry shops. These places generally take about 24 hours to wash and iron your laundry, and their prices are usually very low. See the individual city entries for further details.

HEALTH

Travel health depends on your pre-departure preparations, your day-to-day health care while travelling and how you handle any medical problem or emergency that does develop. While the list of potential dangers can seem quite frightening, with a little luck, some basic precautions and adequate information few travellers experience more than upset stomachs.

Throughout the Gulf the quality of health care is very high. When the Gulf States began to prosper, their rulers invested huge sums of money in hospitals, clinics and long-term health programmes. The result is that countries which only a generation or two ago were ridden by famines and epidemics (which the Bedouin traditionally used as a way of marking time – for example, a child would be said to have been born 'in the year after the year of measles') now enjoy a standard of health care which equals that of the richest countries in the west. In some Gulf countries medical care is free; in others the costs are relatively nominal. For details see the Health section in the individual country chapters.

The flip side of this is that some Gulf countries, particularly Saudi Arabia, are very reluctant to acknowledge outbreaks of infectious diseases. Western embassies tend to be the best sources of up-to-date information on any local contagious diseases.

Travel Health Guides

There are a number of books on travel health:

Staying Healthy in Asia, Africa & Latin America, Dirk Schroeder, Moon Publications, 1994. Probably the best all-round guide to carry, as it's compact but very detailed and well organised.
Travellers' Health, Dr Richard Dawood, Oxford University Press, 1995. Comprehensive, easy to read, authoritative and also highly recommended, although it's rather large to lug around.
Where There is No Doctor, David Werner, Macmillan, 1994. A very detailed guide intended for someone, like a Peace Corps worker, going to work in an underdeveloped country, rather than for the average traveller.

Travel with Children, Maureen Wheeler, Lonely Planet Publications, 1995. Includes basic advice on travel health for younger children.

Pre-Departure Preparations

Health Insurance A travel insurance policy to cover theft, loss and medical problems is a wise idea. There are a wide variety of policies available and your travel agent will be able to make recommendations. The international student travel policies handled by STA or other student travel organisations are usually good value. Some policies offer lower and higher medical-expense options but the higher one is chiefly for countries like the USA which have extremely high medical costs. Check the small print:

- Some policies specifically exclude 'dangerous activities' which can include scuba diving, motorcycling, even trekking. If such activities are on your agenda you don't want that sort of policy. A locally acquired motorcycle licence may not be valid under your policy.
- You may prefer a policy which pays doctors or hospitals direct rather than you having to pay on the spot and claim later. If you have to claim later make sure you keep all documentation. Some policies ask you to call back (reverse charges) to a centre in your home country where an immediate assessment of your problem is made.
- Check if the policy covers ambulances or an emergency flight home. If you have to stretch out you will need two seats and somebody has to pay for them!
- Make sure that the policy you have in mind covers the Gulf. Some insurers, particularly in the USA, still consider the Gulf a danger zone and either will not cover travel there or will insist on exorbitant premiums. It pays to ask these sort of questions in advance rather than discover too late that your policy does not cover the country you are in. If you are working in the Gulf your job will almost certainly include medical coverage of some sort but be sure to find out its exact extent – it may include business trips but not holiday travel, for example.

Medical Kit A small, straightforward medical kit is a wise thing to carry. A possible kit list includes:

- Aspirin or paracetamol – for pain or fever.
- Bandages and Band-aids – for minor injuries.
- Insect repellent, sunscreen, suntan lotion, chap stick and water purification tablets.
- Calamine lotion – to ease irritation from bites or stings.
- Scissors, tweezers and a thermometer (note that mercury thermometers are prohibited by airlines).
- Antihistamine (such as Benadryl) – useful as a decongestant for colds and allergies, to ease the itch from insect bites or stings, and to help prevent motion sickness. Antihistamines may cause sedation and interact with alcohol so care should be taken when using them.
- Antibiotics – useful if you're travelling well off the beaten track, but they must be prescribed and you should carry the prescription with you. Some individuals are allergic to commonly prescribed antibiotics such as penicillin or sulpha drugs. It would be sensible to always carry this information when travelling.
- Loperamide (eg Imodium) or Lomotil for diarrhoea; prochlorperazine (eg Stemetil) or metaclopramide (eg Maxalon) for nausea and vomiting. Antidiarrhoea medication should not be given to children under the age of 12.
- Rehydration mixture – for treatment of severe diarrhoea. This is particularly important if travelling with children, but is recommended for everyone.
- Antiseptic such as povidone-iodine (eg Betadine), which comes as a solution, impregnated swabs and ointment, and an antibiotic powder or similar 'dry' spray – for cuts and grazes.

Ideally, antibiotics should be administered only under medical supervision and should never be taken indiscriminately. Take only the recommended dose at the prescribed intervals and continue using the antibiotic for the prescribed period, even if the illness seems to be cured earlier. Antibiotics are quite specific to the infections they can treat. Stop immediately if there are any serious reactions and don't use it at all if you are unsure if you have the correct one.

Health Preparations Make sure you're healthy before you start travelling. If you are embarking on a long trip make sure your teeth are OK.

If you wear glasses take a spare pair and your prescription. Losing your glasses can be a real problem, although in many places you can get new spectacles made up quickly, cheaply and competently.

If you require a particular medication take an adequate supply, as it may not be available locally. Take the prescription or, better still, part of the packaging showing the generic rather than the brand name (which may not be locally available), as it will make getting replacements easier. It's a wise idea to have a legible prescription with you to show you legally use the medication – it's surprising how often over-the-counter drugs from one

place are illegal without a prescription or even banned in another. If you are travelling to Saudi Arabia it is particularly important that you do this as the Saudis are very strict on the import of prescription drugs. Consult someone at a Saudi embassy beforehand, though be warned that this can be a rather frustrating experience.

Vaccinations

The following vaccinations are recommended for those travelling to the Arab Gulf States:

Cholera Not required by law, but occasionally travellers face bureaucratic problems on some border crossings. Protection is poor and it lasts only six months. It is contraindicated in pregnancy.

Tetanus & Diphtheria Boosters are necessary every 10 years and protection is highly recommended.

Polio A booster of either the oral or injected vaccine is required every 10 years to maintain our immunity from childhood vaccination. Polio is a very serious, easily transmitted disease. The incidence of polio is low in the Gulf.

Typhoid Available either as an injection or oral capsules. Protection lasts from one to five years. There are high rates of infection in most Gulf states. You may get some side effects such as pain at the injection site, fever, headache and a general unwell feeling. A new single-dose injectable vaccine, which appears to have few side effects, is now available but is more expensive. Side effects are unusual with the oral form but occasionally an individual will have stomach cramps.

Hepatitis A The most common travel-acquired illness which can be prevented by vaccination. Protection can be provided in two ways – either with the antibody gamma globulin or with a new vaccine called Havrix.

Havrix provides long-term immunity (possibly more than 10 years) after an initial course of two injections and a booster at one year. It may be more expensive than gamma globulin but certainly has many advantages, including length of protection and ease of administration. It is important to know that being a vaccine, it will take about three weeks to provide satisfactory protection – hence the need for careful planning prior to travel.

Gamma globulin is not a vaccination but a ready-made antibody which has proven very successful in reducing the chances of hepatitis infection. Because it may interfere with the development of immunity, it should not be given until at least 10 days after administration of the last vaccine needed; it should also be given as close as possible to departure because it is at its most effective in the first few weeks after administration – the effectiveness tapers off gradually between three and six months.

Hepatitis B Travellers at risk of contact (see Infectious Diseases) are strongly advised to be vaccinated, especially if they are children or if they have close contact with children. Vaccination is recommended for people living in the Gulf. The vaccination course comprises three injections given over a six-month period then boosters every three to five years. The initial course of injections can be given over as short a period as 28 days then boosted after 12 months if more rapid protection is required.

Tuberculosis TB risk should be considered for people travelling more than three months to the Arab Gulf States. A skin test before and after travel, to determine whether exposure has occurred, may be all that is required as the value of vaccination of healthy adults is uncertain as they usually do not get symptoms. However, vaccination is recommended for children who will be travelling more than three months.

Yellow Fever Protection lasts 10 years and is recommended where the disease is endemic, chiefly in Africa and South America. You usually have to go to a special yellow-fever vaccination centre. Vaccination is contraindicated during pregnancy but if you must travel to a high-risk area it is probably advisable.

Rabies Pre-travel rabies vaccination involves having three injections over 21 to 28 days and should be considered by those who will spend a month or longer in a country where rabies is common, especially if they are cycling, handling animals, caving, travelling to remote areas, or for children (who may not report a bite). If someone who has been vaccinated is bitten or scratched by an animal they will require two booster injections of vaccine. ∎

Immunisations Vaccinations provide protection against diseases.

It is important to understand the distinction between vaccines recommended for travel in certain areas and those required by law. Currently yellow fever is the only vaccine subject to international health regulations. Vaccination as an entry requirement is usually only enforced when coming from an infected area.

Occasionally travellers face bureaucratic problems regarding cholera vaccine even though all countries have dropped it as a health requirement for travel. Under some situations it may be wise to have the vaccine despite its poor protection, eg for the trans-Africa traveller.

On the other hand a number of vaccines are recommended for travel in certain areas. These may not be required by law but they are recommended for your own personal protection.

All vaccinations should be recorded on an International Health Certificate, which is available from your physician or government health department.

Plan ahead for getting your vaccinations: some of them require an initial shot followed by a booster, while some vaccinations should not be given together. It is recommended you seek medical advice at least six weeks prior to travel.

Most travellers from western countries will have been immunised against various diseases during childhood but your doctor may still recommend booster shots against measles or polio, diseases still prevalent in many developing countries. The period of protection offered by vaccinations differs widely and some are contraindicated if you are pregnant.

In some countries immunisations are available from airport or government health centres. Travel agencies or airline offices will tell you where.

Basic Rules

Care in what you eat and drink is the most important health rule; stomach upsets are the most likely travel health problem (between 30 and 50% of travellers in a two-week stay experience this) but the majority of these upsets will be relatively minor. Don't become paranoid – trying the local food is part of the experience of travel after all.

Water The number one rule is *don't drink the water* and that includes ice. If you don't know for certain that the water is safe always assume the worst. The quality of tap water varies widely in the Gulf. In Oman it is absolutely OK, but in Bahrain it is absolutely off limits. See the Health section of the individual country chapters for more details.

Reputable brands of bottled water or soft drinks are generally fine though you should make sure that the seal on your bottle of mineral water has not been broken. Only use water from containers with a serrated seal – not tops or corks. Take care with fruit juice, particularly if water may have been added.

Dairy products in the Gulf are generally manufactured to western standards, though in more remote places you might want to check the 'use by' date and see whether the products are pasteurised and have been stored properly. Boiled milk is fine if it is kept hygienically and yoghurt is always good. Tea or coffee should also be OK since the water should have been boiled.

Water Purification The simplest way of purifying water is to boil it thoroughly.

Vigorously boiling for five minutes should be satisfactory; however, at high altitude water boils at a lower temperature, so germs are less likely to be killed.

Simple filtering will not remove all dangerous organisms, so if you cannot boil water it should be treated chemically. Chlorine tablets (Puritabs, Steritabs or other brand names) will kill many but not all pathogens, including giardia and amoebic cysts. Iodine is very effective in purifying water and is available in tablet form (such as Potable Aqua), but follow the directions carefully and remember that too much iodine can be harmful.

If you can't find tablets, tincture of iodine (2%) or iodine crystals can be used. Four drops of tincture of iodine per litre or quart of clear water is the recommended dosage; the treated water should be left to stand for 20 to 30 minutes before drinking. Iodine crystals can also be used to purify water but this is a more complicated process, as you have to first prepare a saturated iodine solution. Iodine loses its effectiveness if exposed to air or damp so keep it in a tightly sealed container. Flavoured powder will disguise the taste of treated water and is a good idea if you are travelling with children.

Food Salads and fruit should be washed with purified water or peeled where possible. Ice cream is usually OK if it is a reputable brand name, but beware of street vendors and of ice cream that has melted and been refrozen. Thoroughly cooked food is safest but not if it has been left to cool or if it has been reheated. Shellfish such as mussels, oysters and clams should be avoided as well as undercooked meat, particularly in the form of mince. Steaming does not make shellfish safe for eating.

If a place looks clean and well run and if the vendor also looks clean and healthy, then the food is probably safe. In general, places that are packed with travellers or locals will be fine, while empty restaurants are questionable. The food in busy restaurants is cooked and eaten quite quickly with little standing around, and is probably not reheated.

Nutrition If your food is poor or limited in availability, if you're travelling hard and fast and therefore missing meals, or if you simply lose your appetite, you can soon start to lose weight and place your health at risk.

Make sure your diet is well balanced. Eggs, tofu, beans, lentils (dhal in the Gulf's numerous Indian restaurants) and nuts are all safe ways to get protein. Fruit you can peel (eg bananas, oranges or mandarins) is usually safe and a good source of vitamins. Try to eat plenty of grains (including rice) and bread. Remember that although food is generally safer if it is cooked well, over-cooked food loses much of its nutritional

value. If your diet isn't well balanced or if your food intake is insufficient, it's a good idea to take vitamin and iron pills.

In hot climates make sure you drink enough – don't rely on feeling thirsty to indicate when you should drink. Not needing to urinate or very dark yellow urine is a danger sign. Always carry a water bottle with you on long trips. Excessive sweating can lead to loss of salt and therefore muscle cramping. Salt tablets are not a good idea as a preventative, but in places where salt is not used much adding salt to food can help.

Medical Problems & Treatment
Self-diagnosis and treatment of medical problems can be risky, so wherever possible seek qualified help. Although we do give treatment dosages in this section, they are for emergency use only. Medical advice should be sought before administering any drugs.

An embassy or consulate can usually recommend a good place to go for such advice. So can five-star hotels, although they often recommend doctors with five-star prices. (This is when that medical insurance really comes in useful!) You can, however, take some comfort from the fact that the standard of medical care throughout the Gulf is among the highest in the world.

Environmental Hazards
Sunburn It should hardly need saying that this is a potential problem in the Gulf. In the desert or at high altitude you can get sunburnt surprisingly quickly, even through cloud. Use a sunscreen and take extra care to cover areas which don't normally see the sun – eg your feet. A hat provides added protection and in the Gulf can be considered a necessity. You should also use zinc cream or some other barrier cream for your nose and lips. Calamine lotion is good for mild sunburn.

Prickly Heat Prickly heat is an itchy rash caused by excessive perspiration trapped under the skin. It usually strikes people who have just arrived in a hot climate and whose pores have not yet opened sufficiently to cope with greater sweating. Keeping cool but bathing often, using a mild talcum powder or even resorting to air-conditioning may help until you acclimatise.

Heat Exhaustion Dehydration or salt deficiency can cause heat exhaustion. However, life in the Gulf is now so universally air-conditioned that this is less of a problem than you might think. Still, it pays to take time to acclimatise to high temperatures and make sure you get sufficient liquids. Salt deficiency is characterised by fatigue, lethargy, headaches, giddiness and muscle cramps and in this case salt tablets may help. Vomiting or diarrhoea can deplete your liquid and salt levels. Anhydrotic heat exhaustion, caused by an inability to sweat, is quite rare. Unlike other forms of heat exhaustion it is likely to strike people who have been in a hot climate for some time, rather than newcomers.

Heat Stroke This serious, and sometimes fatal, condition can occur if the body's heat-regulating mechanism breaks down and the body temperature rises to dangerous levels. Long, continuous periods of exposure to high temperatures can leave you vulnerable to heat stroke. You should avoid excessive alcohol or strenuous activity when you first arrive in a hot climate.

The symptoms are feeling unwell, not sweating very much or at all and a high body temperature (39 to 41°C). Where sweating has ceased the skin becomes flushed and red. Severe, throbbing headaches and lack of coordination will also occur, and the sufferer may be confused or aggressive. Eventually the victim will become delirious or convulse. Hospitalisation is essential, but meanwhile get patients out of the sun, remove their clothing, cover them with a wet sheet or towel and then fan continually.

Fungal Infections Fungal infections, which occur with greater frequency in hot weather, are most likely to occur on the scalp, between the toes or fingers (athlete's foot), in the groin (jock itch or crotch rot) and on the body (ringworm). You get ringworm (which is a fungal infection, not a worm) from infected animals or by walking on damp areas, like shower floors.

To prevent fungal infections wear loose, comfortable clothes, avoid artificial fibres, wash frequently and dry carefully. If you do get an infection, wash the infected area daily with a disinfectant or medicated soap and water, and rinse and dry well. Apply an antifungal powder like the widely available Tinaderm. Try to expose the infected area to air or sunlight as much as possible and wash all towels and underwear in hot water as well as changing them often.

Infectious Diseases

Diarrhoea A change of water, food or climate can all cause the runs; diarrhoea caused by contaminated food or water is more serious. Despite all your precautions you may still have a bout of mild travellers' diarrhoea, but a few rushed toilet trips with no other symptoms is not indicative of a serious problem. Moderate diarrhoea, involving half a dozen loose movements in a day, is more of a nuisance. Dehydration is the main danger with any diarrhoea, particularly for children for whom dehydration can occur more quickly. Fluid replacement remains the mainstay of management. Weak black tea with a little sugar, soda water, or soft drinks allowed to go flat and diluted 50% with water are all good. With severe diarrhoea a rehydrating solution is necessary to replace minerals and salts. Commercially available oral rehydration salts (ORS) are very useful; add the contents of one sachet to a litre of boiled or bottled water. In an emergency you can make up a solution of eight teaspoons of sugar to a litre of boiled water and provide salted cracker biscuits at the same time. You should stick to a bland diet as you recover.

Lomotil or Imodium can be used to bring relief from the symptoms, although they do not actually cure the problem. Only use these drugs if absolutely necessary – eg, if you *must* travel. For children under 12 years Lomotil and Imodium are not recommended. Under all circumstances fluid replacement is the most important thing to remember. Do not use these drugs if the person has a high fever or is severely dehydrated.

In certain situations antibiotics may be indicated:

- Watery diarrhoea with blood and mucous. (Gut-paralysing drugs like Imodium or Lomotil should be avoided in this situation.)
- Watery diarrhoea with fever and lethargy.
- Persistent diarrhoea for more than five days.
- Severe diarrhoea, if it is logistically difficult to stay in one place.

The recommended drugs (adults only) would be either norfloxacin, 400 mg twice daily for three days, or ciprofloxacin, 500 mg twice daily for three days.

The drug bismuth subsalicylate has also been used successfully. It is not available in Australia. The dosage for adults is two tablets or 30 ml and for children it is one tablet or 10 ml. This dose can be repeated every 30 minutes to one hour, with no more than eight doses in a 24-hour period.

The drug of choice in children would be co-trimoxazole (Bactrim, Septrin, Resprim) with dosage dependent on weight. A three-day course is also given.

Ampicillin has been recommended in the past and it may still be an alternative. People who are allergic to penicillin should not take ampicillin.

Giardiasis The parasite causing this intestinal disorder is present in contaminated water. The symptoms are stomach cramps, nausea, a bloated stomach, watery, foul-smelling diarrhoea and frequent gas. Giardiasis can appear several weeks after you have been exposed to the parasite. The symptoms may disappear for a few days and then return; this can go on for several weeks. Tinidazole, known as Fasigyn, or metronidazole (Flagyl) are the recommended drugs for treatment. Either can be used in a single treatment dose. Antibiotics are of no use.

Dysentery Dysentery is not generally a problem in the Gulf, but should you come down with it, it should be treated as serious.

It is caused by contaminated food or water and is characterised by severe diarrhoea, often with blood or mucus in the stool. There are two kinds of dysentery. Bacillary dysentery is characterised by a high fever and rapid onset; headache, vomiting and stomach pains are also symptoms. It generally does not last longer than a week, but it is highly contagious.

Amoebic dysentery is often more gradual in the onset of symptoms, with cramping, abdominal pain and vomiting less likely; fever may not be present. It is not a self-limiting disease: it will persist until treated and can recur and cause sufferers long-term health problems.

A stool test is necessary to diagnose which kind of dysentery you have, so you should seek medical help urgently. In case of an emergency the drugs norfloxacin or ciprofloxacin can be used as presumptive treatment for bacillary dysentery, and metronidazole (Flagyl) for amoebic dysentery.

For bacillary dysentery, norfloxacin 400 mg twice daily for seven days or ciprofloxacin 500 mg twice daily for seven days are the recommended dosages.

If you're unable to find either of these drugs then a useful alternative is co-trimoxazole 160/800 mg (Bactrim, Septrin, Resprim) twice daily for seven days. This is a sulpha drug and must not be used by people with a known sulpha allergy.

In the case of children the drug co-trimoxazole is a reasonable first-line treatment. For amoebic dysentery, the recommended adult dosage of metronidazole (Flagyl) is one 750-mg to 800-mg capsule three times daily for five days. Children aged between eight and 12 years should have half the adult dose; the dosage for younger children is one-third the adult dose.

An alternative to Flagyl is Fasigyn, taken as a two-gram daily dose for three days. Alcohol must be avoided during treatment and for 48 hours afterwards.

Cholera This is another disease which is now quite rare in the Gulf. Cholera vaccination is not very effective. The bacteria that are responsible for this disease are water-borne, so attention to the rules of eating and drinking should protect the traveller.

Outbreaks of cholera are generally widely reported, so avoid such problem areas.

Hepatitis Hepatitis is a general term for inflammation of the liver. There are many causes of this condition: drugs, alcohol and infections are but a few. Hepatitis is no longer common in the Gulf but it is not unheard of. It *is* common in a number of popular holiday destinations for Gulf-based expats such as Egypt, Kenya and India, for example.

Moreover, the discovery of new strains has led to a virtual alphabet soup, with hepatitis A, B, C, D, E and a rumoured G. These letters identify specific agents that cause viral hepatitis. Viral hepatitis is an infection of the liver, which can lead to jaundice (yellow skin), fever, lethargy and digestive problems. It can have no symptoms at all, with the infected person not knowing that they have the disease. Travellers shouldn't be too paranoid about this apparent proliferation of hepatitis strains; hepatitis C, D, E and G are fairly rare (so far) and following the same precautions as for A and B should be all that's necessary to avoid them.

Viral hepatitis can be divided into two groups on the basis of how it is spread. The first route of transmission is via contaminated food and water (leading to hepatitis A and E) and the second route is via infected blood and body fluids (resulting in hepatitis B, C and D).

Hepatitis A This is a common disease in most Gulf States. Most people are infected as children; they often don't develop symptoms, but do develop life-long immunity. However, the disease poses a real threat to the traveller, as they are unlikely to have been exposed to hepatitis A in developed countries.

The symptoms are fever, chills, headache, fatigue, feelings of weakness and aches and pains, followed by loss of appetite, nausea, vomiting, abdominal pain, dark urine, light-coloured faeces, jaundiced skin and the whites of the eyes may turn yellow. In some cases you may feel unwell, tired, have no appetite, experience aches and pains and be jaundiced. You should seek medical advice, but in general there is not much you can do apart from resting, drinking lots of fluids, eating lightly and avoiding fatty foods. People who have had hepatitis must forego alcohol for six months after the illness, as hepatitis attacks the liver and it needs that amount of time to recover.

The routes of transmission are via contaminated water, shellfish contaminated by sewerage, or foodstuffs sold by food handlers with poor standards of hygiene.

Taking care with what you eat and drink can go a long way towards preventing this disease. But this is a very infectious virus, so if there is any risk of exposure, additional cover is highly recommended. This cover comes in two forms: Gamma globulin and Havrix. Gamma globulin is an injection that gives you the antibodies for hepatitis A, thus providing immunity for a limited time. Havrix is a vaccine that makes you develop your own antibodies, thus giving lasting immunity.

Hepatitis B This is also a very common disease, with almost 300 million chronic carriers in the world. In the Gulf States, in some areas up to 20% of the population carry the Hepatitis B virus. Hepatitis B, which used to be called serum hepatitis, is spread through contact with infected blood, blood products or bodily fluids, for example through sexual contact, unsterilised needles and blood transfusions. Other risk situations include having a shave or tattoo in a local shop, or having your ears pierced. The symptoms of type B are much the same as type A except that they are more severe and may lead to irreparable liver damage or even liver cancer. Although there is no treatment for hepatitis B, a cheap and effective vaccine is available; the only problem is that for long-lasting cover you need a six-month course. Persons who should receive a hepatitis B vaccination include anyone who anticipates contact with blood or other bodily secretions, either as a health-care worker or through sexual contact with the local population, particularly those who intend to stay in the country for a long period of time.

Typhoid Typhoid fever is another gut infection that travels the fecal-oral route – ie contaminated water and food are responsible. Vaccination against typhoid is not totally effective and it is one of the most dangerous infections, so medical help must be sought.

In its early stages typhoid resembles many other illnesses: sufferers may feel like they have a bad cold or flu on the way, as early symptoms are a headache, a sore throat, and a fever which rises a little each day until it is around 40°C or more. The victim's pulse is often slow relative to the degree of fever present and gets slower as the fever rises – unlike a normal fever where the pulse increases. There may also be vomiting, diarrhoea or constipation.

In the second week the high fever and slow pulse continue and a few pink spots may appear on the body; trembling, delirium, weakness, weight loss and dehydration are other symptoms. If there are no further complications, the fever and other symptoms will slowly diminish during the third week. However, you must get medical help before this because pneumonia (acute infection of the lungs) or peritonitis (perforated bowel) are common complications, and because typhoid is very infectious.

The fever should be treated by keeping the victim cool and dehydration should also be watched for.

The drug of choice is ciprofloxacin at a dose of one gram daily for 14 days. It is quite expensive and may not be available. The alternative, chloramphenicol, has been the mainstay of treatment for many years. In many countries it is still the recommended antibiotic but there are fewer side affects with Ampicillin. The adult dosage is two 250-mg capsules, four times a day. Children aged between eight and 12 years should have half the adult dose; younger children should have one-third the adult dose.

People who are allergic to penicillin should not be given Ampicillin.

Worms These parasites are most common in rural, tropical areas and a stool test when you return home is not a bad idea. They can be present on unwashed vegetables or in undercooked meat and you can pick them up through your skin by walking with bare feet. Infestations may not show up for some time, and although they are generally not serious, if left untreated they can cause severe health problems. A stool test is necessary to pinpoint the problem and medication is often available over the counter.

Tetanus Tetanus can strike you down just about anywhere in the world. It is potentially fatal and difficult to treat but is preventable with immunisation. Tetanus occurs when a wound becomes infected by a germ which lives in the faeces of animals so clean all cuts, punctures or animal bites. Tetanus is also known as lockjaw, and the first symptom may be discomfort in swallowing, or stiffening of the jaw and neck; this is followed by painful convulsions of the jaw and whole body.

Rabies Rabies is found in many countries and is caused by a bite or scratch by an infected animal. Dogs are a noted carrier, though there aren't a lot of dogs in most Gulf countries in keeping with the Muslim belief that the dog is an unclean animal. Any bite, scratch or even lick from a warm-blooded, furry animal should be cleaned immediately and thoroughly. Scrub with soap and running water, and then clean with an alcohol solution. If there is any possibility that the animal is infected, medical help should be sought immediately. Even if the animal is not rabid all bites should be treated seriously as they can become infected or can result in tetanus. A rabies vaccination is now available and should be considered if you are in a high-risk category – eg if you intend to explore caves (bat bites can be dangerous) or work with animals.

Meningococcal Meningitis Sub-Saharan Africa is considered the 'meningitis belt' but the disease has appeared in the Gulf several times in recent years. The most serious of these occurrences was in 1987 and appears to have originated with pilgrims who accidentally infected other pilgrims in Mecca during the hajj. Within weeks it was a problem throughout the Gulf, though not every country was willing to acknowledge it. For several years after this outbreak the Saudi authorities required everyone arriving in the country by ship to submit to meningitis jabs before disembarking at Jeddah. Meningococcal meningitis vaccination is not recommended for most travellers to the Gulf, but Saudi Arabia has an entry requirement for all hajj pilgrims to carry a certificate of vaccination. Vaccination provides protection for over a year. Check for reports of current epidemics.

This very serious disease attacks the brain and can be fatal. A scattered, blotchy rash, fever, severe headache, sensitivity to light and neck stiffness which prevents forward bending of the head are the first symptoms. Death can occur within a few hours, so immediate treatment is important.

Treatment is large doses of penicillin given intravenously or, if that is not possible, intramuscularly (ie in the buttocks).

Tuberculosis (TB) There is a world-wide resurgence of tuberculosis and there are high rates of infection in locals in most Gulf States. It is a bacterial infection which is usually transmitted from person to person by coughing but may be transmitted through consumption of unpasteurised milk. Milk that has been boiled is safe to drink, and the souring of milk to make yoghurt or cheese also kills the bacilli.

Typically many months of contact with the infected person are required before the disease is passed on. The usual site of the disease is the lungs, although often other organs may be involved. Most infected people never develop any symptoms. In those who do, especially infants, symptoms may arise within weeks of the infection occurring and may be severe. In most, however, the disease lies dormant for many years until, for some reason, the infected person becomes physically run-down. Symptoms include fever, weight loss, night sweats and coughing.

Diptheria Diptheria can be a skin infection or a more dangerous throat infection. It is spread by contaminated dust contacting the skin or by the inhalation of infected cough or sneeze droplets. Frequent washing and keeping the skin dry will help prevent the skin infection and a vaccination is available to prevent the throat infection. Any treatment should only be given under close medical supervision.

Sexually Transmitted Diseases Sexual contact with an infected sexual partner spreads these diseases. While abstinence is the only 100% preventative, using condoms is also effective. Gonorrhoea, herpes and syphilis are the most common of these diseases; sores, blisters or rashes around the genitals, discharges or pain when urinating are common symptoms. Symptoms may be less marked or not observed at all in women. Syphilis symptoms eventually disappear completely but the disease continues and can cause severe problems in later years. The treatment of gonorrhoea and syphilis is by antibiotics.

There are numerous other sexually transmitted diseases, for most of which effective treatment is available. However, there is no cure for herpes and there is also currently no cure for AIDS. Using condoms is the most effective preventative.

HIV/AIDS HIV, the Human Immunodeficiency Virus, may develop into AIDS, Acquired Immune Deficiency Syndrome. HIV is a major problem in many countries. Any exposure to blood, blood products or bodily fluids may put the individual at risk. In many developing countries transmission is predominantly through heterosexual sexual activity. This is quite different from industrialised countries where transmission is mostly through contact between homosexual or bisexual males, or via contaminated needles shared by IV drug users. Apart from abstinence, the most effective preventative is always to practise safe sex using condoms. It is impossible to detect the HIV-positive status of an otherwise healthy-looking person without a blood test.

HIV/AIDS can also be spread through infected blood transfusions; blood is said to be screened for AIDS in Gulf countries, but most Gulf countries also play down the incidence of AIDS locally. Public education campaigns tend to present the disease as something dangerous but also essentially as a foreign problem.

The disease can also be spread by dirty needles – vaccinations, acupuncture, tattooing and ear or nose piercing can potentially be as dangerous as intravenous drug use if the equipment is not clean. If you do need an injection, ask to see the syringe unwrapped in front of you.

Fear of HIV infection should never preclude treatment for serious medical conditions. Although there may be a risk of infection, it is very small indeed.

Insect-Borne Diseases

Malaria This serious disease is spread by mosquito bites.

Malaria has virtually been eradicated in much of the Gulf. The main area where it has continued to be a problem is Oman and Saudi Arabia. In recent years there have been reports of the disease in both the northern and southern coastal areas of Oman. Travellers to Oman should contact a doctor and/or the Omani embassy in their home country for up-to-date information on the situation.

In Saudi Arabia, malaria is a risk throughout the year in the western and south-western provinces from Najran in the south-west to Ha'il further north. If you are travelling in these areas it is extremely important to take malarial prophylactics. Symptoms include headaches, fever, chills and sweating which may subside and recur. Without treatment malaria can develop more serious, potentially fatal effects.

Antimalarial drugs do not prevent you from being infected but kill the parasites during a stage in their development.

The problem in recent years has been the emergence of increasing resistance to commonly used antimalarials like chloroquine, maloprim and proguanil. Expert advice should be sought, as there are many factors to consider when deciding on the type of antimalarial medication, including the area to be visited, the risk of exposure to malaria-carrying mosquitoes, your medical history, and your age and pregnancy status. It is also important to discuss the side-effect profile of the medication, so you can work out some level of risk versus benefit ratio. It is also very important to be sure of the correct dosage of the medication prescribed to you. It is often advisable to discuss the dosages required for treatment, especially if your trip is through a high-risk area that would isolate you from medical care.

Contrary to popular belief, once a traveller contracts malaria he/she does not have it for life. Two species of the parasite may lie dormant in the liver but they can also be eradicated using a specific medication. Malaria is curable, as long as the traveller seeks medical help when symptoms occur.

Sandfly Bites Avoid sandfly bites by covering up and applying insect repellent, especially between late afternoon and dawn. Sandflies can transmit leishmaniasis, a group of parasitic diseases sometimes seen in travellers. Cutaneous leishmaniasis, which can ulcerate the skin, is a common disease in Saudi Arabia and Kuwait, and visceral leishmaniasis, which affects organs in the body, is found in Saudi Arabia. Both diseases can be treated with drugs.

Typhus Typhus is spread by ticks, mites or lice. It begins with fever, chills, headache and muscle pains followed a few days later by a body rash. There is often a large painful sore at the site of the bite and nearby lymph nodes are swollen and painful. Treatment is with tetracycline, or chloramphenicol under medical supervision.

Seek local advice on areas where ticks pose a danger and always check your skin carefully for ticks after walking in a danger area. A strong insect repellent can help, and serious walkers in tick areas should consider having their boots and trousers impregnated with benzyl benzoate and dibutylphthalate.

Cuts, Bites & Stings

Cuts & Scratches Skin punctures can easily become infected in hot climates and may be difficult to heal. Treat any cut with an antiseptic such as povidone-iodine. Where possible avoid bandages and Band-aids, which can keep wounds wet. Coral cuts are notoriously slow to heal, as the coral injects a weak venom into the wound. Avoid coral cuts by wearing shoes when walking on reefs, and clean any cut thoroughly with sodium peroxide if available.

Bites & Stings Bee and wasp stings are usually painful rather than dangerous. Calamine lotion will give relief or ice packs will reduce the pain and swelling. There are some spiders with dangerous bites but antivenenes are usually available. There are also various fish and other sea creatures which can sting or bite dangerously or which are dangerous to eat.

Scorpions Scorpion stings are a serious cause of illness and occasional deaths in the Gulf States. Shake shoes, clothing and towels before use. Inspect bedding and don't put hands or feet in crevices in dwellings where they may be lurking. A sting usually produces redness and swelling of the skin, but there may be no visible reaction. Pain is common, and tingling or numbness may occur. At this stage, cold compresses on the bite, and pain relief, such as paracetamol called for. If the skin sensations start to spread from the sting site (eg along the limb) then immediate medical attention is required.

Snakes To minimise your chances of being bitten always wear boots, socks and long trousers when walking through undergrowth where snakes may be present. Don't put your hands into holes and crevices, and be careful when collecting firewood.

Snake bites do not cause instantaneous death and antivenenes are usually available. Keep the victim calm and still, wrap the bitten limb tightly, as you would for a sprained ankle, and then attach a splint to immobilise it. Then seek medical help, if possible with the dead snake for identification. Don't attempt to catch the snake if there is even a remote possibility of anyone being bitten again. The use of tourniquets and sucking out the poison have now been comprehensively discredited.

Jellyfish In the Gulf and Red Sea, jellyfish are the most common problem. Local advice is the best way of avoiding contact with these sea creatures which have stinging tentacles. Stings from most jellyfish are simply rather painful. Dousing in vinegar will de-activate any stingers which have not 'fired'. Calamine lotion, antihistamines and analgesics may reduce the reaction and relieve the pain.

Women's Health

Gynaecological Problems Poor diet, lowered resistance due to the use of antibiotics for stomach upsets and even contraceptive pills can lead to vaginal infections when travelling in hot climates. Keeping the genital area clean, and wearing skirts or loose-fitting trousers and cotton underwear will help to prevent infections.

Yeast infections, characterised by a rash, itch and discharge, can be treated with a vinegar or even lemon-juice douche or with yoghurt. Nystatin suppositories are the usual medical prescription. Trichomonas and gardnerella are more serious infections; symptoms are a smelly discharge and sometimes a burning sensation when urinating. Male sexual partners must also be treated, and if a vinegar-water douche is not effective medical attention should be sought. Metronidazole (Flagyl) is the prescribed drug.

Pregnancy Most miscarriages occur during the first three months of pregnancy, so this is the most risky time to travel as far as your own health is concerned. Miscarriage is not uncommon, and can occasionally lead to severe bleeding. The last three months should also be spent within reasonable distance of good medical care. A baby born as early as 24 weeks stands a chance of survival, but only in a good modern hospital.

Pregnant women should avoid all unnecessary medication, but vaccinations and malarial prophylactics should still be taken where possible. Additional care should be taken to prevent illness and attention should be paid to diet and nutrition. Alcohol and nicotine, for example, should be avoided.

WOMEN TRAVELLERS

Travel in the Gulf poses a special set of problems for women – especially unaccompanied women. Many imagine the situation to be much worse than it actually is. This is partly because the strictest country in the region, Saudi Arabia, is the one which receives the most publicity. Outside of Saudi Arabia women can drive cars, eat in restaurants alone or with men to whom they are not either married or related, shop in stores where men are also present etc. Any specific restrictions on visas, travel or general movement are covered in the Women Travellers section of the individual country chapters.

Sexual harassment is a problem almost everywhere in the world. Some women say that this is less of a problem in the Gulf than in other Middle Eastern countries. Certainly the situation in the Gulf is no worse than in, say, Egypt, Tunisia or Morocco. Unaccompanied women will routinely be stared at and will often have lewd comments directed at them. They may be followed and may find strange and unwanted visitors turning up outside their hotel rooms.

Any woman who does not relish being the centre of attention might wish to avoid just about every bottom-end restaurant listed in this book. The exception is Saudi Arabia where, paradoxically, the rigidly enforced segregation of the sexes which so offends many western visitors also serves to afford female diners a degree of privacy difficult to obtain elsewhere in the region.

A few simple rules should be followed whenever possible. Try to stay in better hotels (possibly a moot point as many bottom-end hotels in the Gulf will not rent rooms to single women), do not flirt or make eye contact with strange men, dress conservatively and do not ride in the front seat of taxis. If a person or a situation is becoming troublesome head for a busy place, preferably where a lot of other foreigners and a few policemen are gathered (a shopping mall or the lobby of a big hotel, for example).

Expatriate women who have lived for many years in the Middle East say that the most important thing is to retain both your self-confidence and your sense of humour. Saying that you should not make eye contact with strange men is not the same as saying that you should act timid and vulnerable, and there are obviously times when a cold glare is an effective riposte to an unwanted suitor.

GAY & LESBIAN TRAVELLERS

Homosexual practices are illegal in all of the Gulf States. Penalties include fines and/or imprisonment. Westerners are unlikely to encounter prejudice or harassment as long as they remain discreet; this may not be the case if you become involved with a local.

DANGERS & ANNOYANCES

The Gulf is generally a pretty safe place. Pick-pockets and muggers are all but unknown, and as a region it has largely been spared the political unrest so often associated with other parts of the Middle East.

The main thing you are likely to worry about are the appalling driving habits that almost everyone – local and foreigner alike – display. See the individual country chapters for more specific safety information.

BUSINESS HOURS

The end-of-week holiday throughout the Gulf is Friday. Most embassies and government offices are also closed on Thursday, though private businesses and shops are

Table of Holidays

Hejira Year	New Year	Prophet's Birthday	Ramadan Begins	Eid Al-Fitr	Eid Al-Adha
1417	20.05.96	28.07.96	10.01.97	09.02.97	18.04.97
1418	09.05.97	17.07.97	30.12.97	29.01.98	08.04.98
1419	28.04.98	06.07.98	19.12.98	18.01.99	28.03.99
1420	17.04.99	25.06.99	08.12.99	07.01.00	17.03.00
1421	06.04.00	14.06.00	27.11.00	27.12.00	06.03.01
1422	26.03.01	03.06.01	16.11.01	16.12.01	23.02.02
1423	15.03.02	23.05.02	05.11.02	05.12.02	12.02.03
1424	04.03.03	12.05.03	25.10.03	24.11.03	01.02.04

open on Thursday mornings and many stores will reopen in the evening on Friday. A few companies and embassies, particularly in the UAE, have recently gone to a Friday/Saturday weekend, but this remains the exception rather than the rule.

PUBLIC HOLIDAYS

The Gulf States observe the main Islamic holidays of Eid Al-Fitr, which marks the end of Ramadan, and Eid Al-Adha, which marks the pilgrimage to Mecca. All except Saudi Arabia observe both the Gregorian and the Islamic New Year holidays. In Saudi Arabia the Gregorian New Year is not observed. The Islamic New Year is widely observed in the private sector but is not an official public holiday.

A list of the dates for Muslim holidays up to the year 2004 appears in the table of holidays above. Note that the dates given in the table may vary by several days in either direction as the Islamic calendar is based on cycles of the moon. The Islamic calendar is 11 days shorter than the Gregorian calendar and the holidays mentioned will move back accordingly in subsequent years.

ACTIVITIES

Diving is popular in the Gulf, and there are a number of well-equipped dive centres, particularly in Oman, the UAE and at Yanbu on the Red Sea coast of Saudi Arabia. Kayaks and windsurfers can also be rented at many of the larger hotels and beach clubs in the coastal areas.

Expeditions to the desert in 4WD vehicles are another long-established pastime among both Gulf Arabs and expatriates (see the boxed story on Desert Safaris in the United Arab Emirates chapter, and the individual country chapters for more details).

LANGUAGE COURSES

If you want to learn Arabic, the Gulf is not the place to look. There are a few schools offering Arabic classes, but these tend to be sparsely attended and are offered irregularly. In Saudi Arabia, the courses often come with a heavy dose of encouragement to convert to Islam. You can, however, often learn French or German through those countries' embassies or cultural centres. See the individual city entries for details on language courses, and keep an eye on the local English-language newspapers.

WORK

Labour laws throughout the Gulf are extremely strict. Unless you arrive with a contract in hand it's probably a waste of time – as well as being illegal in most places – to look for a job.

ACCOMMODATION
Camping

The Gulf's only formal camping grounds are those in Saudi Arabia's Asir National Park.

It is also possible to camp out in the desert in some of the Gulf countries (see the individual country chapters).

Hostels

Bahrain, Saudi Arabia and the UAE all have youth hostels. All these countries are HI members and hostel cards are required (though sheet sleeping sacks are not).

Hotels

There are very few truly horrible hotels in the Gulf. Even in the cheapest places it is rare to find rooms which are not air-conditioned or that lack hot water. Mini-fridges and other extras are often standard. The worst hotels listed in this book may seem quite decent if you have recently arrived from Egypt or India. The flip side of this is that no place in the Gulf is really cheap – outside the youth hostels you are going to find few beds for less than US$15 a night. Most places in the Gulf have ample mid-range hotels (US$25 to US$50) and all of the bigger cities are awash in four and five-star accommodation.

FOOD

At the turn of the century half the population of Kuwait was said to be living exclusively on dates and camel milk. The Gulf has never been known for its cuisine. Whenever you see Arab or Arabian food advertised you can safely assume that the place is offering a Lebanese menu.

Lebanese meals are built around a wide selection of appetisers, or *mezze*. *Hummous*, a paste made from chickpeas is the standard dish whose quality is the acid test of any Lebanese restaurant. Fried *kibbe*, balls of spiced ground meat filled with pine nuts, is another Lebanese speciality as is *tabouli*, a parsley salad, often garnished with tomatoes, that is apt to be pretty oily unless you specify otherwise. Any decent Lebanese restaurant should also place a selection of vegetables (lettuce, radishes, onions) on the table as a free appetiser. Main dishes consist of grilled chicken, lamb or beef. Be sure to try *shish taouk*, a skewer of mildly spiced chicken grilled over open coals.

Street food aside, the cheapest meals in the Gulf are almost always found in small Indian/Pakistani restaurants. The menu at these places tends to be very limited: usually *biryani* dishes (chicken, mutton or fish cooked in a pile of mildly spiced rice), chicken and/or mutton tikka and maybe a curry. That's it. In Saudi Arabia, outside of the main cities the only options are usually small, Turkish-run places offering only kebabs and/or chicken with rice. In some places it is possible to get quite cheap South-East Asian food – Thai and Filipino being the most common.

Street food consists mainly of *shawarma*, which is lamb or chicken carved from a huge rotating spit and served in pita bread, often with lettuce, tomatoes or potatoes. In many places you can also find *foul* (pronounced 'fool'), a paste made from fava beans, and *ta'amiya* (or falafel), a mixture of beans deep-fried into a small patty.

For those with more money to spend, almost anything from fish & chips to burritos to sushi is available in the larger cities.

Ice cream is the most popular dessert throughout the Gulf. You will have no trouble finding both local brands and some well-known foreign ones, such as Wall's from Britain and Baskin-Robbins from the USA. The best known Arab dessert is baklava, a pastry made of filo dough and honey. In the Middle East, pistachios are often part of the recipe.

DRINKS

Again, there are practically no indigenous or traditional Arabian drinks, though if you want to try camel's milk you can often find it in supermarkets. *Laban*, a heavy, and often salty, buttermilk is a local speciality.

Western soft drinks, mineral water and fruit juice are the standard fare. In small Indian/Pakistani restaurants, however, tap water may well be the only liquid that is available.

For religious reasons there are no local alcoholic drinks either. Where alcohol is available it has been imported from the west.

Getting There & Away

There are often many more travel agencies in the Gulf than the local market can support and their staff are often, at best, of marginal competence. The problem is the high degree of turnover among employees (which is why I have not recommended any particular travel agencies). Combine this with the fact that most of the agencies make their money from high-volume corporate clients and have little time for people walking in off the street and you can understand why shopping for plane tickets in the Gulf can be a life-short-ening experience.

In any Gulf city your best bet is to check several different places. If you shop around for tickets expect to get similar prices every-where – they are usually controlled either by the local government or by a cartel organised by the airlines and/or the agents themselves. Shopping around will probably save you some, but not a lot of, money and is mainly a form of insurance. It is almost unheard of to find an agency significantly undercutting everyone else in town, but it is not at all uncommon to find a few who are quoting markedly higher prices than the norm. Getting quotes from four to six places guar-antees that you do not wind up paying too much.

AIR

The regionally-based carriers are Saudia (Saudi Arabian Airlines), Kuwait Airways, Gulf Air (based in Bahrain, and co-owned by Bahrain, Qatar, Oman and Abu Dhabi), Emirates (owned by, and based in, Dubai), Qatar Airways and Oman Air. Qatar Airways and Oman Air are both relatively new carri-ers. Qatar Airways was founded in the '90s and Oman Air moved from being a domes-tic-only airline to being an international carrier around the same time.

In addition, all of the major European, Asian and Middle Eastern airlines (with the obvious exception of El Al) serve most of the major cities in the Gulf. There are few direct flights between the Gulf and the USA and service to Africa is a bit spotty.

All of the main cities in the Gulf have excellent air links with Europe, India, Paki-stan and the Far East. The Gulf, however, is still seen by the travel industry primarily as a business destination and, as such, there are very few discount airfares available. Your best bet for cheap plane tickets to or from the Gulf will be to buy them in countries like Egypt, India and Pakistan, which send masses of workers to the region. For more information, see the individual country chapters.

Round-the-World Tickets & Stopovers

The cheapest way to visit the Gulf is often to stop over there when travelling between Europe and Asia, or to include it in a Round-the-World ticket. Dubai and Bahrain, because they are major transport hubs, are the most common stops on Round-the-World tickets.

If you are flying with one of the Gulf-based carriers it is usually possible to stop over in a Gulf capital at little or no extra cost. This would involve stopping off in Dubai while travelling from, say, London to Bangkok on Emirates, or in Bahrain en route from Paris to New Delhi on Gulf Air. Note, however, that Saudi visa regulations make it unlikely that you will manage to get into Saudi Arabia this way (see Transit Visas in the Saudi Arabia chapter for more details). Emirates and Gulf Air often offer stopover packages, including one or two nights hotel accommodation, airport transfers and a short tour all for a fairly reasonable flat fee.

The USA

Of the major US carriers only TWA flies to the Gulf (to Riyadh), but most of the other big US airlines have some form of code sharing agreement with one or more of the local carriers (Delta and Emirates, for example). Gulf Air flies to New York and Houston either directly or via Larnaca (Cyprus), depending on the day of the week. Kuwait Airways flies to New York three times per week (the plane stops in London en route) and Saudia has regular services to New York, Washington and Orlando.

With some shopping around, you might be able to make it from eastern USA to the Gulf for as little as US$1000 return, though this requires some luck and perseverance. Gulf Air and Emirates both sell heavily discounted tickets through 'authorised discounters', usually small travel agencies that specialise in travel to the Gulf or Middle East. The airlines themselves can direct you to such an agency in your area.

If you go this route be sure to ask about add-ons. When I was researching this book,

Emirates was offering not only cheap tickets from the USA to Dubai, but onward 'add-on' tickets from Dubai to Riyadh, Dhahran, Doha or Muscat were available for free! The add-ons to Jeddah and Kuwait were only an additional US$25. The trick was that you could only take one add-on. Such a policy, however, adds greatly to your flexibility in planning a trip. Don't count on an agent to volunteer this sort of information – be sure to ask. Gulf Air often offers similar add-ons between the cities of the airline's owners (eg a free stopover in Bahrain on a ticket to Abu Dhabi).

Australia & NZ

The large Middle Eastern carriers, Gulf Air and EgyptAir, both have regular return flights out of Melbourne and Sydney, via Singapore, to the major Gulf cities starting

---

Air Travel Glossary

Apex Apex, or 'advance purchase excursion' is a discounted ticket which must be paid for in advance. There are penalties if you wish to change it.

Bucket Shop An unbonded travel agency specialising in discounted airline tickets.

Bumped Just because you have a confirmed seat doesn't mean you're going to get on the plane – see Overbooking.

Cancellation Penalties If you have to cancel or change an Apex ticket there are often heavy penalties involved; insurance can sometimes be taken out against these penalties. Some airlines impose penalties on regular tickets as well, particularly against 'no show' passengers.

Check In Airlines ask you to check in a certain time ahead of the flight departure (usually 1½ hours on international flights). If you fail to check in on time and the flight is overbooked the airline can cancel your booking and give your seat to somebody else.

Confirmation Having a ticket written out with the flight and date you want doesn't mean you have a seat until the agent has checked with the airline that your status is 'OK' or confirmed. Meanwhile you could just be 'on request'.

Discounted Tickets There are two types of discounted fares – officially discounted (see Promotional Fares) and unofficially discounted. The lowest prices often impose drawbacks like flying with unpopular airlines, inconvenient schedules, or unpleasant routes and connections. A discounted ticket can save you other things than money – you may be able to pay Apex prices without the associated Apex advance booking and other requirements. Discounted tickets only exist where there is fierce competition.

Lost Tickets If you lose your airline ticket an airline will usually treat it like a travellers' cheque and, after inquiries, issue you with another one. Legally, however, an airline is entitled to treat it like cash and if you lose it then it's gone forever. Take good care of your tickets.

No Shows No shows are passengers who fail to show up for their flight, sometimes due to unexpected delays or disasters, sometimes due to simply forgetting, sometimes because they made more than one booking and didn't bother to cancel the one they didn't want. Full fare passengers who fail to turn up are sometimes entitled to travel on a later flight. The rest of us are penalised (see Cancellation Penalties).

On Request An unconfirmed booking for a flight, see Confirmation.

around A$1629 (low season; A$1829, high season). Middle East Airlines also flies to the Gulf on its way to Beirut. The fare ranges from between A$1525 (low season) and A$1725 (high season).

Alternatively, it is possible to connect with one of the large Asian carriers. For example, Malaysian, Thai, Philippine and Singapore Airlines all have regular return flights out of their home ports to Dubai from around A$1250.

No carrier flies direct to the Gulf States from New Zealand. However, there are a number of combination fares available, eg Air New Zealand and Emirates Airlines offer return fares to Dubai via Asia from around A$2299.

Europe

All of the major European carriers fly to the major cities in the Gulf, usually several times a week, and the Gulf-based carriers usually offer a daily service to London and several flights a week to a handful of other cities (Paris, Frankfurt, Rome and Athens are the most common destinations). Tickets to and from Europe are not especially cheap – getting from London to the Gulf and back often costs UK£400 or more.

There are also a few charter flights each week to Oman and the United Arab Emirates (UAE) – usually Sharjah – and it is sometimes possible to pick up cheap tickets to Dubai and Bahrain on Emirates and Gulf Air respectively. Most of these originate in Britain, Germany or, in a few cases, Switzerland. As tourism picks up around the region it may soon become much easier to make your way to the Gulf at a reasonable cost.

Open Jaws A return ticket where you fly out to one place but return from another. If available this can save you backtracking to your arrival point.

Overbooking Airlines hate to fly empty seats and since every flight has some passengers who fail to show up (see No Shows) airlines often book more passengers than they have seats. Usually the excess passengers balance those who fail to show up but occasionally somebody gets bumped. If this happens guess who it is most likely to be? The passengers who check in late.

Promotional Fares Officially discounted fares like Apex fares which are available from travel agents or direct from the airline.

Reconfirmation At least 72 hours prior to departure time of an onward or return flight you must contact the airline and 'reconfirm' that you intend to be on the flight. If you don't do this the airline can delete your name from the passenger list and you could lose your seat. You don't have to reconfirm the first flight on your itinerary or if your stopover is less than 72 hours. It doesn't hurt to reconfirm more than once.

Restrictions Discounted tickets often have various restrictions on them – advance purchase is the most usual one (see Apex). Others are restrictions on the minimum and maximum period you must be away, such as a minimum of 14 days or a maximum of one year. See Cancellation Penalties.

Tickets Out An entry requirement for many countries is that you have an onward or return ticket, in other words, a ticket out of the country. If you're not sure what you intend to do next, the easiest solution is to buy the cheapest onward ticket to a neighbouring country or a ticket from a reliable airline which can later be refunded if you do not use it.

Transferred Tickets Airline tickets cannot be transferred from one person to another. Travellers sometimes try to sell the return half of their ticket, but officials can ask you to prove that you are the person named on the ticket. This is unlikely to happen on domestic flights, on an international flight tickets may be compared with passports.

Travel Periods Some officially discounted fares, Apex fares in particular, vary with the time of year. There is often a low (off-peak) season and a high (peak) season. Sometimes there's an intermediate or shoulder season as well. At peak times, when everyone wants to fly, not only will the officially discounted fares be higher but so will unofficially discounted fares or there may simply be no discounted tickets available. Usually the fare depends on your outward flight – if you depart in the high season and return in the low season, you pay the high-season fare. ■

Middle East

Every international airport in the Gulf – even very small ones like Al-Ain and Ras Al-Khaimah – has at least one flight a week to Cairo. Beirut, Damascus and Amman are also all easy to reach from anywhere in the Gulf. Air service to Yemen is not as good or as frequent as you might expect, considering its position on the Arabian Peninsula.

Africa

There are only a few flights to Tunis or Casablanca, on either the Gulf carriers or the national carriers of the North African countries. A number of African carriers serve Jeddah and there is frequent service on all of the main Gulf carriers to Nairobi and (with the exception of Saudia) Johannesburg. Addis Ababa is also fairly easy to reach and Tanzania, for historical reasons, has good air links with Oman, but that is about it.

Asia

All of the big Asian carriers have regular services to the Gulf, and almost daily services in the case of the airlines based in the Indian subcontinent. All of the Gulf carriers have frequent service to Bangkok, Singapore, New Delhi, Bombay, Karachi, Lahore, Islamabad, Manila, Hong Kong and Seoul. From the Gulf it is often possible to book relatively cheap air/hotel packages to Thailand, Singapore and other popular Asian holiday destinations. Tickets to and from the subcontinent tend to be fairly affordable because of both high volumes on the routes and because the distances are relatively short.

LAND

It is possible to cross the desert by bus from Turkey, Syria, Jordan and Egypt (via a ferry to Jordan) to Saudi Arabia and Kuwait. See the Getting There & Away sections of the Saudi Arabia and Kuwait chapters for details.

Those wishing to continue beyond Saudi Arabia will need to go to Dammam in the Kingdom's Eastern Province for bus connections. From Dammam, buses go directly to

Bahrain, Kuwait, Abu Dhabi and Dubai. From Dubai you can catch a bus onward to Muscat. To go to Qatar from Dammam, you'll have to catch a bus to Hofuf and then catch a private taxi to Doha (Saudi bus timetables list a Hofuf-Doha bus, but I doubt its existence).

There is no public transport between Saudi Arabia and Yemen, though you can cross the border if you have your own vehicle. I've never heard of anyone hitching that route, but if you can get a Saudi visa there is no reason why it would not, at least in theory, be possible. The border between Yemen and Oman was not open to travellers at the time of writing.

SEA

There are ferries from Egypt, Jordan, Eritrea and Sudan to Jeddah. See the Saudi Arabia chapter for more details.

There are also boats from Bandar Abbas (Iran) to Bahrain and to Sharjah (UAE). For more details see the Getting There & Away sections of those two countries.

DEPARTURE TAXES

Saudi Arabia and Qatar are the only Gulf countries that do not extract some form of departure tax from travellers.

Bahrain charges a departure tax ('passenger service fee') of BD 3 (about US$8) for all departures by air or sea. People driving across the causeway to Saudi Arabia do not have to pay this fee. There is a BD 3 causeway toll, but that applies even if you are only going out to the restaurant on the island in the centre of the causeway.

Kuwait's KD 2 (about US$7.50) departure tax applies only to plane tickets. This ought to have been included in the cost of the ticket when you purchased it. If the tax was not collected at the point of sale you will have to pay it in cash at the airport. Look for 'KWD 2.000' or something similar in the 'tax' box just below the part of the ticket that shows the cities between which you are travelling.

Oman's OR 3 (about US$8) departure tax also applies only to departures by air.

The UAE does things the other way

around. There is no fee charged if you fly out, but those who leave by land or sea must pay a departure tax of Dh 20 (about US$5.50). If, however, you leave the UAE through Hatta or Al-Ain, where the Omanis have a checkpoint but the Emiratis do not, you do not pay the tax for the simple reason that there is nobody standing at the border to collect it.

WARNING

The information in this chapter is particularly vulnerable to change: prices for international travel are volatile, routes are introduced and cancelled, schedules change, special deals come and go, and rules and visa requirements are being constantly amended.

Airlines and governments seem to take a perverse pleasure in making price structures and regulations as complicated as possible. You should check directly with the airline or a travel agent to make sure you understand how a fare (and ticket you may buy) works. In addition, the travel industry is highly competitive and there are many lurks and perks.

The upshot of this is that you should get opinions, quotes and advice from as many airlines and travel agents as possible before you part with your hard-earned cash. The details given in this chapter should be regarded as pointers and should not be a substitute for your own careful, up-to-date research.

Getting Around the Region

Although the Gulf is a relatively small area the visa regulations of the region's various countries often make air the only practical way for anyone other than Gulf Cooperation Council nationals to travel. The United Arab Emirates (UAE), for example, issues most visas for business travellers and tourists at the country's airports only. While Qatar and Oman now issue many visas through their embassies abroad, airport-issued visas are still quite common there too.

This is not to say that overland travel in the Gulf is impossible. There are buses between Dubai and Muscat, and from eastern Saudi Arabia to Bahrain, Kuwait, Abu Dhabi and Dubai. The problem is getting a visa which allows you to make the crossing.

For example, Saudi Arabian and Kuwaiti visas must be obtained in advance. Once you have the visa you can enter the country wherever and however you choose. But UAE visas for most people are issued for pick-up at an airport. Thus, if you can get a Saudi visa (no mean feat), taking the bus from Abu Dhabi to Dammam is easy. If, however, you are in Saudi Arabia and want to go to Abu Dhabi the situation is much more complicated. At the time of writing, only US and German citizens were able to obtain UAE tourist visas through embassies. For travellers of other nationalities the usual practice is to have a hotel sponsor your visa and deposit it at one of the country's international airports (Abu Dhabi, Dubai, Sharjah, Ras Al-Khaimah, Al-Ain or Fujairah) or at Sharjah port (the only port that handles regularly scheduled passenger traffic). This system makes no allowances for people travelling by bus, so you'll probably have to fly.

Much the same can be said for travel between Dubai and Muscat. If you have an Omani tourist visa in your passport, getting from Dubai to Muscat by land involves nothing more than purchasing a bus ticket. Coming the other way is another story. There is no UAE border post on the road used by the bus. That means not only that there is no place to pick up a visa, but there is no Emirati official at the frontier to stamp your passport. If you cross the border this way – even if you already have a valid UAE visa in your passport – you are allowed to remain in the UAE for only 48 hours, after which you will be fined Dh 100 per day when you do try to leave, or when you get caught, whichever comes first.

The crossing points at Sham, between the UAE and Oman's Musandem Peninsula, and at Sila, on the UAE-Saudi border, have checkpoints on both sides. Provided you can obtain a visa in advance, you will not have to worry about the 48 hour rule if you cross at either of these sites. The type of visas that are routinely deposited at airports, however, cannot be left at Sila or Sham.

This system of airport-issued visas also means that hitching across borders with long-distance trucks is only an option for those able to get tourist visas in advance, or those holding UAE residence permits.

The main exception to this rule is Bahrain, which issues tourist and business visas on the Saudi-Bahrain causeway as well as at the airport.

Crossing borders by land is easier with your own vehicle; it simply involves filling out lots of papers at lots of embassies to get your carnet validated. For more details refer to the individual country chapters.

AIR
Air Passes

Gulf Air's appropriately named 'Air Pass' allows you to purchase coupons for travel between Bahrain, Qatar, the UAE and Oman. The coupons cost between US$35 and US$90 per segment, depending on the distance of the journey (Bahrain-Doha is the cheapest, Bahrain-Muscat is the most expensive). This usually works out to between one-third and one-half of the cheapest fare you could purchase in the Gulf (US$35 versus US$69.50 for Bahrain-Doha, US$90 versus US$245 for Bahrain-Muscat). The catch is that you cannot travel between any particular city pair more than once *in the same direction*, not counting transits. In other words, you can make one round trip between, say, Bahrain and Doha but not two. If, however, you have already made that round trip and then want to make a trip to Abu Dhabi, it is OK if your return flight involves a change of planes in Doha, provided that you only transit Doha airport.

Some of the city pairs available are (prices apply in either direction): Bahrain-Doha US$35, Bahrain-Abu Dhabi US$55, Bahrain-Dubai US$65, Bahrain-Muscat US$90, Dubai-Muscat US$55, Doha-Dubai US$55.

The pass must be purchased outside the Gulf Cooperation Council (GCC) countries and you must also have a return ticket to the Gulf on Gulf Air (though the ticket and the pass do not have to be purchased together). The ticket must originate outside the GCC (ie tickets purchased in Saudi Arabia and Kuwait do not make you eligible for the pass), and the pass is not available to anyone who is resident in a GCC country. The pass has a maximum validity of three months. You must have confirmed reservations for all of your intra-Gulf flights before you leave for the region, but those reservations can be changed along the same segments with no penalty. If you want to change your route there is a US$20 re-issue fee, in addition to whatever the difference in the cost of the coupons works out to be. Prior to travelling the pass can be refunded with only a US$20 penalty, but once the first coupon has been used the remainder cannot be refunded.

Airports

In addition to the region's six capitals (Riyadh, Kuwait City, Bahrain, Doha, Abu Dhabi and Muscat), there are international flights to Jeddah, Dhahran and Medina in Saudi Arabia and to Dubai, Sharjah, Al-Ain, Ras Al-Khaimah and Fujairah in the UAE.

It's worth noting that Al-Ain, Ras Al-Khaimah and Fujairah are very small

airports taking relatively few flights each week. Medina is a very bustling domestic airport, but its international side handles only half a dozen or so flights per week (more during the pilgrimage season).

For costs, see the fare tables in the individual country chapters.

BUS

There are four regional bus routes in the Gulf: Saudi Arabia (Dammam/Al-Khobar) to Bahrain (Manama), Saudi Arabia to the UAE (Abu Dhabi and Dubai), Saudi Arabia to Kuwait, and the UAE (Dubai) to Oman (Muscat). Saudi bus timetables also list buses from Dammam and Hofuf to Doha, Qatar, but you'll be hard pressed to find any evidence that these buses actually exist.

The Saudi Arabia to Bahrain route offers five daily departures and, as long as you have organised your Saudi visa in advance, is straightforward.

Travel to Abu Dhabi and Dubai overland is a problem because there is nowhere to pick up your UAE visa. However, going from Abu Dhabi or Dubai to Dammam is not a problem once you have a Saudi visa.

As outlined earlier, travelling to Dubai from Muscat poses the same visa problem as travelling to Abu Dhabi from Dammam (ie there is no place at the border to pick up your visa) with the added twist that there is no UAE border post to stamp your passport on the road used by the bus. Going in the other direction is not a problem, as long as you can get an Omani visa in advance from an Omani embassy instead of picking it up at the airport. If you do obtain such a visa, make sure it is not stamped 'Not valid for entry by road'. Look at the very bottom of the visa. Foreigners living in Oman and wanting to make this trip will need an Omani Road Permit (see the Road Permit section in the Oman chapter for more details).

If you have an Omani visa that allows you to cross by land, it is also possible to travel between Muscat and Abu Dhabi by crossing the border at Al-Ain/Buraimi and taking a domestic bus from Buraimi to Muscat or from Al-Ain to Abu Dhabi. Doing this in either direction, you will clear customs in Oman about 50 km from Buraimi. In the Al-Ain/Buraimi Oasis itself, there is no customs check at the border nor is there any other check on the UAE side, thus the 48 hour rule applies if you are coming up from Muscat.

CAR
Most of the main roads in the Gulf are high-quality two or four-lane highways. Very few roads are unsealed and 4WDs are only necessary for driving around the desert or for other 'off-road' activities. With the sole exception of Kumzar, Oman, which is only accessible by boat, every site covered in this book can be reached *without* a 4WD. If you are interested in off-road driving, pick up one of the numerous locally produced guides on the subject.

Rental
Renting a car in any of the Gulf States is relatively straightforward. Western driving licences are accepted in all Gulf countries except Bahrain, where an International Driving Permit is required. See the Regional Facts for the Visitor chapter or the individual country chapters for more information regarding costs and local regulations.

BICYCLE
In the first edition of this book I wrote something to the effect that long distance bicycling in the Gulf was effectively impossible because of the heat, humidity and because, well, it simply was not done.

However, I received a long letter from a reader who had arrived in Oman from India and Pakistan and had subsequently cycled straight across Arabia to Jordan.

Having established that it is possible to bike across Arabia, I offer the following advice: take extra water bottles. Also bear in mind that bikes used in the Gulf tend to be old clunkers ridden by labourers. Getting any work done on an expensive touring or mountain bike is likely to be difficult if not impossible, so take *lots* of spare parts and know how to repair the bike yourself.

HITCHING
Hitching is never entirely safe in any country in the world, and we don't recommend it. Travellers who decide to hitch should understand that they are taking a small but potentially serious risk. However, many people do choose to hitch, and the advice that follows should help to make their journeys as fast and safe as possible.

Hitching is legal throughout the Gulf and in some places it is extremely common. If, however, you are a white person bear in mind that trying to hitchhike may attract the attention of the police. This is because hitching throughout the region tends to be the preserve of Gulf Arabs and people from Asia. A westerner hitching would be regarded as unusual, and therefore suspicious, by police.

The most common way of signalling that you want a ride is to extend your right hand, palm down. Drivers will usually expect you to pay the equivalent bus or service-taxi fare, though you should be sure of whether, and how much, money is expected before you get in the vehicle.

I would not recommend that women hitchhike at all in this part of the world.

ORGANISED TOURS
Gulf Air, Emirates and a few other airlines offer Bahrain and Dubai stopover packages. These must be purchased in conjunction with an airline ticket and usually include one or two nights hotel accommodation, airport transfers and a half-day city tour.

A number of the big travel agencies, such as Kuoni and Thomas Cook, offer package tours to Oman, the UAE and Bahrain. Generally these are one or two week tours to just one country, including transportation, accommodation, transfers, some meals and sightseeing. The fares vary significantly depending on the season.

Should you arrive on your own and find your own accommodation (this is probably the cheapest way to go – tours seem to use only five-star hotels) full-day, half-day and overnight tours can be booked locally almost anywhere in the Gulf. Cities like Dubai, Muscat and Bahrain have the most to choose from, but even Saudi Arabia and Kuwait, neither of which issues tourist visas, have a few locally based tour operators. Check the relevant city listings for details.

As a rule you are going to pay US$20 to US$30 in local currency for a half-day tour of whatever city you are in. Full-day tours to some place two or three hours away by road (an Al-Ain tour booked from Dubai or a Nizwa tour booked from Muscat, for example) cost US$40 to US$50 in local currency. More elaborate packages, involving 4WD trips into the desert, lunch on a dhow or camping out in a Bedouin tent, run anywhere from around US$90 to US$150. Really elaborate tours can reach the US$200 to US$300 level, even for a two-day one-night trip. In some cases, such as visiting remote sites like Madain Salah in Saudi Arabia, taking a tour may actually be the most cost-effective and hassle-free way to travel.

The problem for independent travellers is that much of the Gulf's nascent tourist industry remains geared toward groups. If you cannot scare up at least four, and possibly as many as 10 or 15 people (depending on the agency and the tour you are interested in) you will have to pay a hefty supplement. Even in busy Dubai and Bahrain, most of the offerings from any given tour company are only available once or twice a week.

There are plans to create tour packages encompassing several Gulf States, but at the time of writing they were not yet up and running.

Bahrain

The only island-state in the Arab world, this tiny country (about the size of Singapore but with a fraction of its population) is unique in several ways. Gulf Arabs and expats mix more easily here than anywhere else in the region. Although Bahrain comprises about 33 islands the country is often referred to simply as 'the island'. It is the easiest of the Gulf countries to visit, and one of the best values for those on a budget.

But while Bahrain is certainly one of the most liberal countries in the Gulf it remains, by western standards, a very conservative place. In comparison to other Arab countries it is less open than Egypt, Jordan or Tunisia, and it certainly does not share those countries' long experience with tourism. Bahrain is a good introduction to the Gulf, though those making their first trip to an Arab country should still be prepared for more than a little culture shock.

In Arabic, *bahrain* means 'two seas'. It is an appropriate designation. Since the dawn of history Bahrain has been a trading centre and, until about a generation ago, virtually all trade came and went by sea. Occupying a strategic position on the great trade routes of antiquity, with good harbours and abundant fresh water, the Bahrainis are natural traders. And they have a reputation for being the hardest bargainers in the region.

Facts about the Country

HISTORY

The island's position has proved to be both a blessing and a curse. It has made Bahrain an outward-looking place and the Bahrainis an open-minded people. It has also meant a lot of other people have been interested in Bahrain. At one time or another Sumerians, Greeks, Persians, Portuguese, Turks, Wahhabis, Omanis and, of course, the British have all taken an interest in the island.

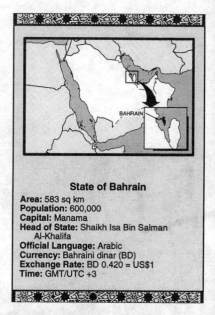

State of Bahrain

Area: 583 sq km
Population: 600,000
Capital: Manama
Head of State: Shaikh Isa Bin Salman Al-Khalifa
Official Language: Arabic
Currency: Bahraini dinar (BD)
Exchange Rate: BD 0.420 = US$1
Time: GMT/UTC +3

Dilmun

Bahrain's history goes back to the roots of human civilisation. The main island is thought to have broken away from the Arabian mainland sometime around 6000 BC and it has almost certainly been inhabited since prehistoric times.

The Bahrain islands first emerged into world history in the 3rd millennium BC as the seat of what became one of the great trading empires of the ancient world. This was Dilmun, a civilisation that was founded during the Bronze Age and continued in some form or other for more than 2000 years. Dilmun evolved here because of the islands' strategic position along the trade routes linking Mesopotamia with the Indus Valley.

What we now call the Middle East had a much more temperate climate 4500 years ago. But even then the land was becoming increasingly arid and Dilmun, with its lush, spring-fed greenery, became known as a holy island in the mythology of Sumeria, one of the earliest civilisations that flourished in the area of what is today southern Iraq. The Sumerians grew out of an earlier (4th millennium BC) people who are referred to as the Ubaid culture. Archaeological finds in Bahrain indicate that the islands were in contact with the Ubaids. Those contacts continued after the founding of Dilmun sometime in the 3rd millennium BC. In its early centuries Dilmun already had strong trading links with the powerful Sumerian city of Eridu (near modern Basra).

Dilmun is mentioned in the Babylonian creation myth, and the *Epic of Gilgamesh* describes it as a paradise to which heroes and wise men are transported to enjoy eternal life. In the epic, the world's oldest known poetic saga, Gilgamesh, King of Uruk, spends much of his time seeking out this sacred island. When he eventually finds it he is met on arrival by Ziusudra, the lone survivor of a flood which had destroyed an earlier generation of men. (Ziusudra is the Sumerian equivalent of the biblical Noah.) Ziusudra, who after the flood had been given the right to live forever in Dilmun, helps Gilgamesh

obtain the flower of eternal youth, but a serpent eats the flower while Gilgamesh is on his way home, leaving him wiser but still mortal.

The greenery of Bahrain was central to the gods worshipped by the people of Dilmun. Bahrain's Barbar Temple, the earliest stages of which go back to about 2250 BC, was dedicated to Enki, God of Wisdom and The Sweet Waters Under the Earth. Enki was believed to live in an underground sea of fresh water on which the world of the surface floated. He was worshipped at an underground shrine built around a sacred well.

Dilmun itself seems to have been founded during the Early Bronze Age, sometime around 3200 BC, and to have come into its own around 2800 BC. Archaeologists divide the civilisation's history into four periods: Formative Dilmun (3200-2200 BC), Early Dilmun (2200-1600 BC), Middle Dilmun (1600-1000 BC) and Late Dilmun (1000-330 BC). Formative and Early Dilmun are the most interesting for the tourist. These periods encompass the construction of many of the island's grave mounds and the Barbar Temple. Middle Dilmun was a period of decline and the Late period saw Dilmun's absorption into the Assyrian and Babylonian empires.

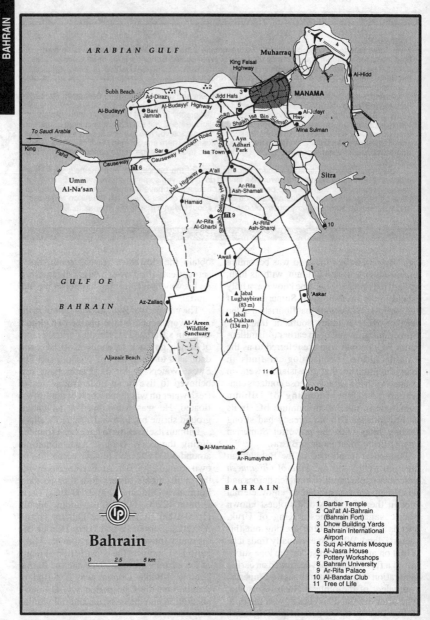

ARABIAN GULF

Muharraq

King Faisal
Highway

Subh Beach

Ad-Diraz

Al-Budayyi'

Al-Budayyi' Highway

Jidd Hafs

Al-Hidd

MANAMA

Bani
Jamrah

Al-Jufayr

Sheikh Isa Bin Sulman Hwy

Mina Sulman

To Saudi Arabia

King Fahd Causeway

Sar

Causeway Approach Road

Isa Town

Ayn
Adhari
Park

Umm
Al-Na'san

6

7

A'ali

8

A'ali Highway

Sitra

Ar-Rifa
Ash-Shamali

Hamad

9

Ar-Rifa
Al-Gharbi

Ar-Rifa
Ash-Sharqi

10

'Awali

GULF OF

BAHRAIN

Az-Zallaq

▲ Jabal
Lughaybirat
(83 m)

▲ Jabal
Ad-Dukhan
(134 m)

'Askar

Al-'Areen
Wildlife
Sanctuary

Aljazair Beach

11

Ad-Dur

Al-Mamtalah

Ar-Rumaythah

BAHRAIN

Bahrain

0   2.5   5 km

1 Barbar Temple
2 Qal'at Al-Bahrain
   (Bahrain Fort)
3 Dhow Building Yards
4 Bahrain International
   Airport
5 Suq Al-Khamis Mosque
6 Al-Jasra House
7 Pottery Workshops
8 Bahrain University
9 Ar-Rifa Palace
10 Al-Bandar Club
11 Tree of Life

From its earliest days Dilmun was a lucrative trading centre. A cuneiform tablet found at Ur, in modern Iraq, records the receipt of 'a parcel of fish eyes' (probably a reference to pearls) sent from Dilmun around the year 2000 BC.

While we know that Dilmun was powerful, it is much harder to say exactly how powerful it was. There is no question that the Early Dilmun civilisation controlled a large section of the western shore of the Gulf, including Tarut Island (now in eastern Saudi Arabia). But there is much dispute over how far north and how far inland that control extended, and whether Dilmun had any influence on the far side of the Gulf, ie modern Iran. At times Dilmun's reach probably extended as far north as modern Kuwait and as far inland as the Al-Hasa Oasis in today's eastern Saudi Arabia.

There is no doubt, however, that Dilmun fell into decline during the Middle period. This was probably connected with the fall of the Indus Valley civilisation (in today's Pakistan), a culture about which little is known but whose disappearance in the middle of the 2nd millennium BC would have stripped Dilmun of much of its activity as a trading port on the route from Mesopotamia to the Indus.

The decline continued over the following centuries. Tablets from the 8th century BC mention Dilmun as a tributary state of Assyria and, by about 600 BC, the once-great trading empire had been fully absorbed by the Babylonians.

From Alexander to Mohammed

After its absorption by Babylon, Dilmun effectively ceased to exist. At the same time the Gulf and eastern Arabia more or less vanish from recorded history for about 200 years. Little is known about what happened in the Gulf between the fall of Dilmun and the arrival of Nearchus, an admiral in Alexander the Great's army. Nearchus set up a small colony on Failaka Island (now part of Kuwait) in the late 4th century BC and is known to have explored the Gulf at least as far south as Bahrain. From the time of

Nearchus until the coming of Islam in the 7th century AD, Bahrain was generally known by its Greek name, Tylos.

The period from about 300 BC to 300 AD appears to have been reasonably prosperous. Pliny, writing in the 1st century AD, noted that Tylos was famous for its pearls. However, few ruins remain from that period. The Bahrain islands seem to have fallen under the sway of the Seleucid Empire, one of the three principal successor states into which Alexander's realm broke up after his death in 323 BC. The Seleucids controlled the swath of land running from modern Israel and Lebanon through Mesopotamia to Persia. Bahrain lay on the outermost edge of this area and may or may not actually have been run by the Seleucids.

The Seleucid Empire, however, was relatively short-lived. Its successor, in what had been the eastern part of the Seleucid lands, was the Parthian Empire. The Parthians were a more explicitly Persian dynasty, though they presented themselves as the protectors of Hellenistic culture and Alexander's legacy. Bahrain almost certainly fell under the Parthians' sway and later drifted into the empire of the Sassanians, who succeeded the Parthians in Persia around the 3rd century AD. The Sassanians formally annexed the islands in the 4th century AD.

It was around this time, the 3rd or 4th century AD, that many of Bahrain's inhabitants appear to have adopted the new Christian faith. Exactly how many, or what percentage of the population they represented, is impossible to determine. The Sassanian Empire was also a centre for Zoroastrianism and, for a time, Manicheism. Zoroastrianism became the empire's official religion in the late 3rd century AD and dissenters were officially persecuted. Though such persecution is known to have continued into the late 6th century, Bahrain seems to have avoided the worst of it. It is certain that the Nestorian sect of Christianity was firmly established in Bahrain, and along much of the Arabian side of the Gulf, by the early 5th century. Church records show that Muharraq and Manama, then known as Samahij and

Tilwun respectively, were the seats of two of the five Nestorian bishoprics which existed on the Arabian side of the Gulf at the time of the coming of Islam. Muharraq also housed a Nestorian monastery. It is uncertain when the two Bahraini bishoprics were finally dissolved, though they are known to have survived until at least 835 AD.

There is also some evidence that during this period the Bahrain islands controlled at least part of the adjacent coast. Sassanian chronicles state that the king settled some of the members of a conquered tribe in Bahrain, namely in Darin. Darin is the main town of Tarut Island which lies north of Bahrain and is much closer to the Arabian mainland. It is also around this time that Bahrain island came to be known as 'Awal', a name which Bahrainis used for the main island until the early years of this century.

The Coming of Islam
Bahrainis pride themselves on the fact that they were one of the first territories outside the Arabian mainland to accept Islam. Around 640 AD the Prophet Mohammed sent a letter to the ruler of Bahrain (possibly a Christian Arab who served as governor on behalf of the Sassanian Persians) inviting him to adopt Islam. In fairly short order the ruler did so, though Christians and Muslims continued to live peacefully together in Bahrain for another two centuries. Even today Bahrain has a tiny community of indigenous Christians.

From the 9th to the 11th centuries Bahrain was part of the Umayyad and, later, Abbasid empires. Its reputation as a stronghold of Shiite Islam was firmly established under the Abbasids whose capital was Baghdad but who derived much of their culture from predominantly Shiite Persia. Though Bahrain in this period had neither the wealth nor the importance it had enjoyed some 2000 years earlier, it appears to have been reasonably prosperous and well run. It was once again on the trade routes between Mesopotamia and the Indian subcontinent. In the middle of the 12th century the great Arab/Spanish geographer Al-Idrisi described the people of

Bahrain as being satisfied with their ruler, who was apparently an independent king owing nominal allegiance to the Caliph in Baghdad. Al-Idrisi referred to the Bahrainis as the people of 'the two banks', which might be a reference to Bahrain and Muharraq islands, or may indicate that Bahrain's ruler still controlled a portion of the mainland coast.

During the Middle Ages Bahrain appears to have changed hands fairly frequently, which is hardly surprising considering its position as a trading centre often on the geographical fringe between two or more competing empires. In addition, the entire Gulf during this period was run by various petty shaikhs who seem to have been constantly at war with one another.

The Omanis were the next major power to take an interest in Bahrain. They conquered Bahrain and Muharraq islands around 1487 and built Arad Fort on Muharraq. This was to supplement the earlier fortifications (the ruins known today as the Islamic Fort at the Qal'at Al-Bahrain site) they had taken over on the north coast of Bahrain Island. Two years earlier the first European known to have visited the islands, a Portuguese explorer named Duarte Barbosa, had noted both the number and quality of the pearls of Bahrain (he called Bahrain, 'Barem').

The Portuguese & the Persians
It was another 36 years before the Portuguese navy conquered the islands as part of their procession up the Gulf from Muscat and Hormuz. As one of the main pearling ports in the Gulf, the islands clearly had economic value. Bahrain's ample supply of fresh water and position about halfway between the Strait of Hormuz and the head of the Gulf gave it military value in the ongoing struggle for control of the area. In the first half of the 16th century Bahrain was on the front line as Portugal and the Ottoman Turks battled for control of the Gulf. The second half of the century was somewhat quieter, as the Portuguese were by then firmly in control.

In the end it was the Bahrainis themselves,

Pearls & Pearling

A report filed in 1900 by a British official in Bahrain stated that half of the island's male population was employed in the pearling industry. This is hardly surprising. Pearling had been a part of the local economy since the 3rd millennium BC. By the early 1800s, when most of the trade routes that had straddled the Gulf were ancient history, pearls and dates were virtually the only things which the region had to offer the rest of the world.

Today pearling has come to be viewed through something of a rose-coloured mist. The fact is that pearl diving was a truly terrible way to make a living. The pearl trade made a few 19th-century Arab families spectacularly rich but for just about everyone else involved it was physically and economically brutal. One can only conclude that it survived as long as it did largely by default – there simply was no other way for most people in the Gulf to earn a living.

The pearling season began each year in late May when the boats would leave Bahrain and the other settlements around the Gulf for the offshore pearl banks. They remained constantly at sea until mid-October. Supplies were ferried out by dhow.

The workers were divided into divers and pullers. A diver's equipment consisted only of a nose-clip and a bag. More fortunate divers might also have had some sort of thin cotton garment which, it was hoped, would provide protection against jellyfish. Rocks were tied to the divers' feet as weights. They would leap into the water with a rope tied around their waists and usually stayed under for about a minute at depths of up to 15m. A tug on the rope meant it was time for the pullers to return the diver to the surface.

Neither the divers nor the pullers were paid wages. Instead, they would receive shares of the total profits for the season. A puller's share was half to two-thirds of a diver's. Boat owners would advance money to their workers at the beginning of the season. The divers were often unable to pay back these loans, got further into debt with each year and, as a result, were often bound to a particular boat owner for life. If a diver died his sons were obliged to work off his debts. It was not unusual to see quite elderly men still working as divers. British attempts in the '20s to regulate and improve the lot of the divers were resisted by the divers themselves, most of whom did not understand the complex accounting system the British had imposed. Riots and strikes became a regular feature of the pearling seasons in the late '20s and early '30s.

In addition to its own long-established pearl trade, by the 19th century Bahrain was also serving as the main trans-shipment point for almost all the pearls produced in the Gulf. From Bahrain pearls were shipped to Bombay where they were sorted, polished and drilled. Most were then exported to Europe.

Around 1930 the Japanese invented a method of culturing pearls and this, combined with the Great Depression, caused the bottom to fall out of the international pearl market. Bahrain has never quite forgiven the Japanese and even now it bans the importation of cultured pearls.

The pearl merchants could all instantly tell the difference between natural and cultured pearls but most other people could not, and didn't care anyway. Today pearls are more common – and far less valuable – than they were 75 years ago. Even if someone wanted to revive the traditional pearling industry today it is doubtful that it would be economically viable. ∎

not the Turks or the Omanis, who drove the Portuguese from the islands in 1602.

In that year the Portuguese governor made the critical mistake of executing the brother of one of the island's richer traders. The trader, Rukn El-Din, proceeded to lead an uprising which soon drove the Europeans from Bahrain. Rukn quickly appealed to Persia for protection, which was a shrewd political move. Aside from the need for help in case the Portuguese decided to come back and punish the Bahrainis, appealing to Persia seemed less provocative than appealing to the Turks, with whom the Portuguese were

in competition for influence in the Gulf. On the other hand it brought Bahrain, once again, firmly back into a Persian empire, which was where it stayed for the rest of the 17th century.

The 18th & 19th Centuries

The Al-Khalifa, Bahrain's ruling family, first arrived in the archipelago in the mid-18th century. They came to Bahrain from Kuwait where they had helped their distant relatives, the Al-Sabah family, become the established power. The Al-Khalifa settled in Zubara, on the north-western edge of the

Qatar peninsula, apparently with a mind towards becoming involved in the region's lucrative pearling trade. Zubara quickly grew into a large town, the ruins of which can still be seen today.

In 1782 or 1783 Shaikh Ahmed Al-Fatih, a member of the Al-Khalifa family, drove out the Persian garrison and occupied the main islands of the Bahrain group, apparently with some help from his Al-Sabah cousins in Kuwait. Bahrain and Muharraq islands were particularly important prizes because their position off the Arabian mainland made them relatively immune to Wahhabi raids. These raids, led by the ancestors of the present Saudi royal family, seem to have been a regular feature of life in Zubara from the late 18th century until the Ottoman suppression of the Wahhabis in 1818. Ahmed ruled until his death in 1796 when his two sons, Abdullah and Salman, took over as joint rulers. Three years later, however, the Omanis returned in force to the islands from which the Portuguese had driven them over 275 years earlier. Salman was forced to retreat to Zubara while Abdullah went into exile on the Arabian mainland.

In 1820 the brothers managed to retake the islands, and a few years of relative tranquillity ensued. Shortly thereafter a treaty was signed with the British, who by then had already been present in the region for over 200 years in the form of the ubiquitous East India Company. This treaty, in which the Bahrainis agreed to abstain from what the British defined as piracy, became the model for similar treaties signed or imposed by the British throughout the Gulf over the next generation. Salman died in 1825 and his son Khalifa continued to rule jointly with Abdullah until 1834 when Khalifa died.

Abdullah ruled alone for a few years. It was during this period that the British began to formalise their presence in the Gulf. India was becoming an increasingly important element of the British Empire and Britain saw security in the Gulf as vitally important to its trade and supply routes to the Indian subcontinent. In 1835 the rulers of Bahrain and the other shaikhdoms of the Gulf had a

peace treaty more or less dictated to them by the Royal Navy. Like the earlier treaty signed with Bahrain, the purpose of this agreement was to end piracy (ie any threat to British shipping) in the region. The British also pressured the shaikhs into outlawing slavery.

But despite the best efforts of the Royal Navy, things did not stay quiet and, around 1840, a string of events began which led to three turbulent decades in Bahrain. A few years after Khalifa's death his son, Mohammed Bin Khalifa, began to challenge Abdullah's authority. Eventually he set himself up in Muharraq as a co-ruler and rival. In 1843 he conquered Zubara and deposed Abdullah, who died in exile five years later. Mohammed ruled unopposed for a few years and, in 1861, signed a Treaty of Perpetual Peace and Friendship with the British. This was the first of the so-called Exclusive Agreements, under which he (and other Gulf rulers who later signed similar documents) ceded to Britain control of foreign affairs in exchange for protection from attack. Other agreements with the British were signed in 1881 and 1891.

Mohammed Bin Khalifa was soon challenged by his cousin Mohammed Bin Abdullah (Shaikh Abdullah's son). Seeking revenge for his father's deposition, Mohammed Bin Abdullah began raiding Bahrain from a base on the mainland. In the midst of this already turbulent situation a war broke out between Bahrain and Qatar, which ended in 1868 with Mohammed Bin Khalifa fleeing to Qatar while his brother Ali proclaimed himself ruler of Bahrain.

In Qatar, Mohammed Bin Khalifa built a new fleet, invaded Bahrain again and killed Ali in 1869. In this, however, he made one key mistake. He buried the hatchet with his cousin, Mohammed Bin Abdullah, and gave him a post in the reconquering force. Once they were back in control of Bahrain Mohammed Bin Abdullah, who apparently had not forgotten who deposed his father, promptly overthrew and imprisoned Mohammed Bin Khalifa.

From their base in Bushire, on the coast of present-day Iran, the British watched all this with, one can only assume, a combination of annoyance and alarm. The topsy-turvy Bahraini politics of 1869 were the last straw. Not long after Mohammed Bin Abdullah's coup, the Royal Navy sailed down from Bushire, deported both of the Mohammeds to Bombay and installed Ali's 21-year-old son Isa as emir. They also leaned on Isa (who reigned until 1932) to appoint a crown prince so as to remove any doubts about the succession. Shaikh Isa's line has ruled Bahrain ever since. The current emir, also named Isa, is his great-grandson.

After installing Isa as emir the British largely stayed out of local politics for the remainder of the 19th century. Their main concern was to keep the Turks, who then controlled eastern Arabia, out of the region. (This was also a concern for the shaikhs, which was one reason why they had signed those agreements in the first place.) Both Turkey and Persia continued to claim Bahrain as part of their respective empires

The Discovery of Oil

Ancient texts contain the occasional reference to oil being found in natural pools, or seepages, in Bahrain. It was traditionally used to fuel lamps and to help make boats waterproof. Seepages, however, do not necessarily imply the presence of crude oil in exploitable quantities.

In 1902 a British official wrote to his superiors that he had heard stories about oil spouting from the sea bed at a point close to Bahrain's shoreline. An engineer was sent to investigate but his report was not promising. Interest among British officials revived in 1908 after oil was found in large quantities in Iran. Still, the Anglo-Persian Oil Company, which then dominated the Middle East's nascent oil industry, seemed more interested in litigation than exploration. They sought to guarantee that no one else had the opportunity to prospect for oil in Bahrain, but at the same time made no attempt to look for it themselves.

The man who spurred the search for oil, not only in Bahrain but also in eastern Saudi Arabia, was Frank Holmes, a New Zealander who had recently retired from the British Army (hence the habit of referring to him as Major Holmes). Virtually every book ever written on oil and the Gulf describes Holmes as eccentric, though few make it clear what was so eccentric about him except for his firm conviction that oil was to be found underneath Arabia. After a great deal of convoluted toing and froing, Holmes' tiny Eastern & General Syndicate was granted a concession to drill for oil in Bahrain in late 1925. The only problem was that neither Holmes nor the syndicate had the sort of money required to launch such an operation.

Holmes spent the next five years trying to round up the necessary funds. When he found a backer in Standard Oil of California (SOCAL, the precursor of today's Chevron) he was then forced to embark on another series of legal contortions. The terms of the concession agreement stipulated that it could not be assigned to any 'foreign' (meaning non-British) company. Eventually SOCAL set up a subsidiary in Canada, which was apparently British enough to get the foreign office in London to agree, and exploration went ahead. Oil in commercial quantities was found in June 1932, the first such strike on the Arab side of the Gulf. Exports began soon afterward and a refinery opened in 1936.

The discovery of oil could not have come at a better time for Bahrain, as it roughly coincided with the collapse of the world pearl market. Until that time pearling had been the mainstay of the Bahraini economy.

Equally important was the fact that oil was discovered in Bahrain before it was discovered elsewhere in the Gulf. The Bahrainis were the first to enjoy the benefits that came from the oil revenues – notably a dramatic improvement in the quality of education and health care. This led to the island assuming a larger role in Britain's operations in the Gulf. The main British naval base in the region was moved to Bahrain in 1935. In 1946 the Political Residency, the office of the senior British official in the region, was moved from Bushire to Bahrain.

The island's oil reserves are quite small and its revenues from oil sales have never approached those of Kuwait, Saudi Arabia or the United Arab Emirates (UAE) on a per capita basis. Today Bahrain produces only a token quantity of oil. In one sense, this has been a boon. Lacking the resources for extravagance, Bahrain has proceeded into the 20th century in a reasonable, measured way. The Bahrainis were forced to think about diversifying their economy far earlier than any of the other Gulf States and this, combined with their long history as a trading nation and lengthy contact with the outside world, has proved an admirable blend of circumstances. ∎

BAHRAIN

well into the 20th century but neither was willing to challenge the British for control of the islands.

This threat to Bahrain's sovereignty from its larger neighbours continued up until 1970. After Persia became Iran, it continued to refuse to recognise Bahrain's existence as anything other than an Iranian province. Teheran threatened military action several times in the 1950s and '60s and refused entry to Iran to travellers whose passports showed evidence of travel to Bahrain. The claim was finally dropped in 1970 after Britain talked the Shah of Iran into accepting the results of a United Nations mission to the island to determine whether or not the inhabitants wanted to be part of Iran. In the wake of Iran's 1979 Islamic revolution, one of Teheran's senior clerics briefly revived the issue, but Iran's spiritual leader, Ayatollah Khomeini, disapproved and the Islamic Republic let the matter drop.

The 20th Century

Shaikh Isa Bin Ali, whom the British had installed in 1869, reigned until his death in 1932. In 1923, however, the British forced him to hand over the day-to-day running of the country to his son, Hamad. Isa, who was then in his mid-70s, was notoriously conservative and opposed even modest reform or modernisation. After his father's death, Hamad ruled in his own right from 1932 to 1942.

Almost immediately upon Hamad's taking power in 1923, modernisation in Bahrain took off. A decade later, when the oil money started coming in, the pace quickened. Schools, hospitals and new mosques were built, much of the country received electricity, and an airport was constructed to serve as a stop on Imperial Airways' London to India route.

In addition to the discovery of oil, the years after WWI also saw another event with long-term significance for Bahrain – the arrival, in 1926, of a new British adviser to the emir, Charles Belgrave. Described in later years by the archaeologist Geoffrey Bibby as 'tall, cool, cheroot-smoking, very,

very efficient', Belgrave (who got the job, believe it or not, by answering an ad in a London newspaper!) was to remain in Bahrain for over 30 years. He was instrumental in setting up the island's educational system, and he appears to have overseen much of Bahrain's early infrastructural development. Because he was, for a time, so powerful, Bahraini officialdom tends to treat him as something of a nonperson these days.

In true empire style Bahrain declared war on the Axis powers one day after Britain in 1939. The Bahrain refinery was then one of only three in the Middle East and its continued functioning was regarded as crucial to the war effort, particularly as both Japan and Germany had been trying to gain toeholds in the Gulf during the 1930s. The war years in Bahrain were generally quiet, the main exception being a botched attempt by the Italian Air Force to bomb the oil refinery on 19 October 1940. They missed.

Shaikh Hamad died in 1942 and was succeeded as emir by his son, Salman. Salman's 19 years on the throne saw a vast increase in the country's standard of living as oil production boomed in Saudi Arabia, Kuwait and Qatar. At that time none of these other areas could match Bahrain's level of development, health or education. As a result, though the country's oil output was tiny compared to that of its neighbours, Bahrain was well positioned to serve as the Gulf's main entrepôt.

The 1950s were unsettled years throughout the Arab world. The rise of the Egyptian leader Gamal Abdel Nasser, his fiery rhetoric and his assaults on the colonial privileges enjoyed by Britain and other western countries in the Arab world, including most areas which were at least nominally independent, galvanised people throughout the Middle East. In the years immediately after WWII, wealthy Bahrainis had begun sending their sons (not, usually, their daughters) abroad to further their education. They studied in Cairo, Beirut or, for the very rich and/or well-connected, London. This new class of well-educated technocrats proved to be particularly resentful of British domination.

In 1952, reform-minded members of the

country's Sunni and Shiite communities formed an eight-person Higher Executive Committee. They sought western-style trade unions, a parliament and, more to the point, demanded that the emir sack Belgrave. Their demands for a more open political system even received some tacit support from the British government (though not, presumably, from Belgrave). Belgrave stayed, but the emir agreed to some of the Committee's demands – a victory which seems to have encouraged them to ask for more.

Matters came to a head in 1956. Early that year stones were thrown at the British Foreign Secretary, Selwyn Lloyd, while he was visiting Bahrain. In retaliation, several members of the Committee of National Union (the Higher Education Committee's successor) were deported. Several people were killed in November of that year in anti-British riots in Bahrain during the Suez crisis. The British landed troops to protect the oilfields, but at about the same time the Saudis, regarding Bahrain as too closely under Britain's thumb, cut off the supply of oil to the refinery (which even then refined significantly more Saudi oil than Bahraini oil). Not long afterwards Belgrave 'retired'. Though the emir appointed another Briton to replace him, the crisis had passed, calm prevailed and Bahrainis went back to their first love – making money.

Shaikh Salman died in 1961 and was succeeded by his son, the present emir, Shaikh Isa Bin Salman Al-Khalifa.

Independence

After Britain announced its intention to withdraw from the Gulf by the end of 1971, Bahrain participated in the attempts to form a federation with Qatar and the seven Trucial States (now the UAE). As the most populous and advanced of the nine emirates, Bahrain demanded greater representation on the council which was to govern the proposed federation. When the other rulers refused, Bahrain decided to go it alone and declared its independence on 14 August 1971 – a decision which also prompted Qatar to pull out of the federation.

A constituent assembly charged with drafting a constitution was elected at the end of 1972. The emir issued the constitution in May 1973, and another election was held later that year for a National Assembly which convened in December. But the assembly was dissolved only 20 months later when the emir decided that radical assembly members were making it impossible for the executive branch to function. Governing is now done by emiri decree, exercised through a Cabinet. In 1975 all trade unions were disbanded. Although allowed to exist under the constitution, the government had never actually sanctioned their formation. All strikes were banned as well.

During the 1970s and '80s Bahrain experienced a huge degree of growth, partly from the skyrocketing price of oil but also because it was still, in the mid to late '70s, well ahead of much of the rest of the Gulf in terms of infrastructure. In recent years its status as an entrepôt has declined somewhat, but its economy has also become more diversified and less oil-dependent. In particular, since the demise of Beirut in the late '70s, the island has established itself as one of the region's main banking and finance centres. There were a few violent pro-Iranian demonstrations in late 1979 and early 1980, but the unrest soon died out.

Despite the economic downturn felt throughout the Gulf in the late '80s, Bahrain remained both calm and prosperous. The country's main shipyard did a roaring trade during the mid-80s, patching up tankers that had been hit by one side or the other in the Iran-Iraq War. In addition, the opening of the Saudi-Bahrain (King Fahd) Causeway in late 1986 gave a boost to both business and tourism.

The 1990s

The early '90s saw a vast improvement in Bahrain's relations with Iran, marked by the resumption of air service between Manama and Teheran. Relations with Iraq, on the other hand, have gone sharply downhill – Bahrainis will not soon forget that Iraq's

BAHRAIN

Saddam Hussein ordered a Scud missile attack on their country during the Gulf War (the missile landed harmlessly in the sea). The post-war monitoring of Iraq's military machine added a new element to Bahrain's traditional role as an entrepôt. Since 1991, it has been through Bahrain that UN officials monitoring Iraq's compliance with the terms of the Gulf War cease-fire have come and gone.

A dispute with Qatar over ownership of the Hawar Islands, of which Bahrain has dejure control, has dragged on for years and remains a diplomatic sore spot between the two countries. In 1995 the Bahraini government expressed annoyance at the Qataris for taking the question of sovereignty over the islands to the International Court of Justice in the Hague. Bahrain's long-held position has been that the dispute should be settled bilaterally or through an Arab mediator.

In recent years, however, the quiet world of Bahraini life has been rocked by sporadic waves of unrest. The trouble began in the fall of 1994 when the emir refused to accept a petition, reportedly signed by some 25,000 Bahrainis, calling for greater democracy. Anger at this incident boiled over into rioting that November with protests centred in the predominantly Shiite villages west of the capital. The main demands of the demonstrators were a restoration of the long-suspended parliament and a broader distribution of the country's wealth among its citizens (unemployment in the Shiite community was estimated at 25 to 30% at the time). In all, at least a dozen people died in the unrest and hundreds were jailed.

There was more unrest in April 1995 and again in late January 1996 when three nights of rioting and arson in villages outside the capital led to yet more arrests. The government, through the state-controlled media, accused Iran of inciting the violence. In February, however, the stakes were raised when a bomb exploded in the lobby of the Diplomat Hotel, injuring several people. Through the spring and early summer, several other bombs either exploded or were discovered and diffused around the country.

GEOGRAPHY

The country is a low-lying archipelago of about 33 islands (including the disputed Hawar group) of which Bahrain Island is the largest at about 50 km long and 16 km wide. The total area of the country is 583 sq km. Jabal Ad-Dukhan, the highest point in the country at 134m above sea level, is in the centre of Bahrain Island. The country's population is heavily concentrated in the northern third of Bahrain Island and on the southern edge of Muharraq Island, the only one of the outlying islands to be inhabited by any significant number of people. Sitra Island has been largely given over to industry. Land reclamation on Sitra and around central Manama has been extensive.

Bahrain, Muharraq, Sitra and Umm Al-Na'san are the only islands in the group of any significant size. Many of the smaller islands are really little more than outcrops of rock, with or without an accompanying sandbar. Several have been tied to Bahrain Island or Muharraq by roads and causeways in such a way that they must be considered extensions of the main islands rather than separate entities.

CLIMATE

This is one area in which Bahrain duplicates all of its neighbours. It can get extremely hot and humid from June to September, with temperatures averaging 36°C during the day. November to March tends to be quite pleasant with warm days and cool (though not really cold) nights. Temperatures vary between a minimum of 14°C to a maximum of 24°C.

FLORA & FAUNA

Bahrain has long been famous for its greenery in the midst of the region's deserts. Recently, however, this has been changing. Though parts of the island are still thickly covered in date palms, the island is a lot less green than it used to be. Some of the trees have been cut down and others have died as increasing demands are made on the underground springs which water them.

As for the fauna, aside from domesticated

donkeys you won't see many animals outside the Al-'Areen Wildlife Sanctuary. Even that old Arabian standby, the camel, is a relatively rare sight in Bahrain.

Al-'Areen Wildlife Sanctuary

The park, a 10-sq-km area in the south-west of Bahrain Island, serves as a conservation area for endangered species indigenous to Arabia, such as the Arabian oryx, though other animals not native to Arabia (eg zebras) have been introduced as well. Access is strictly controlled and there is a limit on the number of people allowed to visit each day. Generally you have to go through the park in a government bus after parking at the entrance. See Around Bahrain Island for more information.

GOVERNMENT & POLITICS

Bahrain is an absolute monarchy though the emir, Shaikh Isa Bin Salman Al-Khalifa, consults often with government ministers and is readily available to citizens. The emir's health has suffered in recent years and much of the day-to-day governing has been carried out by his brother the prime minister, Shaikh Khalifa Bin Salman Al-Khalifa. The Crown Prince, Shaikh Hamad Bin Isa Al-Khalifa, is also the head of the Bahrain Defence Forces. Bahrain is the only Gulf state to have adopted a strict rule of primogeniture within the royal family.

ECONOMY

Bahrain produces fewer than 50,000 barrels of oil per day (for comparative purposes the UAE pumps about two million barrels a day) and refines a large quantity of Saudi oil which arrives via an undersea pipeline. With its relatively limited oil reserves the island has developed a somewhat more diversified economy than many other Gulf States. Bahrain is home to the largest aluminium smelter in the Middle East, a large shipbuilding and repair yard and one of the region's busiest airports.

When Lebanon imploded in the late '70s the Bahraini government made a conscious effort to lure the region's bankers (until then mostly based in Beirut) to Manama and met with a great deal of success. In the late '80s Bahrain's large financial services sector branched out into offshore banking, though it has met with stiff competition from Cyprus and Abu Dhabi in this field.

The '80s also saw the beginning of a calculated drive to attract tourists to the country. In promoting tourism the government sought to broaden Bahrain's tourist base beyond the long-standing flow of people coming down from Kuwait or across from Saudi Arabia on weekends. The tourist office initially focused its attention on the high volume of transit traffic at the airport, but the introduction of longer-range aircraft in the early '90s meant that airlines flying from South-East Asia to northern Europe no longer needed to refuel in the Gulf, and the number of airlines using Bahrain as a refueling stop fell off drastically. The tourist office, in turn, again relied on the weekenders, though the number of long-haul tourists visiting the island continues to rise.

Economically, the Gulf War proved to be a mixed blessing. On one level business was great: Manama's hotels and bars were filled for many months, first by soldiers and sailors on leave and journalists at work, and later by a string of entrepreneurs hoping to cash in on the post-war reconstruction work in Kuwait. But in the longer term the war damaged the country's financial services industry. In addition, the recession which hit the west in the early '90s combined with the fallout of the war to leave the country's financial services industry in a fragile, if slowly recovering, state.

POPULATION & PEOPLE

At the last count, Bahrain had a population of about 600,000 people, of whom some 150,000 are foreign workers. There are many North Americans and Britons working in the island's oil and financial industries. Services are dominated by Filipinos. That said, Manama is probably the most cosmopolitan city in the Gulf.

The Bahrainis themselves are Arabs, though many are at least partially of Persian ancestry. Bahrain's population is 85% Muslim, and around three quarters of the Muslims are Shiites. The Sunni Muslim minority includes the royal family and most of the leading merchant families.

Even before the civil unrest which broke out in late 1994 the government was sensitive about the Shiites, who are generally not as well off economically as the country's Sunnis. You are apt to find that Bahrainis, particularly those working for the government, are not comfortable discussing religion. This is reinforced by the fact that many of the Shiites are at least partially of Persian ancestry, another fact with which the government seems a bit uncomfortable.

EDUCATION

As in most of the other Gulf countries literacy was not widespread until fairly recently. Bahrain now provides free education for all Bahrainis and its American-system International School is considered one of the best in the region – there are even Saudi families from the Eastern Province who send their children across the causeway every day to attend classes there! Though many young Bahrainis still travel abroad to further their education, particularly in the UK and the USA, Bahrain itself has two universities: Bahrain University and the Arabian Gulf University. The latter is managed and funded jointly by the six Gulf Cooperation Council (GCC) states and Iraq.

ARTS

Traditional craftwork continues in several places around Bahrain: dhow building on the outskirts of Manama and on Muharraq, cloth weaving at Bani Jamrah and pottery making at A'ali. The tourist office in Manama has a selection of all of these (except the dhows!), as well as locally made baskets, on sale; or you can drive out and bargain with the craftspeople yourself. The Heritage Centre in central Manama has a number of displays which put these crafts into their original context. As for more expensive traditional arts and crafts, a few goldsmiths still operate

in the Manama souk, though a lot of the work is now done abroad.

Public performances of traditional music and dancing have largely died out, though the tourist office is said to be considering organising shows to keep alive this aspect of Bahraini culture.

SOCIETY & CONDUCT
Traditional Culture

As flashy and modern as central Manama may be, the basic rhythms of life in the island's many villages, and in parts of Manama itself, remain remarkably traditional. Starting from Bab Al-Bahrain in Manama, the further you go back into the souk the more traditional life gets. The same can be said for much of the rest of the country. It is a side of Bahrain that visitors all too often miss.

Dos & Don'ts

Though traditional life can still be seen in Bahrain you should not make the mistake of assuming that you can join in it. Bahrain is relatively liberal as Gulf countries go, but the Gulf itself remains one of the most conservative places on earth. In Bani Jamrah, for example, nobody will object to you taking a photograph of the weavers sitting near the entrance to the village, but that does not necessarily mean that the villagers will be happy if you and your camera go wandering through the village itself. In fact, the weaver's shack in question (complete with a sample catalogue) has been placed outside the main part of the village precisely to send the message that visitors are not particularly welcome inside.

As is the case almost everywhere in the Arab world you should not attempt to photograph women.

Bahrain is still a conservative country where dress is concerned, at least by western standards. In general apply common sense: for women, no miniskirts, short shorts, bikini tops etc. Men should not walk around barechested or in overly tight clothing. Women should probably stick to one-piece bathing suits at the beach, though bikinis are OK around the pool at big hotels.

Conservative dress is particularly in order in rural areas. That means long, loose clothing. Short sleeves are usually OK, even for women, but sleeveless clothes (especially on women) may cause offence in more traditional areas. The spark that touched off 1994's riots was the appearance of scantily clad female joggers in the streets of Suq Al-Khamis as part of a charity 'fun run'. The fact that the race was routed through Suq Al-Khamis at all indicates that somebody had lost sight of a key fact of Bahraini life: Manama and the villages are worlds apart in terms of what is considered acceptable dress and deportment.

Non-Muslims may enter mosques except during prayer time. As in any mosque, both men and women are expected to be well covered (for women this includes covering the head, though a veil is unnecessary) and to take off their shoes at the door. You should bear in mind that while, technically, all mosques are open to visitors, in practice only the Al-Fatih Mosque and the Friday Mosque are visited by non-Muslims with any regularity. You might want to restrict your mosque-viewing to these two and the Suq Al-Khamis Mosque, which is no longer used for prayer.

See Dos & Don'ts in the Facts about the Region chapter for more information.

RELIGION

Bahrain's population is 85% Muslim with indigenous Christian, Jewish, Hindu and Parsee minorities (according to the Ministry of Information). Islam is the state religion. The majority of the Muslims, probably upwards of 70%, are Shiites.

LANGUAGE

Arabic is the official language but English is very widely spoken. As in Saudi Arabia, most of the service personnel are Asian and you can safely assume that they speak English (otherwise they would not be working here). Farsi is also widely spoken,

though it is most often used in the home rather than in public.

See Language in the Facts about the Region chapter for a list of useful Arabic words and phrases.

Facts for the Visitor

PLANNING
When to Go
The best time to visit Bahrain is between November and February, when it's not too hot. Avoid visiting during Ramadan when things slow down significantly. You might also want to stay away during the Muslim festivals marking the end of Ramadan and the annual pilgrimage to Mecca (see Business Hours and Public Holidays & Special Events, later) or over New Year's Eve. At these times the country is swamped, particularly with merrymakers (both Arab and foreign) from Saudi Arabia and Kuwait and hotel rooms become very difficult to find, especially at the bottom end of the scale where the prices sometimes double.

Maps
The Ministry of Information publishes two maps of the country leaving you with something of a Hobson's Choice when it comes to navigation. The *Bahrain Map* (BD 1 at the tourist office) is very comprehensive and includes good inset maps of Manama and Muharraq. It is also very out of date – particularly where the highways outside Manama are concerned. The ministry also publishes a glossy tourist map (BD 1.500 at the tourist office). This is a lot more up to date but it is also a lot less detailed and it, too, is not without errors (notably, the Shaikh Salman Highway is in the wrong place). The blue map is probably your best bet for navigating the back streets of Manama but the glossy map will be more useful if you are looking for the tourist sites outside the capital.

TOURIST OFFICES

There's a tourist office in Bab Al-Bahrain in Manama which organises tours of the city. It has a shop selling maps, postcards, Bahraini handicrafts and assorted touristy kitsch. There is also a tourist information desk at Bahrain airport.

Bahrain does not have any tourist offices abroad, though you can sometimes find some tourist information at Gulf Air's overseas offices.

VISAS & DOCUMENTS
Visas

British citizens do not need a visa to enter Bahrain for periods of up to one month. People of most other western nationalities can obtain a 72-hour transit visa or a seven-day tourist visa on arrival at Bahrain airport or at the Bahraini customs post on the Saudi Arabia-Bahrain Causeway. The three-day visa costs BD 10 and the seven-day visa costs BD 15. Fees can be paid in Bahraini dinars or Saudi riyals. There is an exchange desk in the transit lounge at the airport. For those not driving their own vehicle across the causeway, possession of an onward or return plane or bus ticket is not formally required, but travellers are often asked to produce these and you should expect some delays if you are unable to show one.

A difficulty that some travellers may encounter is that Bahrain does not recognise the concept of naturalisation. For example, an Indian-born Australian or an American who immigrated from Lebanon is still, as far as the Bahraini government is concerned, Indian or Lebanese, respectively, and that means they can't get visas at the airport. Bahraini customs officials are especially strict with nationals of Iran, the Arab world outside the Gulf (especially Lebanon, Palestine and Iraq) and the Indian subcontinent. If your paternal grandparents came from one of these areas of the world you may be OK, but it's a hit-or-miss situation. Calling a Bahraini embassy for advice is of little use as the embassies are often unaware of airport-issued visa regulations.

If you fall into one of the above categories your best bet is to have one of the larger hotels arrange your visa as outlined in the following section.

Whatever your ethnic background, people listing their occupation as writer, journalist, editor etc are generally not admitted to Bahrain unless the Ministry of Information has sponsored their visa. This includes British citizens, and the fact that you may only be on holiday or in transit overnight makes no difference! The ministry usually needs about a week to arrange visas.

Women travelling alone should be aware that the rules on granting visas at the airport to unaccompanied females seem to change fairly frequently. Pensioners probably won't have any problems, but for younger women the safest course is to book a room at a medium-sized (or larger) hotel in advance and have the hotel arrange the visa.

Drivers arriving from Saudi Arabia must sign a Personal Guarantee promising to take the car back out of Bahrain within a specified period of time. Be sure to keep this piece of paper as it must be turned in at customs on the way out. A mandatory insurance fee of BD 1.500 or SR 15 is collected from the driver of every car crossing the causeway.

If your passport has an Israeli stamp you will be denied entry (and they do check).

Hotel-Sponsored Visas To have a hotel arrange a visa for you, send them a fax about three weeks prior to arrival with all your passport data as well as arrival and departure dates and the purpose of your visit ('tourism' is fine). You'll also need to specify the exact flight on which you plan to arrive (airline, flight number, day and time) and include a telephone, fax or telex number where you can be reached. It might be a good idea to double-check everything by telephone. The hotel will act as your sponsor and make all of the visa arrangements for a small fee (usually BD 2 to BD 4, which will be added to your bill). You can then pick up the visa at the airport, port or on the causeway.

Note that as visa rules have loosened up over the last few years hotels have become increasingly reluctant to go through the hassle of arranging visas unless you can give them a good reason to do so. They will gladly extend visas once you are in the country provided, of course, you are staying at their hotel.

Visa Extensions Hotels that can issue visas can also get your visa extended once you are in the country. They generally prefer to have you pick up a 72-hour transit visa on your own at the airport and then, if you want to stay a few more days, they will handle the extension. If you are staying in a cheap hotel and want to extend your stay, your only practical option is to move to a more up-market hotel and stay there. The procedure for extending visas through a hotel is painless and requires nothing from you except a few extra dinars (usually BD 10 for a one-week extension plus a hotel charge of BD 2 to BD 4). It usually takes about two days so don't wait until the morning your visa runs out to hand your passport to the desk clerk at the hotel! Getting a one-week extension of your tourist visa once or even twice should not be a problem but after that things could change. Bahrain is a small place and while it is packed with things to see it still does not take too long to see all of them. The government is very wary of people trying to stay in the country and work on tourist visas. If you came in on a tourist visa and want to stay for more than two weeks you had better be prepared to explain why, because someone is almost sure to ask.

Exit/Re-Entry Visas These are not issued for tourists. Resident foreigners must obtain a re-entry visa before leaving the country on business or holiday. If you live in Bahrain your company ought to take care of this. Resident foreigners who travel frequently can obtain multiple re-entry visas valid for six months.

Other Documents
No special documents are needed to enter or move about the country. Health certificates are not required to enter Bahrain unless you are coming from one of the areas of endemic

yellow fever, cholera etc (eg sub-Saharan Africa). If you plan to rent a car you will need an International Driving Permit.

EMBASSIES
Bahraini Embassies Abroad
Bahraini embassies overseas are of little use to the traveller. They usually handle only residence and work visas, which are only issued after approval has been received from Manama. Addresses of some Bahraini embassies around the world follow.

Iran
　Kheyabun-é Sarvan Khaled Eslamboli, 123 Kuché-yé Nozdahom, Tehran (☎ (21) 626202, 626203)
Kuwait
　Surra District, St 1, Block 1, Building 24, Kuwait City (☎ 531 8530)
Oman
　Al-Kharjiyah St, just off Way 3015, Medinat Qaboos, Muscat (☎ 605074, 605133)
Saudi Arabia
　Diplomatic Quarter, Riyadh, near the Canadian embassy (☎ (01) 488 0044)
UK
　98 Gloucester Rd, London, SW7 (☎ (0171) 370 5132)
USA
　3502 International Drive NW, Washington DC 20008 (☎ (202) 342 0741)

Foreign Embassies in Bahrain
Embassies in Bahrain are listed in the Manama section.

CUSTOMS
You can expect a thorough, though not particularly intrusive, search at Bahrain airport. Non-Muslims are allowed to import two litres of alcoholic beverages. All passengers are allowed to bring in 400 cigarettes or 50 cigars and 250g of loose tobacco. You are also allowed eight ounces (227 ml) of perfume.

You may be asked whether you are carrying a video camera and, if so, this fact is likely to be recorded on your passport to guarantee that you take it out again.

Beyond that, the items on the forbidden list include pornographic material, guns and ammunition and cultured pearls.

MONEY
Costs

If you stay in the souk, walk a lot and have no huge appetite for either food or booze, it is quite possible to get by on BD 10 per day. It is possible to eat for under BD 2. Alcohol will bust your budget quickly – a beer usually costs at least BD 1 and a pint is often BD 1.500 or so. Hard liquor is BD 1.500 or more per shot.

Currency

The Bahraini dinar (BD) is divided into 1000 fils. Notes come in denominations of BD ½, 1, 5, 10 and 20. Coins are 5, 10, 25, 50 and 100 fils. For small transactions most businesses will accept Qatari or Saudi riyals at a flat rate of BD 1 = QR/SR 10. The Bahraini dinar is a convertible currency and there are no restrictions on its import or export.

Currency Exchange

US$1	=	BD 0.420
UK£1	=	BD 0.640
FF1	=	BD 0.081
DM1	=	BD 0.270
A$1	=	BD 0.330

Changing Money

Banking hours are Saturday to Wednesday from 7.30 am to noon. Most banks close at 11 am on Thursday. Some moneychangers keep slightly longer hours and may be open for a while in the late afternoon. Changing money on a Friday will be difficult anywhere except at a big hotel, where the rate is certain to be pretty bad.

The exchange rates on offer at banks and moneychangers, as well as the commissions they charge, can vary widely. Particularly if you are in the centre of Manama (where a large number of banks and moneychangers are concentrated on Government Ave between Bab Al-Bahrain and the Standard & Chartered Bank building) it can pay to spend a few minutes shopping around.

AMEX provides its usual range of cheque-cashing services for card holders and this is probably the easiest way to get money in Bahrain, though some banks will advance cash against Visa cards.

It is also possible to obtain money from local ATM machines. ABN-AMRO Bank's branch on Al-Furdah Ave in central Manama has a cash machine linked to AMEX's Express Cash system. ATMs at Bank of Bahrain & Kuwait branches take cards on the Cirrus and Network systems and the cash machines at British Bank of the Middle East branches are part of both the Plus and Global Access systems.

Tipping & Bargaining

A service charge is added to almost every bill in Bahrain but it generally goes to the shop, not the waiter or waitress. If you're in a good restaurant an appropriate tip would be about 10%. While tips are not expected, especially in cheap places, foreign waiters and waitresses are often paid appalling wages, especially in the smaller places that cater largely to, say, Indian or Sri Lankan labourers. A tip, even a small one, will be much appreciated.

Almost all prices in Bahrain are negotiable up to a point. The trick is finding that point. In many small shops you will probably be offered an immediate discount on the marked price, and you might be able to talk the price of souvenirs on sale in the souk down by an additional 10% or so (but not the ones in the Bab Al-Bahrain government tourist shop; the prices there are fixed). The bargaining range on items like electronic goods varies a lot depending on the market at the time, from almost nothing up to maybe 15%. Hotel rates are almost always negotiable though. There is usually a certain, if small, amount of leeway on plane tickets. This is rarely more than 5%.

Prices of meals, books and organised tours are generally not negotiable.

POST & COMMUNICATIONS
Postal Rates

Domestic postage is 80 fils for each 20g a letter weighs. International postal rates are measured in 10g increments. Postage per 10g to other Gulf countries is 80 fils, to other

Arab countries 100 fils, to Europe and the Indian subcontinent 200 fils, and 250 fils to everywhere else. Postage for aerogrammes is 150 fils to anywhere in the world.

Postcard rates are 60 fils to other Gulf countries, 80 fils to the rest of the Arab world, 150 to Europe and the Indian subcontinent and 200 fils to everywhere else.

Sending parcels by air costs BD 2 for the first half kg to any destination in the Arab world. Each additional half kg costs 300 fils within the Gulf and 500 fils to other Arab countries. The first half kg costs BD 3 to destinations outside the Arab world with each additional half kg costing BD 1 to Europe and the Indian subcontinent and BD 1.500 elsewhere.

Surface parcel rates within the Gulf are BD 2.500 for up to one kg, BD 3.250 for up to three kg, BD 4 for up to five kg and BD 5.250 for up to 10 kg. For other Arab countries the rates for up to 1/3/5/10 kg are BD 2.500/4/5/6; to Iran and the Indian subcontinent the rates are BD 3.500/5/6.500/9; to Europe, Cyprus and Turkey, BD 4/6.500/8/12; to Australia, Africa and South-East Asia, BD 4.500/6/7.500/11; and to the Americas, BD 5/7/9/13.

Sending Mail
Mail to and from Europe and North America takes about a week. Allow 10 days to Australia. The GPO is across Government Ave from Bab Al-Bahrain in Manama.

Receiving Mail
The GPO on Government Ave has poste restante facilities. Address letters to: Your Name, c/o Poste Restante, Manama Post Office (Counter Section), Manama, Bahrain.

Telephone
Bahrain has an excellent telecommunications system. You can direct-dial just about anywhere. When calling Bahrain from the outside world the country code is 973, followed by the local six-digit number. There are no area or city codes. For English-speaking directory assistance dial ☎ 181 for local numbers and ☎ 191 for international numbers.

Bahrain also has one of the most extensive sets of Home Country Direct services in the world. By dialling a special number these connect you directly to an operator in the country in question. You may then make a collect (reverse charges) call or bill the call to a phone company credit card issued in that country. Home Country Direct services available from any phone in Bahrain include:

Australia	800-061
Canada	800-100
Denmark	800-045
Hong Kong	800-852
Ireland	800-353
Japan	800-081
Malaysia	800-060
Netherlands	800-031
Philippines	800-163
Portugal	800-351
Singapore	800-065
South Korea	800-082
UK	800-044
USA	800-001 (ATT)
USA	800-002 (MCI)
USA	800-777 (Sprint)

Payphones take coins, though card phones are equally, if not more, common. For coin phones you need to insert a minimum of 100 fils. Local calls are charged in increments of 50 fils. You can make calls and purchase phonecards at the Telecommunications Office in the Yateem Centre on Al-Khalifa Ave in Manama.

The Bahrain Telephone Company, BATELCO, also has a wide range of information-by-phone services. These run the gamut from the conventional to the bizarre. The conventional ones include Time (☎ 140) and Weather (☎ 268 700). Among the more interesting and novel services are News (☎ 268 912), Sports (☎ 268 222), Healthline (☎ 268 914) and Touristline (☎ 268 444 – for information on Bahrain's tourist spots, hotel activities and advice on souvenir gifts).

Fax, Telex & Telegraph

Fax, telex, and telegraph services are available from the Telecommunications Office in the Yateem Centre on Al-Khalifa Ave in Manama. See the Manama section for more details.

BOOKS
Travel Guides

The best all-round guide to the country's architecture, archaeology and curiosities is *Bahrain: A Heritage Explored* by Angela Clark. It can be found at all hotel bookshops and costs about BD 5. The book, an updated version of Clark's 1981 book, *The Islands of Bahrain*, includes the best general descriptions of the country's archaeological sites (outside of the Al-Khalifa/Rice book which is a bit bulky to haul around). Clark covers every conceivable place of interest though there is nothing on hotels, restaurants, visa regulations etc. Her driving instructions to the sites outside of Manama are sometimes a bit out of date, but one can usually manage to follow them.

Bahrain – A MEED Practical Guide, like the other books in the MEED series, is indispensable for those planning to live in Bahrain. *The Economist Business Traveller's Guides – Arabian Peninsula* is, along with the MEED guide, the best among the many how-to-do-business-with-the-Arabs sort of books on the market.

History, People & Society

Possibly the best book on Bahrain is *Looking for Dilmun* by Geoffrey Bibby, an Anglo-Danish archaeologist who supervised the early professional archaeological work on the island. This is an account of Bibby's digs in Bahrain (which later branched out to include Qatar, Kuwait, Abu Dhabi and eastern Saudi Arabia) and the slow discovery and reconstruction of the history of the ancient Dilmun civilisation. But it also provides a fascinating picture of life in Bahrain and the rest of the Gulf in the '50s and '60s. It's also a pretty good primer on basic archaeological technique.

Archaeology buffs might also want to pick up *Bahrain Through the Ages – The Archaeology* by Shaikha Haya Ali Al-Khalifa & Michael Rice. Hotel bookshops in Bahrain are the easiest place to find this one, which is only available in hardback.

The Merchants by Michael Field includes an interesting chapter on the rise of the Kanoos, Bahrain's most prominent merchant family.

The Bahrain chapter in Jonathan Raban's *Arabia Through the Looking Glass* is quite a good read and contains some pointed observations on expatriate life on the island during the oil boom. He visited in early 1979.

NEWSPAPERS & MAGAZINES

The *Gulf Daily News* is Bahrain's English-language newspaper. It's a bit disappointing in terms of news but hugely useful as a source of 'What's On' information. There is no Friday edition.

All of the larger hotels stock the usual array of international publications: the *International Herald Tribune*, all the main British newspapers, *Time*, *Newsweek*, the *Economist*, as well as major French and German newspapers and magazines. Foreign newspapers and magazines are usually available one or two days after publication.

RADIO & TV

Radio Bahrain broadcasts 24 hours a day on several FM and MW frequencies, of which the main one is 98.5 FM. The fare consists, broadly, of pop music in the morning, feature programmes in the afternoon and light music at night, with quiz shows and documentaries (some locally made, some foreign, which usually means British) mixed in throughout the day. As a community bulletin board and 'What's On' source it can't be beaten.

Channel 55 is Bahrain TV's English programme service. It broadcasts a mix of British and US programmes every day from 5 or 6 pm until around midnight, following which it links up with CNN for one hour before signing off. Bahrain TV also broadcasts BBC World Service TV 24 hours a day on a local UHF frequency.

PHOTOGRAPHY & VIDEO

Film is readily available in Manama, as is processing for colour prints. Slides can often take a few days to get developed and B&W film can be a problem.

Bahrain is fairly relaxed about both tourists and cameras and as long as you don't try to take a picture of something obviously military or obviously taboo (for example women, especially in rural areas) you should have no problems.

As is the case throughout the Gulf many people, particularly the police, are sensitive about videos. You may have trouble bringing a video camera into the country, and you are certain to cause a stir if you try to use it in rural areas.

TIME

Time in Bahrain is GMT/UTC plus three hours. The clocks are not changed for summer time/daylight savings. When it's noon in Manama, the time elsewhere is:

City	Time
Paris, Rome	10 am
London	9 am
New York	4 am
Los Angeles	1 am
Perth, Hong Kong	5 pm
Sydney	7 pm
Auckland	9 pm

ELECTRICITY

The current in Bahrain is 230V AC. British-style three-pin electrical sockets are standard.

WEIGHTS & MEASURES

Bahrain uses the metric system.

LAUNDRY

Laundrettes are virtually unknown in Bahrain, as is the case pretty much everywhere in the Gulf. If you don't feel like doing your washing in the hotel room, the best way to get your clothes cleaned is through your hotel or at one of the numerous small laundries around the centre. Even the small hotels often have a laundry service of some sort and in the cheapies washing a medium-sized load should not cost more than BD 2. Going to a laundry will probably be a bit cheaper, though it may take longer.

HEALTH

Bahrain has a quite highly developed healthcare system and while treatment is not free it is, by western standards, moderately priced. The quality of medical care in Bahrain is very high and there would be no need to evacuate a patient abroad for anything other than fairly serious, specialised procedures. If you are staying in a medium-sized or larger hotel they will almost certainly have a doctor on call or on staff to deal with minor ailments. Otherwise, or for more serious care, contact your embassy for advice. They may refer you to their own doctor or provide you with a list of doctors who speak English. Several of Bahrain's hospitals also offer patient consultations on a walk-in basis. See Medical Services in the Manama section for more details.

Hygiene standards for food preparation in Bahrain are quite high except in a few of the darker corners of the souk. Cases of travellers' diarrhoea almost always originate in the cheaper parts of the souk; if you avoid such places and exercise a little common sense you will probably be OK.

The tap water in Bahrain is not suitable for drinking. It won't kill you, but you won't feel so great after drinking it either. In general stick to bottled water, though coffee or tea made with tap water that has been thoroughly boiled is generally OK.

WOMEN TRAVELLERS

Bahrain is without a doubt one of the easiest countries in the Gulf for women to travel in. The country's long trading history and traditional openness account for its relatively progressive attitude toward women. Though some restaurants have 'family sections', these tend to be used only by Bahraini and Saudi families. Foreigners who do not want to sit there will not usually be forced to do so. Women may drive in Bahrain. Should you find yourself on the receiving end of unwanted advances, remain calm and be firm. If you are not in a public place, seek one out, particularly where someone in authority (a police officer, hotel security person etc) is in evidence.

Women (and men) should still, of course, be aware that Bahrain is a conservative, Muslim country and that many things which would be acceptable in the west will be frowned upon here. Clothing that is overly tight or revealing (miniskirts, halter tops etc) may offend Bahrainis and attract unwanted attention.

Outside of mosques, however, it is never necessary for female visitors to Bahrain to cover their heads, though extra caution should be taken in village areas. Modest shorts or above-the-knee skirts which would be perfectly acceptable in Manama will not go down well in the villages.

USEFUL ORGANISATIONS

While things have been developing quite quickly in recent years, Bahrain is still relatively new to tourism and, as a result, there is very little travel infrastructure. Bahrain's tourist organisations are still geared mostly to people visiting from Saudi Arabia for the weekend and groups who stay in five-star hotels and arrive with everything already organised. Should you find yourself in need of a youth hostel card, you can obtain one from the Bahrain Youth Hostels Association for BD 7 (see the Manama section for more details). Aside from that, however, Bahrain has little in the way of budget travel infrastructure.

DANGERS & ANNOYANCES

Bahrain is a very safe place. Violent crime is quite rare and you can walk around the centre of Manama late at night without fear. This continues to be the case despite the political tensions that have periodically gripped Bahrain since 1994.

The biggest local annoyance is the unshakeable conviction of every taxi driver in the country that any foreign person on foot must want a taxi.

Several bombings in the winter and spring

of 1996 led to heightened security throughout the island and a government crack-down on dissent. Anti-government violence, particularly in Bani Jamrah, Suq Al-Khamis and other villages south-west of Manama, remains a problem, but there was, at the time of writing, no evidence that foreigners were being targeted. For the moment, political unrest remains a cause for concern but not something that would require putting off a trip to Bahrain.

The safest course is to contact your country's foreign ministry for an update on the situation before travelling, and to exercise caution at all times.

BUSINESS HOURS

Shops and offices are generally open from around 8 am until 1 pm. Many shops, particularly in the Manama souk, reopen in the late afternoon from 4 or 5 until 7 pm. Friday is the weekly holiday and many businesses also close early on Thursday. Most western embassies and virtually all government offices are closed all day Thursday (though many Arab embassies will be open on Thursday mornings).

PUBLIC HOLIDAYS & SPECIAL EVENTS

The Islamic holidays of Eid Al-Fitr (the end of Ramadan), Eid Al-Adha (the end of the pilgrimage season) and the Islamic New Year are all observed; for dates see the table of holidays under Public Holidays in the Regional Facts for the Visitor chapter. Secular holidays include New Year's Day (1 January) and National Day (16 December).

Bahrain's large Shiite community also marks the religious festival of *Ashoora*, though this is not an official government holiday. Ashoora marks the death of Hussein, the grandson of the Prophet, at the battle of Karbala in 680 AD. It is the most important religious festival celebrated in Bahrain after the more universal Islamic holidays of Eid Al-Fitr and Eid Al-Adha. Processions, led by men flagellating themselves, take place in many of the country's predominantly Shiite areas. In Manama, the main procession takes place on a series of relatively small streets in the souk about five blocks directly back from Bab Al-Bahrain. You can expect heavy security. The festival takes place every year on the 10th day of the Muslim month of Muharram, the first month of the Hejira year.

ACTIVITIES
Most activities on the island involve clubs, societies and sports organisations. The *Gulf Daily News* and Radio Bahrain are good sources of information on events and gatherings around the island. Although Bahrain is surrounded by water the public beaches are pretty crummy, mainly because the Gulf is so shallow (you can wade as much as half a km out and the water's still only up to your knees); the clubs dredge their beaches. There's no problem for women to swim at the public beaches but they might feel more comfortable at clubs or hotel pools. Otherwise, social life on the island consists mainly of eating and/or drinking out.

WORK
Throughout the Gulf regulations controlling work visas are quite strict. Converting a tourist visa to a work permit can, at least in theory, be done but it is not easy and you might well have to go back home first and pick up your work visa there. It is rather easier for the spouse of a foreigner working in Bahrain to get permission to work. Ultimately, however, working in the country requires that you have a Bahraini sponsor and it is not the sort of place where the casual traveller can expect to pick up short-term work, either legally or illegally.

ACCOMMODATION
Hostel
Bahrain's youth hostel is in the suburb of Al-Jufayr, south-east of Manama's centre. If you are not an HI member, membership cards are available to foreigners for BD 7. See the Manama section for more details.

Hotels
Cheap hotel rooms cost about BD 7/10 for singles/doubles with bath. Rooms without

private baths are a dinar or so less. Cheap hotel accommodation can be a bit hard to come by on weekends, especially during the Eid Al-Fitr holiday which marks the end of Ramadan. See Manama, Places to Stay – bottom end, for details about varying hotel weekend rates.

Like most places in the Gulf Bahrain has a glut of five-star hotels and this can lead to some unusual surprises for the budget traveller. The Bahrain Hilton, for example, has a weekend package (available every Thursday, Friday and Saturday) of one night's accommodation, use of the swimming pool and health club and a free drink at the bar for BD 24 for two people, including the service charge. When you consider that the Hilton will pick you up at the airport and return you there for free, this works out to be almost as cheap as the weekend rates at many of the places in the souk. The Holiday Inn and Delmon Hotel often have similar packages, and they all have to be booked in advance.

FOOD
While a bit thin on Arabic food Bahrain has a bonanza of Asian specialities. From Indian and Pakistani to Thai and Filipino you can find almost any sort of cuisine in the area around Al-Khalifa Rd. Good meals are usually about BD 3, but if you stick to simple things like shawarma you can easily eat for under BD 1.

Cafes & Bars
Cafes tend to be modern, western-style establishments, usually located in the larger shopping centres. A few traditional coffee houses remain, including a particularly good one on Government Ave near the Delmon Hotel, but there are far more places offering cappuccino and cakes than sweet tea and water pipes.

The traditional coffee houses serve mostly tea. Coffee at these establishments usually means Turkish coffee. Traditional Arabian coffee has largely retreated to the hospitality carts of five-star hotels.

Bars are almost all located in hotels,

though a few free-standing restaurants also have bar sections.

Snacks

Bahrain's selection of street food and snacks runs from the traditional to the modern. At the traditional end are shawarma and *sambousa* (samosa), which you are likely to find sold alongside such western fare as burgers, french fries, ice cream and popcorn.

Main Dishes

The cheap restaurant market is dominated by Indian and Chinese food. Many of the tiny Indian places have an extremely limited menu, often consisting mostly of biryanis. Oriental food is a bit more expensive but tends to be a better bet. For one thing the Oriental restaurants often look a lot cleaner. Most of these restaurants offer standard Chinese fare, with variations based on the staff's origin (Thai, Filipino etc).

Desserts

If you want to be indulgent there is always baklava, which is sometimes available in restaurants and can also be found in the Lebanese sweet and nut shops that dot Manama (and every other Gulf city). Otherwise, desserts don't really amount to anything special. Do as the locals do: order ice cream.

Self-Catering

The main problem with self-catering on a budget in Manama is that there are not a lot of places to shop for bread, meat etc in the centre. The small food stores which dot Al-Khalifa Ave and Municipality Ave sell mostly uncooked food (eg rice) and canned or other food requiring some sort of preparation. In other words, this is not a country where buying a loaf of bread and a hunk of cheese is really much of an option. My advice is to spend the extra dinar and get a decent dinner.

DRINKS

Nonalcoholic drinks consist of soft drinks (Pepsi or Coke, 7-Up, orange soda) or fruit juice (not usually fresh unless you are in a big hotel). Alcohol is draft beer and the same selection of the harder stuff that you would find in any bar. Booze is not cheap. Expect to pay at least BD 1 for a can of beer and BD 1.500 for an English pint. Mixed drinks start at around BD 1.500 and head for the sky from there.

ENTERTAINMENT

Bahrain has one of the most lively entertainment scenes in the Gulf. See the Manama section for a full write-up on Bahrain's nightlife.

THINGS TO BUY

Bahrain's specialities, pearls and gold, are good value. Good handicrafts are on sale at the tourist office at Bab Al-Bahrain, which has displays showing where the various items come from on the island. This gives you the option of going out to the village in question and hunting down the craftspeople yourself (though don't expect to save a lot of money this way). Locally produced items include pottery from A'ali, woven baskets from Karbabad and hand-woven cloth from Bani Jamrah. There are also a lot of Arabian souvenirs, such as *dallah* coffeepots, that are manufactured elsewhere for sale in the Gulf. See Things to Buy in the Manama section for details.

Getting There & Away

AIR

The USA & Europe

Though a cheap stopover, Bahrain is a pretty expensive end-destination. While cheap deals to and from the island are sometimes available (particularly in the USA through specially authorised travel agencies – call Gulf Air for a list of these agencies), published fares to and from the island can be absolutely absurd. From the USA you can expect to pay as much as US$2000 return from New York on a regular fare. Special discounted fares through agencies are likely to bottom out at around US$1100. It's often a bit cheaper to originate such a trip in Bahrain, and if some airline has a special offer going it will be widely advertised by travel agencies. But even the special fares are not great. For example, BD 340 to London and BD 325 to Frankfurt (return) are the cheapest prices you are likely to find.

The cheapest published fares to New York are BD 487 one way and BD 624 return in the low season – early January to mid-June and mid-October to mid-December. A high-season return costs BD 675. These fares require a 14-day minimum stay and allow a maximum stay of three months.

Special offers aside, a one-way ticket to London costs BD 372. The cheapest return tickets require a 10-day stay and have a maximum validity of three months. These cost BD 401 in the low season (early January to the end of May and 1 October to mid-December) and BD 506 in the high season. The cheapest one-way/return fares to Rome are BD 309/359 (minimum stay 10 days, maximum three months) and BD 238/314 (six days/three months) to Athens.

Africa, Asia & Australia

Routes to India and South-East Asia tend to be a bit more competitive because of the large number of Asian workers in the Gulf, but you're still looking at special fares priced BD 260 or more to Bangkok and published fares of BD 349/488 for the cheapest one-way/return tickets regularly available (the return fare has a seven-day minimum stay and a three-month maximum). Comparable airfares to Delhi cost BD 191/264 one way/return (seven days/four months) and BD 270/350 (six days/two months) to Nairobi.

The one-way fare to Melbourne is BD 623. A low-season (early February through late August) return costs BD 583 (10 days/four months). During the high season the same ticket goes for BD 672.

Other Arab Countries

Flights to other parts of the Arab world are slightly better value at the published price,

but discounts tend to be harder to find. One-way/return fares to Cairo are BD 159/232 (five day minimum/two month maximum). Tickets to Damascus cost BD 133/179 (five days/two months).

Other Gulf States

Don't look for bargains here either, especially when you consider the tiny distances involved. Here's a sample of the cheapest one-way and return fares from Bahrain, with minimum and maximum stay requirements:

To	One Way	Return	Min/Max
Abu Dhabi	BD 63	BD 51	3/7 days
Dhahran	BD 25	BD 33	2/14 days
Doha	BD 33	BD 26	3/7 days
Dubai	BD 74	BD 60	3/7 days
Jeddah	BD 72	BD 99	2/14 days
Kuwait	BD 42	BD 59	2/14 days
Muscat	BD 116	BD 92	3/7 days
Riyadh	BD 30	BD 42	2/14 days

One-way tickets to Qatar, the UAE and Oman tend to be significantly more expensive than the cheapest available returns. Obviously if you need to go only one way the thing to do is to buy a return and simply throw away the second coupon (airport security being what it is in the Gulf selling the return coupon to someone else is not really an option).

Note, however, that specials are sometimes available to the UAE and Oman. These usually take the form either of 'weekend' fares that allow travel only on Wednesday, Thursday and Friday or of packages involving a couple of nights in a hotel in Dubai or Muscat. Check the windows of the travel agents in the souk for the latest offers.

LAND

Land travel to/from Bahrain is via the causeway to Saudi Arabia, the opening of which, in 1986, spelled the end of passenger dhow service between Bahrain and Alkhobar. You may hear rumours to the effect that only Saudis and Bahrainis can use the causeway. This is nonsense. Except at the weekend crunch periods (Thursday afternoon for traffic to Bahrain, Friday evening for traffic to Saudi Arabia) it tends to be quick and easy. During the weekend crush the bus is a particularly good bet as it has a special lane at customs.

To enter the causeway you must pay a toll of BD 2 or SR 20, regardless of whether you are travelling to Saudi Arabia or only to the island halfway across (where there is a restaurant). At the toll booth on either side you will be asked whether or not you are crossing the border and, if necessary, will be given a landing card to fill out. Drivers entering Bahrain from Saudi Arabia must purchase temporary Bahraini insurance and sign a personal guarantee. For more details see Visas & Documents and Embassies in the Facts for the Visitor section earlier in this chapter.

The Saudi-Bahraini Transport Company runs five buses daily to and from Dammam via Alkhobar. The fare is BD 4 one way, BD 7 return. Bahrain to Dammam or vice versa takes about three hours. They also sell tickets for onward travel to Jordan, Syria, Kuwait and the UAE involving a change of bus in Dammam. For more details see the Manama section.

SEA

There are passenger services between Iran and Bahrain. The boats leave from Mina Sulman on the outskirts of Manama, and there is only one class of service. The trip takes 16 hours and costs BD 36 one way, BD 63 return, plus a BD 3 port tax. Contact International Travel (☎ 250 883) on Al-Khalifa Ave, between Bab Al-Bahrain and the Friday Mosque, for tickets and details. The travel agency can also arrange visas.

LEAVING BAHRAIN

If you depart by air there is an airport Usage Fee of BD 3. This must be paid in cash in Bahraini dinars (Saudi or Qatari riyals are not accepted). Some of the four and five-star hotels will sell pre-paid airport Usage Fee vouchers.

There is BD 2 toll for leaving the country via the causeway to Saudi Arabia and a BD 3 port tax if you leave by boat.

Getting Around

BUS

Bahrain has a fairly straightforward bus system linking most of the major towns to bus stations on Manama and Muharraq. The fare is a flat 50 fils per trip. For a complete list of bus routes see Getting Around in the Manama, Around Bahrain Island and Muharraq sections.

TAXI

Bahrain's taxis are metered, and while you can hire them by the hour for the purpose of seeing areas outside Manama, you should only do this if you really need the cab for an extended period of time or you need to have the cab to wait for a long time at some remote spot (like Qal'at Al-Bahrain or Al-'Areen), where you are unlikely to find another cab to take you on to your next destination.

If you decide to hire a driver by the hour the method is simple: just walk up to a taxi rank and start bargaining. Since few places in Bahrain are much more than half an hour's driving time from anywhere else in the country a fare of BD 5 per hour is perfectly reasonable, particularly if the cab is going to be standing still while you walk around the site. I've never had any trouble bargaining, though the drivers still find the concept a bit novel and may want a complete list of the places you plan to see. Providing an itinerary may prompt them to increase their prices, so I strongly advice against it.

Service-Taxi

Bahrain does not really have service-taxis like those found in other Middle Eastern countries. You will see pick-up trucks, cars and other vehicles with yellow circles on the driver's side door. These are the service-taxis. They often, but not always, follow the same routes as the buses. Unlike other Middle Eastern service-taxis, however, they are not bound to these routes. Drivers are free to go wherever they wish and this can lead to confusion since the route and destination of any given vehicle can change from minute to minute as passengers are picked-up and set down. Service-taxis do not contain meters and passengers normally pay 50 to 100 fils each, depending on the distance travelled.

Few westerners in Bahrain ever travel this way and you may find that the service-taxi picking you up magically becomes a 'special' taxi – with appropriately special fares – as soon as you get in. In any case, taking a service-taxi will save you, at most, a few fils so my advice is that you stick to the bus.

CAR
Road Rules
Bahraini law requires people driving cars or riding in the front seat to use seat belts. There is a BD 10 fine if the police catch you without your seat belt on. Speed limits are rigorously enforced and drunk driving laws are also quite strict. Driving is on the right.

Petrol
Petrol comes in two grades. The lower grade, known as *jayyid*, costs 80 fils per litre; premium, or *mumtaz* (literally 'special'), costs 100 fils per litre.

Rental
Everything in Manama can be seen on foot, but outside of the capital getting around can be a problem if you do not have a car. After all the obligatory extras, you can count on car hire running to BD 15 per day.

Bahrain is the only country in the Gulf where you cannot rent a car on a foreign driving licence. An International Driving Permit is required and must be obtained before you arrive in Bahrain. For more detailed rental information see the Manama section.

WALKING, HITCHING & BICYCLE
While most of Manama and Muharraq can be seen on foot, for about seven months a year it is impractical. You can walk from the Pearl Monument roundabout to the Diplomat Hotel (ie from one end of Manama to the

other) in about 30 to 45 minutes and from the Diplomat to the Muharraq souk in another 20 to 30 minutes. When it is 45°C and humid, however, you may want to think twice about doing this.

Bicycles are not common. Hitchhiking is a bit more problematic. It is not common, but it is not unheard of either. If you find yourself stranded outside of Manama, drivers will often stop and give you a lift. They may or may not expect payment for this but it is considered polite to offer to pay.

LOCAL TRANSPORT
Taxis in Bahrain have meters. Because the meters turn over fairly slowly taxis are quite cost-effective for getting around, especially over distances of two to five km. A flag fall is 800 fils and will take you about 1.5 km. Thereafter the meter ticks over in 100 fils increments every km or so. For all trips from (not to) the airport there is also a BD 1 surcharge.

You should know that the meters are a relatively recent addition to Bahrain's taxis and while the drivers are generally pretty good about turning them on they are none too happy about it. The drivers usually expect some sort of tip at the end of the trip.

Small trucks and other vehicles with a yellow circle painted on the door are unmetered taxis. Save yourself grief by sticking to the metered kind. If you insist on taking an unmetered ride negotiate the fare in advance to avoid problems at the end of the trip. Expect to pay around BD 1 for most trips inside Manama.

ORGANISED TOURS
Bahrain's tourist industry is still largely aimed at stopover and transit passengers and weekend visitors from Saudi Arabia. A number of airlines, starting with Gulf Air, offer short-stay stopover packages in Bahrain aimed at people travelling between Europe and Asia. These generally include a one or two-night stay, some meals and one or more half-day tours. Some of these cost less than US$100, including accommodation, and are pretty good deals. The usual

method of booking a stopover holiday is through the airline on which you will be travelling. Alternatively, you can enter Bahrain on a transit visa and contact a tour company directly. See the Manama section for a listing of tour companies.

Manama

Manama is the very new capital of a very old place – many of the hotels and official buildings along Government Ave sit on reclaimed land. But don't be fooled – only a few blocks inland from the shiny new hotels are sections of the city which have changed little in the last 50 years.

Orientation

Manama's main street is Government Ave, which runs roughly east-west through the city. The central section of this street is the stretch from the Delmon Hotel to the large roundabout by the Hilton and Sheraton hotels. Al-Khalifa Ave runs more or less parallel to, and one block south of, Government Ave. Here you will find many of Manama's cheaper hotels and numerous small restaurants. The hub of all activity is Bab Al-Bahrain and the small roundabout in front of it. The area between Government Ave and the King Faisal Highway contains a collection of government office buildings, banks and hotels. The area south of Government Ave is the souk, or marketplace. The King Faisal Highway runs along the city's (and the island's) northern coast and turns south around the Holiday Inn, changing its name to the Al-Fatih (or Al-Fateh) Highway. The western limit of the centre is the Pearl Monument roundabout, while the National Museum and the causeway to Muharraq mark the centre's eastern boundary.

Exhibition Ave, running south-east from the Shaikh Hamad Causeway to Shaikh Daij Ave and roughly paralleling the Al-Fatih Highway, is the other road you should know. Along it are a number of smaller hotels notable mostly for containing a few of Bahrain's better-known night spots. A few airline and car rental offices and fast-food joints are also in the same neighbourhood.

Information

Tourist Office The tourist office (☎ 231 375) and a government-run souvenir shop are both in Bab Al-Bahrain and are entered from the Al-Khalifa Ave side. They are open daily from 8 am to 1 pm and 4 to 8.30 pm. The shop sells both the older blue *Bahrain Map* for BD 1 and a glossier tourist map for BD 1.500. The latter has less detail but it is more up to date. The shop also sells souvenirs and crafts. The pottery and woven baskets are locally made, but all of the brass and wood work comes from Pakistan while the inlay boxes are Iranian. Organised tours run by government-owned Gulf Tours can be booked through the tourist office.

Foreign Embassies Most embassies are open Saturday to Wednesday from 7.30 or 8 am until noon or 1 pm. Some Arab embassies are also open on Thursday mornings.

Egypt
    Kuwait St, just beyond the Al-Hora Cold Store in the Al-Mahuz District (☎ 720 005)
France
    Diplomatic Area, Al-Fatih Highway, near the National Museum. The building is entered from the Exhibition Ave side (☎ 291 734).
Germany
    Al-Hassaa Building, 1st floor, near Beit Al-Qur'an (☎ 530 210)
Jordan
    Diplomatic Area, Al-Fatih Highway, near the National Museum (☎ 291 109)
Kuwait
    King Faisal Highway, opposite the Holiday Inn (☎ 534 040)
Netherlands (consulate)
    Al-Furdah Ave, Bahrain Commercial Centre, 2nd floor, above the ABN-AMRO Bank office (☎ 224 320)
New Zealand (consular agency)
    Yateem Centre, Level 2 (☎ 223 600)
Oman
    Diplomatic Area, Al-Fatih Highway, near the National Museum. The building is entered from the side facing Exhibition Ave (☎ 293 663).

Manama

ARABIAN GULF

To Muharraq &
Bahrain International
Airport

To Qal'at Al-Bahrain
& Saudi Arabia

To Gulf Hotel,
Al-Jufayr &
Youth Hostel

0   250   500 m

See Central Manama
Hotel District Map

PLACES TO STAY

4   Tylos Hotel
    (Joyce's Bar)
8   Sheraton Bahrain
9   Bahrain Hilton
11 Holiday Inn
12 The Diplomat
25 Omar Khayam Hotel
26 Ramada Hotel

OTHER

1   Pearl Monument
2   Manama Central Market
3   Buses to Saudi Arabia
5   American Mission
    Hospital
6   UK Embassy
7   Bahrain Commercial
    Complex
10 Kuwaiti Embassy
13 German Embassy
14 Beit Al-Qur'an
15 Sail Monument
16 National Museum
17 Omani Embassy
18 Jordanian Embassy
19 French Embassy
20 South Korean Embassy
21 Abu Bakr Al-Sadiq
    Mosque
22 Baisan International
    Hotel (The Warbler
    & Bacchus Bars)
23 Al-Sulmaniya Medical
    Centre
24 Old Palace
27 Al-Qudaybiyah Palace
28 Al-Fatih Mosque

Al-Fatih Highway

Tariq Bin Al-Abd Avenue

Exhibition Avenue

Diplomatic Area
Office Buildings

Vacant Lot

Palace Avenue

Sheikh Sulman Avenue

King Faisal Highway

Ras
Rummaan

Al-Hura

Zubara Avenue

Al-Qudaybiyha Avenue

Shaikh Daij Avenue

Al-Qudaybiyah

Bani Otbah Avenue

Palace Avenue

Awadiya

Dhuwawdah

Khalaf Al-Asfoot Ave

Fadhel

Kanoo

Hammam

Souk

Commercial
Area

Busirra

Zararie

Mukharqah

Isa Al-Kabeer Avenue

Shaikh Mohammed Avenue

Shaikh Hamad Avenue

Shaikh Isa Avenue

Andalus
Garden

Al-Sulmaniya
Garden

Cemetery

Al-Mutanabi Avenue

Al-Sulmaniya Avenue

Al-Sulmaniya Avenue

Kuwait
Avenue

Al-Adliya

Al-Sulmaniya

Al-Sulmaniya Avenue

Lulu Avenue

An Naim

Al-Budayyi Highway

Shuwaifiyah Avenue

Shaikh Salman Highway

Qasari
Garden

Al-Qufool

Delmun
Roundabout

Saudi Arabia
King Faisal Highway, opposite the Holiday Inn
and near the Kuwaiti embassy (☎ 537 722)
UK
Government Ave, opposite the Bahrain Commer-
cial Complex. They also handle Canadian and
Australian affairs (☎ 534 404).
USA
Just off the Shaikh Isa Bin Sulman Highway, in
the Al-Zinj district, next to the Ahli Sporting Club
(☎ 273 300)

Money Several banks are on the side street
that runs from the post office to the parking
lots in front of the Regency Inter-Continental. There are also a number of banks and
moneychangers on Government Ave
between Bab Al-Bahrain and the Delmon
Hotel. You are likely to get better rates from
moneychangers but might wind up paying a
larger commission. It's worth taking a few
minutes to shop around.

AMEX is represented in Bahrain by
Kanoo Travel (☎ 249 346). The office, on
Al-Khalifa Ave just south-west of Bab Al-
Bahrain, is open Saturday to Wednesday
from 8 am to 12.30 pm and 3 to 6 pm, and
on Thursday from 8 am to noon. They are
closed on Friday. They will cash personal
cheques for AMEX card holders but they do
not provide a client's mail service. The big
AMEX office in the Bahrain Commercial
Centre is AMEX's Middle East regional
administrative headquarters; you won't need
to go there unless you have a bill to pay. You
can get cash using AMEX's Express Cash
system from the ATM at the ABN-AMRO
Bank on Al-Furdah Ave, across the street
from the large parking lots in front of the
Regency Inter-Continental.

Other banks in the centre with cash
machines linked into the main international
systems include those at the British Bank of
the Middle East (Plus/Global Access) on Al-
Khalifa Ave across from the back side of the
Heritage Centre, and the Bank of Bahrain &
Kuwait (Cirrus/Network) on Government
Ave across from the Standard & Chartered
Bank building. Bank of Bahrain & Kuwait
also has a cash machine in the departures
area of the airport (before security).

Post The GPO is opposite Bab Al-Bahrain
on Government Ave. It is open daily, except
Friday, from 7 am to 7.30 pm. Poste restante
facilities are available. To receive letters here
address them to: Your Name, c/o Poste
Restante, Manama Post Office (Counter
Section), Manama, Bahrain.

The Ministry of Transportation's Postal
Directorate also runs a philatelic bureau. Call
the bureau on ☎ 523 403 for more information.

Telephone The main Telecommunications
Centre is on the ground floor of the Yateem
Centre shopping complex on Al-Khalifa
Ave. It is open every day from 6.30 am to
11.30 pm. Services include local and international telephone calls, telex, fax and
telegraph. International calls can be direct-
dialled on either coin or card phones or
booked through the operator. There are also
special Home Country Direct phones connecting directly to operators in the USA, UK,
Australia, Japan, the Netherlands and Hong
Kong. You should be aware that booking a
call is much more expensive than calling
direct on the card phones. Phonecards are on
sale at the desk. Cash, AMEX, Visa and
Diners Club are accepted for payment.

Travel Agencies More travel agencies than
one would think the market could possibly
support have offices on either Government
Ave or Al-Khalifa Ave. As in most Gulf
countries, plane tickets are usually cheaper
if purchased through a travel agency, provided you don't mind locking yourself into
particular travel dates at the time of purchase. Also, as in the other Gulf States, prices
are government controlled and do not vary
much between individual travel agents.
However, since not every agency offers
every fare, you should go to three or four
places before making up your mind as to
what really is the cheapest fare. Many of the
travel agencies in the Al-Khalifa Ave area
have signs advertising special deals which
change from month to month. London,
Bangkok and India (usually Delhi or

Bombay) are the most common destinations for these cut-rate fares.

Bookshops The Al-Hilal Bookshop on Tujjaar Ave has a rather eclectic selection of English books ranging from romance novels to technical books to the occasional out-of-print account of some 18th or 19th century explorer's voyages. The books are not cheap but it's as good as the selection gets. Also try the Family Bookshop, near the roundabout next to the UK embassy.

Cultural Centres The main western cultural centres in Bahrain are:

Alliance Française (☎ 683 295), in Isa Town, behind Bahrain University's Polytechnic College, off the 16th December Highway.
British Council (☎ 261 555), in the Ahmed Mansour Al-Ali Building (opposite the BMW showroom) on the Shaikh Salman Highway. The library, on the ground floor, is open Saturday to Wednesday from 9 am to noon and 3 to 6 pm.
USIS (☎ 273 300) has a library (open to all) at the US embassy with US newspapers and magazines. They are open Saturday to Wednesday from 8 am to 4 pm.

Medical Services If you get sick, medical treatment is relatively easy to obtain. The American Mission Hospital (☎ 253 447) offers walk-in consultations for BD 7 (BD 9.500 if you have to see a specialist) plus the cost of any medicine or X-rays required. Similar services are available at the Awali Hospital (☎ 753 434) in Awali, 15 km south of Manama.

Emergency For fire, police or ambulance services dial ☎ 999 from any telephone.

Dangers & Annoyances Bahrain is not a dangerous place. That said, young unaccompanied males should steel themselves for a certain amount of petty harassment. It seems that foreign women encounter far less of this sort of thing than they would in, say, Cairo or Athens, which is not to say that it does not happen. Be firm but maintain your composure and everything will probably be OK.

National Museum
This is the large white building at the northern end of the Al-Fatih Highway, near the Bahrain Island end of the Shaikh Hamad Causeway. The museum is open Saturday to Wednesday from 8 am to 2 pm, and Thursday from 10 am to 5 pm. It is closed on Friday. Admission is 500 fils. Photography is permitted except in the Document Hall and the Dilmun gallery. The collection is exceptionally well displayed, and most exhibits are marked in both English and Arabic. The archaeological displays are particularly good at explaining in lay terms exactly how archaeologists can tell so much from what, to some of us, looks like a bunch of rocks or bones.

The museum, which opened in December 1988, consists of three diamond-shaped halls, each with galleries on both the ground floor and the upper level. These are connected to a large, rectangular building which houses the entrance, an art gallery (to your left as you enter the building), auditorium, classroom, cafeteria and a shop.

Adjacent to the parking lot is an area with reconstructions of a number of **traditional building types**. These include a barasti house and a small mock-village complete with mosque, house with wind tower, souk and several dhows. The museum, and its parking lot, are entered from the Al-Fatih Highway. There is a sign telling drivers where to exit.

The main museum divides Bahrain's history into the Stone Age (5000-3200 BC), Formative Dilmun (3200-2200 BC), Early Dilmun (2200-1600 BC), Middle Dilmun (1600-1000 BC), Late Dilmun (1000-330 BC), Tylos (330 BC-630 AD) and Islám (630 AD-Present).

The organisation of the galleries reflects this division. The easiest way to approach the museum is to start in the Hall of Graves (the gallery nearest the entrance, on the ground floor), work your way through the Dilmun to the Costumes & Traditions galleries and then go directly upstairs and work your way back (from the Travel, Trades & Crafts to Tylos and Islam to the Document Hall galleries).

Sticklers for chronological order may want to move upstairs to Tylos and Islam after viewing the Dilmun gallery, view ethnographic exhibits in the third hall and then finish up in the Document Hall which contains most of the modern material. Before coming to any of this, however, turn left as you pass the ticket desk to reach the **Hall of Dinosaurs** complete with a mechanical, not-quite-lifesize Tyrannosaurus Rex.

Hall of Graves This gallery is dedicated to Bahrain's best known tourist attraction: its grave mounds. There are some 85,000 mounds in the country, covering about 5% of Bahrain's total area. Mound burials in various forms took place from 2800 BC until the coming of Islam in the 7th century AD. The centrepiece of the room is a cross-section of a large 'late type' burial mound. There are also several smaller reconstructed burial sites of other types. Printed displays explain the various types of grave mounds and the differences between them. Grave contents are also on display with signs detailing their functions.

Dilmun The Dilmun gallery has more displays on archaeological technique. It also includes exhibits on seals and engraving, metal casting, pottery, and a thorough outline of temples and temple building. There is a good display on the different stages of construction at the Barbar Temple, which bears careful examination if you are planing to visit the site.

Costumes & Traditions The displays in this gallery cover birth, childhood, marriage, traditional ceremonies, timekeeping, medicine and toys and games. The education display highlights the differences between traditional Koranic schools and the 20th century government schools (founded in 1919). The displays are generally a combination of old photographs, text and life-size dioramas.

Traditional Trades & Crafts This is largely an extension of the Costumes & Traditions gallery on the lower floor. There are large displays on pearling and fishing and smaller ones on weaving and pottery. There's also a reconstruction of an old street in the souk.

Tylos & Islam This gallery is a bit sparse compared with the Dilmun exhibit on the lower floor. Most of the material is from Islamic times, reflecting a dearth of finds from Bahrain's Tylos (Greek) period. A lot of space is devoted to graves and grave architecture (especially gravestones). Note that this gallery has less explanatory material than some of the others. All of the grave inscriptions are translated but little else is. Be sure to see the section on the *qanats*, the large system of underground irrigation canals which were used to transport water from the islands' numerous springs to fields elsewhere. There is also a big display on the country's various forts.

Documents & Manuscripts Most of the signs on the walls (biographies of the rulers of Bahrain etc) are in English but a lot of the material in here is not translated. There is also an interesting display on Arabic writing and calligraphy.

Heritage Centre

The centre occupies a villa on Government Ave across from the Bahrain Commercial Centre. The villa was built in 1937 to house the law courts. The centre is open Saturday to Wednesday from 8 am to 2 pm and Thursday from 10 am to 5 pm, but it's closed Friday. Admission is free and photography is prohibited.

In the parking lot by the main door an old-style canoe and a scale model of an ocean-going dhow are displayed. The courtyard features a reconstruction of a traditional *diwan* (meeting room) under the staircase. The rooms surrounding the courtyard contain photographs of state occasions and the comings and goings of numerous Arab and foreign dignitaries from the island throughout the 20th century. There are also displays on pearl diving, seafaring, folk music instruments, the various uses of the date palm and a reconstruction of the High

Court whose sessions used to be held in the building.

The upper level of the centre houses a series of one-room displays of antique weapons, games, folk medicine, traditional costumes and scenes from everyday life.

You might also want to take a walk around the back side of the building to take a look at the carved door facing Al-Khalifa Ave. This was the main entrance when the building served as Bahrain's High Court and the door has been beautifully preserved.

Wind Towers

Bahrain's pre-electricity form of air-conditioning can be seen in several places in the older parts of town. The towers are designed to catch even slight breezes and funnel the air down into the house (see the boxed story on Traditional Architecture near Society & Conduct in the Facts about the Region chapter).

The easiest one to find is 10 to 15 minutes walk from the Hilton/Sheraton roundabout. With your back to the two hotels follow Palace Ave. Turn right on Road 609 (at the corner with signs for Creative Ads and the Al-Baraka Car Centre). Follow this street for about 200m; it is on the left. The same house also has a well-preserved covered balcony. (If driving, note that Palace Ave is a limited access road and you cannot turn on Road 609 from either lane.)

Friday Mosque

This mosque, built with the island's first oil revenues in 1938, is easily identifiable by its colourful mosaic minaret. The minaret is, in fact, the mosque's most interesting architectural feature, and you're not missing much if you just look at the mosque from the outside. The mosque is at the intersection of Al-Khalifa and Shaikh Isa Aves.

Bab Al-Bahrain

Built by the British in 1945 to house government offices and serve as a formal entryway to the city, the Bab, as it is known locally, now houses the tourist office. The gateway was designed by Sir Charles Belgrave, the long-time British adviser to the rulers of Bahrain. The small square in front of the Bab was once the terminus of the customs pier (which gives some idea of the extent of land reclamation in the area).

Souk

The Bab serves as the main entrance to the souk, which covers roughly the area between Al-Khalifa and Shaikh Abdulla Aves, from Municipality Ave to an area a few hundred metres east of Bab Al-Bahrain. Electronic items and women's clothing seem to be the souk's main stock in trade, aside from gold, but in the great tradition of Middle Eastern bazaars almost anything can be found if you look long and hard enough. Opening hours are from 8.30 am to 12.30 or 1 pm and from 3 to 6 pm daily, with everything closed on Friday.

Beit Al-Qur'an

A striking bit of architecture at the eastern end of Government Ave, Beit Al-Qur'an (Koran House) was opened in 1990 as a museum and research centre. It can be reached from the city centre by bus Nos 1, 2 and 5. The museum is open Saturday to Wednesday from 9 am to noon and 4 to 6 pm and Thursday from 9 am to noon. It is closed Friday.

The museum's centrepiece is a large, and quite striking, collection of Korans, manuscripts, wood carvings etc. Not everything is labelled in English, and a few of the displays are not even labelled in Arabic, but it is definitely worth the trip. If you are unfamiliar with Islam, this centre is a particularly good introduction to the art of Islamic calligraphy. Admission is free, but a donation is requested. The building is entered through the south side.

Look left as you pass through the building's outer lobby and you will see a small mosque with an extremely elaborate *mihrib* (the prayer niche indicating the wall facing Mecca) worked in blue tile.

The first hall is something of a general introduction to Islamic art. Be sure to see the collection of rare astrolabes (tools used by medieval astronomers to chart the sun, moon, stars and other celestial bodies). Also on display are glass and enamelware, manuscripts, tile work and a variety of miniature paintings from Iran, India and Turkey.

From this hall a series of open galleries built around a single long staircase leads you through the development of the Islamic world's highest form of art: calligraphy. Straight ahead of you against the left wall of the first hall of this exhibit is a rare Koran from the 7th century. It is thought to have originated in either Iraq or the Hejaz, and is written in an early form of Kufic script without the dots that are an integral part of modern written Arabic. Another rare Koran, this one from 8th century Hejaz, dominates the centre of this gallery in a display case by itself.

The next level of the exhibit concentrates on illumination, the art of decorating the margins of religious manuscripts. Samples range from 13th century Syria through 18th century Persia to 19th century Turkey. Take some time in this room to see how the styles develop over time.

The level beyond this is noteworthy mainly for some of the museum's odder exhibits – such as a grain of rice and a split chickpea, both from Pakistan and both with Koranic verses and other religious writings on them. The final part of the museum – on the upper level – includes examples of the ornately bound Korans exchanged by Muslim leaders on important occasions and copies of translations of the Holy Book into a wide variety of foreign languages.

Dhow Builders

The most interesting dhow building yard on the Arabian side of the Gulf is in the nondescript-looking sheds just west of the Pearl Monument roundabout. In the same area you can also see fish traps being woven from wire. No admission fee is charged but ask before taking photographs or climbing on the half-built dhows, the latter being a matter of safety as well as courtesy. The dhow yard can be reached by bus No 5.

Al-Fatih Mosque

The Al-Fatih Mosque, also known as the Great Mosque, dominates the Al-Fatih Highway on the coast south of central Manama. You can't miss it: it's the largest building in the country and is said to be capable of holding up to 7000 worshippers.

Non-Muslims are welcome to visit the mosque Saturday to Wednesday from 8 am to 2 pm. It is not open to visitors on Thursday, Friday, national holidays or during prayer time. Visitors should check-in at the small library immediately to the right once inside the main door. Women will be given, and are expected to wear, a hooded black cloak while they are inside the prayer hall. Neither men nor women will be admitted if they are wearing shorts.

The mosque is not on a bus route. The only way to get there (other than on foot) is to take a taxi – about BD 1 from the centre.

Bahrain Crafts Centre

The centre, on Isa Al-Kabeer Ave near the police fort and the intersection with Shaikh Mohammed and Al-Mutanabi Aves, is where many of the Bahraini-made handicrafts on sale in the tourist office come from. You can watch the craftspeople at work, and also make purchases. Call ☎ 254 688 for more information. The centre can be reached from central Manama by bus No 14A.

Beach Clubs

Several of Bahrain's beach clubs are open to visitors upon payment of a dinar or two for a day ticket. Clubs worth trying include the Bahrain Yacht Club, at the southern tip of Sitra Island, and the Al-Bandar Club next door. To get into either club on a Friday you will probably need to be accompanied by a member. Both have swimming and sports facilities, a restaurant and bar as well as small marinas. You can also usually get access to the pools at any of the larger hotels upon payment of a small fee, usually about BD 2, unless they force you to take the lunch buffet as well, in which case it is likely to be a lot more expensive.

Golf

Bahrain's small golf course is in East Rifa, near Awali and just off the Muaskar Highway. It is one of those dirt and sand courses that seem to be unique to Arabia, though a proper grass course is reportedly on the drawing board. Greens fees are BD 3 per day.

Organised Tours

Gulf Tours (☎ 213 460), a division of the government-run Tourism Projects Company, offers a number of itineraries around Manama and the main archaeological/historical sites. These cost BD 7 or BD 8 (BD 5 for children age three to 10 on all trips – there is no charge for children under three years of age) and most of them last three hours. The only tour which is offered every day is 'Bahrain Ancient and Modern', which includes visits to the Al-Jasra House and the nearby government handicraft centre, a quick look at some burial mounds and a trip out on the King Fahd Causeway. The tour departs from the tourist office at 3 pm. All of the other tours are offered once or twice per week. Contact the tourist office for exact schedules.

Gulf Tours also organises lunch and dinner trips aboard dhows or yachts. Lunch and dinner trips on the yacht cost BD 10 per person (BD 5 for children), dhow trips are for dinner only and cost BD 7 (BD 3.500 for children). There is a 20% discount for groups of five people or more. The prices of both the yacht and dhow trips includes a buffet meal.

Other companies offering tours include Bahrain Explored (☎ 211 477) and Sunshine Tours (☎ 223 601).

Places to Stay – bottom end

The *Youth Hostel* (☎ 727 170) is at No 1105, Road 4225 in Al-Jufayr, south-east of the city centre. It is opposite the Bahrain School and just beyond the United Nations Development Programme (UNDP) and UNICEF offices. This is a bit out of the way and if you've got luggage it might be a good idea to take a cab. If you are coming from the airport the route is well signposted.

From the airport or the centre head south on the Al-Fatih Highway and turn left at the Al-Jufayr roundabout. Follow this road past the UN offices and the Bahrain Lawn Tennis Club, and the hostel will be on the left. Beds are BD 2 per night, most of them in two-bed rooms. The toilets and showers are in a separate building. Kitchen facilities are available. The hostel is spartan but clean. There is also a family section, but the management's attitude toward unaccompanied women can best be described as problematic.

All of the following hotels have air-conditioning. Service charges, where applicable, are included in the rates quoted here. Also note that the rates listed are initial quotes and are definitely negotiable, at least during the week. Most of Bahrain's cheap hotels raise their rates over the weekend, which usually means on Wednesday and Thursday nights. If you check in before the weekend and stay through it, you should only be charged the weekday rate, but check first with the management to avoid any misunderstandings.

After a bad patch a few years ago the *Al-Burge Hotel* (formerly the Abu Nawas Hotel) (☎ 213 163, fax 213 512) on Municipality Ave has undergone a modest face-lift and is once again the best cheapie in town. The rooms, which cost BD 8/10 a single/double with bath, BD 6/8 without, are spartan but clean and the staff are friendly. The rooms with attached baths have TVs.

The *Central Hotel* (☎ 233 553) used to be one of Bahrain's better values but has fallen on hard times of late. It is a bit out of the way, in an alleyway off the east side of Municipality Square. The rates are BD 8/12 for singles/doubles, some of which have attached baths.

Just south of Al-Khalifa Ave, the *Al-Kuwait Guest House* (☎ 210 781) has small, spartan, uncarpeted rooms, some with Turkish toilets (the hole-in-the-floor variety), for BD 7/12. Some of the rooms have attached baths and some don't. The clientele seems to be mostly low-income Saudis. Unaccompanied women might want to look somewhere else.

The *Awal Hotel* (☎ 211 321, fax 211 391) has a sign on Al-Khalifa Ave, but the door is on an alley off the main street and nearly opposite the entrance to the west side of the Al-Kuwait Guest House. The hotel is overpriced at BD 15/19.550. The rooms are large but rather musty, and for that sort of money one expects much cleaner bathrooms. A few doors down the alleyway from the Awal is the *Ambassador Hotel* (☎ 277 991). It charges BD 15/20 a single/double. At the southern end of Municipality Square the *Al-Dewania Hotel* (☎ 263 300, fax 259 709), at BD 12.360/15.450 a single/double, is a so-so deal.

The *Seef Hotel* (☎ 244 557, fax 593 363) is just off the north-west side of Government Ave behind the Standard & Chartered Bank building. Singles/doubles cost BD 8/12, all with bath, TV and fridge. The rooms are OK but nothing to write home about. The toilets are all Turkish-style.

On Tujjaar Ave in the souk the *Capital Hotel* (☎ 255 955, fax 211 675) is good value for money at BD 10/14 a single/double, including breakfast. The more expensive *Oriental Palace Hotel* (☎ 233 331, fax 214 141), with rooms at BD 16.100/20.700, is just around the corner.

Further afield, the *Bahrain Hotel* (☎ 227 478, fax 213 509) is good value at BD 9/16 a single/double for simple but very clean rooms, all with private baths, telephones and TVs. The hotel is in two old houses which have been reconstructed. This makes for nice surroundings, but also a lot of walking up and down staircases to get to your room. The hotel is on Al-Khalifa Ave, near the intersection with Road 453 (two blocks east of the Tylos Hotel).

There are also several options in this category outside central Manama. The *Albustan Hotel* (☎ 713 911, fax 712 218), just off Bani Otbah Ave near Guddies supermarket, is slightly dowdy and a bit out of the way but decent enough. Singles/doubles cost BD 12/17. The *Maryland Hotel* (☎ 290 295, fax 594 360), off Exhibition Ave opposite the Abu Bakr Al-Sadiq Mosque, has spacious, comfortable rooms for BD 17.250/23. The

Omar Khayam Hotel (☎ 713 941, fax 713 341) on Abdul Rahman Al-Dakhel Ave, off Exhibition Ave, charges BD 12/15 for singles/doubles.

Places to Stay – middle
Bahrain's mid-priced hotels are a varied lot. A 15% service charge (included, where applicable, in the prices quoted here) can be assumed at this level, as can such amenities as a fridge, TV and telephone. The good news is that the rapid growth of this segment of the hotel market over the last few years has led to a general lowering of prices. Moreover, during slow periods you may be able to bargain a dinar or two off the rates quoted here, but don't count on it. Most hotels in this category do not raise their rates on weekends.

If you want or need to have your entry visa sponsored by a hotel, the cheapest place that provides this service is the *Oasis Hotel* (☎ 229 979, fax 224 421) on Government Ave opposite the Delmon Hotel. At BD 14/18 the rooms are excellent value (the hotel also has two excellent restaurants and a good wine bar) and I would recommend it for unaccompanied women. Another centrally located hotel that will arrange visas is the *Bahrain International Hotel* (☎ 211 313, fax 211 947), a fairly good mid-range option at BD 29.500/35.400.

If you are looking only for a central location it is hard to beat the *Bab Al-Bahrain Hotel* (☎ 211 622, fax 213 661) on Government Ave right next to the Bab itself. It is an extremely clean place with good, medium-sized rooms at BD 20.700/28.750. A few blocks down the street, the *Gulf Pearl Hotel* (☎ 213 877, fax 213 943) is a bit more expensive for singles, at BD 23, but their doubles cost the same as those at the Bab Al-Bahrain Hotel. The *Al-Jazira Hotel* (☎ 211 810, fax 210 726) on Al-Khalifa Ave in the souk is the landmark by which you know you have reached the cheap hotel district. It is quite a good hotel, catering largely to business travellers with small expense accounts. Rooms are BD 21.240/28.320 for singles/doubles, which is a bit pricey but they have

Central Manama
Hotel District

PLACES TO EAT

2 Kwality Restaurant
3 Al-Aswar Sandwiches
5 Al-Osra Restaurant
19 East Restaurant & Coffee
25 Ahmed Abdul Rahim's Coffee House
28 Honey Restaurant
35 Woody's Corner (Restaurant)
38 Cafe Hanan
39 Charcoal Grill Restaurant

OTHER

1 Government House
4 Friday Mosque
6 Gulf Air
7 Manama Centre
8 Kuwait Airways
9 British Bank of the Middle East (ATM)
10 Heritage Centre
11 Saudia Airlines
12 ABN-AMRO Bank (AMEX Express Cash Machine)
13 Dutch Consulate
14 GPO
15 Banks
17 Standard & Chartered Bank
20 Municipality Building
22 Avis Rent-a-Car
24 Manama Bus Station
27 Ebrahim Abu Ahmed Antiques
31 Bradran Persian Store
36 Bank of Bahrain & Kuwait (ATM)
40 Tourist Office
42 Kanoo Travel (AMEX)
43 British Airways
44 Yateem Centre (Telecommunications Office)
47 Souvenir Shops
48 Al-Hilal Bookshop
50 National Bank of Bahrain
51 Al-Awal Exchange (Money Exchange)

PLACES TO STAY

16 Regency Inter-Continental
18 Seef Hotel
21 Delmon Hotel
23 Gulf Gate Hotel
26 Oasis Hotel
29 Al-Burge Hotel
30 Bahrain International Hotel
32 Awal Hotel
33 Al-Kuwait Guest House
34 Al-Jazira Hotel
37 Gulf Pearl Hotel
41 Bab Al-Bahrain Hotel
45 Oriental Palace Hotel
46 Capital Hotel
49 Aradous Hotel
52 Bahrain Hotel
53 Adhari Hotel
54 Central Hotel
55 Sahara Hotel
56 Al-Dewania Hotel

one of Manama's more interesting down-market bars (done entirely in Tudor decor!) and an extremely central location. None of these hotels sponsor visas.

The *Sahara Hotel* (☎ 225 580, fax 210 580), which is on Municipality Square, has singles/doubles for BD 20.700/28.750. The clientele is mostly Gulf Arabs in town for short visits. Across the square, the *Adhari Hotel* (☎ 224 343, fax 214 707) charges BD 17.250/23 but will readily discount its prices. The hotel's bar, the Hunter's Lounge, is popular with US sailors on shore leave, and there are also several other bars and restaurants which are entered from the back and side of the building. The *Aradous Hotel* (☎ 241 011) on Wali Al-Ahed Ave is under the same management as the Adhari and has roughly the same prices. Further west along Government Ave, moving away from the town centre, is the *Tylos Hotel* (☎ 252 600, fax 252 611) with rooms at BD 23/32.200 a single/double. They also arrange visas.

Gulf Gate Hotel (☎ 210 210, fax 213 315) is a relatively new three to four-star hotel with a quiet but central location just behind the Delmon Hotel. Singles/doubles cost BD 20.600/30.900.

Places to Stay – top end

Bahrain has the usual array of top-line hotels. For five-star accommodation you can expect to pay at least BD 30, and probably closer to BD 50, even before the 15% service charge is added on. The rates quoted here are the main rack rates. Corporate discounts of up to 30% are available, but the hotel's generosity in this regard depends on the occupancy rate at the time. Some of these places offer weekend discount packages (see Accommodation in the Facts for the Visitor section earlier in this chapter) for which you have to book in advance. They all arrange visas.

People with money to spend who want something with a bit more character than the average four or five-star hotel should try the *Delmon Hotel* (☎ 224 000, fax 224 107). At BD 31/41 a single/double it's a bit cheaper than the other top-end hotels and good

weekend packages are often available on Wednesday, Thursday and Friday nights. The Delmon opened in 1967, which makes it one of the older hotels on the island and something of a local institution. Its Indian restaurant has a very good reputation.

The main four and five-star hotels in Bahrain are (the rates quoted here include the 3% hotel tax plus any applicable service charge):

Bahrain Hilton (☎ 523 523, fax 532 071), Palace Ave, just north of Government Ave. Singles/doubles cost BD 53.100/64.900.
The Diplomat (☎ 531 666, fax 530 843), across the King Faisal Highway from the National Museum. Singles/doubles cost BD 64.900/76.700.
Gulf Hotel (☎ 713 040, fax 712 088), Bani Otbah Ave, near the intersection with the Al-Fatih Highway. Singles/doubles cost BD 59/70.800.
Holiday Inn (☎ 531 122, fax 530 154), King Faisal Highway, near the causeway to Muharraq. Singles/doubles cost BD 53.100/64.900.
Ramada Hotel (☎ 714 921, fax 742 809), Bani Otbah Ave. Singles/doubles cost BD 47.200/55.460.
Regency Inter-Continental Bahrain (☎ 227 777, fax 229929), King Faisal Highway, near Bab Al-Bahrain. Singles/doubles cost BD 70.800/80.240.
Royal Meridien Bahrain (☎ 580 000, fax 580 333), west of the centre in the Al-Seef district. Singles/doubles cost BD 76.700/88.500.
Sheraton Bahrain (☎ 533 533, fax 534 069), Palace Ave at the intersection with Government Ave. Singles/doubles cost BD 70.800/80.240.

Places to Eat

Cheap & Medium-Priced Very few restaurants in this price category serve alcohol and most of them have the same basic mix of Arabic appetisers and Indian and Far Eastern main dishes. A few western specialities (usually steaks) fill out the menu. While the selections on the menu don't vary much you'll probably find that places staffed by Indians tend to push Indian food, places staffed by Thais will feature Chinese and Thai food etc.

Western-style fast food is also plentiful and affordable; at breakfast time this may be one of your better options. The western fast-food joints are also your best bet if you need a midnight snack – several of the ones around Bab Al-Bahrain and south of the centre along Exhibition Ave are open 24 hours a day.

There are lots of cheap places to eat in the centre, especially on Government Ave and Al-Khalifa Ave around Bab Al-Bahrain. If your taste does not run to burgers and fries try *Charcoal Grill* next to Bab Al-Bahrain. It features a wide selection of Indian, Chinese and Filipino food. Try the mixed fried rice at BD 1.700. Chinese main dishes generally cost BD 1.500 to BD 2 and kebabs BD 1.200 to BD 2, but you can also get sandwiches for 500 fils to BD 1. Nearby, also on Government Ave, *Cafe Hanan* offers a mix of burgers and sandwiches at 300 to 700 fils and Filipino food for BD 1 to BD 1.200. The *Honey Restaurant* (formerly Tharaiya) on Municipality Ave, next to the Al-Burge Hotel, is slightly more expensive. The menu is heavy on Filipino noodle dishes and the food is of average quality. A meal at any of these places costs BD 2 to BD 3. A number of small Indian restaurants, with similar prices, are in the area around the Al-Jazira Hotel.

One block north of Government Ave, the *East Restaurant & Coffee*, next to the Seef Hotel, has Thai food but not much of a selection. Meals cost BD 3 to BD 4.

Further east, immediately across from the entrance to Government House on Government Ave, the *Al-Osra Restaurant* has the usual blend of Arabic, Indian, Chinese and Continental foods. Starters cost 300 to 500 fils and main dishes cost anywhere from 500 fils to BD 3, including an extensive list of curries, most between 500 fils and BD 1. The Indian food is the cheapest, while steaks are the most expensive. The *Kwality Restaurant*, further along Government Ave in the direction of the Hilton/Sheraton roundabout, has a similar menu but, again, the emphasis is on Indian food. The surroundings are nicer, but the food isn't as good as at Al-Osra and the prices are slightly higher.

For a quick snack it is hard to beat *Al-Aswar Sandwiches*, a tiny restaurant on a side street off Al-Khalifa Ave near the Friday Mosque. Large servings of fresh juice cost 250 to 400 fils and burgers can be had for 200 to 500 fils.

One of the best values in Bahrain is at the other end of Government Ave: *La Taverna*, the Italian restaurant on the 2nd floor of the Oasis Hotel. Main dishes cost BD 3 to BD 5 and pasta main courses around BD 2.500. They serve what is arguably the best Italian food in the country. Try the pasta with clams. Across the hall from La Taverna is *Tar-bouche*, a Lebanese restaurant that is also one of the best in town. Meals here also cost BD 3 to BD 5.

For lunch you might want to try the buffet at the *Gulf Pearl Hotel* on Government Ave. The buffet costs only BD 2.200 and you also get 25% off their regular prices for all drinks.

Outside the centre is *Up A Tree Cuppa Tea*, one of Bahrain's most popular small restaurants. Despite the restaurant's somewhat English-sounding name, they specialise in Thai noodle dishes and fried rice, all of which cost BD 2.200 for a large portion and BD 1.500 for a small portion. They also have excellent soups for 900 fils and a selection of home-made cakes for about 500 fils each. They do not serve alcohol or take credit cards. The restaurant is a short distance from the Ramada Hotel, near the intersection of Bani Otbah Ave and Osama Bin Ziad Rd.

There are very few traditional coffee houses left in central Manama. A good one, however, is *Ahmed Abdul Rahim's Coffee House* on Government Ave, south-west of the Oasis Hotel. The sign is only in Arabic but you'll find it hard to miss with all those old men sitting on blue benches sipping tea from tiny glasses. You may join them for 50 fils per cup. Outside the centre the *Public Coffee House* on Isa Al-Kabeer Ave across from the American Mission Hospital is another good bet.

Expensive Outside of the big hotels, which offer the usual selection of Arabic, Continental and Japanese food, there are not too many top-end restaurants in the centre. *The Saddle*, in the Tylos Hotel, is a Tex-Mex restaurant popular with off-duty US servicemen. They have good enchiladas, very good nachos and excellent margaritas. Appetisers start from around BD 1; main dishes mostly from BD 3. Figure on paying BD 6 to BD 8 for a good meal.

Popular up-market places outside the city centre include *Upstairs, Downstairs* in Al-Adliya near the Ramada Hotel for English food and *Señor Paco's* in Al-Mahuz near the British Club for Tex-Mex (of the two Tex-Mex places mentioned here, Señor Paco's is a lot quieter and has better food). Appetisers at Señor Paco's cost BD 1.500 to BD 2 and main dishes cost BD 3.500 to BD 4.500.

You should also keep an eye on the *Gulf Daily News* for cheap lunch specials at the big hotels (or just stick your head into a five-star hotel's bar at lunch time). A typical offer is a buffet lunch (often served in the bar), including a beer or soft drink and dessert, for anywhere between BD 2.500 and BD 5.500, service included. The *Sherlock Holmes Bar* in the Gulf Hotel is often a good bet for lunch deals.

On Fridays most of the big hotels put on all-you-can-eat buffet brunches for BD 6 to BD 8 plus a service charge. If you have an appetite these can be good for a splurge. The best-established is the *Jazz Brunch* at the Diplomat Hotel, featuring live music by the Bahrain Jazz Quartet from 11.30 am to 2.30 pm. Use of the swimming pool for the afternoon is included in the price.

Entertainment

Bahrain's nightlife has improved considerably over the last few years, though it remains a bit thin by western standards. Much still revolves around the bars and lounges in the large and medium-sized hotels, though a few of the hotels (eg the Adhari) increasingly seem to have been taken over by their nightspots.

Cinemas There are a couple of small cinemas in town that show mostly Indian films. For more information check the *Gulf Daily News*.

Bars & Discos Conventional hotel bars range from comfortable-but-generic (the *Clipper Bar* at the Regency Inter-Continental) to the bizarrely thematic (the *Sherlock Holmes Bar* at the Gulf Hotel and the 1st-floor bar at the *Al-Jazira Hotel*, featuring Tudor decor) to the carefully targeted (the *Hunter's Lounge* at the Adhari Hotel).

Bahrain's most interesting bars tend to be attached to otherwise unremarkable hotels, and are often entered through a separate door (hotels have an easier time getting liquor licences than free-standing restaurants, which explains this rather odd state of affairs). You should be aware that many of these bars will turn away any customer who appears to be Arab. This is partly a complicated quirk of Bahrain's liquor licensing laws which has set some of these places up as 'members only' clubs (your BD 1 or BD 2 cover charge representing your 'day membership'), partly a fear that any fight that might break out involving a Gulf Arab could result in the revocation of the all-important liquor licence and partly a racist approach to marketing (ie the assumption that western customers won't want to drink with Arabs).

The Warbler, in the Baisan International Hotel, off the west side of Exhibition Ave on Avenue 2005, is popular with younger western expats. *Bacchus*, also in the Baisan, bills itself as a late-night jazz bar but is more like a late-night disco. Another popular watering hole is *Joyce's* at the Tylos Hotel. *Spats*, a wine bar on the 2nd floor of the Oasis Hotel, and *Henry's*, the bar on the 1st floor of the Mansouri Mansions Hotel, south of the centre at the intersection of Osama Bin Ziad Rd and Al-Adliya Ave, both draw a much more mixed (ie expat and Arab) crowd than most other bars in Bahrain.

The Island's longest-established disco is *Layali* at the Sheraton Bahrain.

Concerts & Theatre Western rock stars occasionally drop in for one-off performances and the five-star hotels regularly bring theatre companies out from the UK (and occasionally France) for three or four-night runs. Arab singing stars also show up now and then.

The best source for information on such events is Radio Bahrain or the monthly brochure *What's On*, published by the government-run Tourism Projects Company. The brochure is available at the tourist office, in the lobbies of most larger hotels and at a number of smaller ones, such as the Al-Jazira.

Things to Buy

A wide selection of local crafts is on sale at the tourist office in Bab Al-Bahrain. The shop also stocks some quite striking wood and brass work, though most of it is not locally made. Prices in the tourist office shop are fixed.

For interesting antiques and regional (though rarely Bahraini) crafts try the Bradran Persian Store (☎ 228 655) on Road 467 (an alley off Government Ave near the Bahrain Islamic Bank). They have a selection of Iranian, Indian and Chinese goods. The shop's speciality, however, is printed tablecloths from Isfahan in Iran. After a bit of bargaining these sell for BD 3 to BD 15, depending on size. If you have a lot of money to spend they also have a good selection of Iranian carpets.

Another good place to look for souvenirs is Ebrahim Abu Ahmed Antique (☎ 270 872). Their main shop is just off Municipality Ave in the centre near the Al-Burge Hotel. They also have a branch shop on Exhibition Ave across the street from the police station. Both shops stock a wide variety of goods, including coffee pots, wooden inlay boxes from Iran, brass and copper work and some jewellery. Their stock also tends to be well labelled, so it is fairly easy to tell the country of origin of most of the items. They carry both genuine antiques and newly minted souvenirs.

Getting There & Away

Air Bahrain international airport is one of the busiest in the Gulf. For flight information call the airport at ☎ 325 555.

The airport's departure area has the usual large duty-free shop, a restaurant, coffee shop and bar, and a newsstand (in the duty-free area). If you need cash on arrival there is a Bank of Bahrain & Kuwait ATM linked into the Cirrus and Plus systems in the departure area before security.

Remember to reconfirm your flight 72 hours in advance, particularly if you are travelling with Gulf Air, Saudia or Kuwait Airways. Most airline offices are open Saturday to Wednesday from 8 or 8.30 am to 12.30 pm and 3 pm to 5 or 5.30 pm (morning hours only on Thursday). The addresses and phone numbers of some of the carriers serving Bahrain are:

Aeroflot
    Exhibition Ave, near the intersection with Gudabiya Ave (☎ 292 838)
Balkan Bulgarian Airlines
    Manama Centre, Government Ave (☎ 214 149)
British Airways
    Al-Khalifa Ave, next to Kanoo Travel/AMEX (☎ 225 303)
Cathay Pacific
    Government Ave, just west of Bab Al-Bahrain; the office is on the 6th floor of the building with the Cathay Pacific sign at street level (☎ 226 226)
Gulf Air
    Manama Centre, Government Ave (☎ 335 777)
KLM
    Manama Centre, Government Ave (☎ 224 234)
Korean Air
    Bahrain Commercial Centre, corner of Government and Al-Furdah Aves (☎ 213 445)
Kuwait Airways
    Manama Centre, Government Ave (☎ 223 300)
Lufthansa
    Manama Centre, Government Ave (☎ 210 026)
Royal Jordanian
    Off the alley that intersects Al-Furdah Ave between the Dairy Queen and the Al-Ahli Centre (☎ 229 294)
Saudia
    Bahrain Commercial Centre, corner of Government and Al-Furdah Aves (☎ 211 550)
Syrian Air
    Bahrain Commercial Centre at the corner of Government and Al-Furdah Aves (☎ 211 360)
Turkish Airlines
    Al-Khalifa Ave, across from the Yateem Centre (☎ 211 896)
Yemenia
    Intersection of Isa Al-Kabeer and Government Aves, next to Kwality Restaurant (☎ 214 313)

Bus The Saudi-Bahraini Transport Company (☎ 263 244) runs five buses daily to/from Dammam via Alkhobar. The fare is BD 4 one way, BD 7 return. Buses leave Bahrain for Saudi Arabia at 8.30 am and noon, and at 3, 6 and 8.30 pm. Buses leave Dammam for Bahrain at 8 and 11 am and at 2, 5 and 8.30 pm.

The trip between Bahrain and Alkhobar takes about two hours with the bus arriving in Dammam about 45 minutes later.

The office also sells other international tickets that involve a change of bus in Dammam. Destinations include Damascus (approximately 48 hours, BD 40), Amman (approximately 36 hours, BD 40), Kuwait (nine hours, BD 21) and Abu Dhabi/Dubai (18 hours, BD 30). The Damascus, Amman and Kuwait tickets all require that you leave Bahrain for Dammam on the noon bus. The Abu Dhabi/Dubai tickets require that you use the 3 pm departure.

The buses come and go from the Central Market buildings on Lulu Ave, between the King Faisal Highway and Government Ave. The ticket office is in the small brown trailer. There are fewer buses each day during Ramadan and more during Eid Al-Fitr and Eid Al-Adha. There are no lockers in the waiting room at the ticket office but the staff might let you stow your gear for a few hours if you are travelling out by bus later that day.

Car All of the big hotels have car rental desks representing the major chains. Rates for compact cars start at around BD 13 per day or BD 70 to BD 80 for a week, including unlimited km. The insurance included usually leaves the renter liable for the first BD 200 of damage in the event of an accident, but you can get around this by purchasing a collision damage waiver for BD 2 per day. Personal accident insurance will probably add another BD 1. To rent a car in Bahrain you need an International Driving Permit. This cannot be obtained in Bahrain if you do not already have one. Foreigners resident in another GCC country can rent a car using a licence from that country.

Some of the well-established international rental agencies include Thrifty Rent-a-Car (☎ 801 100) on Zubarah Ave near the intersection with Exhibition Ave, Avis (☎ 211 770) with an office on Government Ave next door to the Delmon Hotel, and Budget (☎ 534 100) in the Bahrain Commercial Complex on Government Ave.

Getting Around
The Airport Bahrain international airport is on Muharraq Island, six km from the centre. Bus No 1 (which originates in the industrial area of Al-Hidd, off Muharraq) runs between the airport and the central bus station in Manama every 35 minutes from around 6 am until 8.45 pm. The fare is 50 fils and the trip takes about 20 minutes. For late-night departures (which would include most flights to Europe) you will either have to take a taxi or spend many hours camping out at the airport.

A taxi from central Manama to the airport should cost BD 2 or less depending on where you pick it up. For trips into town from the airport there is a BD 1 surcharge, so these tend to cost BD 2 to BD 3.

Bus Bahrain's bus system links routes around Greater Manama with the outlying towns. Fares are a flat 50 fils per trip. The buses run from about 5.30 or 6.30 am until 7.30 or 9.30 pm depending on the route. There is usually a bus every 40 to 60 minutes. Manama's main bus station is on Government Ave between the Delmon and Tylos hotels. See the Muharraq section for routes based on Muharraq Island and the Around Bahrain Island section for all other routes. Manama-based routes and routes passing through Manama are:

Route 1 – Hidd, Bahrain airport, Muharraq bus station, Ras Rummaan, Manama Municipality, Manama Central Market, Manama bus station and vice-versa

Route 2 – Isa Town, Al-Sehlah, Al-Khamis, Al-Sulmaniya, Manama bus station, Manama Municipality, Ras Rummaan, Muharraq

Route 3 – Manama bus station, Manama Municipality, UK embassy, American Mission Hospital, Kuwaiti Building (Shaikh Isa Ave), Radio Station, Al-Jufayr, Mina Sulman

Route 5 – Al-Budayyi', Ad-Diraz, Abu Saybi, Jidd Hafs, Al-Budayyi' Highway, Manama bus station, Manama Municipality, Ras Rummaan, Old Palace Rd, Al-Sulmaniya Ave and vice-versa

Route 7 – East Rifa, West Rifa, Isa Town, Al-Sehlah, Al-Khamis, Al-Sulmaniya Ave, Manama bus station, Manama Municipality, Ras Rummaan, Muharraq

Route 8 – Manama bus station, Manama Municipality, Government House, Mina Sulman, Sitra, Isa Town and vice-versa

Route 14A – Manama bus station, Water Garden, Al-Sulmaniya, Police Fort, American Mission Hospital, Ras Rummaan

Route 14B – Ras Rummaan, American Mission Hospital, Police Fort, Al-Sulmaniya, Water Garden, Manama bus station

Taxi Taxis have meters and are fairly inexpensive because the meters tick over pretty slowly. See Getting Around earlier in this chapter for more information.

Around Bahrain Island

QAL'AT AL-BAHRAIN

Bahrain's main archaeological site, also known as Bahrain Fort or the Portuguese Fort, is a complex containing four separate excavations. At the time of writing the site was undergoing extensive renovation, apparently with the goal of restoring to its original form the ruined Portuguese fortress long familiar to visitors to Bahrain. Despite the construction, and an on-going archaeological dig near the main fort, the site remains open during daylight hours every day. Admission is free.

This was the site of the earliest professional archaeological digs in Bahrain, the ones described so wonderfully in Geoffrey Bibby's *Looking for Dilmun*. When Bibby began digging here in the winter of 1953-54, the Portuguese Fort was the only thing visible. It was obvious, however, that the Portuguese structure was sitting on a tell, a hill formed from the rubble of previous cities. The digging went on well into the '80s and what emerged was a much broader and

more complex pattern of settlement than had been expected. In all, seven layers of occupation were discovered. Bear in mind when looking at both the fort and the excavated areas that the coastline would then have been closer to the ruins than it is today.

The site appears to have been occupied from about 2800 BC, the time when Dilmun was coming into its own as a commercial power. The settlement here was then fairly small. The oldest excavated part of the site is the portion of a defensive wall from the City II period (circa 2000 BC). This was the Early Dilmun period during which the Dilmun civilisation was at the height of its power. The ruins of this wall are all that survive from this era of the site's history. They indicate, however, that this spot on the north coast of the island was regarded as important. (Why else would the previously undefended site have been surrounded with a wall?) The largest visible section of the wall lies just east of the Portuguese ruins.

The excavated remains of Cities III and IV are referred to as the Kassite and Assyrian Buildings. These date from 1500 to 500 BC and lie just south of the Portuguese fortress. The main thing you can see in this area is the ruin of a house with a three-metre-high entryway in the over-monumental style familiar to anyone who has ever spent a few minutes in the British Museum's Assyrian gallery. The house probably dates from the latter part of the City IV period. At the time of writing a team of French archaeologists was digging in this part of the site and the excavated area had almost doubled in size. The on-going dig, however, may mean that access to this part of the site may be limited.

City V was a Hellenistic settlement of which no excavated remains are visible. The area toward the sea contains City VI, the Islamic Fort, of which little remains. This is generally thought to have been built in the 11th century AD though some archaeologists believe it shows characteristics of much earlier construction, indicating that it may have been built on top of (or by making significant alterations to) an earlier structure.

Then there is City VII, the mid-16th

century Portuguese fort surrounded by a dry moat. Two of the bastions are in decent shape and restoration work is in progress.

The site is about five km west of Manama and is easy to reach by car: keep driving on King Faisal Highway past the Pearl Monument roundabout. Take the Al-Budayyi' Highway and turn off it to the right at the roundabout just beyond the exhibition centre (which will be on your left). This turn puts you on Avenue 40 where there is a sign for the Al-Seef district (there is another turn for Al-Seef before you reach the roundabout. Ignore this. It is the access road for the Meridien Hotel). After another 100m take the first left off Avenue 40. Follow the asphalted street through a village until you come to a five-way junction. Look for a dirt track going away to your right over a low hill, which takes you to the fort.

The closest that the buses come is the Al-Budayyi' Highway, from which it would be a very long walk. If you hire a taxi to take you out to the fort do not let the driver leave you there and 'come back in an hour'. The return fare from Manama should be between BD 3 and BD 5.

BARBAR TEMPLE
Barbar is a complex of three 2nd and 3rd millennium BC temples. These were probably dedicated to Enki, the God of Wisdom and The Sweet Waters Under the Earth. In a country as blessed with natural springs as Bahrain this god of fresh waters was, understandably, an important one to the people who lived here.

The excavated complex is viewed from a series of walkways. These give you a great view of everything, though even with a detailed map (such as those in Carter's *Bahrain – A Heritage Explored* or the site guide published by the Ministry of Information) you'll have trouble distinguishing one period from another.

Temples I and II are both from the 3rd millennium BC. In general, the oldest portions of the complex are those closer to the centre, though the entire site was enclosed by a wall during the Temple II period. The

thick wall areas, including the rounded corner one, are from Temple III (early 2nd millennium BC).

To reach the temple take the Al-Budayyi' Highway west from Manama and turn right off the highway at a green sign for Barbar. Follow this road just over half a km; the temple will be on your right, about 50m off the road. The site is open during daylight hours and there is often an attendant there with a guest book, which you will be expected to sign. Admission is free.

The closest bus stop to the Barbar temple is the one near Ad-Diraz Temple, a 20 to 30 minute walk away.

AD-DIRAZ TEMPLE
Ad-Diraz is the other Dilmun-era temple to the west of Qal'at Al-Bahrain. It was excavated in the mid-70s and less is known about it than some of the other contemporary Dilmun temples. It dates from the 2nd millennium BC, and is several centuries younger than the Barbar Temple, from which it differs significantly.

The site is quite small. Its centrepiece is a stone base standing in an area where it would have been almost surrounded by columns. Many of the column bases are still intact. It is thought that the stone base originally supported either an altar or a statue of the god to whom the temple was dedicated. In the centre of the temple is another stone which was almost certainly an altar of some sort. Note the drain hole in the floor, thought to have been used to channel the offerings away from the altar.

Unlike Barbar, the Ad-Diraz Temple is quite close to the Al-Budayyi' Highway. The turn for the temple is clearly signposted as you come from Manama (but not if you are driving in the other direction). It is open during daylight hours and admission is free. To reach the temple take the Al-Budayyi' Highway west out of Manama and look for a white sign with 'Diraz Archaeological Site 300m' written on it in English. The sign, and temple, will be on your right coming from Manama. After the sign turn right onto a small dirt road when you are opposite a bus shelter. The temple is on the small rise immediately adjacent to the road. It is fenced off but you can get a good view of it even if the gate is closed.

Bus No 5 stops near the temple.

BANI JAMRAH

This village, just south of the Al-Budayyi' Highway, near the road's western end, is known for its cloth weavers. The looms themselves are very complex. The weaver sits in a small hollowed-out concrete area inside a shack, drawing the yarn into the loom from a skein placed in a bag secured to a wooden post eight to 10m away. Taking pictures is no problem though the location of the weavers' shacks, which are away from the village and near the main road, implies that tourists are welcome at the shacks but not in the village itself.

Cloth woven in Bani Jamrah is also available for sale at around BD 2.500 per metre. There are many different patterns available, ask to see the catalogue kept in the weaving shack.

To reach Bani Jamrah take the Al-Budayyi' Highway out of Manama. Immediately after you pass the Ad-Diraz Temple you will come to a fork in the road. Keep left. A few hundred metres of driving will take you through a cemetery on Road 4109. While you still have the cemetery on your left you will see a small shack across the road to your right just before you reach the entrance to the village itself. This is the main shack where weaving is demonstrated for visitors.

AL-BUDAYYI' (BUDAIYA)

This small village marks the western edge of Bahrain Island. The beach where the road ends has nice views at sunset and also gives you some idea of the scale of the Saudi-Bahrain Causeway.

SUQ AL-KHAMIS MOSQUE

Approximately 2.5 km south-west of Manama on the Shaikh Salman (or Sulman) Highway, this is the oldest mosque in Bahrain. Reconstruction work has been going on at the mosque for several years and one minaret has now been restored to its original state. The site is open Saturday to Wednesday from 7 am to 2 pm and Thursday and Friday from 8 am to noon. Admission is free.

It is possible to climb the minarets, though I wouldn't recommend this for anyone who is either tall or claustrophobic. The original mosque is believed to have been built in the late 7th century by Umar, one of the first caliphs. As for what you see today, an inscription puts the construction in the second half of the 11th century. It is possible, however, that some fragments of the original mosque remain. Experts say that the building has some architectural features generally unique to 7th and 8th century mosques.

To reach the mosque leave Manama via the Shaikh Salman Highway. Once in the village of Al-Khamis (the site, until the 1960s, of Bahrain's donkey market) you'll see the mosque on the right side of the road as you come from Manama. Alternatively, the mosque can be reached from Manama by bus No 7.

AYN ADHARI PARK

The spring (ayn) for which the park is named, and the entrance to the park itself, are a few km south-west of the Suq Al-Khamis Mosque along the Shaikh Salman Highway. You can also approach the park from the south-east via the Shaikh Isa Bin Sulman Highway. The park is part formal garden, part amusement park (complete with a tiny train chugging among the hedges) and a pleasant respite from Manama's traffic.

A'ALI BURIAL MOUNDS

There are about 85,000 burial mounds in Bahrain. They are, literally, all over the island, though many are concentrated in about half a dozen major mound fields. If you want to look at some excavated ones a permit, though not technically necessary, is a good idea as it makes the guards and/or archaeologists rather more amenable to the presence of your camera. The tourist office can offer advice on this formality. Before visiting a mound field you might also want to visit the National Museum and look at the reconstructed mound in the Dilmun gallery.

The most impressive group of mounds are the so-called 'Royal Tombs' in the village of A'ali, south-west of Manama. These are the largest burial mounds in Bahrain and may or may not have been the tombs of kings. It was one of the great fallacies of 19th century western archaeology to impose European notions of kingship on almost every ancient society. The mounds were originally pronounced 'royal' simply because of their size. The largest are 12 to 15m high and up to 45m in diameter.

A'ali is also the site of Bahrain's best-known pottery workshop. A'ali pottery is on sale in the tourist office shop and at several stalls around the village.

To reach A'ali from Manama, take the Shaikh Salman Highway south past Isa Town, then turn west on A'ali Highway. Continue past the first turn for A'ali and turn off the highway at a small green sign pointing to the left. Once you reach the village turn right on Avenue 42 (there's a small blue street sign) to reach both the mounds and the pottery workshop. If you would like to see some mounds which are not surrounded by lots of houses and a few slag heaps, get back on the A'ali Highway and drive out beyond the edge of town. You'll see one of the island's larger mound fields immediately to your left. Another large mound field is a few km to the north-west at **Sar**. The Causeway Approach Rd runs straight through it. A'ali can also be reached by taking bus No 2 or 7 from Manama to Isa Town and changing there to bus No 9 or 15.

KING FAHD CAUSEWAY

The causeway connecting Saudi Arabia and Bahrain was conceived during the oil boom of the mid-70s and finally opened in late 1986. It is an impressive piece of engineering. Customs and immigration formalities are carried out on an artificial island halfway across the narrow strait separating Saudi Arabia from Bahrain. Two needle-like towers dominate the island, one in Saudi

Arabia and the other in Bahrain. A restaurant in the Bahraini tower offers views splendid enough to make up for the mediocre food. The causeway is well worth both the trip and the BD 2 toll.

AL-JASRA HOUSE

This is one of several historic homes around Bahrain that have been restored to their original condition. This particular one qualifies as historic because it was the birthplace of the present emir, Shaikh Isa Bin Salman Al-Khalifa. He was born here on 3 June 1933. The house was built in 1907 mainly of coral and gypsum, with palm tree trunks used to strengthen the walls. The house is open Saturday to Wednesday from 8 am to 2 pm, Thursday from 10 am to 5 pm and Friday from 3 to 6 pm. Admission is free.

The house is low set and there has been quite a lot of landscaping work around both the outside of the compound and the large courtyard that separates the main gate from the house itself. Many of the rooms have been restored. Their contents are displayed from behind protective sheets of transparent plastic. A map of the house is posted on the wall near the entrance.

To reach the house take the Causeway Approach Rd out of Manama and exit at the turn for Al-Jasra. If you are coming from Qal'at Al-Bahrain and the other sites along the north coast of Bahrain Island continue west on the Al-Budayyi' Highway past Bani Jamrah and turn south on the Al-Janabiyah Highway – look for signs pointing to Saudi Arabia. The Al-Jasra exit is part of the same interchange where the Al-Janabiyah Highway links up with the Causeway Approach Rd.

When you exit the Causeway Approach Rd get onto the Mazare'a Highway. Follow this through a residential area and two roundabouts then turn left at a sign for the Al-Jasra House.

As you pass through the residential area you will also pass a government-run **handicraft centre** on your right a few hundred metres before you reach the house. The centre is adjacent to the bus stop.

The Garden of Eden?
And the Lord God planted a garden eastward in Eden; and there He put the man whom He had formed. And out of the ground made the Lord God to grow every tree that is pleasant to the sight, and good for food; the tree of life also in the midst of the garden, and the tree of knowledge of good and evil.

Genesis 2:8-9

Bahrain's greenery and its depiction in Sumerian mythology as an enchanted place where people lived a life free of death and disease has led some archaeologists and scholars to conclude that it may have been the geographical location of the biblical Garden of Eden. This idea is reinforced by the Tree of Life, the traditional name given by Bahrainis to the lone tree, fed by an underground spring, which stands in the southern, largely desert, part of Bahrain Island.

On one level the identification of Bahrain with Eden may not be as implausible as it seems. Most scholars believe that what we now know as the Old Testament is a product of the mingling of centuries of mostly oral traditions from throughout the Middle East. Trade routes and conquering kings brought the religious traditions of many societies into contact with one another. In the *Epic of Gilgamesh*, Dilmun (Bahrain) is portrayed as an Eden-like paradise. When he arrives there Gilgamesh is met by the Sumerian equivalent of Noah. It is not unreasonable to suppose that, in the centuries before the Book of Genesis was written down, the Hebrew and Sumerian traditions of paradise and the creation became, to some extent, intermingled. Genesis itself actually combines two separate creation stories and includes (chapter 2, verses 10-14) an account of Eden's location which most modern scholars believe to be a later addition, probably by an ancient scholar who was trying to clarify the text.

Those verses say that 'a river went out of Eden...and from thence it was parted and became into four heads' (2:10). It then names the four rivers. One is the Euphrates and another is obviously the Tigris but the identification of the other two is much less clear. Some scholars have identified the other two rivers, named Pison and Gihon, with the Indus and the Nile respectively. Though the Nile flows north and the other three rivers flow south, the idea of all four having a common source would not have seemed as strange then as it does today. The era's geography, such as it was, could envisage the Nile looping up to originate on the northern side of the Mediterranean. This would give the four rivers a common source, probably either somewhere in what is now southern Turkey or in north-central Iraq. Even with an ancient map it is a little hard to see those (or any other) four rivers having a common source at Bahrain.

As the Encyclopaedia Britannica's entry on Eden notes, dryly: 'The attempt to locate a mythological garden is bound to be attended by considerable difficulty'. ■

AL-'AREEN WILDLIFE SANCTUARY
This 10-sq-km preserve in the south-west of Bahrain Island is a conservation area for species indigenous to Arabia, such as the Arabian oryx, although other animals not native to Arabia (eg zebras) have been introduced as well. You have to go through in a special tour bus. The tour takes about 40 minutes. Admission is BD 1 for adults, 500 fils for children under 13 and free for children under four. The sanctuary is open from 7 am to 4.30 pm. Call the sanctuary office (☎ 836116) for more information, including specific tour times.

To reach the sanctuary take the Causeway Approach Rd out of Manama to the Al-Jasra exit, then turn south on the Zaid Bin Omera Highway.

TREE OF LIFE
This lone tree, apparently fed by an underground spring, has been the subject of much speculation. It is the centrepiece of the 'Bahrain-was-the-Garden-of-Eden' theory advanced by some archaeologists, scholars and, most enthusiastically, by the tourist office. For the record no angel, flaming sword in hand, has recently been spotted guarding the tree though the military occasionally uses the area for manoeuvres. It's very hard to find and your best bet is either a resident with a car, a map and a lot of patience or an organised tour.

GETTING AROUND
There are several bus routes based in Hamad Town and Isa Town which can be useful if

you are trying to travel around the island by bus. As always, fares are a fat 50 fils per trip and buses run from around 6 am until early evening. The following list also includes the main buses running between the outer parts of the island and Manama:

Route 2 – Isa Town, Al-Sehlah, Al-Khamis, Al-Sulmaniya, Manama bus station, Manama Municipality, Ras Rummaan, Muharraq

Route 5 – Al-Budayyi', Ad-Diraz, Abu Saybi, Jidd Hafs, Al-Budayyi' Rd, Manama bus station, Manama Municipality, Ras Rummaan, Old Palace Rd, Al-Sulmaniya Ave and vice-versa

Route 7 – East Rifa, West Rifa, Isa Town, Al-Sehlah, Al-Khamis, Al-Sulmaniya Ave, Manama bus station, Manama Municipality, Ras Rummaan, Muharraq

Route 9 – Az-Zallaq, Al-Malikiyah, Karzakkan, Selig, Hamad Town, Buri, A'ali, Isa Town

Route 11 – Hamad Town, West Rifa, East Rifa, Jao, Al-Akr, Ad-Dur and vice versa

Route 12 – Sar, Al-Budayyi', Al-Janabiyah, Al-Hamalah, Dumistan, Karzakkan, Hamad Town and vice-versa

Route 15 – Hamad Town, Buri, A'ali, Isa Town

Muharraq Island

There is no place to stay on Bahrain's second most important island, but there is a lot to see. Most of it is within walking distance of Muharraq's bus station. The bus station is near the end of the causeway to Manama and there are several tea stalls and restaurants in the neighbourhood, as well as a post office. To reach the bus station as you come off the causeway turn right at the first roundabout. The station will be on your right after about 100m.

Bait Shaikh Isa Bin Ali & Bait Seyadi

These two traditional houses are well worth visiting for a look at pre-oil life in Bahrain. To reach them go straight through the roundabout as you come off the causeway from Manama. Follow the road as it swings around to the left, then turn right on Shaikh Abdulla Bin Isa Ave (you should see two small blue-and-white signs pointing the way to the houses). Further up Shaikh

Abdulla Bin Isa Ave you will see two signs pointing to the left, the upper one to 'Sh. Isa Bin Ali House' and the lower one to 'Seyadi House'. Underneath these is a much larger sign for the 'Al-Najah Furniture Show'. The back and side of Bait Shaikh Isa Bin Ali actually occupy this corner, so after turning left you will have the wall of Bait Shaikh Isa Bin Ali immediately to your right. You must follow the wall around to the right to reach the door.

To reach Bait Seyadi from Bait Shaikh Isa Bin Ali (on foot – you can't do this in a car) go straight ahead and a bit to the right as you come out the door of the house and cross a patch of waste ground keeping the mosque to your right and the electrical transformer to your left. This will take you into a narrow alley for about 50m. When you emerge from the alley the minaret of the mosque attached to Bait Seyadi will be right in front of you. The entrance to the house itself is on the far side of the building.

Both houses are open Saturday to Wednesday from 8 am to 2 pm and Thursday from 9.30 am to 5 pm. They are closed Friday. Admission is free.

Walking to either house from the Muharraq bus station should not take more than 10 or 15 minutes.

Bait Shaikh Isa Bin Ali was built around 1800, presumably by one of Muharraq's wealthier citizens. Later in the 19th century the then-emir, Shaikh Isa Bin Ali, acquired the house which he used as both his residence and the seat of government. While the rooms are pretty bare, the different sections of the house are well marked in both Arabic and English with signs explaining their uses. The carved doors and restored plasterwork throughout the house are very interesting and worth a pause for a closer look.

As you enter the building take a minute to look at the large map of the house by the main door. Then continue into the courtyard, where you will see a well. The large room on the right side of the courtyard contains a number of photographs of Shaikh Isa Bin Ali and his family. It also contains a working

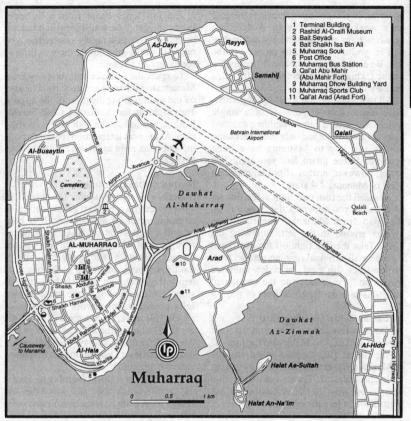

Map legend:
1 Terminal Building
2 Rashid Al-Oraifi Museum
3 Bait Seyadi
4 Bait Shaikh Isa Bin Ali
5 Muharraq Souk
6 Post Office
7 Muharraq Bus Station
8 Qal'at Abu Mahir (Abu Mahir Fort)
9 Muharraq Dhow Building Yard
10 Muharraq Sports Club
11 Qal'at Arad (Arad Fort)

Muharraq

0   0.5   1 km

wind tower – one of the few opportunities still available to sit under a wind tower and marvel at its ability to catch even the tiniest breeze.

Beyond the room with the wind tower a passageway leads to the family's living quarters. Be sure to take a look at the carefully restored reed-and-wood ceilings. Upstairs you will find more living areas.

Bait Seyadi is a smaller house of similar age but the restoration work is not quite as advanced. Still, it's worth the extra few minutes walk. An old mosque is attached to the house.

Qal'at Abu Mahir (Abu Mahir Fort)

This small fort now occupies the south-western tip of Muharraq but was originally on an island a few hundred metres off Muharraq's southern shore. It is only with the huge land reclamation programme of the last 40 years that it has found itself on Muharraq. Along with Qal'at Arad, it used to guard the approaches to Muharraq Bay. Qal'at Abu Mahir dates as far back as the 16th century, though it has been rebuilt several times since then. It is within the grounds of the Muharraq coastguard station so access is sometimes limited. Generally, however, if you present yourself at the gate on a weekday (Saturday to Wednesday) between 7 am and 2 pm and ask nicely they will let you in. You will be escorted to the fort. Be especially careful to ask permission before taking pictures here – it is, after all, a military base.

All that said, the fort itself is not particularly impressive. It consists of a single watchtower with a narrow building attached to its landward side and only the parts facing across the bay to Manama have been restored. If the guard lets you climb the tower, however, it does afford an excellent view of Manama's skyline.

To reach the fort, turn right at the first set of lights as you come off the causeway on the road from Manama. The road then swings around to the left, following the coast. Take the first right off the main road onto a small slip road running parallel to it. Follow this slip road for a few hundred metres and the entrance to the coastguard base will be immediately in front of you.

Muharraq Dhow Building Yard

Muharraq's small dhow yard is on the coast between Qal'at Abu Mahir and the turn-off for the airport. Like the yard on the outskirts of Manama you can see fishing dhows being built and repaired. There is no admission charge, but you should remember to ask permission before taking pictures.

Qal'at Arad (Arad Fort)

The foundations of this fort also date from the 16th century when the site was fortified by the Portuguese, though much of what is visible today was built during the brief Omani occupation of Bahrain at the beginning of the 19th century. Parts of the fort have been beautifully restored and the site is now used for concerts. It is open Saturday to Wednesday from 7.30 am to 2 pm, Wednesday afternoon from 3.30 to 5.30 pm, Thursday from 10 am to 5 pm and Friday from 9 to 11 am and 3.30 to 5 pm. The relatively new 'tower' by the entrance gate has a small display on the fort's history. Admission is free.

The fort looks better from a distance. When you get close you'll see that it has not been nearly as thoroughly restored as you might have thought. Inside there is little to see except an old well.

To reach the fort take the causeway from Manama to Muharraq and keep right (ie stay on the main road) at the turn for the airport. Turn right at the Muharraq Club Service Station, and follow the wall of the sporting club. At the next intersection (past the sporting club) turn right again and follow the road to the end.

Rashid Al-Oraifi Museum

Bahrain's newest museum (it opened in 1994) is really a private art gallery dedicated to the work of its artist-owner. It is built around a collection of Al-Oraifi's paintings, most of which are on Dilmun-related themes. His style is to apply his paint in multiple, heavy layers, a technique that lends the works an almost three-dimensional feeling. A shop in the museum also sells postcards, silverwork and prints of Al-Oraifi's work, though most of the prints are fairly conventional views of sites like the souk and the Friday Mosque rather than the abstract Dilmun images that dominate the museum itself.

The museum is open Saturday to Thursday from 8 am to noon and 4 to 8 pm and Friday from 8 am to noon. Admission costs BD 1.

To reach the museum coming from Manama take the Shaikh Hamad Causeway to the first roundabout. Continue straight through the roundabout and follow the road (Shaikh Salman Ave) as it swings around to the left, and then goes straight. Turn right on Airport Ave (at the second traffic signal past the roundabout) and follow it to Avenue 1. Turn right onto Avenue 1 and go straight, into a small alley, for a few hundred metres. When you reach a stop sign turn left. The museum will then be on your right. Bus Nos 6 and 10 will take you from the Muharraq station to the junction of Airport Ave and Avenue 1, from where you can walk to the museum in a couple of minutes.

Muharraq Souk

The Muharraq souk is a lot less modern than the Manama souk and, for that reason, is rather more interesting. The heart of the souk is the area between Shaikh Abdulla Bin Isa Ave and Shaikh Hamad Ave.

Dhow Trips

Technically you need a permit to take a dhow trip (these are, after all, ocean-going vessels) but if you go down to the wharf at the Muharraq end on the Shaikh Hamad Causeway you might be able to strike a deal with a dhow captain.

A more sensible approach would be to get a group of three or more together and contact a tour operator. See the Manama section for more information.

Getting There & Around

Three bus routes are based at the Muharraq bus station. The buses start around 5.30 am and run until the early evening.

Route 4 – Muharraq bus station, Shaikh Sulman Health Centre, Muharraq Market, Maternity Hospital, Bahrain Club, Muharraq bus station

Route 6 – Muharraq bus station, Shaikh Sulman Rd, Bahrain airport, Maternity Hospital, Ad-Dayr, Samahij

Route 10 – Muharraq bus station, Shaikh Sulman Rd, Maternity Hospital, Bahrain airport, Arad, Halat As-Sultah

Route 13 – Same as Route 4

Bus Nos 1, 2 and 7 run between the Manama and Muharraq bus stations.

Service-taxis also gather at the Muharraq bus station.

Kuwait

Kuwait

Life in Kuwait during the past few decades has rarely been dull. As if being a micro-state with Saudi Arabia, Iraq and Iran for neighbours was not enough, there was the sudden rush of money that, in the 1950s, made Kuwait the prototype of what later came to be known as an oil shaikhdom. That was followed by territorial disputes, breakneck industrial development, a roller coaster experiment with parliamentary democracy, social tensions, the nationalisation of the oil industry, a stock market scandal of mind-boggling proportions, the collapse of the oil market, a rash of Iranian-inspired terror bombings, and eight nerve-racking years of Iran and Iraq bleeding each other white just over the horizon. Kuwaitis are often accused of being arrogant, but anyone who weathers all of that over one generation and comes out smiling deserves some points for endurance.

Then came the invasion. Suddenly, Kuwait was to be the test case for US President George Bush's 'New World Order'. There was a theory, fairly widespread at the time, that the Gulf crisis was destined to be the great defining moment of the post-Cold War world. A couple of years down the line that looked a bit overstated. Returning to Kuwait 10 months after the country's liberation from Iraqi occupation I found it a strangely eerie place. The government seemed obsessed with precisely re-creating the country's appearance prior to the invasion.

A few years later reconstruction was complete and Kuwait looked almost *exactly* as it had before the Iraqis arrived, but the changes in Kuwaiti society had become clearer. The most notable of these is the greater openness that has accompanied the restoration of Kuwait's parliament. Kuwait is, once again, the prototypical oil state, but though it may look the same, much has changed.

The Kuwait of the mid-90s is in many ways a more relaxed, and more interesting, place to visit than the security-obsessed country I first saw in 1988.

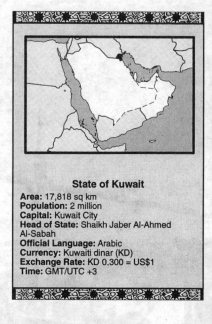

State of Kuwait
Area: 17,818 sq km
Population: 2 million
Capital: Kuwait City
Head of State: Shaikh Jaber Al-Ahmed Al-Sabah
Official Language: Arabic
Currency: Kuwaiti dinar (KD)
Exchange Rate: KD 0,300 = US$1
Time: GMT/UTC +3

Facts about the Country

HISTORY
A Greek Colony in the Gulf
By the standards of Bahrain or Oman, Kuwait is a newcomer to the world scene. The headland now occupied by Kuwait City was settled only some 300 years ago. Prior to that the most important part of what is now the State of Kuwait was the small island of Failaka, which lies just outside the mouth of Kuwait Bay and controls the sea lanes approaching it (a point which, many centuries later, was not lost on the Iraqis, who heavily garrisoned the island). The island also served as a convenient stopover for ancient travellers bound

from Mesopotamia to the Indian Ocean and beyond.

Failaka was inhabited during the Bronze Age, though it is not entirely clear whether it then belonged to the Bahrain-based Dilmun Empire or was a southern outpost of Sumeria. It was the Greeks, however, who put Failaka, which they called Ikaros, on the map.

By 325 BC, Alexander the Great had crossed the Indus River and conquered parts of what is now India. As he prepared to return to Babylon, Alexander ordered Nearchus, a Cretan commander in his army, to build a fleet and return to Mesopotamia by sea, reconnoitring the coast of Persia while Alexander went by land. The fleet was built near present-day Karachi, and Nearchus eventually rejoined Alexander in Babylon. By then the young king was considering a campaign to conquer Arabia, probably with an eye toward the wealth of the frankincense-producing regions in southern Arabia. Nearchus was sent back to the Gulf, this time with the task of scouting the Gulf's Arabian coastline. He launched several different survey vessels, and his troops are known to have travelled at least as far as Hormuz. But the Arabian campaign was never to be. Alexander died at Babylon only days before he planned to depart for Arabia.

By the time Alexander's empire collapsed, a Greek colony had been established on Failaka. Alexander himself is said to have christened the island Ikaros. Though the island was inhabited, when Nearchus arrived its earlier character was rapidly Hellenised. Ikaros became a centre for trade, fishing and pearling. It was no great metropolis, but it seems to have been reasonably prosperous.

The Beginnings of Kuwait

Failaka may have been prosperous but throughout most of the Christian era it was not a place of importance. The adjacent areas of the mainland had even less to recommend them and it was not until the 17th century that anything much happened there.

It is unclear both when Kuwait was founded and when the Al-Sabah, Kuwait's

KUWAIT

ruling family, first arrived there. Official tradition says the family arrived in the area in 1716, though other sources give 1722 or even 'sometime in the 1670s' as the date. What is known is that the Al-Sabah were members of the Utbi tribal confederation and that they, and many others, migrated to the Gulf from the Najd region in central Arabia following a period of drought and famine. The Utbis initially went to Basra (in present-day Iraq) where they appealed for help to the Ottoman authorities. From Basra they are thought to have wandered south to the headland where Kuwait City now stands.

The word *kuwait* is an Arabic diminutive meaning 'small fort'. The term is thought to refer to a fort or storehouse where the local shaikh kept arms and/or food and livestock at the time of the Utbis' arrival. Kuwait at that time was nothing more than a few tents and the storehouse-cum-fort. The land was arid and any agriculture or grazing was negligible. The site did, however, have one clear asset: the bay is one of the best natural harbours on the Arabian side of the Gulf.

The Utbis placed themselves under the protection of the Bani Khalid, then the most powerful tribal confederation in eastern Arabia and the Gulf. They divided among

KUWAIT

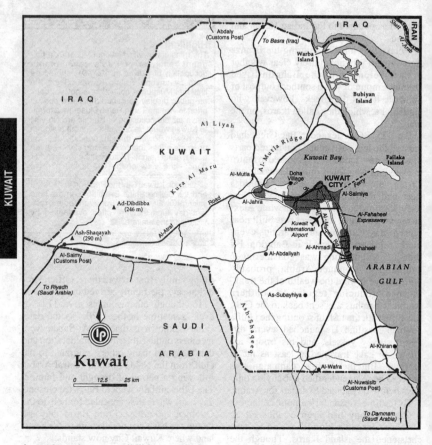

Kuwait

themselves the responsibilities attached to the new settlement: the ancestors of the Al-Sabah family were appointed to handle local law and order and relations with the Bani Khalid. Another family, the Al-Khalifa, was put in charge of the pearl trade, though within a generation it had departed for the better pearling banks of the central Gulf, and by the end of the 18th century had conquered Bahrain where it still rules.

In 1752 the Utbis confirmed the right of the Al-Sabah family to rule Kuwait. Today's ruling family takes its name from an ancestor who was confirmed as ruler in that year and reigned until 1756. He spent this brief period

taking the first steps to establish Kuwait as a major trading centre.

Turks, Persians & Britons

The small settlement grew quickly. A Dutch trader who visited Kuwait in 1756 wrote that it had a fleet of some 300, mostly small, boats. The town could also muster 4000 armed men in times of crisis. The mainstay of the economy was pearling. By 1760, when the town's first wall was built, Kuwait's dhow fleet was said to number 800 and camel caravans based there travelled regularly to Baghdad, Riyadh and Damascus.

The great Danish explorer Carsten Neibuhr

visited Kuwait, which he called Graine, in 1765 and described it as a town of some 10,000 people, though during the summer 70% of its inhabitants would disappear to work the pearl banks or travel with the caravans. According to Neibuhr, in spite of (or maybe because of) the town's prosperity the Utbi and Bani Khalid families still periodically fought over it. Failaka, he said, served as a retreat for noncombatants.

By the early 19th century Kuwait was a thriving trading port. The British traveller WG Palgrave, who visited in 1865, attributed this prosperity to the town's good government.

But trouble was always, quite literally, just over the horizon. It was often unclear whether Kuwait was part of the Ottoman Empire or not. Certainly the Ottomans maintained a claim to the emirate, even after it formally became a British protectorate at the end of the 19th century. Official Kuwaiti history is adamant that the Al-Sabah domains were always independent of the Ottomans. In any event, Constantinople's control of the fringes of its empire had always been pretty nominal and never more so than during the 19th century.

International politics in 18th and 19th-century Kuwait meant playing the Ottomans against the Persians. It was a game at which the Al-Sabah became remarkably adept. As the years went by, the British became involved as well. The East India Company temporarily moved its Basra office to Kuwait twice in the late 18th century (in 1776 and again in 1793-95) to escape the wars between the Ottomans and Persia. In return, the British drove back the Ottomans when they threatened Kuwait in 1795.

During the second half of the 19th century the Kuwaitis generally got on well with the Ottomans. They skilfully managed to avoid being absorbed into their empire as the Turks sought (not entirely successfully) to solidify their control over eastern Arabia, then known as Al-Hasa. They did, however, agree to take the title of provincial governors of Al-Hasa. It was that decision which led to the rise

of Shaikh Mubarak Al-Sabah Al-Sabah, commonly known as Mubarak the Great (reigned 1896-1915), the pivotal figure in the history of modern Kuwait. Mubarak was vehemently opposed to accommodating Turkey. Deeply suspicious of Turkey and convinced (probably correctly) that Constantinople planned to annex Kuwait, he overthrew and murdered his brother, Shaikh Mohammed, did away with another brother (Jarrah) and installed himself as ruler.

In 1899 Mubarak signed an agreement with Britain modelled on the Exclusive Agreements Britain had signed with the other Gulf rulers over the previous four decades. In exchange for the Royal Navy's protection, he promised not to give away territory to, take support from or negotiate with any other foreign power without British consent.

The Ottomans continued to claim sovereignty over Kuwait, but they were now in no position to enforce it. Britain's motive for signing the treaty of 1899 was a desire to keep Germany, then the main ally and financial backer of Turkey, out of the Gulf. The Germans had already built a railway line from Constantinople to Baghdad and an extension to Basra and Kuwait was planned. The treaty was London's guarantee that there would never be a railway link from Europe, via Turkey, all the way to the Gulf.

In 1913 the British confirmed Kuwait's independence from the Ottomans by defining the emirate's border with the Ottoman province of Basra. (When Iraq became independent in 1932, it reluctantly accepted this border but renounced it after Iraq's monarchy was overthrown in 1958.) The Turkish threat faded when Britain occupied Mesopotamia during WWI.

After the palace coup Mubarak's reign was both prosperous and quiet. The population more than tripled (to 35,000 in 1910) and the first schools were opened. Two of Mubarak's four sons went on to become rulers. It is only from these two branches of the royal family that the country's emirs are now chosen.

The 1920s, however, were a different

KUWAIT

story. Around the turn of the century Mubarak had played host for several years to the Al-Saud family. It had been driven from its traditional base in Riyadh and had ended up in Kuwait after wandering along the edge of the Empty Quarter desert for a time. It was from Kuwait that the young Abdul Aziz Bin Abdul Rahman Al-Saud set out, first to reclaim Riyadh, and then to restore the kingdom stretching from the Gulf to the Red Sea which his family had ruled in the late 18th and early 19th centuries.

As he became master of more and more of Arabia, Abdul Aziz never made much secret of his belief that the entire peninsula was, by rights, part of the Saudi kingdom. His years in Kuwait notwithstanding, he eventually turned his attention to the city and unleashed the *ikhwan*, or brotherhood, his much feared army of Bedouin Islamic fundamentalist warriors. Though Abdul Aziz himself was unusually broad-minded the same could not be said of many of his followers, and they took a dark view of what they saw as the loose-living ways of the Kuwaitis.

Kuwait, at that time, had no defensive wall so one was hurriedly erected. The gates along Al-Soor St in modern Kuwait City are all that remain of it today. Hoping to put an end to the Saudi threat to Kuwait, the British, in 1922-23, negotiated a formal treaty under which Abdul Aziz recognised Kuwait's independence. His price, however, was two-thirds of what the ruler, Shaikh Ahmed, had always understood to be his land. The British told Shaikh Ahmed that it was a small price to pay to guarantee the country's independence. The attacks, however, did not stop until some years later (the last one took place in 1930), when Abdul Aziz was forced to crush the ikhwan, who had by then become a threat to his own throne.

The First Oil State

In 1911, the Anglo-Persian Oil Company (the forerunner of today's British Petroleum, or BP) requested permission from the British government to negotiate a concession agreement with the ruler of Kuwait. The British refused, but did go to the trouble of sending an official of their own to inspect the seepages which had attracted Anglo-Persian's attention in the first place.

With much political manoeuvring, in which the British tried in vain to keep US companies out of the region, it was not until 1934 that an oil concession was granted. The contract went to a joint venture owned 50-50 by Anglo-Persian and the US-based Gulf Oil Company. Together, the two companies set up the Kuwait Oil Company (KOC) through which they ran their operations in the emirate.

The first wells were sunk in 1936, and by 1938 it became obvious that the shaikhdom was virtually floating on oil. The outbreak of WWII forced KOC to suspend its activities for several years, but when export operations took off after the war so did Kuwait's economy. Though the state's royalties were slightly lower than those received by Saudi Arabia, Iraq and Iran, the emirate's relatively small population made the revenues huge when calculated on a per capita basis.

The first great rush of oil money came in 1951. In that year Iran's prime minister, Mohammed Mossadiq, nationalised the assets of the Anglo-Iranian Oil Company (as Anglo-Persian was renamed after Persia became Iran in 1935), effectively cutting off the flow of Iranian oil to the company's operations outside the country. Both Anglo-Iranian and its competition rapidly stepped up production elsewhere, including Kuwait, to take up the slack. Between 1946 and 1956 Kuwait's output rose from 800,000 to a staggering 54 million long tons per year.

Emir Abdullah Al-Salem Al-Sabah (reigned 1950-65) became the first 'oil shaikh'. His reign was not, however, marked by the kind of profligacy with which that term later came to be associated. Kuwait's trading wealth had, up to that point, given it a very high standard of living in local terms and had brought with it some degree of development. As a trading city, particularly one with a long history of contact with both the British and the Turks, Kuwait had also developed an open-minded society rather than a xenophobic one. Moreover, when foreign workers began to flood into the country, the Kuwaiti government went out of its way to ease potential tensions by seeing to it that as many of those workers as possible were Arabs.

As the country became dramatically wealthy health care, education and the general standard of living improved on a similar scale. In 1949 Kuwait had only four doctors. By 1967 it had 400. The city wall was torn down in 1957 to make way for the rapid, oil-driven growth.

With this flood of money Kuwait was quickly transformed almost beyond recognition. This, however, was meagre compared to what happened in the '70s. In 1973 Kuwait's oil revenues totalled US$1.7 billion. In 1978 they totalled US$9.2 billion.

Though the fourfold jump in the price of oil between 1973 and 1975 accounted for much of this increase in revenue, another significant factor was the nationalisation of KOC. In 1974 the government bought 60% of the company. In March 1975, with tension between the Arab world and the west still high in the wake of the 1973-74 oil embargo, Kuwait announced that it was taking over the remaining 40% of the company, though this action was not implemented until December of that year.

Independence
On 19 June 1961 the treaty with Britain was terminated by mutual consent and Kuwait became an independent state.

In the years leading up to independence, the Al-Sabah family's position in society had been reinforced by the fact that the early oil

The National Assembly
The Kuwaiti parliament, or National Assembly, has had quite a history. The British first talked the then-ruler, Shaikh Ahmed, into appointing an advisory council in 1921, though he soon dissolved it and returned to ruling alone. A Constituent Assembly, charged with drafting a constitution for the new state, was elected a few months after independence in 1961. The constitution itself was officially promulgated in 1962. Elections for Kuwait's first National Assembly were held later that year and the Assembly first convened in 1963. Though representatives of the country's leading merchant families occupied the bulk of the seats, radicals had a toehold in the body from its inception. The first years of constitutional government were turbulent: leftists in the National Assembly almost immediately began pressing for faster social change and the country had three Cabinets between 1963 and 1965.

In August 1976 the Cabinet resigned, claiming that the Assembly had made day-to-day governance impossible. The emir suspended the constitution, dissolved the National Assembly and asked the crown prince/prime minister of the outgoing government to form a new Cabinet, which he did the following day. When new elections were held in 1981, it was only after the electoral laws had been revised in a way which, the government hoped, would guarantee that the radicals won no seats in the new parliament. While this succeeded after a fashion, the Assembly's new conservative majority proved just as troublesome as the radicals had been. Parliament was dissolved again in 1986. The emir said then that public arguments over policy were dividing Kuwaitis at a time when the country was coming under threat from Iran during the Iran-Iraq War. Some Opposition figures have long contended that the Assembly's real sin was to question the degree to which the Al-Sabah family continued to dominate Kuwait's government.

In December 1989 and January 1990, an extraordinary series of demonstrations took place calling for the restoration of the 1962 constitution and the reconvening of the suspended parliament. The demonstrators challenged the emir's right to rule without the National Assembly and were met by riot police, tear gas and water cannon. In June of that year, elections were held for a Consultative Council which was supposed to spend four years advising the government on possible constitutional changes prior to the election of a new Assembly. Pro-democracy activists demanded the reconvening of the old Assembly and denounced the Consultative Council as unconstitutional.

During the Iraqi occupation of Kuwait, Opposition leaders and the government, meeting in exile in Saudi Arabia, agreed to return to parliamentary rule and the 1962 constitution after the country's liberation. Elections were held in late 1992 and the government and legislature returned to their, by now, traditional roles of bickering over both the details of legislation and the division of power. ∎

revenues were paid directly to the ruler. Many, however, still saw Kuwait as little more than a British colony, including the emirate's large population of Egyptian and Palestinian workers, many of whom rioted during the Suez crisis of late 1956. During those riots some of the country's oil pipelines were blown up.

Abdullah was succeeded by Shaikh Sabah Al-Salem Al-Sabah (reigned 1965-77). The current emir, Shaikh Jaber Al-Ahmed Al-Sabah, served as finance minister under Abdullah before becoming crown prince and prime minister under Sabah.

As Suez had proved, wealth alone could not guarantee stability. The country's labour unions struck in 1967, accusing the government of not giving sufficient support to the Arab and Palestinian cause during that year's Arab-Israeli war. The government sought to placate them, first by briefly cutting off the flow of oil to the west during the war, and later by taking a prominent role in the Arab summit which took place in Khartoum several months after the war. At Khartoum Kuwait promised huge sums of money to the 'frontline' states confronting Israel and to various Palestinian organisations. When war broke out again in 1973, the government sent Kuwaiti troops to fight along the Suez Canal, partly to blunt the criticism it expected in the National Assembly, or parliament.

The 1980s: From Boom to Slump

During the late 1970s Kuwait's economy seemed to be roaring ahead. The country's stock exchange (the first in the Gulf) was among the top 10 in the world by value and bankers were lining up to buy securities denominated in Kuwaiti dinars.

By the mid-80s everything was different. In the winter of 1985-86, the price of oil collapsed and the economies of all the Gulf States were severely affected. But in Kuwait there were other problems as well. In addition to its regular stock market the country had developed a parallel financial market which, while not strictly legal, was allowed to operate openly and with virtually no regulation. The market, known as the Suq

Al-Manakh, operated on a system of post-dated cheques which made it virtually impossible for investors to lose money. In 1982, however, panic ensued when some investors got jittery, tried to reclaim their money and found that the dealers were unable to honour the cheques. Within days the entire system collapsed and hundreds of people became bankrupt. The scandal left behind US$90 billion in worthless post-dated cheques and a mess which the Kuwaiti government has been trying to sort out ever since.

Just as the government began to deal with the fallout from the Suq Al-Manakh fiasco, another problem arose. As the Iran-Iraq War, which had begun in 1980, dragged on into its third year, the emirate's location only a few miles from the frontlines made investors nervous. Though some Kuwaiti companies made a lot of money trans-shipping embargoed goods to Iraq the war was, on the whole, a disaster for the country's economy. It did not help matters much that from 1983 Iran sought to punish (officially neutral) Kuwait for its thinly veiled support for Iraq. From 1983 to 1985 the country suffered a string of Iranian-inspired terror-bombings, including highly publicised attacks on the US and French embassies. These attacks scared off foreigners, exacerbated the Sunni-Shiite division in the population and made the government fanatically security-conscious.

Iraq & Kuwait

Iraq has never really accepted the idea of Kuwait as an independent state: the 1990 invasion was only the latest attempt by Iraq to challenge Kuwait's existence. Minor skirmishes and the occasional major incident have been regular features of Iraqi-Kuwaiti relations since the 1950s. Within hours of Kuwait's gaining independence from Britain in 1961, Iraq reasserted its long-standing claim to the emirate. The emir called in the British who sent a small force to Kuwait. This proved to be enough to deter the Iraqis in the short term, and the force was replaced three months later by a joint Arab League force.

The most serious of the two countries' many border clashes took place in March 1973 when the Iraqis moved an estimated 3000 troops onto Kuwaiti territory, occupied one Kuwaiti border post and shelled another. After a short time Iraq withdrew under pressure from the Arab League (led by Egypt, which was then preparing for war with Israel and regarded the Iraq-Kuwait border dispute as an unnecessary distraction). Even then, however, Iraq's foreign minister went out of his way to assert a claim to Warba and Bubiyan islands.

On the other hand, Iraq had never, not even in 1961, attempted to launch an all-out invasion of Kuwait, and by 1990 the Kuwaitis could reasonably claim that Baghdad was in their debt. Throughout the eight-year-long Iran-Iraq War, Kuwait had been a vital lifeline for both goods flowing into Iraq and exports flowing out. Even after the 1983-85 Iranian-sponsored terrorist bombings and a later Iranian decision to shell Kuwaiti territory, the emirate stood by Iraq politically and contributed enormous sums of money to the Iraqi war effort (partly because Kuwait was concerned that an Iranian victory would spill the Islamic revolution into its territory). At the end of May 1990, the Emir of Kuwait travelled to Baghdad for an Arab summit where, in the traditional Arab manner, he was embraced and kissed by President Saddam Hussein.

Nobody knows exactly when, or why, Saddam decided to invade Kuwait. It is easy to note, in retrospect, that there were signs of trouble. Months before the invasion, for example, the Iraqis had signed a treaty defining once and for all their border with Saudi Arabia. Kuwaiti officials sought a similar treaty and were rebuffed in Baghdad. Some have seen this as the first sign that Saddam was planning to swallow his smaller neighbour. Saddam has never, however, been overly fastidious about international law.

Saddam is known to have badgered the Kuwaitis about money during a closed session of the Baghdad summit. He accused them of waging 'economic warfare' against Iraq by exceeding their OPEC oil production quota which, he claimed, they were doing in an attempt to hold down the price of oil artificially. Both then and after the invasion, the Iraqis also claimed that Kuwait was demanding repayment of the loans it had extended to Baghdad during the war with Iran, a claim which the Kuwaitis have consistently denied. It had been generally understood at the time that the loans were, in fact, gifts.

The first clear public sign of trouble came on 16 July 1990 when Iraq sent a letter to the Secretary-General of the Arab League accusing Kuwait of exceeding its OPEC quota and of stealing oil from the Iraqi portion of an oil field straddling the border. Iraq's foreign minister told an Arab League meeting in Tunisia that 'we are sure some Arab states are involved in a conspiracy against us'. The charge of quota violations was true, as Kuwait had long been one of OPEC's most notorious overproducers, but there was nothing new in this and Iraq itself was hardly blameless on that score. Iraq's accusations over the oil field were harder to pin down but ultimately lacked substance: the Kuwaiti portion of the disputed Rumailah oil field produced a paltry 25,000 barrels per day.

The day after the Arab League meeting, Saddam repeated his accusations in a speech marking Iraq's Revolution Day and vaguely threatened military action against Kuwait and the United Arab Emirates (UAE). Over the next two weeks the Secretary-General of the Arab League, the Saudi Arabian foreign minister and President Hosni Mubarak of Egypt all travelled between Kuwait City and Baghdad seeking to diffuse the growing crisis Iraq had manufactured.

At the end of July 1990, the Kuwaitis were rapidly discovering that all the money they had lavished on development projects around the region over the previous 30 years had not bought them many allies. In addition, Saddam increasingly appeared determined to pick a fight. In the two weeks leading up to the invasion, the various mediators bent over backwards to offer Iraq a graceful way out of the dispute on five or six occasions. Each time Iraq replied by launching another

KUWAIT

verbal salvo in the direction of Kuwait. The Iraqis agreed to attend reconciliation talks with the Kuwaitis in Saudi Arabia in late July but then stalled over the ground rules for the talks, and continued to mass troops just north of the border.

When the tanks came crashing over the border at 2 am on 2 August the Kuwaitis never had a chance. The Iraqis were in Kuwait City before dawn and by noon they had reached the Saudi border. The emir and his Cabinet fled to Saudi Arabia.

The United Nations quickly passed a series of resolutions calling on Iraq to withdraw from Kuwait. The Iraqis replied that they had been invited in by a group of Kuwaiti rebels who had overthrown the emir. The absurdity of this claim was shown up by the failure of the Iraqis to find even one Kuwaiti willing to serve in a quisling government. On 6 August Iraq annexed the emirate.

An emergency summit of the Arab League was held in Cairo on 10 August but Saddam refused to attend. The Iraqis contended that Saudi Arabia's decision a few days earlier to ask the USA for troops to defend the Kingdom was at least as significant a threat to the region's security as Iraq's annexation of Kuwait, and a number of the League's members agreed. The League passed a resolution condemning the invasion but was deeply split.

Western countries, led by the USA, began

The Gulf War – A Chronology

1990

16 July	Iraq sends letter to the Arab League complaining that Kuwait is exceeding its OPEC oil quota and stealing oil from an oilfield straddling the Iraq-Kuwait border.
17 July	Iraqi President Saddam Hussein repeats the charges in a speech marking Iraq's Revolution Day.
26-27 July	Egyptian President Hosni Mubarak and Saudi Arabian Foreign Minister Saud Al-Faisal travel to Baghdad and Kuwait City in separate attempts to diffuse the growing crisis. Iraq agrees to meet Kuwait for reconciliation talks in the Saudi city of Taif on the 31 July.
1 August	Iraq walks out of Taif talks.
2 August	2 am – Iraqi forces invade Kuwait. By the end of the day the country is occupied. Kuwait's emir and his Cabinet flee to Saudi Arabia. In New York, the UN Security Council condemns the invasion and imposes an embargo on Iraqi oil exports.
6 August	Iraq annexes Kuwait.
9 August	King Fahd of Saudi Arabia accepts US offer of troops to defend the Kingdom against a possible Iraqi invasion. The troops begin arriving the following day and number 10,000 by 14 August. Iraq refuses to allow western residents and travellers to leave the country and begins efforts to round up western residents of Kuwait.
10 August	Emergency Arab League summit convenes in Cairo but Saddam refuses to attend. The summit passes a resolution criticising Iraq, but the League is deeply split by Saudi Arabia's decision to allow US troops onto its soil.
18 August	US President George Bush mobilises reserve units of the US military. Iraq announces that it will hold westerners as hostages at military and civilian facilities to guard against a US attack, and threatens to respond to any such attack with chemical and biological weapons.
23 August	Iraq releases some French hostages. Over the next four months all of the hostages are released, usually in small groups of particular nationalities after personal appeals to Saddam by various celebrities and politicians.
10 September	Bush and Soviet President Mikhail Gorbachev, meeting in Helsinki, condemn Iraq's occupation of Kuwait and call for a full withdrawal of Iraqi forces.
Mid-September	Iraqi troop strength in Kuwait reaches 360,000.
Oct-Nov	Amnesty International issues report condemning Iraq for torture and other atrocities in Kuwait as the two sides in the conflict continue to build up their troop strength and dig in.

to enforce a UN embargo on trade with Iraq by stopping and searching ships bound for Iraq and Jordan. In the months that followed US and other forces flooded into Saudi Arabia as the diplomatic standoff over Kuwait deepened. Tens of thousands of refugees, many of them Arabs and Asians who had been working in Kuwait, fled the emirate only to find themselves sweltering in makeshift transit camps on the Iraqi-Jordanian border in the middle of the summer.

The anti-Iraq coalition's forces eventually numbered 425,000 US troops and 265,000 from 27 other countries. They were backed up by an increasingly long list of UN Security Council resolutions calling on Iraq to withdraw from Kuwait. Tales of atrocities

were publicised around the world by Amnesty International, Middle East Watch and Kuwaiti exiles. At the end of November, the US and the UK secured a UN resolution authorising the use of force to drive Iraq out of Kuwait if Baghdad did not pull out voluntarily before 15 January 1991.

With less than a week to go before the expiration of the 15 January deadline, US Secretary of State James Baker met with Iraqi Foreign Minister Tariq Aziz in Geneva. The talks lasted for nearly six hours but came to nothing. In the final hours before the deadline a number of national leaders, including Mubarak of Egypt and French President François Mitterrand, televised appeals to Saddam to withdraw from Kuwait

8 November	USA announces that it is sending an additional 200,000 troops to the Gulf. The anti-Iraq coalition eventually numbers 425,000 US troops and 265,000 troops from 27 other countries. The coalition commands more than 150 ships and 2000 aircraft.
29 November	The UN Security Council authorises the use of force to drive Iraq out of Kuwait if Baghdad fails to withdraw from the emirate by 15 January 1991.
6 December	Iraq releases the last of its foreign hostages.
1991	
9 January	US Secretary of State James Baker and Iraqi Foreign Minister Tariq Aziz hold more than six hours of talks in Geneva in a fruitless attempt to resolve the crisis.
12 January	A joint resolution by the US Congress gives President Bush the authority to use force against Iraq.
17 January	3 am – Coalition forces begin bombing Iraq.
18 January	Iraq launches the first of more than a dozen missile attacks on Israel, with strikes against Tel Aviv and Haifa. The USA sends anti-missile systems, and crews to operate them, to Israel in exchange for an Israeli promise not to retaliate against Iraq.
20 January	Iraq begins pumping oil into the Gulf in an apparent attempt to poison Saudi Arabia's drinking water supply. Within a week the slick is 16 km wide and 56 km long. Eventually it grows to be 64 km wide and 160 km long.
29 January	Iraq attacks, and briefly occupies, the Saudi Arabian border town of Khafji.
12 February	The US military announces that satellite evidence indicates that Iraqi forces are deliberately setting fire to Kuwait's oil wells.
13 February	A US bomb destroys an Iraqi air raid shelter filled with civilians, including many women and children.
24 February	Ground offensive begins.
27 February	Iraqi troops begin withdrawing from Kuwait, setting remaining oil wells on fire as they go. Coalition aircraft trap, and massacre, a retreating column of Iraqi forces near Kuwait's Al-Mutla ridge. Coalition forces enter Kuwait City.
28 February	Bush orders suspension of hostilities bringing ground offensive to an end after only 100 hours.
March	Kuwait's crown prince and emir return from exile and rebuilding begins. Martial law is declared.
November	Press censorship lifted in Kuwait. Last oil well fire extinguished. ∎

before it was too late. Yasser Arafat of the PLO rushed to Baghdad to try to broker a deal.

The deadline passed, the Iraqis did not budge, and within hours waves of allied (mostly US) aircraft began a five-week bombing campaign over Iraq and Kuwait.

The ground offensive, when it finally came, lasted only 100 hours and was something of an anti-climax. Iraq's army, which had been touted in the west for the previous six months as one of the most fearsome military machines on earth, simply disintegrated. While there were relatively few casualties on the allied side, controversy has persisted over the number of civilian and military deaths in Iraq and Kuwait. Numbers from 10,000 to 100,000 or more have been offered.

Liberation & Beyond

When allied forces arrived in Kuwait City on 27 February 1991 they were greeted by jubilant crowds. The city's infrastructure had been almost completely destroyed during the war, though many buildings had survived relatively intact (the same could not be said of their contents which had, in many cases, been looted by the Iraqis).

For the first few days anarchy reigned in the liberated city. Some Kuwaitis turned their fury on what was left of the emirate's large Palestinian population. Yasser Arafat had been widely regarded as a supporter of the invasion, and many Palestinians had remained in the emirate throughout the occupation (in some cases because they had nowhere else to go). Many Kuwaitis thus assumed that all Palestinians had collaborated with the Iraqis and dealt with them accordingly. After liberation a number of people, most of them Palestinians, were convicted by special martial law courts on charges of collaboration.

Kuwaiti society seemed split between those who had stayed throughout the occupation and those who had fled. The government declared martial law but the crown prince, who also served as martial law administrator, did not return from exile in

Saudi Arabia until six days after liberation, and it was another 10 days before the emir himself returned. The royal family was slightly embarrassed by the fact that both the UK and US embassies in Kuwait City were reopened several days before the crown prince returned. By the time the emir returned both British Prime Minister John Major and US Secretary of State James Baker had come and gone.

Amid criticisms that it was moving too slowly, the government set about rebuilding the country, concentrating first on roads and utilities and afterwards on repairing homes and businesses and clearing the country of land mines. Some of the damage inflicted by the retreating Iraqis could only be described as spiteful. As they withdrew from Kuwait, the Iraqis had systematically blown up every oil well in the country and set most of them on fire. For many months thereafter the country was covered in a dense cloud of black smoke from the burning wells, the last of which was extinguished in November 1991, 8½ months after the end of the war.

Even before press censorship was lifted at the end of 1991, a heated debate had begun over the country's political future. In keeping with a promise the Opposition had extracted from the emir during the occupation, the 1962 constitution was restored and elections for a new National Assembly took place in October 1992. The Opposition shocked the government by winning over 30 of the new parliament's 50 seats. In keeping with Kuwaiti tradition the crown prince was reappointed as prime minister. Opposition MPs secured six of the 16 seats in the Cabinet, though the Al-Sabah family retained control of the key defence, foreign affairs and interior ministries. As with past elections the 1992 vote was restricted to the 70,000 or so adult Kuwaiti males holding 'first class' citizenship (those whose ancestors had been resident in Kuwait prior to the 1920s).

By the second anniversary of the invasion Kuwait's government had done an admirable job of erasing many of the physical scars of war and occupation. Kuwait today looks almost exactly as it did before the invasion.

Healing the psychological and personal scars is clearly going to take much longer.

Hundreds of Kuwaitis disappeared during the occupation and many remain unaccounted for, a fact of which visitors to the country are reminded almost daily. Iraq remains a threat. Several times in the years since liberation Iraqi troop movements have prompted Kuwait, the USA or both to mobilise troops. In 1994 Kuwait convicted several Iraqis on charges of attempting to assassinate former US President George Bush when he visited the emirate in 1993. The plot, according to the Kuwaitis, was uncovered and foiled at the last minute.

GEOGRAPHY

Kuwait's 17,818 sq km of land are mostly flat and arid with little or no ground water (much of which is brackish, anyway). The desert is generally gravelly. The country is about 185 km from north to south and 208 km from east to west. Its coastline is unexciting and the desert inland is not particularly

KUWAIT

The Legacy of the Gulf War

A coalition of 28 nations fought to drive Iraq's military out of Kuwait in January and February of 1991. In the months that followed, an equally impressive international effort was required to clean up the mess left behind.

The environmental damage caused by the Iraqis – much of which can only be described as spiteful – was on a truly massive scale. On 20 January 1991, the third day of the war, Iraqi forces opened the valves at Kuwait's Mina Al-Ahmadi and Sea Island oil terminals, intentionally releasing millions of litres of oil into the waters of the Gulf.

The result was an oil slick 64 km wide and 160 km long. Between six and eight million barrels of oil are thought to have been released (though some estimates go much higher) – at least twice as much as in any previous oil spill. At least 460 km of coastline, most of it in Saudi Arabia and Bahrain, was affected.

Releasing the oil appears to have been an attempt by the Iraqis to poison Riyadh's drinking water supply (much of which comes from two desalination plants near Jubail), shut down the Kingdom's offshore oil industry, which was providing fuel to the anti-Iraq coalition, and block an amphibious attack on occupied Kuwait. Some of the smaller releases appear to have been the inadvertent result of coalition bombing raids against targets in Kuwait.

The slick was fought by experts from nine nations, the European Community and the Gulf States themselves. Aramco and other oil companies eventually managed to recover, and reuse, around a million barrels of crude oil from the slick.

Despite a massive rescue effort the slick devastated marine life along much of the coast. While the war was still being fought, stories began appearing about the effect of the slick on the Gulf's large population of cormorants, migratory birds that typically spend the winter months in the Gulf. Dolphins, fish, several endangered species of sea turtles and many other animals died in large numbers as a result of the slick, as did hundreds of hectares of mangroves along the coast.

Though some of Kuwait's famous oil fires may have been set off by allied bombing, the Iraqis began the systematic torching of the emirate's oil wells (of which there were just under 1000 at the time of the invasion) in mid-February. By the time the war ended, two weeks later, nearly every well was burning, including many that had not even been in production at the time of the invasion. The conservative estimate was that at least two million barrels of oil per day were being lost. The resulting cloud literally turned day into night throughout the country.

Like the slick, the oil fires devastated wildlife throughout the region, but they also had a direct impact on public health in Kuwait and the northern Gulf. Black rain and snow caused by the fires were reported as far away as India.

Once the fire on each well was out, the flow of oil itself still had to be controlled. Cleaning up the oil lakes left behind after the fires – in some places up to two metres deep and saturating the sand to a depth of 35 or 40 cm – took much longer than putting out the actual blazes.

Initial reports predicted that it might take as long as five years to put out all the fires, but that proved pessimistic. Another massive international effort, combined with a fair amount of innovation on the part of the firefighters, led to the extinguishing of the last fire after only eight months. The crews did the job so quickly that one well had to be reignited so that the Emir of Kuwait could pull a lever to 'put out the final fire' before a large group of reporters flown in for the occasion in November 1991. ∎

interesting. The only significant geographic feature is the now infamous Al-Mutla ridge where allied aircraft massacred a column of retreating Iraqi forces in the closing hours of the Gulf War.

CLIMATE

In the summer (April to September) Kuwait is hellishly hot. Its saving grace is that it is nowhere near as humid as Dhahran, Bahrain or Abu Dhabi. The winter months are often pleasant but can get fairly cold, with daytime temperatures hovering around 18°C and nights being genuinely chilly. A good medium-weight jacket and a jumper are essential travelling items for a winter visit to the emirate. Sandstorms occur throughout the year but are particularly common in spring.

GOVERNMENT & POLITICS

Kuwait's government is something of a hybrid: not exactly an absolute monarchy, but not really a democracy either. Under Kuwait's 1962 constitution the emir is the head of state. By tradition the crown prince serves as prime minister, making him, at least in theory, head of government. The emir 'appoints' the prime minister who, in turn, appoints the Cabinet (usually reserving key portfolios such as defence, interior and foreign affairs for other members of the ruling family). The constitution allows the emir not only to reign but also to rule, although in practice the current emir leaves day-to-day governance to the crown prince/prime minister.

The ruling Al-Sabah family itself picks the emir from one of two specific branches of the family. These are known as the Jaber and the Salem branches and refer to two of the four sons of Mubarak the Great who ruled Kuwait from 1896 to 1915. The choice of the emir alternates between these two branches (though this pattern has been broken once since Mubarak's death). The current emir, Shaikh Jaber Al-Ahmed Al-Sabah, is from the Jaber branch of the family while the crown prince (who is two years younger than the emir), Shaikh Saad Al-Abdullah Al-Salem Al-Sabah, is from the Salem branch.

The powers of the emir, crown prince and Cabinet are tempered by the 50-member National Assembly. The emir has the power to dissolve the Assembly whenever he pleases, but is required by the constitution to hold new elections within 90 days of any such dissolution – a requirement that, historically, has not always been honoured.

The Assembly was suspended by emiri decree in 1986. It was reinstated in 1992, as part of a deal struck in the fall of 1990 between the emir and crown prince on the one hand and leading Opposition members on the other. Under that agreement the Opposition gave its wholehearted support to the government, then in exile in Saudi Arabia, in exchange for a return to constitutional rule following liberation.

Voting for the Assembly is restricted to adult, male, 'first class' Kuwaiti citizens, though a law approved in the summer of 1994 extended the franchise to the children of naturalised Kuwaitis. Naturalised citizens themselves are not permitted to vote. Whether to extend the franchise to all Kuwaitis, and especially to women, is a subject of heated debate in the country.

As this book went to the printer the most recent elections, held in October 1992, had produced an Assembly determined to assert its powers to question Cabinet members (who are *ex-officio* members of the Assembly) and approve the national budget.

Prior to the Iraqi invasion Kuwait was known for maintaining a markedly independent foreign policy. For many years it was the only Gulf State to have diplomatic relations with the former Soviet Union and its allies. It was a particularly vocal supporter of the Palestinians and was active in the non-aligned movement. In the wake of the invasion it has drawn decidedly closer to the west. Since liberation, defence agreements have been signed with the USA, the UK and France.

The years since liberation have also seen the Kuwaiti government take a somewhat softer line on Arab-Israeli relations. The government quietly supported the 1993 Israel-PLO peace agreement (though some individual members of the National Assembly vigorously condemned it) and was represented by its foreign minister at the March 1996 anti-terrorism summit in Egypt, an event that was also attended by Israel's prime minister.

ECONOMY

Among the Gulf States, Kuwait's oil reserves are second only to those of Saudi Arabia. Oil production is running at about 1.8 million barrels per day (the same as it was before the invasion). Kuwait also has a large petrochemical industry, which was built up from the late '60s onward as a way for the country to keep control of more of the revenues generated by its oil.

Attempts to diversify the economy have met with mixed success. The government sank a lot of money into agriculture in the '70s, particularly into growing alfalfa and into dairy and poultry farming, but most of the country's food has always been imported and there is no sign of that changing in the short term.

Apart from oil, the country is best known for its investment policies. These sometimes bring unwelcome publicity, as when the London-based Kuwait Investment Office began buying large blocks of stock in BP. A British court later forced the KIO to sell some of the stock, though there was a certain delicious irony in the government of Kuwait making even a veiled bid for control of one of the oil companies that had originally made it rich. The government has also sought to diversify the country's role in the oil industry to make it a player on all levels, rather than simply being a producer/refiner of crude oil. It has purchased distribution networks and petrol stations (such as the Q8 chain in the UK) in other parts of the world.

The Fund for Future Generations was established in 1976 as a hedge against the day when oil ran out. For many years 10% of all oil revenues were paid into the fund, the balance of which could not be touched for a minimum of 25 years. At the time of the Iraqi invasion the fund was thought to have held about US$100 billion. It provided an invaluable source of cash during the occupation, when the government used it to support Kuwaitis living in exile and to pay some of the costs of the allied coalition. These

The Water Trade

Kuwait has long been known for its fine natural harbour, but like so many places in the Middle East it is chronically short of water. Today Kuwait has an abundant supply of fresh water and even bottles its own mineral water, but during the first half of this century the rapidly growing town actually imported drinking water from Iraq.

From 1907 until 1950 traders drew fresh water from the Shatt Al-Arab waterway at the head of the Gulf, loaded it onto dhows and shipped it down to Kuwait. The trade peaked in 1947 when it was estimated that 303,200 litres of water per day were arriving in Kuwait by boat. It was a far cry from the 19th century when Kuwait was small enough that, despite its famously arid landscape, it could still meet its needs from rainwater and the area's few wells.

Not surprisingly, Kuwait invested some of its early oil revenues in a mostly unsuccessful search for ground water.

The seaborne trade in fresh water stopped after Kuwait's first desalination plant was built in 1950. But although the desalination capacity now far exceeds the country's demand for fresh water, the government still devotes significant sums of money to research new desalination techniques. Desalination is just about the most expensive way imaginable to acquire fresh water and the technology has not improved over the last 45 years as much as some scientists had hoped. Kuwait's own consumption has risen radically over that period, from 6822 litres per capita in the '50s to 83,380 litres per capita in the mid-80s, according to the government's own figures.

Natural resources are precious and, as any Bedouin can tell you, in the desert water is far more valuable than oil. ■

expenses, and reconstruction costs, are believed to have left the fund with only US$35 to US$40 billion as of early 1995.

In 1961 the government set up the Kuwait Fund for Arab Economic Development, the first such development fund in the Gulf. In the '70s and '80s, Kuwait gave away as much as 10% of its GNP in aid (as against the figure of 0.7% which the UN recommends and which very few developed countries meet).

POPULATION & PEOPLE

While no exact figures are available, Kuwait's population is thought to be around two million, down from about 2.2 million prior to the invasion. Of these about 630,000 (around 32%) are Kuwaitis. As a percentage this represents a slight increase compared with the situation prior to the invasion (at which point Kuwaitis may have numbered as little as 25% of the overall population), but it is still a far cry from what the government would like it to be. Nationalisation of the work force has been a major topic of discussion for years, though only limited progress has been made both before and after the invasion.

Immediately after liberation, the government announced that it would never again allow Kuwaitis to become a minority in their own country. This implied a target population of about 1.2 million, but within months there were indications that the occupation had not blunted Kuwaitis' desire for servants and drivers or made them any more willing than before to do manual labour. As a result, by early 1992 the foreign population of the emirate was thought to have crept back ahead of the native population and within a couple of years it had more-or-less returned to pre-invasion proportions.

What has changed significantly since liberation is the cast of Kuwait's large expatriate population. Prior to August 1990 the country's professional classes were dominated by Arabs in general and Palestinians in particular. Manual labour was largely done by Egyptians. While there were certainly a large number of Indians, Pakistanis

and Sri Lankans in the country pre-invasion, Kuwait never took on the decidedly subcontinental air that cities in Saudi Arabia or the UAE often evince. This was the result of a specific government policy to keep Kuwait as 'Arab' as possible. If the country did not have a Kuwaiti majority in August 1990, it certainly had an Arab one.

After liberation this situation was reversed. Palestinians were the most visible sector of society affected but even the number of Egyptians in the country was drastically reduced, despite Cairo's enthusiastic participation in the anti-Iraq coalition. In the wake of the war, the Kuwaiti government began to encourage the recruiting of non-Arabs in general and South-East Asians in particular, fearing that large populations of expatriate Arabs could pose a security threat during any future crisis. Asians were thought to be more docile politically, less likely to become attached to Kuwait's Arab culture over a number of years and, ultimately, easier to deport if there were ever trouble.

Today, Kuwait's population presents much the same mix one finds in the rest of the Arabian Gulf: labourers from south and South-East Asia, mid-professionals from India, Pakistan, Egypt and Lebanon, and a handful (relative to other foreign communities) of westerners occupying upper-level professional jobs.

EDUCATION

Kuwait has long provided free education to all Kuwaitis and, before the invasion, to many of the foreigners living in the country. As early as the 1950s Shaikh Abdullah was stressing the importance of education, including women's education (an unusual attitude in the Gulf in those days). The University of Kuwait was founded in 1964; since 1980 more than half its students have been women. The government has been trying to channel more young Kuwaitis into the country's eight technical colleges as part of its long-term goal of getting more Kuwaitis into the work force.

ARTS

The arts scene in Kuwait is fairly limited. One gallery of the National Museum used to display the works of local painters but this, along with the rest of the museum, was destroyed by the Iraqis and has not been rebuilt. Sadu House (see the Kuwait City section) is a cultural foundation dedicated to preserving Bedouin art traditions, especially weaving.

SOCIETY & CONDUCT
Traditional Culture

There is not a lot of this left. Even before the Iraqis arrived the Kuwaitis had managed to eliminate most vestiges of life-before-oil in Kuwait City. Weekend picnics in the desert, which were clearly part of the traditional lifestyle, are clearly out of the question because of the lingering danger of mines throughout the country (see Dangers & Annoyances, later).

Dos & Don'ts

Kuwait is a lot more relaxed about matters of public conduct than other Gulf countries. Aside from the obviously immodest by Muslim standards (skirts above the knee, halter tops etc), women can dress as they want and there is never any need for a woman to wear an *abayya* (a long, cloak-like black garment), veil or headscarf. During Ramadan, the Muslim month of fasting, you should refrain from eating, drinking or smoking in public. As always you should never photograph people, especially women, without their permission.

Non-Muslims may enter mosques, even during prayer time, as long as proper dress is observed. Women and men should be well covered by wearing long-sleeved clothing; women must also cover their heads. Be quiet in mosques, do not move around unnecessarily and do not take photographs.

RELIGION

Islam is the state religion and Islamic *sharia* (law) is identified in the constitution as 'a main source of legislation'. Kuwait's brand of Islam is not as strict as that practised in Saudi Arabia, but the country is not as liberal as Bahrain. Most Kuwaitis are Sunni Muslims, though there is a substantial Shiite minority.

LANGUAGE

Arabic is the official language but English is very widely understood.

See Language in the Facts about the Region chapter for a list of useful Arabic words and phrases.

Facts for the Visitor

PLANNING
When to Go

The best time to visit is from mid-October to mid-March, though if you come in summer it is a relief to know that Kuwait is somewhat less humid than the Gulf's other cities (but no less hot).

Maps

The government's drive to reconstruct Kuwait City exactly as it was before the war means that pre-invasion maps are perfectly adequate for finding your way around. The *Oxford Map of Kuwait*, identifiable by the night time photo of the Kuwait Towers on the cover, is the best of the locally available maps. Most hotel bookshops have it. A better map, easy to recognise because of its yellow cover, is published by the Ministry of Information and distributed free at Kuwaiti embassies abroad. I've never seen it on sale in Kuwait.

What to Bring

Aside from the usual Gulf necessities of sunglasses, a hat and long-sleeved, loose clothing, people visiting in the winter months might want to bring at least a medium-weight jacket and a jumper. These are often necessary at night and could prove useful during the day as well.

TOURIST OFFICES

There are no tourist offices in Kuwait and not much in the way of tourist infrastructure. For information on what is happening around town the two English-language newspapers, *Arab Times* and *Kuwait Times*, are your best sources of information.

VISAS & DOCUMENTS
Visas

Everyone except nationals of the other Gulf States needs a visa to enter Kuwait. Kuwait requires everyone entering the country to have a sponsor and it does not issue tourist visas.

Large hotels can sponsor a visa, which is a fairly straightforward process: you send a telex or fax to the hotel with your passport data (date and place of issue, date of expiration, date of birth etc), arrival and departure dates, flight numbers and reason for visit (ie 'business'). The hotels usually prefer a fax copy of the actual passport. Most people will receive a single-entry visa valid for one month and for a one-month stay, though business travellers from western countries that played a large role in the anti-Iraq coalition (eg the USA, UK, France and Canada) are often given multiple-entry visas valid for anywhere between one and 10 years. These allow the holder to come and go at will, though you can still stay in the country for only one month at a time.

The visa processing fee that the hotel has to pay to the immigration department is KD 3.500 and this will certainly be passed on to you. The hotel may also charge you a fee for carrying out this service which could be as little as KD 1 or KD 2 and could be as much as KD 10. Be sure to ask about the costs when you are making your visa arrangements. Hotels also usually require that you stay with them for three nights and some may charge you for whatever the agreed minimum number of nights was if you check out early. It usually takes three to four working days for a hotel to process a visa.

Business travellers visiting a company in Kuwait are sponsored by that particular company, which files various papers with the Ministry of Interior in Kuwait City before the visa can be issued.

Whoever your sponsor is, once you are

informed that your visa has been approved you will have to go to a Kuwaiti embassy to get it (though in some western countries, such as the USA, it is possible to mail your passport in). While visas, once approved, can be picked up at any Kuwaiti diplomatic mission, the pick-up point usually has to be specified at the time the papers are filed. If a company in Kuwait has sponsored your visa you may be asked to show either a letter from the sponsoring company confirming this fact, a letter of accreditation from your own company or both. It is often a good idea to call ahead to see exactly what sort of documentation the people at the embassy want you to supply.

The embassies themselves are of little use to the casual traveller as they only issue visas against instructions from Kuwait. In other words, you cannot simply walk in and apply for a visa.

If your passport contains an Israeli stamp you will be refused entry to Kuwait.

Visa Extensions It is rather difficult to stay in Kuwait for more than one month on a business visa. Even the one-year multiple-entry visas only allow you to remain in the country for a month at a time. People with multiple-entry visas needing to remain in Kuwait for longer than a month have to fly out every 30 days and then come back in (Bahrain is the most common destination). Thus, for business travellers there really is no such thing as an exit/re-entry visa.

Other Documents

Health certificates are only necessary if you are arriving from a part of the world with a disease problem. An International Driving Permit is not usually necessary but it is valid in Kuwait, as are most national driving licences.

EMBASSIES
Kuwaiti Embassies Abroad

Addresses of some Kuwaiti embassies are:

Bahrain
King Faisal Highway, Manama, opposite the Holiday Inn (☎ 534 040)
Oman
Jameat A'Duwal Al-Arabiya St, Medinat Qaboos Diplomatic Area, Muscat (☎ 699626 or 699627)
Qatar
Diplomatic Area, beyond the Doha Sheraton Hotel, Doha (☎ 832 111)
Saudi Arabia
Diplomatic Quarter, Riyadh (☎ (01) 488 3500)
UAE
Diplomatic Area, Airport Rd, Abu Dhabi, behind the Pepsi Cola plant, about 10 km south of the centre (☎ (02) 446 888)
Beniyas Rd, Deira, Dubai, opposite the Sheraton Hotel (☎ (04) 284 111)
UK
45/46 Queen's Gate SW7 (☎ (0171) 589 4533, 581 2698)
USA
2940 Tilden St NW, Washington DC 20008 (☎ (202) 966 0702)

Foreign Embassies in Kuwait
See the Kuwait City section for a list of embassies.

CUSTOMS
Alcohol is banned in Kuwait and before you get it into your head to smuggle in a bottle you should be aware that it is rare for anyone to get past customs without their baggage being searched. The duty-free allowance for tobacco is 500 cigarettes or 50 cigars or half a kg of loose tobacco.

Bans on pornographic material, guns and ammunition apply.

MONEY
Costs
Kuwait is expensive. Accommodation prices are particularly absurd. Rooms at the cheapest hotel in Kuwait City start at KD 12, which is about US$45. On the other hand, bus and taxi fares are reasonable (note: I said 'reasonable', not 'cheap') and it is still possible to feed yourself for around KD 1. A rock-bottom budget would be KD 17.500 per day, but you are likely to find yourself spending rather more than that.

Currency
Kuwait's currency is the Kuwaiti dinar (KD). The banknotes have been changed since the occupation, and the old ones have been demonetised, but you are unlikely to see any of the old bills and there is no need to worry about getting ripped off. Every bank and most moneychangers display posters showing the old and new bills. Pre-invasion coins are still valid.

The KD is divided into 1000 fils. Notes come in denominations of KD ¼, ½, 1, 5, 10 and 20. Coins are worth 5, 10, 20, 50 or 100 fils. The Kuwaiti dinar is a hard currency and there are no restrictions on taking it into or out of the country (nor are there restrictions on the import or export of foreign currencies).

Currency Exchange
US$1	=	KD 0.300
UK£1	=	KD 0.470
FF1	=	KD 0.059
DM1	=	KD 0.200
A$1	=	KD 0.240

Changing Money
For a country with a highly sophisticated financial system Kuwait can be a remarkably frustrating place to change money. Banks tend to charge excessive commissions (and we will not even discuss hotels) but moneychangers, the option of choice elsewhere in the Gulf, often refuse to change travellers' cheques.

Wherever you change money be sure to check the rate against one or two other places and remember to ask about the commissions being charged. Some advice on this subject is offered in the Kuwait City section, but the broad rule is to get whatever you figure you'll need, and as much cash as you are comfortable carrying, in large transactions. The only bright spot in this picture is that even Kuwait's cheap (if you can call them that) hotels take plastic, and this can help reduce the wad of money you have to carry around.

Tipping & Bargaining

Generally a tip is not expected except in fancier restaurants. As in the rest of the Gulf the service charge added to your bill in such places goes into the till, not to the waiting staff.

Bargaining is not as common as you might think. If you ask for a discount at, say, a hotel it is likely to be offered but that initial discount probably represents the bottom line. The main exception to this rule is consumer electronics, but I can't think of a more expensive place in the Gulf to buy such things.

POST & COMMUNICATIONS
Postal Rates

Postal rates for letters or postcards weighing up to 20g are 25 fils within Kuwait, 50 fils to Arab countries and 150 fils to the rest of the world. For cards or letters weighing 20 to 50g postage costs 40 fils domestic, 80 fils in the Arab world and 280 fils everywhere else. Aerograms cost 50 fils for delivery in the Arab world and 150 fils to everywhere else. Mumtaz Post (express service) is available for an additional 200 fils.

Books and other printed matter can be sent at slightly lower rates: 90 fils domestic, 220 fils to Arab countries and 600 fils to the rest of the world for up to half a kg. The rates for sending one kg of printed matter are 160 fils/440 fils/KD 1 and for two kg 220 fils/780 fils/KD 1.300.

The rate for sending a small packet within the Arab world is 220 fils for half a kg and 440 for up to one kg. To countries outside the Arab world the comparable rates are 600 fils and KD 1. Beyond one kg regular parcel rates apply. Ask at the post office for parcel rates as these vary significantly from destination to destination.

Sending Mail

Post boxes are a rare sight around Kuwait City, so you will probably have to brave the lines at the post office if you need to send anything and do not already have stamps. If you are in even a medium-sized hotel it might be a good idea to see whether the front desk sells stamps, or can even mail the letters for you.

Receiving Mail

The post office has not offered poste restante service since liberation so a friend's office or your hotel is probably your best bet.

Telephone

Kuwait has an excellent telephone system and calling pretty much anywhere in the world is quick and easy.

When calling Kuwait from the outside world the country code is 965, and this will be followed by the local seven-digit number. There are no area or city codes.

The USA Direct access code from Kuwait is ☎ 800-288. For MCI CallAmerica, dial ☎ 800-624. These services connect you directly to an operator in the USA. You may then make a collect (reverse charges) call or bill the call to a phone company credit card. Unfortunately the service is not yet available to other countries.

Payphones take 50 and 100 fils coins. Two different types of card phones are in use though neither is seen much outside the telecom offices and post offices, where the relevant cards are sold. Phonecards cost either KD 5 or KD 10.

Fax, Telex & Telegraph

These services are available from the government communications centres, though there are usually long lines there. It's probably easier, but more expensive, to go to a big hotel and send a fax or telex from there.

BOOKS

There are not a lot of good books on Kuwait. *The Merchants* by Michael Field has a chapter on the Alghanims, arguably Kuwait's most important merchant family. Geoffrey Bibby's *Looking for Dilmun* includes several chapters on the archaeological excavations on Failaka Island. It also paints an interesting picture of life in Kuwait in the '50s and '60s.

The New Arabians by Peter Mansfield has a summary on Kuwait's history. Mansfield's

Kuwait: Vanguard of the Gulf (1990) is a more general history of Kuwait, though, as the title implies, it has a very official feel about it. *The Modern History of Kuwait 1750-1965* by Ahmad Mustafa Abu-Hakima is a detailed historical account written by a Kuwaiti scholar based in Canada. It is widely available in Kuwait and is worth a look especially for the old photographs documenting life in Kuwait in the early 20th century.

The hotel bookshops around Kuwait City stock the usual collection of glossy coffee-table books, and the Ministry of Information publishes several books of facts and figures on the country as well as a number of books on the invasion and war. Among these, *The Mother of Crimes Against Kuwait in Pictures* is a rather gruesome collection of photographs of Iraqi atrocities in occupied Kuwait. *Tides of War – Eco-Disaster in the Gulf*, by Michael McKinnon & Peter Vine, looks at the ecological consequences of the oil slicks intentionally released and oil fires intentionally lit by the retreating Iraqis.

See the Facts about the Region chapter for a list of more general books on the Gulf and the Middle East.

Travel Guides

There are practically no guidebooks to Kuwait. Most of the 'guides' you will see on sale in the emirate are little more than advertising circulars. *The Economist Business Traveller's Guides – Arabian Peninsula* is a bit out of date but contains a lot of useful information on business laws and regulations.

NEWSPAPERS & MAGAZINES

Arab Times and *Kuwait Times* are Kuwait's two English-language newspapers. If you are interested in Kuwait's freewheeling (by Gulf standards) political scene *Arab Times* is definitely the superior newspaper. Both provide adequate foreign coverage, largely reprinted from the British newspapers and the international wire services.

The bookshops in the big hotels are the best places to look for foreign newspapers and magazines. These tend to appear about two days late. The *International Herald Tribune*, the main British papers and *Le Monde* are usually available, as are magazines like *Time* and *Newsweek*.

South of the centre on Arabian Gulf St, the supermarket in the Sultan Centre shopping complex stocks a particularly wide variety of foreign newspapers and magazines.

RADIO & TV

Radio Kuwait – aka the 'Super Station' – broadcasts on 99.7 FM, playing mostly rock and roll with a bit of local news and features mixed in. The US military's Armed Forces Radio & Television Service (AFRTS), on 104.3 FM, broadcasts a mixture of music, news and chat shows.

If you are looking for news and do not have a shortwave radio to tune in to the BBC, this is the place to turn. AFRTS carries 'Morning Edition' and 'All Things Considered', the high-quality news programmes produced by the USA's National Public Radio. Because of the time difference the morning programme comes on in the late afternoon and All Things Considered in the dead of night. Neither station can be heard outside Kuwait City.

Channel 2 of Kuwait TV broadcasts programmes in English each day from around 5 pm until midnight. Many hotels, even the smaller ones, have satellite TV, usually offering the package of entertainment, news and sports put out by Hong Kong-based Star TV.

PHOTOGRAPHY & VIDEO

In theory a photography permit is necessary to take pictures of anything in Kuwait. The problem is that the permits must be approved personally by the Minister of Information, which makes them effectively unobtainable for anyone but a working journalist.

In practice this is not something you need to worry about provided you exercise a modicum of common sense. Photographing what are obviously 'tourist' sites (ie the Kuwait Towers, the courtyard of the National Museum or the Red Fort in Al-Jahra) is never a problem and over the years the list of 'sensitive' places has shortened quite a bit. Taking a picture of the Great Mosque, for example, is not a problem today whereas it would have been five or 10 years ago.

Sometimes I have had permits and sometimes I have not, but I have never had any trouble taking pictures in Kuwait, even after the liberation. If you are discreet and do not photograph anything sensitive you should be OK. Also remember that in addition to military areas, the palaces and the airport, all embassies and government buildings are strictly off limits for shutterbugs and that people – especially women – should never be photographed without their permission.

TIME

Kuwait is three hours ahead of GMT/UTC. Summer, or daylight savings, time is not observed. When it's noon in Kuwait City, the time elsewhere is:

City	Time
Paris, Rome	10 am
London	9 am
New York	4 am
Los Angeles	1 am
Perth, Hong Kong	5 pm
Sydney	7 pm
Auckland	9 pm

ELECTRICITY

Electric voltage in Kuwait is 220V or 240V AC. Both the European and the British standard prong configurations are in use (though the latter is more common), and neither necessarily indicates what current is coming out of the wall.

WEIGHTS & MEASURES

The metric system is in use in Kuwait.

LAUNDRY

Laundrettes are unknown in Kuwait. If you don't feel like washing your clothes in your hotel room's sink, your only option is the hotel laundry or one of the many small laundry shops offering 24-hour service to wash and iron clothes.

HEALTH

Health care in Kuwait is on a level with what is available in most western countries. See the Kuwait City section for more information on how to get medical treatment in Kuwait, and the introductory Facts for the Visitor chapter for a more general discussion of health in the Gulf.

The drinking water in much of the country is not good and you would be well advised to stick to bottled water. The tap water will not kill you, but it might not leave you feeling very good either.

WOMEN TRAVELLERS

Harassment of women has been an increasingly serious problem in Kuwait since liberation. The best advice – as offered in a 1992 US embassy circular – is to dress conservatively, not to respond to approaches in the street and to avoid eye contact with men. Women should not travel alone at night in unfamiliar neighbourhoods. If you are followed go to a public place, such as the lobby of a hotel.

A number of embassies keep records of harassment of their female nationals and if you have any problems you might want to report it to your embassy's consular section. They may not be able to do anything on the spot, but foreign governments seem to be putting pressure on the Kuwaiti administration to crack down on sexual harassment.

DANGERS & ANNOYANCES

Although post-liberation Kuwait is not as safe a place as it used to be, Kuwait is still a low-crime city by any reasonable standard. Muggings and having your pocket picked are not among the things you need to worry about in Kuwait. The things that will scare you are much nastier.

You must be aware, above all, of the lingering danger of mines throughout the country. While Kuwait City and the residential sections of other urban centres like Al-Jahra and Al-Ahmadi are clear of mines, much of the desert and, outside the capital, much of the coastline, remain unsafe. Mine clearance has been going on since the end of the war but it is ultimately a somewhat inexact science, particularly in the desert. Sand dunes can shift, covering mines for months, or even years, only to shift again, leaving unexploded mines exposed in what are, theoretically, safe areas. This problem is hardly unique to Kuwait – Egypt, Israel, Libya and a host of other Middle Eastern countries are still dealing with unexploded ordnance left over from the various Arab-Israeli wars and even WWII. Seaborne mines remain a problem, though much less so than in 1992-93. Mines no longer wash up on the beach near the Kuwait Towers every week, which is not to say that it could not happen again.

Since this situation changes from month to month as mine clearance proceeds, the best course before venturing outside the city is to contact your embassy, which will certainly be up on the latest information regarding which parts of the country are safe and which aren't.

If you are going north toward the Iraqi border bear in mind that the border is not very well marked. Despite Kuwait's much publicised construction of a trench, fence, earth wall and various other border fortifications there are still places where it is possible to stray across it unwittingly. If you do so, and get caught, do not expect any help or sympathy from the Iraqis – especially if you carry a US or British passport. Foreigners travelling or working in the border zone have regularly been arrested by Iraqi troops who claimed that they had strayed into Iraqi territory. In several instances such arrests have taken place several km inside Kuwait. If you get into this sort of trouble the UN troops who patrol the border zone have no authority to help you. You'll probably be taken to Baghdad and may be put on trial. The bottom line is that for now you should not go any farther north than the checkpoint on the Al-Mutla ridge without a very good reason.

BUSINESS HOURS

Shops are open Saturday to Wednesday from 8 or 9 am until about 1 pm and from about 4 pm until 6 or 7 pm. Shops in large shopping centres (such as the Al-Muthanna Centre in central Kuwait City or the Sultan Centre on Arabian Gulf St) usually stay open until 9 pm. On Thursdays most businesses will only be open in the morning. Government offices work Saturday to Wednesday from 7 am to 1.30 pm but may close at 11.30 or noon on Thursdays. Friday is the weekly holiday and almost nothing is open during the day, though some shops in the centre and in the souk may open in the late afternoon and early evening.

PUBLIC HOLIDAYS & SPECIAL EVENTS

Secular holidays are New Year's Day (1 January) and National Day (25 February). Liberation Day (26 February) is not an official holiday but everyone seems to treat it as one. In deference to the families of those still missing after the war and occupation, as of 1996 there were no official ceremonies or celebrations marking either National Day or Liberation Day.

Religious holidays are tied to the Islamic Hejira calendar. Eid Al-Fitr (the end of Ramadan), Eid Al-Adha (the end of pilgrimage season), Lailat Al-Mi'raj (the Ascension of the Prophet), the Prophet's Birthday and the Islamic New Year are all observed (for dates see the table of holidays near Public Holidays in the Regional Facts for the Visitor chapter).

ACTIVITIES

The problem of land and seaborne mines has pretty well put what used to be a bustling water-sports culture in Kuwait into the deep freeze. Mines have also put an end to organised desert safaris and 'wadi bashing'.

WORK

With very few exceptions it is not legal to work in Kuwait on a business visa. A business visa cannot be changed to a residence permit in Kuwait. You have to go back to your country of origin and get a residence visa there. Kuwait is currently trying to cut down on the number of foreign workers in the country so residence permits are going to be hard to come by in the foreseeable future.

Coming to Kuwait to look for a job is both illegal and almost certainly a waste of time.

ACCOMMODATION

Getting a bed for the night in Kuwait was never cheap but after the war prices went up by 100 to 150% at most of the country's hotels and they have not returned to earth since. The result is that while the five-star hotels at least provide service for the money they ask, several places (the Kuwait Continental Hotel springs readily to mind) charge five-star prices but offer nothing approaching a five-star level of service. The bottom end of the market has disappeared and, more recently, the mid-range has thinned out. A lot of what's left is grossly overpriced. Standards have remained reasonable – there are no downright filthy hotels in Kuwait. Expect to pay at least KD 15 to KD 20 for a single and KD 23 to KD 25 for a double.

Flat Rental

Rental is only an option if you are going to live in Kuwait, in which case you are likely to be provided with housing anyway. Small one or two-bedroom flats in the parts of the city where most foreigners live start at around KD 400 per month. Flats are a lot cheaper in other parts of the city, notably the mid-to-outer suburbs such as Hawalli, but many of these neighbourhoods are not particularly safe.

FOOD & DRINKS

There is a word for cheap food in Kuwait: biryani. Biryani, not Indian, because while most of Kuwait's cheapest restaurants are Indian, many rarely seem to have anything other than biryanis on the menu. Anyway, the biryanis are pretty good and usually cost under KD 1. Otherwise, the only cheap eats are western fast food: burgers, pizza etc. The selection has improved a bit in the past few years but it is still rather thin.

Cafes, mostly located either in hotels or shopping centres, offer western-style snacks and sandwiches at reasonable prices and the city is well stocked with good, up-market eateries. As usual, most of the latter are in the big hotels, but I have listed several excellent non-hotel places in the Kuwait City section.

All drinks are nonalcoholic. The usual selection includes soft drinks, mineral water, fruit juice, coffee and tea.

ENTERTAINMENT

Dining out and going to the movies are about all you can look forward to in Kuwait. A few restaurants and five-star hotels used to have live music (almost invariably performed by Arabic singers) but this has been informally banned since liberation, apparently out of deference to the families of Kuwaitis still unaccounted for since the occupation and war. There are few other forms of public entertainment. There are several cinemas in Kuwait City. They show mostly Indian, Pakistani and Arabic films, though the occasional English-language movie turns up as well, almost invariably starring Arnold Schwarzenegger or Sylvester Stallone.

THINGS TO BUY

Kuwait is not exactly a shopper's paradise. You can buy traditional Bedouin weavings in Kuwait City at Sadu House, a cultural foundation dedicated to preserving Bedouin art, but there is little else in the way of locally-produced souvenirs on the market. As is the case elsewhere in the Gulf, most of the 'Arabian'-looking items you will see for sale around the country are produced elsewhere.

Getting There & Away

AIR
The USA & Europe

Fares to New York start at KD 348.200 one way and KD 460 for a two-month return (10-day minimum stay). Individual airlines, especially those from what used to be the Eastern Bloc, sometimes have special fares on offer.

The 10-day minimum/three-month

maximum stay return tickets to London start at KD 323.800 and the one-way fare from KD 277.700. Return tickets during the high season (May to August and a couple of weeks either side of Christmas) will cost KD 15 to KD 20 more. As noted above, you might make a tour of airline offices to check for special offers which could save you KD 100 or more.

The cheapest published one-way/return fares to Rome are KD 225.200/258, again with a 10-day/three-month limit on your stay. High season tickets are approximately KD 15 more. Tickets to Athens have no minimum stay and a one-month maximum and cost KD 180 (KD 190 in the high season) for round trips and KD 155 one way.

Asia & Australia

Fares to the Indian subcontinent are among the better deals available out of Kuwait. The cheapest regular fare to New Delhi is KD 191.700 for a return ticket allowing a four-month stay (seven-day minimum). The one-way fare to New Delhi is KD 125.500

Bangkok, often a good deal from other Gulf countries, is fairly pricey at KD 278.200 for a return ticket (seven-day minimum/one-month maximum) but extremely cheap at KD 120 if you only need a one-way ticket.

Australia is an even better deal. Return fares to Melbourne come as low as KD 276.300 in the low season (early September to mid-December and mid-January to May) and KD 287.400 during the high season. These tickets require a 10-day minimum stay and allow you to stay Down Under for up to three months. A one-way fare from Kuwait to Melbourne is KD 243.100.

Other Arab Countries

A one-way fare to Cairo is KD 92.700, the cheapest return costs KD 120.900. No minimum stay is required and the maximum stay allowed on this fare is one month. To Damascus, expect to pay KD 66.500 one way and KD 95.300 return (no minimum/one-month maximum).

Other Gulf States

Sample one-way and return fares to other cities in the Gulf in Kuwaiti dinars include (all returns require a two-day minimum/14-day maximum stay):

Destination	One Way	Return
Abu Dhabi	52.300	72.200
Bahrain	29.800	40.700
Dhahran	29.700	40.700
Doha	37.600	51.700
Dubai	52.300	72.200
Jeddah	69.200	95.900
Muscat	73.300	101.600
Riyadh	41.200	56.700

LAND

Buses operate between Kuwait and Cairo via Aqaba in Jordan and Nuweiba in Egypt. Agents specialising in these tickets (the trip takes about two days) are in the area around the municipal bus station. In Cairo there are a number of agents on Talaat Harb St and Tahrir Square advertising bus transport to Kuwait.

LEAVING KUWAIT

Be sure to be at the airport two hours before departure time. Check-in times are sometimes even longer for long-haul flights to Europe, Asia and North America, but for any flight it would be a good idea to double-check the check-in rules in advance. Before you actually get inside the terminal your car may be searched at a checkpoint on the Airport Rd and all baggage is X-rayed at the entrance to the airport. This can sometimes be a cumbersome process, so allow some extra time for it.

Departure Tax

There is an airport departure tax of KD 2. If this was not added into the price of your ticket at the time of purchase you can expect it to be collected in cash at the airport. Tickets sold outside Kuwait often have not had the tax added in. Look for 'KWD 2.000' or something similar in the 'tax' box just below the part of the ticket that shows the cities between which you are travelling.

KUWAIT

Getting Around

BUS & TAXI

Very cheap inter-city bus service is available to Al-Jahra, Al-Ahmadi, Fahaheel and a handful of other destinations outside Kuwait City. Most inter-city bus fares are 300 or 350 fils. Most of the coaches used by the bus company are reasonably comfortable and well maintained, and local regulations prohibit drivers from picking up extra passengers when the bus is full (ie the bus will never be packed beyond bursting point as sometimes happens in India or Egypt). Note, however, that only the handful of services with route numbers above 500 use air-conditioned vehicles. Tickets are purchased from the driver.

The main bus station is in the centre at the intersection of Al-Hilali and Abdullah Al-Mubarak Sts. There are also secondary stations at the Orthopaedic Hospital to the west of the centre and in Sharq to the east, as well as several smaller lay-bys. See Bus in the Getting Around section of Kuwait City for more details.

There are no service-taxis in Kuwait. There is a taxi rank on Al-Hilali St across from the municipal bus station, but these are simply local taxis whose drivers hang out here when not cruising around looking for fares. While they are not inter-city taxis per se, you could probably negotiate a fare to pretty much anywhere in the country, though the drivers are likely to demand so much money that you might as well rent a car instead. Expect to pay at least KD 10 for a trip to either Al-Jahra or Al-Ahmadi.

CAR

Driving in Kuwait is on the right, and right turns are allowed at red lights. Roads throughout the country are in excellent condition, and the local driving style could best be described as fast and aggressive. If you hold a driving licence and residence permit from another Gulf country you can drive in Kuwait without any further paperwork.

Holders of driving licences from other countries can also drive on their home licences, or on an International Driving Permit, but will also be required to purchase 'insurance' for their licence for KD 10. The cost of the insurance is simply added onto your bill from the rental car company and 'applying' involves nothing more than filling in an extra form when you are doing the paperwork to rent the car. This is mandatory so you really have no choice except to grin and bear it.

Rental

Kuwait is the most expensive place in the Gulf to rent a car. The major agencies (Avis, Europcar, Budget) all charge KD 8 to KD 9 per day for the smallest cars (usually Daewoos). There are local agencies, such as Al-Mulla, which charge cheaper rates. For more details see the Kuwait City Getting There & Away section.

LOCAL TRANSPORT

Bus

Kuwait has an extensive system of local buses. Fares are 100 to 200 fils. You can usually get a route map for free at the main bus station in Kuwait City. See the Kuwait City Getting Around section for a complete listing of bus routes. If you know where you are going the buses can be a good option, but note that while route numbers are displayed on the buses the names of the destinations are not.

Taxi

Most Kuwaiti taxis have no meters. Bargaining the fare in advance may save you some grief at the end of the trip but it may also cost you money. Around town, taxis are orange-coloured. Taxis can be found in ranks near the main bus station, at all of the big hotels and also cruising around the centre. Simply wave your arm at taxis on the street to get them to stop. Few of the drivers speak any English. See Taxi in the Getting Around section of Kuwait City for details of the proper fares and more information on the city's taxi system.

Kuwait City

This is a lovely place to be in: the weather delicious, hot at noon, but too cold to sit in the shade without a *very* warm coat.

So wrote Freya Stark on her arrival in Kuwait in March 1937. Things change. Even before August 1990 'lovely' is not a word I would have used to describe Kuwait City. That said, I have always liked Kuwait. In the years since the liberation it has developed into a remarkably easy-going place, at least compared to what things were like in the late '80s. Inspiring? No. Interesting? Always.

Orientation

Kuwait City could still do with a few more street signs but, in all fairness, there are more directional signs now than there were a few years ago. It is not very difficult to find your way around. The commercial centre is the area from Kuwait Bay inland to Al-Soor St, between the Al-Jahra gate and Mubarak Al-Kabeer St. The coastal road is commonly called Arabian Gulf St and appears that way on some maps. The few signs on the ground, however, say 'Al-Khalij Al-Arabi St' (same thing, only transliterated, instead of translated, from the Arabic). The National Assembly building, what's left of the National Museum, the emir's palace (Sief Palace) and the Grand Mosque all lie along Arabian Gulf St.

The main shopping and commercial area of Kuwait City is Fahad Al-Salem St, which becomes Ahmad Al-Jaber St north of Al-Safat Square, where the commercial centre begins to taper off. The souk is the area between the Municipal Park and Mubarak Al-Kabeer St. Up-market shopping places are clustered along the lower end of Fahad Al-Salem St (near the Sheraton Hotel) and just east of it.

From the centre the city spreads inland, becoming ever broader. The main arteries are a series of numbered ring roads and Arabian Gulf St, which continues far down the coast to Al-Salmiya and beyond.

With the exception of Baghdad St, which is now Bush St, none of the major streets in the city have been renamed since the end of the war.

Information

Tourist Office There being, officially at least, no tourism in Kuwait there is no tourist office.

Embassies Some of the countries with diplomatic missions in Kuwait are:

Bahrain
   Surra district, St 1, Block 1, Building 24 (☎ 531 8530)
Canada
   Da'iya district, El-Mutawakil St, Area 4, House 24, adjacent to the Third Ring Rd (☎ 256 3025)
Egypt
   Surra district, Tariq Ibn Ziyad St, Block 4 (☎ 533 8927)
France
   Mansouria district, St 13, Block 1, Villa 24 (☎ 531 9850)
Germany
   Bahiya district, St 14, Block 1, Villa 13, off Abdullah Al-Salem St (☎ 252 0857)
India
   Diplomatic Area, off Arabian Gulf St south of the centre. Look for a very large red building (☎ 253 0600)
Italy
   Sharq district, Omar Ibn Al-Khattab St, Villa 6 (☎ 244 5120)
Netherlands
   Jabriah district, St 1, Block 9, House 76, near the Fifth Ring Rd and opposite Bayan Palace (☎ 531 2650)
Oman
   Udailia district, St 3, Block 3, House 25, by the Fourth Ring Rd (☎ 256 1962)
Qatar
   Istiglal St, Diplomatic Area, south of the centre off Arabian Gulf St (☎ 251 3599)
Sweden
   Faiha district, Shahba' St, Block 7, Villa 3 (☎ 252 3588)
Switzerland
   Udailia district, St 32, Block 3, House 12 (☎ 255 1872)
UAE
   Istiglal St, Diplomatic Area, south of the centre off Arabian Gulf St (☎ 252 7639)

KUWAIT

UK
Arabian Gulf St, near the Kuwait Towers and Dasman Palace (☎ 243 2046)
USA
Arabian Gulf St, entrance from opposite the Safir International Hotel (☎ 242 4151)

Money Kuwait City has no great central area for banks. You will find them pretty evenly distributed throughout the city. There are a few around Fahad Al-Salem St, a couple near the Science & Natural History Museum on Abdullah Al-Mubarak St and one in the Salhiya Commercial Centre on Mohammed Thunayyan St. People staying in or near the Safir International Hotel (formerly the Kuwait International Hotel and, before that, the Hilton) should use the National Bank of Kuwait branch in the hotel's upper lobby.

Moneychangers can offer slightly better rates than banks (and, usually, lower commissions), but finding one in the centre who will change travellers' cheques can be a problem. Try the Al-Jawhara Exchange Centre in the Souk Al-Watya shopping centre, next to the Sheraton Hotel. It changes travellers' cheques at decent rates with no commission.

AMEX (☎ 241 3000) is represented in Kuwait by Al-Ghanim Travel, on the 2nd mezzanine level of the Salhiya Commercial Centre. It is open Saturday to Thursday from 8 am to 1 pm and 4 to 7 pm, but is closed on Friday. AMEX card holders can cash personal cheques but the office will not hold mail for clients.

Post & Communications The GPO is on Fahad Al-Salem St near the intersection with Al-Wattiya St. It is open Saturday to Wednesday from 7 am to 7 pm, Thursday from 7 am to 3 pm and Friday from 9 to 11 am. The GPO has a card-phone booth from which international calls can be made and phonecards are on sale at a nearby window. Poste restante facilities are not available. The Safat Post Office, at the intersection of Abdullah Al-Mubarak and Al-Hilali Sts, is mainly for post office box holders but counter services are offered as well. It is open the same hours as the GPO.

The main telephone office is at the intersection of Abdullah Al-Salem and Al-Hilali Sts at the base of the telecommunications tower. It is open 24 hours a day. Bring identification for the checkpoint at the door. Card phones (for which cards are on sale) are available for international calls. You can also book international calls and prepay the cost, but this is much more expensive than using the card phones. Telex and fax services are also available.

Travel Agencies Travel agencies in Kuwait operate a comfortable, if strict, cartel. A few years ago virtually every airline office and travel agency in the city was displaying a poster from the Kuwait Travel & Tourism Agencies Association announcing that, in the interest of 'improved customer service', all travel agents were 'agreeing' (in other words, being ordered) to adhere to KTTAA's unified pricing policy. 'That means no discounts', one clerk said when I asked about the signs. He was less candid when I asked how a price-fixing agreement was supposed to provide 'improved customer service'.

Still, as is the case just about everywhere else in the Gulf, there are far too many travel agencies in Kuwait and in their desperation for business most are willing to bargain down the price of tickets, but don't expect a large discount. Since they are cutting into their fairly slim commissions you can't expect to knock more than 5% off a ticket price and the trade-off for that will be locking yourself into the dates and times on the ticket. The farther you are travelling (ie Los Angeles as opposed to Bahrain), the better your chances are of getting some sort of discount. Ask hotel staff or expat acquaintances for advice on finding a competent travel agent.

Fahad Al-Salem St and Al-Soor St (between the Al-Jahra gate and the Radio & TV building) both have lots of small travel agencies. It is pointless to recommend one over another. Despite a theoretical ban on the

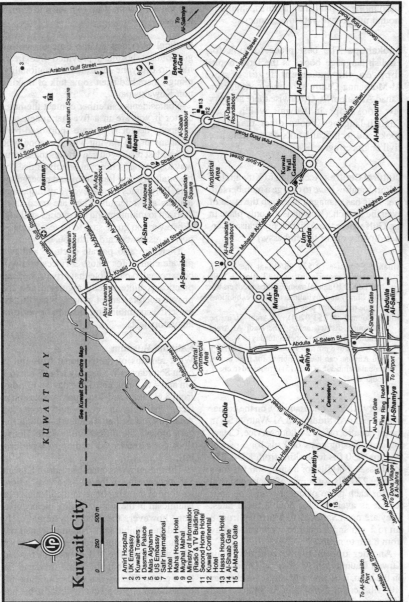

KUWAIT

Kuwait City

0   250   500 m

KUWAIT BAY

See Kuwait City Centre Map

1 Amiri Hospital
2 UK Embassy
3 Kuwait Towers
4 Dasman Palace
5 Mas Aghanim
6 US Embassy
7 Safir International Hotel
8 Maha House Hotel
9 Mughal Mahal
10 Ministry of Information (Radio & TV Building)
11 Second Home Hotel
12 Kuwait Continental Hotel
13 Hassa House Hotel
14 Al-Shaab Gate
15 Al-Maqsab Gate

discounting of published airfares, shopping around might save you some money.

Bookshops The best place to look for English-language books is the large bookshop on the basement level of the Al-Muthanna Centre shopping complex on Fahad Al-Salem St. Otherwise there are very few bookshops in Kuwait which stock English-language books other than textbooks and technical works on subjects like civil engineering.

Cultural Centres According to Kuwaiti law cultural centres have to charge a membership fee. This has managed to cramp the style of even the French. (Kuwait is the only place in the Gulf where the Alliance Française operates directly out of the embassy.)

Alliance Française (π 531 9850), at the French embassy, Mansouria district, St 13, Block 1, Villa 24. The KD 10 annual membership fee covers use of its library and invitations to films, exhibitions and the occasional play or lecture.

British Council (π 253 3204), Al-Arabi St in the Mansouria district, next to the Nadi Al-Arabi stadium. The library is open Saturday to Wednesday from 4 to 8 pm and Thursday from 9 am to 1 pm. Anyone can use the library for free, but an annual membership (KD 15) is required to check books out.

Laundry Al-Shurouq Laundry, on the corner of Abu Bakr Al-Siddiq and Al-Wattiya Sts in the city centre, offers 24-hour service. Cleaning and pressing costs 600 fils for a pair of trousers, 750 fils for a skirt, from KD 1.250 for dresses, 300 fils for a shirt, 500 fils for a blouse, 250 fils for a pair of socks and 200 fils for each piece of underwear. One-hour service is available for double these rates. They are open Saturday to Thursday from 8 am to 1 pm and from 3 to 9 pm and Friday from 8 am to noon.

Another option in the centre is Fajr Kuwait Laundry on Al-Soor St. Depending on the item, it is generally a little bit cheaper (100 fils here or there) than Al-Shurouq and offers the same 24-hour turn-around time. It is open daily from 9 am to noon and from 5 to 9 pm.

Medical Services At the time of writing government hospitals provided free treatment to everyone regardless of nationality, though there had been some talk of making non-Kuwaitis pay.

Nonresidents can either contact the hotel doctor if you are in a five-star hotel, or a company doctor if you are sponsored by a company or are staying with someone who is. As a last resort you can always make your way to the nearest hospital or polyclinic. The hospitals provide long-term and emergency care. Polyclinics handle everyday outpatient matters and referrals. They are open from 7.30 am to midnight and the queues are long. Wherever you go be sure to have your passport or residence card with you.

There are also private doctors, and two private clinics, for whose services you will be expected to pay. Note that private medical practice is quite strictly regulated and the private doctors cannot, among other things, prescribe continuing medication or perform laboratory tests.

National Museum

What remains of the National Museum is open Saturday to Wednesday from 8 am to 1 pm and 4 to 7 pm, and Thursday and Friday from 8 to 11 am and 4 to 7 pm. Admission is free. The museum compound fronts on Arabian Gulf St but is entered through the gate around the corner from Sadu House (look for a short road leading to a parking lot).

The museum was once the pride of Kuwait and its centrepiece, the Al-Sabah collection, was one of the most important collections of Islamic art in the world. During the occupation, however, the Iraqis systematically looted the exhibit halls. Having cleaned out the building they smashed everything and set what was left on fire. It does not look too bad from the street, but the scene inside is far from pretty. The interior of the building has been shored up to prevent its collapse but has otherwise been left as the Kuwaitis found it after liberation. It is the only major building in Kuwait that has not been restored to its pre-war state, and the government has declared that the ruined museum will be maintained as a monument to the memory of the occupation.

Most of the museum's collection was eventually returned by the Iraqis but many pieces had been damaged during their transit to Iraq or had been poorly stored while they were there. At the time of writing, plans for the construction of a new building to house the collection were in motion while teams of restoration experts were attempting to repair the damage to the recovered artefacts.

The museum's ruins are open to the public. From the entry gate head straight in toward the courtyard, go up the ramp and then turn right. This is where the Al-Sabah collection used to be. Another destroyed section of the building is open on the ground level to the left of the entry gate. This is where the archaeological and ethnographic exhibits were. This hall is particularly poignant due to the addition of photographs of some of the things you used to be able to see in the hall. The Planetarium, which was also torched, is open for inspection at the back of the compound.

A hall at the back of the museum complex's courtyard has been restored and is sometimes used for temporary exhibitions.

Sadu House
Sadu House is a small building near the National Museum on Arabian Gulf St. The house is a combination museum and cultural foundation dedicated to preserving Bedouin arts and crafts, particularly weaving (*sadu* is the Arabic word for 'weaving'). The museum contains an interesting display of Bedouin artwork (most of which is for sale) and everyday items used before the oil era both in Kuwait City and by the desert nomads. Especially worth seeing is the Bedouin tent in the building's courtyard. There is also a room in which you can sometimes see weavers at work. Sadu House is the best place in Kuwait to buy Bedouin goods. Large pieces suitable for use as carpets or

wall hangings cost KD 100 to KD 150, pillows around KD 12 and small bags from KD 7 to KD 15.

The house itself is also worth a close look. Though a bit worse for wear (not, by the way, because of the war – it looked this way before the Iraqis showed up) it is built of gypsum and coral. Note the carved decorative work along the roof-level of the courtyard.

The building is open every day except Friday from 8 am to 12.30 pm and from 4 to 7.30 pm. Admission is free.

National Assembly Building
This is the distinctive white building with the sloping roofs on Arabian Gulf St south of the National Museum. The building was designed by Jorn Utzon, the Danish architect who also designed the Sydney Opera House. The two sweeping roofs are supposed to evoke Bedouin tents. The National Assembly remains a fairly sensitive site in security terms and I would not recommend taking photographs of it unless you have a photo permit or are part of an organised group and your guide says it is OK.

Kuwait has long been the only country in the Gulf with a parliament and, for that reason alone, this building occupies an especially important place in the national consciousness. In the late '80s, when the first rumblings of what became Kuwait's 1989-90 democracy movement were heard, the government drove home the message that the old parliament was not returning by changing the building's name to the Permanent Chamber of the Council of Ministers. The Iraqis badly damaged the interior of the building and its restoration became a government priority after liberation. When the National Assembly was reinstated in 1992, the building once again became the home of Kuwait's parliament.

Inside, one of the roofs forms a huge atrium over the parliament's main lobby. The other covers the legislative chamber itself. In addition to the main chamber the complex houses a restaurant and the offices of Kuwait's 50 MPs. Parliamentary sessions are open to the public, though you will have to have your passport or *iqama* (residence permit) to get through the security check at the gate. Check the *Arab Times* to find out when the legislature is in session.

Once inside you will probably be directed to the upper gallery. The lower level – the rows of seats immediately behind the MPs' desks – is generally reserved for diplomats, working journalists, parliamentary staff and visiting VIPs. If they will let you sit down below, however, you should do so. The view is much better.

As amazing as it may sound, simultaneous translation of parliamentary debates into English is available. Ask for a set of earphones as you enter the chamber. If no one offers you a headset go to the lower level of the gallery and try to get the attention of one of the people in the translation booths (on the right side of the lower gallery as you face the Speaker's Chair). If you need a headset but the guards will not let you into the chamber on the lower level ask one of the guards to get one from the translation people for you.

Sief Palace

Sief Palace, at the intersection of Mubarak Al-Kabeer and Arabian Gulf Sts north-east of the National Museum, is the official seat of the emir's court. The oldest parts of the building date from the turn of the century. The Iraqis practically demolished the place and it had to be extensively rebuilt after the war. The huge annexe at the western end of the palace complex is a post-war addition. The interior of the palace is not open to the public. The main thing you can see from the street is the beautiful clock tower.

It would also be a good idea to forget about taking pictures of the palace unless you have a permit. It was considered a sensitive site well before August 1990. Next door, the low-set, very modern building with lots of soldiers around it is the Foreign Ministry. Don't photograph this building either.

The Grand Mosque

This huge, modern mosque opposite the Sief Palace was opened in 1986. It cost KD 13 million to build and the government says that it can accommodate over 5500 worshippers. The central dome is 26m in diameter and 43m high.

The Former Political Agency

About 750m along Arabian Gulf St from Sief Palace (toward the Kuwait Towers) you will find a modest white house with blue trim. From 1904 until the late '30s this was the Political Agency, the British headquarters in Kuwait. Freya Stark spent most of March 1937 here. She adored Kuwait and lavished praise on her host, Gerald de Gaury, but was less impressed by the building, which she referred to as a 'big ugly box'. Viewed straight on it seems quite small, but from the side its true dimensions are clearer. The widow of the last British Political Agent continued to live here for many years, usually spending her winters in the emirate well into the 1980s. The building, which has never been open to the public, was heavily damaged during the Iraqi invasion but has been restored to its pre-war state.

Kuwait Towers

On Arabian Gulf St beyond the UK embassy, the towers are rather hard to miss. Designed by a Swedish architectural firm and opened in 1979, they have become the country's main landmark. The largest of the three towers rises to a height of 187m. The towers fell into disrepair during the Iraqi occupation and were damaged during the war, but they have been restored to their original state.

The upper globe houses a two-level observation deck. The upper level, at 123m, revolves, taking 30 minutes to make a circle. The largest tower's lower globe (at 82m) has a restaurant, a coffee shop and a private banquet room. The lower globe on the largest tower and the single globe on the middle tower are used to store water. The small tower with no globes is used to light up the other two.

The observation deck is open daily from 9 am to 11 pm. In the lower globe the restaurant (which is very expensive) is open until midnight while the (cheaper) cafe closes at 11.30 pm. Admission to the observation deck costs 500 fils. You can go to the restaurants for free. Because the towers overlook the Dasman Palace, cameras with zoom lenses are not permitted and you will have to leave these at the ticket booth.

The towers are not on any main bus route, but they are close enough to the centre that you can walk if the heat is not too bad. A cab should cost around KD 1 from anywhere in the centre, though be warned: the towers can be a difficult place to find a taxi when you want to get back into town.

Tareq Rajab Museum

This museum is at House 16, St 5, Block 12, in the Jabriya district. The house is on a corner two blocks north and one block west of the New English School, near the intersection of the Fifth Ring Rd and the Fahaheel Expressway. It is open Saturday to Thursday from 9 am to noon and 4 to 7 pm, but is closed Friday. Admission is free. There is no sign on the building but it is easily identified by its entrance – a carved wooden doorway flanked by two smaller doors on each side. All four of the door panels are worked in gilt metal. Unfortunately, the museum is not on any bus route. Your best bet is to take a taxi (about KD 1.500 or KD 1.750 from the centre).

The museum, which is housed in the basement of a large villa, is a private collection that was assembled by Kuwait's first minister of antiquities. The focus is on Islamic art. Amazingly, it appears to have survived the occupation and war entirely intact, a fact that makes the collection all the more important considering the fate that befell the National Museum's treasures.

Turn left at the entrance to the galleries and the first thing you will see is a small display of daggers from Oman and Yemen. Immediately beyond this, and sharply left, is a narrow hall with a display of early Islamic manuscripts. The main gallery on this side of the museum is straight ahead as you pass through the daggers. This includes an excellent display of Arabic manuscripts and calligraphy. Be sure to see the talismanic shirts printed with prayers and verses from the Koran. These were worn as undergarments in India in the 17th and 18th centuries. The same hall also has a wide selection of ceramics and pottery from various parts of the Islamic world. A small hall between this gallery and the main entrance contains antique clothes and jewellery.

Traditional costumes and jewellery are displayed in the hall to the right of the entrance. The exhibit is particularly interesting because it covers not only Islam's Arab/Middle Eastern heartland but also much farther flung areas such as the countries of what was Soviet Central Asia (Kazakhstan, Uzbekistan etc).

Science & Natural History Museum

On Abdullah Al-Mubarak St, the museum is open Saturday to Thursday from 8.30 am to noon, but is closed on Fridays and holidays. Admission is free. Though the collection seems to consist largely of stuffed animals, there is some variety. The ground floor also contains animal skeletons, including a few dinosaurs. The Iraqis trashed a transport display which included Kuwait's first municipal bus and one of the first aircraft used by Kuwait Airways. The 1st floor has a display on space exploration and many more stuffed critters.

Old City Gates

Four of Kuwait City's five gates – Al-Shaab, Al-Shamiya, Al-Jahra and Al-Maqsab – lie along Al-Soor St, the street which follows the line of the old city wall (soor is the Arabic word for 'wall'). The Al-Maqsab gate, occupying a small green site between the Sheraton Hotel and Arabian Gulf St, is a relatively recent reconstruction. At the end of the war only its foundations remained intact. The fifth gate (Dasman gate) was near the Dasman Palace by the Kuwait Towers. Despite its ancient appearance the wall, which the gates were part of, was only constructed around 1920. It was built in a hurry as part of the effort to defend the city against the ikhwan, the group of Islamic fundamentalist warriors loyal to Abdul Aziz Bin Abdul Rahman Al-Saud, later the first

KUWAIT

KUWAIT

King of Saudi Arabia. The wall was torn down in 1957.

Covered Souk

The souk, broadly defined, lies between the Municipal Park and Mubarak Al-Kabeer St, from Ahmad Al-Jaber St to Ali Al-Salem St. Moneychangers, gold sellers, electronics merchants etc tend to group into specific areas. The meat and vegetable market, which opens quite early in the morning and is arguably the most interesting part of the souk, is in the very centre of the souk area. The gold souk is just off Ali Al-Salem St.

Post-War Graffiti

The clean-up crews did not leave much of this intact. The Americans, however, have placed a protective plexiglass sheet over 'Thanks for Bush' and a few other slogans painted on the wall of the US embassy compound by grateful Kuwaitis in the days after liberation. The preserved graffiti is on the wall facing the Safir International Hotel.

Exhibition of Kuwaiti Sailing Ships

This small, largely unknown and utterly fascinating tourist site lies far out beyond the edge of the city on the road to Doha Village. It consists of about half a dozen different dhows and other traditional sailing vessels ranging in size from small fishing boats to a large ocean-going dhow. Several of the boats fly the red flag that Kuwait used prior to independence from Britain in 1961. All of the boats have been carefully restored and ramps provide access for curious visitors. It's a long drive out from the city but absolutely worth the trip.

The exhibition is open every day from 8 am to 8 pm. Admission is free.

To reach the site take the Al-Jahra Rd west out of Kuwait City. Follow the signs for Entertainment City and turn onto the Doha Spur Rd. When you reach the roundabout just before the entrance to Entertainment City turn left (by now you will have started to see a lot of small signs for the sailing ship exhibition). The exhibition will be on your left after 3.5 km. There are no buses to this

area of Kuwait. Unless you have a car, a taxi will be your only option. This should cost KD 3 to KD 5 one way, depending on your negotiating skills. Since you do not have a prayer of getting a ride from here, a round-trip costing around KD 8 is probably your best bet. For that price you might be able to get the driver to include a stop in Doha Village.

Beach & Health Clubs

Most of the health clubs at the big hotels are available to nonguests upon the purchase of a membership. Some of the best clubs only sell these by the month, quarter or year but a few are available on a daily basis as well. Your best bet is probably the Safir International Hotel. If you are not staying in the hotel use of the pool and its garden costs KD 4 per day. To use the pool, garden and health club (sauna, squash and tennis courts, weight room etc) costs KD 6.

Some 20 km south of the centre along Arabian Gulf St the Messaliah Families Beach is a good place to go if you have kids along or for unaccompanied women. Admission to the club is 500 fils (250 fils for children under six) and is limited to women and families (ie no unaccompanied men). In addition to a beach and a swimming pool there is a lot of play space for children. There are several fast-food restaurants at the club. If you are travelling without kids be warned that this place can get pretty noisy on Friday afternoons.

As for other beaches, you should be aware that mines remain a problem except at the beach clubs. Explosions are no longer the common occurrence they were in 1991-92, but they do still happen and you would be best advised to confine your swimming to pools.

Boating

If you feel like renting a boat head for the Sultan Centre Restaurants complex about six km south of the centre on the sea-side of Arabian Gulf St. Note that the Sultan Centre Restaurants complex is several km closer to the centre than the main Sultan

Centre shopping complex. In the parking lot you will find a small kiosk. For KD 24 up to 12 people can take a one-hour cruise on a glass-bottomed boat. Two-hour fishing trips for up to six people cost KD 36. Mines are less of a problem at sea than they are on land in Kuwait, but they are still a factor worth considering. Contact your embassy to see whether it has up-to-date information on the situation concerning seaborne mines.

Organised Tours

Orient Tours (☎ 474 2000) is the only company currently running organised tours in Kuwait. It offers half-day tours of Kuwait City and its 'outskirts' for KD 10 on Tuesday and KD 11 on Sunday and Wednesday. This rate presumes a minimum of four people on the tour. If only two or three people are on the tour the prices go up by KD 3 per person. It will not run a tour for only one person. It also offers an all-day trip to the Khiran beach resort on Friday for KD 18 (with a KD 5 supplement if only two or three people take the tour).

The Safir International Hotel offers a free three-hour tour of Kuwait City on Fridays from 10 am to 1 pm for hotel guests only.

Places to Stay – bottom end & middle

All hotels in Kuwait have air-conditioning and private baths. TVs are also standard as are mini-fridges (at the bottom end, though, there might not be anything in them). Many hotels do not have heating in the rooms and you will certainly notice this in December or January. Most of the country's hotels also hit you with a 15% service charge – where applicable this has been added into the rates quoted. The rates listed here are initial quotes but are unlikely to come down by more than KD 1 or KD 2, and that only for people staying four or five days or more.

Kuwait's cheapest hotel is outside the city centre on an unmarked street behind the Safir International Hotel. The *Maha House* (☎ 252 1218, fax 257 1220) charges KD 12/20 for singles/doubles. Anywhere else this hotel would be absurdly overpriced, but in Kuwait it passes for value for money.

Winter travellers should note that the rooms are not heated. That said, it has been renovated and some of the rooms even have kitchenettes. From the centre the hotel can be reached by bus No 15. Get off at the roundabout where you see the Kuwait Continental Hotel and walk toward the sea.

In the centre there are several decent places that, again, pass for inexpensive in Kuwait and cost only a few KD more than the Maha House while offering somewhat better locations. The *Phoenicia Hotel* (☎ 242 1051, fax 242 4402), on the corner of Fahad Al-Salem and Al-Hilali Sts, is, hands down, the best value in the centre at KD 16/20, including breakfast. Farther down Fahad Al-Salam St, the *Carlton Hotel* (☎ 242 3171, fax 242 5848), which has undergone a recent facelift, has slightly larger rooms at KD 17/22. The *Sahara Hotel* (☎ 242 4121, fax 242 4132), between Mohammed Thunayyan and Al-Soor Sts, is slightly better than both the Phoenicia and the Carlton at KD 18/24.

If you are going to pay KD 18 or KD 20 for a room you can do better for your money outside the centre. I would recommend the *Second Home Hotel* (☎ 253 2100, fax 253 2381), just behind the Kuwait Continental Hotel at the Al-Dasma roundabout (the intersection of Al-Istiqlal St and the First Ring Rd). It's a friendly place though no longer the pre-invasion bargain it once was. Rooms are KD 19/23 with the usual small discounts available for longer stays.

Back in the centre, north of Al-Safat Square is the *Oasis Hotel* (☎ 246 5489, fax 246 5490), at the intersection of Ahmad Al-Jaber and Mubarak Al-Kabeer Sts. This is another fairly expensive place with singles/doubles at KD 30/34.

The *Kuwait Continental Hotel* (☎ 252 7300, fax 252 9373), at Al-Dasma roundabout, is excessively overpriced at KD 40.250/46. Some of the troops from the United Nations Iraq-Kuwait Observer Mission (UNIKOM – the UN force that monitors the border area) stay here. Nearby, the *Hassa House* (☎ 257 1659) has two-bedroom apartments it rents for KD 550 per month, but it will also let them out by the

KUWAIT

KUWAIT

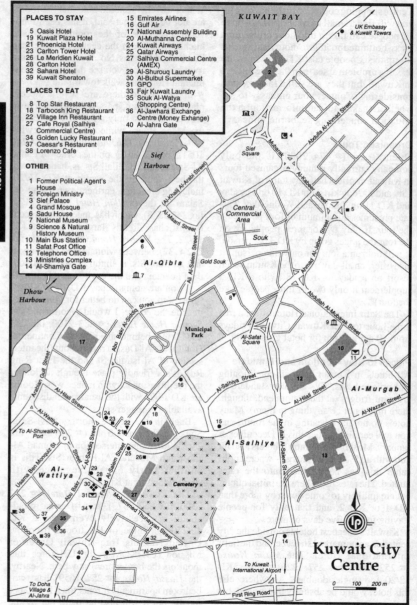

PLACES TO STAY

5 Oasis Hotel
19 Kuwait Plaza Hotel
21 Phoenicia Hotel
23 Carlton Tower Hotel
26 Le Meridien Kuwait
28 Carlton Hotel
32 Sahara Hotel
39 Kuwait Sheraton

PLACES TO EAT

8 Top Star Restaurant
18 Tarboosh King Restaurant
22 Village Inn Restaurant
27 Cafe Royal (Salhiya Commercial Centre)
34 Golden Lucky Restaurant
37 Caesar's Restaurant
38 Lorenzo Cafe

OTHER

1 Former Political Agent's House
2 Foreign Ministry
3 Sief Palace
4 Grand Mosque
6 Sadu House
7 National Museum
9 Science & Natural History Museum
10 Main Bus Station
11 Safat Post Office
12 Telephone Office
13 Ministries Complex
14 Al-Shamiya Gate

15 Emirates Airlines
16 Gulf Air
17 National Assembly Building
20 Al-Muthanna Centre
24 Kuwait Airways
25 Qatar Airways
27 Salhiya Commercial Centre (AMEX)
29 Al-Shurouq Laundry
30 Al-Bulbul Supermarket
31 GPO
33 Fajr Kuwait Laundry
35 Souk Al-Watya (Shopping Centre)
36 Al-Jawhara Exchange Centre (Money Exhange)
40 Al-Jahra Gate

KUWAIT BAY

UK Embassy & Kuwait Towers

Sief Harbour

Sief Square

Central Commercial Area

Souk

Al-Qibla

Gold Souk

Dhow Harbour

Municipal Park

Al-Safat Square

Al-Salhiya Street

Al-Murgab

Al-Wattiya

To Al-Shuwaikh Port

Al-Salhiya

Cemetery

To Kuwait International Airport

To Doha Village & Al-Jahra

First Ring Road

Kuwait City Centre

0   100   200 m

night for KD 30, a very good deal if you have enough people (three to five) to fill the entire apartment.

Places to Stay – top end

All five-star hotels can arrange visas for business visitors. Generally the hotel will require that you stay with them for at least two nights. The maximum stay on this sort of visa is usually one month. Prices quoted here are rack rates, including the service charge. Discounts are usually available.

At this end of the market a pretty good bet is the *Carlton Tower Hotel* (☎ 245 2740, fax 240 1624) which, at KD 44.500/46 including the service charge, is the cheapest place that can arrange a visa. It also boasts a good city centre location on Al-Hilali St just off Fahad Al-Salam St and is a bit cheaper than the other hotels in this category.

Among other top-end hotels are:

Kuwait Plaza Hotel (☎ 245 8890), Fahad Al-Salam St near Al-Muthanna Centre in the city centre. Singles/doubles cost KD 51.750/59.800.
Kuwait Sheraton (☎ 242 2055, fax 244 8032), at the intersection of Fahad Al-Salam and Al-Soor Sts in the city centre, near the Al-Jahra gate. Singles/doubles cost KD 57.500/69.
Le Meridien Kuwait (☎ 245 5550, fax 243 8391), Al-Hilali St in the city centre. Singles/doubles cost KD 57.500/69 – probably the best value for money in this price category.
Messilah Beach Hotel (☎ 562 4111, fax 562 9402), at Messilah Beach, south of the centre on the road to Al-Ahmadi. Singles/doubles cost KD 50.600/55.200.
Radisson SAS Hotel Kuwait (☎ 575 6000, fax 575 2788), on Arabian Gulf St south of Al-Salmiya. Singles/doubles cost KD 64.400/77.050.
Safir International Hotel (☎ 253 0000, fax 256 3797), Arabian Gulf St, Beneid Al-Gar district, opposite the US embassy. This is the favoured haunt of visiting VIPs and western journalists, but it's overpriced at KD 65.550/77.050 for singles/ doubles.

Places to Eat

Cheap & Medium-Priced As always, Indian food is the cheapest. There is an enormous concentration of small Indian/Pakistani restaurants in the area around the bus station – especially down Abdullah Al-Mubarak and

Al-Hilali Sts – and in the souk. The menu never varies: chicken or mutton biryani or fried chicken or chilli chicken. Occasionally samosas and/or some kind of curry are available, but don't hold your breath. A meal rarely costs more than KD 1. Among the better places is the *Top Star Restaurant* in the souk. Enter the souk from the south-west end of Al-Safat Square by the big Citizen sign, take the third alley on the left after the sign and head up the stairs.

Along Fahad Al-Salem St, not far from the Kuwait Plaza Hotel, the *Tarboosh King Restaurant* has kebabs and decent grilled chicken. Half a chicken with rice and soup costs KD 1.500. Also on Fahad Al-Salem St the *Golden Lucky Restaurant* (formerly the New Lucky Restaurant), at the small plaza just by the GPO, is a good bet for those on tight budgets. The menu consists only of biryanis, fried chicken or fish and snacks. The biryanis cost 750 fils to KD 1 and samosas are 100 fils apiece.

One of the best spots for a cheap meal in the centre is the *Village Inn Restaurant*, just off Fahad Al-Salem St behind the Phoenicia Hotel. Though the menu features both Chinese and Indian food the clientele is mostly middle-class Indian expatriates, so you would be well advised to stick to the Indian food (which, anyway, is cheaper). Indian main dishes cost KD 1 to KD 2.

For Chinese food try *Caesar's* on Abu Bakr Al-Saddiq St, not far from the Sheraton Hotel. The restaurant is very popular with both Kuwaitis and expats and you may have to wait for a table, especially on weekends. Main dishes cost KD 1.200 to KD 2.

Cafe Royal, in the Salhiya Commercial Centre, has mostly western food (omelettes, burgers etc) starting from about KD 2. It also offers quite good hot and cold sandwiches for KD 1.500 to KD 1.800 and salads for KD 1.250 to KD 2. Local newspapers are available for customers to read and the cafe is popular with Kuwaitis and expats alike. The location, next to a fountain with a sidewalk cafe atmosphere, is not exactly Paris but come July you'll value the fact that it is indoors. Its position, in one of the city's most up-market shopping malls, also makes it a good spot for a coffee break.

If you are looking for a more traditional open-air coffee house try *Bait Lothan* on Arabian Gulf St just north of the intersection with Qatar St (several km south of the centre). It offers coffee, tea and *shisha* (hookah) pipes in a quiet, open garden. The main building also houses an art gallery. There is no bus service down this part of Arabian Gulf St. A taxi from the centre should cost KD 1.500 to KD 1.750.

Expensive After all these years my highest recommendation in Kuwait still goes to *Mais Alghanim*, a terrific Lebanese restaurant on Arabian Gulf St, between the Kuwait Towers and the intersection with Al-Soor St. It is in a white prefab building, which also contains the local DHL office. The restaurant is at the end of the building closer to Al-Soor St (the large sign is in Arabic only but there's a smaller one in English by the door). Founded in 1953 it is one of the country's older establishments and has long been something of a local institution. Meals cost about KD 3 to KD 4. It is worth going out of your way for. Expect queues for the garden tables in the winter and the indoor (air-conditioned) ones in the summer.

For up-market Indian food try *Mughal Mahal* on Jaber Al-Mubarak St, near the intersection with Al-Hilali St in the Al-Sharq district. Great meals cost KD 4 to KD 5.

If you want to break your budget but don't feel like hotel food try the *New Koreana Restaurant* on the 1st mezzanine level of the Salhiya Commercial Centre. The menu is mostly Korean though there are some Japanese dishes as well. The food is very good and the service magnificent but a meal is likely to set you back KD 8 to KD 10.

Outside the centre the *Steakhouse*, about eight km south of the city centre on Arabian Gulf St, is quite good. The same company runs a complex called the *Sultan Centre Restaurants*, which includes a so-so Mexican place, *Chi Chi's*, that has even managed the trick of making a drinkable nonalcoholic frozen margarita! Plan on spending close to

KD 10 per person. This restaurant complex is about six km south of the centre, on Arabian Gulf St, and a couple of km north of the shopping centre of the same name.

Lorenzo Cafe on Al-Soor St not far from the Sheraton Hotel is probably Kuwait's most up-market western-style coffee house. The coffee (and reportedly most of what goes into the pastries) is imported from Italy. It has excellent cappuccino, espresso and cakes as well as chocolates made on the premises. It is very expensive – and on weekend evenings it is also very crowded – but definitely worth a visit. A cappuccino costs 950 fils and cakes start at KD 1.450 a slice.

Self-Catering The Al-Bulbul supermarket on Al-Wattiya St in the centre is a good bet for do-it-yourself meals. If you are in search of western products you will have to take a car or taxi far down Arabian Gulf St to the Sultan Centre, Kuwait's only big western-style supermarket.

Entertainment

Cinemas The city's handful of cinemas show mostly Indian and Pakistani films, but western movies sometimes turn up as well. The main cinemas in Kuwait City are the Al-Firdaus and Al-Hamrah, both at the Al-Maqwa roundabout (the intersection of Jaber Al-Mubarak and Al-Hilali Sts). There are usually two shows per night; check the *Arab Times* or *Kuwait Times* to see what's on.

Amusement Park Entertainment City, on the western outskirts of Kuwait City, near Doha Village, is Kuwait's only real amusement park. It is not very large by western standards but it is a far cry from the small (and rather rickety-looking) rides that dot the beachfront restaurants at the southern end of Arabian Gulf St in Kuwait City.

The park is open daily from 4 pm to midnight (8 pm to 2 am during Ramadan). Tickets are KD 3.500 for both adults and children. To reach the park take the main road west out of Kuwait City toward Al-Jahra and follow the signs. The park is not accessible by public transport. Getting there by taxi will cost around KD 3, but you may not find it all that easy to get a taxi back into the city.

Things to Buy

In terms of antiques, there's very little to buy in Kuwait. Hotel gift shops often have shiny, imported 'Arabian' gift items. Sadu House is a good place to shop for souvenirs. See the entry on Sadu House earlier in this chapter for an idea of its prices.

Consumer electronics are widely available but the prices are pretty high.

If you are looking for that old but expensive Gulf standby – gold jewellery – try the Souk Al-Watya shopping centre, next to the Sheraton Hotel in the centre.

Getting There & Away

Air Kuwait International Airport is 16 km south of the city centre. There are currency exchange facilities on both the upper (departures) and lower (arrivals) levels. Since the war all carriers have been operating out of Terminal 1. There is no word on when the second terminal will once again be functional. Check-in time is officially two hours but some carriers insist on your being there three hours in advance, so you should call the airline to double-check. Security is tight enough that you should not let this slip too much. Kuwait has always been pretty serious about enforcing the 'only one carry-on bag' rule so this is not the place to try to get three or four pieces of hand baggage through security (unless you are flying in business or 1st class).

Kuwait has never made a serious effort to compete with the massive duty-free shopping complexes run by Dubai and Bahrain. Like much of the rest of the country the airport is functional without being unnecessarily elaborate. The departure lounge has a coffee shop, snack bar, some pay phones and a very modest duty-free operation, but not much else.

For general information, including flight arrivals and departures, call ☎ 433 5599 or 433 4499. Some of the airlines that fly to/from Kuwait are:

Aeroflot
　Fahad Al-Salem St, between the Phoenicia and Carlton hotels (☎ 240 4838)
Air China
　Corner of Ali Al-Salem and Al-Hilali Sts (☎ 243 8568)
Air France
　Hussain Makki Al-Juma Travels, Al-Hilali St, near the Meridien Hotel (☎ 242 0504)
Air India
　Ali Al-Salem St, near the intersection with Fahad Al-Salem St (☎ 243 8185)
Air Lanka
　Al-Soor St, near the Al-Jahra gate (☎ 242 4444)
Alitalia
　Oasis Travel & Tourism, Abu Bakr Al-Saddiq St, near the Sheraton Hotel (☎ 241 4403, ext 103 or 104)
Biman Bangladesh
　Al-Athla Travels, Al-Soor St, between Mohammed Thunayyan St and the Al-Jahra gate (☎ 244 1041)
British Airways
　Corner of Fahad Al-Salem and Ali Al-Salem Sts (☎ 242 5635)
EgyptAir
　Fahad Al-Salem St, just west of Al-Safat Square (☎ 242 1603)
Emirates
　Corner of Al-Hilali and Ali Al-Salem Sts (☎ 243 8690)
Gulf Air
　Ali Al-Salem St, near the intersection with Fahad Al-Salem St (☎ 245 0180)
Indian Airlines
　Al-Soor St, near the Al-Jahra gate (☎ 245 6700)
KLM
　Mezzanine level of the building on the corner of Al-Safat Square and Abdullah Al-Salem St (☎ 242 5747)
Kuwait Airways
　Kuwait Airways tower, Al-Hilali St (☎ 243 3388)
Lufthansa
　Al-Soor St, between Mohammed Thunayyan St and the Al-Jahra gate (☎ 242 2493)
MEA (Middle East Airlines)
　Intersection of Fahad Al-Salem and Ali Al-Salem Sts (☎ 242 3070)
Olympic
　Fahad Al-Salem St (☎ 242 0002)
PIA (Pakistan International Airlines)
　Intersection of Fahad Al-Salem and Ali Al-Salem Sts (☎ 242 1043)
Qatar Airways
　Intersection of Fahad Al-Salem and Al-Hilali Sts (☎ 245 8888)
Saudia
　Al-Sharq district, Ahmad Al-Jaber St (☎ 242 6310)

KUWAIT

Tarom
  Al-Athla Travels, Al-Soor St, between Moham-
  med Thunayyan St and the Al-Jahra gate (☎ 244
  1041)
Turkish Airlines
  Off Fahad Al-Salem St, near the Village Inn
  Restaurant (☎ 245 3820)

Bus Kuwait has only a handful of inter-city bus routes. All long-haul trips cost 300 or 350 fils and, like buses inside Kuwait City, run approximately every six minutes from 5 am to 10 pm (at least in theory; in practice every 15 minutes is probably a better guess). Some of the buses originate at sub-stations in either the Sharq district, east of the centre near the Dasman Palace, or in Al-Jleeb, south-west of the centre, near the airport. Inter-city routes are:

Route 40 – Sharq bus station, Airport Rd, Shuwaikh,
  Kheitan, Subhan, Al-Daher, Fintas, Fahaheel
Route 101 – Main bus station, Airport Rd, Sixth Ring
  Rd, Sabah Al-Salem district, Al-Qurin, Al-
  Ahmadi, Fahaheel
Route 102 – Main bus station, Istiqlal St, Third Ring
  Rd, Cairo St, Fahaheel Rd, Fahaheel
Route 103 – Main bus station, Fahad Al-Salem St,
  Al-Jahra Rd, Al-Jahra, Al-Atraaf, Al-Jahra
Route 105 – Al-Jleeb bus station, Al-Hasawai, Al-
  Shuwaikh, Kheitan, Sabah Al-Salem district,
  Gous St, Al-Saheli St, Fahaheel
Route 502 – Main bus station, Istiqlal St, Khartoum
  St, Fahaheel Rd, Fahaheel

International bus service to Cairo and Dammam (Saudi Arabia) can be booked through any of the small travel agencies around the intersection of Abdullah Al-Mubarak and Al-Hilali Sts.

Taxi While there is a taxi rank across the street from the main bus station, there is no formal service-taxi system operating in Kuwait. You could strike a deal with one of the drivers to go to another city but it would be hit-or-miss.

Car The international car-rental agencies all charge KD 8 to KD 9 per day for the smallest cars. Al-Mulla is the cheapest of the larger local agencies with cars from KD 7.500 per day. These rates usually include unlimited

km, but full insurance will cost an extra KD 2 to KD 4 per day. Discounts on these rates can usually be negotiated, and with some shopping around you should be able to get a car for around KD 8 to KD 9 per day net.

Al-Mulla has offices in the Kuwait Plaza (☎ 245 8600) and Safir International (☎ 250 3869) hotels. Europcar (☎ 484 2988) has its main office in the Shuwaikh industrial area, but it has branch offices in the Sheraton and Continental hotels, and Avis has an office on the corner of Fahad Al-Salem and Ali Al-Salem Sts in the centre.

Getting Around
The Airport Taxis charge a flat KD 4 between the airport and the city. Bus 501 runs between the main bus station off Al-Hilali St and the airport every 30 minutes from 5.30 am to 9 pm. The fare is 250 fils.

Bus The central station for Kuwait's municipal buses is near the intersection of Al-Hilali and Abdullah Al-Mubarak Sts. Large secondary stations are located at the Orthopaedic Hospital (also known as Al-Azam Hospital) on the western edge of Kuwait City and in Sharq, at the eastern edge of the centre. Smaller stations can be found at the Al-Jahra gate and in the districts of Sulaibiya, Al-Jleeb, Kheitan, Jabriya, Messila and Salmiya.

On printed timetables the central station is referred to as 'Mircab bus station'. The main station in the centre has a route map available in both English and Arabic. When you are reading the printed timetables, however, note that the English words 'Origin' and 'Destination' have been reversed at the top of the main column. If you simply remember to read the columns right-to-left, starting with the route number and ending at 'Origin' (or read them as printed below, where the mistake has been rectified) you should be OK.

Buses start running around 5 am and continue until around 10 pm. Officially every route has buses at six-minute intervals, but every 12 to 20 minutes is a more realistic estimate. Fares are 100, 150 or 200 fils depending on how far you travel. Route numbers are displayed on the front of buses but destinations are not. Only the buses numbered 500 and above are operated using modern air-conditioned coaches, though the rest of the bus fleet is reasonably well maintained. The routes below use street names in the centre and along a few major thoroughfares (such as Airport Rd and the ring roads) and district names farther afield.

Route 11 – Sharq bus station (on Dasman Square at the eastern end of the centre), Ahmed Al-Jaber St, Fahad Al-Salem St, Jamal Abdul Nasser St, Al-Sabah Hospital, Orthopaedic Hospital
Route 12 – Sharq bus station, Al-Jahra Rd, Airport Rd, Fourth Ring Rd, Orthopaedic Hospital
Route 13 – Main bus station, Fahad Al-Salem St, Jamal Abdul Nasser St, Airport Rd, Kheitan
Route 14 – Main bus station, Cairo St, Bush St (formerly Baghdad St), Hamad Al-Mubarak St, Ras Salmiya, Messila bus station
Route 15 – Main bus station, Istiqlal St, Fourth Ring Rd, Al-Mogira St, Salem Al-Mubarak St, Ras Salmiya bus station
Route 16 – Al-Jahra gate, Istiqlal St, Hawalli, Fourth Ring Rd, King Faisal Rd, Kheitan
Route 17 – Sharq bus station, Riyadh St, Faiha, Idaliya, Al-Rawdah, Hawalli, Salmiya bus station
Route 18 – Main bus station, Souk, Mubarak Al-Kabeer St, Cairo St, Third Ring Rd, Hawalli, Shuwaikh, Jamal Abdul Nasser St, Orthopaedic Hospital
Route 20 – Sharq bus station, Fahad Al-Salem St, Kheitan, Farwaniya, Omariya, Rabiah, Al-Jleeb bus station
Route 21 – Main bus station, Al-Jahra Rd, Airport Rd, Farwaniya, Al-Jleeb bus station
Route 22 – Sharq bus station, Fahad Al-Salem St, Riyadh St, Third Ring Rd, Airport Rd, Farwaniya, Al-Jleeb bus station
Route 23 – Riyadh St, King Faisal St, Al-Waleed Ibn Abdul Malik St, Ibrahim Ibn Al-Adham St, Kheitan
Route 24 – Main bus station, Abdullah Al-Mubarak St, Al-Maghreb St, Qadisiya, Hawalli, Amman St, Rumaithiya, Salmiya bus station
Route 25 – Al-Jahra gate, Ahmed Al-Jaber St, Dasma, Da'aya, Shaab, Hawalli, Jabriya
Route 26 – Sharq bus station, Fahad Al-Salem St, Shuwaikh, Andalus, Firdous, Sabah Al-Nasser, Sulaibiya
Route 29 – Main bus station, Fahad Al-Salem St, Airport Rd, Shuwaikh, Al-Ghazali St, Hasawi, Al-Jleeb

Route 31 – Sharq bus station, Fahad Al-Salem St, Shamiya, Keifan, Khalidiya, Yarmouq, Kheitan
Route 32 – Sharq bus station, Fahad Al-Salem St, Abdullah Al-Salem St, Nuzha, Al-Rawdah, Qortuba, Surra, Jabriya
Route 34 – Sharq bus station, Fahad Al-Salem St, Airport Rd, Farwaniya, Sixth Ring Rd, Salwa, Salmiya bus station
Route 38 – Al-Jahra gate, Fahad Al-Salem St, Istiqlal St, Hawalli, Bayan, Mishrif, Sabah Al-Salem district, Messila bus station
Route 39 – Sharq bus station, Istiqlal St, Third Ring Rd, Shuwaikh, Ardiya, Abbasiya, Farwaniya, Kheitan
Route 200 – Salmiya bus station, Arabian Gulf St, Hamad Al-Mubarak St, Blagat St, Salmiya bus station
Route 506 – Al-Jahra gate, Fahad Al-Salem St, Istiqlal St, Hawalli, Fourth Ring Rd, Farwaniya, Hasawi, Al-Jleeb
Route 507 – Sharq bus station, Fahad Al-Salem St, Jahra Rd, Shuwaikh, Al-Ghazali St, Al-Jleeb

Taxi Unfortunately, Kuwait has developed one of those taxi systems where there are no meters and the trick is to know what you ought to pay when you get in. Bargaining in advance may save you some grief at the end of the trip but it will probably end up costing you more money. Around town, taxis are orange-coloured.

In general, anything within the city centre is about KD 1. Longer trips just outside the centre (eg from the Sheraton to the Safir International Hotel) cost about KD 1.500. If you bargain, or take the taxi from a rank in front of a five-star hotel, expect to pay double this. You might also try calling Ibrahim Taxi (☎ 244 6720). Its service gets good reviews locally and costs about the same as hailing a cab on the street.

Individual drivers also stop to pick up passengers. This is not a free ride. The driver will expect to be paid the equivalent of a taxi fare for the trip. If you take a lift this way (which unaccompanied women should definitely not do), bear in mind that it is illegal and you could find yourself in trouble if the car is stopped at a police checkpoint. To avoid any misunderstandings you should also negotiate the price with the driver before you get in.

Around Kuwait

FAILAKA ISLAND

The home of Kuwait's main archaeological site, Failaka is definitely worth the trip, though it requires a bit of extra caution. You do not need to be a military genius to figure out Failaka's strategic value during a war. Control the island and you can control seaborne access to Kuwait City. Not surprisingly the Iraqis turned Failaka into a heavily fortified base. After liberation it was found, like much of the mainland, to be filled with mines and it took a long time for the island to be rendered safe enough for the archaeological site to reopen. So, while the site may be open, Failaka is one of those bits of Kuwait where you would be well advised to restrict yourself to well-trod paths.

History

Failaka, which the Greeks called Ikaros, is the best known, and probably the earliest, Hellenistic settlement in the Gulf. It was also the first part of Kuwait to attract the attention of professional archaeologists, who began digging here in early 1958, as documented in Geoffrey Bibby's book, *Looking for Dilmun*. Though it is best known as a Hellenistic site, Failaka's history goes back to the Bronze Age Dilmun civilisation which was centred in Bahrain. The Greeks arrived in the 4th century BC in the form of a garrison placed here by Nearchus, one of Alexander the Great's admirals. A small settlement existed on the island prior to this, but it was as the Greek town of Ikaros that the settlement became a real city or at least a large town.

As you enter the site, the road swings around to the left and ends in front of a group of prefabricated buildings. These are the archaeological museum and the on-site administrative offices.

Visiting the Site

The **mud house** on a small rise between these buildings and the sea contains a display of island life prior to the discovery of oil. The display includes glassware, old navigational equipment and models of traditional Gulf sailing vessels.

Tel Sa'ad, the most ancient of Failaka's three excavated sites, is the excavation next to the building with the ethnographic display. This was a Bronze Age settlement connected with Dilmun. Its centrepiece is the **Temple of Anzak**, the large open area in the centre of the excavation. Anzak was the chief god of Dilmun. Note the column base in one corner of the temple. Beyond the temple, the area toward the sea may have been a fortification of some sort. The area behind the temple (away from the sea) probably also contained houses.

The **inn** is a bit farther up the coast (away from the site entrance) and is easy to spot – just look for the small metal lookout tower nearby. Little of the building remains, but the floor plan is clearly visible.

The **temple** is the centrepiece of Failaka. It, too, is easy to spot from a distance, thanks to the presence of a small sun shelter erected over part of the excavation. It is about 100m inland from the inn. This was the heart of the main Hellenistic settlement. The temple, which was probably dedicated to Artemis, lay at the centre of a square fortress that extended 200m on each side. Two re-erected columns mark the entrance to the temple, which is of the standard Greek two-chamber type. The remains of the altar are also clearly identifiable in front of the temple. Kuwait's most famous archaeological find, the **Ikaros Stele** (which, prior to the Iraqi invasion, was on display in the Kuwait National Museum) was found here. It would have stood to the left of the temple entrance, as one faces the temple from the altar. Surrounding the temple is a large excavated area of houses and fortifications. The entire complex dates from 330 to 150 BC.

To reach the site from the ferry terminal on Failaka, turn right as you exit the terminal building. Almost immediately you will see the mud house, the one which contains the ethnographic display, on a low hill to the right beyond a wall. The entrance is a gate in this wall with seals on either side marked Kuwait National Museum.

Getting There & Away

Ferries to Failaka depart from Ras Salmiya (also known as Ras Al-Ard), on Arabian Gulf St south of the centre. The terminal area can be reached via buses Nos 14, 15, 17, 24, 34 and 200. Before the war ferries to the island operated on an almost hourly basis. At the time of writing there was only one round trip per day.

The ferry keeps an erratic schedule that is updated every month. The outbound run to the island usually leaves at 8 am, but may depart at 8.15, 8.45, 9, 9.15, 9.45 or even 10 am. A printed schedule with exact departure times is available at the ferry terminal and is updated every two weeks.

The ferry trip over to the island takes 90 minutes. The ferry then stays at the island for two hours before making the return trip. This is enough time for a quick look at the archaeological site (which is a short walk from the ferry dock) but not much else. If you miss the ferry back you will be stuck on the island until the following day. Since there are no hotels and the danger of landmines makes camping inadvisable, don't miss the ferry! The fare is KD 1 one way and KD 2 return. If you want to drive onto and off the ferry you must buy a return ticket for KD 37.500. This includes passage for the car and driver, but any passengers will need to purchase regular tickets. Call the ferry company on ☎ 574 2664 for information on sailing times and to see whether frequency has increased from one per day.

AL-AHMADI

Built to house Kuwait's oil industry in the 1940s and '50s, Al-Ahmadi was named after the then-emir, Shaikh Ahmad. It remains, to a great extent, the private preserve of the Kuwait Oil Company (KOC). As with Dhahran in Saudi Arabia and Awali in Bahrain, the visitor driving through Al-Ahmadi's streets has the vague feeling of being in a suburb somewhere in the southwestern USA. Unlike Dhahran (but like

Awali), the gates have long since come down and one need not have a reason to be allowed to drive into 'Little America'.

Al-Ahmadi has shops, supermarkets, banks, travel agents, parks, recreational facilities and a stadium. What it does not have is a hotel. There is a guest house for people having business with KOC but it does not accept non-KOC guests. The town's two sites of note are the Oil Display Centre on Mid 5th St and the Public Gardens.

The **Oil Display Centre** (☎ 398 2747) exhibits are a brief introduction to oil from its formation underground through the prospecting process to extraction, refining, sales and distribution. The display is small but well organised and rather self-congratulatory. The centre is open Saturday to Wednesday from 7 am to 3 pm. Admission is free. At the time of writing it was in the final stages of a complete makeover and was scheduled to reopen in mid-1996.

Al-Ahmadi also has a small, pleasant **pubic garden** that is worth a visit.

Getting There & Away

To reach the town, take the Al-Safr Motorway south out of Kuwait City until you reach the Al-Ahmadi exit. Follow, first, the blue signs for North Al-Ahmadi, and then the smaller white signs for the Display Centre. After the turn for North Al-Ahmadi go left on Mid 5th St (the first roundabout) to reach the Display Centre. To reach the public garden from there, continue along Mid 5th St and turn left on 7th Ave (the first left past the Display Centre). Take the first right turn (onto Mid 7th St) and follow the road until it ends at the entrance to the public gardens. Bus No 101 runs from the main bus station in Kuwait City to Al-Ahmadi (passing by the Oil Display Centre as it enters town) several times an hour. The town, however, really is not worth going out of your way for.

AL-JAHRA

Al-Jahra, an industrial and agricultural town approximately 32 km west of Kuwait City, has a name which lives in Kuwait's history as a battle site, though those with memories of the Gulf War will remember it for a much more recent battle.

History

In 1920 Kuwait's ruler, Shaikh Salem Bin Mubarak, learned that Abdul Aziz Bin Abdul Rahman Al-Saud, the future founder and King of Saudi Arabia, planned to turn his much-feared warriors, the ikhwan, loose on Kuwait. Salem decided to make his stand at Al-Jahra. After being routed by the ikhwan in a battle near the city, the Kuwaiti forces retired to Al-Jahra's Red Fort from where they sought to wear down the more numerous Saudis in a war of attrition. In the meantime, a messenger was sent to the British to invoke the 1899 Anglo-Kuwaiti treaty. A relatively minor British show of force in the waters off Al-Jahra was enough to turn the tide of the siege in the Kuwaitis' favour. The victory also established the Al-Sabah more firmly in Kuwait itself. Two years after the battle of Al-Jahra, Abdul Aziz was prevailed upon to open talks with the Al-Sabah which ended in his recognising Kuwait's independence in exchange for a large chunk of its territory.

Al-Jahra's role in the most recent war over Kuwait is somewhat less romantic. In the final hours of the Gulf War, as Iraqi troops began to evacuate Kuwait City, a huge traffic jam developed just outside Al-Jahra, where the main road from Kuwait City turns north toward the Iraqi border. The convoy stalled on the approach to the Al-Mutla ridge, just west of Al-Jahra, where it was caught by a coalition air attack. The convoy was demolished by the allies and the debris pushed off to the side of the road to rust, where at last report a few bits and pieces of it were still visible – a gruesome collection of the mangled remains of cars, trucks and a few tanks.

Orientation

Al-Jahra's main street is Marzouk Al-Mat'aab St starting from the point beyond the Red Fort where the road loops around to the right at an intersection (marked on maps as a traffic circle, though it's not really that

big) to its intersection with Da'abal Al-Khazaai St, which runs back to the expressway. The stretch of road in question has a number of small restaurants though most have signs only in Arabic.

Red Fort

The town's only site of the more conventional variety is the Red Fort (also known as the Red Palace), famed in Kuwaiti history from the 1920 siege. It is a low rectangular mud fort near the highway. The name is thought to derive from the colour of the walls. The fort is built around a large open courtyard with several annexes on its west side. Small signs (in Arabic and English) scattered around the complex identify the functions of the various parts of the complex, though after a while one empty mud-walled room starts to look pretty much like another. All four of the low towers at the fort's corners can be climbed to get a better view.

The annexe in the fort's south-west corner (through the large wooden door with a number 4 above it) was the harem, the emir's private enclosure. Moving north, the next annexe includes a small mosque. Note the simple, unadorned *mihrib* (prayer niche) in the south wall.

The fort is on Marzouk Al-Mat'aab St next to a park. In the winter it is open daily from 7.30 am to 1.30 pm and 3.30 to 6.30 pm. In summer the hours are 7 am to 1 pm and 4 to 7 pm. The fort is closed throughout the year on Saturday afternoons. At all times the closing hours are flexible. Several times I have arrived when the fort was supposed to be closed and found it open. Admission is free but identification is required. Photography is permitted but videos are not. Call ☎ 477 2559 for more information.

Getting There & Away

Coming from Kuwait City, take the second Al-Jahra exit from the expressway onto Marzouk Al-Mat'aab. The Red Fort is on the right, about 200m south of (ie inland from) the highway, though you can't see it until you are right in front of it. Al-Jahra can be reached via bus No 103, which passes directly in front of the Red Fort.

DOHA VILLAGE

On an arm of land jutting out into Kuwait Bay, Doha Village is the site of several small dhow-building yards and a fishing village of squalid shacks. The dhow yard is not very interesting. If you are planning a trip to Bahrain or to Sur, in Oman, the dhow yards there are far more interesting and easier to get to. The fishers' shacks lie along the road, beyond the concrete walls of the dhow yards.

To reach Doha Village, take the Al-Jahra Rd west from Kuwait City and follow the signs for Entertainment City. When you reach the roundabout just before the entrance to Entertainment City make a left-hand turn (by now you will have started to see a lot of small signs for the sailing ship exhibition). The sailing ship exhibition will be on your left after approximately 3.5 km. Another 700m brings you to a fork in the road; keep left at the fork and you will almost immediately find yourself in the Doha dhow yard.

KUWAIT

Oman

Oman

Long known as the hermit of the Middle East, the Sultanate of Oman is slowly emerging from its shell. Only a few years ago the sultanate required even other Gulf Arabs to obtain visas. But tourism has brought an ever-increasing number of visitors to the country. In 1995 the government estimated that 40,000 tourists visited the sultanate that year.

Oman is quite different from the other Gulf States. Indeed, occupying the southeastern corner of the Arabian Peninsula it, technically, is not a Gulf country at all.

In contrast to the vast desert wasteland of Saudi Arabia or the tiny city-states of the Gulf, Oman is a land of dramatic mountains and long unspoiled beaches. Its capital, Muscat, does not have the nouveau-riche feel that typifies much of the rest of the Gulf. Oman's development since the ascension of Sultan Qaboos Bin Said is all the more striking both because the country's oil reserves are so limited and because under the previous sultan, Said Bin Taimur, the country was almost hermetically sealed off from the outside world. But Said's xenophobic rule was very much the exception in Omani history.

During the 17th, 18th and 19th centuries Oman was an imperial power which vied first with Portugal and later with Britain for influence in the Gulf, the Indian Ocean and along the coasts of India and East Africa.

Tourism is still a new concept for the Omanis and the country has taken a cautious approach to its development. In many ways Oman remains the most traditional country in the Gulf though, at least on the coast, its traditions are often more outward looking than it's given credit for.

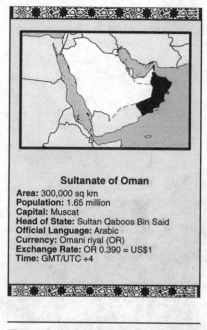

Sultanate of Oman
Area: 300,000 sq km
Population: 1.65 million
Capital: Muscat
Head of State: Sultan Qaboos Bin Said
Official Language: Arabic
Currency: Omani riyal (OR)
Exchange Rate: OR 0.390 = US$1
Time: GMT/UTC +4

Facts about the Country

HISTORY
The Land of Frankincense

As in much of the rest of Arabia the earliest known settlements in Oman date from the 3rd millennium BC. The harbours of Oman's Batinah Coast were on the margins of the trade routes which linked Mesopotamia to the Indus valley. The area did, however, supply a valuable commodity to the rest of the ancient world. An empire known as Magan developed along the Batinah, exploiting the rich veins of copper found in the hills around Sohar. Magan was originally a part of the Akkadian Empire (centred near Sumer, in modern southern Iraq) but it broke away from Akkad's control in the middle of the 3rd millennium BC establishing itself as an independent power. It came to dominate the ancient world's copper trade, supplying the precious metal to the powerful kingdoms of Elam (in modern-day southern Iran) and Sumer, both of whom used it to make weapons and neither of whom possessed any copper deposits of their own.

Magan's copper mines were centred on the inland towns of Lasail and Arja and are thought to have produced between 48 and 60 tonnes per year until the Middle Ages, when the trade finally petered off.

The region's economy declined over the centuries, and sometime around 563 BC Northern Oman was incorporated into the Achaemenid Persian Empire. Later it was dominated by two other Persian dynasties – the Parthians and Sassanians.

It was not until long after Magan's glory days, and not along the Batinah Coast but in the far south of the country, that Oman again became economically important to the ancient world.

The area that now makes up much of Yemen and southern Oman was a rich centre of ancient commerce because it was the source of most of the world's frankincense (see boxed story on frankincense). The frankincense trade made South Arabia wealthy, and brought its inhabitants into contact with merchants from the Mediterranean, the Levant, Persia and India.

Though sailors from Oman are known to have reached India as far back as 100 AD, the northern part of what is now Oman really became important during the first generations of the Islamic era, a period during which Sohar, on the Batinah Coast, was the area's most important settlement.

Omanis pride themselves on being among the earliest converts to Islam. The Prophet sent envoys to the rulers of Sohar, who accepted Islam as did many of their subjects. Among the envoys was Khalid Bin Al-Waleed, who was to become one of early Islam's greatest generals. Shortly after their conversion in the mid-7th century the Omani tribes came under the rule of the Umayyad

Highlights

If you are in Oman for only one day between planes or on a quick business trip, you absolutely must not miss the Mutrah souk. This is undoubtedly one of the best traditional markets left anywhere in Arabia. Those with a little more time, and a desire to learn more about Oman's history, should take in the Sultan's Armed Forces Museum in the capital's Bait Al-Falaj district.

Outside Muscat try to see the old fortress and the market in Nizwa and the fort at Jabrin. Sur, with its fortress and dhow building yard, is the most interesting northern coastal town after Muscat. A circuit of the north's old forts is a good way to see a lot of the country in only a few days.

If you have the time and money, however, the best place to visit outside Muscat is the Musandem Peninsula, the enclave of Omani territory guarding the southern edge of the Strait of Hormuz. The Musandem was, until recently, a military zone and off-limits to tourists. Today all you need is a plane ticket or the taxi fare. For striking scenery there is no place in Oman, maybe none in Arabia outside Yemen, that beats it.

Visitors to the south should be sure to make side-trips to both Job's tomb, with its dramatic views over Salalah, and to the ruins of Khor Rouri, once the centre of the ancient world's frankincense trade. ∎

dynasty. They adopted the doctrines of Ibadi Islam in the late 7th or early 8th century (see Religion at the end of this section). Ibadi Islam in its earliest and strictest form was violently opposed to the idea of the Muslim community being ruled by a hereditary monarch.

Around 746 AD, Talib Al-Haqq led the Omani Ibadis in a revolt against the Umayyads. Despite the inherent disadvantages of a revolt whose leaders came from a relatively remote and isolated part of the Islamic world, the uprising proved to be remarkably successful. The Umayyads had already been weakened by years of internal strife, and the Ibadis swept out of Oman into the rest of Arabia, conquering Medina by 748. Their triumph was short-lived. Within months the Umayyads reconquered Medina, but shortly thereafter their decaying dynasty

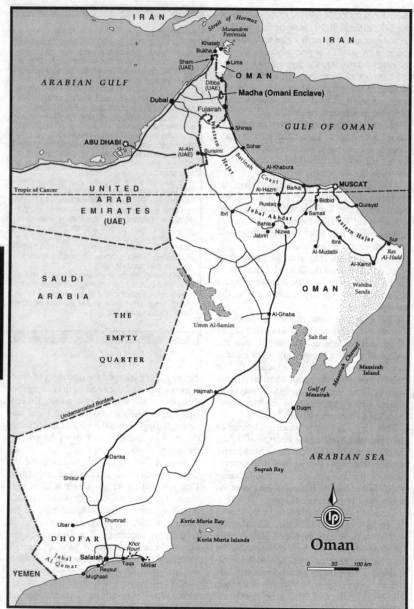

OMAN

Oman

Frankincense

Dhofar, Oman's southernmost region, is one of the few places in the world where the trees which produce frankincense will grow. Frankincense is an aromatic gum which is obtained by making incisions in the trunks of trees of certain species of the *Boswellia* genus. These trees grow only in southern Oman, the Wadi Hadhramaut in Yemen and northern Somalia.

The incense has a natural oil content, which means that it burns well. It also has medicinal qualities. This combination and its relative scarcity made it one of the ancient world's most sought after substances. (The frankincense and myrrh offered as gifts to the infant Jesus were, at the time, far more valuable than the gold.) Frankincense became crucial to the religious rites of almost every people in the known world. The temples of Egypt, Jerusalem and Rome were all major customers. Pliny, writing in the 1st century AD, claimed that control of the frankincense trade had made the South Arabians the richest people on earth.

At the height of the trade in the 2nd century AD, some 3000 tonnes of frankincense was moving each year, mostly by sea, from South Arabia to Greece and Rome. The trade was centred on Sumhuram, which the Greeks called Moscha and which is now known as Khor Rouri. Today its ruins are a short drive from Salalah, the capital of Dhofar and the second-largest city in modern Oman. Though it declined after the 3rd century AD, the incense trade kept South Arabia relatively wealthy well into the 6th century. ■

was overthrown, this time by the Abbasids, who went on to build their new capital at Baghdad.

Unusually, compared to some of the other areas conquered in the first few generations of Islam, the Arabisation of Oman began several centuries before the time of the Prophet. Around the beginning of the Christian era a number of Arab tribes migrated from the western portions of South Arabia (modern Yemen) to what is now southwestern Oman. The coming of Islam in the 7th and 8th centuries accelerated the spread of Arabic as the primary means of communication and within a few generations Oman was the predominantly Arabic-speaking country it is today.

Oman managed to remain independent of the Abbasids. It also remained loyal to the Ibadi strain of Islam which is still dominant in the country today. It was precisely Oman's remoteness from the rest of the Islamic world that allowed the Ibadis to survive as a sect long after they had been suppressed in other parts of the Muslim world.

Building an Empire

The Omani Ibadis elected their first *imam* (prayer leader) in 749. Even at this early stage this represented a break with strict Ibadi doctrine. Still, a hereditary imamate emerged, lasting into the late 9th century. Though the Abbasids then managed to suppress the imamate per se, Oman itself managed to remain relatively free of Abbasid control. Until the Portuguese arrived in the Indian Ocean in 1607 the Omanis had few naval power rivals in the area.

A recurrent theme of Omani history is the split between the country's coastal and inland areas. In the 9th century Nizwa became the capital, indicating that the interior areas had political sway over the coasts. But by the 10th century the balance had shifted and Sohar, on the Batinah Coast, was the largest city. The coastal regions have almost always had the upper hand, both politically and economically, ever since. The coast's trade-derived wealth was formidable. Omani merchants were dealing with China and the Malay Peninsula on a regular basis by the 9th century. Sohar was at its height as a trading centre during this period. In the 10th century the Arab geographer Al-Ishtaraki described Sohar as 'the most prosperous and wealthiest city in the entire region of Islam'.

Sohar was succeeded as the country's principal city by Qalhat (18 km north-west of modern Sur) which prospered until the 14th or 15th century. Though Qalhat was the main city in the country, the kings of the day lived in Hormuz, the island in the middle of the strait with the same name, which is still the geographical key to control of the Gulf.

The Portuguese first appeared in the Gulf in 1506. They quickly realised, as would the

OMAN

British some three centuries later, that control of the Gulf was vital for any European power with imperial designs on India. They occupied Oman in 1507 and, predictably, made Hormuz their main base of operations.

The Portuguese seem to have treated Oman as little more than a way-station on the route to India. Contrary to popular belief, the country is not littered with Portuguese forts. Aside from the Muscat and Mutrah forts and five bronze cannons at Al-Hazm, there are few physical reminders of the 143 years during which they controlled Oman's coastline. This dearth of Portuguese ruins strongly implies that Lisbon's interest in the country did not extend much beyond the protection of its supply lines.

It was, however, the Portuguese who first brought Muscat to prominence when, in 1622, they made it their main base in the region after being driven out of Hormuz. They built up and fortified the town but were not able to hold it. In 1650 Imam Sultan Bin Saif expelled the Portuguese from Muscat and Oman. Omani independence is usually dated from this victory, by which reckoning Oman is the oldest independent state in the Arab world.

The recapture of Muscat marked the beginning of a great expansion of Omani power throughout the Gulf and the Indian Ocean. Almost immediately Omani merchants began to build up their influence along the East African coast. Politically, the Ibadi imamate, though still based in the agricultural area around Jabal Akhdar, controlled much of the country under a new line of imams descended from the Al-Ya'ribi clan.

Four years before the expulsion of the Portuguese the imamate, which then controlled other parts of the coast, had signed its first treaty with the British who were then vying with the Portuguese for influence in the area. The Treaty of 1646, signed with the British East India Company, covered trading rights and allowed British merchants to practice their religion. It also established a separate judicial system for British subjects

and employees of the company. The Dutch East India Company got similar rights in 1670 but was soon forced out of Oman by the British and the French.

Throughout all this, the Omanis retained their independence, which is a lot more than can be said for much of the rest of the Gulf over the next 300 years. Their growing empire in East Africa, where Omani and British merchants competed in much the same way as the British and the Dutch competed in the Gulf, gave the Omanis an economic power base which none of Arabia's shaikhs could match.

Far from finding themselves under the heel of imperialism, by the end of the 18th century the Omanis were ruling their own far-flung empire. At its peak in the 19th century, Oman controlled both Mombasa and Zanzibar and operated trading posts even further down the African coast. It also controlled portions of what are now India and Pakistan. It was not until the British withdrew from India in 1947 that Oman surrendered its last colonial outpost at Gwadar, in what is now Pakistan, near that country's border with Iran.

In 1749, Ahmed Bin Said, the first ruler of the present dynasty (the Al-Busaid), was elected imam. In 1786, with maritime trade becoming more and more important to the empire, the capital was formally moved from the interior to Muscat. It was around this time that the Al-Busaid adopted the title of sultan, which implied temporal authority in a way that the religious title of imam didn't.

Treaties providing for British protection of the sultanate were signed in 1798 and 1800. These involved the British government, as opposed to the East India Company, and unlike the treaties Britain signed with the Gulf shaikhs later in the 19th century, they were neither imposed by force nor did they turn Oman into a protectorate. Oman, for one thing, was better able to defend itself than were the Gulf shaikhdoms. For their part the British were concerned mainly with protecting their own supply lines to India which were then being threatened by the French, who had just occupied Egypt.

The treaties marked the beginning of a special relationship between Britain and Oman which continues to this day. They were later supplemented by similar 'peace, friendship and navigation' treaties in 1891, 1939 and 1951.

The Omani Empire reached its peak in the mid-19th century under Sultan Said Bin Sultan (reigned 1804-56), who added Dhofar to his realm and pushed the sultanate's control far down the East African coast. The sultan commanded an army of 6500 men and a navy which included 15 ships. Traders under his flag sailed the globe. One ship, the *Sultana*, visited New York in 1840 (a portrait of the vessel's captain still hangs in New York's City Hall) and another of Said's vessels called at London in 1842. When he died the empire was divided between two of his sons. One became the Sultan of Zanzibar, whose progeny ruled Said's African colonies well into the 20th century, while the other became known as the Sultan of Muscat and Oman – the coast and interior of today's sultanate which were then regarded as two separate realms ruled by one monarch.

Muscat & Oman

The split between Muscat and Oman had been confirmed in the late 18th century when conservative tribes in the interior elected their own imam. They apparently felt that the sultan in Muscat had grown too liberal and were certainly dissatisfied with the re-introduction of a hereditary monarchy, an act which went against strict Ibadi tradition.

In the 19th century it became common for the positions of imam and sultan to be held by different men. The Imam of Oman increasingly came to represent the political interests of the interior against those of the coast though, in keeping with Ibadi teachings, the post of imam was not always filled. Despite his title the sultan's writ rarely extended very far inland. From 1868 to 1873 one sultan managed to claim both posts, but this was unusual. The result was that Muscat's control of the interior depended to a great extent on the tribes' opinion of the sultan of the day.

Following Sultan Said's death, the division of the empire cut Muscat off from some of its most lucrative domains, causing the country to stagnate economically during the late 19th century. The British exacerbated this situation by pressing the sultan to end the trade in slaves and arms for which Oman had long been known. This left the sultan a great deal poorer and lack of money made the interior even harder to control. This episode also highlighted the extent of the British influence in the sultanate. Many of the sultan's advisors were British and the army itself (known as the Muscat and Oman Levies) was commanded by British officers.

In the early 20th century the imams started holding more and more power in the interior, while the sultans' power decreased.

When Sultan Faisal Bin Turki died in 1913 the interior's tribes refused to recognise his son, Taimur Bin Faisal, as imam. In 1915, with the sultan's control still tenuous and tensions running high, a group of tribes tried to take over Muscat but were pushed back by the British. Things remained unsettled until 1920 when the sultan and the imam signed a treaty at Seeb. Under the treaty, the sultan recognised the imam as a spiritual leader and allowed him limited temporal jurisdiction over the interior without formally yielding his own claim to sovereignty. For the next 35 years the treaty was the main document governing relations between the rival leaders.

The treaty's weakness was that it avoided the one really important question: namely, who had ultimate authority over the inland areas. In 1938 a new sultan, Said Bin Taimur, came to power. When he sought to extend his writ into the interior in the early '50s the British backed him, largely because they believed that there might be oil there. To prospect for it, they needed the sultan to have effective control of the area and Oman's undefined borders with Saudi Arabia and Abu Dhabi to be clearly marked.

The territorial dispute centred on the Buraimi Oasis, which now straddles the border between Oman and the United Arab Emirates (UAE) but was then under Saudi control. In 1952 Said, the British and the

OMAN

imam managed a rare show of unity in ejecting the Saudis from Buraimi. But the Saudis continued to lay claim to the area and, in 1954, Said concluded that the imam had taken the Saudis' side in the dispute. This brought to a head the entire question of sovereignty and the Treaty of Seeb. Said's forces occupied Ibri, cutting the imam off from Buraimi. Having been outflanked on the ground the imam, Ghalib Bin Ali, sought to outflank Said politically by applying to the Arab League for recognition as ruler of an independent state.

In December 1955, Said responded by occupying the imamate's dual capitals of Nizwa and Rustaq. He then annexed the whole of the interior on the grounds that Ghalib had violated the Seeb treaty. The Arab League was generally sympathetic to Ghalib's membership application (an attitude which was probably more anti-British than pro-imamate) but was in no position to help him. The British, by contrast, were very much in a position to help Said, in return for securing oil concessions for British companies.

Ghalib was allowed to go into exile in his home village but his brother, Talib, escaped to Cairo and returned 18 months later to continue the civil war. The revolt was short-lived. With British help the sultan was back in control within three months, though the imam and his brother held out from a base near Jabal Akhdar until early 1959.

Said Bin Taimur (reigned 1938-70) was a fascinating figure, 'an arch-reactionary of great personal charm', in the words of the British writer Peter Mansfield. He was opposed to any sort of change and sought to isolate Oman from the modern world. Under his rule, a country which only a century earlier had rivalled the empire builders of Europe became a medieval anachronism.

Said personally issued all visas. He forbade travel inland by residents of the coast and vice versa. He opposed education, which he saw as a threat to his power. Most Omanis were not allowed to leave the country and the few who managed to get out were rarely allowed to return.

Two of the positive aspects of Said's rule were that he did manage to clear Oman's then-large foreign debts and also managed to bring some semblance of political stability to the country.

What little contact Said had with the outside world came through his British advisors and Muscat's trading families. Some of the traders were foreign and some were Omani, but all had roots in the society going back several generations. Said allowed them to establish commercial empires in Muscat based on hugely lucrative monopolies for the import of the few goods that he, grudgingly, regarded as crucial to his survival. In exchange, the trading families tacitly agreed to stay out of politics and not to import anything which Said felt smacked of progress or the west (eg eye glasses, radios and books). That one of the most prominent of these trading firms still bears the distinctly un-Omani name of WJ Towell & Company testifies that Oman was not always an economic backwater sealed off from the outside world. (WJ Towell & Co was founded in the 1860s by an American adventurer who later sold out to his Scottish assistant who in turn sold the company to his Indian-born assistant.)

Through customs receipts, the merchants also provided Said with most of the country's income of about UK£50,000 per year, a sum which had changed little since the turn of the century. A few merchants were getting rich, but trade had stagnated in the country as a whole and most of the population relied on agriculture or fishing (both concentrated on the north coast) for their livelihood.

Sultan Qaboos

In 1958 Said boarded himself up in his palace at Salalah, which he rarely left thereafter. The formation of a nationalist rebel group, the Dhofar Liberation Front (DLF), in 1962 did little to change this. The DLF's battle against the state, known as the Dhofar rebellion, began in 1965 and was far more serious than Said's earlier clashes with the imamate. Over time (and, after 1967, under

South Yemeni influence) the DLF moved from a pan-Arabist toward a more doctrinaire Marxist ideology. In 1966 a dissident group of Dhofari soldiers almost succeeded in assassinating Said.

The combination of the ever-escalating rebellion and Said's refusal to spend any of the money he had begun to receive from oil exports in 1967 soon began to try even London's patience. In July 1970 Said was overthrown by his only son, Qaboos, in a bloodless palace coup. The British denied any involvement in or advance knowledge of the coup, but this is hard to believe as British officers effectively commanded the army at the time. Said spent the rest of his life living in exile in a London hotel.

Sultan Qaboos Bin Said was only 30 years old when he came to power. He had been educated abroad, including a stint at Sandhurst, the British military academy. Returning to Oman in 1964 he spent most of the next six years under house arrest in Salalah. On assuming power, Qaboos flew to Muscat where he promptly repealed his father's oppressive social restrictions, surrounded himself with foreign – mostly British – advisors and began to modernise Oman's semi-feudal economy.

In a speech delivered on his arrival at Muscat's airport Qaboos said he had seized power after watching 'with growing dismay and increasing anger the failure to use the new-found wealth of this country for the needs of its people'. He added that his government's 'first aim must be to remove unnecessary restrictions under which you, my people, now suffer, and to produce as rapidly as possible a happier and more secure future for all of you'.

There was a certain urgency in Qaboos' programme to bring the country into the 20th century. Oman's oil revenues were, and still are, small and its resources limited. Qaboos saw the need to move quickly if the oil wealth was to have any significant effect on his people's lives. He pushed localisation of the workforce much harder than the rulers of the other Gulf countries. Oman, he knew, needed foreign

aid and know-how, but it could hardly afford the luxury of the armies of foreign labourers who had built the infrastructure of places such as Kuwait.

Despite Qaboos' seeming desire to make a clean break with the past, the Dhofar rebellion continued unabated. In 1973, the sultan asked Iran for help in quelling the rebellion. As the rebels were receiving aid from Marxist South Yemen, the Shah of Iran, who was in the process of grinding down his own country's communist party, was only too happy to oblige. Qaboos also received assistance from several hundred British troops, including elite SAS units. By 1976 the rebels, never very great in number to begin with, had been reduced to a few bands operating out of South Yemen. The rebellion only ended, however, when Oman and South Yemen established diplomatic relations in 1982 and the Aden government cut off its assistance to the rebels.

In foreign affairs Qaboos has carved out a reputation for himself as a maverick. In spite of Oman's past military ties with the Shah he has managed to maintain friendly relations with post-revolutionary Iran. Oman was also one of only two Arab countries (the other was Sudan) which refused to break diplomatic ties with Egypt after it signed a peace treaty with Israel in 1979. In late 1993 the sultan became the first Gulf leader to welcome a representative of Israel to his country when Prime Minister Yitzak Rabin paid a brief visit.

In developing his country, the sultan has shown an acute desire to preserve as much as possible of Oman's traditional character. Old port-cities like Muscat and Mutrah have been modernised without being bulldozed out of existence. The construction of modern housing and office blocks around Greater Muscat has been confined to areas like Qurm or Ruwi, which had few, if any, inhabitants 25 years ago. This pattern has also been reflected in many provincial cities. One of the reasons why Oman has been so slow and cautious in opening up to tourism is this wish to preserve much of the country's traditional culture.

OMAN

GEOGRAPHY

Oman has the most diverse geography of the Arab Gulf States. It is approximately 300,000 sq km in area, although this is a rough estimate since the portion of the border running through the Empty Quarter desert is undefined. Oman occupies the south-eastern corner of the Arabian Peninsula and boasts some 1700 km of coastline. It's territory also includes the Musandem Peninsula, which overlooks the Strait of Hormuz. The Musandem Peninsula is separated from the rest of the country by the east coast areas of the UAE, though Oman controls a tiny enclave of territory entirely surrounded by the UAE in and around the village of Madha. Oman also includes a number of islands, the most important of which is Massirah.

Much of the country's population is concentrated in the strip of land along the coast of the Gulf of Oman, though the largest city, after the capital, is Salalah in the far south on the Arabian Sea coast. The northern coastal strip, known as the Batinah Coast, is a sand and gravel plain separated from the rest of Arabia by the Hajar Mountains, on the other side of which are the seemingly endless sands of the Empty Quarter. The highest peak in the country is Jabal Akhdar (the 'green mountain') at 2980m. The term Jabal Akhdar, however, generally refers to the entire Hajar range as it moves through north-central Oman, rather than to a single peak. Another, lower, range of mountains, the Dhofar Mountains, rise behind the southern coastal plain.

Oman also has two large areas of salt flats. The smaller of the two is Umm Al-Samim, at the 'elbow' where the country's desert border with Saudi Arabia makes a sharp turn. The other is a huge area of the coast opposite Massirah Island and just south of the Wahiba Sands, the sandy desert area popular with tourists and expatriates for 4WD weekend trips.

The mountainous areas of the interior and the Musandem Peninsula are strikingly beautiful and fiercely rugged while the southern coast is tropical in appearance. The Batinah Coast becomes progressively more barren as one moves south along it from the UAE border toward Sur.

CLIMATE

Oman's varied geography makes for a wide range of climatic conditions. Coconuts are grown in the southern coastal areas while the highlands around Jabal Akhdar produce roses and grapes.

Muscat is hot and very humid from mid-March until October and pleasantly warm from October to March. In the Salalah area, humid weather with temperatures approaching 30°C is common even in December. The Salalah area gets drenched by the monsoon rains every year from June to September.

If you are already in Oman and want weather information dial ☎ 1103 for a local forecast.

FLORA & FAUNA

Oman has one of the world's most rigorously green governments. The sultan has devoted much attention to the country's plant life and in early 1990 his horticultural activities even led to a new species of flower being named after him. The government runs a scheme for protecting coastal areas and there are a number of nature preserves, known as National Protected Areas, scattered around the country. The most accessible area is the Qurm Public Park & Nature Preserve, in Greater Muscat.

The sultanate also has a fascinating array of animals ranging from various sorts of molluscs (several new varieties of sea shells have been discovered on Oman's beaches) to a herd of rare Arabian oryx, bred for release into the wild on a special farm owned by the sultan. An area has also been set aside around Ras Al-Hadd, the easternmost tip of the Arabian Peninsula, as a protected breeding ground for the giant sea turtles which live in the Indian Ocean and come ashore in Oman each year to lay their eggs. There is a bird sanctuary in the south of the country, near Salalah, and a sanctuary for the preservation of the Arabian tahr (a kind of wild goat) at a remote inland mountain area known as Jabal

Aswad. The tahr nearly became extinct in the 1970s but are now thriving. The government runs a breeding centre for endangered species at Bait Al-Barakah, west of Seeb, where, in addition to the tahr, Arabian wolves, striped hyaenas and Arabian leopards are raised for eventual reintroduction into the wild. Even the lowly houbara, a bird hunted nearly into oblivion elsewhere in Arabia, is protected in Oman.

Another bird that is protected in Oman is the sooty falcon, a species of grey falcon which nests in Oman every year in April and May. The birds also breed in the Daymaniyat Islands, off the Omani coast, from May to October every year. This site, too, is protected.

To visit any of the conservation areas you will need special permission from the Ministry of National Heritage in Muscat. See the Muscat section later for more information.

You will also need special permission if you want to visit Ras Al-Hadd during the turtle breeding season. Four different species of turtles breed in Oman every year, mostly at Ras Al-Hadd though some also come ashore at Massirah Island. These are the loggerhead turtle, the green turtle, the Olive Ridley and the hawksbill. Only the females come ashore and they do not remain long enough to see their eggs hatch. The newborn turtles that make it from the nest to the sea, eluding various predators along the way, will spend their entire lives at sea until the females among them return to the beach to begin the cycle again.

GOVERNMENT

The government is very much a one-person show. The sultan is the ultimate authority. National Day, for example, is celebrated each year on the Sultan's Birthday (18 November) and not on the anniversary of his assumption of power (23 July). The sultan is also prime minister, foreign minister and defence minister (lower-ranking ministers of state run the latter two ministries on a day-to-day basis). Day-to-day governing is carried out through a Cabinet appointed by the sultan.

The sultan married in 1976 but later divorced. He has no children and no designated heir. Speculation about the succession is not, however, one of Muscat's favourite parlour games. In Oman this simply is not done.

There's an oft-quoted remark by the sultan to the effect that the country is not yet ready for western-style parliamentary democracy and that no purpose would be served by setting up a sham parliament. The implication is that, over a period of time, the country will move toward a less personalised system of government.

In January 1992, an elected Consultative Council, or *majlis ash-shura*, convened for the first time, replacing an appointed State Consultative Council which had existed since 1981. Though a far cry from a western parliament, the Council is widely seen as a first step toward broader participation in government. It mainly comments on draft laws and other such topics as the sultan chooses to put in front of it.

ECONOMY

In 1970, when development in much of the rest of the Gulf was already well under way, Oman still had only 10 km of surfaced road (between Muscat and Mutrah). There were only three primary schools in the country and no secondary schools. There was one hospital which was run by US missionaries. Today, Oman has a modern system of roads, housing and health care to rival that of any other Gulf state.

Though the economy is essentially oil-based, Oman's oil production is relatively modest by Gulf standards. Agriculture in the inland areas and fishing on the coast continue to be important sources of income for much of the population.

The government has been more successful than any other in the region at 'localising' its economy, that is, replacing foreigners with Omanis wherever possible. It is far more common to see Omanis in service positions or doing manual jobs than it is to see other Gulf Arabs doing similar jobs.

OMAN

POPULATION & PEOPLE

Oman's population is estimated to be about 1.2 million, concentrated in Muscat and along the Batinah Coast. While Omanis are Arabs, the country's long trading history has led to a great deal of mingling and intermarriage of Omani Arabs with other ethnic groups. There has been an Indian merchant community in Muscat for at least 200 years and, in the north, it is also common to find people who are at least partly of Persian or Baluchi ancestry.

EDUCATION

Free primary and secondary education are one of the mainstays of Oman's modernisation programme. Sultan Qaboos University on the outskirts of Muscat is the country's main post-secondary institution.

The government has also been working hard in recent years to eradicate illiteracy, which remains high among older people living in the interior.

ARTS

Oman has devoted a great deal of effort to preserving its traditional arts, dance, music and culture. While it is possible that you may come across traditional dancing simply while driving down a road, the best place to observe such things is usually at one of the many museums scattered around greater Muscat. There are no regular programmes of, for example, folk dancing, though occasional performances are announced in the local press, usually timed to coincide with some sort of official cultural exchange programme.

For information on Omani craftwork see Things to Buy later in this chapter.

SOCIETY & CONDUCT
Traditional Lifestyle

Despite the modern appearance of Muscat's Qurm, Khuwair, Ruwi and Medinat Qaboos districts, much of the country, including parts of the capital area, remains intensely traditional. Every spring the sultan spends several weeks driving around the country on a 'meet the people tour'. This is covered extensively on Omani TV. A few minutes viewing one of the reports will show you the extent to which the day-to-day life of the average Omani, living in a town in the interior or a fishing village on the coast, is close to what it would have been centuries ago. Omanis seem to be adept at assimilating what they want or need of modern life, enjoying its benefits without letting the new technology adversely affect their own lives and values.

Most Omanis wear traditional dress on a day-to-day basis though, contrary to a widely held belief among foreigners, the law does not require that they do so. The law does mandate, however, the wearing of traditional dress at work by all Omanis employed by the government (a not insignificant portion of the employed population).

For men, traditional dress consists of a loose *dishdasha*, or floor-length shirt-dress. These are usually light blue in colour though white, brown and other colours are sometimes seen. Omani men also wear brimless, circular hats with abstract patterns embroidered on them in a variety of colours. Sometimes the hats are replaced by a turban, particularly in coastal areas.

Women's dress is far more colourful than the simple black cloaks common in much of the rest of the Gulf region. Colourfully printed dresses are wrapped with even more colourfully printed shawls and veils. The patterns and colour schemes of both the dresses and the shawls/veils varies by region.

Dos & Don'ts

Many Omanis, even in Muscat, still live in very traditional circumstances, and they're generous and welcoming to foreigners. However, as Oman has only been open to the outside world just over 25 years, a degree of sensitivity is required. Taking photographs anywhere in Oman is a sensitive matter and taking pictures of women is almost always out of bounds. In rural areas it is important to dress modestly. The taboos are no different from those that apply in other Gulf States (see Dos & Don'ts in the Facts about the Region chapter).

Also note that outsiders are definitely not welcome in the Lewara quarter of Muscat's Mutrah district, where many of the capital's Shiite Muslims live. There are usually a couple of people sitting in the gateway which leads from the Mutrah Corniche into the Lewara quarter and their manner tends to be polite but firm.

Non-Muslims are not permitted to enter mosques in Oman.

RELIGION

Most Omanis follow the Ibadi sect of Islam. The Ibadis are one of the Muslim world's few remaining Khariji sects, and are a product of Islam's earliest fundamentalist movement.

In 657 Ali, the fourth caliph and the Prophet's cousin and son-in-law, agreed to peace talks with his main rival for the leadership of the Muslim community. The Kharijis (seceders) were originally followers of Ali but broke with him over a point of principle. They believed that by agreeing to discuss the leadership question he had compromised on a matter of faith. This compromise, they held, rendered him unworthy of both their loyalty and the leadership itself.

Various Khariji sects developed over the next 200 years, all generally adhering to the principle that Muslims should follow the adult male who was best able to lead the community while upholding the law. If the leader failed to uphold the law he could be replaced almost instantly. Most Kharijis also rejected out of hand the idea that any person could have an hereditary claim on the leadership of the Muslim community. The various Khariji sects differed largely in their interpretation of the term 'upholding the law' and how strictly pure the leader had to be to remain worthy of the community's loyalty. The leader, or imam, was to be chosen by the community as a whole. The Ibadis were among the more moderate of the Khariji sects.

The Ibadis are one of the few Khariji sects which has survived into the 20th century. They take their name from Abdullah Bin Ibad Al-Murri Al-Tamimi, a theologian who was probably from Najd, in modern Saudi Arabia, but who did most of his important teaching while living in Basra (in present-day southern Iraq) during the late 7th century. His teachings seem to have caught on in Oman partly because they touched the right political chords at a time when the Omani tribes were rebelling against the Damascus-based Umayyad caliphate. Ibadism came to thrive on the edges of the Muslim world – the only other place where a really strong Ibadi dynasty was ever established was western Algeria in the 8th century.

A hereditary Ibadi imamate emerged in Oman from the mid-8th to the late-9th century, when it was suppressed by the Abbasid Empire which had replaced the Umayyads as the predominant power in the Muslim world. This adoption of a system of hereditary rule is one of the elements which distinguishes Ibadism from the more strict (and now defunct) Khariji sects, though Ibadis still retain the broad Khariji rejection of any embellishment of the basic pattern of worship laid down by the Prophet.

In one form or another the imamate continued in the more remote parts of Oman's interior until well into the 20th century (see the History section earlier in this chapter).

LANGUAGE

Arabic is the official language though English is widely spoken in business circles. In the northern coastal areas you can find traders and sailors who also speak Farsi and/or Urdu, in addition to a large number of expatriates from the Indian subcontinent.

See Language in the Facts about the Region chapter for a list of useful Arabic words and phrases.

Facts for the Visitor

PLANNING
When to Go

Mid-October to February or mid-March, when the weather is most temperate, is the best time to visit. The monsoon season in the

OMAN

south is from June to September, and while you probably do not want to be in Salalah during the rains, it is definitely worth a visit in October when everything in Dhofar is still lush and green.

Maps

The best map is the Bartholomew *Map of the Sultanate of Oman*. It has a light blue cover with a picture of the Seeb clock tower on one side and palm trees on the other. Unfortunately it is pretty hard to find, and it's even harder to get hold of a copy in English. Its inset maps of Salalah and the various districts of Greater Muscat are excellent and the road map of the country as a whole is by far the most up-to-date one.

The Oxford *Map of Oman*, available in most hotel bookshops in Muscat, is not quite as good but you can navigate well enough with it. When using either of these maps remember that a lot of the roads shown as 'projected' have now been built. Use the country map at the beginning of this chapter to double-check the extent of road construction at press time with whatever either of these maps shows.

The Bartholomew *Map of the Arabian Gulf* is OK on northern Oman. The larger Bartholomew *Map of the Arabian Peninsula* makes a nice wall-hanging (as do a number of other similar maps) but the scale is too large for it to be of much use as a road map.

What to Bring

Sunglasses and a hat are the first essentials, plus a good sunscreen for anyone who burns easily, especially in the southern part of the country. These, and anything else you might need, are all readily available in Muscat. See the Regional Facts for the Visitor chapter for more general notes on essentials for any Gulf trip.

TOURIST OFFICES

There are no tourist offices in Oman. See the Muscat section for information on tour companies and programmes offered by the various large hotels.

VISAS & DOCUMENTS

Visas

Unless you are a citizen of another Gulf country you need a visa to enter Oman. Omani visa regulations have eased considerably since the first edition of this book. It is now generally possible for citizens of western countries (North America, Western and Central Europe, Japan, Australia, New Zealand etc) to obtain business and tourist visas at most Omani embassies overseas. Applying for the visa in your home country, or in a foreign country where you hold a permanent residence or a work visa, is not necessary but does seem to speed up the procedure, as does making your application in person rather than by post.

Wherever you apply you will need to produce several (probably four) photographs and fill out two or three copies of the application. Showing an onward or return ticket does not appear to be a requirement, though I've heard of a few people being asked to produce these, particularly in New Delhi. Visas are not cheap. Costs will vary according to your nationality, but the standard two-year multiple-entry tourist visa will generally cost around US$35 to US$40 in the local currency.

Business visas are usually valid for between three months and one year (again, depending on your nationality) and allow multiple entries. They also require a supporting letter from your company and, possibly, from any company you plan to visit while in Oman. Business visas cost around US$60.

Processing either kind of visa usually takes between three and six working days. Tourist visas often allow you to remain in Oman for as long as six months at a stretch. Business visas generally limit travellers to three weeks per stay.

When filling out the visa application pay careful attention to the section asking where you plan to enter Oman. You are not bound to the entry point or points you declare here, but if you check only Seeb airport there is the possibility that you will receive a visa allowing entry and exit by air only.

You may be told by the embassy that an

ordinary tourist visa is not valid for entry by land unless it specifically says so. However, I had no trouble entering and leaving Oman by land several times through three different border posts while researching this edition of this book. The guards at the posts all said that any tourist visa was valid at any post unless it specifically had something to the contrary (like 'By Air Only') written on it.

If your passport shows any evidence of travel to Israel you will be denied entry to Oman.

Hotel-Sponsored Visas If you don't carry a western passport or are not conveniently close to an Omani embassy it is also possible to obtain a visa through most of the country's four and five-star hotels. This process usually takes about a week, though if you hold a passport from a country that provides Oman with a lot of low-cost labourers (Egypt, Pakistan, India) it could take substantially longer. The main drawback to this method is its expense.

The procedure for getting a visa through a hotel it is pretty straightforward. Fax the hotel, make a reservation and send them a copy of the first page (the part with your photo and personal data) of your passport. You might also have to provide a list of countries visited in the last year and you may be asked to mail four photos to the hotel, so try not to do all this at the last minute. Be sure to give the hotel your exact arrival details and a contact number so that they can let you know when your visa is ready. Obviously the hotel is going to charge you for this service, though the cost is likely to be pretty nominal compared to what you are going to pay for the room. The hotel will usually require a three-night minimum stay. The trick of moving to a cheaper hotel – common in the UAE – is not a good idea. It is illegal and the odds on your getting caught are pretty high. Outside of the city in which your visa-issuing hotel is located you can, of course, stay wherever you wish.

The hotels are not actually issuing visas; they are issuing No Objection Certificates

(NOCs). See below for more information on NOCs.

Hotel-sponsored visas do have their drawbacks. Cost aside, the most obvious one is that they are only available through Seeb airport in Muscat. You cannot get a visa through a hotel and then enter the country by land for the simple reason that your visa will be waiting for you at the airport and not at one of the overland crossing points. You should also bear in mind that hotel-sponsored visas are invariably single-entry visas. This means that if, for example, you get your visa through a hotel, make a side trip to the Musandem and then get stuck in Khasab because your return flight to Muscat has been cancelled, you are out of luck – your visa will not allow you to return to the capital by road as this would involve leaving and then re-entering Oman.

If you are going the hotel-sponsored visa route it is absolutely essential that you obtain some written acknowledgment from the hotel that your visa has been approved. If you cannot produce a fax on the hotel's letterhead, or some other official-looking document, quoting a visa or NOC number there is a very good chance that you will not be allowed to board your flight to Muscat.

No Objection Certificate (NOC) The NOC was once the great hurdle that had to be cleared before most travellers could enter Oman. With the government's move toward a relatively straightforward system of tourist and business visas these have largely fallen by the wayside for all but expatriate workers planning to move to Oman.

An NOC is essentially an official piece of paper stating that neither your Omani sponsor nor the government has any objection to your plans to visit the country. Once the NOC is issued you will be informed of its number and your airline will get a telex from the immigration department quoting the number and authorising them to allow you to board your flight to Muscat. Without this telex you almost certainly will not be allowed to board the plane. Having made it to Muscat and stood in the usually huge

OMAN

queue at the NOC window, you will be given a small slip of paper which you take to passport control and trade for a visa all before you have retrieved your luggage.

Visa Extensions In theory these are available to tourists and businesspeople through their hotel/sponsor but you are going to have to come up with a good reason why you need it (especially if you have a tourist visa allowing you to stay in the country for six months!). If you have come in on a tourist visa issued by an Omani embassy you will have to go to the Immigration and Passports Directorate in Muscat.

Exit/re-entry visas are not available for tourists and are not necessary for resident expatriates.

Other Documents
Site Permits A permit from the Ministry of Culture & National Heritage in Muscat is needed to visit most archaeological sites, old forts etc. The permits are free and issued without fuss at the ministry, which is adjacent to the Natural History Museum in the Ministries area of Medinat Qaboos. Head for the 2nd floor of the main building and ask for the forts and castles division. You will have to bring your passport or, if you live in Oman, your residence permit, and you may be asked to specify the date of your visit.

In theory the people in the permit office can also tell you which forts are closed for restoration. However, several places I was told were closed proved to be open. At other sites where restoration work was going on the guards were willing to give me limited access. Consult expats and other travellers as well as the ministry for the latest information as you plan your trip to the interior. Note that the general rule seems to be that groups of more than four or five people have to call ahead to make arrangements to visit a fort or an archaeological site.

Road Permits If you are a foreign resident of Oman you will need a road permit to enter or leave the country by land. This includes trips between the main part of Oman and the

Musandem Peninsula, since these require crossing through the UAE. At the time of writing it was only possible to drive into the UAE as the border with Yemen was closed. Road permits are easily obtained in three to five days through your sponsor. The only problem is that permits are not issued to single women. That means that unmarried female travellers, even expatriates, cannot drive to Dubai for the weekend. More importantly, it also means that they cannot ride up to Dubai with their married friends in their car, let alone catch a ride with a single male friend. This is the only such travel restriction on single and/or unaccompanied women in the sultanate.

Visitors (of either sex) holding a tourist visa do not need a road permit to enter or leave Oman by land.

EMBASSIES
Omani Embassies Abroad
Following is a list of some Omani embassies abroad:

Austria
   Waehringerstrasse 2-4, 1090 Vienna (☎ (222) 316 452)
Bahrain
   Diplomatic Area (near the National Museum), Al-Fatih Highway, Manama (☎ 293 663)
France
   50 Ave de Lena, 75116 Paris (☎ (1) 47 23 01 63)
Germany
   Lindenallee 11, D-5300 Bonn-2 (☎ (22) 835 7031)
Kuwait
   Udailia, St 3, Block 3, House 25, by the Fourth Ring Rd, Kuwait City (☎ 256 1962)
Netherlands
   Koninginnegracht 27, 2514 AB Den Haag (☎ (70) 361 5800)
Qatar
   41 Ibn Al-Qassem St, Villa 7, Hilal District, Doha, fronting on the C Ring Rd (☎ 670 744)
Saudi Arabia
   Al-Ra'id District, behind the petrol station opposite the main gate of King Saud University, Riyadh (☎ (01) 482 3120)
UK
   44B Montpelier Square, London SW7 1JJ (☎ (0171) 584 5332/3)

OMAN

USA
   2342 Massachusetts Ave, NW, Washington DC, 20000 (☎ (202) 387 1980/1)
   866 United Nations Plaza, Suite 540, New York NY (☎ (212) 355 3505)

Foreign Embassies in Oman
See the Muscat section for a list of embassies in the capital.

CUSTOMS
Non-Muslims arriving at Seeb airport can bring in one bottle of booze. Those arriving by road are not permitted to import alcohol. Do not press your luck on this or assume that you can talk your way around it. I've heard a lot of stories about booze being confiscated at the border – especially at the Musandem crossing points.

The customs regulations allow travellers to import a 'reasonable quantity' of cigars, cigarettes and tobacco. There are no unusual regulations regarding things like cameras, computers or cassette players.

Video tapes are another story. The customs officers are extremely concerned about these and you can expect to have any videos you try to import held at customs and scrutinised for several days.

MONEY
Costs
It is not possible to travel truly cheaply in Oman. Budgets of OR 15 per day in Muscat and OR 20 to OR 25 outside the capital, where cheap hotels are much rarer, are about as low as you are likely to achieve. Finding a free bed, however, can cut these figures by one-half to two-thirds.

Accommodation is the main barrier to seeing Oman on a budget. Once you get around that problem many other aspects of daily life are quite cheap. A bus or microbus ticket from Muscat to any provincial city in the north of the country costs, at most, a few riyals and a bus ticket to Salalah can be purchased for as little as OR 5 one way. You can fill your stomach for as little as 600 baisa at one of the country's innumerable cheap Indian restaurants. Admission to

museums, forts and other places of interest is generally free.

Oman does not have middle-range hotels and restaurants, so once you leave the low-budget category you are likely to see costs head for the stratosphere fairly rapidly. Even staying in a relatively modest hotel and eating in medium-priced restaurants you could easily see costs hit OR 50 per day.

Currency
The Omani riyal (OR) is divided into 1000 baisa (also spelled baizas). Notes come in denominations of 100 and 200 baisa, and OR ¼, ½, 1, 5, 10, 20 and 50. Coins are 5, 10, 25, 50, and 100 baisa, though the 25 and 50 baisa coins are the only ones you are likely to see on a regular basis. The notes have both English and Arabic script but the numbers on the coins appear only in Arabian characters. The riyal is a convertible currency and there are no restrictions on its import or export. Foreign currency can also be taken into or out of the country freely.

Currency Exchange

US$1	=	OR 0.390
UK£1	=	OR 0.590
FF1	=	OR 0.075
DM1	=	OR 0.250
A$1	=	OR 0.300

Up-to-date foreign exchange rates are available by phone 24 hours a day by dialling ☎ 1106.

Changing Money
Banking hours are Saturday to Wednesday from 8 am to noon and Thursday from 8 to 11 am. Moneychangers keep the same hours and also usually open from around 4 to 7 pm. Some of the moneychangers, particularly the ones in and around Muscat's Mutrah souk, are also open for an hour or two on Friday afternoon from 4.30 or 5 pm.

ATMs are widespread, though few of them appear to be tied into the big international systems. The exception is the British Bank of the Middle East, some of whose machines accept cards on the Plus system.

OMAN

National Bank of Oman's ATMs are tied into the Global Access network.

Tipping & Bargaining

Tipping is not expected in cheaper places while more expensive restaurants tend to add a service charge to all bills (though this often goes to the restaurant not the waiting staff).

Most prices are fixed in Oman. This applies to restaurants, hotels and taxis. The only things you can expect to haggle over will be souvenirs in the souk. Even in the souk, however, bargaining can be a frustrating experience. Shopkeepers tend to be inclined to offer a small discount from the marked price but not much else. The price of a souvenir turban is not likely to move by more than a few hundred baisa. Even if you are spending OR 100 on old silver jewellery or daggers you are likely to find that the shopkeeper offers an initial discount of 10 to 15% off the marked price and then refuses to budge.

Consumer Taxes

A 5% municipality tax is applied to all hotel and restaurant bills.

POST & COMMUNICATIONS
Postal Rates

Sending a postcard costs 30 baisa inside Oman, 50 baisa to other Gulf and Arab countries and 150 baisa to the rest of the world. Postage for letters weighing 20g or less is 50 baisa inside Oman, 80 baisa to other Gulf countries and 100 baisa to the rest of the Arab world. Postage on letters to everywhere else is 200 baisa for the first 10g, 350 baisa for 20g and OR 1 for anything between 20g and 50g.

Domestic small packet rates are 300 baisa for packets weighing up to half a kg and 600 baisa for packets between 500g and one kg. To other Gulf Cooperation Council (GCC) countries the comparable (half kg/one kg) small packet rates are 800 baisa/OR 1.500 and to other Arab countries OR 1/2. Mailing small packets to countries outside the Arab world costs OR 2/4.

Parcel rates for up to one kg are OR 1

within Oman. Elsewhere surface/air rates are: Gulf countries OR 2/3, other Arab countries OR 3/3, rest of world OR 4/6 for a one kg parcel. Sending a five kg parcel costs OR 3 domestically, OR 6/10 to other Gulf countries, OR 10/15 within the Arab world and OR 15/20 elsewhere.

Sending Mail

Post offices are open weekdays from 7.30 am until 2 pm. They close at 11 am on Thursday and are closed all day Friday.

Receiving Mail

You can use the poste restante service at the GPO in Ruwi or the branch post office in Muscat to receive mail. Have your mail addressed to: Your Name, Poste Restante, Ruwi Central Post Office, Ruwi, Sultanate of Oman, or to the Muscat Post Office, Muscat, Sultanate of Oman. AMEX clients can also receive mail through the AMEX office in the capital. See the Muscat section for details.

Any parcels you receive while in the sultanate will incur a 250 baisa charge for presentation to customs and you may be required to come collect them at the post office and have them cleared through customs there. The authorities are particularly sensitive about books and other printed matter and about videos. The latter are liable to be held for inspection for several days. Parcels received post restante incur an additional 50 baisa handling charge.

Telephone, Fax & Telegraph

There are central public telephone offices in both Muscat and Salalah and in a few smaller cities and towns as well. With the exception of the call booking office in Muscat, however, these mainly offer card phones, and card phones are pretty easy to find almost anywhere. They also offer fax, telex and telegraph services. Your best bet for phoning home is to get a phonecard or two and call from a payphone. Overall Oman's telephone system is excellent and you should have little trouble when making international calls.

Direct-dial rates are 300 baisa per minute to other GCC countries, 600 to 750 baisa per minute to most other Arab countries (excluding North Africa), India, Pakistan and East Africa; 900 baisa per minute to North Africa and OR 1 per minute to everywhere else.

The number for directory assistance is ☎ 198 and the operators usually speak English. For the correct time dial ☎ 140, for weather information dial ☎ 1103.

When calling Oman from the outside world the country code is 968, followed by the local six-digit number. There are no area or city codes.

BOOKS
Travel Guides
Oman – A MEED Practical Guide is comprehensive but in need of an update. *The Economist Business Traveller's Guides – Arabian Peninsula* is a very useful how-to-do-business-with-the-Arabs sort of book.

There are a large number of specialist guides to Oman published by companies based in either Muscat or Dubai. All are widely available in Muscat for OR 5 to OR 6. The *APEX Explorer's Guide to Oman* is absolutely indispensable for anyone planning a spot of 'wadi bashing'. In addition to detailed route descriptions and invaluable driving tips it also features a section on taking photographs in the desert and notes on what to see if you feel like dropping OR 300 on a tour of Muscat by helicopter. *Off-Road in Oman* by Heiner Klein & Rebecca Brickson covers much of the same territory.

Somewhat more specialised titles include *Snorkelling and Diving in Oman* by Rod Salm & Robert Baldwin, *Birds of the Batinah of Oman* by RA & GE Honeywell, *Whales and Dolphins Along the Coast of Oman* by Robert Baldwin & Rod Salm, *Seashells of the Sultan Qaboos Nature Reserve at Qurm* by Kathleen Smythe, *Field Guide to the Geology of Oman* by Samir S Hanna, and *Musandem – Architecture and Material Culture of a Little Known Region of Oman* by Paolo M Costa, as well as a large number of coffee-table books.

History
There are few good history books devoted specifically to Oman. Michael Field's *The Merchants* has a fascinating chapter on the growth of modern Oman built around the story of WJ Towell & Co, one of Oman's biggest family-owned trading companies. *The Arabs* by Peter Mansfield has a brief but useful chapter on Oman.

People & Society
Oman has been thoroughly covered by a variety of travellers. *Travels in Oman – On the track of the early explorers* by Philip Ward combines a modern travel narrative with the best of the 18th, 19th and early 20th century travellers' accounts of the country. *Sultan in Oman* by James Morris is a travelling journalist's account of a visit to Oman in the 1950s, though you should be aware that it is banned in the country.

Some of the action in Wilfred Thesiger's 1959 classic *Arabian Sands* takes place in and around Salalah, which Thesiger visited at the end of one of his journeys into the Empty Quarter. The final section of the book is an account of a trip around Oman's northern interior.

NEWSPAPERS & MAGAZINES
The *Times of Oman* and the *Oman Daily Observer* are the local English-language newspapers. Foreign newspapers and magazines are available only in the bookshops in Muscat's five-star hotels and in a few other places frequented by the western community (supermarkets in Medinat Qaboos and the Family Bookshop outlet in Qurm, for example) and are usually about three days old. Outside of Muscat you can forget about finding foreign papers except, maybe, at the Salalah Holiday Inn and the Salalah Family Bookshop.

Oman Today is a magazine-cum-handbook published every two months and widely available throughout the sultanate for 500 baisa. Each issue has a comprehensive listing of clubs, activities, restaurants and entertainment, including visiting musical or theatrical acts. It is mainly aimed at the expat

OMAN

community. A less thorough listing of activities in Oman can be found in *What's On*, a monthly publication based in the UAE and available in the sultanate.

RADIO & TV

Omani TV has a daily newscast in English at 8 pm and shows English-language movies two or three nights a week (usually around 11 pm). Hong Kong-based Star TV is also widely available in the sultanate, even in relatively small hotels. Star's offerings include an entertainment channel, a sports channel, the BBC's World Service Television and Channel V, which shows music videos. Many hotels also have Zee TV, an Indian satellite channel, and one or more of the international Arabic satellite services (Egyptian TV, Dubai TV, MBC and ART).

The Sultanate of Oman FM Service is the local English-language radio station. It broadcasts on 90.4 FM every day from 7 am until 9 pm, with news bulletins at 7.30 am, and 2.30 and 6.30 pm. The fare is mostly classical music interspersed with light entertainment.

The main source of information for the expat community is the seemingly omnipresent BBC World Service. *Oman Today* lists the frequencies on which one can pick up the BBC in Oman.

PHOTOGRAPHY & VIDEO

Oman is a very security-conscious place. Don't photograph anything even vaguely military (though forts still in use by the police are generally OK if, like the three forts in Muscat and Mutrah, they are also recognised tourist attractions). Do not photograph people, especially women, without asking their permission first. Tourism is still relatively new to Oman so exercise caution, tact and discretion at all times. Video cameras are a particularly sensitive subject.

TIME

Omani time is GMT/UTC plus four hours. When it's noon in Muscat, the time elsewhere is:

City	Time
Paris, Rome	9 am
London	8 am
New York	3 am
Los Angeles	12 midnight
Perth, Hong Kong	4 pm
Sydney	6 pm
Auckland	8 pm

ELECTRICITY

The electricity voltage in Oman is 220/240V AC with British-style three-pin plugs.

WEIGHTS & MEASURES

Oman uses the metric system. In the souks silver jewellery is often sold according to weight, measured in tolas. Tolas are sometimes called 'thallers' after the Maria Theresia Dollar, an 18th century Austrian coin which became the model for Arabia's common currency of the 19th and early 20th century. One tola is equal to 11.75g.

LAUNDRY

There are no laundrettes. If you are not a wash-it-in-the-sink sort of person it's fairly easy to get your laundry done through even the cheapest hotels, though it might take 48 hours. A moderately sized load will cost OR 1 or OR 2. You can also find small laundries in Muscat and Salalah that will clean your clothes in 24 hours or so.

HEALTH

Since his ascension to power Sultan Qaboos has made improving health care and hygienic standards in Oman one of his main priorities. The result today is one of the most squeaky-clean countries you could ever hope to visit. Even the smallest restaurants in the souk are usually held to quite high standards of cleanliness. The tap water is drinkable throughout the country and no special vaccines are necessary, though a Cholera and a gamma globulin (or Havrix) as a Hepatitis A preventative are always a good idea if you are planning extensive travel off the beaten track in the interior. Malaria, virtually endemic only 30 years ago, is no longer a huge problem, but you may want to consider anti-malarial medications, particularly if you plan to travel extensively in the south. See Health in the Regional Facts for the Visitor chapter for more information.

WOMEN TRAVELLERS

Oman is one of the easiest countries in the Gulf for women to travel in. Still, the usual advice for the region applies: avoid wearing clothing which is overly tight or revealing. Trousers are OK as long as they are loosely cut, though some expatriate women prefer long dresses. There is no need for a foreign woman to wear a headscarf, though in rural areas you will certainly gain respect by doing so. Shorts are always a bad idea outside the big hotels and the interior is even more conservative than the coast.

DANGERS & ANNOYANCES

Oman is a very orderly society and harassment, of both women and men, is far less of a problem here than in some of the other Gulf States. In general you should find it a reasonably open and easy place to travel so long as you dress properly and avoid doing anything which the police might construe as spying, such as photographing police stations, airports or military facilities.

BUSINESS HOURS

Businesses are open daily from 8 am to 1 pm and 4 to 7 or 7.30 pm except Friday. Most businesses are also closed on Thursday afternoons. Many of the shops in Muscat's Mutrah souk are open during the early evening hours on Friday. Shops in the Mutrah souk and in some of Muscat's more up-market shopping malls stay open until 8 or 9 pm most nights.

Banks are open Saturday to Wednesday from 8 am to noon (11 am on Thursday). The moneychangers in and around the Mutrah souk keep much the same hours as other businesses. Government offices are open from 7.30 or 8 am until 2 pm from Saturday to Wednesday and until 1 pm on Thursday.

PUBLIC HOLIDAYS & SPECIAL EVENTS

Secular holidays which are observed in Oman are New Year's Day (January 1),

National Day (November 18) and the Sultan's Birthday (November 19). You should be aware, however, that National Day and the Sultan's Birthday are somewhat fluid, and also tend to be celebrated twice.

Just as the US government has a habit of setting holidays and then celebrating them on the Monday nearest the appointed date, National Day and the Sultan's Birthday have a way of moving around by up to a week in either direction. Moreover, since most government employees are required to spend National Day participating in the lavish official ceremonies marking the occasion, the entire country is usually given two or three days off from work to mark National Day a week or so after the actual event. For the visitor the main significance of this is that everything (and, be warned, I do mean everything) closes down twice. I once got trapped in Khasab because the air force closed the control tower at the local airport in observance of national day, thereby cancelling all flights!

The National Day festival features all sorts of highly visible official celebrations. A few of these are usually open to the public, and a quick glance at the local newspapers or a little time spent listening to Radio Oman around National Day will let you know which of the celebrations you can attend. Most of the official functions are by invitation only, but these are usually carried live on television.

The Islamic holidays of Eid Al-Fitr, Eid Al-Adha, the Islamic New Year and the Prophet's Birthday are all observed (for the dates see the table of holidays near Public Holidays in the Regional Facts for the Visitor chapter). Observance of the two Muslim Eids is more traditional than what you will see on National Day. The event is often marked with spontaneous dancing in the streets, even in Muscat.

ACTIVITIES

The variety of terrain in Oman makes weekend mountain and desert motoring particularly worthwhile. The *APEX Explorer's*

OMAN

Guide to Oman is essential reading for anyone planning to see the country by 4WD.

Water sports are becoming the recreational mainstay of some of the five-star hotels. The main ones in Muscat all either have a beach of their own or have arranged to use somebody else's, and sport small fleets of sailboats, windsurfers, pedal boats etc. Several have diving gear available for guests to rent.

All of the big hotels also have health clubs which you can join. The Al-Bustan Palace boasts the fanciest and most expensive of these with an annual fee of OR 235 for singles and OR 350 for couples. The cheapest health club is at the Ruwi Novotel where a year's membership will set you back only OR 80 (couples OR 100).

Oman Today has complete listings of the various clubs, societies and ethnic cultural associations in Oman. The Muscat section includes information on and telephone numbers for a number of beach clubs and other places to spend your time and money.

WORK

One of the quickest ways to make yourself unpopular with the authorities is to start looking for work while visiting the country on a tourist visa. The rules on imported labour are still pretty strict. If you want to work in Oman you should go back home and apply for a job from there.

Assuming that you do have a contract and a job, your company will usually send you the NOC number before you fly out and you'll get a short-term visa at the airport. This will later be modified by your sponsor into a residence visa. Exit/re-entry visas are not necessary for expatriates, who usually receive two-year multiple-entry visas.

ACCOMMODATION
Camping

There are no formal camping grounds in Oman. Camping in the mountains or the desert is more a matter of finding a good spot and setting up shop. Be careful, however, not to intrude on land that may belong to someone and be sure not to choose a camp

site which might cause problems. Do not, for example, camp in the shadow of a village, especially if you plan to drink. This might offend the locals and you could, unwittingly, be on someone's land.

There are also certain practical and safety related aspects of camping in the desert which you should be aware of. The first is to always have more than one vehicle if at all possible and never to leave the city without letting someone know where you are going and when you plan to return. Anyone planning to make an overnight trip of this sort should pick up *Staying Alive in the Desert* by KEM Melville.

Hotels

Muscat has a range of hotels to suit most budgets, all of which are quite clean. Outside of the capital most hotels are still fairly clean but you will find your choice of accommodation severely limited. Most of Oman's main provincial towns have only one or two hotels. Even Salalah, the largest city in the country after Muscat, only has around half a dozen places to stay. In Muscat you can spend anything from OR 5 to OR 70 on a single room. In Salalah the selection bottoms out at around OR 8 for a single and OR 12 for a double.

FOOD

Eating cheaply in Oman almost always means eating Indian. There is little in the way of traditional cuisine. Muscat and Salalah are full of small Indian restaurants where the food is good, if not too varied.

Muscat also has a number of up-market Indian and Lebanese restaurants and the usual collection of western-style fast-food establishments, especially fried chicken places. The big hotels offer the usual selection of international fare.

DRINKS

Small restaurants are likely to offer you a choice of little more than Coke, Pepsi or water. Larger restaurants have a wider variety of soft drinks as well as fruit juice, sometimes freshly squeezed. Alcohol is available only in larger hotels and expensive restaurants.

ENTERTAINMENT

There is a disco at the Muscat Inter-Continental Hotel and most of the other large hotels have lounge acts of some sort in their bars. *Oman Today* and the UAE-based *What's On* magazine are your best sources for this sort of information.

THINGS TO BUY

Oman is unquestionably the best place in the Gulf to go souvenir shopping.

Daggers

Oman's most distinctive product is the *khanjar*, also spelled *khanja*, the curved dagger worn by Omani men on important occasions, and in rural areas they are still sometimes worn every day. Traditionally the handles of these daggers were made from rhino horn, though today they are almost always made from either plastic or wood.

If a shopkeeper tells you that the handle of the dagger he is trying to sell you is made from rhino horn consider three things. First, virtually every country in the world strictly prohibits the import of anything containing rhino horn. Second, do you really want to help promote the illegal slaughter in East Africa of an endangered species? And third, is it real rhino horn, anyway? The fact is that if the shopkeeper is asking less than OR 800 for the dagger it is *not* made from rhino horn.

Khanjars with plastic or wooden handles (the only ones you are likely to see) sell for anywhere between OR 30 and OR 500, depending on the extent and quality of the decoration on the dagger, scabbard and belt. As a rule, however, anything under OR 50 tends to be pretty nasty – either very shoddy or very beaten up or both. That said, unless you really know what you are doing you should not invest more than OR 115 (about US$300) in a khanjar. When the bargaining starts remember that many shops catering to tourists throw in a display box for free but charge up to OR 10 extra for a belt and OR 20 for a frame. If you do not want the box

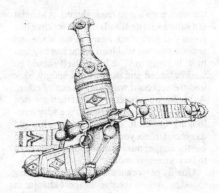

A Sayidi khanjar dagger with its distinctive five rings.

(and they are quite bulky) make this clear during the bargaining and get a few riyals knocked off the price. Paying cash is usually a bit cheaper than using a credit card. Khanjars are cheaper in Muscat than in Nizwa.

Khanjars come in two basic designs: regular khanjars are identified by two rings along the central part of the scabbard – the line followed by the belt when one is attached. *Sayidi* khanjars have five rings. A generation or two ago these were a sign that the wearer was a member of the ruling Al-Busaid family, but today anyone can wear either style. Regular khanjars are decorated entirely, or nearly entirely, using thin silver thread. The intricacy of the thread pattern, and the skill with which it is executed, are among the main determinants of value. The uppermost part of the scabbard may, however, be a single, carefully tooled sheet of silver. Sayidi khanjars are often covered entirely in silver sheet with little or no thread used. If the lower part of the scabbard is covered in sheet silver it should also wrap around the back side of the tip of the scabbard. It is rare to see the silver wrap around more of the back than the tip of the scabbard, but this is a sign of value.

The most important things to look for in assessing a khanjar's quality are weight and

OMAN

the workmanship on the scabbard. A khanjar is a substantial item and ought to feel like one when you pick it up. Remove the blade and see whether the scabbard alone has any heft to it. It ought to. The blade itself should be well-balanced and ought to fit snugly back into the scabbard with a minimum of effort. As blades are subject to wear, if they are used you should not be surprised to see very new-looking blades in the handles of fairly old daggers. Unless you are actually planning to use the dagger this is not something you need to be concerned about.

Quality of workmanship is also fairly easy to judge. Ask to see the cheapest khanjar in the shop, and then look at one of the OR 300 models and you'll get the idea quickly. Good silver is not shiny to the point of being white, as evidenced by the fact that the daggers tend to get less shiny as one moves up the price scale. The same applies to khanjars covered

entirely in sheet silver. It is fairly easy to tell good work from sloppy work if you just take a minute or two to examine several pieces side by side. If you are considering a khanjar covered entirely in sheet silver take the blade out of the scabbard and look across the slit into which the blade goes. This will give you some idea of how thick the silver is.

Some khanjars have a second knife inserted in a small scabbard attached to the back of the main scabbard. I wouldn't pay too much of a premium for one of these – the knives in question are often cheap steak knives that have had a bit of silver wrapped around the handle.

Do not believe anything anyone tells you regarding the age of individual pieces. Few khanjars are really more than 20 to 40 years old, and quality, not age, should be your main criterion anyway.

If you really want to make your passage

OMAN

Kohl Boxes (*mkahalah*)

These are usually the cheapest silver pieces available at OR 8 to OR 20. There are three basic types. Men's khol boxes are thin silver cylinders 5 to 10 cm in length connected by a small chain to a silver applicator rod that looks a bit like a big toothpick. The women's model is smaller and wider with a flat bottom and a smaller applicator. Women's khol boxes may be as small as a thimble or as big as a shot glass. Men's boxes usually have screw-off tops connected to the chain, while women's have tops that simply pull off. You may also see khol boxes made from plastic bottles with a narrow top and a bulb-shaped bottom and covered in beads. These are khol boxes from Dhofar, the southernmost region of Oman. They tend to be a lot cheaper than the silver variety – only OR 2 or OR 3 for the small ones, especially if you buy them in Salalah. ■

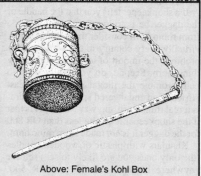

Above: Female's Kohl Box

Below: Male's Kohl Box

GORDON ROBISON

GORDON ROBISON

Oman

Top: Mutrah's long sweeping Corniche is one of the most attractive in Arabia.
Bottom: The bright, colourful dresses and shawls worn by many Omani women are a dramatic contrast to the black cloak common elsewhere in the Gulf.

GORDON ROBISON

Oman

The lush A'Thowarah Oasis, not far from Nakhal, is a popular Omani picnic spot.

through airport security a nightmare, you can explore the selection of guns and swords that are also on sale in many silver shops.

Jewellery

Silver jewellery is easier to pack than a khanjar, tends to be more affordable and is less likely to freak out the people running the X-ray at the airport.

Traditional jewellery ranges from small silver boxes designed to hold kohl (traditionally used as make-up by both men and women) to huge belts or chest-pieces. It is often very intricately designed. Thin layers of gold or bronze, coloured glass and old coins are all used to decorate the basic silverwork. Silver jewellery is almost always sold according to weight, measured in tolas (see Weights & Measures earlier in this section).

Shopkeepers looking for a sale are apt to make great claims for the age of their wares. Bear in mind, however, that most of this stuff was made as wedding jewellery. As it was (and still is) considered an insult for a bride to be given used jewellery to wear on her wedding day the tradition has long been that a woman's jewellery is melted down and sold for its weight after her death. For this reason very little of the jewellery you will see on sale in the souks of Muscat and Nizwa is more than 50 to 60 years old. Much of what is available is worn and battered so try to go shopping when you have a few hours to look closely at the various offerings. You should be able to get one or two really nice pieces for OR 30 to OR 50. A particularly common Omani necklace design is a rectangular box that opens at one end (a small paper containing verses from the Koran would normally have been inserted into the box) and is decorated with gold leaf laid on top of the silver.

If you plan to do any shopping for antique jewellery *Oman Silver* by Ruth Hawley might be a good investment, particularly since most of the shopkeepers in Muscat's silver souk have well-thumbed copies.

Some of the more common types of jewellery include:

Maria Theresia Dollar (Thaller).
On the back side of the coin is the double-headed eagle of Austria-Hungary.

Prayer Holders ('aud saleeb) These are small to medium-sized cylinders into which wood or a piece of paper containing verses from the Koran or incantations against evil spirits are placed. The larger ones, which may be 20 to 25 cm in length, were sometimes used to carry messages between VIPs. Depending on the thickness of the silver and the quality of the work they can cost anywhere from OR 20 to OR 60.

Maria Theresia Dollars These are commonly known as thallers and are on sale in many jewellery shops. Along with the Indian rupee these were the common currency of the Gulf for much of the 19th and early 20th centuries. The coins remained legal tender in Oman until 1968. Regardless of when they were minted, all Maria Theresia dollars bear the date 1780 (presumably the date on the original which the 19th century Arabian silversmiths used as a model). As with the jewellery, you can safely assume that the ones you'll see on sale are nowhere near that old. They contain about 20g of solid silver and sell for about OR 3 a piece.

Gunpowder Horns (tilaheeq)

For some reason gunpowder horns have become very popular over the last few years. Maybe because they are more substantial than a khol box but cheaper than a khanjar. Their popularity has meant that a lot of cheap ones have recently appeared on the market

OMAN

OMAN

Coffeepots

One of the Middle East's most distinctive craft items is the traditional Arabian coffeepot, or dallah.

Coffee originated in Arabia, in the Yemeni highlands (in the peninsula's south-western corner). The English word 'mocha' is actually a corruption of the word 'makha' – the name of the Yemeni port through which most of the coffee was exported to Europe during the Middle Ages.

Among the Bedouins, offering coffee is an important sign of hospitality, and its preparation, involving the roasting and grinding of the beans and their mixing with cardamom, is an important ceremony.

The most common type of Arabian coffeepot has a large, almost bulb-like, lower section. These coffeepots do not narrow significantly at the middle before opening out again at the top. This design is common throughout the Gulf and the Levant. There are also certain regional variations of the basic design. Wrapping the handle in leather, possibly interspersed with small decorative bits of metal, for example, is a style typical of coffeepots made in Syria.

In the Arab Gulf States, Omani coffeepots are particularly easy to spot. They tend to be taller than the ones found elsewhere in the region, and are much narrower through the mid-section. The Omani design is most easily identified, however, by the sharply defined ridge just above the base.

The Omani style of coffeepot is also widely used in the United Arab Emirates, but is rarely seen in Saudi Arabia or the Northern Gulf. Many shops in Muscat are now selling silver coffeepots that are very expensive – OR 70 and up. Copper ones are harder to find but are still pricey at around OR 40. ∎

---

while the good ones have rapidly appreciated in price. A cheap gunpowder horn is likely to cost between OR 20 and OR 30, and a good one is nearly as much as a cheapish khanjar dagger, around OR 50 (especially for the ones that have some gold leaf worked into the decoration).

As with khanjars you should look for solidity and workmanship when picking out a powder horn. The top should come on and off cleanly and should not be flimsy. The mechanism for releasing the powder out through the spout at the narrow end should work, at least on the newer ones.

Clothing

Other things to buy include caftans. The turbans worn by virtually every Omani man also make good presents, generally costing about OR 10.

Pottery

Locally made pottery, usually in the form of incense burners, can be purchased in Dhofar. See Things to Buy in the Salalah section for details.

Getting There & Away

AIR

There are no bucket shops in Muscat, though you might save 10% or so by shopping around. If you are headed east it is often possible to get discounts on flights to Bangkok. The fares quoted here are the cheapest regular, published single and return prices (the returns are usually excursion tickets). Travel agents are usually willing to discount the regular fares quoted below if you are willing to lock yourself into particular travel dates. Also, this does not take account of any special deals or promotional offers which one airline or another may have going at any given moment. Since not every travel agent handles every airline you should be sure to visit several, or stick to the biggies like AMEX/Zubair Travel to make sure you're getting all the relevant information on the routes you are interested in.

Finally, as always in the Gulf, ask a lot of very specific questions about dates and ticket restrictions and ask for specific quotes on different carriers. Do not count on the agent simply to volunteer the lowest fare.

The USA

Return fares to the eastern USA from Muscat generally cost OR 600 to OR 650 depending on the season and how badly the agent wants to sell the ticket. The high season is mid-June to mid-October and about 10 days either side of Christmas.

The UK

Although you might think that flights to London would be fairly cheap because of the sheer number of British expats in Oman, this is not the case. At OR 512 for a return ticket, it is almost the same price as flying to New York and more expensive than a low-season return to Melbourne. One-way fares are about OR 375. If you want to fly to London at Christmas time it would be wise to book very early, say, in August or September.

That said, the rates mentioned above are the 'regular' fares and London, because it is a popular route, is one on which packages and special offers are particularly common.

Europe

The basic return excursion fare to Rome is OR 428 (minimum stay 10 days, maximum stay three months). A similar ticket to Athens costs OR 348. One-way fares are OR 325 to Rome and OR 264 to Athens. Summer is the best time to look for special fares to these and other European cities.

Australia

Low-season (February to August) return fares to Melbourne are OR 505. The high-season (September to January) fare will cost you OR 584.

India & Africa

New Delhi, at OR 191 for a return ticket allowing a four month stay, is one of the better deals available out of Muscat. The one-way fare is OR 143. Nairobi, at OR 309 return (minimum stay six days, maximum stay two months), OR 239 one way, is less of a bargain and Johannesburg at OR 612 for the same sort of return ticket is in the same price category as far-off New York. The one-way fare to Johannesburg is OR 462.

The Middle East

The cheapest regular return ticket to Cairo costs OR 288 (five day minimum stay, two months maximum). A one-way fare is OR 194. The same type of ticket to Damascus costs OR 288 return, OR 174 one way.

Other Gulf States

A sample of one-way and cheap return fares from Muscat to other Gulf cities, with the minimum and maximum stay requirements follows:

To	One Way	Return	Min/Max
Abu Dhabi	OR 62	OR 49	3/7 days
Bahrain	OR 106	OR 85	3/7 days
Dhahran	OR 81	OR 114	2/14 days
Doha	OR 91	OR 72	3/7 days
Dubai	OR 58	OR 46	3/7 days
Jeddah	OR 130	OR 180	2/14 days
Kuwait	OR 93	OR 130	2/14 days
Riyadh	OR 93	OR 130	2/14 days

Note that to the other Gulf States, and particularly to Dubai and Abu Dhabi, cheap 'weekend fares' are often available. Restrictions vary, but these usually allow outbound travel on a Wednesday or Thursday with the return on Friday or Saturday.

LAND

Entering or leaving by land means travelling between Oman and the UAE as the border with Yemen is not open to travellers. Tourists do not require any documents beyond their passport and visa.

Foreign residents of Oman need a road permit (see Documents earlier in this chapter) to enter or leave the country by land. This includes leaving Oman in transit, for example crossing UAE territory to get from Muscat to Khasab. Note, however, that road permits are not issued to single women.

SEA

At present there are no scheduled seaborne passenger services to or from Oman, though cruise ships occasionally call at Muscat.

LEAVING OMAN

Departure formalities at Muscat's Seeb international airport are fairly straightforward. The airport is efficient and the staff are not overstretched, so things tend to move along smoothly. You should appear at the airport at least an hour in advance of departure time. Bear in mind that it takes a good 30 minutes by taxi or an hour by bus to reach the airport from Mutrah.

If you are leaving by road and you have a tourist visa be prepared for some minor delays at the border. Tourist visas are still relatively new, and most people holding them still come and go by air, so the border guards may be unfamiliar with your visa. This is unlikely to slow you down for more than a couple of minutes.

Departure Tax

There is a tax of OR 3 for all departing international passengers at Seeb airport in Muscat.

Getting Around

AIR
Domestic Air Services

Oman Aviation flies two times per day between Muscat and Salalah for OR 27 one way, OR 50 return, and from Muscat to Sur three times per week for OR 14 one way, OR 28 return. There are four flights per week to Khasab in the Musandem, two of which go via Dibba. The fare to both Khasab and Dibba is OR 20 one way, OR 40 return. There are also four flights each week to Massirah Island (OR 17 one way, OR 34 return).

BUS

Inter-city buses are operated by the Oman National Transport Company (ONTC) which has daily services to most of the main provincial towns.

The main bus station is on Al-Jaame St in Ruwi, Muscat; tickets are sold in an office there. Outside Muscat and Salalah there really aren't any stations as such. An inter-city bus may stop at the edge of town along the main highway or, in the case of larger towns like Nizwa or Sohar, it will make a pass through the town like a local bus, stopping whenever someone is standing by a bus stop sign (of which there will be one every couple of hundred metres) before swinging back onto the highway. Tickets are available from the bus driver.

Complete timetables for all routes are posted at the Ruwi station. In provincial towns there is usually a small signboard with the timetables for the routes from that town posted at the stop. Tickets for all inter-city services are available in advance, at least in Muscat, but reservations are accepted only for the express services to Salalah. It is generally a good idea to book seats to Salalah a day or two in advance.

Costs

With the exception of Salalah none of the main inter-city routes costs more than OR 4 each way. The fare to Salalah is OR 8 one way, OR 16 return. See the Muscat section for more detailed information on costs and the frequency of ONTC's services.

TAXI & MICROBUS

Oman has an extraordinarily comprehensive system of service-taxis and microbuses. The taxis are invariably orange and white, the microbuses are white. Both have an orange medallion painted on the driver's door. This medallion includes, usually in large letters, the name of the vehicle's home governate or, in the case of vehicles from Muscat, district. Unfortunately, it is written only in Arabic. If you can read Arabic look for the medallion first as it provides an excellent guide to where the vehicle is headed. Both taxis and microbuses congregate at main road junctions and often, but not always, at a central spot in most towns. They also spend a lot of time cruising around looking for passengers.

Unlike service-taxis in other Middle Eastern cities Oman's service-taxis and microbuses do not wait until they are full to leave, though how empty the driver will be willing to travel is a judgment call. For example, if you have arrived at a main road junction and want to cover the last 10 or 15 km into a particular village the driver of a 14 passenger microbus may set off with only you in the vehicle, reasoning that he can pick up a lot of local business in the other villages he will have to pass through. If he expects things to be slow between your starting point and your destination he may opt to wait until he has more passengers. Taxis, since most of them only carry four passengers, are more likely to wait around for extra passengers before setting off. This is a very cheap way to get around, provided you are in no particular hurry.

You can also, of course, take a taxi or microbus 'engaged' (ie privately) by paying for all of the seats in it. If it is late at night or you are asking the driver to travel a very long distance he may demand a premium over the simple x-seats-times-the-usual-fare formula. Remember, engaged rates are for the vehicle, not per person.

Women should have no problem using the microbuses or taxis – Omani women and expatriate women from the Indian subcontinent use them all the time. Be aware, however, that foreign women, especially foreign women unaccompanied by a man, remain an unusual site throughout Oman.

CAR
Road Rules
Vehicles drive on the right-hand side of the road. Traffic laws are enforced fairly strictly in Oman, especially in Muscat.

All of the crazy driving habits you may have acquired in Saudi Arabia, Kuwait or the UAE should be unlearned before you get behind the wheel in Oman unless you want to part with a lot of money in fines. These include driving as fast as you please, not giving way when you enter a roundabout and making liberal use of the horn.

Seat belt use is mandatory for passengers in the front seat of cars. The fine for not wearing one is OR 10. Right turns are not allowed at red lights.

Speed limits in Oman are posted on all roads and highways. Drivers, however, are not stopped for speeding in Oman. Instead, speeders are 'intimidated by telephone and post' by the police (I quote from a Royal Oman Police circular on policy regarding speeding) and, if unreachable, are forced to pay their fines before a passport, residence permit, new car registration or any other

government document can be issued. Car rental companies usually make renters sign a statement to the effect that they are aware of this policy.

Petrol
Petrol comes in two grades: super and regular. It costs around 118 baisa per litre for super and 112 baisa for regular.

Rental
Renting a car in the sultanate is fairly easy but it is not cheap. Most foreign drivers' licences are accepted for people on business or tourist visas as are international driving permits. Resident expats must obtain an Omani licence. This can usually be issued against a foreign driving licence without any further test being administered. You will probably have to leave a credit card imprint with the rental company, even if you are planning to pay cash at the end of the day and if you are cited for speeding or any other traffic violation this will be charged to your credit card, possibly several weeks after you turned in the car.

Rates for small cars start at about OR 12 per day plus OR 2 to OR 3 per day for insurance. You can plan on spending about OR 90 to OR 100 net to rent a car for a week. Rentals usually include 100 or 150 free km per day but beyond that you will probably be paying at least 70 baisa per km. This adds up pretty quickly considering how spread out the capital is, let alone driving anywhere else. If you are renting a car for a week or more you may be able to negotiate a discount of up to 25% and a higher number of free km per day.

Note that some car rental companies charge an extra OR 2 to OR 4 if you pick up or drop off the car at Seeb airport in Muscat.

HITCHING
While Omanis thumb rides all the time, especially in rural areas, it is not a common practice for foreigners. On the other hand it is not illegal. I've met people who have happily spent days thumbing their way around Dhofar. However, you might attract

the unwelcome attentions of the police by doing so. For more information see Hitching in the Getting Around the Region chapter.

LOCAL TRANSPORT
Bus, Taxi & Microbus
Only Muscat has a local bus system. Local taxis tend to be pretty thick on the ground throughout the country as are 14-passenger microbuses. In smaller areas in particular it is difficult, if not impossible, to distinguish between local and inter-city taxis and microbuses. Most drivers wear both hats and are always willing to consider driving you wherever you want to go, for a price.

ORGANISED TOURS
Organised full and half day tours are available in both Muscat and Salalah. See the respective city entries for details.

Muscat

Muscat is a port the like of which cannot be found in the whole world where there is business and good things that cannot be found elsewhere.

So wrote the great Arab navigator Ahmed Bin Majid Al-Najdi in 1490 AD. Five centuries later Muscat still enchants visitors in a way that no other city in the Gulf can even begin to. Maybe this is because Muscat does not have that slightly artificial feel which typifies so much of the rest of the region.

History
Muscat's history dates from at least the 1st century AD and it was probably mentioned by Ptolemy, who referred to a 'concealed harbour', a description which aptly fits the old section of Muscat if you approach it from the sea. But while it was settled at this time it was neither large nor important. Even well into the Islamic era it was eclipsed by Sohar and Hormuz which, lying in the midst of the strait of the same name, was by far the most important port in the area for many centuries.

Muscat began to grow during the 9th century when ships bound to India from more northern ports began calling there to take on fresh water, but it first gained importance during the 14th and 15th centuries. However, even then it was little more than a small trading post, albeit an important one. Muscat was an outpost of the powerful kings of Hormuz and, eventually, it became their entrepôt. It was in this role that, inevitably, it attracted the attentions of the Portuguese who conquered the town during the 16th century.

It was not, however, until 1622, after they themselves had been driven out of Hormuz, that the Portuguese made Muscat their main stronghold in the area. It was around this time that the town walls (a refurbished version of which still stand) were built. But by then Lisbon's era in the Gulf was drawing to a close. Muscat was Portugal's last stronghold in the region and the Omani reconquest of the town in 1650 effectively ended the Portuguese era in the Gulf.

Since the mid-18th century Muscat has been the seat of the Al-Busaid dynasty, the current ruling family of Oman. It has seen the growth and, later, the partition of a maritime empire that once controlled much of the coast of East Africa.

Despite the splendour of this history, the Omani capital languished in an almost medieval torpor for most of this century. During the 1960s, as the economies of the other Gulf States roared ahead, life in what was then known as Muscat and Oman seemed to slip further and further behind.

All of that changed in the wake of the 1970 palace coup which brought Sultan Qaboos Bin Said to power. The advantage that Muscat gained from a late start at modernisation and development was the opportunity to learn from the mistakes of others. The result is a capital which has retained much of its traditional architecture and beauty, while making great strides toward modernisation in a remarkably short span of time.

Orientation
You will sometimes hear Muscat referred to as the 'three cities' or the 'capital region'.

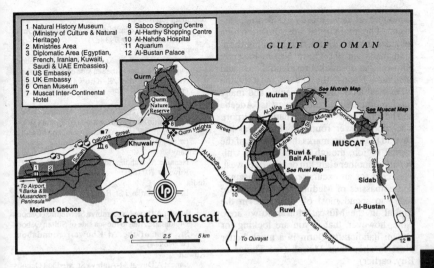

1 Natural History Museum
  (Ministry of Culture & Natural
  Heritage)
2 Ministries Area
3 Diplomatic Area (Egyptian,
  French, Iranian, Kuwaiti,
  Saudi & UAE Embassies)
4 US Embassy
5 UK Embassy
6 Oman Museum
7 Muscat Inter-Continental
  Hotel

8 Sabco Shopping Centre
9 Al-Harthy Shopping Centre
10 Al-Nahdha Hospital
11 Aquarium
12 Al-Bustan Palace

Greater Muscat

OMAN

Greater Muscat covers a huge area from Seeb airport in the west to the sultan's palace in the east. Moreover, the various districts of the city do not mesh seamlessly into one another. On the contrary, they are often separated by low hills and ridges which serve, to a certain extent, to compartmentalise the capital's various districts.

The 'three cities' are Muscat, Mutrah and Ruwi. Muscat is the old port area. It is the site of the sultan's palace and is a fascinating place to wander around but it has few shops and, except for the old city walls, there is not much to see. The real attraction is the traditional feel of the place. Mutrah, three km north-west of Muscat, is the main trading and residential port area. Its long, sweeping Corniche is one of the most beautiful spots in Arabia, and its souk one of the best. Behind the Corniche is a labyrinth of streets and alleys into which few tourists ever venture save for quick trips into the main part of the souk. When expats talk about 'going down to the Corniche' they are referring to Mutrah.

A few km inland from Muscat and Mutrah lies Ruwi. A generation ago this was an undeveloped valley; today it is the capital's modern commercial district. The Ruwi valley actually includes the districts of both Ruwi and Bait Al-Falaj (which derives its name from the fort that now houses the Sultan's Armed Forces Museum and was once virtually the only building in the valley). Part of this area is also formally known as Mutrah Al-Tijari, or Commercial Mutrah. But in general the whole area is referred to as simply Ruwi. Ruwi is laid out as a fairly straightforward grid and even now it is far from completely built up. Two roads connect the Ruwi valley to Mutrah, one a highway sweeping around to the west to end on the Mutrah Corniche at the roundabout by the Mina Hotel and the Mutrah bus station. The other road is Mutrah High St, which takes in the small district of Mutrah Al-Khubra and ends at the gate to the inland side of the Mutrah souk. If you are travelling by car take the highway as Mutrah High St is narrow, often jammed and eventually dumps you into that maze of streets and alleys that is the inland portion of Mutrah. There is no direct link between Ruwi and Muscat.

Immediately south of Muscat lie the small villages of Sidab and Al-Bustan and, further south, the huge Al-Bustan Palace Hotel.

Along the coast to the west of Mutrah are

a number of new, mostly residential, districts. The main ones are Qurm, which includes the Gulf Hotel, five or six big shopping malls and the Qurm Nature Reserve; Khuwair, an up-market residential area, and Medinat Qaboos, the site of most of the ministries, a couple of museums and many foreign embassies. Further west is 'Adeeba and beyond that is Seeb international airport. The clock tower roundabout, several km beyond the airport, marks the outskirts of the capital region, though Sultan Qaboos University is another eight km or so further west.

Except for an excursion to the museums and embassies of Medinat Qaboos you are likely to spend most of your time in the capital in the Muscat-Mutrah-Ruwi area. Note, however, that if you are looking for Omani handicrafts Qurm is a much better place to shop than Mutrah (see Things to Buy, earlier).

If you are out in the Qurm-Medinat Qaboos-Khuwair area on foot you should be aware that there are only two pedestrian passages across Sultan Qaboos St along this entire 15 or 20 km stretch of road. One is the bridge over the highway at the exit near the Muscat Inter-Continental Hotel, the other is a pedestrian subway under the street in the Ministries area (if you are trying to reach the Natural History Museum and were let off on the wrong side of the road the latter of these two is closer to it).

Information

Foreign Embassies

Embassies are open from Saturday to Wednesday. Some Arab embassies are open on Thursday morning as well.

Australia
  See entry under UK.

Austria
  Just off A'Noor St in Ruwi at Way 309 (☎ 793145 or 793135)

Bahrain
  Al-Kharjiyah St, just off Way 3015, Medinat Qaboos (☎ 605074 or 605133)

Canada
  See entry under UK.

Denmark (consulate)
  WJ Towell & Co building, 1st floor, next to Oman Aviation, Ruwi (☎ 793887)

Egypt
  Jameat A'Duwal Al-Arabiya St, Medinat Qaboos Diplomatic Area to the sea side of Sultan Qaboos St, west of the Al-Khuwair roundabout (☎ 600411)

France
  Jameat A'Duwal Al-Arabiya St, Medinat Qaboos Diplomatic Area to the sea side of Sultan Qaboos St, west of the Al-Khuwair roundabout (☎ 604310 or 604222)

Germany
  Near the Al-Nahdha Hospital on Al-Nahdha St in Ruwi (☎ 702164)

India
  Bank Al-Markazi St, Ruwi (☎ 706894)

Iran
  Jameat A'Duwal Al-Arabiya St, Medinat Qaboos Diplomatic Area to the sea side of Sultan Qaboos St, west of the Al-Khuwair roundabout (☎ 696944)

Kuwait
  Jameat A'Duwal Al-Arabiya St, Medinat Qaboos Diplomatic Area to the sea side of Sultan Qaboos St, west of the Al-Khuwair roundabout (☎ 699626 or 699627)

Netherlands
  OC Centre, 7th floor, Ruwi St, Ruwi, near the Ruwi Novotel Hotel (☎ 705410)

Qatar
  Al-Maamoura St, Bait Al-Falaj, behind the Al-Falaj Hotel (☎ 701802)

Saudi Arabia
  Jameat A'Duwal Al-Arabiya St, Medinat Qaboos Diplomatic Area to the sea side of Sultan Qaboos St, west of the Al-Khuwair roundabout (☎ 601744)

Switzerland (consular agency)
  At the Swissair office, United Travel, 1st floor, Bank Al-Markazi St, Ruwi, next to the Emirates Airlines office (☎ 750379)

UAE
  Jameat A'Duwal Al-Arabiya St, Medinat Qaboos Diplomatic Area to the sea side of Sultan Qaboos St, west of the Al-Khuwair roundabout (☎ 600302)

UK
  Jameat A'Duwal Al-Arabiya St, Medinat Qaboos Diplomatic Area to the sea side of Sultan Qaboos St, west of the Al-Khuwair roundabout (☎ 693077). This embassy handles emergencies for Australian and Canadian citizens.

USA
  Jameat A'Duwal Al-Arabiya St, Medinat Qaboos Diplomatic Area to the sea side of Sultan Qaboos St, west of the Al-Khuwair roundabout (☎ 698989)

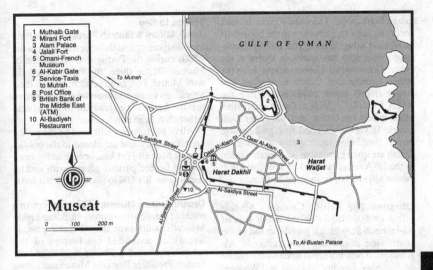

1 Muthaib Gate
2 Mirani Fort
3 Alam Palace
4 Jalali Fort
5 Omani-French Museum
6 Al-Kabir Gate
7 Service-Taxis to Mutrah
8 Post Office
9 British Bank of the Middle East (ATM)
10 Al-Badiyeh Restaurant

GULF OF OMAN

To Mutrah

Al-Saidiya Street

Qasr Al-Alam St.
Qasr Al-Alam Street

Harat Waljat

Harat Dakhil

Al-Saidiya Street

To Al-Bustan Palace

Muscat

0   100   200 m

OMAN

Money Most of the big banks are in Ruwi along Markaz Mutrah Al-Tijari St. There is also a branch of the Standard & Chartered Bank next to the Ruwi bus station and a plethora of moneychangers (plus a few banks) along Souk Ruwi St.

In Mutrah you will find a number of moneychangers on the Corniche around the entrance to the souk and also inside the souk (head straight into the souk and keep left when the main path forks by a fountain).

In Muscat you will find a branch of the British Bank of the Middle East with an ATM, as well as several other banks near the post office and the Al-Kabir gate.

AMEX (☎ 708035) is represented by Zubair Travel & Services Bureau in Ruwi; open daily, except Friday, from 8 am to 1 pm and 4 to 6 pm. The office can't change cash or travellers' cheques. Client's mail should be addressed to: American Express – client's mail, PO Box 833, Ruwi, Oman.

Post The GPO is right on the dividing line between Ruwi and Bait Al-Falaj at the northern end of Markaz Mutrah Al-Tijari St. It is open Saturday to Wednesday from 8 am to 2 pm and 3.30 to 5.30 pm. On Thursday, Friday and holidays they keep a shorter 8 to 11 am schedule. There is a philatelic department on the upper floor.

There is a branch post office in Mutrah near the Mina Qaboos port services building, just off the main road linking the roundabout near the Mina Hotel with Ruwi. It is open only Saturday to Wednesday from 8 am to 2 pm and 4 to 6 pm. Muscat's post office is near the Al-Kabir gate. It keeps the same hours as the Mutrah branch.

Telephone & Fax The telephone office is in Ruwi on Souq Ruwi St near the intersection with Street 37. Two international call cabins are on the upper floor. You can also send faxes from a desk in the main lobby. The office is open daily from 7.30 am to 9.30 pm.

Travel Agencies The capital's greatest concentration of travel agents is in and around Markaz Mutrah Al-Tijari St in Ruwi.

Bookshops There really aren't any decent English-language bookshops in the Muscat-Mutrah-Ruwi area. In fact, outside Muscat and Salalah there simply are no foreign-language bookshops. The easiest place to look for books, newspapers etc is in the bookstalls at Muscat's big hotels. The Family Bookshop chain also has stores in Qurm at the Qurm Commercial Centre, across from the Sabco Commercial Centre in Muscat. The larger hotels stock publications like the *APEX Explorer's Guide to Oman* and coffee-table books on Oman and the other Gulf States. If you want good foreign-language novels then bring them with you. Books in Oman are quite expensive – a paperback that in the USA sells for US$4.95 will cost OR 6 (about US$15.60) or more in Muscat.

Libraries The British Council's Muscat office (☎ 600548) is on the south side of Al-Inshirah St, which is parallel to and on the south side of Sultan Qaboos St, in Al-Khuwair. Their library is open to the public on Saturday, Sunday, Monday and Wednesday from 11 am to 8.45 pm and on Tuesday from 2 to 8.45 pm. They are closed Thursday and Friday. Though the library focuses mostly on reference works and information for people wanting to study in Britain there is also a very thorough section of books on the Middle East in general and Oman in particular. They also have current newspapers and magazines available for reading.

Medical Services Large hotels generally have a doctor on call, if not on staff, and this should be your first stop if you get sick. You may or may not be charged for a consultation with a hotel doctor. Expatriates usually have some sort of medical plan through their company and this would be the place you should go first if visiting an expat.

If you need hospitalisation this will probably be free, though if things get really serious you are likely to find yourself on the first plane headed home. The Al-Nahdha Hospital on the outskirts of Ruwi (on the left as you head from Ruwi toward Khuwair) is the main medical centre in the 'three cities' area.

Emergency Dial ☎ 999 for the police, an ambulance or to report a fire.

Things to See

Jalali, Mirani & Mutrah Forts All three forts took on more or less their present form in the 1580s during the Portuguese occupation of Muscat. Of the three, the Portuguese built only Mutrah Fort from scratch, though their alterations to the other two were so extensive that the forts can be said to be of Portuguese rather than Arab construction.

All of the forts are still used by the police and/or military and are closed to the public, though Mutrah Fort has, occasionally, been opened to foreign tour groups with special permission. It's OK to photograph the forts.

Omani-French Museum This museum, in a restored turn-of-the-century building inside Muscat's walls near the Al-Kabir gate, is largely an extended celebration of the sultan's state visit to France in 1989 and the French President François Mitterrand's state visit to Muscat in 1992, There are also several galleries detailing relations between the two countries in the 19th and early 20th centuries. The museum's upper level includes an interesting display on shipbuilding and scale models of different types of ocean-going vessels.

The house itself was built in 1896 by a niece of the then-sultan and enlarged in 1906 when it became the office and residence of the French consul in Muscat. Sultan Qaboos gave the building back to the French government in 1989, at which point it was converted into a museum. The museum's signs are in French and Arabic but a shortened English version of the text also appears on many of the exhibits.

The museum is open Saturday to Wednesday from 8.30 am to 1.30 pm. Admission is free. If you are coming into Muscat from Mutrah the museum is quite easy to find, as there are a lot of signs pointing the way. Once you pass through the Al-Kabir gate it is about 50m in and to your right.

National Aquarium Muscat has by far the best aquarium in the Gulf. It is south of old Muscat between Sidab and Al-Bustan. The turn is well signposted. Visiting hours are not

The Ship Sohar
This sailing vessel occupies the roundabout near the entrance to the Al-Bustan Palace hotel. The ship was built in Sur's dhow yard under the supervision of the Ministry of National Heritage to commemorate the voyage of Abdullah Bin Gasm, an Omani trader who reached Canton, China in the 8th century AD. The boat was built using the materials, methods and tools of Bin Gasm's era. In November 1980 the *Sohar* set sail for Canton, where she arrived eight months later. The ship is built largely of palm bark and rope. No nails were used in her construction. ■

posted, but presumably the opening times are roughly similar to those of the capital's other main museums: Saturday to Wednesday from around 8 am to 2 pm. Admission is free.

All of the specimens on display are native to Omani waters and most are accompanied by thorough descriptions in English. In addition to fish, crustaceans and coral there is a display of Omani sea shells in the lobby and a separate room with an open tank containing sea turtles.

Things to See – Medinat Qaboos
Oman Museum The Oman Museum is in the Ministries area; look for a small, white building next to the much larger, brown Ministry of Information building on a hill overlooking the rest of Medinat Qaboos. The museum is open Saturday to Wednesday from 7.30 am to 2.30 pm. It is closed Thursday and Friday. Admission is free. A free guidebook in English and French is on offer, but it's little more than a condensation of the wall signs.

The museum is small but well organised and is well worth the trek to Medinat Qaboos.

Displays on the ground floor cover the history, geography and geology of Oman from the third millennium BC onwards with an emphasis on trade routes and the country's trading history. There is also a display on shipbuilding detailing the designs

of different types of ocean-going dhows. One section of this floor charts the growth of Muscat and there is also a display on agriculture in the sultanate, including a large section on *falaj* (irrigation channel) systems and how they work. The 1st floor has a small display on Islam, consisting mostly of manuscripts, a fair to middling display of Omani arts and crafts, and an excellent room on architecture in the sultanate with an emphasis on forts.

To reach the museum by car take the exit off Sultan Qaboos St marked for the Muscat Inter-Continental Hotel (the same exit that has signs for the Children's Museum). If you are coming from the direction of Ruwi or Mutrah go around the roundabout at the exit and take Al-Ilam St across the bridge over Sultan Qaboos St then turn right on Al-Inshirah St. If you are approaching from the other direction (say, from the Natural History Museum or the embassies area in Medinat Qaboos) take the exit marked for the Inter-Continental Hotel, turn right on Al-Ilam St and then left on Al-Inshirah St before you cross over the bridge.

Once you are on Al-Inshirah St go 850m and take the 5th left, onto Way 1595, then go 400m and turn left onto Way 1526. After another 250m turn right onto Way 1530. From there, go 550m and turn right at a sign for the Oman Museum (actually this is nearly a 180° turn). Another 150m brings you, at last, to the door.

You can also reach the museum by taking bus No 23 to the exit where there is a sign for the Muscat Inter-Continental Hotel, and then walking. However, as it is a long way and all uphill, I strongly recommend taking a taxi if you don't have access to a car.

Children's Museum This museum (☎ 605369), near the Foreign Ministry off Sultan Qaboos St (it's well signposted), is open Saturday to Wednesday from 8 am to 2 pm and Thursday from 9 am to 1 pm. It is also open Monday evenings from 4 to 8 pm for families only. It is closed on Friday; admission is free. The museum is a practical, science-oriented place with lots of hands-on displays. You do not have to be a child to have fun here.

Natural History Museum This is a museum you should definitely try to visit before heading out of the capital. The museum is on Al-Wazarat St, which runs parallel to Sultan Qaboos St on the side toward the sea, in the Ministries area. Look for a small green sign with a drawing of a lynx (the museum's symbol) indicating the exit. The museum is open Saturday to Wednesday from 8 am to 2 pm and Thursday from 9 am to 1 pm. It is also open Sunday and Friday afternoons from 4 to 7 pm.

The first hall to the right as you enter the museum contains a brief region-by-region description of Oman's geography, geology, flora and fauna. To the left, the main gallery has lots of stuffed specimens of the fauna. Going out the main door of the museum and turning right takes you to the whale hall, which is dominated by a skeleton of a sperm whale and includes a short film on whales. There is also a small botanical garden near the museum's parking lot.

Everything at the museum is labelled in both English and Arabic.

To get there by public transport, take bus No 23. Look for the museum off the road on the right as you come from Ruwi.

Things to See – Mutrah
Mutrah Fish Market The fish market is at the northern end of the Mutrah Corniche near the Mina and Corniche hotels. In addition to fish, meat is also sold here and you will sometimes find shell merchants. The best time to come is early in the morning. The market usually opens around 6.30 am.

Mutrah Souk The Mutrah souk is without a doubt the most interesting souk in the Arab Gulf States. Be sure to stop for a drink at the teahouse on the left-hand side of the main entrance. Most visitors head immediately for the dozen or so shops specialising in **antique silver jewellery**. To reach these turn up the first alley on your right (more or less opposite the teahouse) after entering the souk through the main gateway on the Mutrah Corniche. You will go up a slight incline, passing through a portion of the cloth souk, before reaching the small group of shops selling antique silver.

Another place worth wandering around is

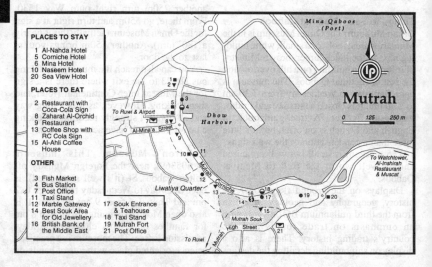

PLACES TO STAY
1 Al-Nahda Hotel
5 Corniche Hotel
6 Mina Hotel
10 Naseem Hotel
20 Sea View Hotel

PLACES TO EAT
2 Restaurant with Coca-Cola Sign
8 Zaharat Al-Orchid
9 Restaurant
13 Coffee Shop with RC Cola Sign
15 Al-Ahli Coffee House

OTHER
3 Fish Market
4 Bus Station
7 Post Office
11 Taxi Stand
12 Marble Gateway
14 Best Souk Area for Old Jewellery
16 British Bank of the Middle East
17 Souk Entrance & Teahouse
18 Taxi Stand
19 Mutrah Fort
21 Post Office

Mina Qaboos (Port)

Mutrah

0   125   250 m

To Ruwi & Airport

Dhow Harbour

Al-Mina'a Street

Mutrah Corniche

Liwatiya Quarter

To Watchtower, Al-Inshirah Restaurant & Muscat

Mutrah Souk

High Street

To Ruwi

the **spice souk**. To reach this head directly into the souk from the entrance on the Corniche and make a sharp turn (nearly a U-turn) to your left after about 100m when you reach a fountain with large mock-ups of Omani jewellery in it.

As with any good Arab souk, however, the best thing to do is simply to wander at will. The Mutrah souk is not really very big and you are in no danger of getting lost, though there may be moments when it does not look that way.

Watchtower At the eastern end of the Corniche, above and behind the Al-Inshirah restaurant, a restored watchtower looks out over Mutrah. The climb is steep and involves more than 100 stairs, but the view from the top is worth it. The tower's staircase can be reached either by going through the restaurant or by walking down past the restaurant's service entrance (on the right hand side as you face the building).

Things to See – Ruwi

National Museum You could easily miss the National Museum (☎ 701289), on A'Noor St near the intersection with Al-Burj St, but it is definitely worth a look. The museum is open Saturday to Wednesday from 7.30 am to 2.30 pm. It is closed Thursday and Friday. Admission is free. Photography is strictly prohibited.

On the ground floor, the entry area contains what are best described as odds and ends – a plaque commemorating the dedication of Muscat's first hospital in 1909 sits near Omani-made pottery that is for sale (at very good – fixed – prices). Going up the stairs you will pass several excellent examples of the ornately decorated wooden chests for which Oman is known (and which Arab craftspeople in the former Omani colonies along the East African coast still make).

The real exhibit area is on the upper floor, a single large hall with a number of small rooms off to its sides. Much of the central area of this main hall is given over to cases displaying Omani silverwork of various kinds, making the museum an ideal place to

visit before any souvenir-hunting expedition you may be planning. Starting from the right, you will find, first, a room containing kitchen utensils followed by a room displaying traditional women's dresses and by another room done in the style of a typical sitting room or bedroom in an old Omani home.

This brings you to the large mural covering the entire rear wall of the main hall. The mural shows trade routes throughout Oman's history and also has scale models of several different types of trading vessels.

Starting down the rooms on the other side of the main hall you will find first a room displaying different kinds of coffeepots (again, a good place to look before you shop) along with guns and Chinese porcelain, some of which was once owned by the (Omani) Sultan of Zanzibar. Next is a room devoted to the ruling Al-Busaid (Al-Bu Said) family, including jewellery and khanjars once owned by various members of both the Muscat and Zanzibar branches of the family. The final room on this side of the main hall is devoted to space and includes two small Omani flags carried to the moon and back by American astronauts.

Sultan's Armed Forces Museum This museum is open Sunday, Monday, Wednesday and Thursday from 8.30 am to 1 pm. On Thursday the museum is also open from 4 to 6 pm. Admission is 500 baisa for adults, free for children under 18. You are usually required to go through the museum with a guide (even if the two of you do not share a common language) and photography is strictly prohibited.

The museum, run by the Omani Army, is in the Bait Al-Falaj Fort, which gives its name to the Bait Al-Falaj district. The fort is one of the oldest buildings in Muscat. It was built in 1845 as a royal summer home, was restored extensively in the early 1900s and served as the headquarters for the Omani army from WWI until 1978. The museum is quite well presented and the lower floor is definitely worth a visit.

The museum is divided into sections on

Pre-Islamic Oman, Oman & Islam, the Portuguese in Oman, the Al-Ya'aribah (Al-Ya'ribi) dynasty, the Al-Busaidi (Al-Busaid) dynasty, the establishment of the armed forces and the 'incident at Jabal Akhdar and Dhorfur (Dhofar) mutiny' (the insurrections which the current sultan had to put down during his early years on the throne).

The ground floor's exhibits provide an excellent outline of Omani history, while those on the upper level are more specifically military in nature. Leaving the fort's main door and turning left around the building you will pass a low stone enclosure on your right. This contains the fort's falaj. Beyond this is the remainder of the military exhibit – a re-creation of a field command post, a large collection of military vehicles and weapons and a Cadillac Fleetwood that once belonged to the sultan.

Ruwi Souk The Ruwi souk is a good place for shopping, but it is not exactly a tourist attraction. Like the rest of Ruwi it is a modern creation. Those in search of gold jewellery should try Souk Ruwi St.

Clock Tower During the day, little distinguishes Ruwi's clock tower, just off Al-Jaame St, from the dozens of other such structures around the Gulf. You have to stop by after dark for the full effect. The base of the tower on the side facing Al-Jaame St is made up entirely of TV screens and once the sun goes down they blare out Oman TV's signal to any and all passers-by; loudspeakers are strategically positioned around the adjacent square. It's reminiscent of George Orwell's *1984*.

Activities
Pick up a copy of *Oman Today* for information on Muscat's various sporting clubs and societies.

Beaches One of the Muscat area's more popular public beaches is at Jussa, south of the Al-Bustan Palace Hotel off the Qantab Rd. It is a popular picnic spot for Omani families, especially on public holidays.

Beach Clubs Many of the large hotels will let outsiders use their beach facilities for a fee. While a bit expensive (it is free if you are staying in the hotel) these beaches should definitely be considered by unaccompanied women, who are far less likely to suffer from harassment here than at a public beach. Women with a male escort who simply do not like being stared at might want to consider forking out for the hotels too.

The Al-Bustan Palace has far and away the best facilities, though the entrance fee is pretty steep at OR 6 (OR 10 on Thursday and Friday). For this you get access to their pool, spa, sauna and a large private beach. The complex also includes a restaurant, beachside cafe and two bars. Kayaks can be rented for OR 3 per hour and windsurfers for OR 4 per hour. Snorkelling equipment is OR 2 per hour.

Getting onto the beach at the Muscat Inter-Continental is a bit cheaper at OR 4 on weekdays and OR 5 on Thursday and Friday (OR 3 for children under 18 years), but both the facilities and the beach itself are a lot less impressive. Windsurfers cost OR 2.500 per hour, and you can use the squash and tennis courts for OR 1 per hour. There's also a swimming pool.

Diving The Oman Dive Centre (☎ 950261) is in Jussa, south of the Al-Bustan Palace Hotel. Day memberships cost OR 2 and one 45-minute dive with full equipment costs OR 10. The fee for two dives is OR 19. If you bring your own gear these fees drop to OR 5.500/10.500. Half-day snorkelling trips are also available for OR 4.500.

To reach the centre take the Qantab exit off the road from Al-Bustan to Ruwi then take a right at the turn-off for Jussa and follow the signs to the dive centre.

Ice Skating Muscat's ice rink (☎ 696492) is on Al-Khuwair St, 2.5 km west of the Khuwair roundabout. The rink is open Saturday to Wednesday from 9 am to 10 pm,

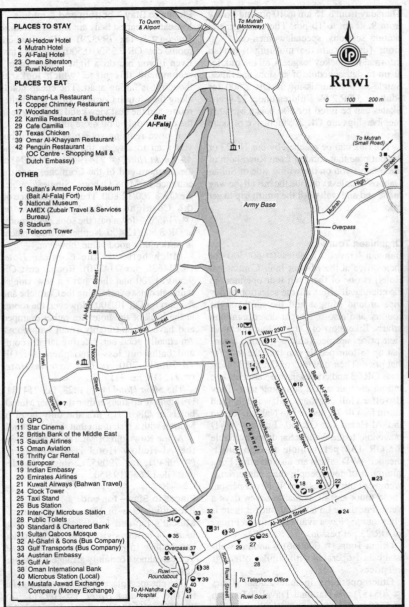

Ruwi

0   100   200 m

To Qurm & Airport

To Mutrah (Motorway)

To Mutrah (Small Road)

Bait Al-Falaj

Army Base

Overpass

PLACES TO STAY

3   Al-Hedow Hotel
4   Mutrah Hotel
5   Al-Falaj Hotel
23 Oman Sheraton
36 Ruwi Novotel

PLACES TO EAT

2   Shangri-La Restaurant
14 Copper Chimney Restaurant
17 Woodlands
22 Kamilia Restaurant & Butchery
29 Cafe Camilia
37 Texas Chicken
39 Omar Al-Khayyam Restaurant
42 Penguin Restaurant
    (OC Centre - Shopping Mall &
    Dutch Embassy)

OTHER

1   Sultan's Armed Forces Museum
    (Bait Al-Falaj Fort)
6   National Museum
7   AMEX (Zubair Travel & Services
    Bureau)
8   Stadium
9   Telecom Tower

10 GPO
11 Star Cinema
12 British Bank of the Middle East
13 Saudia Airlines
15 Oman Aviation
16 Thrifty Car Rental
18 Europcar
19 Indian Embassy
20 Emirates Airlines
21 Kuwait Airways (Bahwan Travel)
24 Clock Tower
25 Taxi Stand
26 Bus Station
27 Inter-City Microbus Station
28 Public Toilets
30 Standard & Chartered Bank
31 Sultan Qaboos Mosque
32 Al-Ghafri & Sons (Bus Company)
33 Gulf Transports (Bus Company)
34 Austrian Embassy
35 Gulf Air
38 Oman International Bank
40 Microbus Station (Local)
41 Mustafa Jawad Exchange
    Company (Money Exchange)

Al-Mujamma Street

Al-Burj Street

A'Noor Street

Ruwi Street

Mutrah High Street

Storm Channel

Bank Al-Markazi Street

Markaz Mutrah At-Tijari Street

Bait Al-Falaj Street

Way 2307

Al-Furqan Street

Al-Jaame Street

Souk Ruwi Street

Ruwi Roundabout

Ruwi Souk

To Al-Nahdha Hospital

To Telephone Office

Overpass

OMAN

Thursday from 8.15 am to 10 pm and Friday from 9.30 am to 10 pm. There are general skating sessions, special women-only sessions (usually in the mornings) and an informal ice hockey league. Call the rink for an up-to-date schedule of sessions and times. Single-session admission is OR 2.500 for adults and OR 2 for children under 12 years. Skates can be hired for 500 baisa. Monthly memberships are OR 30, inclusive of skate hire.

The rink can be reached by bus No 23 or 26, but note that coming from Ruwi both of these leave you on the wrong side of Sultan Qaboos St unless you ride the bus all the way to the end and wait until the return trip to get off.

Organised Tours

Bahwan Travel Agencies (☎ 600500 for their office at the Muscat Inter-Continental Hotel) is one of the main tour operators in the country. It offers a large selection of day trips around Muscat and the north of the country and also overnight desert camping safaris. Like most of Oman's tour operators their prices are per vehicle – which means that up to four people can take the tour for that price. Their day tour of Greater Muscat costs OR 23 and comes in two varieties – an antiquities tour and a shopping tour. They also offer a full-day tour to Nizwa, Bahla and Jabrin for OR 70, and one to Nakhal, Rustaq and Al-Hazm for OR 50. Full-day 4WD excursions to the Wahiba Sands are available for OR 133 per vehicle though other, cheaper, 4WD safaris are also on offer. For a minimum of four people they can arrange evening dhow cruises for OR 10 per person. These tours are all available seven days a week. For those on a tighter budget there is a bus tour to Nizwa available only on Friday for OR 23 per person.

Orient Tours (☎ 605066) is another well-established operator with similar offerings and prices.

Other operators include Zubair Tours (☎ 705457) and National Travel & Tourism (☎ 566046, fax 566125) in Wattiyah.

Places to Stay – bottom end & middle

Muscat's cheapest beds are at the *Al-Hedow Hotel* (☎ & fax 799329) in Ruwi where rooms cost OR 7.350/10.500, including tax. Even if you are on a tight budget I can't recommend this place, which looks as though it is falling apart. The cheap hotels along the Mutrah Corniche offer both better rooms and the best views and atmosphere in the city for only a bit more money.

If price remains your main concern but you want to stay on the Corniche try the *Al-Nahda Hotel* (☎ 714196, fax 714994) at the northern end of the Corniche, near the entrance to Mina Qaboos. Singles/doubles are OR 8.700/12.800. The cheapest place on the Corniche is the *Sea View Hotel* (☎ 714555), down past the souk, with rooms at OR 8.600/12.400. Neither of these places is particularly good value, however.

Much better is the *Corniche Hotel* (☎ 714636, fax 714770). Rooms cost OR 9.500/14.700 and they have a few singles with balconies overlooking the Corniche and the port for OR 10.500. However, the rooms at the back of the hotel are rather cramped and have uncomfortably small bathrooms. An equally good bet, offering larger rooms and baths but less atmosphere for OR 10.500/14.700, is the *Naseem Hotel* (☎ 712418, fax 711728).

The *Mina Hotel* (☎ 711828, fax 714981) is a bit more up-market than the other Mutrah hotels at OR 12/15. It's the only hotel in Mutrah with a restaurant that serves alcohol.

At the Ruwi end of Mutrah High St near the Al-Hedow Hotel is *Mutrah Hotel* (☎ 798401, fax 790953). Singles/doubles cost OR 13.650/19.950.

Places to Stay – top end

Everything else in Muscat is expensive. Muscat's top-end hotels can all sponsor tourist or business visas. The prices quoted here include 15% tax and the service charge. You can almost certainly arrange a discount of some sort.

The cheapest place that can arrange a visa is the *Al-Falaj Hotel* (☎ 702311, fax 795853) on Al-Mujamma St in Bait Al-Falaj.

Rooms cost OR 31.500/37.800. A bit more expensive, but very centrally located, is the *Ruwi Novotel* (☎ 704244, fax 704248) on Ruwi St. It charges OR 33.600/38.850. Also in Ruwi is the *Oman Sheraton* (☎ 799899, fax 795791) with singles/doubles costing OR 66.700/75.900.

The *Al-Bustan Palace* (☎ 799666, fax 799600) is a long way from anything else in the capital region, but it's worth the drive just for a look at its massive atrium lobby. Nestled away in its own cove south of Muscat, the hotel was built in the early '80s as the venue for a GCC summit meeting. The hotel is a small resort with an emphasis on water sports. Singles/doubles start at a whopping OR 102/119.600. If you want to live like an emir you can always stay in the Grand Deluxe Suite for a mere OR 776.

In Medinat Qaboos the *Muscat Inter-Continental Hotel* (☎ 600500, fax 600012) is another self-contained mini-resort with its own beach, but it's not as grand as the Al-Bustan Palace. Rooms can be had for a mere OR 58.650/64.400 (more if you want a sea view).

Out by the airport is the slightly tatty *Seeb Novotel Muscat* (☎ 510300, fax 510055) with rooms at OR 41.400/49.450.

Places to Eat – cheap & medium-priced

Mutrah Of the several small restaurants at the northern end of the Mutrah Corniche, the best is the place with the green-and-red-on-white *Restaurant* sign near the roundabout near the Mina Hotel. It is fairly spartan, and sometimes water is the only drink available, but the biryanis are quite good and cost only 500 baisa per helping. Stand-up snacks are available from the kiosk at the bus station on the Mutrah Corniche. A short distance inland from the roundabout, the *Zaharat Al-Orchid* coffee shop and restaurant has excellent shawarma and also offers cheap sandwiches, burgers and fresh juice. Oddly there are two restaurants with this name a few metres apart. The better of the two is the one further inland.

The semi-circular building on the Corniche between the Naseem Hotel and the entrance to the souk, sporting an RC Cola sign with the words *Coffee Shop* emblazoned on it is a particularly good place for cheap, quick meals. Try the chickpeas masala for 200 baisa.

Inside the Mutrah souk you should definitely make your way to the *Al-Ahli Coffee House*. The house speciality is fresh juice at 300 to 400 baisa per glass. They also offer an excellent mixed juice 'cocktail' for 600 baisa. Burgers and sandwiches are available for 300 to 500 baisa apiece. To reach the coffee house from the Mutrah Corniche entrance to the souk go directly into the souk and keep right at the first fork (the one with the fountain). Follow this street until you reach a T-junction by the Muscat pharmacy. Turn left at this junction and the coffee house will be on your right after 25m.

The only cheapish restaurant in Mutrah that serves alcohol is *Albahr* (which is Arabic for the sea), the restaurant at the Mina Hotel. If you are not staying in the hotel, however, they won't serve booze unless you order a meal. The view of Mutrah is great and the Indian food is excellent. Main dishes cost about OR 3, plus drinks. The hotel's street level *coffee shop* is also a popular local gathering spot, particularly on cool evenings when both Omanis and foreigners can be found munching shawarma or falafel and sipping tea in front of the hotel.

Of course, the one place you must not miss under any circumstances is the *teahouse* at the entrance to the Mutrah souk. Sweet tea is 75 baisa a cup, served as you sit on stone benches on either side of the entry archway. No visit to Muscat would be complete without a pit stop here.

Muscat The pickings here are pretty slim. Try the *Al-Badiyeh Restaurant* to the south of the post office. The menu is mostly mid-priced Indian. Most main dishes cost OR 1 to OR 2.

Ruwi There are several good bets in Ruwi, such as the *Kamilia Restaurant & Butchery* just off Al-Jaame St. The fare here includes biryanis at OR 1.500 and grilled dishes, such

OMAN

as kebabs, for OR 1.800, including soup and salad. Chinese main dishes cost OR 1.200 to OR 1.500. Outdoor tables are available during the winter. The view of the parking lot is hardly romantic but the breeze is nice. A cafe serving shawarma and an ice-cream shop, both also run by Kamilia, are part of the same complex.

Across Al-Jaame St from the Ruwi bus station *Cafe Camilia* is a good spot for a quick snack with sandwiches and shawarma for 200 baisa.

Texas Chicken at the corner of A'Noor and Al-Jaame Sts has good chicken and burgers, but you should really visit to try their excellent, and cheap, Chinese and Filipino noodle dishes costing OR 1.200 each. The *Penguin Restaurant* in the OC Centre at the Ruwi roundabout is part of a local fast-food chain serving burgers and fried chicken. A bit more up-market, but still fairly cheap, is the *Omar Al-Khayyam Restaurant*, across Al-Jaame St from Texas Chicken, near the Oman International Bank. It has both Chinese and Indian food, including a wide selection of Indian vegetarian dishes, most of which are OR 2 or less.

If you want to have a drink with dinner and do not want to pay handsomely for the privilege try *Woodlands*, an Indian restaurant off Bank Al-Markazi St. The food is pretty good and moderately-priced with most main dishes at OR 1.500 to OR 2.200 and a few under one riyal. Most of the food is fairly spicy.

Ruwi and Qurm are the places to go for western fast food.

Places to Eat – expensive All of the following restaurants serve alcohol unless otherwise noted.

A good choice if you need an up-market restaurant for a business meeting is the *Copper Chimney Restaurant*, just off Markaz Mutrah Al-Tijari St in Ruwi. They have some of the best Indian food in Muscat and the surroundings are quite dignified. Dinner is fairly expensive at OR 5 to OR 7, but the food is great. The *Cooper Chimney Chinese Restaurant*, on the floor immedi-

ately above the main Cooper Chimney restaurant, is even more expensive with meals running at OR 10 per person and up. A much better bet for Chinese food is *Shangri-La* at the Ruwi end of Mutrah High St, near the Mutrah Hotel. They offer what may be the best Chinese food in Oman. Main dishes mostly cost OR 3.500 and up, but the portions are very large.

Al-Inshirah, a seafood restaurant on the Mutrah Corniche specialising in Thai dishes, is very expensive at OR 10 or more per person, but it offers a great view as compensation.

Entertainment
Muscat is rather thin when it comes to entertainment. There are discos at the Muscat Inter-Continental Hotel and at the Oman Sheraton Hotel and many of the big hotels have lounge acts of some sort in their bars.

The Star Cinema (☎ 791641) shows both western and Indian films (though rather more of the latter). Tickets are OR 1 and 800 baisa. It is the unmistakable round building in Ruwi near the GPO.

Things to Buy
One result of the growth of tourism in Oman has been that while the Mutrah souk remains a great place to wander around and soak in the atmosphere, it has become a pretty pricey place to shop for Omani handicrafts.

The best place to look for both khanjars and silver jewellery is, oddly enough, a shopping mall out in Qurm. Inside the Sabco Commercial Centre is an area with dagger and jewellery shops called, appropriately, 'the souk', which includes a government-run handicrafts centre with fixed prices. The government shop's khanjars go for about OR 70 each. This, and the fact that most people shopping in Qurm are expats who have more time on their hands than the average tourist, has held down prices at the other shops in the area.

Those with a lot of money to spend should visit Antique World (☎ & fax 566503) on the ground floor of the Al-Harthy Complex shopping mall in Qurm. The shop specialises in antique khanjars and other handicrafts as well as more generic Middle Eastern collectibles, such as David Roberts lithographs.

See Things to Buy in the Facts for the Visitor section in this chapter for detailed information on things to buy in Muscat's various markets.

Getting There & Away

Air Seeb international airport is 37 km from Muscat or Mutrah. The departure tax is OR 3 for international trips (there is no departure tax for domestic flights). Note that domestic flights other than those to Salalah are not shown on the arrivals and departures monitors.

Domestic and international flights use the same check-in and departure areas. Domestic passengers can purchase goods in the duty-free shop with the exception of alcohol. Like virtually every airport in the Gulf, Seeb offers 1000-ticket car raffles. Seeb duty-free is not, however, the place to do your last-minute souvenir shopping. The handicrafts are hugely overpriced and the khanjars are quite low-quality.

The departure lounge also offers a post office, bank, restaurant and snack bar. For airport flight information call ☎ 519223 or ☎ 519456.

See Domestic Air Services in the Getting Around section in this chapter for details of domestic flights out of Muscat.

Some of the airlines flying out of Muscat are:

Air India
    Markaz Mutrah Al-Tijari St, Ruwi (☎ 708639)
Air Lanka
    Mezoon Travel, Al-Burj St, Bait Al-Falaj (☎ 796680)
Air Tanzania
    Oman Aviation office, just off Markaz Mutrah Al-Tijari St, Ruwi (☎ 704004)
Biman Bangladesh
    At the intersection of A'Noor and Al-Jaame Sts in Ruwi, in the same building as Texas Chicken (☎ 701128)
British Airways
    Al-Jaame St (access from Markaz Mutrah Al-Tijari St), Ruwi (☎ 702244)

EgyptAir
    At the intersection of Bank Al-Markazi and Markaz Mutrah Al-Tijari Sts, Ruwi, next door to the Emirates Airlines office (☎ 796134)
Emirates Airlines
    At the intersection of Bank Al-Markazi and Markaz Mutrah Al-Tijari Sts, Ruwi (☎ 786600)
Ethiopian Airlines
    Ruwi St, Ruwi, just south of the Ruwi roundabout (☎ 796976)
Gulf Air
    Musandam Building, Ruwi St, near the Ruwi roundabout (☎ 703555)
Iran Air
    Bank Meli Iran building, Al-Burj St, Ruwi (☎ 787423)
KLM
    Qurm Commercial Centre, Qurm, 1st floor, entrance from the back of the building (☎ 566737)
Kuwait Airways
    Bahwan Travel Agencies, Markaz Mutrah Al-Tijari St, Ruwi (☎ 707119)
Lufthansa
    Al-Burj St, Bait Al-Falaj (☎ 708986)
MEA (Middle East Airlines)
    Mezoon Travel, Al-Burj St, Bait Al-Falaj (☎ 796680)
Oman Aviation/Oman Air
    Just off Markaz Mutrah Al-Tijari St, Ruwi (☎ 707222)
PIA (Pakistan International Airlines)
    Markaz Mutrah Al-Tijari St, Ruwi, next to the Saudia office (☎ 792460)
Royal Jordanian
    Mezoon Travel, Al-Burj St, Bait Al-Falaj (☎ 796680)
Saudia
    Markaz Mutrah Al-Tijari St, Ruwi (☎ 789485)
Syrianair
    Al-Jaame St, Ruwi, behind the Oman International Bank (☎ 703662)
Swissair
    Bank Al-Markazi St, Ruwi (☎ 703303)
Thai Airways International
    Bahwan Travel Agencies, Markaz Mutrah Al-Tijari St, Ruwi (☎ 705934)

Bus The Ruwi bus station (☎ 708522) is the main depot for inter-city buses in the sultanate. There is a waiting room at the bus station. Luggage can be stored in the cargo area (around the side of the ticket office).

There are three buses per day to Buraimi (3¾ hours on the morning express bus, six hours on the regular afternoon buses, OR 3.600) at 7 am, and 1 and 3 pm. The Buraimi

OMAN

buses travel via Barka (one hour express, 1½ hours regular, 900 baisa) and Sohar (2¾ hours for the morning express bus, four hours for the afternoon buses, OR 2.200).

Buses for Ibri (4½ hours express, 5¼ hours regular, OR 3.200) leave daily at 8 am (express), 2.30 pm (express) and 4 pm (regular). Ibri buses travel via Fanja (one hour express or regular, 600 baisa), Samail (about 1½ hours for either service, 900 baisa), Nizwa (2½ hours express, three hours regular, OR 1.600), Bahla (three hours express, 3½ hours regular, OR 2) and Jabrin (four hours express, five hours regular, OR 2.200). There are also extra regular buses to Nizwa via Fanja and Samail at 6 and 10 am and 6 pm. You can also reach Fanja on the Sur buses.

Other inter-city routes include: Rustaq (three hours, OR 1.800) daily at 6 pm, via Barka (1½ hours, 900 baisa) and Nakhal (two hours, OR 1.500); and Sur (4¼ hours express, 5½ hours regular, OR 3.400) via Al-Kamil (3½ hours express, 4½ hours regular, OR 2.500) daily at 7.30 am (express), 2.30 pm (express) and 4.30 pm (regular).

Salalah is the only route on which ONTC has competition. ONTC's buses leave daily at 7 am and 7 pm with an extra bus at 6 pm from mid-June through mid-September. All their Salalah buses leave one hour later during Ramadan. The trip takes 12 hours, including a couple of rest stops. The fare is OR 8 one way and OR 16 return. There is also a 'family fare' of OR 40 which includes return transportation for two adults and two children. From mid-June through to mid-September the family fare can only be used on the day buses and it is not valid for travel during and for two days before and after Eid Al-Fitr and Eid Al-Adha. Note that there is no computerised reservation system. Any return reservation you make to or from Salalah should be reconfirmed directly with ONTC as soon as you arrive, especially if you are travelling on a weekend or a holiday.

Booking a day or two early is not necessary but would be a good idea if you really want to travel on a particular bus.

The competition comes from three companies, all of which have offices in the area behind the Sultan Qaboos Mosque in Ruwi. Gulf Transports, just off A'Noor St, has buses to Salalah daily at 7 am and 5 pm for OR 8 one way and OR 14 return. Al-Ghafri & Sons (☎ 707896) has buses at 6.30 am and 4.45 pm at the same prices. Bin Qasim Transport (☎ 785059), next door to Al-Ghafri, has a daily bus at 3 pm for OR 5 one way, OR 9 return.

ONTC's coaches on the Salalah route are very high-quality, relatively new, European-made vehicles with toilets on board. Al-Ghafri and the others use older, Egyptian-made buses, some with toilets. Whomever you travel with you must have your passport available for inspection at a checkpoint about mid-way through the trip.

The only international bus service is to Dubai. Buses leave twice a day, at 7.30 am and 4.30 pm, from the Ruwi bus station. During Ramadan the late bus leaves at 5.30 pm. The trip takes six hours. In Dubai the buses come and go from Airline Centre on Al-Maktoum Rd in Deira, Dubai. The fare is OR 9 one way, OR 16 return. A family fare of OR 36 is also available, which covers return transportation for two adults and two children. The fare is not valid for travel during and for two days before and for two days after either Eid Al-Fitr or Eid Al-Adha.

Taxi & Microbus Greater Muscat has two main service-taxi stands for both taxis and microbuses. One is in Ruwi across Al-Jaame St from the main bus station while the other is out at the Seeb clock tower (formally the Sahwa Tower) roundabout, beyond the airport. Most of the taxis and microbuses out at the clock tower wait around in a parking lot on the far side of the clock tower as you approach it from Muscat. A few can often be found at other edges of the roundabout, but the main lot should be your first stop. A shared taxi from Ruwi to the clock tower costs 500 baisa. Microbuses charge 300 baisa for the same trip. From Mutrah the taxi/microbus fare is 700/300 baisa.

There is a lot of traffic along main routes

to places like Rustaq, Sohar, Nizwa and Ibri. Taxis and microbuses to Sur and Buraimi are harder to come by and drivers going to Salalah exist more in theory than in practice.

Some sample taxi/microbus fares are: Barka OR 1/300 baisa, Sohar OR 2.500/1.700, Rustaq OR 2/800 baisa, Nakhal OR 2/1, Samail OR 1/500 baisa, Nizwa OR 1.500/1, Ibri OR 3/2, and Sur OR 3.500/3. Only taxis make the trip to Buraimi, at OR 5 per person. To take any vehicle 'engaged' (ie all by yourself) multiply the number of seats by the fares listed here and be prepared to bargain. The driver won't go below the seats-times-fare formula but he may insist on a premium, particularly if you want to travel after dark.

Car There are several rental agencies in the area around the Ruwi roundabout as well as the usual desks in big hotels and at the airport. I was able to negotiate a fairly good rate for a long term (10 day) rental with Europcar (☎ 700190) but it took quite a lot of haggling. Thrifty Car Rental (☎ 784275) was also competitive, though not as willing to bargain over the number of free km. Among local agencies Mark Rent-a-Car (☎ 562444) offers competitive rates and well-maintained vehicles.

These, and most other car rental offices in Muscat, charge an extra OR 2 to OR 4 if you pick up or drop off the car at the airport.

Getting Around

The Airport To get a bus to the city centre turn left as you come out onto the street from the arrivals area and walk about 200m until you are down at the departures end of the terminal building. The bus stop is across the street from the building itself, adjacent to the road that brings cars into the airport from Sultan Qaboos St.

Buses leave the airport for Ruwi and Mutrah at 6.44 and 7.10 am and thereafter at 20 and 54 minutes past the hour until 8.54 pm. On Friday buses leave the airport at 7.02 and 7.42 am and then at nine, 20 and 50 minutes past the hour until 9.20 pm. The route also passes the Ruwi bus station and

the Qurm roundabout. The trip takes about 50 minutes and the fare is 200 baisa. Route 28 also passes the airport but it stops only at the Seeb airport roundabout on Sultan Qaboos St.

Bus Nos 23 and 24 leave for the airport from the Mutrah bus station at 20 and 50 minutes past the hour from 6.20 am to 9.50 pm daily, except Friday. On Friday (and on holidays) there is an additional bus at 5 minutes past the hour, but the buses do not start running until 7.20 am.

Taxis between the airport and the centre cost OR 6 to/from Ruwi and Mutrah and OR 5 to/from Qurm, Medinat Qaboos and Khuwair. If you share a service-taxi you should pay 500 to 700 baisa.

A few of the inter-city buses and the express buses from Salalah and Dubai also stop at the airport on their way into and out of Muscat.

Bus ONTC's system of local buses covers greater Muscat fairly thoroughly. Fares are either 100 or 200 baisa (300 baisa to Sultan Qaboos University), depending on the distance travelled. Destinations are displayed on the front of the buses in Arabic and English, but the bus numbers are only in Arabic numerals. The main bus station (☎ 708522) is on Al-Jaame St in Ruwi (the same place that the inter-city buses leave from) and there is a secondary station by the roundabout near the Mina Hotel in Mutrah. Bus Nos 2, 4, 23, 24, 28, 31 and 32 all run between the Mutrah and Ruwi stations for 200 baisa. Generally speaking, most buses run two or three times an hour from around 6.30 am until around 10 or 10.30 pm. Printed schedules in English are available at the Ruwi bus station.

Bus routes within Greater Muscat are:

Route 1 – Ruwi bus station, Al-Jaame St, Ruwi roundabout, Ruwi St, Al-Burj St, Star Cinema, Bait Al-Falaj St, Oman Sheraton, Al-Wadi Al-Kabir roundabout, Al-Wadi Al-Kabir St, Al-Wadi Al-Kabir West, Al-Wadi Al-Kabir East. Returns via Al-Wadi Al-Kabir St, Al-Wadi Al-Kabir roundabout, Bait Al-Falaj St and Al-Jaame St to the Ruwi bus station

OMAN

Route 2 – Mutrah bus station, Mina Qaboos, Al-Mina'a roundabout, Al-Mina'a St, Jibroo, Bait al-Falaj roundabout, Bait Al-Falaj St, Al-Jaame St, Ruwi bus station, Ruwi roundabout, Hamriya roundabout, Al-Nahdha St, Al-Nahdha Hospital, Wadi Adei roundabout, Wadi Adei St. Returns via Wadi Adei St, Wadi Adei roundabout, Al-Nahdha Hospital, Al-Nahdha St, Hamriya roundabout, Ruwi roundabout, Ruwi St, Al-Burj roundabout, Jibroo, Al-Mina'a St, Al-Mina'a St, Mutrah bus station

Route 3 – Ruwi bus station, Ruwi roundabout, Hamriya roundabout, Al-Nahdha St, Al-Nahdha Hospital, Wadi Adei roundabout, Wadi Adei St. Returns via Wadi Adei St, Wadi Adei roundabout, Al-Nahdha Hospital, Al-Nahdha St, Hamriya roundabout, Ruwi roundabout, Ruwi St, Al-Burj roundabout, Al-Burj St, Bait Al-Falaj St, Al-Jaame St

Route 4 – Mutrah bus station, Mina Qaboos, Al-Mina'a roundabout, Al-Mina'a St, Jibroo, Bait Al-Falaj roundabout, Ruwi St, Al-Burj roundabout, Al-Burj St, Bait Al-Falaj St, Al-Jaame St, Ruwi bus station, Ruwi roundabout, Hamriya roundabout, Al-Nahdha St, Al-Nahdha Hospital, Wadi Adei roundabout, Wadi Adei roundabout, Watayah roundabout, Maidan Al-Fateh St to Khoula Hospital in Qurm Heights. Returns by the same route as far as the Ruwi roundabout and then continues via Al-Jaame St, Bait Al-Falaj St, Al-Burj St, Al-Burj roundabout, Ruwi St, Bait Al-Falaj St, Jibroo, Al-Mina'a St and the Al-Mina'a roundabout.

Route 23 – Mutrah bus station, Bait Al-Falaj roundabout, Mutrah business district, Ruwi bus station, Al-Nahdha St, Qurm roundabout, Sultan Qaboos St, Al-Khuwair roundabout, Ministries area, Al-Ghubra roundabout, Sultan Qaboos St, Seeb airport, Seeb clock tower, A'Seeb St, Al-Mawalah roundabout, Al-Hail, A'Shamaliyah St, Al-Khoudh roundabout, Wadi Al-Bahais St, Seeb souk and vice versa. On Friday and holidays the bus by-passes the Al-Ghubra roundabout.

Route 24 – Mutrah bus station, Bait Al-Falaj roundabout, Mutrah business district, Ruwi bus station, Al-Nahdha St, Qurm roundabout, Sultan Qaboos St, Al-Khuwair roundabout, Ministries area, Al-Ghubra roundabout, Bausher roundabout, Al-Ghubra St, Royal Hospital, Azaiba roundabout, Sultan Qaboos St, Seeb airport, Seeb clock tower, A'Seeb St, Al-Mawalah roundabout, Al-Khrais St, Al-Raudah St, Al-Hail North, Al-Adiyat St, Wadi Al-Bahais St, Seeb souk and vice versa. On Friday and holidays the bus by-passes the Al-Ghubra roundabout.

Route 25 – Ruwi roundabout, Hamriya roundabout, Al-Nahdha St, Al-Nahdha Hospital, Wadi Adei roundabout, Watayah roundabout, Qurm roundabout, Sultan Qaboos St, Dohat Al-Adab St, Al-Kulaiah St, Baushaer roundabout, Al-Ghubrah St, Sultan Qaboos Sports Complex, Royal Hospital, Ghala roundabout, Ghala St, Way 5221, Way 6041, Al-Omran St, Way 6421, Azaiba Heights

Route 26 (runs Friday and holidays only) – Ruwi roundabout, Hamriya roundabout, Al-Nahdha St, Al-Nahdha Hospital, Wadi Adei roundabout, Watayah roundabout, Qurm roundabout, Sultan Qaboos St, Al-Khuwair roundabout, Ministries area, Al-Ghubrah roundabout, Al-Baushaer roundabout, Al-Ghubrah St to Al-Baushaer Social Housing

Route 27 – Mabailah Housing Section 6, Al-Khuwair St, A'Sharadi St, Wadi Al-Arush St, Wadi Bahais St, Seeb souk

Route 28 – Mutrah bus station, Bait Al-Falaj roundabout, Mutrah business district, Ruwi bus station, Al-Nahdha St, Qurm roundabout, Sultan Qaboos St, Seeb airport roundabout, Seeb clock tower, Al-Mawaloh roundabout, Al-Hail Al-Jadeeda, Al-Khoudh Social Housing

Route 29 – Same as Route 27 except that it starts from the Mabailah Industrial Estate.

Routes 31 & 32 – Mutrah bus station, Bait Al-Falaj roundabout, Mutrah business district, Ruwi bus station, Al-Nahdha St, Wadi Adai roundabout, Al-Amarat St, Earth Satellite Station, Ibn Sina'a St, Seih A'Dhabi St, Wadi Hatat Section 2, Wadi Hatat Section 3, Hail Nahdha St, Medinat Al-Nahdha

Taxi Muscat's taxis, like all others in Oman, are orange and white. As in so many other Middle Eastern countries, a pernicious fare system operates in Muscat. If you bargain you will inevitably pay two or three times what you ought to, but the only way to pay the proper fare is to know it before you get into the cab and not to raise the subject of money at all – just hand the driver the proper sum at your destination.

Regular taxis also function as local service-taxis, usually travelling from ranks in various parts of the city. Local service-taxis also come disguised as pick-up trucks and microbuses. There is one rank on the Mutrah Corniche, and another in Ruwi opposite the bus station. Drivers usually stand by their vehicle shouting the destination or cruise around the neighbourhood looking for the last couple of passengers when they are almost full.

A taxi between Mutrah and Ruwi costs OR 1 in either direction if you take it by yourself ('engaged'), or 200 baisa if shared. The same trip in a microbus costs 100 baisa. Muscat to Mutrah is OR 1 engaged and Muscat to Ruwi OR 1.500 engaged. There are no shared taxis between Muscat and Ruwi. Mutrah to Qurm is OR 3 engaged or 300 baisa shared, and Ruwi to Qurm OR 2 engaged or 300 baisa shared.

Microbus In Mutrah, local microbuses cruise the Corniche, particularly the end near the Mina Hotel and the Mutrah bus station, while in Ruwi they park en masse in a lot across Al-Jaame St from the main bus station. They do not wait until they are full to begin their journey and may even set off on a heavily travelled route (such as Mutrah to Ruwi) with only one or two people on board. Mutrah to Ruwi costs 100 baisa, Mutrah to Muscat 150 baisa and no microbus journey within greater Muscat should cost more than 300 baisa, including trips to the airport. The only significant exception to this rule is trips to the main microbus station at the Seeb clock tower (beyond the airport). This trip is 500 baisa.

Microbus drivers within the city generally go wherever the spirit moves them. Before you get into the bus simply ask the driver 'Ruwi?', 'Medinat Qaboos?', 'Khuwair?', or whatever. He may not have originally planned to go there but will now that he has a paying passenger.

Car If you are driving bear in mind that the parking situation in both Muscat (ie the old port area) and Mutrah is pretty bad. Inside Muscat's walls in particular much of the space has been given over to reserved parking for official vehicles.

AROUND MUSCAT
A'Rusayl

On the road from Muscat to Nizwa, about 10 km past the Seeb clock tower and just before you reach the exit for A'Jifnain, you will pass two small forts. Until the ascension of Sultan Qaboos the fort closer to Muscat marked the boundary between Muscat and Oman. The fort has undergone some limited restoration work and is worth a quick photo stop if the traffic on the highway is not too heavy.

A service-taxi/microbus from the Ruwi station in Muscat to A'Rusayl costs 600/300 baisa. Regular ONTC buses make the trip for 300 baisa. Any of these will drop you in the village, several km from the fort, though you will pass the fort on your way into town.

Fanja
The town of Fanja, 75 km from Mutrah and just off the highway from Muscat to Nizwa and Sur, is well known as a good place to shop for **pottery**, though you should be aware that most of what you are going to find on offer is from Iran, not Oman.

The best place to look is by the BP petrol station on the edge of the main souk area. Look for people selling the pottery out of the back of small trucks. OR 1 to OR 3 buys some of the larger plain pieces or the smaller painted ones, such as incense burners.

If you arrive by microbus this is probably the area where you will be dropped. Microbus drivers charge 700 baisa for the trip to or from the Ruwi taxi and microbus stand. Service-taxis charge OR 1 for the trip. Regular buses (one hour, 600 baisa) bound for places further afield (such as Nizwa) stop in Fanja.

Northern Oman

BARKA
The small town of Barka, some 80 km west of Mutrah and Ruwi, makes an excellent day trip outside the capital, or an easy stopover on the way from Muscat to Sohar.

Orientation & Information
Barka is a well signposted turn-off on the main road from Muscat to Sohar. If you are

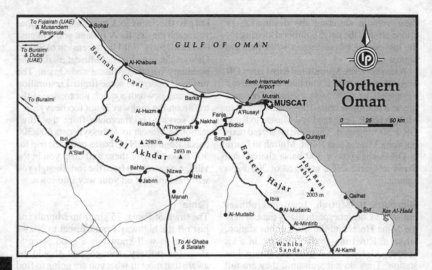

taking a microbus it will probably drop you at this junction and you will have to pick up another microbus to cover the extra few km to the centre. Barka Fort will be on your right as you enter town, just before reaching a major intersection at which a number of banks and a few small restaurants can be found. This is also where the taxis and microbuses hang around. Barka's post office is another 1½ km west of this intersection. There is no phone office in the centre but there are payphones and a number of shops sell phonecards.

Barka Fort

Coming into Barka from the main Muscat-Sohar highway you will pass Barka Fort, on your right, 400m before you reach the town's main intersection. The fort is open every day from 7.30 am to 6 pm. Admission is free. Technically, permits from the Ministry of National Heritage in Muscat are required to enter the fort, though this seems to be only loosely enforced. Photography is permitted inside the fort but videos are not.

As you enter the fort's main court look right. The door with spikes is approximately 300 years old. Going through this door and up the stairs to the right you will find a small

courtyard. The door on the left leads to the office of the *wali* (governor), a room now displaying several khanjars and other weapons as well as some jewellery. The door at the end of the office leads to a hall that served as a waiting room.

Other doors off the small courtyard lead to a bathroom (an old one, not a functioning one) and to the living quarters for the wali and his family, which occupy both this floor and the one above it. Be sure to see the master bedroom, which includes a display of china and porcelain. It is located on the upper level. The living area also includes a small prayer room, easily identified by the *mihrib* (niche indicating the wall facing Mecca) in its west wall.

Below the prayer room and to the left is a large open courtyard from which you can have access to one of the fort's defensive towers. Inside the tower (only one tower is open to visitors – the one directly across the courtyard if you enter it from the prayer room) is a well. You can also see several rooms that were used to store weapons and ammunition, and an underground prison. A staircase in the centre of the tower leads to the top, from where you will have a good view over the entire town.

Adjacent to the tower, the fort's main courtyard has a well and a mosque.

Bait Nua'man

This restored house, one of the largest in the area, gives you an idea of how the wealthier residents of Oman's coast lived several generations ago. Permits from Muscat are required for entry, but be warned that the site does not keep the same regular hours as the fort.

To reach Bait Nua'man from Barka Fort continue along the road that brought you into Barka from the main highway and go 4.8 km beyond the fort. This will bring you to a left turn onto a paved road. Take this turn (if you reach a roundabout you've gone too far) and follow the road 1.9 km. Bait Nua'man will be on your right.

Places to Eat

If you are in need of a meal try the *Sawahil Al-Bathna Restaurant*, on the main intersection across the street from the Commercial Bank of Oman. Look for a small restaurant with a lot of Lipton tea ads pasted to the door. Biryanis cost 500 baisa each.

Getting There & Away

There are four buses per day between Barka and Muscat's Ruwi bus station (one hour express, 1½ hours regular, 900 baisa). The express bus leaves Ruwi at 7 am. Regular buses leave at 1, 3 and 6 pm. The express bus from Barka to Ruwi leaves daily at 4.40 pm. Regular buses leave at 8.30 and 11.30 am, and 7.30 pm. The buses all come and go from the roundabout where the road into Barka meets the Muscat-Sohar highway.

Taxis and microbuses can be found both around the main intersection and at the junction of the Barka road with the Muscat-Sohar highway. A shared taxi from the Seeb clock tower taxi stand to Barka costs OR 1 per person and around OR 8 engaged. Microbuses charge 300 baisa per person for the trip from the Seeb clock tower roundabout to Barka.

SOHAR

Sohar, home port of the fictional Sinbad the sailor, is one of those places where history casts a shadow over modern reality. A thousand years ago it occupied three times its present area and was the largest town in the country.

By those standards Sohar today is something of a disappointment. The fort and its small museum are quite good. The town might be a candidate for a miss if you are pressed for time. If time is not a factor, or if you can combine Sohar with the Batinah Coast's other sites (Barka, Rustaq, Nakhal etc) it makes a good turn-around point for a two or three day swing out of Muscat and back and it definitely should not be missed.

History

Sohar's history stretches back to the 3rd millennium BC, when it was the seat of the Magan Empire and a major centre of the Batinah Coast's copper trade with powerful

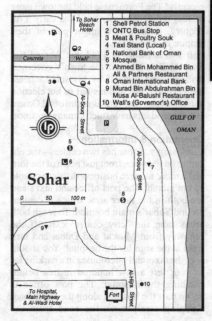

Map key:
1 Shell Petrol Station
2 ONTC Bus Stop
3 Meat & Poultry Souk
4 Taxi Stand (Local)
5 National Bank of Oman
6 Mosque
7 Ahmed Bin Mohammed Bin Ali & Partners Restaurant
8 Oman International Bank
9 Murad Bin Abdulrahman Bin Musa Al-Balushi Restaurant
10 Wali's (Governor's) Office

Sohar

empires further afield, including Sumer. It may be the 'Omana' mentioned by Pliny in the 1st century AD, and it is almost certainly the 'Emporium Persicum' ('Persian Market') near the Strait of Hormuz mentioned in a 5th century Byzantine text. The city, by then, was extremely rich – the Prophet Mohammed was buried in a silk shroud from Sohar.

From the 7th to the 13th centuries AD Sohar was the most important port and trading centre in Oman, rising to prominence as the frankincense trade in the south of the country died out. The 10th century Arab geographer Makdisi wrote glowingly of Sohar as a rich and beautiful city.

The city prospered during the Middle Ages and was incorporated into the Kingdom of Hormuz in the 14th century. In September 1507 the Portuguese bloodlessly captured the city, the governor surrendering to them because his overlords in Hormuz apparently had sent neither reinforcements nor the governor's own wages any time recently! The Portuguese held the town more or less uninterruptedly until the early 17th century, making it a major part of their empire in the Gulf.

It was at Sohar in 1744 that Ahmed Bin Said Al-Busaid, then the town's governor, distinguished himself by his stand against the Persians. His actions led to his election at Nizwa later that year as imam of all Oman. His descendants have ruled Oman ever since.

Orientation & Information

Confusingly, Sohar has two centres – the old centre on the waterfront just north of the fort, and a more modern business district a couple of km inland. The post office and taxi stand are both in the latter area, which is centred around Sohar's main hospital. To reach both areas take the 'city centre' exit off the highway from Muscat and Dubai and turn right at the sign for the hospital. You should spot the taxis and microbuses in a parking lot to your left a few hundred metres before reaching the hospital. The post office is 250m past the hospital along the same road. Keeping straight on the road from the

highway instead of taking the hospital turn brings you to the fort and the coast road. The distance from the highway to the fort is about 2.5 km. The modern business district around the hospital is about one km off the highway.

Sohar Fort

Sohar Fort is a large, whitewashed, slightly irregular rectangle with a single tower rising from its courtyard. It is a dramatic sight after the earth-coloured forts that dominate the rest of Oman. The fort is open Saturday to Wednesday from 7.30 am to 2.30 pm. On Thursday and Friday it is open from 8 am to noon and from 4 to 6 pm. Admission is free and no permit from Muscat is required.

The first fort on the site is thought to have been built in the late 13th or early 14th century, though much of what you see today dates from the first half of the 17th century. The fort was extensively restored by the Omani government in 1992.

The fort's museum is in the tower. The rooms on the ground floor include displays on Oman's geology and geography and on ancient history. There is an especially interesting section covering the ancient copper trade that was centred on the Batinah Coast. Also on this floor is the tomb of Sayyid Thuwaini Bin Said Bin Sultan Al-Busaid, the ruler of Oman from 1856 to 1866. He was the son of Sultan Said Bin Sultan, the 19th century ruler under whom Omani power reached its height. After Said's death the empire was divided between his sons. Thuwaini, buried here, became ruler of Oman and its dependencies on the coast of what is now Pakistan. His brother, based in Zanzibar, became ruler of Oman's large coastal empire in East Africa. Sultan Thuwaini died at Sohar in 1866 while preparing a military expedition to reclaim the Buraimi Oasis from ancestors of the present Saudi royal family who had seized control of it.

The three rooms on the museum's 1st floor continue the story of Sohar's development as a trade centre from the centuries before Islam into the Middle Ages. Room seven includes information on the history of a number of

Oman's important forts with an emphasis, naturally, on the development of Sohar Fort itself.

The 2nd floor is empty, but it does provide access to the tower's roof. The sweeping view across Sohar and the sea is well worth the climb.

At the far end of the courtyard from the main entrance you can see the excavated remains of the 13th century houses on whose ruins the original fort was built.

Fish Souk

Fishing remains one of Sohar's main industries and if you are around either at dawn or at dusk a visit to the fish souk, where the day's catch is on sale, can be fun. The souk is on the coast two km north of the town centre.

Places to Stay & Eat

There are only two places to stay in Sohar. The *Al-Wadi Hotel* (☎ 840058, fax 841997), just off the main highway coming from Muscat, is the cheaper of the two at OR 23.100/31.500 for singles/doubles. It has small beach-cabin-like rooms surrounding its swimming pool but is ultimately a bit of a disappointment, considering the price. Nevertheless, it remains a lot cheaper than the *Sohar Beach Hotel* (☎ 843701, fax 843776) where rooms cost OR 28.750/ 34.500, including tax and the service charge. If you can afford the extra money this is one case where the more expensive hotel is definitely the better value for money.

To reach the Al-Wadi Hotel coming from Muscat, turn left at the second Sohar roundabout, the one whose centrepiece looks like a mosque's dome on stilts. The hotel is about 10 km west of the centre. The Sohar Beach Hotel is about six km north of the centre on the coastal road. From the centre just follow the coast north. From the highway follow the big green signs.

There are a number of good cheap restaurants within easy walking distance of the fort. Two worth trying are *Ahmed Bin Mohammed Bin Ali & Partners Restaurant* and *Murad Bin Abdulrahman Bin Musa Al-*

Balushi Restaurant. Both have biryanis, curries and similar fare for around 500 baisa per serving. If you're in town when the weather is nice the Ahmed Bin Mohammed restaurant has a few tables outside overlooking the coastal road and the sea.

For more up-market dining and booze you will have to go to one of the hotels.

Getting There & Away

Bus There are three buses per day between the Sohar Hospital and Muscat's Ruwi station. Buses to Muscat leave daily at 9 am, and 2.55 and 5 pm. The 2.55 pm bus is an express bus and takes 2¾ hours to reach Ruwi. The other buses are regular services and take four hours to make the same trip. The fare on either service is OR 2.200. Buses from Ruwi to Sohar leave daily at 7 am (express) and at 1 and 3 pm (regular).

The daily express buses from Dubai to Muscat and vice versa make a meal stop in Sohar at the Penguin Restaurant on the main highway just south-east of the turn for the centre (look for a small commercial complex that also includes a Shell petrol station and a Land Rover dealership). From there you can get a nonstop lift into Muscat for OR 5 or to Dubai for OR 4. Tickets can be purchased from the driver but you would be well-advised to phone ahead to the Ruwi bus station in Muscat (☎ 708522) to make a booking so that the driver knows to look for you when he reaches Sohar. The Muscat-bound buses come through daily at approximately 10.30 am and 8.30 pm. The Dubai-bound buses arrive at around 9.30 or 10 am and 6.30 or 7 pm.

Taxi & Microbus Microbuses and taxis arrive and depart from a parking lot across the street from the hospital and 150m to the north of it. A few can also be found at the roundabout where the highway from Muscat meets the road coming up from the town centre. Microbuses charge OR 1.700 for the trip to the Seeb clock tower roundabout, OR 2 to Ruwi. Taxis charge OR 2.500 to the clock tower and OR 3 to Ruwi. Expect to pay around OR 15 if you take a taxi engaged.

There is no direct taxi or microbus service to Rustaq and Nakhal. Expect to pay about OR 15 one way to take a taxi to either city engaged. To make the trip without taking a taxi or microbus engaged you'll have to take a Muscat-bound vehicle as far south as one of the two road junctions leading to Rustaq and Nakhal and get another ride from there.

For CR 25 the taxis will take you to Dubai (engaged only).

NAKHAL

Nakhal is an otherwise nondescript town dominated by one of Oman's more dramatic forts. The **fort** in question rises from a hill in Nakhal's small town centre. It is open daily from 7 am to 5 pm. Admission is free. A permit from the Ministry of National Heritage in Muscat is required to visit the fort, at least in theory.

Entering the fort go upstairs and turn left at a large carved door. This will take you to a small courtyard with a cannon. The wali's winter reception area is the small room to your left. Beyond this is the fort's kitchen area and, still further on, the fort's east tower, which can be climbed for a good view over the town.

Back near the wali's office a short flight of stairs leads up and into the main part of the fortress passing several storerooms and the fort's prison. When you reach another staircase go up, heading straight rather than turning left. This leads to the living quarters of the wali and his family. Some attempt has been made to restore the various rooms – bedrooms and a women's *majlis*, or meeting room – to their original form. A U-turn at the top of the stairs leading into these living quarters takes you to the more strictly military part of the fort, from where a passageway leads back to where you started.

As you enter the village the fort is two km beyond the turn for Nakhal off the main road, on the right. There are several small restaurants in the area immediately below the fort.

Getting There & Away

There is only one bus per day between Muscat and Nakhal. The bus leaves the Ruwi station in Muscat daily at 6 pm arriving at 7.55 pm. The return trip leaves Nakhal every morning at 8 am, arriving in Ruwi at 10 am. Since there is no place to stay in Nakhal this could be a bit awkward. If you do arrive or leave by bus the fare to or from Ruwi is OR 1.500. The bus stop is at the junction of the main road from Barka and the small road that leads onward to Nakhal's centre.

You'll find microbuses and taxis both at the junction with the main road and in the area below the fort. Microbuses charge OR 1 for the trip to the Seeb clock tower and 300 baisa to/from the Barka roundabout on the Muscat-Sohar highway. Taxis charge about OR 2 for the same trip, though most in the area appear to specialise in short local runs for a couple of hundred baisa (such as between the main road and the town).

A'THOWARAH

A few km beyond Nakhal lies the lush spring known as A'Thowarah. The spring emerges into a wadi here to form a stream and a small oasis. It is a perfect place for a stroll or a picnic. Put your hand into the stream close to the point where it rises from the rocks – the water is surprisingly warm even in winter.

To reach A'Thowarah from Nakhal turn right onto Nakhal's main paved street as you leave the fort (if you are coming in off the main road from Muscat and Barka just continue past the fort). After about 500m you will start to see directional signs for A'Thowarah. The distance from the fort to the spring is 2.3 km, but be exceedingly careful if you are driving as the road winds through a populated area laced with date gardens and falajes.

At the spring you will find a couple of small shops selling water, soft drinks and snacks.

AL-AWABI

Al-Awabi, a village on the road from Nakhal to Rustaq and Al-Hazm is noteworthy only for its small **fort**.

The fort has not been restored and different parts of it are in various stages of disrepair. The building is basically square in design and has only one watchtower/bastion. The part of it that includes the door facing the road appears to be a later addition. The fort is not open to the public.

The fort is 2.4 km off the Nakhal-to-Rustaq road and is worth a quick look if you have your own car. Coming from Nakhal take the first Al-Awabi turn-off (the second Al-Awabi turn-off if you are coming from Rustaq) and then just follow the road through the village. However, I would not recommend breaking your microbus journey here simply for a look at the fort, especially since it might take a while for you to find another bus or taxi and get moving again.

RUSTAQ

Some 175 km south-west of Muscat, Rustaq (Rostaq) is best known today for its imposing **fort**, though for a time in the Middle Ages it was Oman's capital.

A permit from Muscat is necessary to enter the fort, which was under restoration at the time of writing. To enter the fort you go up a ramp, passing through the large area between the inner and outer walls until you reach a second gate (note the niche above the light bulb at this second gate – it is from here that the hot oil would have been poured down on any attacking army) and then go up a flight of stairs and through an archway. At this point the first door on your left leads to the fort's prison. Inside, a low and narrow hole in one wall leads to what was once the women's section of the prison. Having made your way back out of the prison area head straight and then look down to the left to see the spring which rises inside the fort. This natural supply of fresh water would have left the fort's defenders particularly well positioned to withstand a siege. A nearby staircase leads down to a washing basin.

Upstairs, over the second door on the left, at the top of the stairs, you'll see slits for archers to shoot from. Once upstairs (moving anti-clockwise around the court) the first room was for the guards while the second leads to a windowless 'final punishment' prison. The third room was another guard room, from where there's a good view of the surrounding date palms and mountains. The fourth room was a Koranic school, one room of which contained a small mosque. Just off this room is a well with a stone-cut basin for the ablutions Muslims must perform before prayer. At the back of the school complex another staircase leads up to the lower of two roofs. Turn right, then walk straight to reach the library. The small room to the right of the library was reserved for the imam. The closet-sized room next to this was the prayer room of the imam's wife. A storeroom (which looks a lot like the library in its present state) at the rear of the roof level includes the entrance to an underground passage. Local legend has it that this used to connect Rustaq with the fort at Al-Hazm.

One of the fort's turrets is sometimes open to visitors. Try to get the guide to take you up it. The view is worth the climb.

There is a small souk near the entrance to the fort. It is good for shopping though in size and variety it is only a pale shadow of Nizwa or Muscat. The best time to visit is early morning, especially on Fridays.

Rustaq's only other site is a small, very new-looking, white mosque on the edge of town next to which is a natural spring. There are no hotels in Rustaq though the town has a few small restaurants. In late 1995, however, it was not just the fort but also much of the town that was torn up for repair work.

Getting There & Away

There is one bus a day to Muscat from Rustaq. The bus originates in the town, departing at 7.05 am and arriving at Muscat's Ruwi station three hours later. The daily bus from Muscat to Rustaq leaves Ruwi at 6 pm. The fare in either direction is OR 1.800.

Microbuses can be found a few hundred metres from the fort on the main road to Nakhal and the coast. Microbus fares from Rustaq include: Nakhal, 500 baisa; the junction with the coastal highway, 400 baisa; Sohar, OR 1; and Muscat-Ruwi, OR 1 (800 baisa to the Seeb clock tower). The fare to Muscat in a shared taxi is OR 2.

The Hejira Calendar

Islamic religious observances throughout the Arab Gulf States – and in all official business in Saudi Arabia – are scheduled according to the Hejira calendar. In English, Hejira dates are usually followed by the letters AH (for *anno hejiri*) to distinguish them from dates computed according to the Gregorian calendar used throughout much of the rest of the world.

The Hejira calendar begins in the year 622 AD, taking as its starting point the Prophet Mohammed's hejira, or migration, from Mecca to Medina.

The Prophet was forced to flee Mecca because his preaching had angered the city's rulers. At around the same time, supporters in Medina (or Yathrib, as the city was then called) invited him there to act as a judge in commercial disputes.

The Hejira calendar is based on cycles of the moon, which makes it about 11 days shorter than the solar-based Gregorian calendar. Moreover, Hejira months are held to begin only when the new moon is actually sighted – not simply when the calendar says it ought to be sighted – so heavy rain or cloud cover can lead to the start of a new month being postponed a day or two.

This is most clearly evident every year when Ramadan, the Muslim month of fasting comes around (see the boxed story on Ramadan near Islam in the Facts About the Region chapter). While many Middle Eastern countries (including all of the Arab Gulf States) defer to the scholars based at the Grand Mosque in Mecca to determine when, exactly, Ramadan begins and ends, some other countries, particularly in North Africa, rely on observations by their own scholars. The result is that Ramadan can begin and end a day or two earlier in one country than it does in the next.

Because the Hejira year is some 11 days shorter than the Gregorian year, Islamic holidays move backwards through the Gregorian calendar making a cycle every 33 years or so.

For the traveller the Hejira calendar is important mainly because the construction dates carved over the doorways of many older buildings are given in AH, not AD. That means that a mosque built in 1350 is about 70 – as opposed to 650 – years old.

In most Muslim countries the Hejira calendar is used to mark religious observances. Sometimes it may appear alongside the Gregorian date at, say, the top of a newspaper, but the Muslim calendar is not widely used in everyday life.

The exception to this rule is Saudi Arabia where the Hejira calendar alone is used for all official business. Your passport will be stamped with a Hejira date, any official document you receive will carry a Hejira date and many Saudis, you may find, have only a vague idea what year it is according to the Gregorian calendar. You may not notice this in the big cities, where Gregorian dates are widely used because of the large expatriate community, but you will notice it rapidly once you venture into rural areas (particularly if you can speak or read Arabic). ■

AL-HAZM

The town of Al-Hazm is little more than a fort surrounded by a few houses off the road from Muscat to Rustaq, but it is well worth the stop.

To visit the **fort**, which does not appear to be actively used by the local police but remains under their jurisdiction, you will need a permit from the Ministry of Culture & National Heritage (obtained at the Natural History Museum in Muscat). You will probably also be given a (non-English speaking) police officer as a guide when you visit the fort.

Before you enter take a look at the falaj which flows underneath the fort. It is still in use, irrigating the gardens surrounding the fort.

Entering the fort itself note the carved doors. The inscription on the left-hand door dates its construction to 1162 AH (circa 1750 AD, see the boxed story about the Hejira calendar, above). The inscription on the right identifies as the fort's builder Imam Sultan Bin Saif II, a member of the Al-Ya'ribi dynasty who reigned from 1706 to 1719.

As you enter the fort move around to your right to see the well, which is about 25m deep. At the end of the corridor beyond the well is a room with a huge stone pillar in its centre.

When you get to the centre of the fort you will again encounter the falaj. An inscription to the right of it dates this part of the fort to 918 AH (1512 AD). The imam's tomb is just beyond the hole in the wall.

There used to be a small mosque in a room upstairs and to the right. The room is easily identified by its mihrib, or prayer niche. Another flight of stairs nearby leads to a room which may once have been used as a Koranic school. Nearby, another doorway leads to a room directly above the main gate. Note the holes through which callers were scrutinised. The holes were also used for pouring hot oil onto the heads of unwelcome visitors. If you keep climbing up through the bastions you will pass a set of antique cannon and cannon balls bearing the crest of the Portuguese monarchy. These cannon and the Muscat forts are virtually the only physical remnants of Oman's century and a half of Portuguese rule. Keep going all the way to the top of the tower for a good view of the surrounding countryside.

Al-Hazm is 20 km north of Rustaq and 24.5 km south of the Muscat-Sohar highway. Coming from the coast make a right turn at the Al-Hazm roundabout at a sign for Hazm. Follow this road for 1.5 km and then turn at a sign for 'Qal'at Al-Hazm'. It is impossible to miss.

AL-KAMIL

The small town of Al-Kamil, 60 km south-west of Sur, is a good stopping place if you are on the lookout for traditional architecture in its pre-restoration state. There are a number of fascinating buildings in the town centre, including a **fort** with a simple square design and three tapered watchtowers. The only parts of the fort that have been restored are the main gateway on the east side and a portion of the north-eastern corner. The (new) lavishly carved door in the east wall is worth a look.

The town is full of other interesting mud-brick buildings. Of note is a large **house** about 150m east of the fort. The house includes a four-storey tower that lends it an almost Yemeni feel. Tall houses are common in Yemen but, forts aside, are unusual in Oman. Just south of the fort – across the large open lot – a yellowish archway leads to another open lot surrounded by a number of interesting buildings. Fifty metres to the right of the archway as you stand facing it is a restored watchtower.

While Al-Kamil is certainly worth a stop you should bear in mind that it is not really a 'site' on Oman's established tourist trail. Foreigners are still a fairly rare sight here and you would be well-advised to maintain a low profile.

To reach the fort from the main road turn off the Muscat-Sur road at the second Al-Kamil exit if you are coming from Muscat (the first if you are coming from Sur). This is the spot at which there is a sign parallel to the road that says 'Sur 60 km', as opposed to the one further on that says 'Sur 61 km'. From this turn go 650m and turn left onto a paved road at a pharmacy (which will be on your right). If you reach a roundabout you have gone too far. After turning by the pharmacy, Al-Kamil's post office will be on your left after 100m. The fort is just beyond the post office.

The Muscat-Sur buses stop in Al-Kamil about 45 minutes before reaching (or after leaving) Sur. The fare between Al-Kamil and the capital is OR 2.500.

SUR

Sur (Sour) has a lot going for it, starting with a nearly ideal location. It is a fairly quiet place but has great beaches (most easily accessible via the Sur Beach Hotel) and several interesting things to see. Sur is only 150 km down the coast from Muscat as the crow flies, though by road it is a bit over twice that distance. That makes it a bit too far for a day trip but it is still worth the effort. Sur is one of Oman's highlights.

Orientation & Information

Sur's commercial centre, containing the taxi stand and bus stop, the cheaper of the town's two hotels, and a few restaurants, is a few km north-east of the government buildings that make up its administrative and historical centre. The post office is on the roundabout between the Sinesla Fortress and the main mosque. If you arrive from Muscat (or from the airport) you will pass the fortress on your left as you head into both the administrative and the commercial centres. The Sur Beach Hotel can be reached either by following the

OMAN

signs on the Muscat Rd (these will take you to the hotel by-passing the centre entirely) or by going into the commercial centre and turning as indicated on the map. The dhow builders' yard and ferry to Ayega are on the coast beyond the commercial centre as you approach it from Muscat.

Sinesla Fortress

Sur's main fort is relatively simple in construction: a squareish defensive wall with towers at the four corners on a hill overlooking the town. Look carefully and you will notice that the two watchtowers facing the sea are slightly taller than the two that face inland.

Entering the fort through the main gate look to your right and you will see a mosque noteworthy for having both indoor and outdoor prayer areas. The small building in the centre of the courtyard was a storeroom, the building to the left of the entrance was a prison. To the extreme left of the entrance you will find a wooden door at ground level – a cistern for water storage. Both of the towers facing the sea are open to visitors. The larger one has cannon and guns. The smaller one was a lookout post and has no gun emplacements.

You'll need a permit from the Ministry of Culture & National Heritage in Muscat to visit Sinesla. The fort is open daily from 7.30 am to 6 pm. Admission is free.

Bilad Fort

The more impressive of Sur's two forts is just over six km inland from the town centre on the road headed back toward Muscat. It is open daily from 7.30 am to 6 pm. A permit from Muscat is required to visit the fort, at least in theory. Though there are no explanatory signs the fort is well worth a visit. The fort is approximately 200 years old and its basic design – lots of open space, little in the way of accommodation – implies that it was constructed as a defensive centre rather than an administrative one.

Like many Omani forts Bilad is built around a single large courtyard, but the overall design of the fort is quite irregular.

Sur

Not to Scale

1 Taxi Stand
2 National Bank of Oman (ATM)
3 Oman Orient for Travel & Tours (Oman Air)
4 Sur Hotel
5 Arabian Sea Restaurant
6 Al-Shath Restaurant
7 Bus Stop
8 New Souk

To Sur Beach Hotel (5.3 km)

To Sinesla Fortress, Bilad Fort & Muscat

To Dhow Builders' Yard (3 km)

The two main towers are unlike anything else you will see in Oman, featuring extra high lookout posts above the main portion of the tower. In the courtyard itself the small building next to the well was a mosque. Note the mihrib carved into one of its outer walls, providing guidance for the faithful too numerous to fit into the mosque itself. The building built into the outer wall of the far right corner from where you enter the fort was the governor's office and quarters.

To reach Bilad Fort take the Muscat road from the centre. After six km turn right just past a green sign with a white drawing of a fort (in Arabic the sign says 'Bilad Fort – Sur') with an arrow pointing to the right. The turn is not signposted if you approach it from the direction of Muscat. From the turn-off go 300m and you will see the fort directly in front of you.

Marine Museum

This is not your standard Omani museum. The marine museum is actually a project of the local youth club. It is, however, open to the public and it should not be missed. The highlight of the small exhibit is a collection of photographs of Sur in 1905. These were taken by the French consul in Muscat during

Oman's Forts

Some of Oman's best known sites are its forts. Contrary to popular belief, very few of these are of Portuguese construction. Though styles changed over the centuries a few architectural characteristics are common to many of Oman's forts. For example, though most Omani forts are built around a large rectangular courtyard, few of them are symmetrical. After looking at only a handful of buildings it is easy to distinguish those built mainly for defensive purposes from those built as administrative centres. The larger forts usually include extensive living quarters for the wali, or governor, and his family. These often included a school and a private mosque.

To get the most out of a tour of Oman's forts, look for the features that are unique to each building. Compare the huge drum-shaped tower of Nizwa Fort with the high white-washed tower of Sohar Fort that, unusually, rises from inside the courtyard. Both of these are large complexes, and stand in sharp contrast to the low-set, defensive look of forts such as Bukha. ■

GORDON ROBISON

GORDON ROBISON

Top: Nizwa Fort, built in the mid-17th century by Sultan Bin Saif.
Bottom: The distinctive white-washed Sohar Fort.

Oman's Forts *cont*

Top: Bilad Fort's main towers have unusually high lookout points.
Bottom: Bukha Fort against a dramatic mountain backdrop.

a visit to the town and they are a striking contrast with the Sur of today. Other photographs in the display chart the growth of Sur from the turn of this century through to the mid-1970s.

The museum also has an exhibit on ships and shipbuilding and on life in coastal Oman. Another room contains traditional regional costumes, navigational charts, and photographs of some of the region's antiquities, most of which can only be reached by 4WD. In this second room be sure to pause for a look at the set of photos of the Sinesla Fortress prior to its restoration.

In the clubhouse adjacent to the museum you can also see a large scale model of Sur and its surroundings.

The museum is inside the Al-Arouba Sports Club and is open daily from approximately 8 am to noon and 4 to 7 pm. Admission is free. The club is across the road from the side of Sinesla through which the fort's compound is entered and about 100m closer to the centre. Look for a stone wall with sports figures painted on it.

Dhow Builders' Yard

Sur's dhow yard is one of the town's highlights. It is still quite active and at any given time a dozen or more dhows may be under construction. Since this is a working yard rather than a tourist site per se there is no ticket booth, and certainly no requirement that you have a permit. Photography is permitted in the dhow yard but, as always, ask people's permission before taking their picture. The dhow yard is just over three km from the centre toward Ayega.

Ayega

Just beyond the dhow yard is a small ferry that will carry you across the narrow sound to Ayega, a village where many of the dhow builders live. The two-storey sand-coloured building near the Ayega ferry landing is the house reserved for the sultan whenever he comes to visit. The ferry crossing is free and takes about two minutes.

Places to Stay & Eat

Cheapish beds can be found in the town centre at the *Sur Hotel* (☎ 440090, fax 443798). Singles/doubles are OR 13.800/ 26.200, all with bath. The rooms are sparsely furnished but adequate. If you think you may be using the air-conditioner make sure it works before you take the room. Sur's up-market hotel is the somewhat over-priced *Sur Beach Hotel* (☎ 442031, fax 442228). Its rooms cost OR 25.300/32.200. The hotel is 5.3 km north of the centre. It is the only place in town that serves alcohol.

The *Arabian Sea Restaurant* on the ground floor of the same building as the Sur Hotel (though the entrance faces the other side of the block) is a good enough place to eat. Most main dishes cost OR 1 to OR 1.500, though you can also get sandwiches for 200 to 500 baisa. Several similar small restaurants are in the area near the hotel.

Getting There & Away

Air The airport is south of the town centre on the Sur-Muscat road. The telephone number for flight information is ☎ 440423. Oman Air has three flights a week between Muscat and Sur. The fare is OR 14 single, OR 28 return.

Oman Air does not have an office of its own in Sur, but tickets can be purchased, and return flights reconfirmed, through Oman Orient for Travel & Tours (☎ 440279), located in the town centre.

Bus There are three buses per day between Muscat and Sur. Express buses (4¼ hours) leave Sur for Muscat daily at 6 am and 2.30 pm. On Friday and holidays the later bus departs at 4.30 pm. The regular bus (5½ hours) leaves every day at noon. From Muscat express buses leave Ruwi for Sur at 7.30 am and 2.30 pm. The regular bus departs at 4.30 pm. The fare in either direction is OR 3.400.

Taxi Service-taxis for Muscat (OR 3.500 to the Seeb clock tower roundabout) tout for passengers in the parking lot around the corner from the Sur Hotel. You will also find microbuses headed in the same direction for OR 3 per person, but these are not really the major modes of public transport along the Sur route.

SAMAIL

From the main Muscat-Nizwa road Samail appears to be little more than a bus stop, one that people usually head straight past. But turning off the road is a great short side trip for those with the time to spare. Ten km from the junction with the main road is **Samail Fort**, nestled between a wadi and an oasis of palm trees on one side and a hill of dark, loose stone on the other. The hill virtually blocks the view of the fort from the road.

The fort itself is irregularly shaped. It has only one bastion, though there are also two **watchtowers** on the hilltops a few minutes walk from the fort itself (the watchtowers are the main thing you will see from the road). Even though you cannot get into the fort it is worth stopping for a look, and making the climb up to the watchtowers for a view out over the oasis. The climb is steep and there is a fair amount of loose stone, but it is not long and most people should be able to handle it.

To reach the fort turn off the Muscat-Nizwa road (a left turn if you are coming from Muscat) at the big green sign welcoming you to the Samail Wilayat. If you are coming from Nizwa you will not be able to see this sign, so look for a sign saying 'Samail 4 km' and pointing right. At the junction itself there is a small green sign for the Al-Meratib Institute which you can see coming from either direction. Follow the road for 10 km through the villages of **Al-Qrain** and **Al-Ulaiya**, both of which also have forts that are visible from the main road, though neither one is restored. You will reach a junction with a road going off to the right and a sign saying 'Luzugh 10 km', pointing in the direction you are travelling. At this point you should be able to see one of the watchtowers on the hill above you and to the left. About 250m beyond the sign turn left onto a dirt track between two whitewashed walls. The fort will be on your left.

The Samail road junction is a stop on the bus route from Muscat to Nizwa (it appears in the printed timetables as 'Samail Hospital'). The trip takes 1⅓ hours express and just over 1½ hours regular. The fare to Samail is 900 baisa, see the Nizwa and Muscat Getting There & Away sections for departure times.

Microbuses bound from Muscat's Seeb clock tower roundabout to Nizwa will drop you at the Samail road junction for 500 baisa (800 baisa from Ruwi). The shared taxi fare from the Seeb clock tower is OR 1. From Nizwa to Samail the microbus fare is 700 baisa and taxis charge OR 1.500. From the junction to the fort the microbus fare is 200 to 300 baisa each way. Microbuses park around the junction and if none are there just wait, because a local microbus comes by every few minutes.

NIZWA

Only 45 years ago Wilfred Thesiger was forced to keep well clear of Nizwa. As the seat of the imams who then ruled much of the country's interior it had a reputation for ferocious conservatism. Thesiger's Bedouin companions were convinced he would have little chance of emerging from the town alive. Today, visitors need have no such worries; Nizwa has rapidly emerged as one of Oman's major tourist centres. It is probably the country's most popular destination after Muscat.

Most tourists visit Nizwa on day trips from Muscat, 172 km away, and spend only an hour or two in the town. By public bus Nizwa is a fairly easy day trip from the capital. Those with time to spare, however, should pause for a day or so to get the real feel of the place. In addition to its aesthetic charms Nizwa is also the centre for Oman's jewellery and craft industries. Most of the khanjars you see on sale in Muscat's Mutrah souk are manufactured here. Prowl the back alleys of the souk and you may even find a group of Indians or Pakistanis hard at work dagger-making under the watchful eye of an Omani craftsman.

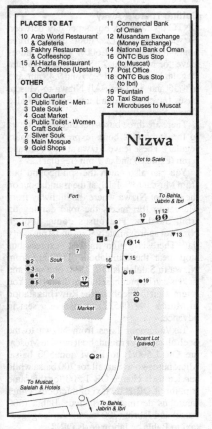

PLACES TO EAT
10 Arab World Restaurant
   & Cafeteria
13 Fakhry Restaurant
   & Coffeeshop
15 Al-Hazfa Restaurant
   & Coffeeshop (Upstairs)

OTHER
1 Old Quarter
2 Public Toilet - Men
3 Date Souk
4 Goat Market
5 Public Toilet - Women
6 Craft Souk
7 Silver Souk
8 Main Mosque
9 Gold Shops
11 Commercial Bank
   of Oman
12 Musandam Exchange
   (Money Exchange)
14 National Bank of Oman
16 ONTC Bus Stop
   (to Muscat)
17 Post Office
18 ONTC Bus Stop
   (to Ibri)
19 Fountain
20 Taxi Stand
21 Microbuses to Muscat

Nizwa

Not to Scale

OMAN

Orientation & Information

Nizwa's main visual landmark is the large, blue-domed mosque which is on your left if you enter the town from the direction of Muscat. The souk is the area immediately around the mosque. Past the mosque the main street swings around to the right into the town's modern business area. The taxi stand and bus stop are both by the parking lot in front of the mosque.

The post office is located in the souk. It is open Saturday to Wednesday from 9 am to 2 pm and Thursday from 8 to 11 am. You can change money at any of the several banks in the city centre.

Nizwa Fort

Visually, Nizwa's Fort is hardly the most breathtaking set of battlements in Oman but it has an impressive history. The fort was built in the mid-17th century by Sultan Bin Saif, the first imam of the Al-Ya'ribi dynasty. For the next 300 years it was the primary seat of the imamate, serving as a combination palace, seat of government and prison. It is open daily from 7.30 am to 4 pm (until 5 pm from June to September). Admission is free but you will need to have a permit from Muscat. Still photography is permitted inside the fort.

Be sure as you enter to take a moment to study the large map of the fort by the main doorway. The fort is actually quite a large complex of buildings – much larger than it looks from the street. A small guidebook in English is sometimes available at the entrance for free.

Once inside the fort be sure to go all the way through to the back to have a look at the fort's garden and its falaj irrigation system.

Old Nizwa

If you go out the door of the fort, turn right and go about 100m you will enter what remains of old Nizwa, a small maze of narrow alleys, mud homes and some craft workshops. You can also get a great view of this area from the fort's tower.

The Souk

The town's other great attraction is its souk. Despite having been moved into more modern quarters a few years ago the souk retains much of its colour, and its vitality. The bad news is that the souk's popularity with package tours has made it one of the worst places in the sultanate to shop for souvenirs. Everything in the silver souk is outrageously overpriced, especially the khanjars. Even worse, because most people visiting with groups have only an hour or so to spend here, the merchants are often not interested in serious bargaining –, there will always be another group along later. The result is that Nizwa-made jewellery and khanjars actually cost more here than they do in Muscat and much of what is on display in the souk is often either of poor quality or in poor condition.

The best thing to do is to avoid the silver souk altogether and spend your time wandering among the merchants buying and selling fish, meat, fruits and vegetables or household goods. There is a special souk area for dates, and even a goat souk.

Places to Stay & Eat

Nizwa's two hotels will both put a dent in your budget. By far the better deal is the *Falaj Daris Hotel* (☎ 410500, fax 410430) where singles/doubles cost OR 21/28.350, including tax and service. The hotel is on the Muscat road, 4.5 km from the town centre. It's on the left if you are coming from the capital. About 20 km from the centre and on the right if you are coming from Muscat is the *Nizwa Hotel* (☎ 431616, fax 431619), where the rooms go for OR 34.500/40.250. You can probably bargain a few riyals off the rack rate at either hotel. The restaurants and bars at the two hotels are the only places in Nizwa that serve alcohol.

For a quick snack in town there's a shawarma stand at the *Fakhry Restaurant & Coffeeshop* on the right-hand side of the main street (coming from Muscat), next to the Habib Bank office. Look for an Orange Crush sign in Arabic. Shawarma cost 150 baisa apiece. For full meals try the *Arab World Restaurant & Cafeteria*, which is across the street and down the road a bit under a large Pepsi sign. A meal usually costs OR 1 to OR 2 with good chicken and kebab dishes leading the menu. Note that most of the items on the menu come with a lot of side dishes included. There is another restaurant with the same name a couple of km outside the centre on the road to Muscat.

Near Nizwa's taxi stand is *Al-Hazfa*, a particularly good bet. They have excellent chicken and mutton biryanis and curries for 600 baisa and the portions are fairly large to boot. The restaurant is on the 1st floor of the small complex of shops facing the mosque and the souk. There are also a number of small coffee shops in and around the souk.

Getting There & Away

ONTC operates six buses per day between Nizwa and Muscat (2½ hours express, three hours regular, OR 1.600). Express buses leave for Muscat at 7.45 am and 5.45 pm. Regular buses leave at 5.55 and 9.45 am, and at 1.55 and 3.55 pm. All Nizwa-to-Muscat buses travel via Samail and Fanja and also stop at Seeb airport.

There are three buses per day from Nizwa to Ibri (around 2 hours express, 3¼ hours regular). These leave Nizwa at 10.30 am and 5 pm (express) and at 7 pm (regular).

You can also catch the southbound bus from Muscat to Salalah at the roundabout on the edge of Nizwa where the highway from Muscat to Ibri meets the road coming up from Salalah. The buses come through Nizwa at approximately 9 am and 9 pm every day. There is a sign marked 'express bus stop' near the roundabout. The fare from Nizwa to Salalah is OR 7.200 one way and tickets can be purchased from the driver. You might want to telephone the Ruwi bus station in Muscat (☎ 708522) to reserve a seat in advance.

Taxi/microbus fares from Nizwa to the Seeb clock tower roundabout outside Muscat are OR 1.500/1, to Ruwi add 500 baisa. Microbuses go to Samail for 700 baisa while service-taxis charge OR 1.500 for the same trip. Ibri is OR 2, by taxi or microbus. Other microbus destinations include Bahla (500 baisa) and Jabrin (700 baisa). An 'engaged' taxi to Bahla or Jabrin costs OR 8.

BAHLA

At the time of writing the huge **fort** that dominates the small town of Bahla, 40 km west of Nizwa, was undergoing restoration. Parts of Bahla Fort are thought to be pre-Islamic in origin and when work on it is complete the site, which lies smack on the main road from Nizwa to Jabrin and Ibri, should be a major tourist attraction.

Between the bus stop and the fort you can see a **well**, which is still in use. Behind the fort you will find a portion of Bahla's **city wall**. West of the town centre, there are more

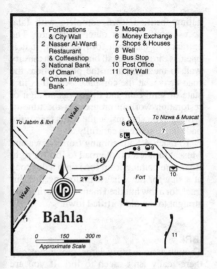

1 Fortifications
& City Wall
2 Nasser Al-Wardi
Restaurant
& Coffeeshop
3 National Bank
of Oman
4 Oman International
Bank
5 Mosque
6 Money Exchange
7 Shops & Houses
8 Well
9 Bus Stop
10 Post Office
11 City Wall

To Jabrin & Ibri

To Nizwa & Muscat

Fort

Bahla

0   150   300 m
Approximate Scale

fortifications guarding the approach to the town across the adjacent wadi.

As a town Bahla can be a bit confusing. The fort is in the old town centre, several km west of the newer buildings, such as the wali's office, that make up Bahla's administrative core. The main residential districts, however, are in the area around the fort where you will also find a bus stop (Bahla Suk on ONTC's timetables), the post office, two banks and a couple of small restaurants.

The only hotel in the area is the *Bahla Motel* (☎ 420211, fax 420212) 5.4 km east of the centre on the road coming from Nizwa. They have large, if somewhat pricey, rooms at OR 17.250/23 for singles/doubles. Near the fort you can get a bite to eat at the *Nasser Al-Wardi Restaurant and Coffeeshop* which offers the usual chicken or mutton curries for 600 baisa each. Half a roasted chicken with rice costs 900 baisa.

Buses for Bahla leave Muscat daily at 8 am, and 2.30 and 4 pm. The first two buses are express services and arrive in Bahla in just over three hours. The 4 pm bus is a regular service and takes just over 3½ hours to make the trip. The fare from Muscat is OR 2. The buses travel via Nizwa, leaving Nizwa for Bahla at 10.30 am, and 5 and 7 pm. The

bus fare from Nizwa should be no more than 300 baisa. Microbuses charge 500 baisa for the trip to Bahla from Nizwa. An 'engaged' taxi should cost around OR 8 but you might be able to knock a riyal or two off that with some hard bargaining.

JABRIN

Jabrin (Jibreen) is another stop on the Old Forts Route. It is just over 50 km from Nizwa on the Ibri road and is pretty easy to visit from Muscat in one day, even using pubic transport (provided you get an early start). If you are stretching the trip out overnight you should plan to stay either in Nizwa or at the Bahla Motel as there is no hotel in Jabrin. As for Jabrin itself there really is no town to speak of – just a **fort** standing on a plain, though there is a housing development nearby. The fort, however, is dramatic. It is large and imposing and its location commands the entire plain and surrounding hilltops for quite some distance around.

To reach the fort from Nizwa follow the Ibri road for 45.5 km then turn at a sign for Jabrin. After another four km the pavement ends at a small roundabout. Turn right, go 500m, and you will reach the fort. In theory you will need a permit from Muscat to enter the fort, though they seem to be pretty loose about this. The fort is open daily from 8 am to 5 pm. Admission is free.

Many of the rooms inside the fort are labelled, most of them in English. Jabrin is worth visiting if only for the restoration job, which is one of the best in Oman. It is a much more dramatic place than Nizwa and its restored state gives one some sense of what it looked like in its prime. Various household items and furnishings are on display throughout the fort.

Despite its imposing battlements, the fort was originally built as a palace. Its construction was ordered in 1671 by Imam Bal'arab Bin Sultan Al-Ya'ribi, who is also buried there. The design was only later modified to fortify the building.

Entering through the main door you will come to a dramatic, high-walled courtyard through which the falaj containing the fort's

OMAN

water supply used to flow. A door to your right leads to the fort's kitchen area (through which the falaj also flowed) and to several storage rooms. Going left out of the main courtyard takes you to two large, empty rooms that made up the fort's servants' quarters. From these a staircase to the left leads up to a prison (complete with manacles still hanging on the wall).

This second level of the fort includes the imam's majlis, or formal public meeting room, and a dining hall. In the majlis be sure to take a look at the recesses built into the floor beside the windows to allow the fort's defenders to shoot at attackers from a standing position, and also to duck incoming fire.

Continuing on to the next level brings you to a series of small, open courtyards on the fort's roof around which are some living quarters and a school. When you reach the roof go to your right, continue on to another roof section and look for a staircase leading down through a door in the middle of this second roof area. This takes you to the private living quarters of the imam and his family. The ceiling paint here is particularly impressive. Most of the rooms are filled with various sorts of household items as well as a smattering of weapons.

Stairs continue down from this level through more family rooms to the guard's quarters. On a very narrow staircase, and shortly before you reach the guard's rooms, you will find another small staircase leading to the imam's tomb. From there a short walk through the fort's gunpowder store and another low passage will bring you back to the main entrance.

Buses from Muscat to Ibri and vice versa stop at the road junction for Jabrin. The trip from Muscat takes four hours by express bus and five hours on a regular bus and costs OR 2.200.

A'SLAIF

A few km east of the uninteresting city of Ibri is the very interesting village of A'Slaif. Though the village's residents now live in modern houses, above them looms a fascinating fortified town complete with falaj access shafts in its outer courtyard. The entrance to the main fortified area, if it is open, is through a small black door in the city wall to the right from the place where the road arrives at the complex. A'Slaif is in a state of semi-ruin and there was no sign of restoration work in progress at the time of writing. The area inside the walls is in quite bad shape, so tread carefully.

To reach A'Salif coming from Nizwa and Muscat turn left off the road to Ibri (or right if you are coming from Ibri) onto a dirt road at a sign for the village. Following this dirt track for a few hundred metres will bring you straight to the old fortified town.

IBRI

Though it is a fairly large provincial city there really isn't much to Ibri. If you are driving into Oman from the UAE via Buraimi it may be the first large Omani town you pass through after clearing customs.

Most of Ibri's services are on a road perpendicular to the main Muscat-Buraimi road. these include the bus stops, a couple of petrol stations, the post and phone offices and a few small grocery stores. At the junction of these two roads you will find the taxi and microbus stand and Ibri's lone hotel, the surprisingly good *Ibri Tourist Guest House* (☎ 491400, fax 491554). They charge OR 12.600/16.800 for singles/doubles, including tax. If you need to change money, there are several banks around this intersection.

There are three buses per day from Muscat to Ibri (4½ hours express, 5¼ hours regular, OR 3.200). Express buses leave the Ruwi bus station at 8 am and 2.30 pm. The regular bus departs at 4 pm. Express buses bound for Muscat leave Ibri at 5.55 am and 3.55 pm. The regular bus departs Ibri at 7.35 am. All buses travel via Nizwa.

Microbuses charge OR 2 to Muscat while taxis cost OR 3 for the same trip, in both cases to the Seeb clock tower – not to Ruwi. A microbus or taxi to Nizwa should cost between OR 1.500 and OR 2, depending on the driver's mood and how busy things are.

OMAN

BURAIMI

The long-disputed Buraimi Oasis straddles the border between Oman and Abu Dhabi in the UAE. Both the Omani and the Emirati sides of the oasis are covered in this book's UAE chapter. This is because the Omani portion of the oasis is effectively in a customs union with Abu Dhabi.

Approaching the oasis from the Omani side requires that you pass through out-going Omani customs (and, if you are an expatriate living in Oman, that you possess a Road Permit – see Other Documents in the Facts for the Visitor section in this chapter). Once through this checkpoint (53 km from the border) you can pass freely between the Omani town of Buraimi and the city of Al-Ain, in the UAE. You can also continue up the road to anywhere else in the UAE. Approaching the oasis from the UAE side does not involve a customs check or require any documentation beyond that ordinarily required to enter the UAE.

There are three buses per day between Buraimi and Muscat (3¾ hours express, six hours regular, OR 3.600). The express bus leaves Muscat every day at 7 am and regular buses leave at 1 and 3 pm. Buses from Buraimi to Muscat depart at the same times, except that the express bus to Muscat is the 1 pm trip while the regular trips are at 7 am and 3 pm. Microbuses do not make the trip between Buraimi and Muscat but taxis do, at least in theory, for OR 5. See the Buraimi section of the United Arab Emirates chapter for more details.

AL-GHABA

Al-Ghaba is not much more than a cross-roads 342 km south of Muscat on the road to Salalah. The main reason you are likely to stop here is to get petrol on the way south. If you are travelling by bus, the southbound Salalah Express stops here for about an hour for meals. The rest house has 10 tolerable rooms for OR 6/10 a single/double. The fare in the restaurant is chicken or the curry-of-the-day served on an ample pile of rice for OR 1.

Southern Oman

SALALAH

Salalah, Oman's second city, is the capital of the country's southern region and the birthplace of Sultan Qaboos. It is also a striking change from Muscat. It catches the Indian summer monsoon (virtually the only corner of Arabia which does) and, as a result, it is cool, wet and green from mid-June to mid-September just as the rest of Arabia is going through the worst of the summer heat.

Salalah is also the capital of the province of Dhofar, which has a population of about 300,000.

Though Salalah has a small museum the real attraction of the area is its temperate climate, the striking mountain scenery just after the monsoon and the beautiful beaches of white sand that stretch for miles along the coast. It is also a good base for exploring the villages and archaeological sites of Oman's southern region.

Orientation & Information

Salalah's centre is at the intersection of

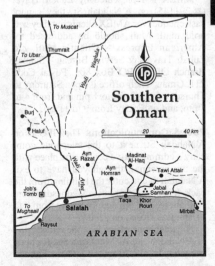

A'Nahdah and A'Salam Sts. Both the bus station and the Redan Hotel are a 10 to 15 minute walk from this intersection, and the gold souk is right around the corner. Most of the city's businesses are either along, or just off, one of these streets.

The Holiday Inn has a free map of the Dhofar region available at the front desk. This can be useful if you plan to do any touring by car.

Money There are several banks and a few exchange houses around the intersection of A'Nahdah and A'Salam Sts. I've had good experience with Oman United Exchange Company, who were willing to bargain a bit over the rate. As always in Oman, travellers' cheques draw a less favourable rate than cash, though the difference is unlikely to work out to much more than 500 baisa or so per US$100. For those who arrive by bus and need cash immediately there is a branch of the Commercial Bank of Oman on 23rd July St just south of the new souk.

The British Bank of the Middle East's branch on A'Salam St has an ATM linked into the Global Access cash machine network.

AMEX is represented by Zubair Travel (☎ 291145) on A'Nahdah St, they cannot cash cheques for AMEX clients but they will hold mail. Mail should be addressed to: American Express – Client's Mail, c/o Zubair Travels & Service Bureau – Salalah Branch Office, PO Box 809, Postal Code 211, Oman. Their office is open Saturday to Thursday from 8 am to 1 pm and from 4 to 7 pm, and on Friday from 9 to 11 am.

Post & Communications The GPO is on A'Nahdah St, next to the telephone company's administrative centre (the place with the big antenna), though you have to exit A'Nahdah St and enter the building from the back. It is open Saturday to Wednesday from 7.30 am to 1.30 pm and Thursday from 9 to 11 am. It is closed on Friday.

The telephone office is at the intersection of A'Nahdah and Al-Montazah Sts. It's open every day from 7.30 am to 12.30 am. Fax and telex facilities are also available but these close down around 9 pm.

Bookshops Although the pickings are small, the best places to find foreign-language books, newspapers etc are in the bookstalls at the Salalah Holiday Inn or at the Family Bookshop on A'Nahdah St near the intersection with A'Salam St.

Laundry A small shop on A'Salam St, about 100m east of the Oman Cinema, with only the word 'Laundry' in large letters on the sign offers in-today out-tomorrow washing for most clothes for around 100 baisa per item. It is open daily from 7.30 am to 1 pm and 3.30 to 11 pm. Another small laundry (similar prices) can be found further down A'Salam St across from the Redan Hotel.

Museum
Salalah's museum is in the Cultural Centre on A'Robat Rd (access is from the back side, via A'Nahdah St). There is no English lettering on the building, but it is the huge white second building west of the intersection of A'Robat Rd and A'Nahdah St. When you enter the main door the museum is to your left. The doors on the right lead to a theatre. The museum is open Saturday to Wednesday from 8 am to 2 pm. Admission is free.

As you pass through the lobby look at the exhibit of Wilfred Thesiger's photographs of Salalah and other parts of Arabia in the 1940s and '50s. Most of the photos are from his book *Arabian Sands*.

Entering the main part of the museum from the Cultural Centre's lobby you will find yourself in one large room. Immediately to your left are stones with inscriptions in the ancient script known as South Arabian. This blends into a display of locally-made pottery. The pottery exhibit will lead you to a large room containing models of half a dozen different types of sailing ships and several display cases containing Omani jewellery. Be sure to see the display of 11th and 12th century Chinese coins found at Al-Balid, near Salalah. The same room also has displays of traditional wooden chests, khanjars

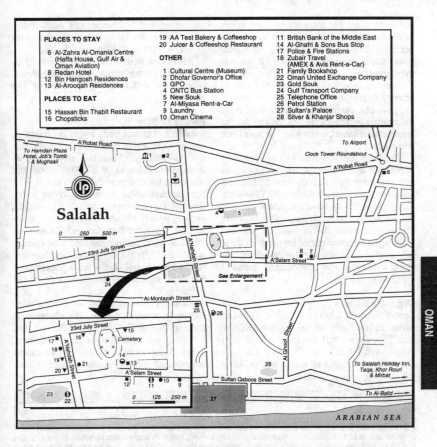

Salalah

0   250   500 m

PLACES TO STAY

6 Al-Zahra Al-Omania Centre
   (Haffa House, Gulf Air &
   Oman Aviation)
8 Redan Hotel
12 Bin Hangosh Residences
13 Al-Arooqah Residences

PLACES TO EAT

15 Hassan Bin Thabit Restaurant
16 Chopsticks

19 AA Test Bakery & Coffeeshop
20 Juicer & Coffeeshop Restaurant

OTHER

1 Cultural Centre (Museum)
2 Dhofar Governor's Office
3 GPO
4 ONTC Bus Station
5 New Souk
7 Al-Miyasa Rent-a-Car
9 Laundry
10 Oman Cinema

11 British Bank of the Middle East
14 Al-Ghafri & Sons Bus Stop
17 Police & Fire Stations
18 Zubair Travel
   (AMEX & Avis Rent-a-Car)
21 Family Bookshop
22 Oman United Exchange Company
23 Gold Souk
24 Gulf Transport Company
25 Telephone Office
26 Petrol Station
27 Sultan's Palace
28 Silver & Khanjar Shops

OMAN

and other weapons and scale models of both a bedouin tent and a reed house like those once used by coastal dwellers. Further along the wall, to your right, are displays of traditional clothing and basketry.

With the exception of the Thesiger exhibit, most of the museum's displays are labelled only in Arabic.

New Souk

There is nothing special about this souk. Meat, fish, fruit, vegetables and, occasionally, livestock are on sale. Mixed in among these are a handful of stalls selling khol

boxes, pottery and other locally-made handicrafts. The souk is also the home of the bus station and a few modern shops, most of which sell textiles.

Al-Balid

The ruins of Al-Balid, site of the ancient city of Zafar, lie about 4.5 km east of the city centre on the coast, just west of the Salalah Holiday Inn. Zafar's heyday was in the 11th and 12th centuries AD when it was an active trading port. Coins from as far away as China have been found at the site. There is a fence around the site and, in theory, you need a permit to enter, but there are so many holes in the fence and places where it has simply been torn down that this is hardly a problem. I was taken there permit-less by a government guide.

There is not much to see. The site is heavily overgrown and is likely to impress only serious students of archaeology. Near the mound which dominates the site are the remains of a large building said to have been a mosque.

To reach the site start in the centre on A'Nahdah St. Follow the street south to the intersection with Sultan Qaboos St then turn left (there is a sign for Al-Hafah). Go 400m, turn right at the corner of the palace wall and follow another street straight to the beach (a distance of about 300m from the corner). Follow the beach road east for just over three km until it ends at a small roundabout. Al-Balid's fence will be immediately ahead of you and to the left.

Organised Tours

Orient Tours (☎ 235333, fax 235137) has an office in the lobby of the Salalah Holiday Inn. They have a half-day tour to Taqa, Tawi Attair, Ayn Homran and other sites around Salalah for OR 60 for up to four people. They

also offer slightly cheaper OR 40 half-day tours (again, for up to four people) and an all-day 4WD trip to Ubar for OR 100.

Al-Miyasa Rent-a-Car (☎ & fax 296521), on A'Salam St next door to the Redan Hotel, offers three different, slightly cheaper day tours.

Places to Stay

Salalah's cheapest beds are to be found at two small hotels in the city centre, both near the Al-Ghafri & Sons bus stop. The *Al-Arooqah Residences* (☎ 292935) is both the nicer and the cheaper of the two at OR 8/12 for singles/doubles, most with private baths. The hotel is on an upper floor of the building beside which the Al-Ghafri buses stop. Across the street *Bin Hangosh Residences* (☎ 298079) is not as good, and a bit pricier, at OR 10/15, but it is still cheaper than any of the local hotels. Look for a 'Residences for Rent' sign on the left hand side of the building.

Salalah's remaining four hotels are all significantly more expensive. The cheapest of these is the *Redan Hotel* (☎ 292266, fax 290491) on A'Salam St in the centre. Singles/doubles are OR 14/17. The location is good and the rooms are large and clean.

Ubar

In early 1992 a group of US explorers announced that they had found the remains of Ubar, one of the great lost cities of Arabia. According to legend Ubar was a sort of Arabian cross between Atlantis, and Sodom and Gomorrah. Scholars are fairly certain that the place *did* exist, that it came to control the frankincense trade, and that, as a result, it grew incredibly wealthy. That is about all that is known for sure. The Koran says that God destroyed Ubar, causing it to sink beneath the sands, because the people were decadent and had turned away from religion.

Predictably some scholars have disputed the expedition's claim to have found Ubar. At the time of writing, excavations at the site were proceeding slowly and little had been turned up that was anywhere near old enough to date from Ubar's golden age.

Reaching the site requires a 4WD. Take the main highway north from Salalah to Thumrait. Slightly more than 10 km beyond Thumrait turn left at a sign saying 'Shasrar 72 km'. Shasrar is the village where the site is located. When you enter the village the site will be to your right and the Wali's office to your left. Go to the Wali's office if the site is locked up. It might also be a good idea to stop by the Salalah museum before making the trip – the site is more likely to be open if the people at the museum let the people in Shasrar know you are coming.

Be warned: though archaeologists are very excited about Ubar the site has a reputation with tourists for being something of a disappointment. If you do not have a 4WD (expensive) day tours to Ubar can be booked through several agencies in Salalah. See Organised Tours in the Salalah section for details. ■

The *Haffa House* (☎ 295444, fax 294873) in the Al-Zahra Al-Omania Centre at the clock tower roundabout just outside the city centre charges OR 28.750/32.200. The *Hamdan Plaza Hotel* (☎ 211025, fax 211187), on the main road leading west out of the city, is a relatively new five-star place with rooms for OR 32.200/40.250. On the coast, just beyond Al-Balid, the *Salalah Holiday Inn* (☎ 235333, fax 235137) charges OR 37.950/ 47.725, including tax and the service charge. It has a pool, private beach, health club and two bars.

Places to Eat

At the bottom of the price scale you would be hard-pressed to do better than the *AA Test Bakery & Coffeeshop* (formerly the Antco Bakery) on A'Nahdah St. They have very good samosas for only 50 baisa apiece and also offer cheap sandwiches and other quick snacks. A few doors away, the *Juicer & Coffeeshop Restaurant* has good shawarma for 200 baisa each, as well as soft drinks and juice. Cheap but substantial Indian meals are available at the *Gareez Restaurant* on A'Salam St next to the Redan Hotel.

Chopsticks, a Chinese restaurant, is a bit more up-market. The food is only passable and the service is awful but at least it offers an affordable change from cheap Indian food and shawarma. Main dishes cost OR 1 to OR 2. Moderately up-market Indian food can be had at the *Hassan Bin Thabit Restaurant* on 23rd July St. Main dishes cost OR 1 to OR 1.500, but you can also get simple curries for 500 to 700 baisa. For anything much fancier you'll probably have to head for the Salalah Holiday Inn which has a couple of restaurants all of which serve the basic hotel menu of European dishes (steaks, sandwiches, pasta, omelettes etc) and Oriental (usually Lebanese) food.

Entertainment & Activities

What social life there is in Salalah centres on the Holiday Inn. For the latest information get a copy of *Oman Today* or just stop by the hotel when you are in town. Outsiders can join the hotel's health club on a monthly

basis. Use of the pool for the day costs OR 3 for nonguests. The hotel also has a nightclub with live entertainment, usually a lounge band and a belly dancer, and a disco on weekends.

Things to Buy

Among Dhofar's most distinctive souvenirs are the small, bead-covered plastic bottles used by women to carry khol for decorating their eyes. These are a far cry from the silver khol boxes used by both men and women in the northern part of the country, and also a lot more affordable. They can be purchased in the new souk for OR 3 to OR 5, depending on size.

Other locally made crafts available in the new souk include pottery incense burners. These cost OR 1.500 to OR 10 depending on size with the easily-packable ones all coming in at OR 5 or less. The OR 10 ones would make excellent doorstops.

If you are looking for khanjars, there is a small street near the sultan's palace with a number of small shops selling daggers and swords. In the city centre, several shops in the gold souk also have khanjars as well as a limited selection of old silver jewellery.

Getting There & Away

Air Salalah's small airport is served only by Oman Aviation (☎ 295747). Their office is on the 1st floor of the Al-Zahra Al-Omania Centre by the clock tower roundabout. There are two flights per day to Muscat. The fare is OR 27 one way and OR 50 return.

Bus Buses leave the ONTC office in the new souk for Muscat every day at 7 am and 7 pm with an extra bus at 6 pm from mid-June through to mid-September (12 hours, OR 8 one way, OR 16 return). Departures are one hour later during Ramadan. There is also a 'family fare' of OR 40 which includes return transportation for two adults and two children. From mid-June through to mid-September the family fare can only be used on the day buses and it is not valid for travel during and for two days before and after Eid Al-Fitr and Eid Al-Adha. Because

OMAN

there is no computerised reservation system it is a good idea to reconfirm your return reservation to or from Muscat as soon as you arrive. You can store luggage in the ONTC ticket office at the new souk.

Al-Ghafri & Sons (☎ 293574) also run buses to Muscat every day at 7 am and 4.45 pm. Departures are from their office on A'Salam St. In Muscat the buses arrive at the company's office near the Ruwi bus station. At OR 8 one way and OR 14 return, the fare is a bit cheaper than ONTC, but the buses are older and clunkier.

Taxi & Microbus Salalah's taxis and microbuses hang out in front of the British Bank of the Middle East on A'Salam St in the centre. Taxis will generally only make inter-city trips on an 'engaged' basis, which is invariably expensive (OR 10 to Taqa, for example). Microbus fares from Salalah include: Taqa, 300 baisa; Mirbat, 500 baisa; Mughsail, OR 1; Thumrait, OR 1; and Muscat, OR 8.

Getting Around

The Airport There are no buses to/from Salalah airport. The taxi fare between Salalah airport and the city centre is about OR 1 but is negotiable.

Taxi & Microbus Local taxis and microbuses also gather in front of the British Bank of the Middle East on A'Salam St in the centre. The taxis do not seem to spend much time cruising around looking for fares. Generally a microbus ride inside the city costs around 200 baisa and a taxi ride about 500 baisa. To further flung destinations like the Holiday Inn, OR 1 should be sufficient.

Car If you want to rent a car in Salalah try Al-Miyasa Rent-a-Car (☎ 296521) on A'Salam St next door to the Redan Hotel (look for the large 'Car Rent' sign). They offer small cars for OR 14, including insurance and 200 free km per day. Additional kms are 50 baisa each, but you can probably bargain a couple of riyals off the daily rate, even if you only need the car for a day or two.

As for the larger agencies, Budget (☎ 235160) has a desk at the Holiday Inn, there is an Avis office at Al-Zubair Travel (☎ 291145) on A'Nahdah St and Thrifty has an office in the Al-Zahra Al-Omania Centre. The rates at all of the larger agencies are the same as in Muscat.

AROUND SALALAH

There are very good **beaches** all along the road to Mughsail once you're about five km out of Salalah. The road runs along the beach and all of the beaches are open to the public, including women (though women should not wear bikinis). The water is generally calm but the wind can sometimes kick up a lot of sand. Overnight camping on the beach is not allowed. If you do not have a car and decide, for some reason, to forego microbuses, you should not have too much trouble hitching rides, though they are often for only a few km at a time. It's too hot and humid to cycle most of the time, and there is nowhere to hire a bike.

MUGHSAIL

Mughsail (Mugsail) is 45 km west of Salalah. It offers beautiful unspoilt beaches as well as some spectacular scenery on the drive out. This includes several **frankincense** groves which are located 15 to 25 km out of Salalah. Most are along the right hand side of the road if you are coming from Salalah. When young or not flowering they are mostly small, gnarled and less than impressive.

Mughsail itself is a fishing community and you can often see the fishers' boats pulled up on the shore while their camels wander about on the beach. The government has built a series of sun shelter pavilions along much of the beach but aside from that it is essentially untouched by development.

Because there are few houses in Mughsail the place is easy to miss. Heading west out of Salalah you'll know you're there when you reach a small green police fort on the inland side of the road. The fort is mid-way along Mughsail's beach. Around it you will find Mughsail's few shops.

OMAN

Job's Tomb

In religious terms the mortuary known as Job's Tomb (and referred to in Arabic simply as '*Nabi Ayoub*' – Prophet Job) is probably the most important site in Dhofar. Regardless of your religious convictions the tomb – situated on an isolated hilltop overlooking Salalah – is a must-see both for the beautiful drive up to its mountain site and for the excellent view over Salalah that the parking lot affords on a clear day.

Entering the enclosure itself (open more or less around the clock, admission free) you will pass a mosque on your left. This, like all mosques in Oman, is closed to non-Muslims. A footpath from the gate goes past the mosque and through some trees ending at a small white building with a gold-coloured dome. This is the tomb itself. The tomb is open to everyone but mosque-decorum must be observed: shoes must be removed and women are expected to cover up. Inside you will find a single, remarkably long grave set into the floor and covered in ornate shrouds embroidered with verses from the Koran.

Near the parking lot the *Prophet Ayoub Region Restaurant* offers food and scenery from its spot on the hillside overlooking Salalah and the Arabian Sea.

The tomb is just over 30 km from Salalah's centre. To reach it take the main road west from the centre toward Mughsail and turn right at the sign for Ittin when you are on the outskirts of Salalah, just after passing the Hamdan Plaza Hotel. From the turn-off follow this road for 22 km and then turn left off the main road at a sign that says 'Al-Nabi Ayoub 1½ km'. After 1.4 km you will come to a fork in the road. Keeping right takes you to the restaurant, going left takes you to the parking lot outside the tomb enclosure. There is no public transport to or from the tomb. ∎

If you continue beyond Mughsail on the road toward the Yemeni border the landscape gets even more spectacular.

Microbuses charge OR 1 in either direction for the trip between Salalah and Mughsail.

AYN RAZAT

Ayn Razat is a spring rising in a landscaped garden approximately 25 km north-east of Salalah. It makes a pleasant stop for half an hour or so if you are making a tour of the sites east of Salalah. To reach Ayn Razat head east out of Salalah and follow the signs. From the roundabout where Ayn Razat is signposted it is another 10.5 km.

AYN HOMRAN

Seven km off the Salalah-Taqa road is Ayn Homran, a small, spring-fed oasis much of which is now taken up by a government-run agricultural project. There is also a small **park** and the entire area is dominated by a **watchtower** on a hill overlooking the spring. A paved road leads from the main highway into the oasis. This ends in a parking area, just beyond and to the right of which is a natural pool.

TAQA

The village of **Taqa**, 36 km east of Salalah, is definitely worth a stop. It is said to be one of the few places where the sewn boats which were common to the region in the early years of Islam are still made and used, though I have never managed to confirm this claim by observation. What Taqa definitely does have is a **castle** and, nearby, a **cemetery** where you can see the grave of Sultan Qaboos' mother, Maizoun Bint Ahmed Al-M'ashti, who died in August 1992.

The castle is easy to find – just follow the brown and white signs once you enter Taqa. It is open Saturday to Wednesday from 7.30 am to 2.30 pm. Admission is free and no permit is required. Once inside you will find a cramped courtyard surrounded by rooms. Most of the rooms have signs in English indicating what they were once used for. The castle itself was used as the local wali's office until 1984.

To reach the graveyard from the castle turn left out of the castle's door and walk toward the main road. Between the castle and the road is the **Mosque of Shaikh Al-Affif**. The graveyard is in front of the mosque, and fronts on the main road. Standing facing the mosque and the graveyard look all the way to your left. At the left-hand corner of the graveyard nearest the road you will see several particularly ornate graves each marked by two stones. Among these is a single grave with three stones, this is the grave of Sultan Qaboos' mother. Immediately to the right of it is the grave of her brother. The next grave to the right is her father, the sultan's grandfather.

There is no place to stay in Taqa, though you can pick up a meal at any of several small restaurants and coffee shops around the castle. Microbuses pick up and drop their charges on the town's main road a few hundred metres west of the turn for the castle. The fare from Salalah to Taqa is 300 baisa. Taxis will only make the trip from Salalah 'engaged'. This will probably cost around OR 10.

KHOR ROURI

Centuries ago Khor Rouri was an important port holding down the southern end of the frankincense route. It was then known as Sumhuram. From this small bay, boats and rafts took the frankincense to Qana, 640 km down the coast in what is today Yemen, on the first stage of its journey to the bazaars of Damascus and the temples of Rome. Today, little remains of the city except the ruins of a palace-cum-fort sitting atop a mound of rather nondescript looking rubble. The setting, however, is dramatic enough to make the site worth going out of your way for. The ruins have the Dhofar Mountains rising behind them and overlook a sheltered harbour guarded by twin cliffs. The calm is almost unearthly, but it is strangely easy amid that calm to imagine a time 18 or 20 centuries ago when this quiet bay was one of the most important ports on earth.

In theory a permit from the Salalah museum is needed to visit the site. The museum may also want to send a guide out to the site with you to unlock the gate. This usually means that you have to go to the museum one day and make arrangements to visit the site the following day, but in my experience the gate to the site is often unlocked and there are enough holes in the

fence that you should not have any trouble getting in if the attendant is nowhere to be found. The site is in slightly better condition than Al-Balid and individual rooms among the ruins are easier to make out, though it would take an archaeologist to find out what any given room was used for. The steel cage near the left-centre of the fort (as you face the sea) marks the site of an old well. Nearby (down and to the right, still facing the sea) you can see inscriptions on some of the stones.

To reach the site take the road from Salalah toward Mirbat and turn at the Khor Rouri sign, about seven km beyond Taqa's centre. There is another turn-off further down the road, but the first turn, coming from Salalah, is the easier of the two to navigate. The site is 2.5 km off the main road along a bumpy dirt track. Follow the track for 2.1 km to a fork. Keep right at the fork and you will see the mound and the fence on your right after another 400m.

The microbus fare from Salalah should be 300 to 400 baisa, but you will have to walk to the gate from the main road. Returning to Salalah or continuing on to Mirbat from Khor Rouri requires hiking back to the main road and flagging down a microbus headed in the appropriate direction.

JABAL SAMHAN

Jabal Samhan is a high plateau 41 km by road east of Salalah. It's worth the diversion (on a clear day) for the striking views over the surrounding countryside especially during the green months of the late summer. To reach it, turn at the sign just west of Khor Rouri saying 'Tawi Attair 18 km' and follow the road to the end, up a steep incline.

MIRBAT

The town of Mirbat (Mirbaat), just over 70 km east of Salalah, is about as far east of Salalah as you can go without a 4WD. The town's small **fort** has a lonely, end-of-the-road feel about it as it overlooks both the town and the coastline trailing off back toward Salalah. Brown and white signs in English will point you toward the fort as you enter town. Note that it is not the first fort you will see. The one visible from a great distance as you approach Mirbat is a police fort that is still in use.

Mirbat's other noteworthy site is the **Bin Ali Tomb**, a small and quite photogenic mosque built in a style typical of Yemen's Hadhramaut region. The tomb is one km off the main road. It is the larger of the two white tombs in the cemetery – the one closer to the parking area. You will see the tomb off to the right as you approach Mirbat on the road from Salalah. There are also some nice **beaches** about six km west of Mirbat. Look for the government-built picnic pavilions.

Beyond these two sites there is very little to Mirbat itself. There are no hotels and only a handful of restaurants. If you are looking for a meal try *Restaurant* – the place with the Pepsi sign – on the main road a few hundred metres beyond the town's centre. Reasonably good biryanis can be had for 600 baisa.

Mirbat's taxi stand is in the centre at the small parking lot by the 'Departments Store' and a newish stone mosque with several small blue domes. Microbuses from Salalah charge 500 baisa for the trip.

THUMRAIT

There is not much to the town of Thumrait, 80 km inland from Salalah on the road to Muscat, but the contrasts in scenery make it worth the drive if you have the time and a car. The first half of the drive is spent climbing to and through the mountain plateau overlooking Salalah. The second half of the route takes you along the plateau itself and finally into the desert area behind it. The plateau is strikingly green in the late summer and early autumn right after the monsoon season but rapidly reverts to desert once the rains are over. Microbuses charge OR 1 for the trip from Salalah.

Musandem Peninsula

Separated from the rest of Oman by the eastern border of the UAE, and guarding the southern side of the strategically important Strait of Hormuz, the Musandem Peninsula was until recently a military zone and largely off limits to tourists. Though the military is still a major presence throughout Musandem the area is now open to visitors, and it is one of the highlights of the country. Musandem is a land of stark beauty. It is the least developed part of the Gulf's least developed country; an area of fjords, small villages and dramatic, mountain-hugging roads. Musandem remains one of Arabia's least accessible areas, but also one of its most memorable. It is definitely worth the effort.

And effort is indeed required. There are no paved roads in Musandem outside of the town centres in Khasab, Bukha and the Omani portion of Dibba. There are only a handful of flights into Khasab each week, all on tiny planes. If you are a foreign resident of Oman you need a road permit to enter Musandem overland. Public transport within Khasab, between towns or back down to the

UAE and Muscat exists more in theory than in practice and some of the region's settlements are accessible only by boat. It is also very expensive, even by Omani standards.

The good news is that the widely-held belief that you cannot move about outside of Khasab without a 4WD is not true. You may even hear that the road between Khasab and the border post at Tibat (on the road to Ras Al-Khaimah and Dubai) is impassible without a 4WD. This is nonsense – as shown by the large number of non-4WD cars with Dubai and Ras Al-Khaimah number plates driving around Khasab on any given day. That said, without a 4WD your options in Musandem are a bit limited. The road up from Dibba via Rawdah, for example, *does* require a 4WD, so with a normal car Tibat is really the only way in. This section lists pretty much all of the places in Musandem you can visit using a regular car. For detailed information on destinations requiring a 4WD consult *Off-Road in Oman* or the *Apex Explorer's Guide to Oman*, both of which are widely available in Muscat.

KHASAB

Musandem's capital is small but far from sleepy. Its port bursts with activity, much of it involving the smuggling of American cigarettes to Iran, and its souk is filled with both visitors from other parts of Musandem and an ever-increasing number of tourists. The waterfront is a beautiful spot for a sunset stroll with its carefully-restored fort framed by bare, rugged hills. It is also a good base for exploring the region. Starting from Khasab you can easily visit both Bukha and Khor Najd in a single day.

The bad news is that Khasab is something of a one-horse town commercially. There is one hotel, one car rental company, one tour operator and they all charge predictably monopolistic prices.

Orientation & Information

For such a small place Khasab is surprisingly spread out. The town's commercial centre is the port and the small souk a km or so south-east of it. The souk consists mainly of

merchants who sell cigarettes to the Iranian smugglers who crowd the port every day, along with a couple of restaurants and small groceries and the Khasab Travel & Tours office. Another 1.5 km to the east is the town's 'new souk'. This consists of a few more restaurants and groceries, the post office, a couple of banks, Khasab's lone car rental agency and the Oman Air office. Most of Khasab's houses are just north, or still further east, of the new souk. The Khasab Hotel and the airport lie a short distance to the south.

Though it is remote, Khasab's telephone and postal systems are just as efficient as those found throughout the rest of Oman. Changing money is also pretty much the same as it is anywhere else – that is to say it is a somewhat slow and bureaucratic process at banks, and quick (but with bad rates) at the hotel.

Khasab Fort

There is nothing especially remarkable about Khasab Fort. The design, though a bit odd, will be familiar to anyone who has already looked at the rest of Northern Oman's forts. What sets this one apart is the setting.

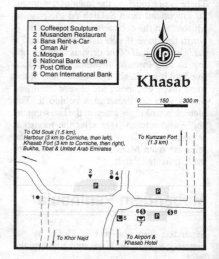

1 Coffeepot Sculpture
2 Musandem Restaurant
3 Bana Rent-a-Car
4 Oman Air
5 Mosque
6 National Bank of Oman
7 Post Office
8 Oman International Bank

Khasab

0   150   300 m

To Old Souk (1.5 km),
Harbour (3 km to Corniche, then left),
Khasab Fort (3 km to Corniche, then right),
Bukha, Tibat & United Arab Emirates

To Kumzan Fort
(1.3 km)

To Khor Najd

To Airport &
Khasab Hotel

Though some distance from the modern port and souk, the fort dominates the bit of coast that provides access to Khasab's older sections. None of the corner towers, however, match each other or the large fifth tower in the centre of the fort's courtyard.

Though the fort has been restored, little effort has gone into making it tourist-friendly beyond hanging khanjars in a few of the rooms. Its opening hours are a bit erratic. Government office hours (Saturday to Wednesday from 7.30 am to 2.30 pm) are your best bet. If the fort is open no permit is required to visit it. Admission is free.

Kumzan Fort

Kumzan Fort is a ruin, but it is worth the diversion if only for the contrast with Khasab Fort. It was built by a local imam approximately 400 years ago and originally had 22 rooms inside its walls. Though little remains of the fort today two of its towers are still standing.

To reach the fort go east out of the roundabout by the Oman Air office (a right turn if you are coming from the Khasab Hotel, straight if you are coming from Khasab Fort and the port) in the new souk area and turn left onto a paved street after 300m. Follow this street for another 1.3 km as it winds through a residential area. The fort will be on your left.

Khasab Port

What is interesting about the Khasab port is not so much the main dhow jetty and customs administration building, but the little bay next to the main port where, on any given day, a hundred or so speedboats from Iran are anchored or pulled up on the shore. These Iranians are smugglers who make the short trip over from Bandar Abbas (about two hours using the souped-up boats and outboard motors needed to outrun the Iranian Coast Guard) to purchase goods that are expensive or hard to find at home. The Omani authorities charge them a couple of riyals for the privilege of tying up in Khasab for the day and then let them go shopping in the souk. A quick walk through the souk will show you what the Iranians are in the market for. Maybe half of all the shops in the souk are bulk cigarette merchants. The Iranians buy enormous quantities of cigarettes ('Only American cigarettes', one boat captain told me), wrap the boxes up in plastic and, after dark, head back across the strait. You will occasionally see other goods being loaded onto the boats but cigarettes are the main business, and the smugglers are remarkably open about it. During the day they wander around Khasab chatting and getting in the odd bit of personal shopping. Every shop and restaurant in Khasab accepts Iranian riyals without question and aside from tourism (and with tourism still in its infancy) it appears to be the town's economic mainstay.

Beach

There is a small beach just outside Khasab. Follow the road from the port toward Bukha. The beach is at a lay-by on the right exactly one km after the point where the pavement ends.

Organised Tours

Khasab Travel & Tours (☎ 830464), in the old souk, offers group trips by boat to the Sham fjords. A full day tour, including lunch, costs OR 25 per person (OR 12 for children under 12). Their shorter half-day boat trip costs OR 15 (OR 8 for children). For OR 50 a head they will take you all the way to Kumzar and back. These tours only leave when the people who run the company decide that there are enough people to make it worth their while. They were a bit fuzzy when I asked about numbers, but critical mass appears to be from four to six people.

Places to Stay & Eat

The only hotel in the entire Musandem is the *Khasab Hotel* (☎ 830267, fax 830989). At OR 18.975/32.200 for singles/doubles, including the tax and service charge, it is rather overpriced. The rooms are pretty basic but they are clean, there's a pool and the hotel has Musandem's only bar. Do not expect any discount on the rack rate unless you are staying for five days or more. Because the hotel is small, calling ahead for reservations is a very good idea.

In the new souk the *Bukha Restaurant* has biryanis that are more subtly spiced than what one usually finds down in Muscat. These cost 600 baisa per serving. Kebabs are available in the evening and the place is popular with the Iranian cigarette smugglers – always a good sign. For roasted chicken try the *Musandem Restaurant* in the new souk area. Half a chicken costs 600 baisa. Rice is 300 baisa a portion.

Getting There & Away

Air Oman Air's office (☎ 830543) is on the new souk's main roundabout, between the Khasab Hotel and the port area. They fly to Muscat four days a week. Fares are OR 20 one way and OR 40 return, a price you will find hard to beat by going overland unless you have your own car. Two flights a week go via Dibba, to which the fares are the same as those to Muscat. The trip takes about 90 minutes nonstop and two hours via Dibba using 20 seat twin-prop planes. These cruise at around 2800m providing passengers with a spectacular view of the Musandem Peninsula. That alone is worth OR 20.

You should be aware that the Khasab airport is actually an air force base at which Oman Air is allowed to land a couple of times a week. This means that Khasab flights are subject to cancellation whenever the air force feels like it, such as during National Day when the air base simply shuts down for a couple of days. This, and the extremely small size of the planes used on the Khasab route, means you should make visiting the Oman Air office and reconfirming return reservation to Muscat your first priority upon arrival. The airport itself is on the southern edge of town, a few km beyond the Khasab Hotel.

Taxi The 10-passenger 4WD pick-up trucks that serve as the Musandem's service-taxi system gather in Khasab's old souk, near the port. The drivers say they travel to Bukha and Tibat for OR 1 per passenger but there does not appear to be a lot of action. It's most

likely you will have to take a vehicle 'engaged'. The standard engaged rates are: Bukha OR 5, Tibat or Khor Najd OR 10, Dibba OR 25, Muscat OR 70.

Though it is only about 70 km from Ras al-Khaimah to Khasab there are no service-taxis making the run on a regular basis. The Khasab pick-up drivers charge OR 15 for an 'engaged' trip to Ras Al-Khaimah (about two hours if there are no hold-ups at the border). If you are travelling to Ras Al-Khaimah (or Muscat) make sure the driver is an Omani (most of them are but it doesn't hurt to double-check) and that he has his identity card and car papers as these will be needed at the border. If you are going to Ras Al-Khaimah you should also make sure you and the driver are both clear on where he is taking you. If you want to go to the city of Ras Al-Khaimah make sure the driver understands that, otherwise you may find yourself dumped just across the border in Sham, which is part of the Emirate of Ras Al-Khaimah but a good 40 km north of the city of the same name.

It's also worth noting that getting out of Khasab by road is a lot cheaper than getting in. All things considered, OR 15 is a pretty reasonable one-way fare. Travelling from Ras Al-Khaimah to Khasab is an entirely different story. Ras Al-Khaimah's service-taxi drivers demand Dh 200 for the trip to Khasab, though for Dh 40 they will take you to the Sham border post from where you can try to hitch a ride into Khasab. To leave the UAE by road you will also have to pay a Dh 20 road tax (this does not apply when you enter the UAE by road). Foreign residents of Oman need a road permit to leave and re-enter Oman by land. Tourist visa holders do not need road permits.

The upshot of this is that if you are trying to get from Muscat to Khasab by public transport the cheapest way to do it is by air. If you are in Khasab and need a lift back to Muscat asking around in the bar at the Khasab Hotel is your best bet. The problem you are likely to run into is that most of the people propping up the bar at the hotel are expats, many of whom may not be aware that tourists do not need road permits. This may make them reluctant to take you when they discover that you have no road permit.

Car Rental Khasab's only car rental operation is Bana Rent-a-Car (☎ 830678) on the new souk's main roundabout. Their rates are pretty outrageous – OR 10 to rent an ageing small car (a Daewoo Racer, for example) for use in Khasab only. If you want to take the car to Bukha the rate goes up to OR 15, Khor Najd sends it to OR 20. You could, of course, lie to them about where you plan to take the car, but I would not recommend it. Most of their cars are in poor condition but they will give you one of the better ones if they know you're going outside the town. Moreover, if you tell them you are staying in Khasab this fact will be written into your rental agreement – meaning that any accident or damage outside the town is not covered by the insurance. To further guarantee that you stay in Khasab they will try to give you only 50 km per day free with very high per km charges beyond that. There is also no grace period for late returns unless you specifically arrange one in advance, they demand a OR 50 cash deposit for all rentals (I was able to bargain this down to OR 35 only by proving to the clerk's satisfaction that OR 35 was all the money I had) and they only take cash – no plastic.

Renting a car in Muscat and driving it to Khasab is not really an option because of the need to cross the UAE. You can get permission to do this from Muscat's car rental agencies but it sends the cost of both the rental and the insurance through the ceiling.

Getting Around
The Airport Khasab may have the only airport in the world that is completely devoid of taxis. The Khasab Hotel will meet your flight if you have a reservation there and can also give you a lift to the airport when it is time to leave. Either of these services costs OR 3. If someone offers you a lift into town but expects to be paid for the service do not agree to pay more than OR 2 as the distance is only a few km.

Taxi The Musandem's only form of public transport are open 4WD pick-up trucks with benches in the back. These are the local service-taxis, though it is rare to see one actually going anywhere with passengers in it. Mostly they just seem to hang around Khasab's old souk and wait for people who need 'engaged' trips to other towns. Should one of these vehicles actually be moving, the driver will charge a couple of hundred baisa for a lift within the town.

TAWI
About 10 km from the spot near Khasab port where the pavement ends lies the village of Tawi, home to a handful of prehistoric **rock carvings**. These are easy to miss because there are only a few of them and they are at ground level by the track running through the village, but they are worth a quick diversion if time is not a major concern.

To reach the carvings turn inland off the Khasab-Bukha road at Quida onto a dirt track. Coming from Khasab the track is just beyond the sign with the village's name but before you pass any of Quida's houses. Follow this track up the Wadi Quida for 2.3 km. The carvings will be to your left on two rocks at a point where the track bends sharply to the right just before a large white house. Across the track from the carvings is an ancient **well** that is still used by Tawi's residents.

AL-HARF
This small village roughly mid-way between Khasab and Bukha is noteworthy for only one thing: the view. The drive from Khasab to Bukha involves crossing a mountain. Al-Harf is the village at the point where the road crests. Along the road are several places where you can pull over and admire the view. Legend has it that on a clear day you can make out the Iranian coast from Al-Harf. It is definitely worth a stop.

BUKHA
Bukha has the distinction of being the only place in Musandem outside Khasab and Dibba with paved streets or, more accurately,

OMAN

a paved street. It also has two forts. The more interesting of the two is **Bukha Fort**, on the coast. If you are coming from Khasab the fort is the first thing you will arrive at. The other fort, which is in ruins, is on a hill a short distance inland and north of Bukha Fort. The town's residential and commercial centre is another km further down the road. The town's administrative buildings, such as the post office, and its petrol station are two km south of the town centre on the road toward Tibat. Being only 27 km from Khasab by road, it makes an easy and scenic day trip.

Bukha Fort has towers at three of its corners. It is fairly photogenic, but is not usually open to the public. The **ruined fort** is really little more than a single large tower inside a walled enclosure. More fortifications can be seen three km north of Bukha in the village of **Al-Jadi** which has one restored watchtower dominating the southern edge of its beach and another overlooking the settlement from a hilltop to the north.

Bukha's centre consists of a bank, a few small shops and a restaurant all stretched out along the single paved road. For a meal try the *Saeed Abdullah R. Al-Shehi Restaurant* which has good mutton curry at 800 baisa for a large portion. Look for a white sign with green English lettering. If you go one km beyond the fort (coming from Khasab) and turn left onto the asphalt into the town centre the restaurant will be on your left after 250m.

KHOR NAJD

Khor Najd (Khor A'Najd) is the only one of the Musandem's fjords that can be reached from Khasab in an ordinary car, though it needs to be a car in fairly decent repair considering how steep (both climbing and descending) the last portion of the drive is. It is 24.5 km by road from Khasab's centre, about a 45 minute drive. The best view of the area is your first view of it – from the point where the road from Khasab finally cuts through the mountains. The small beach below is better suited to camping than swimming, and is a popular weekend spot with both Omani and Emirati families, particu-

larly since it has a concrete ramp for launching boats.

To reach Khor Najd go west from the new souk roundabout and turn off the pavement after 350m at the corner where you see a coffeepot-shaped sculpture (the 24.5 km mentioned above is measured from this point). After 200m the road forks, keep left and follow the road for another 3.4 km (the airport perimeter fence will be on your left) until you reach an intersection with a sign reading 'Dabba 110 km'. Go straight through this intersection and just over 8.5 km later you will see a green sign pointing to, among other places, 'Khor A'Najd 10 km'. Turn left, follow this road for another 5.6 km and then turn left again. After another 1.5 km you will come to a three-way fork in the road, take the centre road and you will soon begin a steep ascent. After 2.3 km you will reach the outlook, and your first view of Khor Najd. Another (even steeper) 2.8 km descent brings you to the water's edge.

KUMZAR

For the truly adventurous, few Arabian excursions can top a trip to Kumzar. Set on an isolated cove at the northern edge of the Musandem Peninsula, Kumzar is accessible only by boat. The village's residents do not speak Arabic. Their language, known as Kumzari, is a mish-mash of Farsi, Hindi, English and Arabic (for the record, Arabic is widely understood in Kumzar. English, however, is an entirely different matter).

The village's only 'sight' is a **well** half a km or so up the wadi that serves as Kumzar's main 'street'. The well, which is now brackish, was Kumzar's sole source of water until the government built a small desalination plant next to the harbour in the '70s. Even today most of the town's water is delivered through communal taps – note the incredibly long hoses running from the taps into houses throughout the village. The old **stone houses** are also interesting to look at, quite unlike anything you will see in the rest of Oman. The houses appear to get older as one moves further up the wadi.

Kumzar's small waterfront has a narrow

beach on a pretty bay where speedboats and fishing boats are tied up. There are a few small grocery stores. If you need a bite to eat try the *Abdul Aziz Bin Mohd. Bin Jafar Restaurant*. The fare is pretty basic, but their concrete balcony is a good spot for a cup of tea.

The main attraction of a visit to Kumzar is really the spectacular scenery on the boat trip out and back. Once you arrive, bear in mind that visits by foreigners are still not an everyday occurrence in Kumzar and an exceptional degree of discretion is required. Ask permission before taking pictures, and be prepared to be stared at by everyone and followed around by a small army of children wherever you go.

Water-taxis travel between Khasab and Kumzar most days, charging OR 3 per head. This can be a pretty harrowing trip. Most of the speedboats used as water-taxis have no seats and maybe 15 cm clearance between the deck and gunwale. There's really nothing to hold onto once the boat heads out into the open ocean, nor is there any safety gear. The water-taxis won't leave until they have crammed 15 or so people into the boat, which tends to make the two hour trip to Kumzar an extremely nerve-wracking experience. Also, there is no guarantee that you will be able to get back the same day.

Alternatively, you could hire the entire boat. The captains on the dock in Khasab will start by asking OR 30 for a one-way trip, but with a little tenacity you should be able to get someone to take you over to Kumzar, wait around there for two or three hours and then

bring you back for OR 40. If you can split this cost among four or five people you will have a faster (it takes about one hour each way with three to five people on the boat instead of 15 to 17) and probably safer trip, not to mention a more comfortable ride and a guaranteed lift back. It's not cheap, but it does have its advantages. If you catch a water-taxi over, you could find yourself stranded and wind up paying OR 30 or more to get back to Khasab. Mostly it depends on how much time you have to burn. If you do get trapped you can probably camp on the beach at the edge of the village. Khasab Travels & Tours also offers an all-day trip to Kumzar for OR 50 per person if you can scare together a large enough group of people.

Madha

The other Omani territory separated from the rest of the country is the Madha enclave near the UAE's Fujairah. This is a tiny area consisting of a few villages spread out over a small patch of semi-desert. The Madha governate is completely surrounded by UAE territory and if it were not for a sign on the road saying it's part of Oman you would not know the difference. There are no customs controls, just a sign saying you've crossed the border. However, your UAE car insurance is not valid once you cross into the enclave. See Madha in the East Coast section of the UAE chapter for more details.

OMAN

Qatar

Qatar

In Albert Hourani's book *A History of the Arab Peoples*, Qatar ranks a grand total of two references (Bahrain has seven, Kuwait 17). Arthur Goldschmidt's *A Concise History of the Middle East* mentions the country only once – its listing in a population table. The index to John Bagot Glubb's *A Short History of the Arab Peoples* does not list Qatar at all and, to add insult to injury, Glubb did not even bother to mark the place on the book's maps.

Qatar has always had a way of falling off the outside world's radar screens. Most foreign maps of Arabia drawn prior to the 19th century do not show the Qatar peninsula. The British writer Peter Mansfield once remarked that even quiz show champions were likely to have trouble finding the place. I would only add that if few westerners can locate Qatar even fewer can pronounce it correctly. The stress is on the first syllable. The first vowel is short, the second one silent: 'QaT-r'.

But things have been changing and, considering its size, Qatar has made news remarkably often over the last few years. The country first issued tourist visas in 1989, and after a slow start it has begun to reap the benefits of that new openness. Though Qatar remains a far cry from the tourist centres of the UAE, it's really not all that bad. Give Qatar a chance...you may be surprised.

Facts about the Country

HISTORY
Beginnings
Archaeological digs have shown that the Qatar peninsula was inhabited during the Stone Age when the region's climate was milder than it is today. But the archaeologists have found little evidence of habitation between the most ancient of times and the modern era. Qatar does have its share of

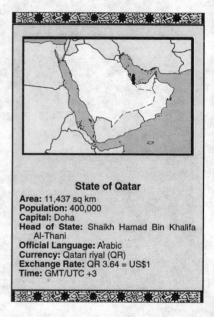

State of Qatar
Area: 11,437 sq km
Population: 400,000
Capital: Doha
Head of State: Shaikh Hamad Bin Khalifa Al-Thani
Official Language: Arabic
Currency: Qatari riyal (QR)
Exchange Rate: QR 3.64 = US$1
Time: GMT/UTC +3

ancient grave mounds but there are no known sites connecting it to the Bahrain-based Dilmun Empire. Apparently the landscape was little more inviting then than it is now.

Qatar is the only significant place in the Gulf to have no Portuguese ruins of any sort. Since the Portuguese conquered, or at least attacked, just about everywhere else in the Gulf this strongly implies that 16th-century Qatar was either uninhabited or very nearly so. Qatar is not mentioned in any substantial way by the various European travellers who reached the Gulf between the 16th and early 18th centuries.

For most of its recorded (ie recent) history Qatar has been dominated by the Al-Thani family who arrived in the mid-18th century and became the peninsula's rulers about 100 years later. The Al-Thani family is a branch of the Tamim tribe and is thought to have arrived in Qatar from southern Najd in central Arabia. Originally they were nomadic Bedouins, but the region's sparse vegetation led them to settle in the peninsula's coastal areas where they became fishers and pearl divers.

By the mid-18th century Qatar was well established as a pearling centre. Activity was then centred on Zubara, in the north-west, which was under the control of the Al-Khalifa family (who are now the rulers of Bahrain). Since that time, and even into the present day, tension between the Al-Khalifa and the Al-Thani has been a constant feature of Qatar's history. The Al-Thani fought several long battles with the Al-Khalifa for control of the peninsula, and did not get full control of Zubara itself until 1937. Today, Zubara is firmly under Qatari control and the principal territorial dispute between the two countries concerns the Hawar Islands, which lie just off Qatar's western coast.

Doha was never a trading port of the importance of Kuwait or Manama. Throughout the 19th and early 20th centuries Qatar remained shockingly poor, even by pre-oil Gulf standards. Seemingly bleak and remote places like Zubara were so hotly contested precisely because they controlled access to the one thing which provided enough money to feed the local populace: the pearl beds.

The Rise of the Al-Thani

Qatar's first Al-Thani emir was Shaikh Mohammed Bin Thani, who took effective control of most of the peninsula from the Al-Khalifa and established his capital at Al-Bida, today's Doha, in the mid-19th century. To strengthen his position vis-à-vis the other tribes in the area, he signed a treaty with Britain in 1867. At the time, he was almost certainly seeking British protection from the Al-Khalifa.

Shaikh Mohammed died later that year and was succeeded by his son, Jasim (sometimes also spelled Qasim). From the 1870s onward Jasim, who reigned until his death in 1913, became a master at maintaining his own independence by playing the British off against the Turks.

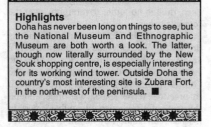

Highlights
Doha has never been long on things to see, but the National Museum and Ethnographic Museum are both worth a look. The latter, though now literally surrounded by the New Souk shopping centre, is especially interesting for its working wind tower. Outside Doha the country's most interesting site is Zubara Fort, in the north-west of the peninsula. ■

In 1872 he signed a treaty with the Turks allowing them to place a garrison in Doha, though he never allowed it to grow very large and, reportedly, refused to take any money from the Ottomans. The presence of Turkish troops did, however, provide Jasim with a certain amount of cachet locally. As the nominal representative of the Ottoman sultan, Jasim was a powerful figure in eastern Arabia during the late 19th and early

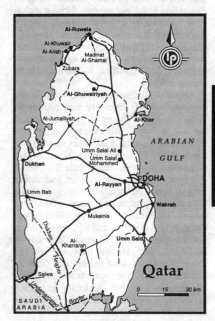

QATAR

20th centuries, exercising significant influence, though not quite sovereignty, over the region's tribes.

But being the Turk's man also had its drawbacks. The Ottomans maintained only a small presence in the region while the British, who were the dominant power in the Gulf, were on the ground in force. Though in practical terms Qatar was independent, this state of affairs also meant that it was, in a sense, surrounded by hostile forces. Over the years the small Turkish garrison in Doha began to seem more destabilising than reassuring. In 1893, Jasim fought a small battle against the Turks but when he died, on the eve of WWI, the Turks were still in Doha.

Jasim's successor, Shaikh Abdullah, oversaw the withdrawal of the Ottoman garrison in 1915 after Turkey entered WWI on the side of Germany. The British almost certainly had a hand in this withdrawal, and in 1916, they signed an Exclusive Agreement with Abdullah modelled on the agreements they already had in place around the Gulf. According to the agreements, Britain undertook to protect the local ruler in exchange for a promise that the ruler would not have any dealings with other foreign powers without British permission. The 1916 agreement was extended and modified by another treaty signed in 1934.

Abdullah's expulsion of the Turks was a combination of necessity and prudence. With Britain and Turkey on opposite sides in the war, and the British controlling the rest of the Gulf, switching alliances seemed like a wise move. On a local level, Abdullah also had to worry about Abdul Aziz Bin Abdul Rahman Al-Saud, the founder and future king of Saudi Arabia, who was then in the process of conquering most of eastern Arabia. The Turks were in no position to help Qatar in the event of a Saudi attack, even assuming they wanted to do so. Qatar's 1916 agreement with Britain only obliged the Royal Navy to defend the emirate from an attack by sea, but the commitment to Abdullah and his line that the treaty embodied almost certainly caused Abdul Aziz to decide against invading Qatar.

Oil

Even before the collapse, around 1930, of the pearl market, life in Qatar was rough. With poverty, hunger, malnutrition and disease all widespread, the emir welcomed the oil prospectors who first arrived in the early 1930s. In 1935, he granted a concession to Petroleum Development (Qatar), or PDQ, the forerunner of today's state-run Qatar General Petroleum Corporation (QGPC). PDQ was a subsidiary of the Iraq Petroleum Company (IPC) which, in turn, was owned by a collection of US, British and French oil interests.

The prospectors struck oil in 1939 but, because of WWII, production did not begin for another 10 years. It was only then, in 1949, that the British finally posted a Political Agent to Doha. Until that time the country had been covered by the Political Agent based in Bahrain.

At that point things began to move very quickly. The new British agent was followed, a few years later, by a financial adviser sent to help the emir deal with the unprecedented sums of money he suddenly found himself holding. Even then, the Qataris were shrewd enough to maintain some balance. As he and his father had done in politics prior to WWI, Abdullah carefully balanced the sources of the advice he received. An Egyptian named Hassan Kamil was hired to offer the emir additional financial advice, and he stayed on as adviser to subsequent emirs for several decades.

Abdullah abdicated on account of his advancing age in 1949. He was succeeded by his son Ali (reigned 1949-60) who presided over the first stages of Qatar's oil boom. The quantity of oil produced in Qatar was not in itself huge but the country's tiny population made it instantly wealthy on a per capita basis. Much of the early revenue was devoted to establishing the basics of modern life: Qatar's first school opened in 1952 and health-care facilities were immediately upgraded, though a full-scale hospital did not open until 1959.

Shaikh Ali had little interest in the day-to-day business of government with the result that by the mid-50s his nephew, Khalifa Bin Hamad Al-Thani, was, to a great extent, running the country. At the beginning of the '60s Ali abdicated in favour of his son, Ahmed, but the new emir was as uninterested in the government as his predecessor had been. By all reports, Ahmed spent most of his reign pursuing *la dolce vita* abroad and when he was at home seemed more interested in falconry than affairs of state. With Ahmed's ascension, Khalifa became deputy ruler and prime minister.

Between local politics and the development of the country, Khalifa was very active. As quiet as Qatar usually is, it was not entirely spared from the turmoil which swept the Arab world during the '60s, including a general strike in 1963. With time, however, the ever-increasing flow of oil money seemed to blunt many people's political ambitions. Attempts by some Qataris to form leftist political groups in the '70s never gained significant support, and the country has been stable ever since.

Independence

When the British announced that they would leave the region by the end of 1971, Qatar entered talks with Bahrain and the Trucial States (now the United Arab Emirates, or UAE) on forming a confederation. When Bahrain pulled out of the talks because it did not think that the governmental formulas gave it sufficient weight, Qatar followed Bahrain almost immediately.

It was somehow indicative of his style of government that Shaikh Ahmed proclaimed Qatar's independence, on 1 September 1971, in Geneva rather than Doha. At that point his demise probably became inevitable. Khalifa took power in a palace coup on 22 February 1972. It seems that the real impetus for Ahmed's ouster lay with a broad circle of male members of the ruling family, and in the end, Ahmed's mistake was to lose their confidence. After his overthrow, Ahmed went into exile in Dubai.

Khalifa was well prepared to take over. By the time of the coup he had been Qatar's de facto ruler for more than 15 years and had

already at one time or another run the departments of foreign affairs, oil & finance, and education & culture. He had also headed both the police force and the secret police. One of his first moves as emir was to crack down on the extravagant ways of certain members of the royal family.

The years following Khalifa's palace coup were marked by political stability. As was the case throughout the Gulf, the dramatic rise in oil prices after 1974 gave the government more than enough money to build one of the world's great all-encompassing welfare states.

Still, Qatar has been affected by the political turbulence of its neighbours. Like the other small states of the Gulf, Qatar viewed Iran's 1979 revolution with great alarm. In 1983 the government announced that it had discovered a cache of weapons and foiled a plot to overthrow it. The Hawar Islands dispute with Bahrain has been another consistent, if low-level, cause of tension. In 1995 Qatar asked the International Court of Justice in The Hague to settle the dispute over the islands along with another maritime border disagreement with Bahrain.

The 1990s

Since independence, Qatar has retained its close defence ties with Britain and has increased defence cooperation with both the USA and France. US and Canadian troops were stationed in Doha during the Gulf War.

For many years Qatar's foreign policy closely followed the lead of Saudi Arabia, but in the '90s that began to change. Early in the decade Doha ruffled some feathers around the Gulf (including those of Riyadh) by seeking closer ties with Iran. In 1991, the Qataris and Iranians signed an agreement under which Iran will supply Qatar with fresh water via an undersea pipeline, a project which has been viewed with reservations by some of Doha's Gulf Cooperation Council (GCC) neighbours. In 1993, following the peace agreement between Israel and the Palestine Liberation Organization, Qatar became the first Gulf country to have open diplomatic contact with the Jewish state

QATAR

when the two countries' foreign ministers met in New York. In late 1995 Qatar became the first Gulf state to start an economic relationship with Israel, agreeing to supply Tel Aviv with natural gas, albeit through a third party.

In June 1995 Shaikh Khalifa, then holidaying in Switzerland, was unexpectedly replaced as emir by his son Shaikh Hamad Bin Khalifa Al-Thani, until then the crown prince and defence minister.

GEOGRAPHY

The Qatar peninsula, shaped a bit like a thumb, juts northward into the Gulf from the east coast of the Arabian Peninsula. It is about 160 km long and 55 to 80 km wide. The country's total area (including its small islands) is 11,437 sq km. The desert tends to be flat (the highest elevation in the country is only about 40m above sea level) and gravelly. There is virtually no natural vegetation.

CLIMATE

Summer (May to September) temperatures in Qatar generally average 35°C, but it is not uncommon for them to get up to 50°C. The 90% humidity also means that Qatari summers can be ferociously hot . The winter months are much milder with pleasant, cool evenings. Sandstorms are common throughout the year, especially in the spring. Though it does not rain much in Qatar the few weeks of wet, or wettish, weather in December and January can be pretty miserable, in no small part because few of the country's roads have any drainage to speak of.

FLORA & FAUNA

Qatari fauna is limited to birds such as the houbara and to animals that are pretty hard to spot, such as the sand cats and bats. The emir is said to have a private herd of Arabian oryx though neither these nor much of anything else are to be seen roaming freely. You will, of course, see camels but not a lot of them. Qatar's lack of natural vegetation has meant that it never acquired a large population of Bedouins and thus, by Arabian standards, no large herds of camels. Falconry

remains a popular sport among the well-to-do Qataris, though falcons themselves are a rare sight in the wild.

The National Museum in Doha has displays on the region's marine life, including a tank where live sea turtles can be seen.

GOVERNMENT & POLITICS

Qatar is ruled by an emir: Shaikh Hamad Bin Khalifa Al-Thani who supplanted his father, Shaikh Khalifa Bin Hamad Al-Thani, in June 1995. The emir can appoint and dismiss Cabinet ministers at will, though turnover in the Cabinet doesn't often occur. Laws are announced in emiri decrees. Though he is, in theory, an absolute monarch the emir must always retain the support and confidence of the other members of the ruling family. Retaining this support requires not only good government but ongoing and wide-ranging consultation with the Cabinet, other members of the ruling family and representatives of the country's larger merchant families.

Much of this consultation is informal, though some of it takes place at the regular *majlis* (court) which the emir and other members of the ruling family hold. Any member of the public (usually the men) can address the emir or some other senior figure about any issue during these sessions. Regular, formalised consultation also takes place through an Advisory Council whose 30 members are appointed by the emir. The Council can comment on proposed laws though it can neither change the proposals nor propose new laws on its own.

Qatar has one of the most all-embracing welfare state systems in the world. Qataris are entitled to free education and health care and free, or nearly free, housing. The prices of food, electricity and water are heavily subsidised.

ECONOMY

Qatar has an oil-based economy, though in recent years natural gas has been moving to the fore. The country's oil reserves may well run out early in the 21st century but its North Field is one of the largest natural gas fields in the world and can probably produce for a

Oil – A Primer

The modern world is built on more or less unlimited access to cheap oil. Oil and its by-products are everywhere. Look at the cover of this book. The laminated cover that helps Lonely Planet guides stand up to hard travel is made by applying a thin layer of plastic – one of oil's most visible by-products – over the paper.

Humankind has known about oil since ancient times. Asphalt or bitumen, the residue left behind after oil's liquid and gaseous parts have evaporated, was used in ancient Egypt as a waterproofing agent. Oil gathered from natural springs or seepages was used for centuries as insulation, as building material and as an ingredient in medicines.

Our oil-based society, however, traces its beginnings to the 1850s when scientists in the USA and Canada figured out how to distil crude oil into kerosene. Kerosene rapidly replaced whale oil as the illuminant of choice throughout Europe and the Americas – it was cheaper, and burned more efficiently.

At about the same time, oil prospectors in the US state of Pennsylvania attached pumps to drills used to bore for salt, creating the first oil wells. These made it possible to bring vastly larger quantities of crude onto the market. Previously, oil had been gathered from natural springs and seepages, or dug out of the ground by hand.

Further growth was spurred by the invention, around 1900, of the internal combustion engine. Until that time petrol had been a waste product of the then-primitive refining process. The use of engines on cars and countless other mechanised devices, and the need for oil as a lubricant in those same engines, led to a demand for petrol that far outstripped supply.

The supply problem was solved in 1909 when scientists in the US state of Indiana discovered how to 'crack' oil – heating it under pressure to break down its larger molecules in ways that made the oil easier to refine. Until then only 15% to 20% of a barrel of oil could be turned into anything other than asphalt. Cracking immediately raised that figure to around 45% and subsequent technological advances have brought it to between 80% and 90% today.

Refining essentially breaks oil into its constituent parts. Some of these are sold more or less as is, while others are refined further or go through other processes until they become the range of products we today derive from oil.

The business of oil is divided into upstream and downstream operations. The former refers to exploration and production while the latter includes everything from refining to retail sales in the form of petrol or other products.

Oil as a commodity is traded on the international financial markets. The value of any individual barrel is determined by both the laws of supply and demand, and by the quality of the oil itself. The oil price you hear quoted in financial news reports every day usually refers to one of several 'benchmark' grades of crude such as Dubai Light, Saudi Arabian Light, North Sea Brent or West Texas Intermediate, names that refer to major oilfields where particular grades are dominant.

Oil trades almost exclusively in US dollars, and is sold by the barrel. One barrel is equal to 42 US gallons (159 litres). The 42-gallon barrel was established as a standard unit in 1866 in Pennsylvania though today oil is neither stored nor shipped in barrels of this, or any other, size. ■

century or more. The government has tried to diversify the economy but, as elsewhere in the Gulf, this has met with only limited success. Steel, fertilisers and petrochemicals are the country's main non-oil products. Most of Qatar's industry is based at Umm Said, south of Doha. Qatar is a member of the Organization of Petroleum Exporting Countries (OPEC).

POPULATION & PEOPLE

About 400,000 people live in Qatar, of whom about 25% are Qataris. This makes it the smallest country in the Arab world by popu-

lation. Most Qataris are of Najdi (central Arabian) ancestry, though there are also a number of families of Persian descent.

The foreign population represents a mix of people from Asia, the Indian subcontinent and the Arab world (Egyptians, Palestinians, Syrians, Jordanians, Lebanese). Britons make up the largest contingent among the country's western expatriate population.

EDUCATION

The country's first school opened only in 1952 but progress since then has been fast. The University of Qatar opened in 1977 but before then hundreds of Qataris were sent to Egypt, Lebanon and the west to further their education. All education, including university, is free for Qataris. Foreign children living in Qatar usually attend international schools which teach a particular national curriculum.

ARTS
Traditional Dancing
On Friday afternoons during the summer (May to September) various troops performing traditional dances can be seen around Doha and Al-Khor. Montazah Park, just beyond the C Ring Rd in Doha, is a good place to go on an early summer evening to see traditional dancing. Shows usually start around 5 pm.

Theatre & Art
Qatar's National Theatre (☎ 831 333) is on the Corniche in the Ministry of Information & Culture building in Doha. The 500-seat auditorium is used for the performance of Arabic plays and also serves as the venue for visiting foreign companies. Depending on the event, tickets are QR 25 to QR 50 and can be obtained from the box office. To find out what's on enquire at a big hotel or stop by the theatre.

The Al-Sadd Art Gallery (☎ 427 333) features shows by both Qatari and foreign artists. It is open Saturday to Thursday from 9 am to noon and 4 to 8 pm. The gallery is outside the centre on the ground floor of another Ministry of Information & Culture building, this one on Al-Sadd St, near the Shebastan Restaurant.

SOCIETY & CONDUCT
Dos & Don'ts
Qatar is more liberal than Saudi Arabia but a far cry from Bahrain or Dubai. Qataris are quite accustomed to the presence of large numbers of foreigners with different habits in their midst, and virtually everyone in the country has travelled abroad at one time or another. Still, Qatar is a very conservative place by western standards and the usual

social taboos that exist in the Gulf certainly apply here as much as anywhere else.

Dress conservatively and do not wear shorts in public except at the beach or at a hotel's swimming pool. Women should always cover their shoulders and avoid clothing that is overly tight or revealing.

If you are offered coffee or tea in someone's home or at a business meeting – it would be unusual if you weren't – it is considered very impolite to refuse.

RELIGION
Most Qataris adhere to the austere Wahhabi sect of Islam which also dominates in Saudi Arabia. Qatari Wahhabism, however, is less strict than the Saudi variety. For example alcohol, which is strictly prohibited in Saudi Arabia, is available in Qatar and there is no prohibition on women driving cars.

LANGUAGE
It may cross your mind in Doha that Urdu, the Pakistani language, would be more useful here than Arabic. In fact many of the thousands of Pakistanis in Qatar have been living here for a very long time and they tend to speak good Arabic. In Doha, as is the case in every other capital city in the Gulf, you should have no trouble getting by with English.

See Language in the Facts about the Region chapter for a list of useful Arabic words and phrases.

Facts for the Visitor

PLANNING
When to Go
Because the heat is so fierce in the summer and sandstorms are so common in the spring and winter, the best time to visit Doha is in November or late February and early March. During these times you are most likely to get bearable temperatures with a minimum of wind. In December and January there might also be some rain. The rains themselves are not all that heavy, but

they often cause problems on the roads. It rarely rains for more than a few days, however, so this need not be much of a consideration in planning your trip.

Maps

Most of the available maps of Doha leave much to be desired. The Oxford map is hopelessly out of date and on too small a scale, while the *Business & Tourist Map of Doha City* (QR 20, available in most bookshops) has too many drawings of buildings and too few streets, especially around the city centre. The *Tourist Map of Doha*, published by Gulf Air and available free at most big hotels, is an improvement on either of the above. The best map available is the one compiled by Doha's municipal government, but you have to go down to the municipality to get one.

What to Bring

A hat and sunglasses are absolutely essential during the summer. In winter, a light windbreaker and a light sweater for the evenings are a good idea.

TOURIST OFFICES

Despite having been open for tourism since 1989, Qatar still has very little tourist infrastructure. The big hotels (either the information desk or any signboards for groups that may be posted in the lobby) and the agencies listed under the Organised Tours heading in the Doha section are your best bet for up-to-date tourist information.

VISAS & DOCUMENTS
Visas

Nationals of GCC countries and British passport holders with right of abode in the UK do not need a visa to enter Qatar. The following information applies to everyone else, except Israelis.

Tourist visas are available to people of any nationality and can be obtained either through Doha's larger hotels for collection at the airport or in advance through Qatari embassies overseas. The latter option tends to work best for people from western countries. If you hold a passport from a country

in the developing world the hotel-sponsorship route is probably your best bet.

If you are a writer or journalist the visa application forms direct you to apply for sponsorship to the Ministry of Information & Culture in Doha, which can usually come up with a visa (for airport collection) in about a week. A writer or journalist seeking a tourist visa through a hotel or an embassy is likely to be referred to the ministry, even if you really are only on holiday.

Though Qatar has led the other Gulf countries in opening up to trade with Israel, at the time of writing, it still barred entry to Israeli passport holders (except in exceptional circumstances, such as an official invitation from the government) and to anyone whose passport bears an Israeli stamp. Depending on the state of the peace process, you may want to check with a Qatari embassy to see whether this ban remains in effect.

While visas are now fairly easy to obtain, they are issued in a manner which guarantees that a stay in Qatar is not likely to be cheap.

Hotel-Sponsored Visas To obtain a Qatari visa, you need a sponsor who is responsible for your actions while you are in the country. The most common way to obtain a tourist or business visa is to have a hotel sponsor you. This is a fairly straightforward process but you will be required to stay in the hotel sponsoring you for as long as you are in the country. It is possible to transfer your sponsorship from one hotel to another but you'll still be staying in the top-level hotels. Trying to get a cheap hotel to assume responsibility for you once you are already in Doha is probably a losing venture. Trying to get a cheapie to sponsor you in the first place is a complete waste of time.

Having decided to spend some money, here's what you do. Contact the reservations department of one of the big hotels (fax numbers for hotels which will sponsor tourist visas are listed in the Doha section) with your passport details, reason for visit (business, tourism etc), your arrival and departure dates and flight information. The last item is important as you will be picking your visa up at the airport. It usually takes between four days and a week to process visa requests.

The hotel should send back a telex or fax acknowledging your reservation and quoting your visa number. If the acknowledgment you receive does not include the visa number you should contact the hotel again and ask for it. If you don't have a proper visa number (ie one matching the list that the airline has received from Qatari immigration), you may not be allowed to board the plane. Gulf Air is particularly strict on this score. This system makes it impossible to enter the country overland or by sea.

At Doha airport, head for the window where visa forms are distributed. Once you have your form just get in line for passport control; the immigration officer does the rest.

Tourist visas are valid for 14 days and cost QR 105. Seven-day business visas cost QR 120. The hotel or company sponsoring you may have paid this fee in advance. If you are sponsored by a hotel the visa fee will probably be added to your bill along with a service charge. If the visa fee has not been prepaid then you will have to pay it yourself at the airport. There is a bank next to the visa desk.

Transit Visas It is possible to obtain a 72-hour transit visa on arrival at Doha airport if you are holding an onward ticket. You are likely to find, however, that the airlines are extremely reluctant to board passengers whose tickets show an overnight transit in Qatar but who do not have a tourist visa.

Exit/Re-Entry Visas These are necessary for resident foreigners who want to leave the country and return later and must be obtained by the sponsor. Tourists or business people need a new visa each time they enter the country.

Visa Extensions Tourist visas can easily be extended for an additional 14 days and business visas for seven days. Renewing a tourist visa costs QR 200. Visa renewal is handled by the hotel or company acting as your

sponsor. If you obtained your visa through an embassy you may have to go to the Passports & Immigration Directorate in Doha (☎ 443 300) and handle the process yourself, but if you are in a five-star hotel you may be able to convince the hotel to take care of it for you.

EMBASSIES
Qatari Embassies Abroad
Qatari embassies may or may not issue tourist visas depending on your nationality and the location of the embassy where you apply. The surest bet is to hold a passport from the US, Canada or a West European country and to apply in your home country, or at the Qatari embassy in the nearest neighbouring country. Canadians, for example, should contact the Qatari embassy in Washington or the UN mission in New York as there is no Qatari embassy in Ottawa. Western expats living in another GCC country should have little trouble obtaining a Qatari visa in the country where they reside. If getting a visa at the embassy is viable you will probably have to fill out two or three forms and supply an equivalent number of photographs. Business travellers may be asked to supply a letter from the company they will be visiting. Fees, if applicable, vary by nationality. Processing time for tourist visas is usually two or three working days. Anyone who works in the news business still has to go through the Ministry of Information & Culture in Doha and pick up their visa at Doha airport.

Addresses of some Qatari embassies and consulates abroad are:

Austria
    Strudlhofgasse 10, A-1090 Vienna (☎ (1) 319 6639)
Belgium
    71 Ave ED Reesevelt, Brussels (☎ (2) 640 2900)
Egypt
    10 Themar St, Mohandessen, Giza, Cairo (☎ (2) 360 4693)
France
    57 Quai D'Orsay, 75007, Paris (☎ (1) 45 51 90 71)
Germany
    Brunnen alle 6, 53177 Bonn (☎ (228) 957 520)

India
  G-5 Anand Niketun, New Delhi 110021 (☎ (11) 611 7240)
  Bajaj Bawan, Nariman Point, Bombay 400021 (☎ (22) 202 7192)
Iran
  Bozorgrah-é Afrigha, 4 Kheyabun-é Gol Azin, Teheran (☎ (2) 2221255)
Japan
  6/16/22 Shirogame Minato KU, Tokyo 108 (☎ (3) 3446 7561)
Jordan
  Jabal Amman, 11183, Amman (☎ (6) 648346)
Kuwait
  Diplomatic Area, Istiglal St, Kuwait City (☎ 251 3599)
Lebanon
  Shouran, Dibss Bldg, Beirut (☎ (1) 865271)
Oman
  Al-Maamoura St, Ruwi, Muscat (☎ 701802)
Pakistan
  20 Khayaben-E-Iqbal, Margala Rd, F-6/3 Islamabad (☎ (51) 214 635)
  16th Khayaben Hafiz, PH 5 Defence, Karachi (☎ (21) 586 2171)
Russia
  Koroviy Val 7, Apartment 196-198, Moscow (☎ (95) 230 1577)
Saudi Arabia
  Takhassosi Rd, near the Euromarché supermarket, Riyadh (☎ (1) 482 5544)
  Mohammed Bin Abdul Aziz St, Area N-23, Al-Andalus district, Jeddah (☎ (2) 665 2538)
Syria
  20 Al-Madfas Place, Awat Blvd, Damascus (☎ (11) 333671)
Switzerland
  1218 Grand Saconnex, Geneva (☎ (22) 798 8500)
Tunisia
  2 Rue Dr Burnet, 1002 Tunis (☎ (1) 285600)
Turkey
  Karace Sok 19, Gazi Osman Pasha, Ankara 06610 (☎ (312) 441 1364)
UAE
  Al-Muntasser St, 26th district, Abu Dhabi (☎ (2) 435 900)
  Trade Centre Rd, Al-Mankhool district, Bur Dubai, near the Bur Juman Centre, Dubai (☎ (4) 452 888)
UK
  1 South Audley St, London, W1Y 5DQ (☎ (0171) 493 2200)
USA
  600 New Hampshire Ave NW, Suite 1180, Washington, DC, 20037 (☎ (202) 338 0111)
  747 3rd Ave, 22nd floor, New York, NY 10017 (☎ (212) 486 9355)

Yemen
  Al-Siteen St, Faj Attan, Sana'a (☎ (1) 217488)

Foreign Embassies in Qatar
See the Doha section for the addresses of embassies in Qatar.

CUSTOMS
Arriving at Doha airport you are apt to find visa collection and customs fairly fast and efficient and passport control quite slow. This is mainly because the passport control officers are left with the job of filling out the several forms required to process each visa.

You are not allowed to import alcohol into Qatar and, in my experience, booze is the main thing that the customs officers are on the lookout for. Books, photographs and, especially, videos in your possession may also come in for careful scrutiny, though I have never had any problems in this respect. Pork products are also prohibited. There is no limit on the number of cigarettes and cigars or the amount of loose tobacco you can bring in.

MONEY
Costs
Since the first edition of this book was published most of Doha's cheap hotels have vanished, along with the city's youth hostel. You can still eat cheaply in Doha, but cheap beds are now much harder to come by. The result is that on an absolutely rock-bottom budget – that is, staying in the cheapest hotels, eating in the cheapest restaurants and walking almost everywhere – you might be able to live in Doha on QR 100 a day. Unless you can get a tourist visa through a Qatari embassy you will not be able to do this, however. The cheapest hotel that sponsors visas (the Oasis) charges about QR 300 per night, though you could probably get a discount on that rate. So even if you still walked a lot and ate cheaply it would be hard not to spend QR 300 or more per day.

Currency
The Qatari riyal (QR) is divided into 100 dirhams, which are also commonly referred

QATAR

to as *halalas*. Notes come in QR 1, 5, 10, 50, 100 and 500 denominations. Coins are 25 and 50 dirhams. The Qatari riyal is fully convertible so there is no black market and there are no exchange controls. Many shops will also accept Saudi riyals at par for small transactions.

Currency Exchange

US$1	=	QR 3.64
UK£1	=	QR 5.61
FF1	=	QR 0.70
DM1	=	QR 2.39
A$1	=	QR 2.87

Changing Money

Moneychangers will generally provide you with slightly better rates than banks, though changing travellers' cheques at a moneychanger can often be a trying experience. The trick is finding a moneychanger willing to take your brand of cheques. It often helps to have your original sales receipt available, as some places will not change cheques without seeing the receipt first.

If you have a credit card or an ATM card it is also possible to get money from cash machines throughout the country. All British Bank of the Middle East cash machines are tied into the Cirrus, Plus, ETC and Global Access systems. The ATMs at Commercial Bank of Qatar branches are also tied into Cirrus and Plus as well as the Diners Club system.

Tipping & Bargaining

A service charge is usually added to restaurant bills in Qatar but this rarely goes to the waiting staff. Local custom does not require that you leave a tip after a meal though it would certainly be appreciated.

The sort of traditional shops where serious bargaining usually takes place in the Gulf are becoming fewer and farther between in Qatar. Small discounts are sometimes offered to customers in modern clothing stores and you can almost always negotiate a bit off the price of electronic goods, rental cars and hotel room, but the price of everything else is usually fixed.

Consumer Taxes

Aside from a 5% hotel tax (which the cheapest places appear to ignore) there are no consumer taxes in Qatar.

POST & COMMUNICATIONS
Postal Rates

Sending a postcard or a letter weighing up to 10g domestically costs 15 dirhams. To other GCC countries the rate is 25 dirhams, to other Arab countries 50 dirhams, to Iran and the Indian subcontinent 80 dirhams and to the rest of the world QR 1. The comparable rates for 20/30g letters are 30/45 dirhams domestic, 50/75 dirhams to the GCC, QR 1/1.50 to the rest of the Arab world, QR 1.60/2.40 to Iran and the subcontinent and QR 2/3 to everywhere else.

Parcel rates vary from destination to destination. Parcel postage is by the kg, and after the first kg the rate generally goes down a bit. Sample rates for sending a one-kg parcel by air/sea are: Australia QR 63/40, Canada QR 54/40, France QR 57/50, Germany QR 46/50, New Zealand QR 67/41, UK QR 47/38, USA QR 53/41.

Sending Mail

Most hotels sell stamps and there are several post offices around Doha, including one in The Centre, the capital's main shopping mall.

Receiving Mail

Poste restante is not available in Qatar and AMEX does not hold clients' mail. If you are staying in a four or five-star hotel it will probably be willing to hold mail for a short time prior to your arrival (assuming, of course, that you have a reservation). Otherwise you'll just have to wait and get your letters somewhere else.

Telephone

The telephone system in Qatar is excellent and direct-dialling overseas calls rarely takes more than one attempt. Phonecards worth QR 20, QR 50 and QR 100 can be purchased at the Main Telecommunications Centre in Doha though as yet there are few card phones outside the Telecommunications Centre itself.

For directory assistance dial ☎ 180, and if you prefer to book an international call rather than direct-dial, call ☎ 150. Dialling ☎ 140 will get you the correct time, while ☎ 144 connects you to a brief taped summary of the day's news.

If you direct-dial international calls reduced rates apply from 8 pm to 7 am and all day on Friday and holidays. The regular/reduced rates per minute to other Gulf countries are QR 3.60/2.50; to the USA or Australia, QR 9.20/6.40; to the UK, Germany or France, QR 9/6.80; to Egypt, QR 6.40/4.60; and to Jordan, QR 6.80/4.80.

The USA Direct access code from Qatar is 0800-011-77. This connects you to an ATT operator in the USA and allows you to make either a collect call or to bill the call to an ATT phone credit card. Calls to third countries via USA Direct are not permitted from Qatar.

When calling Qatar from abroad the country code is 974. There are no area or city codes. To make international calls from Qatar dial '0' followed by the country and city codes and the local number.

Fax, Telex & Telegraph
These services are available at the Main Telecommunications Centre in Doha or through the business centre of any big hotel. As with the telephones, the service is very good.

BOOKS
The literature on Qatar is a bit thin. One of the few books on the market which focuses entirely on Qatar is Helga Graham's *Arabian Time Machine*. Subtitled 'Self-Portrait of an Oil State' the book is a collection of interviews with Qataris about their lives and traditions both before and after the oil boom and about how Qatari society has coped with its sudden wealth.

Peter Mansfield's *The New Arabians* has a fairly short chapter on Qatari history. A better bet might be *The Merchants* by Michael Field, which has lots of good

general information on the Gulf in pre-oil days. It also has a chapter devoted to the Darwish family, one of Qatar's more prominent merchant clans.

'The Day Before Tomorrow', the Qatar chapter in Jonathan Raban's *Arabia Through the Looking Glass*, is probably the best section of this wonderful book. During a short visit in 1979, Raban managed to speak to a particularly interesting cross-section of people: Qatar's leading playwright, a local TV producer and a Jordanian officer working for the Qatari army, in addition to the usual collection of somewhat jaded western expats.

See the introductory Facts for the Visitor chapter for a more general list of books on the Gulf and the Middle East.

Travel Guides
Qatar – A MEED Practical Guide is badly in need of updating but is still a useful book for anyone planning to live in Qatar. *The Economist Business Traveller's Guides – Arabian Peninsula* is a useful how-to-do-business-with-the-Arabs sort of book.

NEWSPAPERS & MAGAZINES
The *Gulf Daily News* is the local English-language newspaper. The best place to find foreign newspapers and magazines (which usually arrive a day or two after publication) is at The Centre shopping complex on Salwa Rd.

RADIO & TV
Qatar FM broadcasts programmes in English from early morning until late evening, with an eclectic musical selection. Its signal goes out on 97.5 FM and 102.6 FM. It broadcasts short news bulletins every few hours. If you have a shortwave radio you can usually pick up the BBC on one of the following frequencies: 15.070, 9.410, 11.760 and 21.470.

Qatar TV's second channel (channel 37, UHF) broadcasts programmes in English from late afternoon until about midnight seven days a week. With a good antenna you can usually also pick up the English-language stations broadcasting from Abu

QATAR

Dhabi, Saudi Arabia, Dubai and Bahrain. They all show a selection of British and US entertainment programmes, movies and documentaries. If the Bahrain station (channel 55, UHF) is coming in well try channel 57, UHF, where Bahrain TV carries BBC World Service Television 24 hours a day. Most hotels, except for the smallest ones, have satellite dishes and pipe the Star TV package into every room. This includes an entertainment channel (mostly old US shows, but not as old or as heavily censored as the ones on the local stations), a sports channel, a music video channel, BBC World Service Television, and one or two Indian/Pakistani satellite services.

PHOTOGRAPHY & VIDEO

Film is easy to find in hotels and shopping centres all over town, though getting anything other than colour prints developed can be a hassle. There are no restrictions on taking pictures aside from the usual ban on military sites (including the airport) and the courtesy and caution which are always required when taking pictures of people in the Gulf.

TIME

Qatar is three hours ahead of GMT/UTC. The clocks don't change during the summer. When it's noon in Doha, the time elsewhere is:

City	Time
Paris, Rome	10 am
London	9 am
New York	4 am
Los Angeles	1 am
Perth, Hong Kong	5 pm
Sydney	7 pm
Auckland	9 pm

ELECTRICITY

The electric voltage is 230 volts AC. Qatar uses British-style sockets.

WEIGHTS & MEASURES

Qatar uses the metric system.

LAUNDRY

There are no laundrettes, but most of the small hotels in the souk also offer laundry service for guests. There are a number of small laundry shops around the centre. See the Doha section for addresses and prices.

HEALTH

Unless you are arriving from an area where cholera, yellow fever or some similar disease is endemic, vaccination certificates are not required for entry into Qatar.

Like other Gulf countries the standard of health and health care in Qatar is very high. There is no need to take malaria prophylactics nor do you need any shots beyond the usual regimen that any traveller should have (mainly DPT or a tetanus booster and gamma globulin).

Qatar's tap water is generally OK to drink, though anyone with a very sensitive stomach should probably stick to bottled water.

If you do get sick, hospital care is free in Qatar. See the Doha section for hospital information and the Health section of the introductory chapters for more general health-related travel information.

WOMEN TRAVELLERS

Though most Qataris follow the Wahhabi sect of Islam, the country does not have the sort of restrictions on women and their movements for which Saudi Arabia (the heartland of Wahhabism) is known and there is no local equivalent of Saudi Arabia's religious police, the *matawwa*. Still, one must accommodate oneself to the local style of life. Women wearing very tight or revealing clothing will attract leers and comments in public places. A woman should always travel in the back seat when taking a taxi. Women should also avoid making eye contact with men whom they do not know as this is often misinterpreted as a come-on. Single women may also find that they are unwelcome in the cheapest tier of hotels and restaurants.

DANGERS & ANNOYANCES

Qatar is a very safe country. The main thing to watch out for in Doha is the driving. Much of the city's traffic system is defined by a series of roundabouts. There are often no lights to control entry to these roundabouts with the result that, when traffic is heavy, people have to force their way into a moving stream of vehicles. When traffic is light the situation is worse; many drivers simply sail straight into the roundabout without slowing down at all.

BUSINESS HOURS

Shops and offices are open from around 8 am until noon and may reopen in the late afternoon from 4 or 5 until 7 pm. Some of the modern western-style shopping centres stay open until 9 pm. Friday is the weekly holiday and many businesses also close early on Thursday. Embassies and government offices are closed all day Thursday.

PUBLIC HOLIDAYS & SPECIAL EVENTS

The Islamic holidays of Eid Al-Fitr (the end of Ramadan), Eid Al-Adha (the end of the pilgrimage season) and the Islamic New Year are all observed. For dates refer to the table of holidays near Public Holidays in the Regional Facts for the Visitor chapter.

Qatar's National Day is on 3 September. Embassies and government offices are closed but most private businesses stay open. There are no other secular holidays.

ACTIVITIES

Although there are several sporting clubs in and around Doha where members can play squash, racquetball, tennis etc, they are of little use to tourists as none of them offer day memberships. For the visitor the best options are the health clubs at the big hotels. These tend to be scaled-down versions of the bigger clubs though some, notably the one at the Doha Sheraton, are pretty big in their own right. You can usually use the club if you are staying in the hotel. Nonguests can often use hotel swimming pools for a small fee.

The Doha Golf Course & Club – Qatar's first and only golf course – was scheduled to open in late 1996. At the time of writing neither the fees nor the exact rules governing who would be able to use the course had been announced.

The best place for beaches is south of

Doha along the road to Umm Said, though the quality of these beaches is nothing to write home about.

Desert excursions (or 'wadi bashing'), as always, are a popular pastime. If you have no friends or acquaintances to invite you along, desert outings can be booked through the local tour companies. Most 'wadi bashing' excursions head for areas south-west of Doha along the road to Salwa.

WORK

Qatar is not the sort of place where you can expect to pick up a few months of casual work waiting tables or teaching English. To obtain a work visa one usually has to have a job, and a signed contract, in hand before arriving in Qatar. It is possible, however, to arrive in the country on a tourist visa, look for a job and then have one's employer pick up the sponsorship and convert the tourist visa into a residence visa. This is usually an option only for people with specialised professional skills.

ACCOMMODATION

There are no hotels outside of Doha which, considering the size of the country, is not really a problem. You could easily start in Doha, drive first to the UAE border then north to the tip of the peninsula and back down to Doha again all in a morning.

It is fairly easy to find good hotels for around QR 100, and QR 200 will buy you splendid accommodation, but the visa and sponsorship rules are such that you probably won't be staying in any of these places unless you obtained a visa through an embassy in advance. The Oasis is the cheapest hotel that sponsors tourist visas and a single there costs about QR 285 per night, including the service charge (though you can almost certainly arrange some sort of discount). On the other hand the facilities at all of these places are quite good.

FOOD

Qatar does not have an indigenous cuisine worth mentioning. Apart from the restaurants at the big hotels (which offer fairly predictable fare), Doha itself is filled with the usual collection of western fast-food places and small Indian and Pakistani restaurants offering little more than curries and biryani dishes. At the Pakistani restaurants you can eat for about QR 10 while western fast food is a bit more expensive.

Meals at the big hotels cost at least QR 50 and usually closer to QR 100 during the frequent 'theme' nights held in the hotel restaurants.

DRINKS
Nonalcoholic Drinks
Fruit juice and soft drinks are about all that you will find in the average Qatari restaurant. The cheaper the restaurant the slimmer your selection is likely to be. In the cheapest places in the souk nothing more than tap water, which is OK for drinking, may be available.

Alcohol
You can't bring alcohol into the country but you can get it legally if you are staying in a large hotel or if you are a non-Muslim expat and your sponsor agrees.

All of the larger hotels have one bar and one restaurant that serve liquor. These operate according to certain fairly strict rules. The hotels are not allowed to advertise the availability of alcohol or the location of the bar. If you see a sign in the lobby that advertises entertainment in the something-or-other lounge without any indication of where the lounge is, that usually means you are looking at an ad for the bar. Ask at the reception desk to find out its location, or just get in the lift and hit the button for the top floor (the latter method is not foolproof but it works surprisingly often).

The bars and 'wet' restaurants are open only to hotel guests and those who have purchased memberships. You will have to show either a room key or a membership card at the door. You might be able to talk your way in if you are not a member or a hotel guest, but that depends entirely on how accommodating the people checking IDs are feeling. Legally, they are not supposed to let you in. Sometimes this is enforced strictly and sometimes it is not. Memberships are usually pretty nominal – around QR 100 for a year, which makes them cost-effective for

Weaving
Iran, Turkey, Pakistan and Afghanistan are famous for their carpets. Among the Bedouins of Arabia, however, it is weaving that has a time-honoured place in the local culture.

Where carpets are knotted, rugs and other Bedouin work are made on a loom. In settled areas, such as the Bahraini village of Bani Jamrah, these can be quite large, elaborate affairs. Looms used by those Bedouin who still live as nomads are small and can be easily taken apart for transport.

Traditionally, weaving (*sadu* in Arabic) is the job of a household's women. Bedouin women are responsible for weaving and maintaining the tents in which the family lives, including interior walls and some ground-coverings. With time, they may also produce saddlebags and decorative bridles for the family's camels, clothing for other members of the family (woollen vests, for example) and pillows for the family's use. Traditionally, goat hair was the favoured material for the tents and camel or goat hair for other purposes.

Today, however, a Bedouin family is more likely to purchase a canvas tent from a tent shop, which may also sell many furnishings for such dwellings. Even in government-run centres designed to preserve the traditional arts (such as those in Abu Dhabi, Kuwait and Bahrain) it is more common to see saddlebags, pillows and other items woven from imported cotton or synthetic fibres.

In most 'traditional' souks or markets much of the woven material one sees these days has been produced with western shoppers in mind. Saddlebags, bridles, runners and tent walls remain popular items among the Bedouin, but few Bedouin have any use for the western-style bags with shoulder straps that are an increasingly common sight in weaving shops. In the Gulf's cities, many of the woven items one finds for sale are actually imported, usually from Egypt or Syria. ■

those in the country for, say, a month but stuck in either a company flat or in a 'dry' hotel.

Non-Muslims living in the country who have a monthly income above a certain level are given a permit allowing them to purchase a certain amount of alcohol each month. The purpose of this system is to allow western and well-to-do expats to have alcohol while keeping it out of the hands of Asian and subcontinental expatriates. It is illegal for a non-Muslim to offer or serve alcohol to Muslims.

THINGS TO BUY

You are not likely to find much in the way of Arabian souvenirs in Doha. If you are flush with money there are a couple of stores in the centre and in the large hotels specialising in Persian carpets. Much of the Arabian stuff you will see (eg incense burners) is actually made in Pakistan or Syria.

If this interests you, try Arab Heritage at the intersection of Jasim Bin Mohammed and Al-Jasra Sts. It has a good selection of weavings (mats, wall hangings and bags woven on a loom) and mosaic work, mostly from Syria, at decent prices. Medium-sized woven goods can be purchased for around QR 65. Another store with no name, but with a similar selection of goods, is immediately across the street. There is also a small shop at the National Museum selling much the same selection of stuff.

Getting There & Away

AIR

Qatar is one of the four part-owners of Gulf Air (along with Bahrain, Oman and Abu Dhabi) and recently launched its own national carrier – Qatar Airways. At the time of writing Qatar Airways was still relatively new. It operates services to Abu Dhabi, Dubai and Kuwait several days a week, sometimes with more than one flight per day. It has one to three flights a week to Amman, Beirut, Damascus, Cairo, Khartoum, Sana'a

and Sharjah. Its only European destinations are Athens and London. It also flies to a number of cities in India and Pakistan.

The USA & Europe

Flying to Doha from North America is absurdly expensive. Going the other way tends to be cheaper but you are still looking at a minimum of US$1200 or so after some shopping around for discounted fares and special offers. The cheapest regular tickets from Doha to New York are APEX fares requiring a 14-day minimum stay and allowing a three-month maximum stay. These cost QR 6180 (about US$1700) in the low season (early January to mid-June and mid-October to mid-December). The same ticket during the high season costs QR 6680. The one-way fare to New York is QR 4640. Gulf Air has a one-stop flight from Doha to New York once a week.

There is daily service between Doha and the UK, both direct and via Bahrain, on Gulf Air and several times a week on Qatar Airways. In addition, most of the major West European airlines fly to Doha between one and three times a week. The cheapest regular tickets to London are excursion fares requiring a 10-day stay and allowing a three-month maximum stay. These cost QR 4030. The one-way fare to London is QR 2860.

To Rome (10 days/three months) a return ticket costs QR 3270 and a one-way QR 2400. Return fares to Athens start at QR 2510 (six days/three months) with one-way tickets available for QR 1850.

Your best bet for finding a good fare out of Qatar is to ask friends and acquaintances whether they know a good travel agent or to trudge around to eight or 10 of them yourself. The fares quoted here are regularly published tariffs, and special deals to specific cities are often available.

Africa, Asia & Australia

A one-way ticket to Nairobi costs QR 2670 and a return QR 3470 (six-day minimum/ two-month maximum). India, often a good buy from the Gulf, is no great bargain from Doha. The one-way fare to New Delhi is QR

1870 and a seven-day/four-month return costs QR 2600. Flying to South-East Asia costs as much as, or even more than, going to Europe. The best return to Bangkok is QR 4880 (seven days/three months) with one-way tickets costing an astounding QR 3490.

At QR 6230 the one-way fare to Melbourne is actually higher than the low season return (QR 5830, 10 days/four months). A high season return is QR 6700. Low season fares apply roughly from February to August.

Other Arab Countries

As is often the case out of the Gulf, your best bet for flying out to another Arab country is Syria. A one-way ticket to Damascus costs QR 1210 with returns available from QR 1610 (five days/two months). The one-way fare to Cairo is QR 1320. A five-day/two-month return costs QR 1940.

Other Gulf States

Flying around the Gulf is never cheap and Qatar is no exception to this rule. Following are samples of the cheapest one-way and return fares with minimum and maximum stay requirements:

To	One Way	Return	Min/Max
Abu Dhabi	QR 450	QR 350	3/7 days
Bahrain	QR 340	QR 250	3/7 days
Dhahran	QR 250	QR 330	2/14 days
Dubai	QR 570	QR 450	3/7 days
Jeddah	QR 760	QR 1060	2/14 days
Kuwait	QR 480	QR 670	2/14 days
Muscat	QR 960	QR 760	3/7 days
Riyadh	QR 390	QR 540	2/14 days

As you may already have noticed there are several destinations – notably Bahrain, Abu Dhabi and Dubai – to which the one-way fare is higher than the cheapest return. It may prove more cost effective to buy a return ticket and throw way the second coupon. You cannot count on the counter staff at an airline or travel agency to bring this fact to your attention, so be sure to ask.

The fares listed here are the lowest regularly published prices. There are several other more expensive fare categories, the general rule being that the longer you stay and the more flexibility you want the more expensive it gets. There also may be promotional fares to individual cities available from time to time. If you are travelling on Wednesday, Thursday or Friday Gulf Air sometimes has 'weekend fares' to popular watering holes like Bahrain and Dubai. When available, these usually cost around QR 20 or QR 30 less than the regular excursion fare, but they restrict you to travel on certain flights on Wednesday, Thursday and Friday only. Again, be sure to ask to see if this would fit into your schedule.

LAND

There are no buses or taxis to Saudi Arabia or the UAE. In theory, one can drive one's car, but this is really only a viable option for those holding residence visas or tourist visas issued overseas (which are still not the norm). Tourist and business visas usually have to be picked up at the airport and it is not possible to arrange to get them at the frontier.

SAPTCO, the Saudi Arabian bus company, lists buses from Dammam to Doha in its timetables but I have been unable to unearth any evidence that these buses actually exist.

SEA

At the time of writing there were no scheduled passenger sea services to or from Qatar. I've been hearing for years now about plans to start a jetfoil service between Bahrain and Dubai via Doha. I'll believe it when I see it.

LEAVING QATAR

You must arrive at Doha airport at least 45 minutes prior to the scheduled departure time of your flight, though in my experience an hour or more would be a better bet. Long-haul flights to Europe sometimes have a two-hour check-in time, so it would be a good idea to double-check with your airline in advance. Check-in procedures tend to be slow and inefficient and if there is the slightest confusion about whether your visa for your destination is in order you can expect even more delays. Once you have checked in, passport control and security tend to move smoothly. There is no departure tax.

Remember to reconfirm your flight at least 72 hours before departure; Gulf Air is especially picky on this score.

Getting Around

Qatar does not have a bus or service-taxi system, so regular taxis and rented cars are your only options for getting around the country. Though the taxis have meters you should probably negotiate the fare in advance for any trip outside Doha.

CAR
Road Rules
Driving in Qatar is on the right side of the road and visitors are well advised to be on their toes, particularly when negotiating Doha's lethal system of roundabouts. I'm not sure whether right turns are, in fact, legal at red lights but everybody makes them and if you find yourself blocking someone who wants to make one you are likely to be subjected to a fierce blast of the horn.

Petrol
There are two grades of petrol. Regular petrol is called Mumtaz. It is 90 octane and costs 55 dirhams per litre. Super is 97 octane and costs 60 dirhams per litre.

Rental
You can rent a car on most foreign driving licences. Licences from other GCC countries are accepted only from GCC nationals and from foreigners who can show a residence visa from the country whose licence they are presenting. This rule, however, only applies for the first seven days that you are in the country. After that you will need a temporary licence issued by the traffic police. To obtain this you will need a letter from your sponsor, two photographs and QR 50. Most of the larger car-rental companies, and a few of the

biggest hotels, will take care of this for you. Whether a car-rental agency charges a fee for this service is likely to depend on the length of time you rent the car. I would not recommend wading into this bureaucratic task on your own.

With a little shopping around you can rent a car for about QR 120 per day, or even QR 100, including all the extras, if you are taking it for a week or so.

See the Doha section for more details on costs and car-rental agencies.

HITCHING
Driving north out of Doha you will sometimes see men, almost always Qataris, trying to thumb lifts. I have never seen a foreigner hitching in Qatar and such a sight would almost certainly attract the attention of the local police, though it is probably not, strictly speaking, illegal.

WALKING
In this climate, walking outdoors for more than a couple of hundred metres is not really an option for much of the year. You can walk around Doha but be prepared for people to give you lots of funny looks and for every taxi driver to slow down on the assumption that you are searching for a lift.

Doha

Around the Gulf, Doha has earned the unenviable reputation of being the dullest place on earth. You will be hard-pressed to find anyone who'll claim the place is exciting. That said, there's nothing *wrong* with Doha; the bay is pleasant and there are enough interesting sites around town to keep a traveller occupied for a day or two.

Orientation
Like some other cities in the Gulf, modern Doha is laid out in honour of the private car. The older section of Doha and much of the main business area lies between the A Ring Rd and the coast. To the extent that there is

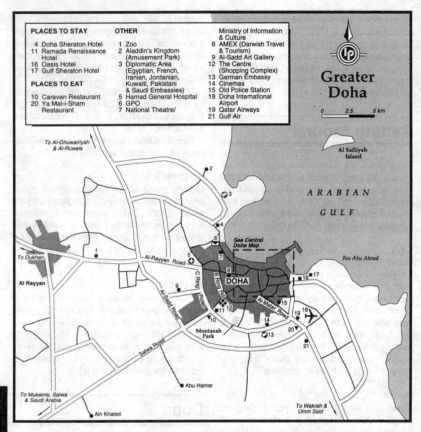

PLACES TO STAY
4 Doha Sheraton Hotel
11 Ramada Renaissance
   Hotel
16 Oasis Hotel
17 Gulf Sheraton Hotel

PLACES TO EAT
10 Caravan Restaurant
20 Ya Mal-i-Sham
   Restaurant

OTHER
1 Zoo
2 Aladdin's Kingdom
   (Amusement Park)
3 Diplomatic Area
   (Egyptian, French,
   Iranian, Jordanian,
   Kuwaiti, Pakistani
   & Saudi Embassies)
5 Hamad General Hospital
6 GPO
7 National Theatre/

Ministry of Information
& Culture
8 AMEX (Darwish Travel
   & Tourism)
9 Al-Sadd Art Gallery
12 The Centre
   (Shopping Complex)
13 German Embassy
14 Cinemas
15 Old Police Station
18 Doha International
   Airport
19 Qatar Airways
21 Gulf Air

Greater
Doha

0   2.5   5 km

Al Safliyeh
Island

ARABIAN

GULF

To Al-Ghuwairiyah
& Al-Ruweis

To Dukhan

Al Rayyan

Al-Rayyan Road

Ras Abu Aboud

See Central
Doha Map

DOHA

Al-Matar Road

Montazah
Park

Salwa Road

To Mukeinis, Salwa
& Saudi Arabia

Abu Hamer

Ain Khaled

To Wakrah &
Umm Said

QATAR

a city centre it is probably the string of large buildings along the Corniche between the Qatar National Bank and the Emir's Office. The area inland from the waterfront includes a post office, Doha Fort, the Ethnographic Museum, a new shopping centre, what's left of the old souk and several large banks. The main business district is farther inland, and beyond this lie the residential districts. The roundabout where Jasim Bin Mohammed, Al-Asmakh, Al-Musheireb and Ali Bin Abdulla Sts come together is the best focal point for the budget traveller. This places you near both the souk and what pass in Doha for

cheap hotels. Several points of interest are within easy walking distance as are both the post office and the Telecommunications Centre. Doha is relatively easy to navigate as the area inside the A Ring Rd is not very large.

Information
Foreign Embassies Some of the countries with embassies in Doha are:

Egypt
   Diplomatic Area, beyond the Doha Sheraton
   Hotel (☎ 832 555)

France
    Diplomatic Area, beyond the Doha Sheraton Hotel (☎ 832 283)
Germany
    Al-Jazira Al-Arabiya St, behind the University Bookshop (☎ 876 959)
Iran
    Diplomatic Area, beyond the Doha Sheraton Hotel (☎ 835 300)
Jordan
    Diplomatic Area, beyond the Doha Sheraton Hotel (☎ 832 202)
Kuwait
    Diplomatic Area, beyond the Doha Sheraton Hotel (☎ 832 111)
Lebanon
    Intersection of Al-Rayyan Rd and Suhaim Bin Hamad St (☎ 444 468)
Oman
    41 Ibn Al-Qassem St, Villa 7, Hilal district, fronting on the C Ring Rd (☎ 670 744)
Pakistan
    Diplomatic Area, beyond the Doha Sheraton Hotel, near the Iranian embassy (☎ 832 525)
Saudi Arabia
    Diplomatic Area, beyond the Doha Sheraton Hotel (☎ 832 030)
UAE
    Khalifa Town district, off Al-Khor St (☎ 885 111)
UK
    Al-Istiqlal St in the Rumailiah district, near Murmar Palace, opposite the Qatar Bowling Centre (☎ 421 991). It also takes care of Australians and New Zealanders.
USA
    At the intersection of Ahmed Bin Ali and Al-Jazira Al-Arabiya Sts, opposite the TV station on the northern outskirts of Doha (☎ 864 701)
Yemen
    Al-Jazira district, near the Al-Sadd roundabout (☎ 432 555)

Money Moneychangers' offices in the souk will provide you with slightly better rates than banks. There are ATMs at the British Bank of the Middle East branch on Abdulla Bin Jasim St, across from the Emirates Airlines office, and at the Commercial Bank of Qatar branch on Grand Hamad St. The Commercial Bank of Qatar also has an ATM in the arrivals area of the airport. See Changing Money in the Facts for the Visitor section for details of the ATM systems that the different banks are tied into.

AMEX is represented in Doha by Darwish Travel & Tourism (☎ 422 411) on Al-Rayyan Rd between Al-Bidda St and the B Ring Rd. Look for the complex dominated by a building with a large Apple Computer logo. It is on the left if you are coming from the centre. It is open Saturday to Thursday from 8 am to 12.30 pm and from 3.30 to 7 pm (Thursdays only until 6 pm). Cheques are cashed for card holders but it will not hold mail for AMEX clients.

Post The GPO is on the Corniche between the National Theatre/Ministry of Information & Culture and the Doha Sheraton Hotel. It is open from 7 am to 8 pm daily except Friday when it's open from 4 to 6 pm. All parcels and registered letters posted to Doha are available here for collection.

For sending mail, the old GPO at the intersection of Abdulla Bin Jasim and Al-Bareed Sts is more convenient. It is open Saturday to Thursday from 7 am to 1 pm and from 4 to 7 pm and Friday from 8 to 10 am. During Ramadan its hours are 8 am to noon and 8 to 10 pm.

There is also a small post office in The Centre, the shopping mall on Salwa Rd. This post office is open Saturday to Thursday from 9 am to 12.30 pm and from 4 to 8 pm.

Telephone The Main Telecommunications Centre is on Al-Musheireb St, near the intersection with Al-Diwan St. It is open 24 hours a day and also offers fax, telex and telegram services. International calls can be direct-dialled from card phones (QR 20, QR 50 and QR 100 cards are available), though you don't get the same cheap rates people get by calling from home. Calls can also be booked through the operator with a three-minute minimum charge. Collect (reverse charges) calls are not available. See the Facts for the Visitor section for more information on available telephone services and the rates for international calls.

Travel Agencies There are an astonishing number of travel agencies all over town and, because of the high turn over among their staffs, it is impossible to recommend any in particular. Your best bet is to ask the locals if they can recommend one.

Bookshops Doha has hardly any foreign-language bookshops and, unusually, even the newsstands of five-star hotels do not provide their usual, if expensive, selection of foreign-language novels. Try the bookshop in The Centre, the shopping mall on Salwa Rd. It has a selection of English-language books heavy on spy novels and romances.

Cultural Centres Some of the foreign cultural centres in Doha include:

Alliance Française (☎ 417 548), Ibn Naeem St, just off Ibn Seena St. It is open Saturday to Wednesday from 9 am to 12.30 pm and 5 to 7 pm, till 8 pm on Monday. It is closed all day Thursday and Friday and on Sunday morning.

The American Cultural Center (☎ 351 279), Muaither St, just off Suhaim Bin Hamad St, behind the Sherazad Restaurant. Its library is open Saturday to Wednesday from 7.30 am to 3.30 pm.

The British Council (☎ 426 193), Ras Abu Ayoub St opposite the Hardees fast-food restaurant. The Council's library is open Saturday to Wednesday from 10 am to noon and from 4 to 7.30 pm.

Laundry Al-Baker Laundry (☎ 442 704) on Al-Asmakh St is slow but cheap. It will have your clothes back the next day only if you drop them off by 7 am, otherwise it takes two days. Prices for washing and ironing include: T-shirts QR 2, jeans or other trousers QR 3, men's dress shirt QR 2, blouse QR 3, women's dress QR 5 or more, and underwear QR 1. It is open every day (including Friday) from 6.30 am to 12.30 pm and from 3 to 10.30 pm.

Medical Services Medical care is free in Qatar even for visitors. If you get sick, the best thing to do is ask your hotel (or a company doctor if you are visiting someone) to refer you to a hospital. The Hamad General Hospital (☎ 446 446) on Al-Rayyan Rd between Suhaim Bin Hamad (C Ring Rd) and Mohammed Bin Thani Sts offers treatment for tourists on a walk-in basis.

Emergency For fire, police or ambulance services dial ☎ 999.

National Museum

The Qatar National Museum is on the Corniche at the eastern end of town near the intersection with Al-Muthaf St. The museum is open daily except Saturday from 9 am to noon and from 3 to 6 pm (4 to 7 pm in the summer). It is closed Friday mornings. Admission is QR 2.

Before entering, take a moment to look at the building. Most of the complex which the museum now occupies once served as a palace for Shaikh Abdulla Bin Mohammed, Qatar's ruler from 1913 to 1951.

Once inside, turn right and walk through a short passageway to reach the aquarium (stuffed fish on the upper level, live ones in the basement) and the artificial lagoon with its display of dhows. As you walk around the lagoon on your way to the aquarium building stop to take a look at the sea turtles in their open-air tank. The aquarium building's upper level also includes a display on pearls and pearling.

The geology and archaeology exhibits are in the building on the far side of the central courtyard, opposite the main entrance. The archaeology display, which occupies most of the ground floor, includes the usual collection of arrowheads, potsherds, flint etc. The section on seafaring and traditional celestial navigation methods is particularly interesting. The lower level of this building is a jumbled collection of displays on desert life, Islam and astronomy as well as an exhibit on the oil industry. Each room is quite well laid out but there appears to be no pattern to the floor as a whole.

The courtyard is surrounded by a series of rooms displaying artefacts showing the traditional lifestyle of the Qatari people, as well as crafts and a reconstruction of the state majlis from the museum's palace days.

Also in the courtyard are three residential buildings added to the palace complex at different points over the last 75 or so years. At the time of writing most of the space in these buildings was still under restoration.

Ethnographic Museum

Located in the central courtyard of the new souk shopping complex, between Al-Asmakh St and Grand Hamad St, the museum is open Sunday to Thursday from 9 am to noon and from 3 to 6 pm and Friday from 3 to 6 pm. It is closed Saturday. Admission is free.

The museum is in a restored traditional Qatari house from the early 20th century, which provides a look at what life in Qatar was like before the oil era. Signs explain the function of the various rooms in the house and their importance in the life of the family.

Of particular interest is the building's wind tower. In addition to being one of the better preserved wind towers in the Gulf, it is one of Qatar's few remaining examples of this form of traditional Gulf architecture. When inside the museum be sure to spend a few minutes sitting under the wind tower to appreciate the ingenuity involved in designing this pre-electricity form of air-conditioning.

Doha Fort

The Doha Fort is on the corner of Jasim Bin Mohammed and Al-Qalaa Sts (enter from the Jasim Bin Mohammed St side). Officially, the fort is open Sunday to Friday from 8.30 am to noon and 3 to 7 pm (till 6 pm on Friday), but the hours seem pretty erratic. It is closed Saturday. Admission is free.

The interior of the fort consists of a large, paved courtyard with a fountain. The displays run the gamut from model dhows to paintings of Qatari life. Moving to your right from the entrance, the first of the rooms surrounding the courtyard contain weavings, paintings with Qatari themes and, farther down, several examples of carved stone and wood, including a very interesting carved wooden door. The rooms on the opposite side of the courtyard have displays on goldsmithing, rope-making and stonecarving in addition to displays of textiles, weaving and other traditional crafts. There is also a small exhibit on fishing, shipbuilding and seafaring in general. The roof provides a nice view of the courtyard.

In all, the fort is worth a quick stop if you are not pressed for time, but most of the topics dealt with by the exhibits are covered much more thoroughly in the National Museum.

Postal Museum

If you are a stamp collector this place should figure near the top of your to-do list in Doha. The museum is adjacent to the old GPO on Al-Bareed St. It is open Saturday to Thursday from 4 to 6 pm, though these hours appear to be loosely interpreted.

Old Police Station

This tiny fort-like building on the corner of Al-Matar Rd and Al-Waab St, between the B and C Ring Rds, was once a police post on the outskirts of Doha but is now little more than a curiosity within the city's urban sprawl. The small whitewashed building (on the left if you are coming from the centre) is easy to miss. You can't go in, but a peek through the windows confirms that you're not missing much: the interior is empty.

Zoo

Doha's zoo, on the Dukhan Rd west of the city, is far from the centre of town. It is open Sunday to Friday from 3 to 9 pm. The general public is admitted only on Thursday, Friday and Sunday. Monday and Wednesday are for families and Tuesday for women and children under nine. Admission is QR 5 for adults, QR 2 for children under nine.

Amusement Park

While it is, on the whole, oriented toward fairly young children, Aladdin's Kingdom at the West Bay Lagoon also has the distinction of being the only amusement park in the Gulf with a serious roller coaster. The park is open Sunday to Thursday from 3.30 to 9 pm and Friday from 2.30 to 8 pm, but is closed on Saturday. Monday and Wednesday are for women only and Tuesday is for families only. Admission is QR 35 for both adults and children.

To reach the park take the Corniche to the roundabout by the Al-Salam Plaza, a short distance before you reach the Doha Sheraton Hotel. Turn left out of this roundabout and follow the signs to West Bay Lagoon. The park is just over five km from the roundabout.

Organised Tours

Doha's tour companies are still largely oriented toward groups. Qatar Holidays (☎ 495 585 or 495 567) offers half-day city tours for QR 60. It also has excursions to camel races (half day, QR 60), a beach club (half day, QR 70), dhow trips (half day, QR 175, including lunch), a tour to Al-Khor and other sites in the north of the country (full day, QR 175 including lunch) and an all-day desert safari (QR 300, including lunch). Its office in the the Gulf Sheraton Hotel's lobby is open Saturday to Wednesday from 8 am to 5 pm and Thursday from 8 am to 1 pm.

Doha Tours (☎ 495 585, fax 495 912) has similar offerings and prices. It's probably a good idea to call both companies as each excursion will only be offered once or twice a week, not every day.

Places to Stay – bottom end & middle

There is no longer a youth hostel in Doha and half of Doha's cheap and medium-priced hotels have also disappeared in the past few years. That leaves only a handful of sort-of cheap hotels. On the up side, none of these places have increased their prices much. All of the rooms at these hotels have air-conditioning, TVs and private baths. None can sponsor visas and all are 'dry'.

If you are looking for the cheapest beds in town head for the *Venice Hotel* (☎ 412 473, fax 412 476) at the intersection of Al-Muthaf and Al-Meena Sts. At QR 80/100 for singles/doubles it is OK as far as it goes, but bear in mind that an extra QR 30 will get you a significantly better room (in a better location) elsewhere in town.

For example, the *New Capital Hotel* (☎ 445 445, fax 442 233), on Al-Musheireb St between Aghadir St and the Telecommunications Centre, quotes a rack rate of QR 264.50/299, including the service charge, for singles/doubles. However, 19 times out of 20 it will discount this to QR 125/150 net if you just ask. At the lower rate it is a very good deal. This is the cheapest place in town for those who crave a swimming pool. It also has satellite TV.

Next door, the *Qatar International Hotel* (☎ 321 761, fax 442 413) is very clean and modern but not quite as good as the New Capital. It charges QR 120/150 and it's Doha's favoured haunt for Russian tourists.

Not far from the souk, the *Qatar Palace Hotel* (☎ 421 515, fax 321 515) falls somewhere between the New Capital and the Qatar International in terms of quality. Rooms are QR 160/200 plus a 15% tax and service charge, but it will readily discount this to QR 120/160 net. The hotel is on Al-Asmakh St near the intersection with Al-Areeq St.

Places to Stay – top end

These are the places that can arrange your visa. They are also the hotels large enough to have bars. All add 17% in taxes and service charges to the bill (this has been included in the quoted prices). As elsewhere in Doha, the glut of hotel space means that most will readily offer discounts on the rates listed here.

At the very top of the scale sits the *Doha Sheraton* (☎ 833 833, fax 832 323), built for 1984's Gulf Summit (an event which it also hosted in 1990). Dominating the north side of Doha Bay the hotel, constructed as a flat-top pyramid, has become the country's main architectural landmark. The lobby is enormous and has a small, but well-laid-out, display of 17th and 18th-century Islamic antiquities. Singles/doubles are QR 819/936 and the hotel has a pool and health club. If you can't afford to stay here at least drop by and take in the sweeping view of Doha and the bay from the rooftop restaurant.

Not to be confused with the Doha Sheraton is the *Gulf Sheraton Hotel* (☎ 432 432, fax 418 784) on Ras Abu Aboud St at the eastern end of the city. This used to be simply the Gulf Hotel, which is how most people

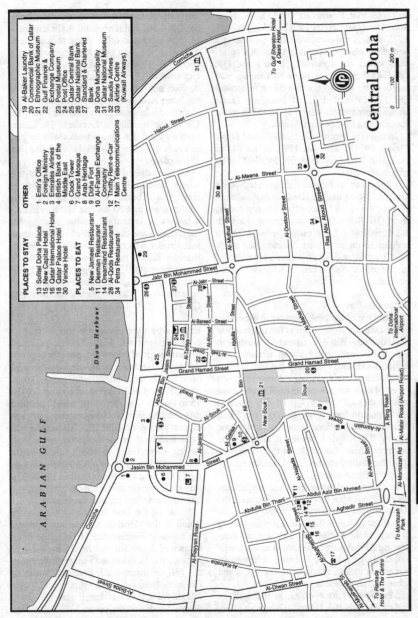

Central Doha

0   100   200 m

ARABIAN GULF

Dhow Harbour

QATAR

To Gulf Sheraton Hotel & Oasis Hotel

To Doha International Airport

To Montazah Park

To Ramada Hotel & The Centre

PLACES TO STAY
13 Sofitel Doha Palace
15 New Capital Hotel
16 Qatar International Hotel
18 Qatar Palace Hotel
30 Venice Hotel

PLACES TO EAT
5   New Jameel Restaurant
11 Desman Restaurant
14 Dreamland Restaurant
28 Al-Qods Restaurant
34 Petra Restaurant

OTHER
1   Emir's Office
2   Foreign Ministry
3   Emirates Airlines
4   British Bank of the
    Middle East
6   Clock Tower
7   Grand Mosque
8   Arab Heritage
9   Doha Fort
10 Al-Fardan Exchange
    Company
12 Thrifty Rent-a-Car
17 Main Telecommunications
    Centre
19 Al-Baker Laundry
20 Commercial Bank of Qatar
21 Ethnographic Museum
22 Gulf Finance &
    Exchange Company
23 Postal Museum
24 Post Office
25 Qatar Central Bank
26 Qatar National Bank
27 Standard & Chartered
    Bank
29 Doha Municipality
31 Qatar National Museum
32 Saudia Airlines
33 Airlines Centre
    (Kuwait Airways)

Corniche

Haloul Street

Al-Meena Street

Al-Muhal Street

Al-Dostour Street

Ras Abu Aboud Street

Jabr Bin Mohammed Street

Al-Jabr Street

Al-Bareed Street

Al-Ahmed Street

Al-Teeb Street

Al-Tarbiya Street

Grand Hamad Street

Souk Waqif

Abdulla Bin Jasim Street

Al-Souk

Al-Jasra

New Souk

Souk

A Ring Road

Al-Asmakh Street

Al-Matar Road (Airport Road)

Al-Montazah Rd

Al-Areeq Street

Abdul Aziz Bin Ahmed

Aghadir Street

Abdulla Bin Thani

Al-Najada Street

Al-Oistat

Jasim Bin Mohammed

Al-Kahraba

Al-Rayyan Road

Al-Maymoun Street

Al-Diwan Street

Al-Bidaa Street

Al-Maslamah St

Corniche

still refer to it. Rooms are QR 585/702. Next door the *Oasis Hotel* (☎ 423 453, fax 431 171) attracts business travellers on a budget and is the cheapest hotel in Qatar that sponsors visas for tourists. Rooms are QR 287/345 but with a little bargaining you ought to be able to get that down to around QR 220/280 net. Fans of Jonathan Raban should note that he stayed at the Oasis while researching his book on Arabia.

In the city centre, the *Hotel Sofitel Doha Palace* (☎ 435 222, fax 439 186) on Abdul Aziz Bin Ahmed St asks QR 345/460 for its singles/doubles.

Farther out, at the intersection of Salwa Rd and the C Ring Rd, the *Ramada Renaissance Hotel* (☎ 417 417, fax 410 941) has rooms from QR 363/410. The occupancy rate here is clearly low – I was once upgraded from a regular room to a suite because, the clerk said, I was a 'regular customer'. I had stayed in the hotel only once before, two years earlier!

Places to Eat

Cheap One of the best cheapies in the centre is the *Desman Restaurant* at the intersection of Abdul Aziz Bin Ahmed and Al-Musheireb Sts. It has very good cheap Chinese and Indian food and, unusually for this kind of small place, draws a lot of customers for both types of cuisine. Soups cost QR 5 and most main dishes are QR 5 to QR 10. The portions are large and the service is good. Note that there is another place with the same name nearby. The food, however, is better at the one listed here. Just look for the one across from the Sofitel entrance and you are sure to get the right restaurant.

Another good bet in the same neighbourhood is *Dreamland Restaurant* (formerly the Arsh Bilqees Restaurant), on the corner of Masafi St (a small side street running along the side of the Sofitel Doha Palace and connecting Abdul Aziz Bin Ahmed and Aghadir Sts) and Aghadir St. It has a selection of biryanis, mutton, chicken etc for QR 6 and other Indian dishes at similar prices.

New Jameel Restaurant, at the western end of Abdulla Bin Jasim St, has fresh juice, fairly simple food (a plate of curry with bread for QR 4.50) and ice cream. A similar menu of shawarma and other quick meals can be found at the *Al-Qods Restaurant* on the corner of Al-Ahmed and Al-Jabr Sts in the city centre. The restaurant's sign is only in Arabic, but it is across from the entrance to the Souq Al-Jabor shopping centre.

Affordable western-style meals (QR 10 to QR 30) can be eaten at the cafe in The Centre on Salwa Rd. Ice-cream freaks will be glad to know that there is a *Baskin-Robbins* next to the cafe.

On the edge of the centre, but definitely worth the trip, is the *Petra Restaurant* on Ras Abu Aboud St between Jabr Bin Mohammed and Al-Meena Sts. It is mainly a takeaway restaurant (it has seating for, maybe, six) and the only drinks available are soft drinks which come out of a vending machine next to the cash register. For falafel sandwiches (QR 2), shawarma (QR 3), foul and other such dishes, however, you can't beat the food. A whole roasted chicken costs QR 15.

Expensive One place you should make a point of trying is *Ya Mal-i-Sham*, a Lebanese restaurant on Al-Matar Rd, directly opposite the main entrance to the airport (the pink neon sign is hard to miss). Mezzes and soups cost QR 5 to QR 15 and main courses are QR 15 to QR 25. The fare is the usual Lebanese mix of chicken, kebabs, mixed grill and pigeon plus good Gulf fish. It's not the best Lebanese food in the Gulf, but aside from paying three times as much to eat in the sterile surroundings of a big hotel it is certainly the best Lebanese food in Doha. The service is friendly and from the 2nd floor you have a great view of, um, the airport.

Some of the best food in Doha is to be found at the *Caravan Restaurant*, opposite the Ramada Renaissance Hotel at the intersection of Salwa Rd and the C Ring Rd. The restaurant is built around a huge all-you-can-eat (30 or more main courses) buffet of Chinese, Thai, Japanese, Filipino and Indian dishes for QR 33 at lunch and QR 39 at dinner (both are net prices – including the ubiquitous service charge – but do not include beverages). Most of the dishes are also available à la carte, but that will cost you at least QR 30 so you might as well take the buffet. The restaurant is very popular. Do not let its location amid a bunch of US fast-food places put you off.

Spending more than about QR 50 on dinner means eating in a hotel. The Doha Sheraton and Ramada hotels are reputed to have the best food in town with the formal *restaurant* at the top of the Sheraton topping the list. Lunch or dinner in one of the big hotels will cost QR 75 or more. The Ramada's *coffee shop*, though utterly devoid of atmosphere, is generally considered one of the best eateries in town. It runs a series of 'speciality' nights (Indian, Far Eastern etc) with very large buffets at around QR 85 per person. If you want to have an alcoholic drink with dinner you will have to stay in one of the hotels large enough to have a bar, or your stay must be long enough to make purchasing a membership worthwhile. The lone restaurant serving booze in each of the big hotels is usually hidden away on an upper floor along with the bar.

Self-Catering The best place for do-it-your-self shoppers is the supermarket in the complex known as The Centre, on Salwa Rd near the Ramada Renaissance Hotel. Unless you have cooking facilities this is not likely to save you a lot of money over the cheaper Indian restaurants.

Entertainment
Cinema & Theatre There are a couple of cinemas in town but they show only Pakistani and Indian films. Once in a blue moon the British Council may bring a travelling theatre company through town. Doha, however, is the kind of place where going out means dinner out and that's about it. Some of the big hotels offer light entertainment (ie live background music) with their theme-night dinners. Check the *Gulf Daily News* or the lobbies of the hotels themselves to find out what's on.

Arabic plays and the occasional foreign

troop can be seen at the National Theatre on the Corniche. The Ministry of Information & Culture has an art gallery in Doha (Al-Sadd Art Gallery) and sponsors displays of traditional dancing in summer. (See Arts in the Facts about the Country section.)

Bars Though the limited sale of alcohol in large hotels has been legal in Qatar since late 1993 the numerous, and strict, rules governing the bars (such as a de facto ban on advertising) has lent these places a rather pleasing informal quality. A few of the bars still feel like speakeasys. The bar at the Sofitel, for example, continues to use picnic coolers to store the ice and keep the beer cold and makes do without a cash register (staff keep the money in a metal box by the door). At the other end of the spectrum the bar in the Gulf Sheraton has a fairly well-established feel about it.

Bars are only open to people with a room in the hotel and to 'members'. An annual membership usually costs around QR 100. Room keys and membership cards are checked at the door and you should not bank on being able to talk your way in without one or the other.

Getting There & Away
Air Doha has a small, serviceable airport. The departures area was extensively redone in the early and mid-90s but this largely added space for people to move around, not thousands of sq metres of duty-free shopping. There is a cafeteria, a small duty-free shop, a gift shop and a couple of snack stands.

Some of the airlines flying in and out of Doha are:

Air India
    Airline Centre, Ras Abu Aboud St (☎ 418 423)
British Airways
    Airline Centre, Ras Abu Aboud St (☎ 321 434)
EgyptAir
    Trans Orient Travel, Al-Matar Rd, near the airport (☎ 458 301)
Emirates
    Abdulla Bin Jasim St, across from the British Bank of the Middle East (☎ 425 577)

QATAR

Gulf Air
Al-Matar Rd, near the airport entrance (☎ 455 444)
Iran Air
Jasim Bin Mohammed St, across from the clock tower (☎ 323 666)
KLM
Airline Centre, Ras Abu Aboud St (☎ 321 208, 321 209)
Kuwait Airways
Airline Centre, Ras Abu Aboud St (☎ 424 112)
Lufthansa
Next to the Emir's Office, off Jasim Bin Mohammed St (☎ 418 666)
MEA (Middle East Airlines)
Oasis Hotel, Ras Abu Aboud St (☎ 320 294)
PIA (Pakistan International Airlines)
Airline Centre, Ras Abu Aboud St (☎ 426 290)
Qatar Airways
Al-Matar Rd, just before the entrance to the airport if you are coming from the centre (☎ 430 707)
Royal Jordanian
Airline Centre, Ras Abu Aboud St (☎ 431 431)
Saudia
Ras Abu Aboud St, opposite the Airline Centre (☎ 430 888)

Bus There are no international or domestic bus services. There used to be a small white shed in the parking lot by the old GPO marked 'Public Transport Office' but a parking garage now occupies that spot, thus ending the long-standing pretence that a bus system existed. There aren't any service-taxis either, which is quite unusual in the Middle East.

SAPTCO, the Saudi Arabian bus company, lists regular buses from Dammam to Doha, but nobody in Dammam could tell me where in Doha these buses picked up or dropped off passengers and I was unable to locate a SAPTCO agent in Qatar.

Car Rates at all of the big car-rental agencies start at around QR 130 to QR 150 per day for a small car including insurance and unlimited mileage. You might be able to bargain this down to about QR 100. The rental desks at the airport are also a good bet, particularly if you need a car on the weekend or at an odd hour of the afternoon or evening. Car-rental arrangements can also be made in the lobbies of most medium-sized hotels and in all of the big ones.

Thrifty Rent-a-Car (☎ 433 800) has an office in the shopping complex attached to the Hotel Sofitel Doha Palace (if you are facing the main entrance to the hotel it is around the wall to your left). EuroDollar Rent-a-Car (☎ 321 313) is on Al-Rayyan Rd in the same complex as AMEX. Look for a large building with an Apple Computer logo. Avis (☎ 495 578) has an office in the Gulf Sheraton Hotel. Europcar (☎ 438 404) has an office on Al-Rayyan Rd as well as desks in the Sheraton and Sofitel hotels. All of these agencies also have desks at the airport.

Getting Around

The Airport A taxi between the airport and the centre will cost QR 10 to QR 15.

Taxi There are lots of taxis in the city so you should not have too much trouble finding one. Flag fall is QR 2 and the meter adds QR 1 per km in 10 dirham increments.

Around Qatar

If you are heading south out of Doha, toward Wakrah or Umm Said, take the airport road (Al-Matar Rd) and just keep going. The main road to all points north is 22nd February Rd which, as you leave the city, becomes Shimal Rd.

WAKRAH

Sixteen km south of Doha on the Umm Said Rd, Wakrah is little more than a lay-by with a small **museum** and some good beaches just south of the town.

The museum, however, keeps somewhat unpredictable hours. I've tried to get in on a number of occasions and have never found it open. Behind the museum are the ruins of what is thought to be a palace.

UMM SAID

Umm Said is Qatar's answer to Dhahran in Saudi Arabia or Al-Ahmadi in Kuwait – it is the oil company town, the centre of operations for QGPC and the country's various gas and petrochemical-related industries. You cannot get into either the industrial or residential areas without a reason to do so (ie an appointment in one of the industrial facilities or an invitation to someone's home in the case of the residential compounds).

UMM SALAL MOHAMMED

The attraction of Umm Salal Mohammed (Umm Silal Mohammed), the first town north of Doha, is its **fort**. The town appears to the left of the road about 25 km north of Doha. The turn is marked by a green sign in English. Coming from Doha you will have to make a U-turn and then turn right (look for a white sign).

Once you have made it from the main road into the town you will come to a roundabout. To reach the fort, take the first right out of the roundabout and drive straight through the town for 1.4 km. It's on the left. The fort is open when someone is around to unlock the door (mornings are your best bet). It is a relatively small whitewashed rectangular building with two towers, one of which rises to a height of four storeys. Near the fort is a small **mosque** with an old minaret that has recently been restored to its original state.

Taking another right turn immediately after turning out of the roundabout and following this road for a km will bring you to some ruined mud-brick fortifications.

UMM SALAL ALI

This town is 37.5 km north of Doha and the only site is a field of **grave mounds.** The mounds are very old, probably dating from the 3rd millennium BC. (All of the region's burial mounds, whatever their age, are pre-Islamic in origin. Islam forbids cairn burials.) It is hardly on the scale one finds in Bahrain but if you haven't seen a mound field yet Umm Salal Ali (Umm Silal Ali) is worth a quick diversion. See Around Bahrain Island in the Bahrain chapter for more information on burial mounds.

A green sign in English marks the turn. As at Umm Salal Mohammed, you must make a U-turn and then a right if you are coming from the direction of Doha. A small mound field lies just north of the town and more mounds are scattered in among Umm Salal Ali's buildings.

There is no place to stay in Umm Salal Ali, though the town does have two small *restaurants* and a grocery store.

AL-KHOR

A small town 67 km north of Doha, Al-Khor is the home of a small **museum**. In theory the museum is open daily except Friday mornings and Saturday afternoons from 8 am to noon and from 4 to 7 pm (3 to 6 pm in the winter). In practice I have never found the door unlocked.

The only other things of note are the ruins of a **mosque** and number of old **watchtowers** scattered around the centre, several of which have been restored to their original form. It is impossible to date the original construction of the watchtowers with any precision but like much of the rest of the town it is unlikely that they date from before the 20th century, though the towers visible today are likely to have been built on the ruins of earlier, similar, structures. An Arabic inscription inside the mosque says that it was built in Ramadan 1372 AH (1953 AD). From the mosque, the view of the ocean is splendid and the setting is quite peaceful. If you have the time, Al-Khor is a pleasant day trip out of Doha.

There's no place to stay in Al-Khor, but the *Ain Helaitan Restaurant & Coffeeshop*, on the Corniche between the ruined mosque and the museum, is a good place for a snack. The Turkish coffee (QR 2) is excellent as are the kebabs, though the latter are a bit pricey at QR 15.

Coming from Doha, the turn for Al-Khor is 16 km north of Umm Salal Ali. It is not very well marked. Look for the 'Al-Khor Exchange' sign. To reach the museum follow the main road into town until you reach a roundabout near the coastline with a sign pointing left to the Corniche. Turn left and proceed along the coast for about 650m. The museum is the white building on the right.

The ruined mosque is another 700m along the coast on the landward side of the road, but if you're driving you'll have to go a km or so past it before you can make a U-turn.

ZUBARA

Near Qatar's north-western coast, 105 km north of Doha, Zubara (Zubarah) occupies a place in Qatari history. Its **fort** was built in 1938 as a border police post. The design is a small four-bastion structure around a courtyard. It was used by the military until well into the 1980s. Today, well-to-do Qataris occasionally travel up here on expeditions, but that's about it.

Nothing you'll see around here even hints at the place's history. Until about 100 years ago, Zubara was the main settlement in Qatar. For almost 200 years it was controlled by the Al-Khalifa, Bahrain's ruling family, but hotly contested by them and Qatar's Al-Thani family. The fort you see today was built shortly after the Al-Thanis wrested the settlement from Bahraini control once and for all.

Several of the rooms around the fort's courtyard have displays of items, mostly potsherds, found at or near the fort. You can also climb one of the towers for a rather bleak view of the surrounding desert. There is a well in the fort's courtyard.

Two km beyond the fort are the ruins of some much older **coastal fortifications**. A rough dirt road to the ruins starts at the rusty gate next to the fort – the attendant will open it for you – and leads down the hill and to the right. Low brick fortification walls and the excavated remains of a city are clearly visible but there are no explanatory signs of any sort. According to Geoffrey Bibby, the archaeologist, the fortifications at Zubara are built directly on the coastal rocks, indicating that they are the site's first and only level of occupation. Bibby speculated that the buildings are probably from the 18th century, though he found some potsherds at the site that indicated that it might have been occupied a century or so earlier.

To reach Zubara, turn left at the police post 68 km north of Doha (there's a small sign in English) and follow the road. You can't miss the fort. On a clear day you'll see it from a distance of almost seven km as there's absolutely *nothing* around it.

AL-RUWEIS

The Qatar peninsula's northernmost point offers little to the traveller. There are a few small grocery stores and *restaurants* and a causeway out to the fishing village on **Ras Abu Amran** island but that's about it.

If you've got a car, a couple of hours to kill and it's not too hot, try the drive between Al-Ruweis and the Zubara fort. The road passes several abandoned coastal villages, most notably **Al-Khuwair** and **Al-Arish**. The roads/tracks to these places shown on the *Oxford Map of Qatar* are mostly nonexistent, but you can easily spot the abandoned villages from the main road and you shouldn't need a 4WD for the short trek across the desert to reach them. The towns were abandoned in the 1970s. The shells of houses and shops clustered around a ruined central mosque can be a bit spooky.

GETTING AROUND

The following are only estimates of what you should pay by taxi (return trip with a minimum of waiting time at the site – say, half an hour) to the destinations outside Doha:

Wakrah	QR 40
Umm Said	QR 75
Umm Salal Mohammed	QR 75
Umm Salal Ali	QR 100
Al-Khor	QR 150
Zubara	QR 225
Al-Ruweis	QR 250

It is highly debatable whether a taxi to Umm Salal Ali is worth it, compared to the cost of renting a car for the day. In the case of Al-Khor, Zubara and Al-Ruweis you're just throwing away money by taking a taxi.

Saudi Arabia

Saudi Arabia

Arabia has intrigued travellers for centuries. Vast and mostly arid, it is the cradle of the Islamic religion, the Arab race and the Arabic language – a language considered holy by Muslims.

Today's Saudi Arabia (or the 'Kingdom' as both Saudis and foreigners invariably call it) retains that mystique, in part because it is so incredibly difficult to visit. The tragedy is that so many of the people who do manage to get in dismiss the entire idea of touring the Kingdom and never make any attempt to see or experience what it has to offer. The Kingdom has an abundance of places to go and things to see, from the spectacular ruins of Madain Salah in the north-west, to the forests and traditional architecture of the south-western Asir region and the vast datě groves of the Eastern Province's Al-Hasa Oasis.

Seeing many of these places involves a fair amount of effort and paperwork; the climate is often harsh and the social regulations governing life in the Kingdom strike the average visitor as more than a bit Draconian. Still, Saudi Arabia offers the traveller the rare opportunity of exploring a country where tradition and modernity are still working out their accommodation with one another. It is a truly unique society, and if you have the opportunity to experience it to the full, that opportunity should not be wasted.

Facts about the Country

HISTORY
Traders' Crossroads
Leaving aside the vast desert wilderness of the Empty Quarter, Saudi Arabia – historically, socially and geographically – can be divided into three regions. The eastern and western coasts of the country, along the Gulf and the Red Sea respectively, were important stations along the trade routes of antiquity.

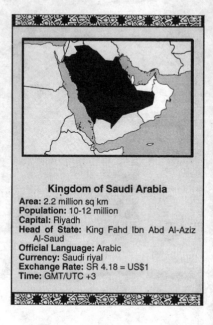

Kingdom of Saudi Arabia
Area: 2.2 million sq km
Population: 10-12 million
Capital: Riyadh
Head of State: King Fahd Ibn Abd Al-Aziz Al-Saud
Official Language: Arabic
Currency: Saudi riyal
Exchange Rate: SR 4.18 = US$1
Time: GMT/UTC +3

Until modern times the third region, the deserts of north-central Arabia, was a remote and rarely visited area containing Bedouin camel herders and, in the oases, small farming settlements.

Until the 18th century the history of what is now Saudi Arabia is largely the history of the coastal regions. In the Gulf this history goes as far back as any yet recorded. Parts of what is now eastern Saudi Arabia were first settled in the 4th or 5th millennium BC by migrants from what is now southern Iraq. These people were known as the Ubaids. The geography of the Gulf was quite different then and throughout Arabia the climate was far less harsh than it is today. Archaeologists have shown that many of the ancient sites now lying on the coast of the Gulf were once islands. Other sites that are now surrounded by large expanses of desert were once coastal regions or sat on the shores of lakes. Some sites, such as Tarut Island, have been inhabited almost continuously since Neolithic times.

The Ubaids were in contact with the Bahrain-based Dilmun Empire, which appears to have controlled a large portion of the Saudi coast – the tell on which Tarut Fort sits has yielded Dilmun-era pottery. Though apparently ruled from Bahrain during this period, the Eastern Province does not contain the large number of grave mounds for which Bahrain is known.

Civilisation appears to have come to the western part of the Arabian Peninsula somewhat later. Cave paintings have been found in north-central Arabia but the earliest major site in the west of the peninsula is Al-Faw, a city on the edge of the Empty Quarter which was an important stop on the caravan route from Yemen to the Mediterranean. Al-Faw reached its peak between about 200 BC and 400 AD. Finds from the excavations at Al-Faw can now be seen in the museum at Riyadh's King Saud University.

References to the Arabic language and to the 'Arabs' as a definable people first appear in Assyrian texts dating from the middle of the 9th century BC and referring to tribes in and around what is now northern and northwestern Saudi Arabia. Taima, Domat Al-Jandal (aka Jof) and Al-Ula are among these proto-Arab settlements, some of which became significant local powers. For a decade in the middle of the 6th century BC Taima was even the capital of the powerful Babylonian Empire.

The best known of the western Arabian kingdoms was that of the Nabataeans. Their empire, centred on Petra (now in southern Jordan), stood astride the main frankincense route from Yemen's Wadi Hadhramaut to Damascus. Madain Salah, north of modern Medina, was the empire's second most important city. By levying a 25% toll on all goods passing through their territory, the Nabataeans became extremely rich. The empire thrived in the 1st century BC, at one point stretching as far north as Damascus,

---

Highlights

Visitors to Riyadh should not miss the museum and, if at all possible, should find a few hours for a trip to Dir'aiyah. In Jeddah the main attractions are the old city and its souks, particularly the Souk Al-Alawi. People with an extra few days should head either south-west for Abha and the Asir National Park or north-west for a look at the spectacular ruins of Madain Salah. In the Eastern Province try to visit the Aramco Exhibit in Dhahran.

The Kingdom's most spectacular archaeological sites are at Madain Salah, in the north-west of the country, and at Domat Al-Jandal in the far north. Getting to either of these places requires some effort (Madain Salah in particular is a long way from anywhere), but it is absolutely worth it and if you can make time for either you should do so. ■

---

but declined in the 1st century AD when the Romans began transporting the frankincense by ship. (See the Frankincense boxed story in the Oman chapter for information about the importance of frankincense.) In 106 AD the Nabataean kingdom was incorporated into the Roman Empire.

The Romans appear to have taken a political interest in Arabia only once. In 25 BC Aelius Gallus, a Roman general, led a force of some 13,000 men south through what is now western Saudi Arabia in an attempt to conquer the frankincense-producing regions of Wadi Hadhramaut and Dhofar, in modern Yemen and Oman, respectively. His army rolled through what is now Medina and later conquered Najran but had to turn back at Marib (now in Yemen) because of thirst.

The Coming of Islam

The decline of the frankincense trade after the 3rd century AD moved Arabia to the margins of the ancient world.

The Gulf, the Arabian side of which lay on the edge of Persia's Sassanian Empire, retained some importance as a trade route between Mesopotamia and India. A large Christian community grew up there during the 4th and 5th centuries, and there were

SAUDI ARABIA

bishops based in the town of Darin on Tarut Island, and in Qatif on the mainland. There may also have been bishoprics in the Al-Hasa Oasis and near Jubail. Though Christianity seems to have been the largest religion in the area by the late 5th century, the strong Persian influence in the region has led some scholars to believe that Zoroastrianism was also widespread.

Central Arabia, the area now known as Najd, was populated largely by pagan nomadic tribes. Most of these nomads worshipped spirits which they believed were embodied in animals or things around them (rocks, trees etc), though some Christian communities existed in the oasis villages as did a few monasteries. In the western part of the peninsula, now known as the Hejaz, there were large Jewish communities, particularly at Yathrib (today's Medina). The Kaaba at Mecca was an important centre of pagan pilgrimage, its focus then, as now, being the black stone, thought to be a meteorite, lodged in one corner of the structure. The Kaaba itself was then filled with idols which were later cast out by the Prophet Mohammed. Today the Kaaba sits in the centre of the courtyard of the Grand Mosque, and it is toward this ancient stone structure (a house originally built by Adam and later by Abraham, according to Muslim belief) that all Muslims face while praying. The house and the black stone represent a focus for Muslim spirituality, but are not objects of worship in and of themselves.

With the exception of a few trading centres along the Gulf and a few oasis settlements along the caravan routes in the west, Arabia at the dawn of Islam was an isolated and dangerous wilderness ruled by a multitude of local warlords. Though two large Christian empires (the Ethiopian and the Byzantine) lay nearby, monotheism had not taken root very deeply. Life in the Gulf revolved around pearl diving and fishing. In the Hejaz the most important settlements were Yathrib (Medina), which was mostly agricultural, and Mecca, whose prosperity was based upon a combination of trade and pagan pilgrimage.

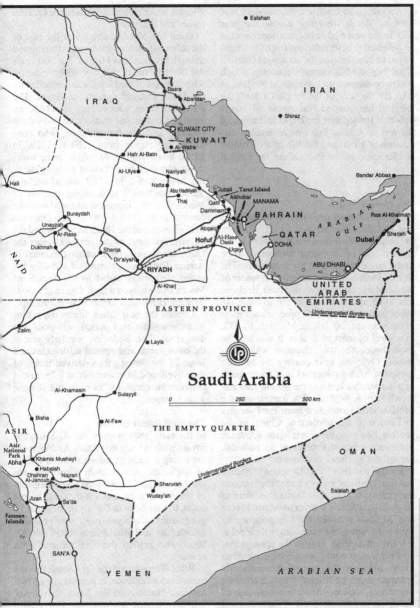

SAUDI ARABIA

According to tradition, Mohammed was born in Mecca sometime around the year 570. In the year 610 he began to receive what he believed to be revelations from God, conveyed to him through the archangel Gabriel. Thus began Mohammed's ministry, which was to continue until his death, at Medina, in 632. By the time of the Prophet's death the religion he founded had swept all others before it throughout the Hejaz and much of the rest of Arabia. For a more detailed discussion of Islam and the life of the Prophet see Religion in the Facts about the Region chapter.

The Centre Shifts

After Mohammed's death many of the tribes that had allied themselves to him militarily, becoming at least nominally Muslim in the process, did not consider themselves to be under any obligation to his successors. The first of Mohammed's successors as leader of the Muslim community, Abu Bakr, declared this to be apostasy and set out to force the tribes back to Islam. This process took most of the next year but left the Muslims, by 633, in control of most of Arabia. It also laid the groundwork for the conquests which followed. Over the next century the Muslim armies of Arabia swept out to conquer much of what we now know as the Middle East and North Africa. Within a few generations the Muslim world stretched from the Pyrenees in Europe to the borders of China. In the process, however, the new religion's Arabian birthplace soon lost much of its political, though not spiritual, importance.

By the middle of the 7th century, Islam's political centre of gravity had shifted outside the peninsula – first to Damascus, later to Baghdad and Cairo – never to return. Mecca and Medina retained their importance as spiritual centres, but increasingly their political importance lay only in the prestige that a Muslim ruler could acquire by controlling them. Most of the rest of the peninsula returned to its traditional ways, a constant tug of war between the Bedouin nomads of the desert and the residents of the towns and villages which dotted the coasts, the caravan routes and the oases.

From 961 Mecca came under the rule of the Sherifs, descendants of Mohammed through his grandson Hassan. For 300 years the Sherifs ruled the city independently while the rest of the Hejaz was controlled by the Shiite Fatimid dynasty of Egypt. The Fatimids were succeeded, in 1169, by another Cairo-based dynasty, the Ayyubids (Saladin and his descendants), who controlled the region from 1169 to 1229. In 1250, however, the Ayyubids were overthrown by their own class of slave-soldiers, the Mamelukes. In 1269 the Mameluke Sultan Baybars I took direct control of Mecca. The city remained under Mameluke control until 1516-17 when the Ottoman Turks conquered the Hejaz and reinstated the Sherifs. For most of the next 400 years the Ottomans showed only marginal interest in Arabia. Eventually, control of virtually the entire Hejaz was ceded to the Sherifs of Mecca who enjoyed a high degree of autonomy under nominal Ottoman overlordship.

Outside the holy cities, life in the peninsula throughout this period was poor and dangerous. The Bedouins regularly raided the oasis towns and coastal settlements and some of the desert tribes derived much of their livelihood from ambushing pilgrim and commercial caravans. Famine and disease were common.

The First Saudi Empire

In the early 18th century the Al-Saud, the royal family of modern Saudi Arabia, were the ruling shaikhs of the small oasis village of Dir'aiyah (near modern Riyadh) in the southern Najd. The Al-Saud were members of the Aneza tribe and are thought, at that point, to have been in Dir'aiyah for about 10 generations. Dir'aiyah itself was probably founded by a Bedouin ancestor of the Al-Saud who settled there in the mid-15th century.

What is now called the First Saudi Empire grew from an alliance, cemented circa 1744, between Mohammed Bin Saud, the ruler of Dir'aiyah, and Mohammed Bin Abdul

Wahhab (born 1703). Mohammed Bin Abdul Wahhab first came to prominence as a judge in Najd in the 1740s. He preached, and applied, a simple, unadorned and strict form of Islam derived from the Hanbalis, the most conservative of the four main schools of Sunni Muslim jurisprudence. The result of this alliance was Wahhabism, a back-to-basics religious movement which was originally aimed at the Bedouin tribes of Najd. Many of the Najdi Bedouins had long been only nominally Muslim and by the early 18th century it is said that some tribes had even gone back to worshipping rocks, trees or the tombs of local saints.

Mohammed Bin Abdul Wahhab's religious fervour and Mohammed Bin Saud's military skill proved to be a potent combination which outlived its two founders. After conquering most of the tribes of Najd and converting them to Wahhabi doctrine, the Saudi-led forces swept out across the peninsula. By 1806, when the empire reached its greatest extent, it included most of the territory of today's Kingdom of Saudi Arabia as well as a large section of what is now southern Iraq.

In 1802 the Saudi-led Wahhabis took Mecca, which they immediately set about purifying according to Wahhabi doctrines. They stripped the Kaaba of its traditional ornamental draperies and destroyed the tombs of saints. But in their zeal the conquerors made a fatal mistake: they turned away the annual pilgrim caravans from Cairo and Damascus, accusing the pilgrims of being infidel idolaters. These two caravans were, at the time, the means by which most of the people participating in each year's hajj arrived in the holy city. They included not just Egyptians and Syrians but Muslims from all over Europe, North Africa, the Middle East and even Central Asia. They were, at least in theory, under the protection of the Ottoman sultan. While Ottoman rule in Mecca had always been, at best, nominal, the Wahhabi refusal to allow the pilgrims to enter Mecca was an affront which the sultan could hardly afford to ignore.

The sultan was in no position to send an army against the Wahhabis and had to ask Mohammed Ali (in theory his viceroy in Egypt but, in practice, an independent ruler) to do so. This expedition, led by Mohammed Ali's son, Ibrahim Pasha, lasted from 1812 to 1818. The Wahhabis were initially driven out of the Hejaz and then systematically chased back to Najd. Dir'aiyah fell in 1818 and Abdullah, the reigning head of the House of Saud, was captured and taken back to Constantinople, where he was later executed. The rest of the Al-Saud were driven from Dir'aiyah and retreated to Riyadh, 30 km to the south, which has been regarded as the clan's capital ever since.

Rebuilding the family fortunes proved to be a slow process. A second Ottoman-Egyptian expedition was sent to Najd to smash the Al-Saud and other local warlords in 1838. In 1843 Faisal Bin Saud, then the head of the family, managed to drive the Ottoman-Egyptian forces out of Najd and restore Saudi rule over Dir'aiyah. But when Faisal died in 1867 his sons squabbled over the succession. With the Al-Saud divided internally the Ottomans sought to gain control of Najd by offering their support to the rival Al-Rashid family. The Al-Rashid set themselves up in Hail, 640 km north-west of Riyadh. In 1891 Mohammed Bin Rashid drove the Al-Saud from Riyadh and became the undisputed ruler of Najd until his death in 1897.

The Rise of Abdul Aziz
After their expulsion from Riyadh some of the Al-Saud family wound up in prison in Hail while others retreated to the desert and the edges of the Empty Quarter. Part of this second group eventually migrated to Kuwait where the ruling shaikh took them in.

It was in Kuwait that the next head of the family came of age. Abdul Aziz Bin Abdul Rahman Al-Saud was a remarkable man. He combined deep personal piety with an intuitive grasp of military strategy and diplomacy which bordered on genius. In later years he would be known throughout the Arab world as The Lion of Najd and to the world at large as Ibn Saud, King of Arabia.

In 1902 Abdul Aziz set out to restore the family fortunes, and almost immediately succeeded in recapturing Riyadh from the Al-Rashids in a swift night-time attack with a force of about 30 men. He rapidly took control of the rest of southern Najd before pausing to consolidate his power.

Alarmed by the loss of Riyadh the head of the Al-Rashid family, usually referred to as Ibn Rashid, appealed to the Ottomans for help, claiming that Abdul Aziz was getting support from the British. This was not true though Ibn Rashid may well have believed it. By 1905 Ibn Rashid had been reinforced by more than 5000 Turkish troops. These, however, proved undisciplined. Abdul Aziz simply avoided them – letting them fester in the sun and cause trouble in Hail while he turned his attentions elsewhere. By 1906 the Saudis were consistently winning their skirmishes with the Al-Rashid and gaining ever more tribal support. They soon moved out of Najd toward the Gulf and, in 1912-13, drove an Ottoman garrison out of the Al-Hasa Oasis. From there, however, Abdul Aziz could go no further: the Gulf shaikhdoms were under British protection and the British had made it clear that they were not willing to see their clients overthrown.

When WWI broke out Ibn Rashid declared his support for the Ottomans, a move which led Abdul Aziz to seek British help for the first time. In December 1914 he signed a treaty with the British ceding them a measure of control over his foreign policy in exchange for an annual subsidy and their recognition of his sovereignty over Najd.

Throughout his conquest of the peninsula Abdul Aziz's fighters were drawn mostly from the *ikhwan* (brotherhood), a society of Bedouin warriors that he founded in 1912. The ikhwan were nomads who had been resettled in oasis farming villages. This made them easy to round up as a fighting force, and easy to drill in Wahhabi religious doctrines. Eventually, there would be 100 ikhwan colonies. The ikhwan's zeal was supplemented by Abdul Aziz's diplomacy, which was built around alliances with the tribes he con-

quered. Abdul Aziz would often marry a daughter of his conquered rival. After a fairly brief period the bride was usually returned to her family loaded with gifts. The children these unions produced became links binding together the Al-Saud and the other family.

In 1930, Abdul Aziz had to suppress the brotherhood for fear of losing his own throne after many of his former warriors came to believe Abdul Aziz, through his rather modest contact with foreigners (mostly the British), had opened Arabia to too many outside influences. By that time the ikhwan had also angered the British by raiding across the border into Iraq, Kuwait and Trans-Jordan. They ignored Abdul Aziz's orders to stop this practice, thus putting him in a difficult position.

Britain, Turkey & the Hejaz
Though Ottoman forces, under Ibrahim Pasha, had driven the Saudis out of the Hejaz in the early 19th century, Ottoman prestige there never quite recovered. Throughout the 18th and 19th centuries the Ottoman Empire was in decline, losing territory either in Europe or to Europeans almost every year. With so many problems in Greece, the Balkans and North Africa, the Hejaz was never at the top of Constantinople's agenda.

The loss, during the 19th century, of virtually all of the empire's European provinces changed the nature of the Ottoman state. For the first time in several centuries an Ottoman sultan found himself ruling an empire which was overwhelmingly eastern and Islamic. If, however, the sultan was going to stress his realm's Islamic identity (and around the end of the 19th century a conscious decision to this effect was taken in Constantinople) then day-to-day control of the Hejaz, and especially of the holy cities, was essential.

In 1900 Sultan Abdul Hamid II (reigned 1876-1909) announced that a railway would be built from Damascus to Medina with a later extension to Mecca. The ostensible purpose of the project was to make it easier for pilgrims to reach the holy cities, but trains are equally good at carrying troops and Abdul Hamid's real motive for the project was to bring the Hejaz back under firm Ottoman control. The Hejaz Railway to Medina began operation in 1908.

With the outbreak of WWI in 1914 the Turkish army officers who were the power behind the throne in the Ottoman Empire prevailed on Sultan Mohammed V to declare a *jihad*, or holy war, calling on Muslims everywhere to rise up against Britain, France and Russia. This alarmed the British, who vastly overestimated the sultan's virtually nonexistent influence over India's large Muslim population. To counter him they negotiated an alliance with Hussein Bin Ali, the Grand Sherif of Mecca. In 1916 Sherif Hussein agreed to lead an Arab revolt against the Turks in exchange for a British promise to make him King of the Arabs after the war – a promise which the British never seriously intended to keep.

A New Kingdom

Throughout WWI and during the years immediately following it Abdul Aziz concentrated his energies on finishing off Al-Rashid rule in the northern Najd, and on conquering Asir (the small kingdom lying between the Hejaz and Yemen) and the remaining portions of what is now Saudi Arabia's Eastern Province. It was only then that he turned his attention to the Hejaz. In 1924, with Abdul Aziz's forces already in control of Taif and threatening Mecca, Sherif Hussein abdicated as King of the Hejaz (a title he had awarded himself during the WWI revolt against the Turks). He went into exile in Cyprus where he died in 1931. On the same day (16 October) that Hussein departed from Jeddah the first of the ikhwan entered Mecca unopposed, wearing pilgrim garb and carrying no weapons. Abdul Aziz himself did not enter the holy city until early December. He, too, arrived dressed as a pilgrim.

Abdul Aziz set about conquering Medina and the rest of the Hejaz while laying siege to Jeddah. He also bent over backwards to show the rest of the Muslim world that he was a fit custodian of the holy cities, largely by ending the practice of fleecing pilgrims. Jeddah surrendered in December 1925. The

following month Abdul Aziz formally assumed the title of King of the Hejaz in addition to his previous title as the Sultan of Najd. In 1932 he combined the two crowns and renamed the country the Kingdom of Saudi Arabia.

The Al-Saud were once again the rulers of Arabia, but their kingdom was still desperately poor. It has been estimated that in the 1920s the country's total revenue was just over UK£200,000 per year, almost a third of which came from Abdul Aziz's British subsidy. Finances had always been a problem. Arabia was far from rich and tradition required that Abdul Aziz, as the ruler, share whatever wealth came into his possession while also lavishing gifts on both allies and conquered rivals. Thus when the oil prospectors first came calling Abdul Aziz thought they were wasting their time looking for oil in his country, but he was in no position to turn down the money they offered.

In 1920 Frank Holmes, a New Zealander who had served with the British Army, was the first to approach Abdul Aziz about an oil concession. Holmes' Eastern & General Syndicate was granted a concession in 1923 but the company failed to find sufficient backing for exploration and the concession lapsed after two years.

After oil was discovered in commercial quantities in Bahrain in 1932, the companies showed renewed interest in Saudi Arabia. Abdul Aziz's own interest in oil had also revived. The Kingdom's financial crisis in the early '30s was severe. The market for pearls collapsed around 1930 when the Japanese discovered how to culture them and the Great Depression led to a drop in demand for Saudi Arabia's other export product, dates. The Kingdom's only other significant source of income was the pilgrimage to Mecca which, like the date market, had been badly hit by the Depression. The total number of pilgrims dropped from about 100,000 per year in the early 20th century to only 20,000 in 1933.

Thus in May 1933 Abdul Aziz granted an oil concession to Standard Oil of California (SOCAL – the precursor of Chevron), which paid him a much needed cash advance of UK£50,000 against future royalties. Drilling began in 1935 but oil was not found in commercial quantities until 1938. By then SOCAL had sold half its interest in the concession to the Texas Oil Company (now Texaco). In 1944 SOCAL and Texaco formed the Arabian American Oil Company, or Aramco, to run their operations in the Kingdom. In 1948 Aramco sold some of its shares to Standard Oil of New Jersey (now Exxon) and Socony Vacuum (Mobil). Aramco was phenomenally successful (it is said never to have failed to make a profit) and for many years was the largest US firm operating outside the USA.

Though oil was discovered in Saudi Arabia in 1938, WWII forced production to shut down almost immediately. After the war, however, things took off and by 1950 the Kingdom's royalties were running at about US$1 million per week which, at the time, was an unbelievable sum of money for Abdul Aziz.

By 1960 81% of the Saudi government's revenue came from oil. This was reinforced over the years by the government's rising stake in the oil industry. Saudi Arabia started its relationship with the oil companies on the basis of a royalty agreement but in 1950 Abdul Aziz demanded and got 50-50 profit sharing with Aramco. In late 1972 the Kingdom took a 25% stake in the oil company and its assets. That share was increased to 60% in 1974 and 100% in 1980. After taking full control, the Saudi government formally changed the company's name from Aramco to Saudi Aramco.

After Abdul Aziz

Abdul Aziz died in 1953 and was succeeded by his son Saud who immediately embarked on a reign of profligacy. With his garish palaces and habit of riding around the desert in a Rolls Royce tossing gold coins to the Bedouins, Saud soon became the embodiment of tasteless excess. His habits were particularly destructive because the country was still largely the king's personal fief. Oil revenues were paid directly to the monarch.

There was no distinction between the king's private funds and the state treasury. Although Abdul Aziz had set up a Council of Ministers shortly before his death, there was still no real system of government in the modern sense of the term. Under King Saud this arrangement was not proving very workable.

In March 1958 the family forced Saud to surrender his powers, but not the crown, to his younger brother Prince Faisal, then foreign minister. Faisal immediately began to modernise the country's administration and set about trying to get the Kingdom's finances back in order. Thanks to Saud, the government was now in debt to Aramco.

But the idea of Saud as a figurehead did not fit with the conception that he, and many others, had of the Saudi monarchy. In December 1960 Saud regained his powers with the help of the Kingdom's small clique of western-educated technocrats. This group threw its support behind Saud on the understanding that, in return, he would institute some form of representative government. Faisal resigned as prime minister. Saud, though in declining health, returned to his free-spending ways.

From late 1962 Saudi Arabia found itself involved in a bloody proxy war against Egypt, with the two countries supporting opposite sides in Yemen's civil war. There was general agreement within the royal family that a republican government in Yemen posed a threat to the Saudi monarchy, but the family also increasingly came to believe that Saud, with his poor health and lack of financial sense, was incapable of dealing with the situation. On 3 November 1964, after a long internal struggle, the family forced Saud to abdicate. He went into exile, living mostly in Athens until his death in 1969.

King Faisal

One of Faisal's first acts as king was the final abolition of slavery in Saudi Arabia. It was a sign of things to come. Over the 11 years of his reign the Kingdom was to move a long way toward becoming a modern country.

An essential first step in this was ending

the costly Egyptian-Saudi proxy battles being fought in Yemen. In 1965 Faisal invited Egyptian President Gamal Abdel Nasser to Jeddah for talks on the conflict. Both sides eventually agreed to suspend aid to their respective clients and pull out their troops (which, in Egypt's case, numbered more than 50,000), but the agreement collapsed in a climate of mutual mistrust. It was only Egypt's defeat in the 1967 Arab-Israeli War that brought the Saudi-Egyptian War in Yemen to an end (though the Yemeni Civil War itself continued until April 1970).

However, relations between the two countries did not really begin to improve until after Nasser's death in 1970. Faisal's relations with Nasser's successor, Anwar Sadat, were much better and when the 1973 Arab-Israeli War broke out the Riyadh-Cairo axis was an important political element before, during and after the conflict.

The wealth which came Saudi Arabia's way in the '60s brought with it increased political clout. The Kingdom participated in the brief attempt by Arab states to cut the flow of oil to the USA and Britain during the 1967 war, and while the oil weapon proved ineffective then, the Arab world's oil producers learned a number of lessons which proved useful later. The west, in contrast, seems to have drawn precisely the wrong conclusions, coming to believe itself immune from the threat of an embargo.

In the run-up to the 1973 war the USA was given ample warning that the situation, both politically and economically, would be different from 1967. Faisal said repeatedly that if the USA continued to support Israel it could not expect an endless flow of cheap Arab petroleum. The warnings were ignored and when Arab states, led by the staunchly pro-western Saudis, announced the embargo in October 1973, no one was more shocked than the Americans. The embargo initially covered all of the western oil-importing countries. The list, however, was quickly pared back until only the USA and the Netherlands, the European country which the Arabs judged to be most vocally pro-Israel, were subject to the boycott. Its effect was

largely psychological (at the time the USA imported less than 10% of its oil from Saudi Arabia), but if the goal was to get the west's attention it certainly succeeded. By the time the sanctions were lifted less than a year later, the Arab Gulf States in general, and Saudi Arabia in particular, had found their way onto the west's psychological map of the world. The press coverage was far from favourable, but the Arabs were no longer being ignored.

The price of oil increased fourfold and Faisal, who controlled 30% of overall production within the Organisation of Petroleum Exporting Countries (OPEC – the worldwide oil producers' cartel) and 35% of the non-Communist world's proven, exploitable reserves, immediately became a force to be reckoned with on the world stage.

If Abdul Aziz had been astonished by the money oil earned him in the '50s, the sums it now brought to his son were truly staggering. Between 1973 and 1978 Saudi Arabia's annual oil revenues went from US$4.35 billion to US$36 billion. Amid the flood of money, however, Faisal and his oil minister, Ahmed Zaki Yamani, emerged as OPEC's main voices for moderation and price stability. They both realised that pulverising the economies of the west was not in their interest. The west not only bought the oil but it was also where much of Saudi Arabia's substantial financial surplus was invested.

The Boom

A building boom began in Saudi Arabia as money was poured into utility and infrastructure projects and the construction from scratch of a petrochemical industry.

Faisal, however, did not live to see it. In 1975 he was assassinated by a nephew, who was said to have been deranged. The motive for the killing was never fully explained and has provided grist for the region's conspiracy theorists ever since. He was succeeded by his half-brother, Khalid, with another half-brother, Fahd, as crown prince.

It is difficult today to appreciate the extent to which Saudi Arabia was modernised during King Khalid's reign (1975-82). Most accounts of Riyadh and Jeddah in the late '70s describe the cities in terms of huge construction sites. The physical growth of these cities was staggering. For example, in the early '70s Riyadh's old airport, which today appears to be fairly close to the centre, was well outside the city. People visiting Riyadh or Jeddah after an absence of only a few years often found the cities changed beyond recognition.

The accomplishments of this period were genuinely astonishing, though the result today is a certain degree of overcapacity.

In the late '70s everyone seemed to be making easy money; some Saudis, however, were troubled by the outside influences that were now flooding into the Kingdom. The royal family has always walked a fine line between those of their subjects who want Saudi Arabia to join the modern world and those who fear any contact with modernity. The country's Islamic identity has never been a subject of debate. Rather, the tension has always been between those, including most of the senior members of the royal family, who believe that modernisation and Islam are generally compatible and those who reject this idea.

This tension in Saudi society became clear in November 1979 when some 300 radicals seized control of the Grand Mosque in Mecca. Booming their demands out through the mosque's public address system, the group, mostly Saudis though some foreigners were also involved, criticised the royal family and the Kingdom's modernisation. The zealots may have assumed that the populace would rally to their call, but this did not happen. It took government troops 10 days to retake the mosque, an operation in which over 250 people died, including 117 of the radicals. Another 63 people were captured when the mosque was retaken. Six weeks later they were executed.

At about the same time riots broke out in and around Qatif, a predominantly Shiite town in the Eastern Province. These were related to long-standing grievances among the country's Shiite minority, and the timing was connected to the Shiite holiday of *ashoora*, the public observance of which had long been banned in the Kingdom. Saudi National Guard forces suppressed the disturbances, killing at least 12 people and arresting hundreds more.

King Fahd

King Khalid died in June 1982 and his half-brother Fahd became the fourth of Abdul Aziz's sons to rule Saudi Arabia. Fahd was well prepared for the job. Khalid's health had long been poor and for much of his reign Fahd, then crown prince, had been the country's ruler in all but name.

The seizure of the Grand Mosque, the riots in Qatif and the Iranian revolution had all given the monarchy a scare. The threat from Iran in particular, which was openly hostile to King Fahd and the Al-Saud family, led Fahd to deepen his country's defence ties with the USA, Britain and France.

The competing tenants of Wahhabism and Shiite Islam (each sect regards the other as heretic), combined with the more basic fact that Iran's revolution overthrew a monarchy in favour of a republic, created a tense relationship between Saudi Arabia and Iran following the 1979 revolution.

The low point in Saudi-Iranian relations probably came in 1987. In July of that year, as the hajj reached its climax, demonstrations broke out in Mecca. The details are hotly disputed but it is fairly clear that some of the 150,000 Iranian pilgrims then in Mecca had arrived with the intention of staging demonstrations against the USA and Israel. The Saudis have long demanded that the hajj be kept free of politics. This stance is in keeping with Wahhabi doctrine but is anathema to the Iranians. The demonstrations in front of the Grand Mosque degenerated into a stampede. The Iranians later accused Saudi authorities of firing on the crowd; the Saudis denied this and, in response, produced a small mountain of weapons they said had been confiscated from Iranian pilgrims during the 1986 and 1987 pilgrimages. At least 400 pilgrims, most of them Iranians, were dead by the time the square in front of the mosque was cleared, and for several years thereafter the Iranians boycotted the pilgrimage.

In the wake of Iraq's invasion of Kuwait in 1990, Saudi Arabia worried that it might be Baghdad's next target and asked the USA to send troops to defend the Kingdom. Saudi Arabia eventually found itself playing host to over 500,000 foreign (mostly US, British and French) troops. During the war Iraqi troops briefly occupied the Saudi border town of Khafji, only to be driven out after two days by a combined Saudi-Qatari force, backed up by US Marines.

Once the war was over and the troops had gone home, the one clear legacy of the crisis was the demand for political change. In November 1990, apparently in response to criticism that he had not consulted widely enough before inviting in the foreign troops, King Fahd announced that plans were under way for a consultative council, or *majlis ash-shura*.

In March 1992 the king announced that the council would be appointed before the end of the year and outlined its duties. After some delays the body finally convened in 1993. Like similar councils in some of the other Gulf States it is a consultative body without any actual legislative authority. In many ways its creation simply codifies and formalises the wide-ranging system of consultation which has always existed in Arabian society.

In late 1995 King Fahd became ill (US government spokespeople said he had suffered a stroke, though the Saudis themselves denied this) and temporarily surrendered power to his half-brother, Crown Prince Abdullah. The king resumed his duties in February 1996, but doubts about his health persisted.

November 1995 also brought with it an unsettling reminder of the tensions that remained in Saudi society nearly five years after the Gulf War. That month a bomb exploded at a building in Riyadh where US soldiers trained members of the Saudi National Guard. Six people died in the blast and security was tightened throughout the capital.

GEOGRAPHY

Saudi Arabia is about 2.2 million sq km in area, most of it desert. In geological terms the Arabian Peninsula is an extension of north-eastern Africa.

Western Saudi Arabia is dominated by a mountain chain running the entire length of the country and generally becoming higher and broader as one moves south towards Yemen. The Kingdom's tourist resorts are in this area: Taif, in the mountains above Mecca, and the forests of the Asir region stretching from Al-Baha to Abha. The scenery throughout the Asir region is particularly striking, with evergreen forests overlooking desert wadis. In many places the mountains drop sharply to the Red Sea coastal strip. To the east, however, they gradually turn into a series of low hills before merging into the deserts of the central Arabian plateau.

About half of Saudi Arabia is taken up by the Rub' Al-Khali, or Empty Quarter. This is the largest sand desert in the world, an area about the size of France. The region is so fierce that even the Bedouins, who call it simply the Sands, are reluctant to venture into it. North of the Empty Quarter the great deserts of central Arabia stretch into Iraq. This is the region known to earlier generations of westerners as Arabia Deserta. Much of it is gravel desert, sometimes with a thin covering of sand or a bit of scrub growth. The extreme north-west of the Kingdom contains Arabia's second great sand desert, the Nafud.

The Eastern Province is a low-lying area which contains a number of *sabkhas* (salt flats). The desert here tends to be thin and crusty and because of the low elevations the air often seems particularly thick and damp. The main geographical feature of the east is the gigantic Al-Hasa Oasis, centred on the town of Hofuf, with its miles upon miles of date palms.

CLIMATE

Summers in the Kingdom are unbelievably hot. Daytime temperatures rise to 45°C or more from mid-April until October throughout the Kingdom, with high humidity in the coastal regions. In the summer it gets 'down' to 38°C or so overnight on the Red Sea coast. In places like Jizan, this weather continues well into November. Even in December or January it can be uncomfortably hot.

In the dead of winter (December-January) temperatures in the main cities will drop into the teens during the day and even hit single digits in some places, particularly in the central desert regions, overnight. In the coastal areas it rains regularly, less often in Riyadh.

FLORA & FAUNA

A drive across Saudi Arabia's deserts will provide you with wonderful opportunities for viewing desert scrub growth and tamarind trees. In the forested areas of Asir there are various sorts of evergreens.

Aside from camels you are not likely to see much wildlife. The desert is full of nocturnal creatures such as hedgehogs and sand cats (a small species of cat typified by very large ears and tufts of hair on the feet. The large ears help the cats hear approaching enemies while the extra hair on the soles of their feet makes it easier for them to walk over loose sand), and there are wild monkeys (hamadryas baboons, to be precise) in the forests of the Asir region.

The Riyadh museum and the regional museums scattered around the country all have good displays on all the interesting wildlife in the Kingdom that you will probably never see.

Asir National Park

Saudi Arabia's only national park sprawls over a large portion of the south-western Asir region. See the Abha section for complete details of the park and its facilities.

GOVERNMENT & POLITICS

In theory Saudi Arabia's king is an absolute monarch, but in practice the system is not quite that simple. Abdul Aziz, the founder of the present Saudi dynasty, was a traditional Arab tribal leader. He acquired power and territory through conquest but maintained them through diplomacy. The system of government in the Kingdom today is a blend of this traditional system and modern ideas of administration. Thus, while much of the country's day-to-day life is supervised by a system of extremely bureaucratic ministries, every Saudi citizen also retains the right to take any grievance, be it a lost camel or a complex commercial dispute, directly to the king.

Important decisions are rarely taken by the king alone. Before acting he usually consults the Cabinet, senior members of the royal family and the country's religious and business establishments.

King Fahd's creation, in 1993, of a consultative council was, in part, a move to formalise and modernise this traditional system of give-and-take between the ruler and the various elements of Saudi society. The council's members are appointed by the King. About the time the council was announced (in 1992), King Fahd told a newspaper that elective democracy was not an appropriate system of government for Saudi Arabia or the other Gulf States. The council can comment on proposed laws and recommend changes but does not have any legislative authority.

After King Fahd, the next person in line for the throne is his half-brother Prince Abdullah, who heads the National Guard and who temporarily assumed the king's powers during Fahd's illness in the early part of 1996. In theory the succession passes down the line of King Abdul Aziz's sons with the family collectively deciding which prince is best suited to take charge. In 1992 King Fahd announced plans to formalise this system through an electoral college of 400 sons and grandsons of Abdul Aziz.

Saudi Arabia has no constitution. King Fahd and his predecessors have often said that the Koran is the only constitution that the country needs. Much of the legal system is based on a straight application of the *sharia* (Islamic law) as interpreted by the Hanbali school of Islamic jurisprudence, the most conservative of Sunni Islam's four main legal schools.

Date pickers need to be both agile and strong because date palms can reach a height of 23m and more than 1000 dates may grow on a single branch.

ECONOMY

Prior to the discovery of oil, the peninsula's economy revolved around the hajj in the west, date farming and pearling in the east and tribal raiding in the centre.

After WWII oil quickly replaced these traditional pursuits as the main source of income. In the early '70s Saudi Arabia embarked on a long-term diversification programme. Economic development schemes focused on heavy industry, petrochemicals and agriculture. Today the Kingdom churns out huge amounts of steel and cement, boasts one of the world's largest petrochemical industries and is a net exporter of wheat.

All of this costs money (wheat does not grow in the desert without very expensive human assistance), and money in Saudi Arabia usually means oil. The Kingdom has long had to strike a balance between deriving most of its income from oil and oil-related industries and its long-standing commitment to price stability in the world oil market. This has led to some enormous adjustments in its output over the years. In 1979 the country was pumping about eight million barrels of oil per day (bpd). In 1983 it dropped to five million bpd but in early 1992 it was back up to 8.5 million bpd and plans were in the works to expand capacity to 10 million bpd.

The result is that when the bottom drops out of the oil market, as happened in 1986 when oil fell below US$10 per barrel, spending plans have to be radically redefined. Similarly, if the oil price skyrockets, as happened in 1973-74 and again in 1979-80, impossible projects suddenly become possible. In either case the resulting shock waves are felt throughout the economy.

This is not simply a question of how much money the government can channel into infrastructure and agriculture projects each year. Much of the diversification drive of the '70s and '80s created industries related to oil, whether directly or indirectly. Many of the country's private businesses are service companies whose main clients are either the government, the government-owned oil and petrochemical industries or their employees. To a greater extent than most Saudis like to admit, the national economy still fluctuates with the price of oil.

POPULATION & PEOPLE

Because of its size and its history Saudi Arabia is a much less ethnically homogeneous place than is generally thought. The central Najd region was cut off from most of the rest of the world for many centuries and the population there is quite homogeneous. Pure-blooded Najdis often have long faces and sharply defined features. The Hejaz, on the other hand, presents one of the most mixed populations imaginable. For 14 centuries Muslims have been arriving in the Hejaz from all over the world and until earlier this century many of them stayed on. Hejazis may be as dark skinned as sub-Saharan Africans or as pale as some northern Europeans. As people became more mobile this diversity increasingly applied to the Saudis as a whole. One can even encounter a handful of Saudis with distinctly Chinese features. Natives of the Gulf area fall somewhere between these extremes. The communities of what is now eastern Saudi

Arabia were not, until recently, as cosmopolitan as the traditional trading centres of Bahrain or Sharjah, though they did have some contact with Iran and India in the century or so before the discovery of oil. Saudis of the south-western Asir region are distinctly Yemeni in appearance and dress.

The Kingdom has a fairly large population of nomads. They are known as Bedouins, or Bedu in common parlance, and as camel-nomads in anthropological terms. Because many of them wander freely across international borders in search of forage for their animals, nobody knows how large this population is.

The expatriate population is quite varied. Every medium-sized or larger city has huge contingents of Egyptians, Indians, Pakistanis and Filipinos. In Riyadh and Jeddah there are significant communities of almost every western, Arab and Asian nationality.

Exactly how many people live in Saudi Arabia is unclear. The government says there are 15 million Saudi citizens, but most private estimates put the overall population closer to 12 million, of whom about seven million are thought to be Saudis.

EDUCATION

The growth of the Saudi educational system over the last two generations has been as striking as the development of the country itself, though at times it has been far from smooth. Virtually every innovation had to be fought for by reformers.

Educating women was particularly problematic – the first girls' school was opened in 1956 by the wife of the future King Faisal. Even then it had to be disguised as an orphanage. In September 1963 the news that a girls' school was shortly to open in Buraydah touched off riots there. From these difficult beginnings there has grown a system of free primary and secondary education for all Saudi citizens. By 1985 there were nearly two million children (including almost 800,000 girls) in the Kingdom's primary and secondary schools. There are around 100,000 students in Saudi Arabia's seven universities. The Saudi education system is

strictly segregated at all levels (in some university courses male professors lecture their female students through video systems) and foreign children are not allowed to attend Saudi schools.

Most of the larger foreign communities in the Kingdom (Indian, Pakistani etc) run schools following their own systems. Children of western expatriates usually attend US or British-system international schools, or are educated at boarding schools in other countries.

SOCIETY & CONDUCT

Possibly the most enduring western myth about Saudi Arabia is the belief that all Saudis are incredibly rich. It is true that few, if any, Saudis are destitute but there is a great deal of distance between the two extremes.

Bedouins

The Bedouins' essential way of life has hardly changed since the time of the Prophet. That said, they're extremely adaptable people. Water may now be carried in plastic containers instead of animal skins and Bedouin families may take radios with them across the desert. Even in Riyadh it is not unusual to see a Bedouin man driving a small Japanese-built pick-up truck, from the back of which his camel is serenely observing the world.

You will see Bedouins everywhere in the Kingdom, but the only time you are likely to meet them is if you happen upon one of their encampments while driving in the desert. Should this happen, it is important that you approach the situation with tact and discretion. Although most Bedouins are hospitable there are some who want nothing to do with foreigners. Do not go marching up to a Bedouin camp uninvited. If the residents want to invite you in for coffee or tea it will be obvious, regardless of any language barrier which may exist. If you are invited into someone's tent follow the guidelines outlined under Dos & Don'ts in this section as well as in the Facts about the Region chapter. Within reason, foreigners' faux pas usually provoke amusement, not anger, among Bedouin hosts.

Dos & Don'ts

Saudi Arabia is still one of the most insular societies on earth and a certain degree of tact and discretion is called for, even in big cities.

Dress conservatively. Shorts in public are absolutely out of the question. Women should always cover their shoulders and should not wear clothing that is overly tight or revealing. Take things offered to you with the right, not the left, hand and avoid showing the soles of your feet to people.

Do not attempt to photograph people without their permission. Men should not photograph Saudi women or even ask permission to photograph them, and foreign women should think twice before doing so. Do not take pictures of, or attempt to enter, mosques, as this is strictly forbidden.

When offered coffee or tea in someone's home or at a business meeting, it is considered very impolite to refuse.

Life under Saudi Arabia's strict brand of Islam takes some getting used to. Alcohol and pork are illegal, and so are theatres and cinemas. Women are not allowed to drive and must be accompanied by their husband or a male relative to travel by bus or train (domestic flights on Saudia, the Saudi national airline, are exempt from this rule). At prayer time all shops must close and even TV programmes are interrupted. The only exceptions are the restaurants in some five-star hotels. What follows are some notes on a few of the trickier aspects of day-to-day life. See under Women Travellers in the Facts for the Visitor section for information directed specifically at female visitors and residents.

Alcohol Booze is illegal in Saudi Arabia which is not to say that it does not exist. Illegal alcohol comes in two varieties: imported and home-made. The former is alcohol (usually whisky) which has either been smuggled in or procured through one of the embassies.

Home-made firewater comes in several varieties. The most common, and the most potent, is *siddiki* (Arabic for 'my friend'), sid for short. This is a very pure distilled spirit, frequently 96 to 98% alcohol when it comes out of the still, at which point it is almost always cut 50-50 with water. Don't drink it straight. Even after it has been diluted sid is still very potent. If properly made it has very few impurities so it hits you a lot harder than regular booze. The most common mixer is 7-Up. If improperly made, sid can make you blind or even kill you.

Home-made wine and beer are also common, and almost anyone can tell you how to take the local nonalcoholic beer or grape juice and ferment it.

Only a fool would try to bring alcohol into the country or to move the stuff around. If you get caught, plan on spending a minimum of three months or so in prison, possibly a lot longer. This is flexible and depends a lot on both the nature of your offence and on how badly your sponsor wants to get you out. As with drugs in western countries, possession is one thing while dealing is another thing entirely. Flogging is also part of the standard punishment, though this is rarely applied to westerners. When released from prison you will be deported and blacklisted.

The Religious Police Formally known as the Committee for the Propagation of Virtue and the Prevention of Vice, the *matawwa*, or religious police, have a fearsome reputation as a squad of moral vigilantes out to enforce Islamic orthodoxy as they understand it. This is not exactly true. The system of recruiting and training matawwa has become a bit more formal over the years. The religious police are part of the complex system of give-and-take involving liberals and conservatives through which the Al-Saud maintain order in the country.

Matawwa activity tends to come in waves. The clearest sign that one of these waves is sweeping over a city is a shopping centre in which almost every door carries a notice asking women not to enter the premises. For their part, men should bear in mind that Saudi law makes the five daily prayers

SAUDI ARABIA

mandatory for all Muslims. If you are a Muslim, or if the matawwa think you are a Muslim, you may be ordered into the nearest mosque on pain of arrest. They have also been known to stop couples in public and demand proof of marriage.

The best way to deal with the matawwa is to steer clear of them. However, if you do find yourself facing an angry-looking religious policeman the first thing to do is to keep calm. The second thing to do is be polite but firm. Above all, do not turn the situation into a confrontation. If the matawwa are asking something reasonable of you – not using a pay phone during prayer time, for example – do it.

Afterwards report the incident to your embassy. In recent years most western embassies have taken to keeping a log of matawwa activity directed against their nationals. These things tend to go in cycles and after enough Saudis and enough embassies have complained to the government the authorities crack down on the matawwa in a given area.

Ramadan Ramadan, the month during which Muslims fast from dawn until dusk, is marked throughout the Muslim world but nowhere with as much fervour as in Saudi Arabia. Do not make the mistake of thinking that a Ramadan visit to a place like Egypt has prepared you for Ramadan in the Kingdom. As is the case everywhere in the Muslim world, life in the Kingdom moves more slowly during Ramadan, at least during the day. Non-Muslims must always remember, however, that in Saudi Arabia public observance of the fast is mandatory. This is applied very broadly. In an office where there are no Muslim staff, for example, everyone must still forego their morning coffee on the off chance that a Muslim might enter the room (people in such situations often clear out a desk drawer and keep the coffee cup in there). If you are caught smoking, drinking or eating in public you can be sent to prison, usually until Ramadan is over. That extends to smoking while riding in a car.

RELIGION
Islam

Most Saudis are Sunni Muslims who follow the Wahhabi sect of Islam. The country also has a Shiite minority which constitutes between five and 10% of the population. Most of the Shiites live in the Eastern Province, where they may account for as much as a third of the population, though there are also small Shiite communities in the Asir region, near the Yemeni border.

No non-Muslim may hold Saudi nationality and the public profession of all other faiths is banned. Non-Muslims may not enter mosques in Saudi Arabia. Non-Muslims are also barred from the area surrounding Mecca (about 25 km from the city in all directions) and may visit only the outskirts of Medina. Although it is not clear what the penalties for violating, or attempting to violate, these bans are, my advice is to drop any idea of testing the Saudis on this one.

See the Facts about the Region chapter for a more general discussion of Islam.

Wahhabism Wahhabism takes its name from Mohammed Bin Abdul Wahhab (1703-92), a preacher and judge from the central Najd. He began to preach in the 1740s in response to what he saw as an ever-increasing lack of respect for Islam among the Bedouin tribes of central Arabia. By the mid-18th century many of these Bedouin tribes were only nominally Muslim and a few are said to have returned to pagan religious practices. Abdul Wahhab preached a return to Islam's origins and traditions as interpreted by the Hanbali school of Islamic jurisprudence. This meant strict adherence to the Koran and the Hadith (accounts of the Prophet's words and actions) as interpreted by Islam's leading scholars.

Wahhabism is a rather austere form of Islam. It frowns on tobacco as well as alcohol and pork, and well into this century tobacco smoking was illegal in what is now central Saudi Arabia. Wahhabis reject such concepts as sainthood and forbid the observance of holidays such as the Prophet's birthday, which most other Muslims celebrate. Even the term Wahhabi makes strict followers of the sect uncomfortable because it appears to exalt Mohammed Bin Abdul Wahhab. Strict Wahhabis prefer the term *muwahidin*, which translates as unitarian, because they profess only the unity of God.

LANGUAGE
Arabic is the official language of Saudi Arabia. English is the universal language of commerce in the Kingdom and you should have no trouble getting by with it in all of the main cities and towns.

Facts for the Visitor

PLANNING
When to Go
The best time to visit Saudi Arabia is between November and February when the climate over much of the country is at its mildest. During these months it can be fairly cold at night in desert areas like Riyadh, though the weather in Jeddah tends to be mild. Sandstorms are, however, always a possibility and there is no way to predict their occurrence.

The Asir Mountains are at their best a bit earlier and a bit later than the rest of the country – during the main winter months they are often locked in fog which makes driving dangerous and robs you of the views which are the area's main attraction. Try to visit Taif and Abha in September-October or March-April. During the summer all of the hotels in the mountain areas tend to be booked solid.

If possible, stay away from the Kingdom during Ramadan. If you don't like crowds it would also be a good idea to avoid Jeddah for two or three weeks either side of the hajj.

Maps
The best maps of Saudi Arabia are those drawn by Zaki Mohammed Ali Farsi, commonly known as the Farsi Maps. They are available at most bookshops and hotels in the Kingdom for about SR 20 each. The series

includes city maps of Riyadh, Jeddah, the Eastern Province (Dammam/Alkhobar), Abha & Khamis, Taif, Mecca and Medina. There is also a road map covering the entire country. The Riyadh, Jeddah, Eastern Province and Mecca city maps and the national map are also available in the form of 'A to Z' atlases, each of which is about the size of a phone book. These go for SR 40 to SR 80. All are, to varying extents, out of date but still usable. Just remember that roads shown as 'projected' have often been finished.

Most of the other professionally drawn maps of the country, including both the Bartholomew and Oxford maps, are hopelessly out of date.

What to Bring
Sunglasses and a hat are absolutely essential. Your clothing should be long and loose. The sun is very intense and people tend to burn quickly in Saudi Arabia so it is a good idea to bring along a thin, long-sleeved garment of some sort, in addition to your sunscreen, especially in July and August.

For the winter months, particularly in desert areas such as Riyadh, Medina and Hail, you will want a jumper and a light to medium-weight jacket. The climate in Asir in the winter can be genuinely foul, and warm clothing will definitely be in order.

TOURIST INFORMATION
Even though Saudi Arabia does not issue tourist visas, tourist information does exist. There is a small but growing tourist industry catering to Saudis, Gulf Arabs (the only people who can get into the Kingdom without a visa) and resident expatriates. This industry exists mostly in and around Abha and Al-Baha and, to a lesser extent, Hofuf. Its services consist of weekend packages, sometimes including tours, run by the larger hotels. Look for ads in the *Arab News* and *Saudi Gazette* announcing promotions at the various hotels and consult the city headings in this chapter for further information.

A new and noteworthy entry in the field of Saudi tourism is Golden Eagle Services, a Riyadh-based company that offers tour packages to Madain Salah and other destinations around the Kingdom.

VISAS & DOCUMENTS
Visas

Visas are very, very difficult to obtain. Saudi Arabia has a well-deserved reputation as one of the hardest places in the world to visit. All persons entering the Kingdom must have a Saudi sponsor – in effect, someone who will vouch for your conduct during your stay in the country. Tourist visas are not available and hotels are unable to sponsor business travellers. Your options consist of visitor, residence or transit visa and, for Muslims, hajj and *umrah* visas. Once you are in the country your sponsor has sole control over everything affecting your visa. Only a Saudi can apply for an entry visa, a visa extension, an exit visa or an exit/re-entry visa. If you need to extend your stay in the country you will have to do it through your sponsor.

From the first of Ramadan each year Saudi embassies in Muslim countries issue only hajj visas until the hajj is over about three months later. There's no longer a ban on issuing visas to people whose passport contains an Israeli stamp, but this could cause you problems with some border guards who may not be aware of the new regulations.

A final note: all official business in Saudi Arabia is conducted according to the Muslim Hejira calendar. Any Gregorian date you see on a document is there solely for the foreign community's convenience. The Hejira calendar is 11 days shorter than the western calendar, though this can vary by a day either way. A visa valid for a stay of one month is valid for a Hejira month, not a Gregorian month. This means, for example, that if you have a one-month visa and you stay for a month according to the western calendar you will have overstayed your visa by a day or two – and you will be in trouble.

Visitor Visas To obtain a visitor visa (ie a business visa) you will need a formal invitation telex from the company or Saudi individual sponsoring you. This really means that you need to have your visa number. An 'invitation' is essentially an acknowledgment that your sponsor has obtained a visa on your behalf and that authorisation to issue this visa has been sent to the Saudi embassy in a particular city. At that point all you have to do is appear at the embassy bearing your visa number. If you do not have a visa number do not bother going to the embassy. Visas are filed by number, not name. No number, no visa. If you show up with the number in the morning, you can usually pick up your visa the same afternoon. Visitor visas can be picked up at any Saudi diplomatic mission, though the pick-up site has to be specified when the visa application is filed by the sponsor in the Kingdom.

Residence Visas In addition to all the paperwork which your sponsor will have to file in the Kingdom, to obtain a residence visa you have to produce copies of your employment contract and academic or professional qualifications. Then you have to fill out, and have translated into Arabic, several lengthy forms detailing your own and your family's background. You will also have to submit the results of an extremely comprehensive medical examination (the embassy will provide the form for your doctor to fill out), including a blood test which shows you to be HIV negative. It usually takes a couple of months to pull all of this paperwork together at both ends. Eventually your sponsor should inform you of your visa number, against which you can collect an entry visa. This will be converted into a residence visa once you arrive in the country. At that point you will almost certainly have to surrender your passport to your employer and you will be issued with an *iqama*, or residence permit. Residence visas are issued only in your home country or in a country in which you have permanent residence.

Transit Visas Transit visas are the only remotely easy option for entry into the Kingdom. Their validity ranges from 24 hours to seven days, depending on the manner in which you are transiting the

SAUDI ARABIA

country. In all cases they must be obtained in advance.

Airport Transit Visas The 24 and 48-hour transit visas are for people passing through Saudi airports. These are issued by Saudi embassies after you have shown them your airline tickets and convinced the people at the embassy that when it came to purchasing these tickets you had absolutely no choice other than an overnight transit in Saudi Arabia. If, for example, you are flying Saudia from Cairo to Nairobi via Jeddah the embassy is going to want to know why you can't take a nonstop EgyptAir or Kenya Airways flight. There is a fairly good chance that your request for a transit visa will be turned down, so before buying a plane ticket you should consider carefully whether you really want to run the risk of being trapped in the transit lounge at Riyadh, Jeddah or Dhahran airport for a day or two. If you do get this sort of transit visa you will have to surrender your passport to the immigration authorities at the airport and collect it again on the way out.

Road Transit Visas Road transit visas are fairly straightforward. People driving between Jordan and either Kuwait or Yemen are usually issued three-day transit visas. As a general rule these are only issued at the Saudi embassies in Amman (Jordan), Kuwait City and San'a (Yemen). You have to go to the embassy with your carnet and proof that you already have a visa for the country at the other end of the road. People driving between Jordan and Bahrain or the UAE often get seven-day transit visas. If you are coming from Oman you will have to pick up the transit visa in Abu Dhabi.

In theory it is possible to hitch a ride on any of these routes, though in practice you probably will not get a transit visa unless you are already attached to a vehicle. So your best bet is to link up with a driver in, say, Amman and apply with that person for the transit visa.

Transit visas for travel between Kuwait and Jordan usually restrict the traveller to transiting the Tapline (Trans-Arabian Pipeline) service road. If you have this sort of visa you should banish any thought of getting off the Tapline road and heading down to Riyadh for a few days. In the unlikely event that you make it to Riyadh (or Jeddah, or anywhere else) and back to the Tapline road without getting caught at one of the numerous checkpoints, you are almost certain to be spotted when trying to leave the country.

Hajj & Umrah Visas For hajj visas there is a quota system of one visa for every 1000 Muslims in a country's population. Exactly how this system is administered varies from country to country though, as a rule, it is fairly difficult to get a hajj visa outside your home country.

Umrah visas are issued to any Muslim requesting one. To obtain the visa, you must apply either in your home country or in a country where you hold permanent residence. All you need is to show a round-trip plane ticket to Jeddah. If you are not from a Muslim country or do not have an obviously Muslim name, you will be asked to provide any official document that lists Islam as your religion. Converts to Islam must provide a certificate from the mosque where they went through their conversion ceremony.

Umrah visas are valid for one week and only for travel to Jeddah, Mecca and Medina and on the roads connecting them to one another. If you are travelling by road, they allow you to travel on the road between the holy cities and the border.

Exit/Re-Entry Visas People in the Kingdom on a visitor visa do not need an exit visa to leave the country. Foreigners holding residence permits need exit/re-entry visas to leave and re-enter the Kingdom. A final exit visa is issued to people leaving at the end of a work contract. Both types of visa must be obtained on your behalf by your sponsor.

Generally, exit/re-entry visas for people employed in the Kingdom are good for a single trip and allow you to stay out of the country for two months. Dependents and people whose sponsors submit proof that

SAUDI ARABIA

they need to stay away for more than two months for work-related reasons can get six month exit/re-entry visas. A multiple exit/re-entry visa, usually valid for six months, is issued to workers only in special cases where the sponsor specifically requests it and can show that a need for such a visa exists. They are also sometimes issued to children of people working in the Kingdom where the child is attending school in Bahrain or the UAE.

As with other visas the dates on exit/re-entry visas refer to Hejira, not Gregorian, months. If you have a six month exit/re-entry visa its validity is about a week shorter than it looks according to a western calendar. On a two month exit/re-entry visa the difference will be one to three days. Do not expect a lot of flexibility from immigration officials at the airport on this score, even if you are only a day late in re-entering the country.

Visa Extensions These must be obtained by your sponsor.

Other Documents
Travel Letters Technically, foreigners living in the Kingdom need the permission of their sponsor to travel outside of the city in which they reside. In practice this is only enforced for travel between provinces. This permission takes the form of a letter from your sponsor approving your travel plans. This is handled by a company or a ministry's Government Affairs Department which also handles all visa-related paperwork. The maximum validity of a travel letter is one Hejira month.

Foreigners on a visitor visa can travel anywhere in the Kingdom, except Mecca and Medina for non-Muslims, with only their passport. The problem you may encounter is that a lot of the people who ought to be aware of this fact aren't. While researching this book I always had trouble purchasing domestic air tickets because the Saudia counter staff would insist on seeing my nonexistent travel letter. However, the security people at the airport always knew the rules so I never had any trouble actually

getting onto a plane. For this same reason people on a visitor visa who make overland trips should expect delays at checkpoints around the country. The guards at the checkpoints often do not know the rules and insist on seeing a travel letter. Don't worry about this. Usually the guards will take your passport to their officer and you will be on your way within five to 10 minutes. Similarly, you can expect a worried look from clerks at small hotels, youth hostels and any hotel outside a big city when they find out that you have a passport but no travel letter. It is highly unlikely, however, that you will be turned away from a hotel because of this.

Site Permits To visit virtually any fort, ruin or archaeological site in the Kingdom you must first obtain a permit. The only exceptions are the Masmak Fortress in Riyadh, Dir'aiyah and the Najran Fort. Permits for all sites except those in the area between Dammam and Jubail are issued by the Department of Antiquities at the Riyadh Museum. Permits for all Eastern Province sites except those in and around the Al-Hasa Oasis are issued at the Regional Museum of Archaeology & Ethnography in Dammam.

In Riyadh you have to file the application one morning and return a day or two later to collect the permit. In Dammam they can often issue permits the same day provided you arrive before 10 am. Resident foreigners will have to bring along their iqama and, if the site involves a trip to a province other than the one where they live, a travel letter will also be required. People in the country on a visitor visa require only a passport.

Once you get to the place you plan to visit it is often necessary to take the permit to the local branch of the antiquities office. Most of the Kingdom's archaeological sites do not have permanent attendants so this is often the only way to get the gate unlocked. In some places, notably Al-Hasa, you may also have to trek around to a couple of offices to get the permit validated before anyone will open up the site for you. As government officials stop work around 1.30 or 2 pm you have to get an early start.

Note that some sites such as the south Dhahran archaeological sites or the Hanakiyah rock carvings, east of Medina, are in military areas. To visit these you will need a guide arranged by the antiquities authority in charge of permits in that area. This is complicated and can probably be ruled out for a lone sightseer.

While researching the second edition of this book I was told by officials at the Ministry of Education's antiquities division that plans were moving ahead for a limited abolition of the permit system at some of the Kingdom's more popular sites. This would involve lifting the requirement that visitors have permits and, instead, setting up ticket booths. The tentative list of sites slated to open up in this way included Riyadh's Murabba Palace (Masmak, presumably, would get a ticket booth as well), Dir'aiyah, Madain Salah, the Najran Fort, the two forts in Hail and Qasr Ibrahim in Hofuf. The plan also involves instituting admission charges at the Kingdom's museums. Exactly when, or if, this will happen is anyone's guess.

EMBASSIES
Saudi Embassies Abroad
Some of Saudi Arabia's embassies overseas include:

Australia
  12 Culgoa Circuit, O'Malley, Canberra 2606 ACT (☎ (06) 286 2099)
Bahrain
  King Faisal Highway, Manama; opposite the Holiday Inn and near the Kuwaiti embassy (☎ 537 722)
Iran
  59 Kheyabun-é Bokharest, Teheran (☎ (2) 624294)
Jordan
  1st Circle, Jebel Amman, Amman (☎ (6) 641076)
Oman
  Jameat A'Duwal Al-Arabiya St, Medinat Qaboos Diplomatic Area, Muscat; the embassy is to the sea side of Sultan Qaboos St, west of the Al-Khuwair roundabout (☎ 601744)
Qatar
  Diplomatic Area, beyond the Doha Sheraton Hotel, Doha (☎ 832 030)

Syria
  Al-Jala'a Ave, Abu Roumaneh, Damascus (☎ (11) 334914)
UAE
  Karamah St near the intersection with Dalma St, Abu Dhabi (☎ (2) 465 700)
UK
  30 Belgrave Square, London SW1 (☎ (0171) 235 0303)
USA
  601 New Hampshire Ave NW, Washington DC, 20037 (☎ (202) 342 3800)

Foreign Embassies in Saudi Arabia
See the Riyadh and Jeddah sections for listings of embassies and consulates in the country.

CUSTOMS
It is standard procedure for Saudi customs officers to search every bag thoroughly, but the searches are rarely malicious. Many books on Saudi Arabia open with horror stories about the customs check at Riyadh or Jeddah airports. For the record, I've been through Saudi customs dozens of times at airports, on the causeway to Bahrain and at Jeddah Islamic Port and only once, in all that time, has the search been ill-tempered. On several occasions I've been more or less waved through.

The import of anything containing alcohol or pork is strictly forbidden. Customs officers also pay close attention to any books, magazines or photographs you are carrying. Video tapes are often held at the airport for a day or two for screening by censors. Anything that is deemed pornographic (which, in Saudi Arabia, could even include vacation photos of your family and friends at the beach) or politically sensitive may be immediately confiscated.

MONEY
Costs
Saudi Arabia is not a cheap place, but it is possible to travel there relatively cheaply if you put your mind to it. Filling your stomach for SR 15 or less is never a problem. Beds are not quite so cheap, generally bottoming out at SR 55 to SR 90 in hotels. Youth hostels

charge only SR 8 per night but they can be difficult to reach. It is possible to cross the peninsula for less than SR 200, which is not bad considering that it's about 1600 km by road.

Travelling around the Kingdom can be done on about SR 50 a day, though SR 100 is a more realistic low-budget estimate (SR 200 if you don't stay in the youth hostels).

Currency

The Saudi riyal (SR) is divided into 100 *halalas*. It is a hard currency, and there are no restrictions on taking either riyals or foreign currency into or out of the country. Notes come in SR 1, 5, 10, 50, 100 and 500 denominations. All of the notes except for the SR 500 have King Fahd's picture on the front (the SR 500 note shows King Abdul Aziz). Some older money with King Faisal's picture is still in circulation, though it is becoming a pretty rare sight. The King Faisal-era notes are larger than the current ones and are differently coloured but they are still valid. Coins come in 5, 10, 25 and 50 halalas and SR 1 denominations.

Currency Exchange

The riyal is pegged to the US dollar, so while the US$/SR rate rarely moves by more than a halala or so either side of SR 3.75, the exchange rates against other western currencies are changing constantly.

US$1	=	SR 4.18
UK£1	=	SR 6.43
FF1	=	SR 0.80
DM1	=	SR 2.74
A$1	=	SR 3.29

Changing Money & ATMs

Banking hours are generally Saturday to Thursday from 8 am to noon. These hours can vary locally by half an hour or so in either direction. Moneychangers are among some of the Kingdom's larger banking operations and often offer slightly better rates than banks, though if you are only changing a few hundred dollars you are unlikely to notice the difference.

Two of the Kingdom's largest financial houses, the Al-Rajhi Banking & Investment Corporation and the Al-Rajhi Commercial Establishment for Exchange (which are, by the way, completely different companies) will change only Visa travellers' cheques, not AMEX or Thomas Cook. Some banks will not change travellers' cheques at all, some will only change brands they sell. Others will only cash cheques for account holders. Changing cash is never a problem.

There is not much of a pattern to this, though a few things can be stated with certainty: first, always have with you the original purchase receipt for the cheques, whatever brand they may happen to be, because without it few banks will exchange them. Second, try not to get stranded in the boondocks without money. As you move away from the Jeddah-Riyadh-Dhahran corridor changing money tends to become an increasingly frustrating and time-consuming experience.

If you want to get money out of an ATM your best bet is the Saudi Cairo Bank. Every branch (and there's one in every Saudi city of any size) has an ATM linked into the Cirrus and Plus networks.

Tipping

Tips are not generally expected by waiters in Saudi restaurants. The service charge added to your bill is not an automatic tip but goes straight into the till. Most waiters in the Kingdom, even in expensive hotel restaurants, are paid very small salaries and a few extra riyals would certainly be appreciated.

Foreign drivers of the white limousine taxis generally expect a small tip while the Saudis who drive most of the Kingdom's yellow cabs usually do not.

Bargaining

In Saudi Arabia the price of almost anything is negotiable up to a point. Travel agents, though not the airlines, are almost always willing to knock a few riyals off the initial price they quote you for a ticket. Hotels, too, will usually offer some sort of discount on the room rate if you ask. You can assume that food prices, in both supermarkets and restaurants, are fixed but most consumer goods are, to some extent, negotiable. Bargaining, however, frequently means asking for a discount and being offered it. After that initial offer the price may not go any lower. In a Bedouin market or the souks of Najran and Hofuf, more serious bargaining often takes place but the lengthy haggling sessions which are part of the west's mythology of Arabia are largely a thing of the past.

POST & COMMUNICATIONS
Postal Rates
Airmail postage for letters sent to addresses outside the Arab world is SR 1.50 for the first 10g and SR 1 for each additional 10g. Within Saudi Arabia and to other Arab countries postage is 75 halalas for the first 10g and 50 halalas for each additional 10g. Postcard postage is SR 1 outside the Arab world and 50 halalas inside the Kingdom and to other Arab countries.

Small packets (up to one kg) sent by air to destinations outside the Arab world cost SR 6 for the first 100g and SR 3.50 for each additional 100g. The rate for small packets sent by air to addresses inside the Kingdom or in other Arab countries is SR 3 for the first 100g and SR 1.75 for each additional 100g.

Up to five kg of printed matter can be sent by airmail for SR 4.50 for the first 100g, SR 2.50 for each additional 100g. Rates within the Kingdom and to Arab countries are SR 2 for the first 100g and SR 1.25 for each additional 100g.

Registering a package or letter costs SR 3 internationally and SR 2 inside the Arab world.

Sending Mail
The lines in Saudi post offices tend to be rather long, especially at the end of the month when many foreign workers are sending their salaries home to their families.

Any parcel you want to mail abroad must be brought to the post office open so that Saudi customs can inspect it. If the parcel includes video tapes these will have to be viewed by customs before you can mail them

out. Outside the main cities that could take a while.

Bear in mind also that postcards are a rare sight outside the main cities. The result is that you may find the card passed around the post office while the officials try to make up their minds whether that picture of camels is permissible to send through the mail. You are then likely to be charged the letter, not the postcard, rate for mailing the card. This is annoying, but the difference in price is only a few halalas and arguing, in my experience, is pointless.

Receiving Mail
This can be a problem. There is no door-to-door postal service in Saudi Arabia and mail is delivered only to post office boxes. There are no poste restante facilities and AMEX does not hold mail. The best approach is to find a sympathetic friend who will let you get mail through his or her company, or to make do without. Resident expats usually get their mail through their sponsoring company. If you are in the country on a visitor visa your sponsor's address is probably your best bet.

Telephone
Saudi Arabia has an excellent telecommunications system. Almost every town has a telephone office through which international calls can be made. Some of the telephone offices also offer fax, telex and/or telegraph service. Long-distance calls can also be made from payphones but this requires a lot of SR 1 coins – the payphones are surprisingly antiquated in comparison with the high-tech standards of the rest of the phone system. Moreover, they constantly beep throughout the call, which can get pretty annoying.

Should you need change for the phone, look for the ubiquitous change men who hang around the main banks of payphones in every town. You will recognise them by the sound they make – they announce their presence by making clinking noises with their piles of SR 1 coins. They change these for bills taking a 10% commission – ie you get nine SR 1 coins for a SR 10 note.

For directory assistance or other operator services in English dial ☎ 905.

At the time of writing, Saudi Telecom was upgrading the payphones and some more modern ones had begun appearing around the Kingdom. Card phones were also becoming an increasingly common sight, though the phonecards themselves were not yet widely available in shops.

USA Direct service is widely available in the Kingdom. The access code is 1-800-10. This service connects you to an ATT operator in the USA, allowing you to make either a collect (reverse-charge) call or to bill the call to an ATT credit card. You can only make calls to the USA using this system. Calls to other countries are not permitted.

The country code for calls to Saudi Arabia is 966. This is followed by an area code for the individual city and the local seven-digit number. The dialling-out code for international calls is 00 followed by the country code, city code and number. To make a long-distance call within the Kingdom dial 0 followed by the city code and number.

Fax, Telex & Telegraph
In addition to the telephone centres, you can send faxes or telexes from the business centres in most big hotels and from some of the larger copy shops. The latter offer a much better deal.

BOOKS
Guidebooks
There are very few guidebooks to Saudi Arabia on the market. Berlitz publishes a pocket guide to the country, though this is often outdated and of rather limited use. *The Economist Business Traveller's Guides – Arabian Peninsula* is the best among the many how-to-do-business-with-the-Arabs sort of books on the market.

Anyone interested in desert driving in central Arabia should pick up *Desert Treks from Riyadh* by Ionis Thompson. The book is a comprehensive guide to 4WD fun within a few hours of the Saudi capital. The book is

widely available at bookshops in the Riyadh area.

Travel
CM Doughty's *Travels in Arabia Deserta*, originally published in 1888, is one of the seminal works of Arabian travel literature. If you don't feel like ploughing through its 1400 pages, Penguin publishes an abridged version. Doughty's writing inspired, among others, TE Lawrence whose *Seven Pillars of Wisdom* (1926) is both a classic of modern literature and an extraordinarily self-serving account of the Arab revolt in Hejaz and Trans-Jordan during WWI. *Revolt in the Desert*, also by Lawrence, is a shortened version of Seven Pillars. Richard Burton's *Personal Narrative of a Pilgrimage to Al-Madinah & Meccah*, originally published in 1855, remains one of the few accounts of the holy cities written by a non-Muslim. Burton, travelling in disguise, joined the 1853 hajj caravan from Cairo. The pantheon of Arabian travel classics is completed by Wilfred Thesiger's 1959 memoir, *Arabian Sands*, in which he recounts his two journeys across the Empty Quarter in the late 1940s. *Fool's Paradise* (Vintage Books, New York, 1988), by Dale Walker, is an interesting description of travel in modern Saudi Arabia.

History, People & Society
Robert Lacey's *The Kingdom* is the best work on modern Saudi Arabia. *The House of Saud* by David Holden & Richard Johns focuses on the royal family and is also interesting. Peter Mansfield's *The New Arabians* contains a shorter and slightly more propagandist history of the country.

The Merchants by Michael Field includes an interesting chapter on the Alirezas, one of the Hejaz's most prominent merchant families. In a similar vein you might also want to look for *At the Drop of a Veil* by Marianne Alireza, a Californian who married into the Jeddah-based merchant family in the 1940s.

General
The Kingdom of Saudi Arabia is a Ministry of Information-sponsored coffee-table book

packed with wonderful photographs. Another book in the same vein is *Aramco and its World*, a PR piece put out by Saudi Aramco that features great photography, a good short history of Saudi Arabia and Arabian society and a very readable primer on oil and the oil industry.

Bookshops
The selection of English-language books available in the Kingdom is rather limited. Hotel bookshops and a few bookshops in the Kingdom's larger cities tend to stock mostly spy novels, a bit of pulp fiction and a few classics, often Dickens and Hemingway.

NEWSPAPERS & MAGAZINES
The *Arab News*, *Saudi Gazette* and *Riyadh Daily* are the country's English-language newspapers. *Arab News* is the largest and most widely read and is particularly interesting for its 'Islam in Perspective' column in which a leading Saudi religious scholar answers readers' questions about Islamic beliefs and practices. All of these papers tend to have fairly good foreign news coverage.

Major foreign newspapers and magazines are widely available in the Kingdom's main cities, usually at the big hotels and the large, western-style supermarkets. Periodicals usually appear two or three days after publication, by which time they have received a very thorough going-over by Saudi censors. Scantily clad women are made modest with a black felt pen. Advertisements for alcoholic beverages and articles which are regarded as politically sensitive (which includes almost anything dealing with Saudi Arabia) are ripped out of each and every copy on sale. Before buying a foreign publication you might want to flip through it quickly to see how much has been removed.

RADIO & TV
Channel 2 of Saudi Arabian TV broadcasts exclusively in English, except for a French-language newscast every night at 8 pm. The programmes are a mixture of old and heavily edited US shows and locally made documentaries and talk shows. The news in English is broadcast every night at 9 pm.

In the Eastern Province your TV choices are wider. Channel 3 is Aramco's TV station. It tends to be a more up-to-date version of Channel 2 (ie two-year-old instead of 10-year-old American programmes). It also broadcasts a lot of US sports. Viewers in the Dammam-Alkhobar area can also usually pick up the English-language stations from Bahrain (one channel carrying entertainment programmes in the evening, and an all-news channel carrying BBC World Service 24 hours a day), Qatar and, if the weather is good, Abu Dhabi.

Radio broadcasts in any language other than Arabic are rare. In the Eastern Province Radio Bahrain (98.5 FM) comes in fairly clearly. Aramco also has a station that broadcasts mostly country music. Almost everywhere else in the country you will have to stick to short-wave frequencies. In Jeddah, Riyadh and the Dhahran area you can also receive the USA's Armed Forces Radio & Television Service (AFRTS) broadcasts on FM.

PHOTOGRAPHY & VIDEO
What used to be the rule of thumb for travel in Communist countries is still a good guide in the Kingdom: never point your camera at anything that might be considered a target for bombing, blowing up or shooting at during a war.

In Saudi Arabia this always extends to mosques and includes archaeological sites, though in the latter case it is not enforced with any degree of uniformity. You should never go wandering through a souk or a Bedouin market with a camera around your neck. Keep it out of sight in a bag and ask permission before you start snapping.

Bear in mind that the Saudis are even more sensitive about videos than they are about still cameras. Videos are prohibited at some archaeological sites (notably Madain Salah), and using a camcorder pretty much anywhere is an excellent way to attract the attention of the police.

Film is easy to find in the Kingdom's main

cities, but check that it has not passed its expiry date. There are numerous shops specialising in one or two-hour photo processing, but most of these places can only handle colour prints. Slides or B&W film tend to take a lot longer, sometimes a week or more, and the results are often less than satisfactory.

TIME

The time in Saudi Arabia is GMT plus three hours. Clocks are not changed for summer time so the time difference vis-a-vis many other countries changes a couple of times a year. When it's noon in the Kingdom, the time elsewhere is:

City	Time
Paris, Rome	10 am
London	9 am
New York	4 am
Los Angeles	1 am
Perth, Hong Kong	5 pm
Sydney	7 pm
Auckland	9 pm

ELECTRICITY

Both 220V and 110V AC are found in various places in the Kingdom, though the latter is the more common of the two.

WEIGHTS & MEASURES

The metric system is used in Saudi Arabia.

LAUNDRY

There are no laundrettes in Saudi Arabia. You can either do your washing in the hotel sink, send it to the hotel laundry or look for one of the small (usually Indian-run) laundry shops that are to be found in the centre of most Saudi cities.

HEALTH

The standard of health care in Saudi Arabia is very high and almost any ailment can be treated inside the country. Many diseases which were once endemic, such as malaria, are now virtually unknown in the Kingdom. Though a cholera shot and a gamma globulin booster might not be a bad idea if you are planning to spend a lot of time far off the beaten track, there are no special precautions which need to be taken before visiting Saudi Arabia.

Health care for foreign visitors in the Kingdom is organised through their sponsor. Saudi law requires that employers provide comprehensive health coverage for all of their employees, and if you are working in the Kingdom your company will probably have a standing relationship with a particular hospital or clinic to which you will be referred for treatment. Visitors in need of medical attention should contact their sponsor. At a pinch, most big hotels have a doctor on call.

There are occasional outbreaks of diseases, such as meningitis, because of the extremely crowded conditions at the hajj. It is something which you should be aware of but should not worry about.

The quality of drinking water varies greatly in the Kingdom. Even in Riyadh and Jeddah it may be necessary to obtain 'sweet water' for drinking and cooking from a central source. This varies even from neighbourhood to neighbourhood within a given city. On the whole you should probably stick to bottled water.

See the Facts about the Region chapter for a more general discussion of health in the Gulf.

WOMEN TRAVELLERS

Men and women are strictly segregated in Saudi society and the trend over the last few years has been toward increasingly rigorous enforcement of this rule.

Restaurants usually have a family section where women, whether accompanied or not, must sit. Restaurants which do not have a family section often will not serve women, and there has been a trend in recent years to bar women entirely from some smaller shops and fast-food outlets. This varies from place to place and enforcement is generally much tighter when a particular city is experiencing a lot of matawwa activity. It does, however, work both ways. Some shops specialising in women's clothing are off limits to men. Museums and some shops have special women-only hours and banks catering only to female customers are becoming increasingly common.

Municipal buses have separate sections for women – at the back, screened off from the rest of the bus. Unaccompanied women cannot travel by inter-city bus or train and some taxi companies will not give them rides. A woman leaving the country usually has to be accompanied to the airport by her husband even if he is not travelling. Unmarried female expatriates, such as nurses, are often driven to the airport by a company representative carrying a letter authorising their departure. On arrival in the Kingdom they must be met at the airport by the sponsor or his representative. Domestic travel by air requires a letter from one's sponsor for female expatriates. No special documents are necessary for women to enter the country on a visitor visa, but unaccompanied female visitors are still unusual enough that you can certainly expect delays at the airport security checkpoints.

An unaccompanied woman cannot check into a hotel without a letter from her sponsor, and it would probably also be a good idea for the sponsor to contact the hotel in advance. Saudi Arabia's youth hostels are entirely off limits to women.

The dress regulations for women are not nearly as fearsome as has sometimes been portrayed. Obviously skirts above the knee and tight pants are out. Strictly speaking, it is not necessary for a foreign woman to wear the *abayya* (a long, black cloak-like garment) and a floor-length skirt. In practice, however, this often proves to be the path of least resistance (generally a good path to take in Saudi Arabia). In places where the matawwa are active it might be a particularly good idea. In the main cities (Riyadh, Jeddah and Dhahran/Alkhobar) and in smaller places which either have, or see a lot of, foreigners (Jubail, Yanbu, Taif, Abha, Hofuf) there is no need for foreign women to cover their heads, let alone wear a veil. In more remote or conservative areas (Jizan, Hail, Najran, Sakaka, Tabuk) it is advisable for foreign women to cover their heads. The only place where I have ever heard of foreign women having to wear veils is Buraydah.

Women who are, or appear to be, of Arab descent are likely to be held to far tighter standards of dress than western or Asian women, especially outside the main cities.

Reports of sexual harassment vary widely but leers and obscene comments, usually in Arabic, seem to be fairly common. Women in closed public spaces, like aeroplanes, should expect rather a lot of this sort of thing. Though men will stare they are less likely to touch. The general atmosphere of harassment is less intense than in places like Egypt, Tunisia or Morocco. This works both ways, as for every Saudi man who looks on you as a sex object there is another who is genuinely alarmed by the thought of even being in the same room with you.

In general it is best to remain stoic in the face of comments and to shout at, not punch, anyone who gropes you. The social opprobrium that comes from having touched a woman in public is one of your most effective weapons in these situations.

DANGERS & ANNOYANCES

Saudi Arabia is a very safe country and street crime is almost unknown. Petty theft, particularly things being stolen out of cars, is another matter. This is fairly common and, as a rule, you should not leave anything sitting on the seat of a parked car in any of the main cities.

The main thing that you will have to worry about is the rather frightening way that people drive. As a rule the driving gets crazier as one moves farther west in the country.

Men, particularly younger men, should be prepared for a certain amount of sexual harassment from other men. It is not uncommon to be propositioned in a restaurant or followed around by someone.

BUSINESS HOURS

Banks and shops in Saudi Arabia are open Saturday to Wednesday from 8 or 8.30 am until 1 or 1.30 pm. Many shops, and some banks, reopen in the late afternoon from about 4 to 7 pm. Big shopping centres, particularly in Riyadh, Jeddah and Alkhobar, may stay open until 10 pm. Few businesses are open on Thursday afternoons and almost everything is shut up tightly on Friday.

At prayer time everything closes; even Saudia stops answering its telephone numbers for reservations. The length of the prayer break can be anything from 20 minutes to an hour. If you are already inside a restaurant and eating, the staff may let you hang around and finish your meal, or they may throw you out. This usually depends on whether or not the religious police have recently been active in the area. In any event, if they do let you stay in the restaurant they are unlikely to let you leave before the place officially reopens.

PUBLIC HOLIDAYS & SPECIAL EVENTS

Wahhabism is so strict on matters of observance that no holidays other than Eid Al-Fitr and Eid Al-Adha are observed in the Kingdom (for the dates see the table of holidays near Public Holidays in the Regional Facts for the Visitor chapter). Saudi National Day is 23 September though it is not widely observed.

Much of the country, and virtually the entire government, also shuts down for two to three weeks at hajj time each year. People tend to be more preoccupied with the pilgrimage and its logistics the farther west you get. In the Eastern Province there is little change in the rhythms of life, whereas in Jeddah, and especially Mecca and Medina, the hajj consumes everyone's time for several weeks both before and after the actual week of the pilgrimage.

The Kingdom's only cultural and folkloric festival, the Jinadriyah National Festival, takes place every year at a special site about 45 km north-east of central Riyadh. See the Riyadh entry for more details.

Some of the larger western companies occasionally manage to bring in classical musical groups, though you will have to be pretty well connected to the expat grapevine to hear about these.

ACTIVITIES

Desert drives, or 'wadi bashing', are popular throughout the country and it is usually fairly easy to find someone in the local expat community who can give you advice on where to go for a picnic in the desert. There are also a couple of locally produced guidebooks on the subject (see the earlier Books section). Water sports are less common, largely because most western beach wear is considered unacceptable in the Kingdom.

LANGUAGE COURSES

It is possible to study Arabic while living or working in the Kingdom, but you have to look hard for courses. The few schools that offer Arabic classes often have to scrape around to get enough students. Free, or very cheap, Arabic lessons organised by various Islamic groups are often advertised in the English language press, though these often include a heavy dose of encouragement to convert to Islam. More to the point, the Arabic taught in such courses may be Koranic Arabic, which is far removed from everyday street Arabic. See Language Courses under Riyadh and Jeddah for further listings.

ACCOMMODATION

Places to stay range from youth hostels to five-star hotels. No matter how cheap the hotel you can count on it having air-conditioning, although a few of the cheaper places in the mountains have ceiling fans.

Saudi law requires the presentation of proper documents to check in at any hotel or hostel. For visitors this means a passport. Expatriates will require their iqama and a travel letter from their sponsor. Small hotels and youth hostels often will ask you to go out and make a photocopy of these documents if you did not arrive with copies in hand. People with a visitor visa will need photocopies of the first page of their passport and of their entry visa. Expatriates should have a copy of the page of the iqama that has the photograph on it and a copy of the travel letter. Large hotels will do this for you.

Women travelling alone need a letter from their sponsor to check into any hotel, and it is usually a good idea for the sponsor to contact the hotel in advance to double-check the arrangements.

Camping

The only formal camping grounds in Saudi Arabia are those in the Asir National Park. Sites in the park are allocated on a first come, first served basis. Camping in the desert is also popular. This should never be attempted alone or without proper equipment. The best idea is to look for travelling companions who are already experienced desert campers and accompany them.

Hostels

Saudi Arabia's youth hostels (*bayt ash-shabab* in Arabic) are a treat. They are almost always spotless, rarely crowded and are among the best in the world – a single or double room with a private bath is often standard. Stays are limited to three nights, though the management tends to be flexible about this. Unfortunately, the hostels are often located way out of town and it is not always possible to get there from the airport or bus station by public transport. The other drawback is that Saudi hostels are open only to men.

Saudi Arabia is an IYHF member and hostel cards are always required. Foreigners can purchase cards for SR 30 per year. This can be done at any hostel but the process is a lot smoother in Riyadh, Dammam and Jeddah than anywhere else. In addition to the fee you will need two passport-sized photographs, a copy of your passport or iqama and, for residents, a letter from your employer. The *Saudi Arabian Youth Hostels Federation Handbook* is available for free at all of the bigger hostels and many of the smaller ones. It contains complete listings of the Kingdom's 19 hostels and their facilities.

Hotels

Hotels usually bottom out at about SR 50 for a single without bath and around SR 70 for rooms with private bath. What you get for this price varies wildly. Always look at the room before saying yes. Bargaining is usually, though not always, an option. A lot will depend on how full the hotel is at the time. The rule of thumb seems to be that the more the room costs the better your chances are of getting a discount. In any event you should always have a clear understanding with the management of what the room rate is before you agree to stay.

The major international hotel chains are amply represented in the Kingdom. Singles/doubles in four and five-star hotels cost between SR 250/350 and SR 550/650. Some big hotels, the Abha Inter-Continental for example, have quite good weekend packages on Wednesday and Thursday nights.

FOOD

Eating cheaply in Saudi Arabia usually means eating either western-style fast food or Indian food served in rather dingy surroundings. Outside the main cities grilled chicken and *foul* (a fava beans dish) are the most common cheap meals. For a quick, and very cheap, meal try *shawarma*, beef or chicken carved from a large spit and rolled up in pita bread with some or all of the following: lettuce, tomatoes, hummous and hot sauce. They usually cost SR 3 each, and two of them and a drink make a decent meal.

For more up-market dining, every big city has a selection of moderately priced Oriental restaurants. Filipino and Thai food are the cheapest whereas Chinese food tends to be the most expensive. This is because there are many more low-paid Filipino and Thai workers than Chinese in the Kingdom. Thus, Chinese food is largely an up-market business catering to well-off Saudis and expats. The bigger cities also have a selection of up-market Lebanese, Indian and western eateries.

Traditional coffee houses, in which everyone drinks tea, not coffee, are becoming rarer. There are a few in Jeddah and in some of the provincial cities but most have yielded to western-style cafes situated in shopping malls.

Silver Jewellery

'Silver' jewellery is rarely made of pure silver. Other metals such as nickel are often included in the mix both to keep pieces affordable and to strengthen them. Silver is fairly heavy, and in its pure form looks a bit dull when placed beside pieces with a high nickel content, even when polished. Look for quality and consistency in the crafting, particularly in the detailed work around the edges of individual pieces. Much of what is available consists of very large pieces that have been chopped up and reconfigured into five or six different necklaces. There is no reason not to buy a necklace that was once a piece of something larger, but larger pieces should be examined carefully to ensure that they have not, in turn, been pieced together from a bunch of smaller cast-offs. Ultimately, Bedouin silver is something you purchase for aesthetic reasons, not as an investment, so when you go shopping buy what you like the look of.

Red coral beads are one of the main traditional decorations used on necklaces and other Bedouin jewellery, though most of the red coral you will see today is fake.

Some of the main styles of silver jewellery include:

Qiladah

Qiladah These are triangular pendants with a single stone – usually red but sometimes blue – set into the centre. Sometimes you will also see two slightly overlapping triangles. The design is also known as the 'Hand of Fatimah', after the Prophet's daughter, and it is similar in concept to the hand-shaped charms hung in most Egyptian homes to ward off the evil eye. The *qiladah* is also sometimes used as a head ornament.

Banager

Banager A *banager* is a bracelet, though the term can be extended to include armlets *(asawir)* and anklets *(khalakhil)*. Bracelet styles are extremely varied. They can be small and tightly wound, large and extremely heavy, wide and flat and fastened with a hinge, or large and hollow, making the resulting piece extremely light despite its size. Here, too, things are not always what they seem. A very heavy silver piece may consist of a relatively thin layer of silver wrapped around a copper core. Again, buy on appearance and artisanship – not for investment purposes.

Hazm *Hazm* (belts) are the biggest and heaviest jewellery pieces. They are also among the most expensive – expect to pay at least SR 500 for a good one and possibly as much as SR 800. Belts come in two basic styles. The first consists of small silver links 'woven' together. The second type (the one you will see many of the Bedouin women in the Najran souk wearing) is made up of large individual silver pieces strung together over a cloth or mesh belt. Look for uniformity in the links. As with a good *iqd* this will indicate that the belt in question was crafted as a single piece rather than assembled out of stray pieces. Also look for a belt with a clasp which works properly. Ideally, the clasp should be a small silver pin attached to the buckle by a short chain.

Kirdan *Kirdan* are collars or chest pieces made of silver mesh and decorated with a variety of different bangles. These can be very large, though most of the ones you are likely to find will probably be about 20 to 25 cm wide and 10 to 15 cm deep.

Hazm

Ilagah

Ilagah These are essentially the feminine version of an *agal* (the ropes that Saudi men use to keep their headdresses in place), and are among the hardest pieces to find. A normal *ilagah* consists of twin silver chains *(silsilah)* that lay atop the woman's head while another two or three-strand chain runs down her back. The latter will have between one and three bell-shaped ornaments. A variant on this style includes an additional two long chains which would have hung down over the wearer's ears.

Iqd Also known as *oqd*, *iqd* is the generic word for a necklace. The most traditional type is a large piece consisting of five panels – triangular ones at either end and three rectangular panels hung in-between. From each of the three centre panels hangs a *hirz*, or charm case. These are small cylinders containing scraps of paper with verses from the Koran and other charms meant to bring good luck. The hirz is usually soldered shut, though you will also occasionally find ones that can still be opened. A hirz usually has small chains, beads or other ornamentation hanging off it. The hirz and the panels to which they are connected are often broken out of the main necklace and sold separately. Since they can also be reassembled, it is important to look carefully at any five-panel iqd you are considering buying. The design should be identical on all five panels. If it is not, the necklace was probably assembled from pieces of several others.

Hirz that can be opened are usually larger pieces intended to be worn as necklaces in their own right. Another common design is a rectangular hirz hung horizontally and decorated with three oval stones. These are designed to be worn separately.

Many necklaces also incorporate Maria Theresia Dollars, or *thallers*. These silver coins were the common currency of the Gulf for much of the 19th and early 20th centuries. Regardless of when they were minted all Maria Theresia dollars bear the date 1780 (presumably the date on the original coin which the 19th century Arabian silversmiths used as a model). The coins, like most silver jewellery, are rarely more than 50 or 60 years old.

Kaffat *Kaffat* are forehead bands, woven in silver and generally about 20 cm long. While finding one is easy, finding a good one is not. Look for the closeness of the weave and the quality of the craftwork. ∎

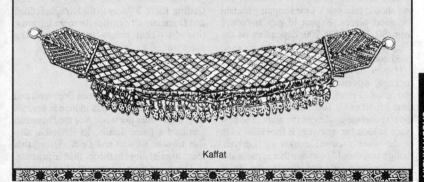

Kaffat

DRINKS

The selection consists of soft drinks, mineral water and fruit juice. 'Saudi champagne', which you will sometimes see on menus and which can generally be ordered by name, is a mixture of apple juice and Perrier.

ENTERTAINMENT

Almost every form of public entertainment is banned in Saudi Arabia. This includes cinemas, theatres and even lounge singers in hotel restaurants. The exceptions are sporting events and the annual folklore festival near Riyadh. Soccer and camel racing are the most popular spectator sports. Unless you read Arabic, however, it is very difficult to keep up with the soccer scene in the Kingdom because the English-language newspapers tend to ignore it. The games are played at the local stadiums and tickets tend to be fairly cheap (around SR 10), though you'll need to have some Arab friends to know when the matches are scheduled to take place. Camel races take place throughout the winter months. The best place to see them is in Riyadh, where there is a large camel track just outside the city centre.

THINGS TO BUY

Among the best buys in the Kingdom is silver Bedouin jewellery. Although this is a Yemeni speciality, you can find a good selection in the souks of Khamis Mushayt and Najran and at a few shops in Riyadh and Jeddah. Bedouin jewellery is wonderful and one should take one's time shopping around for good pieces. Expect to pay anywhere from SR 100 to SR 700, depending on the size and intricacy of the work, for pieces in good condition.

If you have plenty of space in your luggage, woven Bedouin bags make great souvenirs. Prices, after bargaining, range from SR 50 to SR 1000, again depending on the size and the quality of the work. The best place to look for weavings is the Hofuf souk or the weekly camel market in Nairiyah, though you should be aware that as more and more foreigners are now visiting the Hofuf souk the merchants there have taken to importing mass-produced weavings from Syria to keep up with demand.

Most of the other Arabian souvenirs you will see in shops around the Kingdom – incense burners, for example – come from somewhere else, usually Pakistan. The exception is the small pottery incense burners for sale in Jizan.

Gold jewellery is also good to buy as the work can be quite striking and the pieces are relatively inexpensive.

Getting There & Away

AIR

A return plane ticket from the USA to Saudi Arabia is likely to cost over US$1000, even if purchased from a bucket shop. From Europe it is not a lot cheaper. Flying out of Saudi Arabia to North America, Europe and the Far East is usually much cheaper. Fares fluctuate wildly, and cheap fares are usually available only through travel agents, not the airlines.

Youth/student fares are often available for international travel out of the Kingdom but they are rarely, if ever, the cheapest way to fly. Don't count on the travel agent to tell you this. If you ask for a youth fare (the cutoff age is usually 26) without mentioning other options, most of the Kingdom's travel agents will simply quote a price and will not point out the cheaper fares, if they exist. See Getting There & Away in the Riyadh, Jeddah and Dammam city entries for more information on ticket prices to and from the Kingdom.

LAND
Other Gulf States

SAPTCO runs buses between Dammam and Abu Dhabi and Dubai (six to nine hours, SR 170) three times per week. See the Dammam section for more details. Its timetable also lists trips to Kuwait and Doha (Qatar) that seem to exist more in theory than in practice.

There are five buses per day between Bahrain and Dammam/Alkhobar. The trip takes about three hours and costs SR 40 one way and SR 70 return. See the Dammam section for more details.

Egypt

There are daily bus services from Riyadh, Jeddah and Dammam to Cairo via Aqaba (Jordan) and via Dhuba, on the Kingdom's northern Red Sea coast. From Riyadh the trip to Cairo takes 36 to 40 hours and costs between SR 350 and SR 400 depending on who you travel with and where you cross the Red Sea. Jeddah-Cairo costs SR 290 to SR 320 and takes about 36 hours. From Dammam the trip takes about 48 hours and costs SR 410 to SR 455. All of these prices include the ferry crossing between Saudi Arabia or Jordan and Egypt. Buses are operated both by the government-run Saudi Arabian Public Transport Company (SAPTCO), and by a number of private foreign carriers.

From Cairo, all buses to Saudi Arabia leave from the Alexandria Bank building on Kasr El-Nil St. One-way tickets are E£250 to Riyadh, E£220 to Jeddah and E£300 to Dammam. These can be obtained from Marrakech Travel (☎ 354 6046) at the corner of Tahrir St and Tahrir Square in Cairo.

See the Riyadh, Jeddah and Dammam sections for more details.

Jordan & Syria

SAPTCO has buses from Riyadh, Jeddah and Dammam to both Amman and Damascus. The service is daily out of Riyadh and several times per week out of Jeddah and Dammam. A ticket to either city costs SR 200 regardless of where your trip starts or finishes. The trip to Amman takes about 20 hours from Riyadh and Jeddah. Damascus is about a 30 hour trip. From Dammam the journey times are 24 hours to Amman and 36 hours to Damascus. Jordan is a particularly competitive route out of Riyadh and some comparison shopping at the travel offices around the Riyadh bus station could save you SR 50 or so.

You can also travel to Jordan and Syria on the Istanbul-bound buses run by the Turkish

companies. They offer slightly cheaper fares than SAPTCO to Amman, but not to Damascus.

See the Riyadh, Jeddah and Dammam sections for more details.

Turkey

After a lull following the Gulf War, service between Riyadh and Istanbul has picked up again. Both SAPTCO and a clutch of Turkish companies offer service several times a week. The one-way fare is SR 260. You may initially be quoted fares in the SR 340 to SR 360 range, but these are fares for Turkish citizens that include the cost of Syrian and Jordanian transit visas. Since virtually everyone using these buses is Turkish the people running the line sometimes forget that they do not offer this visa service to other nationalities. If you're not Turkish you are expected to arrange your Syrian and Jordanian visas yourself, in advance.

SAPTCO says it takes only 48 hours to get from Riyadh to Istanbul, but I would recommend that you take that claim with a very large pinch of salt. Several Turkish bus companies offer service three times a week from Jeddah to Istanbul for SR 260 and claim a rather more believable journey time of 72 hours. The buses travel via Ankara (60 hours, same fare). The Dammam-Istanbul fare is SR 300 on SAPTCO. See the Riyadh, Jeddah and Dammam sections for more details.

SEA

Egypt

The car ferry connecting Jeddah with Suez is the main seaborne route in and out of the country. The trip takes about 36 hours if the boat travels directly between Suez and Jeddah and about three days if it stops in Aqaba, Jordan. At the time of writing, there was no service between Jeddah and Aqaba, but you should keep this in mind should the service resume. Unfortunately you cannot always count on being accurately informed of the route the boat is taking. The food on these boats is pretty dreadful so you might want to bring your own (enough to last for the longer trip). The trip is very long and very dull, and the heat and humidity on the Red Sea can become fierce. Fares range from SR 225 on the deck to SR 500 in 1st class. All of the boats to Egypt take cars as well. Fares for small cars start at SR 500.

See the Jeddah Getting There & Away section for details.

Jordan

At the time of writing there was no regular boat service between Jeddah and the Jordanian port of Aqaba. You might be better advised to take the bus. The shipping agencies along Al-Mina'a St in Jeddah which sell tickets to Egypt and Sudan also sell tickets to Aqaba when there are tickets to sell. See Getting There & Away under Jeddah.

Sudan

Regular passenger shipping services operate between Jeddah and Port Sudan. If you try this, be sure that your visa allows it – many Sudanese visas issued to foreigners now come stamped 'By Air Only', and Sudanese customs officials are not flexible in such matters. Once in Port Sudan you will have to register with the security police and obtain a travel permit to continue on to Khartoum or anywhere else. This process usually takes at least several days. The trip to Port Sudan takes 10 to 12 hours and costs between SR 300 and SR 400 depending on the class of ticket you buy. For details see the Jeddah Getting There & Away section.

Eritrea

You can also travel by boat between Jeddah and Musawwa. The trip takes 18 to 20 hours and costs SR 300 to SR 400. For more details see the Jeddah Getting There & Away section.

LEAVING SAUDI ARABIA

Departing from the Kingdom through Riyadh, Jeddah, Dhahran or Medina airports is fairly straightforward. You should be at the airport two hours before the scheduled departure time. Flights to India, Pakistan and Egypt tend to be filled with workers who are taking home small mountains of electronic

goods and presents. Check-in procedures for these routes tend to be very slow, mostly because of the time needed to figure out everybody's excess luggage bills, so it might be a good idea to arrive even earlier.

On flights to London and New York at Christmas time, and to Cairo during peak periods (such as the January school vacations), Saudia and EgyptAir often require that passengers obtain their boarding passes three days in advance, presumably to prevent overbooking. Check with the airline to see whether this rule is still in force. In any event always reconfirm your flight.

Departure Tax

There is no departure tax for international flights leaving Saudi Arabia.

Getting Around

AIR

All domestic air services in the Kingdom are operated by Saudia (Saudi Arabian Airlines), which is quite reliable. The most frequent and efficient service is on the Jeddah-Riyadh-Dhahran corridor.

Because of the size of the country, air travel is the main mode of transport. Considering the distances involved, Saudia's domestic services, though no great bargain, are reasonably priced. There are, however, a few quirks in the system. There are no flights, for example, on some regional routes like Abha-Najran and Abha-Jizan that would seem like obvious city pairings. Flying between these cities involves backtracking to Jeddah which is both expensive and time-consuming.

The table of fares in this section shows the air routes between the Kingdom's main cities. All of the fares shown are one-way economy class and are quoted in Saudi riyals. Round-trip fares are double the one-way fare. Some of the routes shown in the table may require a change of aircraft in either Riyadh or Jeddah.

For more detailed information on direct

Airfares

	Riyadh	Jeddah	Dhahran	Medina	Hail	Taif	Abha	Jizan	Najran	Tabuk	Sakaka
Riyadh		240	140	240	190	240	270	310	270	380	270
Jeddah	270		410	130	240	100	180	190	240	270	290
Dhahran	140	410		370	330	380	410	450	410	520	400
Medina	240	130	370		140	230	310	320	370	180	190
Hail	190	240	330	140		430	*420	500	460	210	100
Taif	240	100	380	230	430		140	190	*340	370	510
Abha	270	180	410	310	*420	140		*370	*420	450	540
Jizan	310	190	450	320	500	190	*370		140	460	580
Najran	270	240	410	370	460	*340	*420	140		650	540
Tabuk	380	270	520	180	210	370	450	460	650		140
Sakaka	270	290	400	190	100	510	540	580	540	140	

* Direct flights are not available on all routes and a change of planes (probably in either Jeddah or Riyadh) may be required.
Note that in Saudia's published timetables 'Sakaka' appears as 'Jouf'. ■

air connections to and from each city, see the various individual city listings. You can also stop by any Saudia office for an up-to-date timetable.

BUS

Getting around by bus is probably your best bet if you are not pressed for time and do not have a car. Bus fares are one-half to two-thirds of the equivalent airfare. In Asir, where there are few flights between the main towns and flying often requires going back to Jeddah, the bus will probably be just as quick and the fare may be only about 20% of what a flight would cost. The view is also likely to be a lot better.

SAPTCO operates comfortable, air-conditioned buses that usually run on time. On longer routes the buses have an on-board toilet and in all cases the buses make rest stops every couple of hours.

You can buy bus tickets only on the day of departure or one day in advance. There are no seat reservations but when you purchase a ticket your name will be added to a passenger list for the specific bus you request. This ensures that the buses do not get overbooked. When purchasing tickets you will also have to show identification and, for residents, a travel letter.

Women are not allowed to ride inter-city buses unless they are accompanied by their husband or a male relative.

SERVICE-TAXI

Service-taxis usually cluster around the bus station in each city and cover most of the destinations the buses go to at the same prices. They leave when full, which could mean anything from five to 11 passengers, depending on the size of the vehicle.

TRAIN

Saudi Arabia has the only stretch of railway track on the entire Arabian Peninsula – one line from Riyadh to Dammam, via Hofuf and Abqaiq. Trains leave three times a day in each direction every day except Thursday, when there is only one train. Note that the noon train does not stop in Abqaiq in either direction. The regular schedule is:

From Riyadh (daily except Thursday)

departs Riyadh	8.00 am	1.10 pm	6.20 pm
departs Hofuf	10.40 am	3.50 pm	9.00 pm
departs Abqaiq	11.22 am	---	9.42 pm
arrives Dammam	12.05 pm	5.12 pm	10.25 pm

From Riyadh (Thursday only)

departs Riyadh	9.24 am
departs Hofuf	12.04 pm
departs Abqaiq	12.46 pm
arrives Dammam	1.29 pm

SAUDI ARABIA

From Dammam (daily except Thursday)

departs Dammam	7.00 am	12.13 pm	5.20 pm
departs Abqaiq	7.46 am	---	6.06 pm
departs Hofuf	8.32 am	1.42 pm	6.52 pm
arrives Riyadh	11.05 am	4.15 pm	9.25 pm

From Dammam (Thursday only)

departs Dammam	9.00 am
departs Abqaiq	9.46 am
departs Hofuf	10.32 am
arrives Riyadh	1.05 pm

Classes

Saudi trains have both 1st and 2nd-class carriages. There is also a restaurant car. Sandwiches, coffee, tea and soft drinks can be purchased from vendors in the passenger section.

Reservations

The trains are not very crowded but it still pays to buy your ticket a day or so in advance, or in the morning for the evening train. The process of scrutinising people's IDs both when tickets are purchased and when going through security before boarding can be a bit slow. Also note that the ticket windows in the stations close at prayer time, meaning you'll have to get the ticket early if departure and prayer times coincide.

Costs

At SR 60 one way, a 1st-class train ticket between Riyadh and Dammam costs the same as the bus and delivers a much more comfortable ride. At SR 40 one way, a 2nd-class ticket is the cheapest way to travel between Riyadh and the Eastern Province. Children under 12 travel for half price.

CAR & MOTORCYCLE

Despite its large public transport system, Saudi Arabia remains a country which glorifies the private car to an extent rivalled only by the USA. It is possible to get around in a Saudi city without your own wheels but it's a real pain in the neck, especially in Riyadh. Even if you save money by taking buses between cities there is a lot to be said for renting a car at each destination.

Motorcycles are a fairly rare sight on Saudi roads.

Road Rules

Saudi Arabia's most famous rule of the road is the one which says that women are not allowed to drive. Aside from that, however, there is nothing particularly surprising. Driving is on the right side of the road. Right turns are allowed at red lights unless specifically forbidden. Indeed, if you don't plan to turn right, get over into one of the left lanes or someone is likely to come up behind you and lean on their horn until you move. The speed limit is usually 120 km/h on open highways, and 50 or 60 km/h in towns. While citations for speeding are rare, be aware that they also involve a night in jail.

Rental

If you are in the country on a visitor visa you can rent a car on a driving licence from most western countries. There does not seem to be a firm list of which countries' national licences are accepted and which are not. If you carry a passport from an African, Arab, East European or Asian country (aside from Japan or Singapore) it might be prudent to show up with an International Driving Permit in hand. Licences from other GCC countries are only accepted from GCC nationals and people who can show that they live in the country that issued the licence.

Rental rates are government controlled, with mandatory insurance and collision-damage waiver. In addition, all companies seem to rent the same line of cars so there's not much point in shopping around. If you are going to be taking the car to different parts of the country it is a good idea to stick to the larger agencies. If you get into trouble or decide to drop the car off early, a company with offices around the Kingdom can prove much more useful than a small, local agency.

Rates start at SR 110 for a Toyota Corolla or similar. That includes insurance and 100 free km per day. Additional km are 40 halalas each. A discount of 20, 25 or 30% on this price is almost always available for the asking, and since it has usually been agreed on among the rental companies, shopping around for discounts is about as pointless as shopping around for rates.

Technically, the law requires that anyone renting a car produce a letter from their sponsor guaranteeing the cost of the rental and that this letter be stamped by the Chamber of Commerce. In practice, a credit card imprint is usually sufficient, and some companies will accept a cash deposit.

Motorcycles and 4WD vehicles are difficult, if not impossible, to rent.

Petrol

Saudi Arabia is a famously cheap place to fill up your gas tank. There is only one grade of petrol in Saudi Arabia and it sells for 60 halalas per litre almost everywhere. The exceptions are some stations in remote locations which may sell petrol at 63 or 64 halalas per litre.

Purchase

Expats usually buy cars from other expats, if only to save time on the paperwork. Company cars are still a fairly standard perk for most foreigners in the Kingdom, language teachers excepted.

BICYCLE

Bicycles, like motorcycles, are a rare sight in the Kingdom.

HITCHING

Hitching is common in the Kingdom among less well-off Saudis and among Indians, Pakistanis, Filipinos etc. It is rare enough among westerners that anyone trying it would be likely to attract the unwelcome attention of the first policeman who happened by. In the Hejaz and Asir regions, hitchers are usually expected to pay the equivalent of the bus fare along the same route.

WALKING

Saudi Arabia is a car-oriented society. Distances within cities are long and walking can be considered downright weird. I was once questioned by the police for taking a stroll around the neighbourhood where I was living at the time. In any case the heat makes walking any significant distance a chore during most of the year.

BOAT

There are no domestic boat services along either the Gulf or the Red Sea coasts.

LOCAL TRANSPORT
The Airport

Getting to the airport in a Saudi city is not always straightforward. In Riyadh there are no buses, only very expensive taxis. In Jeddah only one of the airport's two terminals is served by bus. In Dhahran buses run to the airport frequently, though when the new Dhahran airport opens this may not be the case. See the individual city entries for more information.

Bus

Full-scale municipal bus systems operate in Riyadh, Jeddah and the Dammam-Alkhobar area of the Eastern Province. Smaller scale local services operate in cities like Taif and Abha. Local fares are always SR 2. Riyadh and Jeddah also have confusing minivan systems which operate more or less along the main SAPTCO bus routes. These also charge SR 2 per trip.

Taxi

Taxis in the Kingdom's main cities have meters. See the individual city entries for details on the prices of flag falls and per km charges. On the whole, Saudi Arabia is a pretty cheap place to take a taxi.

ORGANISED TOURS

A few of the big hotels in Abha and Hofuf organise city tours and the Medina Sheraton runs a very popular weekend tour to Madain Salah and the Hejaz Railway. There is also one private-sector tour operator based in Riyadh offering trips to Madain Salah and other destinations around the country. See the relevant city sections for more details.

Riyadh

Riyadh (Riyad, Riad, Ar-Riyadh) rises from the desert like a high-tech oasis of glass, steel and concrete. There are freeways, office towers, housing that stretches off beyond the horizon, big hotels, bigger hospitals and one of the biggest airports in the world – none of which was here 30 years ago.

While Riyadh, and the nearby oasis town of Dir'aiyah, are the ancestral home of the Al-Saud family, it is only in the last generation that Riyadh has become the centre of government in the Kingdom. Though technically Saudi Arabia's capital since the nation's establishment in 1932, it was eclipsed by Jeddah until quite recently. The ministries, embassies and just about everything else were headquartered in Jeddah well into the 1970s.

History
Riyadh is an oasis city built on the remains of an earlier settlement known as Hajer. The name Riyadh has been in use since at least the 12th century AD, though the city's founding is usually dated to sometime around 1746 when a wall was built around several of the existing settlement's buildings. This walled area became what is now the old city's core – the area around the Masmak Fortress.

Riyadh became the Al-Saud's capital after 1818 when the family was driven out of Dir'aiyah by soldiers loyal to the Ottoman sultan. The village was not part of the family's ancestral territory but it had fallen under their control in the mid-18th century, as the First Saudi Empire was being built. After making Riyadh their capital, the Al-Saud spent most of the 19th century using it as a base for a seemingly endless series of tribal wars, most notably with the Al-Rashid clan, whose base was the northern city of Hail. In 1891 the Al-Saud were forced to abandon the city to the Al-Rashid and wandered for a time along the edges of the Empty Quarter before migrating north to seek refuge in Kuwait.

It was from Kuwait that the young Abdul Aziz launched his now famous raid on the family capital, beginning the string of conquests which would eventually restore the Al-Saud as masters of most of the Arabian Peninsula. Between Abdul Aziz's conquest of the city in 1902 and his death in 1953 very little changed in Riyadh. Even the advent of Saudi Arabia's oil era had little immediate effect on the city. Most government affairs continued to be carried out from Jeddah until the 1970s and it was not until the end of that decade that many of the foreign embassies finally moved to what had long been Saudi Arabia's capital more on paper than in practice.

Throughout the 1950s and '60s, change came to Riyadh in a slow, measured way but during the '70s the pace accelerated dramatically. Even by Gulf standards Riyadh is a very new city – almost nothing that you can see in Riyadh today predates WWII and a great deal of it is less than 20 years old.

Orientation
In addition to being new and spotlessly clean, Riyadh is a sprawling mess that you'll only find easy to navigate if you can read Arabic. Unfortunately, most of the usable maps of the city are also available only in Arabic.

The first thing you should do is get a copy of the Farsi map and learn the names of the main districts. Because most of the road signs are only in Arabic, directions in Riyadh are often given in relation to landmarks, but this system relies on your having some knowledge of the main districts. Al-Bathaa is the central, older portion of town immediately adjacent to which are Masmak, Al-Murabba and Al-Wazarat. North of these areas lie Olaya and Sulaymaniyah, the main residential and business areas for the capital's business community.

To the extent that Riyadh has any centre at all it is the Al-Bathaa district, more or less the area around Al-Bathaa St and Al-Malek (King) Faisal St between Al-Washem and

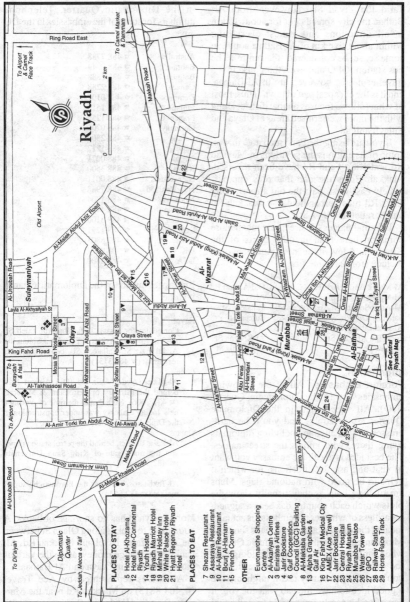

Riyadh

To Airport
& Camel
Race Track

0   1   2 km

Ring Road East

To Camel Market
& Dammam

Makkah Road

Old Airport

Al-Malek Abdul Aziz Road

Al-Uroubah Road

Sulaymaniyah

Layla Al-Akhyaliyah St

Mosa Ibn Nosayr Street

Olaya

King Fahd Road

Al-Amir Mohammad Ibn Abdul Aziz Road

Al-Amir Soltan Ibn Abdul Aziz Street

Aziz Ibn Masoud Ibn Jalawi Street

Al-Amir Abdul

Olaya Street

Al-Takhassosi Road

To
Burayidah
& Hail

To Airport

Al-Amir Torki Ibn Abdul Aziz (Al-Awal) Road

Makkah Road

Umm Al-Hamam Street

Al-Malek Khaled Road

To Di'raiyah

Diplomatic Quarter

To Jeddah, Mecca & Taif

Al-Uroubah Road

Al-Ihsa Street

Salah Al-Din Al-Ayubi Road

Al-Malek (King) Abdul Aziz Road

Al-Dhahran Street

Al-Wazarat

Ma'ahad Al-Edarah

Al-Wesham Al-Jami'ah Street

Al-Mather Street

Al-Batha'a Street

Faisal Street

Omar Ibn Al-Khattab

Al-Amir Faisal Ibn Torki Ibn Abdul St

Al-Malek (King) Fahd Road

Abu Feras
Al-Hamdani
Street

Al-Murabba

Al-Batha'a

Al-Malek Saud Street

Amro Ibn Al-A'as Street

Al-Imam Faisal Street

Al-Imam

Al-Imam Torki Ibn Abdula Street

Abdul Aziz Ibn Mohammad

Al-Wesham Al-Jami'ah Street

Omar Al-Mokhtar Street

Tariq Ibn Ziyad Street

Abdula Street

Al-Khari Road

Al-Amir Salman Ibn Abdul Aziz

See Central
Riyadh Map

PLACES TO STAY
5 Hotel Al-Khozama
12 Hotel Inter-Continental
   Riyadh
14 Youth Hostel
18 Riyadh Marriott Hotel
19 Minhal Holiday Inn
20 White Palace Hotel
21 Hyatt Regency Riyadh
   Hotel

PLACES TO EAT
7 Shezan Restaurant
9 Assaraya Restaurant
10 Al-Ajami Restaurant
11 Bourj Al-Hamam
15 French Corner

OTHER
1 Euromarche Shopping
   Centre
2 Al-Akariyah Centre
3 Emirates Airlines
4 Jarir Bookstore
6 Gulf Cooperation
   Council (GCC) Building
8 Al-Maktaba Garden
13 Alpha Graphics &
   Gulf Air
16 King Fahd Medical City
17 AMEX (Ace Travel)
22 Jarir Bookstore
23 Central Hospital
24 Riyadh Museum
25 Murabba Palace
26 War Tower
27 GPO
28 Railway Station
29 Horse Race Track

SAUDI ARABIA

Tariq Ibn Ziyad Sts. However, from Al-Bathaa the city spreads out for about 10 km in all directions and almost everything within about five km of Al-Bathaa could, in some sense, be considered 'the centre'. The bus station, GPO and everything else that a traveller needs, however, are in Al-Bathaa, and it is the cheapest part of town. Thus, most of what follows focuses on that district along with the more westernised areas of Olaya and Sulaymaniyah.

If you are using the Farsi map note that on some of its editions the positions of Makkah Rd and King Fahd Rd have been reversed. Makkah Rd is the one that runs approximately east-west, past the old airport. King Fahd Rd runs perpendicular to Makkah Rd and parallel to Olaya St.

Informal names for streets are much more common here than in other parts of the Kingdom. A few of the more important ones include (formal name first):

Al-Malek Abdul Aziz Rd:	Old Airport Rd
Al-Malek Faisal St:	Al-Wazir St
Al-Amir Soltan Ibn Abdul Aziz St:	Tallateen St
Salah Al-Din Al-Ayoubi Rd:	Sitteen St
Al-Imam Faisal Ibn Torki Ibn Abdulla St:	Al-Khazan St
Al-Ihsa St:	Pepsi Cola St

Information

Foreign Embassies All of the following embassies are in the Diplomatic Quarter (DQ). All street signs in the Diplomatic Quarter are in Arabic and you'll be hard-pressed to find anyone, including diplomats living there, who knows the street names. The best idea is to call the embassy you want to visit and ask for directions, for which it helps to be good with national flags. Maps are of little help as they usually show the plots which each country has been assigned, regardless of whether the embassy is actually located there (for example, all maps show the Mexican embassy in the Diplomatic Quarter when, in fact, it is in an office building near the old airport). Allow time to get lost. If you're getting about by taxi it might also be a good idea to have the cab wait for you. It can often be nearly impossible to find a taxi

in the Diplomatic Quarter. Telephone numbers for some of the embassies in the DQ are:

Australia	☎ 488 7788
Bahrain	☎ 488 0044
Belgium	☎ 488 2888
Canada	☎ 488 2288
Denmark	☎ 488 0101
Finland	☎ 488 1515
France	☎ 488 1255
Germany	☎ 488 0700
Ireland	☎ 488 2300
Italy	☎ 488 1212
Jordan	☎ 488 0071
Kuwait	☎ 488 3500
Netherlands	☎ 488 0011
New Zealand	☎ 488 7988
Norway	☎ 488 1904
Pakistan	☎ 488 4111
Sweden	☎ 488 3100
Switzerland	☎ 488 1291
UAE	☎ 482 6803
UK	☎ 488 0077
USA	☎ 488 3800

Embassies outside of the Diplomatic Quarter include:

Egypt
Consulate (for visas): Ja'far Ibn Abi Taleb St, Al-Sulaymaniya district, off Al-Amir Soltan Ibn Abdul Aziz St (Tallateen St), behind the KFC restaurant (☎ 465 3131)
India
Al-Malek Abdul Aziz Rd (Old Airport Rd), behind the Ministry of Petroleum & Minerals (☎ 477 7006). Note that at the time of writing a new Indian embassy was under construction in the Diplomatic Quarter.
Oman
Al-Ra'id district, behind the petrol station opposite the main gate of King Saud University (☎ 482 3120)
Qatar
Al-Takhassosi Rd, near the Euromarche supermarket (☎ 482 5544)

Money Riyadh has no shortage of banks. A good place to look is along Olaya St between the Al-Khozama Hotel and Makkah Rd. All banks here change money, as do the various moneychangers in Olaya and Al-Bathaa.

AMEX is represented by Ace Travel (☎ 464 8813) on Makkah Rd near the Marriott Riyadh Hotel and the junction with

Al-Ma'ther St. It is open Saturday to Thursday from 9 am to 1.30 pm and 4.30 to 8 pm, closed Friday. Cheques are cashed for card holders through a nearby bank. Lost AMEX cards can be replaced in one day, but the AMEX client's mail service is not available.

Post The GPO, on Al-Malek Abdul Aziz Rd, near the intersection with Al-Bathaa St, is open Saturday to Wednesday from 7.50 am to 2.50 pm and from 4 to 10.30 pm. Mumtaz Post (express mail) service is available Thursday from 7.30 am to 1 pm. The post office is closed Friday. There is no poste restante service.

Telephone & Fax There are several sets of international call cabins around the city. The most central ones are by the Al-Foutah Garden at the intersection of Al-Dhahirah and Al-Imam Faisal Ibn Torki Ibn Abdulla Sts. There are also call cabins on Jareer St, near the intersection with Salah Al-Din Al-Ayoubi Rd.

If you need to send a fax try Alpha Graphics (☎ 464 1600) on Olaya St just south of the intersection with Makkah Rd. They charge SR 12 per minute to the USA, UK and Germany, SR 17 to Australia and SR 5 to other Gulf countries. Unlike hotel business centres there is no three minute minimum and portions of a minute are charged as such, not rounded up.

The telephone code for Riyadh is 01.

Travel Agencies Riyadh has lots of travel agencies, but I am always reluctant to issue recommendations on this score because of the high turnover rate at these places. If you need to talk to a travel agent AMEX is probably your best bet in the first instance.

Bookshops The best selection of English, French and German books is at the Jarir Bookstore. They have two branches in Riyadh. One is on Olaya St just south of the intersection with Mosa Ibn Nosayr St, the other is on Al-Ihsa St in the Al-Malaz district.

Cultural Centres Some of the cultural centres in Riyadh include:

Alliance Française (☎ 476 6436), Al-Dhobbat, just behind the Hyatt Regency Hotel and the Saudi Industrial Development Fund building. It has a library, from which you can borrow books after paying a SR 50 membership fee. Membership also entitles you to attend films, exhibits and other cultural programmes. These are held about three times a month.

British Council (☎ 462 1818), Level Two, Tower B of the Al-Musa building, on Olaya St, opposite the King Fahd library. Library membership costs SR 160 for six months.

Medical Services Though Riyadh has an abundance of hospitals many of the best known ones are either reserved for the royal family, the military or some other class of VIPs, or they are highly specialised. Embassies can usually steer their nationals toward doctors in emergencies. Expats will have a company doctor.

The Dallah Hospital (☎ 454 5277) at the intersection of King Fahd Rd and Al-Imam Saud Ibn Abdul Aziz Ibn Mohammad Rd takes emergency cases on a walk-in basis.

Emergency Dial ☎ 999 for the police, ☎ 997 for an ambulance, ☎ 998 to report a fire.

Site Permits Permits for visits to all forts and archaeological sites in the country, except for those in the Eastern Province, can be obtained at the Riyadh Museum. Permits for sites in the Eastern Province are issued at the museum in Dammam (except for sites in Hofuf, for which permits must be obtained in Riyadh). The only exceptions to this rule are the Masmak Fortress, Dir'aiyah and the Najran Fort, for which permits are not required.

For permits, which are issued free, bring your passport or iqama. If you are a foreigner resident in Saudi Arabia and the permit you are requesting involves a trip outside the province in which you live you will also need a travel letter from your sponsor approving your plans. The office which issues permits

SAUDI ARABIA

is at the back of the museum compound. Enter from a side street at the green sign marked 'Ministry of Education, General Department of Antiquities & Museums'.

Riyadh Museum

Start your tour of Riyadh at the museum (☎ 411 2576) in the Department of Antiquities building on Al-Imam Abdul Aziz Ibn Mohammed St in the Umm Seleem district, near the Central Hospital. It's open Saturday to Wednesday from 8 am to 2 pm and admission is free. An office by the main hall exit door sells pamphlet-sized guides to the museum and other sites of interest around the Kingdom. The guide to the museum itself costs SR 15 but is a waste of money – it merely repeats the text on the signs on the wall.

After you enter through the main gate the **Ethnographic Hall** is immediately to your right. Its centrepiece is a large model of the Masmak Fortress. The rest of the display includes carved and painted doors from Qassim (the region immediately north of Riyadh) and Qatif (a largely Shiite town in the Eastern Province which was once the major port on the Arab side of the Gulf). Also on display are clothes, musical instruments, weapons, cooking utensils, several beautiful woven bags and some jewellery.

The **main hall** is straight on from the main gate. The displays are well laid out with signs in both English and Arabic. The introductory display contains some items from archaeological digs in the Eastern Province. Turn right and follow the displays around the main hall, moving from the Stone Age to early Islam. The galleries are particularly thorough on geography and archaeology. The last room of the exhibit has an interesting display on Islamic architecture.

Masmak Fortress

This was the citadel in the heart of Old Riyadh and the residence of the Al-Rashid garrison that Abdul Aziz and his small band overcame in January 1902 to regain control of the city. During the raid one of the future king's companions heaved a spear at the door

with such force that the head is still lodged in the doorway (look just to the right of the centre panel of the small door set into the main door). The fortress is built of dried mud. It is now used as a museum honouring Abdul Aziz and his unification of the various regions that make up the Kingdom of Saudi Arabia.

Masmak is open Saturday to Wednesday from 8 am to noon and from 4 to 8 pm. Sunday and Tuesday are for families only. Admission is free and permits are not required. You should, however, be aware that Masmak is a standard stop on all VIP itineraries in the Kingdom and the presence of even a relatively minor personage (such as a newly arrived ambassador) will mean that the fortress is closed to everyone else. The Saudi Arabian Department of Antiquities publishes a fairly good guide to the fortress. The guide, which costs SR 5, can be purchased at the Riyadh Museum.

Masmak was built around 1865 on the site of an earlier fortification that had existed since the early 19th century. It was extensively renovated in the late 1980s and converted into the museum you see today in the early '90s.

Once inside you will find a nicely reconstructed traditional diwan (sitting room or formal reception area) on the ground floor. An open courtyard at the rear of this level has a well which still works, and is surrounded by six interestingly painted doors. On both the ground floor and the upper level large red arrows guide you through the story of both Abdul Aziz's military career and the accompanying growth of Riyadh. The first few rooms of this display contain a fascinating collection of photographs of the city taken between 1914 and 1919.

The display continues on the upper level with placards describing the Kingdom's modern accomplishments in such fields as medical services, finance and telecommunications.

Murabba Palace

This combination fortress/palace was built by King Abdul Aziz in 1946 (an inscription over the main door dates it to 1365 AH). Permits are required here and it's open Saturday to Wednesday from 8 am to 2 pm. The Saudi Arabian Department of Antiquities publishes a fairly good guide to the palace which can be purchased at the Riyadh Museum for SR 5.

The palace's lower level consists of a courtyard with a date palm growing in its centre and surrounded by a number of closed rooms.

The upper level has a display of traditional clothes and crafts. Note the enormous camel saddle in the room immediately to your left at the top of the stairs. Another part of this level is the hall which was Abdul Aziz's formal reception area for guests. It contains mostly chairs and carpets though some old rifles are also on display.

King Faisal Centre for Research & Islamic Studies

The King Faisal Centre has a gallery of manuscripts and Islamic art in its complex behind the Al-Khozama Hotel in Olaya. The centre usually has an exhibit focusing on some aspect of Islamic art or culture, though not always. Admission to the exhibits is free. The upper floor of the hall houses a small permanent exhibition on the treatment and preservation of old books and manuscripts.

King Saud University Museum

King Saud University, on the western edge of Riyadh near the Diplomatic Quarter, has a small museum displaying finds from the university's archaeological digs at Al-Faw and Rabdhah.

Al-Faw, on the edge of the Empty Quarter, is a pre-Islamic site which reached its peak between 300 BC and 300 AD. The beautiful miniature bronze statues discovered there and displayed in the museum show both Egyptian and Nabataean influences. Rabdhah, about 100 km east of Medina, was a station on the Zubaydah Pilgrims Road which linked Mecca and Medina with Persia and Iraq. (See the boxed section under Birkat Al-Khurabah later in this chapter.)

The museum is open from Saturday to Wednesday (mornings only), but to visit it you must first make an appointment through the university's public relations office (☎ 467 8135). They may make the appointment for you, or you may be referred directly to the museum's curator (☎ 467 4942). It usually takes only a day to arrange a visit for one or two people, but larger groups will require several days notice.

The museum is worth the effort. Many of the displays are labelled only in Arabic but this is unlikely to be a problem as a member of the museum staff is almost certain to be assigned to guide you around.

Al-Bathaa Souk

Riyadh's main covered souk has been a victim of the city's rush into the 20th century. Small portions of it remain, however, particularly immediately east of Al-Bathaa St for a few blocks either side of Abu Ayoub Al-Ansari St.

Camel Market

Around 30 km from the centre on the outskirts of the city is one of the largest camel markets in the Middle East. Unlike most of the Kingdom's other camel markets the Riyadh market is open seven days a week. Trading is heaviest in the late afternoon. The permanent nature of the market has served to give it a rather squalid look, but it is still a fascinating place to wander around.

To reach the market take the Dammam Rd to the Thumamah exit – the last one before the road heads off east across the desert. You will see the market stretched out along the north side of the road.

Al-Thumairi Gate

On Al-Malek Faisal St, near the Middle East Hotel, is an impressive restoration of one of the nine gates which used to lead into the city before the wall was torn down in 1950. Other reconstructed bits of the city wall are scattered around the general area.

Across the street, opposite the hotel, is the new Al-Thumairi Gate, a more modern structure vaguely resembling a triumphal arch.

Al-Foutah Garden

There isn't much greenery in central Riyadh so Al-Foutah Garden, though not exactly lush, is a welcome change.

Maktaba Garden

This is another patch of green, this time in Olaya at the intersection of Olaya St and Al-Amir Soltan Ibn Abdul Aziz St. The park is only open to families. Admission is SR 2 for adults, SR 1 for children under 12.

Language Courses

The Centre of Languages & Scientific Services (☎ 456 7380) offers Arabic classes. The Al-Imam Islamic University, on the road to the airport, also offers Arabic classes for expatriates, though these tend to include a fairly heavy element of pressure to convert to Islam.

The German embassy (☎ 488 0700) regularly organises (German) language courses. Contact the embassy for information.

Special Events

Saudi Arabia's one, big, institutionalised cultural occasion is the Jinadriyah National Festival. It is organised every year by the National Guard and takes place at a special site 45 km north-east of central Riyadh. The festival includes traditional dancing, art and craft shows, camel racing, lectures and poetry readings. It usually lasts one or two weeks and takes place in February. Note that since Ramadan will coincide with part, or all, of February until about 1998, the festival may be moved to another time during those years.

Places to Stay – bottom end

The *youth hostel* (☎ 405 5552) is on Shabab Al-Ghansani St, a side street between Al-Malek Fahd Rd and the junction of Al-Amir Sa'ad Ibn Abdul Aziz and Abu Feras Al-Hamdani Sts in the Al-Namodhajiyah district. Beds are SR 8. The hostel is neither on any bus route, nor within walking distance of the bus station (count on paying SR 15 for a taxi).

The cheap hotels are all clustered in the vicinity of the bus station. The prices quoted here include the service charges, where applicable. In most cases it should be possible to bargain SR 10 to SR 15 off the quoted price, particularly if you are staying for more than a few days. All these hotels have air-conditioning.

The *Middle East Hotel* (☎ 411 1994) on Al-Malek Faisal St is a bit out of the way but certainly the cheapest place in town after the youth hostel. Singles/doubles are SR 45/70, none with private bath but including breakfast. While the rooms are very small and a bit cramped and the toilet is nothing to write home about, the price is hard to beat.

The *Cairo Hotel* (☎ 401 4045) on Abu Ayoub Al-Ansari St, just off Al-Bathaa St, is drab but clean though some of the rooms are windowless. Rooms are SR 65/100 with bath, fridge and telephone, but the window-less ones are rather cell-like and those with windows are not a lot better. The *Sageer Hotel* (☎ 405 2871, fax 403 1644), in an alley opposite the Cairo Hotel, offers rooms of a similar standard with bath for SR 65/90. Look for the sign with Arabic writing and a red arrow with the word 'Hotel' written on it in English pointing to the right up the alley. Further down Al-Bathaa St, the *Al-Jazeera Hotel* (☎ 412 3479, fax 412 4993) has good rooms at SR 71.50/110.

West of Al-Bathaa St there are several good-value hotels along Al-Imam Faisal Ibn Torki Ibn Abdulla St (Al-Khazan St). The *Al-Rawdah Hotel* (☎ 412 2278) and *Al-Medina Hotel* (☎ 403 2255) are opposite each other about a block from the intersection with Al-Bathaa St. Both charge SR 55/83 for rooms without bath and SR 66/99 with bath. Be warned, though, the air-conditioners at the Al-Rawdah are ancient. The Al-Medina is the better deal of the two.

Hotel Alrajehi (☎ 412 3557, fax 412 3291), up an alley behind the Al-Rawdah Hotel, is a bit more up-market but particularly good value at SR 72/120 for rooms with bath, including breakfast. On Al-Bathaa St, the *Al-Haramain Hotel* (☎ 404 3085) has clean rooms with TV for SR 77/116 with bath, SR 66/99 without.

Places to Stay – middle

Riyadh's mid-range hotel market has expanded in the last few years as a couple of the cheapies have undergone facelifts. On Al-Bathaa St the *Mamora Hotel* (☎ 401 2111, fax 401 0167) is excellent value at SR 80/120 for singles/doubles. Next door the *Asia Hotel* (☎ 403 5127, fax 401 0167) is under the same management but gives you less for more at SR 82.50/126.50.

Another good bet is the *Riyadh Hotel* (☎ 402 8777), on Omar Al-Mokhtar St, where the staff are friendly but the rooms are a bit dark. Singles/doubles cost SR 80/120.

The *Abalkhail Hotel* (☎ 405 6660), two short blocks off Al-Bathaa St behind the Asia Hotel, is an interesting place. The large, clean rooms are good value at SR 85/130 but the atmosphere throughout the hotel is extremely religious. There's even a shelf filled with religious books in every room.

Also good value is the *Safari Hotel* (☎ 405 5533), on a side street off Al-Bathaa St. Singles/doubles are SR 120/170 though you might be able to talk them down to SR 80/120. The Safari would be a good choice for a married couple or a family with children. The *Al-Bathaa Hotel* (☎ 4052 000)

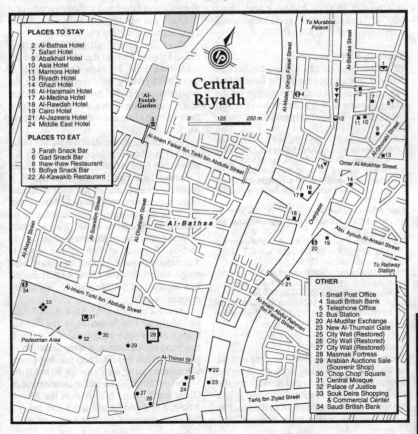

PLACES TO STAY
2 Al-Bathaa Hotel
7 Safari Hotel
9 Abalkhail Hotel
10 Asia Hotel
11 Mamora Hotel
13 Riyadh Hotel
14 Ghazi Hotel
16 Al-Haramain Hotel
18 Al-Medina Hotel
18 Al-Rawdah Hotel
19 Cairo Hotel
21 Al-Jazeera Hotel
24 Middle East Hotel

PLACES TO EAT
3 Farah Snack Bar
6 Gad Snack Bar
8 Ihaw-Ihaw Restaurant
15 Bofiya Snack Bar
22 Al-Kawakib Restaurant

OTHER
1 Small Post Office
4 Saudi British Bank
5 Telephone Office
12 Bus Station
20 Al-Mudifar Exchange
23 New Al-Thumairi Gate
25 City Wall (Restored)
26 City Wall (Restored)
27 City Wall (Restored)
28 Masmak Fortress
29 Arabian Auctions Sale (Souvenir Shop)
30 'Chop Chop' Square
31 Central Mosque
32 Palace of Justice
33 Souk Deira Shopping & Commercial Center
34 Saudi British Bank

Central Riyadh

SAUDI ARABIA

looms over the street of the same name. The rooms, all with TV and fridge, are quite large and cost SR 225/290. This is another good family choice, partly for the very large rooms and especially because it is the cheapest place in Riyadh with a swimming pool. Nearby, the *Al-Oroba Hotel* (☎ 405 5959, fax 405 5619) is very nice but no great bargain at SR 165/214.50. When things are slow and the prices drop to around SR 100/150 this is good value. The *Ghazi Hotel* (☎ 402 2287, fax 405 4001), on Al-Ghorabi St just off Al-Bathaa St, has good rooms and a nice atmosphere. Rooms cost SR 110/165.

Outside the centre the *White Palace Hotel* (☎ & fax 478 7800) on Al-Malek Abdul Aziz Rd (Old Airport Rd) has a good location and is very good value at SR 145/190.

Places to Stay – top end

All of the rates quoted include the service charge. These are rack rates – the basic prices – and a discount is usually available for the asking, though how big the discount is will depend on how busy the hotel is.

Hotel Al-Khozama – Olaya St, in Olaya, near the intersection with Al-Amir Soltan Ibn Abdul Aziz St (Tallateen St) (☎ 465 4650, fax 464 8576). Widely reputed to have the best hotel food around. The quality of the service makes up for the rather small rooms. Singles/doubles cost SR 402.50/517.50.

Hotel Inter-Continental Riyadh – Al-Ma'ther St (☎ 465 5000, fax 465 7833). Singles/doubles are SR 517.50/673.

Hyatt Regency Riyadh – Al-Malek Abdul Aziz Rd (Old Airport Rd) (☎ 479 1234, fax 477 5373). Singles/doubles are SR 517.50/575.

Minhal Holiday Inn – airport end of Al-Malek Abdul Aziz Rd (☎ 478 2500, fax 477 2819). Singles/doubles are SR 402.50/563.50.

Riyadh Marriott Hotel – Al-Ma'ther St, near Makkah Rd (☎ 477 9300, fax 477 9089). Singles/doubles are SR 517.50/673.

Places to Eat

Cheap & Medium-Priced The area around the bus station is packed with small coffee shops, shawarma stands and restaurants, the latter mostly being of the chicken and kebab variety. A meal, consisting of half a chicken and a huge pile of rice, costs between SR 7

and SR 10. Near the Middle East Hotel and the Al-Thumairi Gate you will find *Al-Kawakib*, a particularly good place for roasted chicken and rice. Half a chicken with a big plate of rice costs SR 8. Back on Al-Bathaa St try the *Bofiya Snack Bar* for good, quick snacks (shawarma, juice etc). The sign is in Arabic but look for the orange and yellow stripes.

Another good place for shawarma, pastries and something that resembles pizza is *Farah*, on Al-Bathaa St just across from the Al-Bathaa Hotel. Look for a sign in Arabic with red and white lettering and a picture of a hamburger. *Gad* is a similar place nearby; there's also a larger and swisher version of it in Olaya just off Al-Amir Soltan Ibn Abdul Aziz St, near the King Faisal Centre.

There are several dozen places selling cheap Filipino food on the streets behind the Al-Bathaa Hotel. Try *Ihaw-Ihaw* a couple of short blocks along the street separating the Al-Bathaa and Safari hotels. Their 'budget lunch' consisting of rice, one selection from their cafeteria line and a drink is a bargain at SR 7.

Al-Amir Soltan Ibn Abdul Aziz St (Tallateen St) in Olaya is a good place to look for affordable food of all types. Good, cheap Lebanese food can be had at *Al-Ajami*, a cafeteria-style restaurant just over a km east of the intersection with Olaya St. Mezze cost SR 5 to SR 10 apiece and kibbe can be ordered by the piece at SR 2 each. Note, however, that the restaurant has no family section. A notch or two up the scale is *Assaraya*, a popular Turkish restaurant, also on Al-Amir Soltan Ibn Abdul Aziz St. Excellent kebabs cost SR 12 to SR 15. It's highly recommended.

French Corner on Al-Amir Abdul-Aziz Ibn Mosa'ad Ibn Jalawi St is the Riyadh branch of a popular Kingdom-wide chain. It has good coffee drinks, a wide selection of pastries for SR 5 to SR 7 and full, but generally unimpressive, meals for SR 20 to SR 40.

Italian Caffe Corner at the intersection of Olaya and Al-Amir Mohammad Ibn Abdul-Aziz Sts is a good place to sit and enjoy a coffee, cappuccino, juice or ice cream while watching the traffic roll by. Indoor seating is limited, however, and there is no family section. Cappuccino costs SR 6 per cup.

Riyadh also seems to have more western fast-food eateries than any other city in the Kingdom.

Expensive One of the better bets is *Da Pino*, an Italian restaurant in the Al-Khozama Centre next to the Al-Khozama Hotel on Olaya St in Olaya. Main dishes are SR 30 to SR 40 for pasta and SR 50 to SR 70 for meat, but it is the best Italian food in Riyadh.

Riyadh's best Chinese food is at the *Gulf Royal Chinese Restaurant* on Mosa Ibn Nosayr St across from the Al-Akariyah Centre. Main dishes cost from SR 25. Nearby, the *Bangkok Seafood Restaurant* has decent but overpriced Thai-style seafood. A modest meal here rapidly heads for SR 100 per person.

A good bet for Indian food is *Shezan*, just off the south side of Al-Amir Soltan Ibn Abdul Aziz St between Olaya St and King Fahd Rd. Main dishes cost SR 20 to SR 40. One of Riyadh's better up-market Lebanese restaurants is *Bourj Al-Hamam* on Al-Takhassosi Rd, about one km south of the intersection with Makkah Rd. Mezze cost SR 5 to SR 15 apiece. Main dishes are SR 20 to SR 40.

On the hotel circuit, the Al-Khozama Hotel on Olaya St has, overall, the best food in town. Try the *Caravan Stop Restaurant* just off the lobby.

Entertainment

Riyadh's nightlife is notoriously thin, even by Saudi standards. Even the souks do not stay open as late as they do in Jeddah or Alkhobar. On most nights your only option, if you don't know anyone in Riyadh, is to dine out. The embassies sometimes bring in musical or theatrical groups for performances, but you'll have to be plugged into the expat grapevine to hear of these as they are rarely advertised.

If you can read Arabic it is fairly easy to keep up with the Kingdom's soccer scene and to find out how to get tickets both to club games and to international matches. Unfortunately the English-language press, while it publishes the results of the games, is not very good about giving potential fans advance notice of upcoming events.

Things to Buy

Spices and the occasional woven item can be found if you wander deep into the Souk Al-Bathaa. The best place in Riyadh to buy Yemeni silver and other Arabian souvenirs is Arabian Auctions Sale, near the Masmak Fortress. Prices for the silver are OK, but you can do better in Jeddah or Najran. A number of smaller shops dealing in (mostly imported) souvenirs are located in and around Al-Thimiri St, near the fortress.

Getting There & Away

Air King Khalid international airport (the airport code is RUH) is a long way from the city – nearly 40 km from Al-Bathaa. There are four commercial terminals and a royal terminal. Of the four commercial terminals No 1 is not in use, No 2 is for domestic flights, No 3 for Saudia international flights and No 4 for foreign airlines.

Riyadh is Saudia's base of operations and there are frequent flights to just about everywhere in the Kingdom. Sample one-way economy fares include: Jeddah SR 270, Dhahran and Hofuf SR 140, Gassim (Buraydah) SR 130, Hail SR 190, Taif and Medina SR 240, Abha and Najran SR 270, Jizan SR 310, and Tabuk SR 380. See the fare table in the Getting Around section for more details.

International fares vary significantly from month to month. Here's a sample of Saudia's best one-way and return fares, with minimum and maximum stay requirements. To London, New York and Athens the round-trip fare shown is low season. High season is roughly mid-December to early January and June to August. Expect to pay more then. Use these prices only as bench marks. With some shopping around you can probably beat them:

To	One Way	Return	Min/Max
Abu Dhabi	SR 641	SR 889	2/14 days
Athens	SR 2517	SR 2591	0/90 days
Bahrain	SR 299	SR 414	2/14 days
Bangkok	SR 1668	SR 3336	0/1 year
Cairo	SR 1518	SR 1834	0/60 days
Doha	SR 423	SR 587	2/14 days
Dubai	SR 707	SR 980	2/14 days
Kuwait	SR 600	SR 830	2/14 days
London	SR 4057	SR 4177	0/90 days
Muscat	SR 1089	SR 1510	2/14 days
Nairobi	SR 2136	SR 2781	6/60 days
New Delhi	SR 1613	SR 2564	7/120 days
New York	SR 4695	SR 5294	7/30 days

Airline Offices Some of the airlines serving Riyadh are:

Air France
    Al-Malek Abdul Aziz Rd, near the White Palace Hotel (☎ 476 9666)
Biman Bangladesh Airlines
    Makkah Rd, near the junction with Al-Ma'ther St (same complex as AMEX; ☎ 462 3376)
British Airways
    King Faisal Centre, Olaya (behind the Al-Khozama Hotel, between Olaya St and Makkah Rd), street level (☎ 464 5550)
EgyptAir
    Salah Al-Din Al-Ayoubi Rd (☎ 478 4004)
Emirates
    Mosa Ibn Nosayr St, across from the Al-Akariyah Centre, Olaya (☎ 465 5485)
Ethiopian Airlines
    Al-Malek Abdul Aziz Rd, near the White Palace Hotel (☎ 478 2140)
Garuda
    Mosa Ibn Nosayr St, across from the Al-Akariyah Centre, Olaya (☎ 465 5898)
Gulf Air
    Olaya St, just south of the intersection with Makkah Rd (☎ 462 6666)
Kuwait Airways
    King Faisal Centre, Olaya (behind the Al-Khozama Hotel, between Olaya St and Makkah Rd), 1st floor (☎ 463 1218)
Lufthansa
    King Faisal Centre, Olaya (behind the Al-Khozama Hotel, between Olaya St and Makkah Rd), street level (☎ 463 2004)
MEA (Middle East Airlines)
    King Faisal Centre, Olaya (behind the Al-Khozama Hotel, between Olaya St and Makkah Rd), street level (☎ 465 8468)
Olympic
    King Faisal Centre, Olaya (behind the Al-Khozama Hotel, between Olaya St and Makkah Rd), 1st floor (☎ 464 4596)

PIA (Pakistan International Airlines)
    Makkah Rd, near the intersection with Olaya St (☎ 465 9600)
Royal Jordanian
    At the corner of Al-Amir Soltan Ibn Abdul Aziz St (Tallateen St) and King Fahd Rd (☎ 462 5697)
Saudia
    The main reservations office is at the intersection of Al-Amir Torki Ibn Abdel Aziz (Al-Thani) and Olaya Sts far to the north of the centre (☎ 488 4444). Starting at the intersection of Olaya St and Al-Uroubah Rd, counting that traffic signal as number one, go north (away from the centre) to the sixth traffic signal, just over five km.
Swissair
    Al-Malek Abdul Aziz Rd, near the White Palace Hotel (☎ 476 6444)
Syrianair
    King Faisal Centre, Olaya (behind the Al-Khozama Hotel, between Olaya St and Makkah Rd), street level (☎ 465 4231)
Turkish Airlines
    Olaya St, between Al-Amir Soltan Ibn Abdul Aziz St and Makkah Rd (☎ 463 1600)
TWA
    Salah Al-Din Al-Ayoubi Rd (☎ 477 5830)

Bus – domestic The bus station just off Al-Bathaa St is SAPTCO's inter-city depot. You'll need identification to buy a ticket and the lines tend to be long. Unaccompanied women are not allowed to travel by bus.

There are 11 buses every day to Jeddah (13 hours, SR 130) via Taif (10 hours, SR 100). These buses go around Mecca and are OK for non-Muslims. The same buses used to go through Mecca, forcing non-Muslims to change at Taif. If you are a non-Muslim bound for Jeddah it would be prudent to double-check that the routing has not changed again.

Other routes include: 11 daily to Dammam (4½ hours, SR 60); three daily to Hofuf (four hours, SR 45) with an extra bus on Thursdays. To Buraydah (4½ hours, SR 60) there are nine buses every day. There are three buses per day to Hail (eight hours, SR 100), 10 daily to Abha (13 hours, SR 125), two daily to Jizan (18 hours, SR 160), three daily to Najran (12 hours, SR 115), three daily to Bisha (12 hours, SR 135), two daily to Tabuk (17 hours, SR 200), and two daily to Sakaka (14 hours, SR 175).

For Muslims only, buses leave for Mecca

(10 hours, SR 115) five times per day and for Medina (12 hours, SR 140) three times daily.

Bus – international SAPTCO's international services have expanded greatly in the last few years and increased competition has led to price cuts on some routes. The Saudi company competes on most of these routes with various foreign passenger and freight services, many of which have offices near the bus station.

In general, the companies running buses headed for Turkey via Jordan and Syria have offices between the SAPTCO station and Al-Bathaa St while the bus companies serving Egypt are on the far side of the station as you approach it from Al-Bathaa St. The companies operating buses to Syria and Jordan are scattered around the entire area. All of the foreign companies can usually undercut SAPTCO's price, and might throw in a few meals as well. The Amman and Cairo routes are particularly competitive. On the other hand, SAPTCO's buses are often newer and may be more comfortable. If you are travelling to Turkey remember to ask for the non-Turks price, the one that does not include Syrian and Jordanian transit visas (if you're not a Turkish citizen you are expected to get these on your own in advance).

Information on SAPTCO's international services can be obtained in the terminal building. There is an international ticket window, and a timetable is posted on the wall in Arabic. A printed timetable, again in Arabic, is available for the asking. SAPTCO buses to Istanbul cost SR 260 (non-Turks price), Cairo SR 350 via Dhuba, SR 395 via Aqaba, Jordan. Tickets to Amman or Damascus cost SR 200. There is twice-weekly service to Kuwait (SR 150). SAPTCO will also sell you a through ticket to Bahrain (SR 100), Doha (SR 125) or Abu Dhabi (SR 195), but these routes require a change of bus in Dammam if you're going to Bahrain and in Hofuf if you are headed to Qatar or the UAE.

Service-Taxi These also leave from the SAPTCO station. Service-taxis used to be a northbound traveller's best bet, but the increased frequency of SAPTCO's service means that the bus is probably a better bet these days though in the early morning (before 8 am) taxis for Buraydah usually fill up fairly quickly. The fare is SR 60. It's more difficult to get a service-taxi to the Eastern Province and Jeddah, though drivers do operate on these routes and charge slightly more than SAPTCO buses. Expect to pay SR 150 to Jeddah, SR 70 to Dammam, SR 55 to Hofuf and SR 120 to Hail. All service-taxis leave when they are full. Most carry either five or seven passengers.

If you are facing the bus station with your back to Al-Bathaa St the taxis to Buraydah and Hail will be to your right and all the others to your left.

Note that drivers headed for Jeddah are unlikely to take non-Muslims, especially if they have already filled some of the seats with Muslims, because it would mean taking the long detour around Mecca.

Train The railway station is on Al-Amir (Prince) Abdul Aziz Ibn Abdullah Ibn Torki St, 2.5 km east of the bus station. Trains leave for Dammam via Hofuf and Abqaiq three times daily, except Thursday when there is only one train. Daily departures are at 8 am, 1.10 pm and 6.20 pm. The lone Thursday train leaves at 9.24 am. The journey to Dammam takes about four hours. Fares in 1st/2nd class are SR 60/40 to Dammam, SR 52/34 to Abqaiq and SR 45/30 to Hofuf. The ticket office is open from 6 am to 10 pm. Women are not allowed to travel by train without a male escort. For information call ☎ 473 1855, 473 1811 or 473 1845. Note that the 1.10 pm train does not stop in Abqaiq.

To reach the station from Al-Bathaa go up Omar Ibn Al-Khattab St, following the 'Railway Station' signs.

Car Rental Prices are fixed by the government and the depth of any available discount is agreed in advance by the companies so shopping around does little good. The

328 Riyadh – Getting Around

annoying thing about renting a car at the airport is that there are only a couple of companies in each terminal, so comparison shopping (more for model availability than price) involves an inordinate amount of hiking back and forth. Expect to pay SR 110 per day, including insurance, for the smallest cars available (usually Toyota Corollas) from all the companies. With whatever discount they are offering at the time that should drop the net price to SR 90 to SR 100. Most big hotels also have a car hire desk and you can find a number of car hire offices along Olaya St near the Al-Khozama Hotel.

Getting Around

The Airport There is no bus service to King Khaled international airport. The buses and minibuses marked 'Airport' go to the old airport via Al-Malek Abdul Aziz Rd. Your only option to get to the 'real' airport is a taxi. A cab to the airport could cost anything from SR 30 to SR 70, depending on where in the city you start. From the airport the white limos have a set tariff of SR 50 or SR 60 to most districts in the city though a few of the areas closer to the airport are only SR 45. The yellow cabs have a rank separate from the limos at each terminal. They tend to insist on the same fares as the limos, and if the drivers will not bargain you might as well take one of the limos, which are almost always more comfortable. The limo drivers also usually have a better idea where they are going.

Bus SAPTCO buses and private minibuses cover most of the city. Fares on either are SR 2. There is no route map. Both the buses and the minibuses have their routes posted in the front window, though on the latter this may be only in Arabic. The small (and packed) minibuses follow more or less the same routes as the buses, and the route numbers are applicable in either direction.

Sorting out these routes is difficult because SAPTCO's timetables tend to use old unofficial names and to be inconsistent about these names. Here are some of their main Riyadh routes (using the actual names of the main streets the routes follow):

No 1 – Mosa Ibn Nosayr St, Al-Malek Abdul Aziz Rd, Al-Bathaa St as far as the Ring Rd South

No 5 – Al-Foutah Garden, Al-Sowailim St, Salam St, Al-Amir Abdullah Ibn Abdul Rahman Ibn Faisal St, Dirab Rd, Al-Shafa district; returns to centre via Al-A'sha St, Al-Frayyan St, Al-Dhahirah St

No 7A – Al-Bathaa St, Al-Malek Faisal St, Al-Malek Saud St, Al-Nasiriyah St, Al-Ma'ther St, Al-Jawhrah Bint Ibn Maamar St, Al-Malek Khaled Rd, Umm Al-Hamam St, Al-Uroubah Rd, King Saud University

No 8A – Al-Bathaa St, Al-Washem St, Al-Malek Saud St, Al-Nasiriyah St, Al-Takhassosi Rd

No 9 – Al-Bathaa St, Al-Amir Abdul Aziz Ibn Moad'ad Ibn Jalawi St, Al-Ma'ther St, Olaya St, Al-Imam Saud Ibn Abdul Aziz Ibn Mohammad St, Al-Takhassosi Rd

No 9A – Al-Bathaa St, Al-Amir Abdul Aziz Ibn Moad'ad Ibn Jalawi St, Al-Ma'ther St, Olaya St, Al-Imam Saud Ibn Abdul Aziz Ibn Mohammad St

No 9B – Al-Bathaa St, Al-Amir Abdul Aziz Ibn Moad'ad Ibn Jalawi St, Al-Imam University

No 10 – Khaled Ibn Al-Waleed Rd, Obadah Ibn Al-Samit St, Makkah Rd, Al-Ihsa St, Omar Ibn Abdul Aziz St, Salah Al-Din Al-Ayoubi Rd, Al-Jami'ah St, Al-Bathaa St

No 10A – Prince Bandar Ibn Abdul Aziz St, Khaled Ibn Al-Waleed Rd, Obadah Ibn Al-Samit St, Makkah Rd, Al-Ihsa St, Omar Ibn Abdul Aziz St, Salah Al-Din Al-Ayoubi Rd, Al-Jami'ah St, Al-Bathaa St

No 12B – Al-Rabwah, Omar Ibn Abdul Aziz Rd, Fatimah Al-Zahra' St, Jareer St, Salah Al-Din Al-Ayoubi Rd, Al-Dhahran St, Omar Ibn Al-Khattab St, Al-Malek Abdul Aziz Rd, Al-Bathaa St, Al-Imam Faisal Ibn Torki Ibn Abdullah St; returns via Al-Malek Faisal St instead of Al-Bathaa St

No 15 – Ka'b Ibn Zohayr St, Abdul Malek Ibn Hisham St, Al-Swaidi St, Al-Derib St, Al-Bathaa

No 17 – Al-Bathaa St, Tariq Ibn Ziyad St, Al-Amir Salman Ibn Abdul Aziz St, Al-Kharj Rd, 2nd Industrial City

No 110 – Al-Bathaa St, Al-Malek Abdul Aziz Rd, Omar Ibn Al-Khattab St, Al-Dhahran St, Salah Al-Din Al-Ayoubi Rd, Al-Naseem

Taxi There are two kinds of taxis: white-and-orange and yellow cabs. In both cases a flag fall is SR 3 after which the meter ticks over in 50 halala increments at SR 1 per km. Most yellow cabs are driven by Saudis, with the driver usually being the owner. The white cabs with an orange stripe down the side are driven by non-Saudis (usually Filipinos, Egyptians or Indians) and tend to be better maintained. The drivers in the white cabs are more likely to speak English.

AROUND RIYADH
Dir'aiyah

Riyadh's most interesting site is outside the city. On the capital's northern outskirts, about 30 km from Al-Bathaa, lie the ruins of Dir'aiyah, the first capital of the Al-Saud clan and the Kingdom's most popular and easily accessible archaeological site (no permits required). The site is open Saturday to Thursday from 7 am to 6 pm and Friday from 1 to 6 pm. Admission is free. Still photography is permitted but video cameras are not.

The site was settled in 1446 by an ancestor of the present royal family. Dir'aiyah reached its peak in the late 18th and early 19th centuries during the First Saudi Empire, in particular under Saud the Great (ruled 1803-14). This prosperity didn't last long. The Ottoman sultan sent an army to the Hejaz in the early 19th century to recapture the holy cities and crush Saudi power in the peninsula. In 1818 they reached Dir'aiyah which surrendered after a six-month siege. Abdullah, Saud's son and successor, surrendered and was eventually executed. Dir'aiyah was razed and what was left of the Al-Saud and their followers moved to Riyadh. Reconstruction of Dir'aiyah's ruins began in 1981.

Entering through the main gate, the office on the left has a small display of clothes, weapons and handicrafts. A larger visitor centre has been on the drawing board for about a decade. The **Palace of Salwa** is the impressive building towering up behind the office. Actually it was a complex of several palaces, some residential and some used for administrative purposes.

Across the street from the office is the partially restored **Mosque of Al-Turaif** which was once connected to the palace complex by a bridge. The bridge allowed the ruler to come and go from the mosque in relative security and was built in the wake of an unsuccessful assassination attempt on

Saud the Great, then the ruler of the growing First Saudi Empire, in 1803.

To reach the main area of the ruins continue straight past the office and turn left, as indicated on the sign reading 'To the Eastern Palaces', around the wall which will eventually appear in front of you. This is the **Palace of Fahd**. Following this wall will soon take you past the **Palace of Abdullah Bin Saud**, also partially rebuilt. It is on the right. Abdullah Bin Saud was the last ruler of the First Saudi Empire, and led the resistance to the six month Ottoman siege of 1818. After surrendering to the Turks he was taken back to Constantinople and executed.

Following the street straight takes you to the somewhat nondescript ruins of the **Palace of Thunayyan Bin Saud** (Abdullah's uncle and the brother of Saud the Great). Turn right here and continue past the ruined **Palace of Mishaari** toward the **Palace of Nasser**, which will slowly appear directly ahead of you. Before you reach this, however, the **Palace of Sa'd Bin Saud** will appear to your right. This is Dir'aiyah's largest restored building. Be sure both to get a look at the well-restored painted door, and to go around the left side of the palace as you

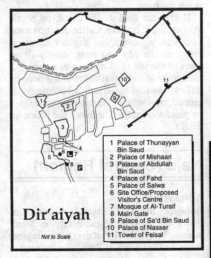

1	Palace of Thunayyan Bin Saud
2	Palace of Mishaari
3	Palace of Abdullah Bin Saud
4	Palace of Fahd
5	Palace of Salwa
6	Site Office/Proposed Visitor's Centre
7	Mosque of Al-Turaif
8	Main Gate
9	Palace of Sa'd Bin Saud
10	Palace of Nasser
11	Tower of Feisal

Dir'aiyah

Not to Scale

SAUDI ARABIA

stand facing it. The left side and back are much more interesting than the front.

Following the path that runs between the Palace of Sa'd Bin Saud and the Palace of Nasser takes you out of the main area of restoration. After about 150m a white sign pointing to the right indicates the way to the **Tower of Feisal**, a restored defence tower in the (also much restored) city wall. The tower is named after the member of the Al-Saud family charged with defending Dir'aiyah against the 1818 siege. Feisal died during the siege and the tower was subsequently named in his honour. At one time Dir'aiyah's perimeter wall was 15 km long. This is a good spot to pause for a look out over the date palms of the modern oasis before making your way back to the gate.

Getting There & Away To reach Dir'aiyah from Riyadh, leave the city centre following the signs for the airport. Once you're on the expressway to the airport look for signs to Dir'aiyah. Once you exit the expressway you should see the ruins in the distance to your left. Follow the road until you reach a T-junction. Turn left, and left again when you reach a roundabout. Go straight, and look for the small white signs indicating a right turn to reach the ruins.

If you can find it, *Dir'aiyah*, by Stevie Wilberding & Isabel K Cutler, contains some excellent photographs, a good historical essay on the city and three short walking tours of the site (half an hour to an hour). It used to be widely available but has become difficult to find in Riyadh's bookshops. A pirated, photocopied, version can sometimes be purchased at the Dir'aiyah site office for SR 15.

Najd (Central Region)

BURAYDAH
Buraydah has the unenviable reputation of being the least hospitable city in Saudi Arabia. The main city of the Qassim region, it lies 330 km north of Riyadh on the road to

Hail. It is the only place in the Kingdom where all foreign women are required to be veiled.

Geographically, the desert plains running north from Qassim are also the Kingdom's agricultural heartland, though Hail is more important than Buraydah as an agricultural centre. It is a place most people pass through as there's not much to see and do.

However, if you do stop here, take a walk through the residential areas two or three blocks on either side of Khobib St, between the communications tower and the Riyad Bank building. A few examples of interesting traditional Najdi mud-brick houses are still around to be seen. Foreigners are still a slightly unusual sight here so try not to draw too much attention to yourself.

Orientation & Information
Buraydah's main road is Khobib St, also known as Commercial St, which runs north-south through the city. At the northern outskirts of town it becomes the Medina road. There are few street signs in either Arabic or English, and the Arabic signs only give the names of the intersecting streets. The main intersections are at First St and, farther north, the intersection dominated by the Riyad Bank building.

Coming from Riyadh the service-taxi and bus stations are both in a one-storey brown building on the east side of Khobib St at the last set of traffic lights before the communications tower, which is clearly visible atop a small hill on your left. The Saudia office is farther up Khobib St on the west side.

You can change money at the Saudi American Bank on Khobib St, just north of the bus station. There's also an office of the Al-Rajhi Banking & Investment Corporation a few hundred metres farther north. There is a Saudi Cairo Bank with a Cirrus/Plus-linked ATM on Khobib St near the Riyad Bank.

There are international call cabins at the communications tower on the west side of Khobib St, a few hundred metres north of the bus station.

The telephone code for Buraydah is 06.

Places to Stay

Buraydah has an excellent and accessible *youth hostel* (☎ 381 3007) at the Sporting City, 12 km north of the town centre. From the bus station take bus No 2 (every 30 minutes, SR 2) all the way to the end of the line. It's about a 30-minute ride. The bus stops at a T-junction near the sports complex. Turn left, then follow the complex's wall around to the right to reach the gate. Beds are SR 8 per night.

The *Al-Gassim Hotel* (☎ 324 1858, fax 325 1854) is the only place to stay in the town itself. Singles/doubles cost SR 110/165 with bath, SR 99/148.50 without. It is on the west side of Khobib St, one long block beyond the Riyad Bank building. The rooms are quite clean and big, some have Turkish toilets.

The *Al-Dubaikhy Hotel* (☎ 381 3566), 10 km north of the centre on the Medina road, is slightly cheaper at SR 83/121 for rooms with bath, SR 72/110 without. The rooms are simple but clean and some have a fridge and TV. This place, however, is not a good idea if you do not have a car – taxis demand SR 20 for the trip from town and, once the driver has left, you are likely to find that getting back into the centre is a bit of a problem.

The upper end of the local market is the *Al-Salman Hotel* (☎ 323 5984, fax 324 0373), with rooms at SR 288/373 including the service charge. To reach it follow Khobib St almost to the big, golf-ball-like water tower, turn right (there's a sign in Arabic) and follow the road through four traffic lights. You'll see the hotel. Alternatively, you can call from the bus station and they will send a car to get you.

Places to Eat

Khobib St has a number of small restaurants between the bus station and the Riyad Bank building. The fare is mostly Turkish but there are some Indian/Pakistani places as well. On the west side of Khobib St, just down the hill from the telephone office, try the *Middle East Restaurant* (there is no sign in English – look for a pink sign with white writing and a picture of a chicken). They have good, cheap foul and grilled chicken. Similar fare

can be had at the *Madina Restaurant* by the bus station.

Getting There & Away

Saudia flies to Buraydah (which its timetables list as Gassim) several times a day from Riyadh (SR 130 one way, economy class) and once or twice a day to/from Jeddah (SR 290). Direct flights also operate several times a week to Dhahran (SR 270), Medina (SR 160), Arar (SR 210), Hail (SR 100), Sakaka (Jouf, in the timetables) (SR 180) and Tabuk (SR 290).

SAPTCO runs 10 buses a day to Riyadh. The trip takes four hours by the new road and 6½ hours by the old road and costs SR 60. It also has three daily buses to Hail (four hours, SR 40) at 2, 8.45 and 11.30 pm. The first and last buses continue on to Tabuk (10 hours, SR 140). There are four daily buses to Medina (seven hours, SR 80) at 2.30 am, 2, 10.30 and 11 pm.

Service-taxis charge the same as the buses to Riyadh and Medina but ask SR 60 for the trip to Hail. They tend to fill up fairly slowly with the exception of regional service-taxis making the half-hour trip to Unayzah (SR 5). Local taxis cluster near the bus station and at a rank on Khobib St at the base of the communications tower hill.

HAIL

Hail (pronounced Hay-El), 640 km northwest of Riyadh, was formerly the seat of the Al-Rashid family, the Al-Saud clan's most formidable rivals. It is now the centre of the Kingdom's vast agricultural programme, and most of Saudi Arabia's wheat crop comes from the area around Hail.

Orientation

Hail's main street, the one coming from Riyadh and Buraydah, runs north-south and centres on Commercial District Square by the Saudi Hollandi Bank building. Old Hail is roughly east of this street and the newer areas are west of it, except for the Al-Qashalah Fortress. There's another square bearing the same name north-east of the one just described. This second square looks

PLACES TO STAY
12 Hail Hotel

PLACES TO EAT
5 Habbr Restaurant
11 Lahore Restaurant
15 Wajabat Sera'a Restaurant
16 Fast Food (Al-Waja)

OTHER
1 Minibus Stop
2 Saudia Airlines
3 Service-Taxis
4 Saudi Hollandi Bank
6 Al-Bank Al-Saudi Al-Fransi

7 Taxi Stand
8 Payphones
9 National Commercial Bank
10 Al-Rajhi Commercial Establishment for Exchange
13 Telephone Office
14 Fire Station
17 Bus Station
18 Police Station
19 Ministry of Education
20 Governate
21 School
22 Portion of Ruined City Wall
23 'Airif Fort

more like a parking lot and is dominated by the fruit and vegetable souk. You are unlikely to get the two squares mixed up. The bus station is at the Al-Qashalah Fortress, three blocks south of Commercial District Square.

Information
To change money, head for Saudi Hollandi Bank or the offices of other main banks or moneychangers in the vicinity of Commercial District Square. Al-Bank Al-Saudi Al-Fransi, the National Commercial Bank and Al-Rajhi Commercial Establishment for Exchange all have offices within a few

minutes walk of the square. The local branch of the Saudi Cairo Bank is on the southern edge of the centre, near the Al-Jabalain Hotel.

Hail's post office is well south of the centre on the Medina road. The Saudia office is next to the Saudi Hollandi Bank building. International call cabins can be found at the telecom office next to the fire station. The telephone code for Hail is 06.

Before doing any sightseeing your permit, which must be obtained in Riyadh, has to be validated at the antiquities section of the Ministry of Education office in town (ask for *maktab al-athaar*). The office is on the 1st floor and is open Saturday to Wednesday from about 8 am until 1 pm. These are also more or less the hours during which you can visit the sites. The staff are quite friendly and will probably insist on accompanying you to the sites. Ask permission before you start taking pictures at the forts, even if you have a permit. The office distributes a small booklet on the region's antiquities for free, but it is available only in Arabic.

Al-Qashalah Fortress
This mud fortress is impressive but somewhat younger than it looks. It was built in the 1930s and was used mostly as a barracks for Abdul Aziz's troops in Hail. As Hail had traditionally been the seat of the rival Al-Rashid clan, the king may have thought it prudent to build a new garrison for his troops rather than take over the quarters of the Al-Rashid shaikhs whom he had only recently conquered. (It was typical of Abdul Aziz's approach to rivals that, having conquered, he would try to co-opt rather than dispossess them.)

The entrance is through the south gate. Inside there's a large courtyard which has been cut in half by a wall to create a separate area for the King's police and soldiers. The entire courtyard is surrounded by a two-storey gallery, the lower half of which is whitewashed, as are a few of the pillars on the upper lever. The lower half also contains some interesting ornamental work. The small building in the courtyard contains a display of artefacts from Hail and the surrounding desert region. On the east side of the courtyard is a small mosque. A foundation stone dates the mosque's construction to 1362 AH (1943 AD). To reach the mosque, turn right once you enter the courtyard then pass through another gate, also to your right.

A sign outside the fort says it is open only Sunday, Monday and Tuesday from 9 to 11 am. What it does not say is that the fort is also open only when the museum's manager (as opposed to the guard) is present. If you arrive during the posted hours and the manager is present you can get in without a permit from Riyadh. At other times a permit and a guide from the local antiquities office are required.

Photos are permitted in the fortress itself but not inside the museum.

'Airif Fort

Built about 200 years ago, 'Airif Fort was a combined observation post and stronghold. From the nearby fragments of Hail's wall it appears to have been situated just outside the city proper. It also appears to be the fort sketched by Lady Anne Blunt when she and her husband Wilfred visited Hail in 1889. After climbing up the hill and going through the main gate into the fort, look to your right for an open hall filled with low pillars. A niche in the south wall identifies it as a small mosque, partially open to the sky.

At one end of the large main courtyard of the fort is a doorway leading to a smaller inner court that has both upper and lower levels and gives you access to 'Airif's main watchtower.

Other Attractions

Two restored towers in Barazan Square adjacent to Hail's central mosque are all that remains of another of Hail's palaces.

About 25 km south-east of the city, **Jabal Yathrib** is the site of rock inscriptions dating from the 5th and 6th centuries BC. As with the sites in Hail, you will need a permit from Riyadh which must be validated in Hail. Someone from the antiquities office in Hail will accompany you to the sites but you will

probably be expected to provide transport (4WD recommended).

Places to Stay

The *youth hostel* (☎ 533 1485) is at the stadium, a 20 to 30-minute walk south of the bus station. Beds are SR 8. The hostel entrance is on the side of the complex, not the main road. Alternatively, walk into town from the bus station (about 10 minutes) and catch a minibus from the parking lot in front of the Saudi Hollandi Bank building. These leave when they are full so be prepared to wait. The fare is SR 2.

The *Hail Hotel* (☎ 532 0180, fax 532 7104) is on King Khalid St but there are no street signs anywhere in the vicinity. The hotel is a lot better than it looks from the street. Singles/doubles with bath cost SR 132/171, though they will readily discount that to SR 120/155. Rooms without a private bath cost SR 121/159.50. To reach the hotel walk west from Commercial District Square and turn left at the first set of traffic lights. The hotel will then be on your right.

The *Al-Jabalain Hotel* (☎ 533 2294, fax 532 1166) is south of the city centre beyond the youth hostel. There is no sign in English but for sheer size the place is pretty hard to miss. Rooms, including the 10% service charge, are SR 230/299 for singles/doubles.

Places to Eat

The *Lahore Restaurant*, opposite the Hail Hotel, is a decent, fairly clean place with the usual selection of chicken dishes and curries. The shakshoka (mildly spiced scrambled eggs) makes a good, cheap breakfast at SR 5. Another good bet is *Wajabat Sera'a*, a small Indian place opposite the Al-Bank Al-Saudi Al-Fransi which offers cheap samosas (50 halalas each) and other quick eats. Look for a black sign with yellow lettering and a picture of a chef. For shawarma and fresh juice try *Fast Food* (in Arabic the sign says *Al-Waja*) on the Main Rd across from the southern edge of the park. Look for a red sign.

If you are truly desperate for western food try the *Habbr* hamburger place on the corner of Commercial District Square. Be warned, it's not very good.

Getting There & Around

Hail's small airport is south-west of the centre. There are two or three flights a day to/from Riyadh (SR 190 one way, economy class), daily service to Jeddah (SR 240) and one or two flights a week to Dhahran (SR 330), Buraydah (Gassim) (SR 100), Medina (SR 140), Arar (SR 140), Sakaka (Jouf) (SR 100), Rafah (SR 100), Tabuk (SR 210) and Turaif (SR 200).

SAPTCO runs three buses a day to Riyadh (eight hours, SR 100) via Buraydah (four hours, SR 40). Departures are at 4 and 8 am and at 7 pm. There are two buses per day to Medina (six hours, SR 65) at 9.30 am and 6.30 pm and two buses per day to Tabuk (8½ hours, SR 100) at 3.30 am and 6.30 pm.

Service-taxis tout for passengers in the parking lot behind the Habbr restaurant on Commercial District Square and in another parking lot behind the Saudia office. Southbound, however, the bus is by far your best bet.

For getting around locally without waiting for the minivans in Commercial District Square to fill up, there are usually metered taxis in front of the Saudia office. There is also a taxi rank diagonally across the intersection from the minibus stop.

JUBBA

Jubba, 100 km north-west of Hail, is the only settlement of any size in the Nafud, the smaller of Saudi Arabia's two great sand deserts. Serious desert buffs often claim the Nafud (the desert Peter O'Toole and Omar Sharif cross during the first half of *Lawrence of Arabia)* is much more scenic than the Empty Quarter. This may well be true, but the road to Jubba, unlike the road to Sharurah, is nothing to write home about. The town itself is a different story. Jubba is the site of one of Saudi Arabia's most important archaeological sites: the 3rd millennium BC **Thamudite rock carvings** at Thanabit, on the edge of town.

Even by Saudi standards visiting the site is inordinately complicated. That said, the carvings are fascinating and make an easy day trip from Hail (there is no place to stay in Jubba). After obtaining a permit in Riyadh and having the Hail antiquities office check this permit and issue you a permission slip to enter the site, you will have to drive to Jubba and locate the home of Hejab Al-Mutlaq, the site guard. Jubba gets only a handful of visitors so Mr Al-Mutlaq, rather than spending his days at the gate, waits at home for people to arrive bearing permits.

To reach the Al-Mutlaq home, keep straight as the highway from Hail enters the town and becomes a local street. Half a km after the divided road ends, the street opens up into a small square; continue straight ahead following this street around to the left until you arrive at a small fork. Keep right at the fork and follow the road for 600m as it becomes narrow and winds about. Look for two petrol pumps on your left, then a small black sign with white writing. Make a right turn 100m past the sign onto a sand and dirt track just beyond a low mud wall. Follow this track through an area of mud houses. After 450m the track forks; keep left. After another 100m you will see a white house in front of you and to the left. That's it. You'll have to make a left turn to reach the front door and a place to park. The house is 3.7 km from the spot where the divided highway into town ends.

Mr Al-Mutlaq will probably guide you to the site but, just in case, you can reach the gate from his front door as follows: turn left out of the front door of the house and follow the dirt road for 450m until you reach a T-junction. Turn left at this junction. The road will swing to the left and then to the right to leave you pointed in the same direction that you were originally headed. At 300m from the T-junction you will find yourself in front of a white house; from here head straight for 900m. This will bring you to a large open area. The site gate is on the far side of this area, about 300m away and to the right. Be careful driving these last 300m, as the track is quite sandy in places.

As for the carvings themselves, after passing through the gate turn right around the first main outcrop of rock. Follow the rock face for about 30m and look up. About four metres above ground level – and relatively easy to climb up to – is an animal figure surrounded by writing. Other, similar, figures are distinguishable below this and to the left but these are harder to make out.

To the right of these figures, and a bit higher up, is more writing surrounding a lion-like figure. Look for more writing on the underside of the nearby overhang.

On the far side of the site from the gate you can also see several antelope figures and some human figures, one of which is life-size.

LAYLA

The town of Layla is a way-station on the route from Riyadh to Najran, Abha and the Empty Quarter. South-east of the town are the so-called **Layla Lakes**, a popular spot for water-skiing and other weekend activities with those who do not mind the long drive from Riyadh and have the 4WD needed to reach them.

For anyone else Layla is a place to get petrol or a meal, or to stay overnight if you don't have the energy to keep driving. There are several small *rest houses* at both the northern and southern ends of town. Most have signs only in Arabic, but they are easy enough to spot, being part of large complexes that also include a gas station, restaurant and supermarket. The rest houses rent rooms by the hour, usually charging about SR 15 per hour, though if you are staying the entire night you can probably negotiate some sort of discount. Accommodation in all of these places is pretty basic.

SULAYYIL

Though it is some 570 km from the capital, Sulayyil is technically still part of Riyadh emirate, or province. Earlier this century the author/diplomat/explorer/spy Henry St John Philby was excited by the opportunity to visit the town, which he used as a jumping-off point for his exploration of the Wadi Dawasir. Today it holds no particular allure, except as the closest vestige of civilisation to the important archaeological site at Al-Faw, 120 km to the south-west. A few of the town's old mud-brick buildings have survived along the backstreets, but that's about it. To reach the old buildings turn off the main north-south highway when you see a water tower to the east of the road with a top that resembles a juice extractor. Drive to the area on the far side of this tower and look around the backstreets. Prepare to be underwhelmed.

There are a couple of *rest houses* like those around Layla at the northern and southern ends of town. The latter are slightly better. The rest houses ask SR 10 to SR 15 per hour. If you need a cheap place to sleep try the *Al-Darees Resthouse*, the sign is only in Arabic but it is next to the first petrol station on the left after the road narrows from four lanes back to two if you are moving south through the town. The bus stop is at another rest house about 10 km south of the centre.

About 32 km south of Sulayyil there is a *SASCO Rest House* which, though more expensive, is also a dramatic improvement over what is on offer in the town. Two-bed rooms cost SR 120 for a single or double, and a suite with two bedrooms, two bathrooms a sitting room and a kitchen goes for SR 240. There is also a restaurant, supermarket and a mechanic's shop on the premises. The SASCO facility is much the better bet for couples or families.

AL-FAW

The remote location of Al-Faw belies its importance. Al-Faw was once a great trading centre, and the artefacts recovered at excavations here are among the most important finds in the Kingdom. Historically it is probably a more important, if less dramatic, site than Madain Salah. A number of finds from the digs here can be seen in the museum at King Saud University in Riyadh.

The site is about 120 km from the centre of Sulayyil and 106 km north of the point where the road south from Sulayyil forks with one branch going to Najran and the other to Shararah. Look for a large radio tower. There are two petrol stations on the east side of the road just north of this tower. The track leading to the site is immediately south of the southern petrol station (the second one, if you're coming from Sulayyil). From the petrol station go 900m until you arrive at a small white house. The site is in the fenced-off area immediately behind the house. The track from the main road to the site is passable with a regular car, but barely just. If you get stuck in the sand don't say I didn't warn you.

As you face the house and site you will see another compound about 400m off to your left. This is where the archaeologists stay during the winter excavation season. It is also where the site attendant lives, so you'll have to go there to find him to get into the site. Most of the excavated area is in the small grey building inside the fenced-off area. Bring a torch. You must also have a permit from the antiquities office at the Riyadh Museum to visit the site. The site does not have formal opening and closing hours, but it is a good idea to show up before noon.

Jeddah

The white town hung between the blazing sky and its reflection in the mirage which swept and rolled over the wide lagoon.

TE Lawrence

Once a modest port living mostly off the pilgrim trade, Jeddah (Jiddah, Jidda) has evolved into one of the Arab world's most important commercial centres. Jeddah has also managed the feat, rare in today's Arabia, of building around, rather than over, its history. One of its nicest aspects is that a surprising amount of Lawrence's white mirage has survived into our era.

But while historical Jeddah still exists, it is dwarfed by the modern metropolis. Within its walls Jeddah occupied about one sq km

of land. Today it is approximately one thousand times that size.

It has been called the 'Paris of Arabia' and if this title seems a bit overstated, it is difficult to deny Jeddah its place as the most interesting and friendly of the Kingdom's big cities.

History

According to tradition, Jeddah was settled in the 3rd century BC by an ancestor of the Prophet Mohammed. Less poetically, it is known that a Persian fleet campaigning against Ethiopia and Yemen in the 6th century AD, shortly before the Prophet's birth, landed in the region.

Jeddah has long served as Mecca's outlet to the sea. Mecca was a thriving commercial centre long before the coming of the Prophet. It was an important stop on the caravan route from Yemen to Egypt and Syria and a local centre of pilgrimage for the tribes from the surrounding deserts. The spread of Islam made the holy city a religious centre for people from the four corners of the earth, many of whom arrived by sea, and Islam soon transformed Jeddah into a thriving metropolis in its own right. The city first became important during the caliphate of Othman Bin Affan, early in the Islamic era, though the oldest known description of the city dates from 933 or 934 AD (322 AH). Until well into this century Jeddah's port was one of the main gateways to Arabia for pilgrims bound for Mecca. Hundreds of thousands of people would land each year at Jeddah and make the two-day overland journey to Mecca. Jeddah is still the main gateway to the holy city, though today it is the city's airport, rather than its seaport, that welcomes the bulk of the hajjis.

In approximately 1080 AD Jeddah was destroyed after the city's leaders fell foul of the rulers of Mecca, to whom they were subject. Travellers' accounts from the following century describe Jeddah as having a low standard of living, though by the 13th century its fortunes had reversed themselves and the town was again prosperous. At this time it was under the control of Egypt's

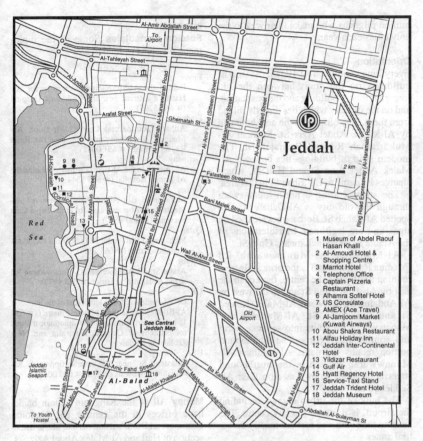

Jeddah

Red
Sea

Jeddah
Islamic
Seaport

To Youth
Hostel

Al-Balad

See Central
Jeddah Map

Old
Airport

To
Airport

Al-Amir Abdallah Street

Al-Tahleyah Street

Al-Andalus Street

Arafat Street

Ghematah St

Al-Madinah Al-Munawwarah Road

Al-Amir Fahd (Sitteen Street)

Al-Makarounah Street

Al-Amir Majed Road

Al-Haramain Road (Al-Haramain Road)

Ring Road Expressway

Falasteen Street

Bani Malek Street

Khaled Ibn Al-Waleed Street

Wali Al-Ahd Street

Corniche Road

Al-Andalus Street

Hail Street

Al-Kournaish

Dahaban Street

Al-Amir Fahd Street

Al-Malek Khaled Street

Makkah Al-Mukarramah Rd

Ba Kahshab Street

Ali Al-Murtadi St

Abdallah Al-Sulayman St

Al-Falah Street

Al-Mina'a Street

Al-Dahab (Zahab) Street

1	Museum of Abdel Raouf Hasan Khalil
2	Al-Amoudi Hotel & Shopping Centre
3	Marriot Hotel
4	Telephone Office
5	Captain Pizzeria Restaurant
6	Alhamra Sofitel Hotel
7	US Consulate
8	AMEX (Ace Travel)
9	Al-Jamjoom Market (Kuwait Airways)
10	Abou Shakra Restaurant
11	Alfau Holiday Inn
12	Jeddah Inter-Continental Hotel
13	Yildizar Restaurant
14	Gulf Air
15	Hyatt Regency Hotel
16	Service-Taxi Stand
17	Jeddah Trident Hotel
18	Jeddah Museum

0   1   2 km

Mamelukes. The Portuguese attacked Jeddah in 1541 but failed to take the city, and it is from this era – 1517 AD – that the oldest known picture of the city, one made by a Portuguese artist, dates.

Jeddah is in the Hejaz. The entire Hejaz came under nominal Turkish control in the 16th century, though the local rulers retained a great deal of autonomy. The first foreign consuls arrived during the first half of the 19th century.

After the Wahhabis, under Abdul Aziz, took control of the city in 1925, the foreign presence (which had increased notably during WWI) began to expand even further.

Foreign representatives to the new king's court were posted to Jeddah, rather than to the official capital, Riyadh, because of the latter's relative inaccessibility. Diplomatically, this was easily finessed as Najd and the Hejaz were, technically, two separate states which simply happened to have the same king until 1932. After that it was more a matter of convenience. The embassies stayed in Jeddah until the early 1980s, and as late as the mid-70s a sizeable chunk of the Saudi bureaucracy was headquartered here rather than in the official capital. Today, the city's forte is commerce, though it still remains the principal port of entry for the more than two million pilgrims who make their way to the holy cities each year.

Orientation

Everything centres on Al-Balad: the strip of buildings on the coast between the old foreign ministry building and the bus station, and on the old city which lies directly inland from them. The old city is the area bounded by Al-Malek Abdel Aziz St, Makkah Al-Mukarramah Rd and Ba'najah St. The modern strip of buildings lies between Al-Malek Abdel Aziz St and Hail St, which changes its name to Ba'ashan St in this area.

The street cutting a north-south swath through the old city is Al-Dahab St, also spelled Al-Zahab St. Both names are used on signs and are legitimate transliterations of the Arabic name, which means Gold St.

Al-Madinah Al-Munawwarah Rd (Medina Rd, for short) is the principal street running north from the centre, flanked to the east by Al-Amir Fahd St and to the west by Al-Andalus St. Between Al-Malek Khaled St and Falasteen St, Al-Madinah Al-Munawwarah Rd splits into separate north and southbound streets. The southbound portion retains the name Al-Madinah Al-Munawwarah Rd while the northbound street is officially known as Abo Bakr Al-Seddeeq St.

The bulk of the urban sprawl, including the airport, is north of the city centre. The areas to the south and east are mostly industrial zones.

As in Riyadh, there are a number of streets with commonly used, but unofficial, names. The most important one to know is Al-Amir Fahd St, which is commonly called Sitteen St or King Fahd St. Al-Dahab St is sometimes referred to as King Faisal St. The names of several main streets are commonly anglicised. These include Falasteen St (Palestine St) and Al-Malek Abdel Aziz St (King Abdul Aziz St). Note also that the term 'Corniche' is commonly applied to the entire coastal road as it passes through the city, including those areas where it, formally, has a different name (such as Hail St, Ba'ashan St or Al-Falah St.

Information

Foreign Consulates Some of the diplomatic missions in Jeddah are:

Egypt
  Behind the Al-Mousadiyah Centre in the Al-Hamra'a district, near the Children's Hospital (☎ 660 5205)
France
  Adham Commercial Centre, 9th floor, Al-Madinah Al-Munawwarah Rd, near the Hyatt Regency Hotel (☎ 651 0082)
Germany
  Al-Iman St in the Al-Hamra'a district, behind the Al-Hamra Hospital (☎ 665 3344)
Jordan
  Mohammed Bin Abdul Aziz St, just off Al-Madinah Al-Munawwarah Rd at the Pepsi Cola overpass (☎ 660 7630)
Qatar
  Mohammed Bin Abdul Aziz St, Area N-23, Al-Andalus district (☎ 665 2538)
Turkey
  Arafat St, off Al-Madinah Al-Munawwarah Rd in the Al-Hamra'a district (☎ 665 4873)
UK
  Off Al-Andalus St, one block east of the Sheraton Al-Bilad Hotel, in the Al-Shate'e district (☎ 654 1811). The British also handle diplomatic matters for citizens of Canada, Australia and New Zealand in Jeddah.
USA
  Falasteen St, near the intersection with Al-Andalus St, Ruwais district (☎ 667 0080)

Money All of the Kingdom's main banks have offices in the centre. The National Commercial Bank's main office, at the intersection of Hail and Al-Malek Abdel Aziz Sts, is hard to miss – it's the tallest building in Jeddah. There is also an Al-Rajhi Banking & Investment Company branch on Al-Malek Abdel Aziz St opposite the Shaheen Hotel, and a Saudi British Bank branch in the shopping arcade at the Red Sea Palace Hotel. There are a large number of moneychangers along Al-Qabel St in Al-Balad between Al-Malek Abdel Aziz St and the tunnel that goes underneath Al-Dahab St.

AMEX is represented by Ace Travel (☎ 665 1254), on Falasteen St near the intersection with Al-Hamra St. They can replace lost and stolen cards and cash personal cheques for card holders but will not hold client's mail. The office is open Saturday to Wednesday from 9 am to 1.30 pm and 4.30 to 8 pm. On Thursday it's open only during the morning hours, and on Friday it is closed.

Post & Communications The GPO is the large red and white building opposite the bus station, between Ba'ashan and Al-Bareed Sts. The entrance is on the Al-Bareed St side of the building. The GPO is open Saturday to Wednesday from 7.30 am to 9.30 pm. On Thursday only the Mumtaz Post (express mail) windows are open from 7.30 am to 2 pm. The post office is closed on Friday.

There is also a post office in the Hamra'a district just off Al-Madinah Al-Munawwarah Rd a short distance south of the Al-Amoudi Centre and on the opposite side of the road.

The telephone office is on Abo Bakr Al-Seddeeq St in the Al-Sharafeyyah district, just south of the intersection with Falasteen St. The telephone code for Jeddah is 02.

Travel Agencies Central Jeddah is full of tiny travel agencies of dubious competence. Most companies have a travel agent they work through and expats may be obliged to use that company. In general I stick to Ace Travel if I have to buy an international ticket, and I buy my domestic plane tickets directly from Saudia. There are no bucket shops and current regulations in the Kingdom make it unlikely that you'll get any significant discount by going through a travel agent anyway.

When you are quoted a fare, however, always remember to ask for a discount. A reduction of up to 12%, more or less, may be forthcoming, though this is likely to leave you locked into your travel dates.

Bookshops The Al-Mamoun Bookshop, on the 1st floor of the Corniche Commercial Centre, has a reasonable selection of English books. You will find a better selection at the Jarir Bookstore on the south side of Falasteen St between Makarounah and Al-Amir Majed Sts.

Cultural Centres The British Council (☎ 672 3336) is on the 4th floor of the Middle East Centre on Falasteen St, next to the Marriott Hotel. The Saudi French Centre (☎ 682 3319) is on Al-Qurayash St in the Al-Salamah district near the Al-Ansar Hospital.

Emergency Dial ☎ 999 for the police, ☎ 997 for an ambulance, ☎ 998 to report a fire.

Dangers & Annoyances Jeddah is notorious for having the craziest driving habits in the Kingdom. Riding or driving through the city can be a pretty nerve-wracking experience.

Jeddah Museum

Jeddah's Regional Museum of Archaeology & Ethnography is in an awkward location near the Al-Khozam Palace and the Islamic Development Bank, but if you have not already been to the Riyadh Museum (the displays are quite similar) it is worth the trip. The museum is open Saturday to Wednesday from 8 am to noon. Admission is free.

To the right of the entry hall is a room with displays on the age and geology of the earth along with pottery and other prehistoric relics from various parts of the Kingdom. There are also displays on ancient trade routes, the domestication of the camel and the development of Arabic script.

Next, head upstairs. Turning left at the top of the stairs takes you to a room with displays on calligraphy, the Zubaydah Road and Islamic architecture (a particularly useful section if you are new to the region and want to learn more about mosques). Next, proceed through the door in the right-hand wall of the exhibit hall to a room with displays on Jeddah's architecture, including a large, scale model of the Naseef House. Beyond this hall are several restored sitting rooms, a display on King Abdul Aziz and an exhibit of clothing and Bedouin silver. The museum finishes with two small rooms featuring weapons and household items.

To reach the museum from Al-Balad take

Makkah Al-Mukarramah Rd south to the intersection with Al-Amir Fahd St and turn right. Go past the water tower, which will be on your left, to the first traffic light (a distance of about 900m) and turn left. Look for a small white sign pointing left to the Islamic Development Bank's office. Follow this street for 150m to a T-junction. Turn right and follow the road for another 350m (during which it will make a 90° turn to the left), at the end of which the road forks. Keep left and the museum will be on your right after another 300m.

Walking Tour & Old City Walls

Many of Jeddah's sites lie along the course of the old city walls, which were torn down in the late 1940s. The walls ran along Al-Malek Abdel Aziz St, Makkah Al-Mukarramah Rd and Ba'najah St. A circuit of these streets should take under an hour on foot.

Along the route are the three reconstructed old city gates, which are all that remain of the wall. They are the North City Gate on Maydan Al-Bayal, Bab Makkah at the intersection of Makkah Al-Mukarramah Rd and Ba'najah St, and Bab Sharif on Ba'najah St near a hospital and now opening onto a large parking lot.

Near the North City Gate are several good examples of traditional Jeddah architecture in various states of preservation.

The old city is now a protected urban area. Buildings there cannot be torn down unless they are dilapidated beyond repair, in which case they must be replaced with something of a similar size and architectural style. Many of the older houses within the old city walls are constructed not of stone but of coral quarried from reefs in the Red Sea.

Shorbatly House

Just east of the North City Gate, this house is one of the best known examples of the city's traditional architecture. During the '80s it was restored to something approaching its original state and plans were announced to turn it into a museum. The museum, however, eventually went into a different building (see next entry) and the Shorbatly House has been allowed to deteriorate once again. In the immediate area around it you will see several other old houses, also in various states of disrepair.

Municipality Museum

The museum is in the restored traditional house opposite the headquarters of the National Commercial Bank. There is no sign in English but the house is impossible to miss. The museum is open Saturday to Wednesday from 7.30 am to 1.30 pm. Admission is free, but you must first make an appointment with the curator (☎ 642 4922). I have managed to talk my way into the museum without an appointment on two separate occasions, but there is no guarantee that you will be equally lucky, so it's probably a good idea to call ahead if at all possible.

The house, which is approximately 200 years old, is the only surviving building of the WWI-era British Legation in Jeddah. TE Lawrence stayed at the Legation when he visited in 1917, though there is no way of knowing whether he actually stayed in this particular house as the Legation then included several other buildings as well. Like many Jeddah buildings of that era it is built of coral quarried from the Red Sea.

The photographic display at the far end of the entrance hall includes aerial photographs of Jeddah in 1948, 1964 and 1988 that dramatically illustrate the city's growth. In the main portion of the hall, in the display case that will be to the left as you enter the building, there is a sword presented by Britain's King George V. This, like much else in the museum, is only labelled in Arabic. The other cases in the entry hall include several old Korans and several interesting Persian astrolabes.

The room to the left of the entry hall has a large photograph of King Abdul Aziz surrounded by his family. The present king (Fahd) can be seen standing in the back row to the right of his father. The room to the right of the entry hall has a display of pottery and glassware from various parts of the Islamic world.

The rest of the house is a combination of exhibits (silver, old weapons etc) and rooms done up in traditional style. It is very ornate, with lots of Egyptian and Syrian furniture with mosaic inlay work and presumably reflects the way in which Jeddah's wealthier citizens would have lived until only a generation ago.

Naseef House

Along the old city's main thoroughfare, Souk Al-Alawi, stands one of the city's most famous houses. The Naseefs are one of Jeddah's old-line merchant clans. In the 19th and early 20th centuries their family home was one of the most important houses in Jeddah. The larger of the two trees to the left of the house's front door was, as recently as the 1920s, the only tree in all of Jeddah and thus an indicator of the family's wealth and importance. After conquering the city in 1925 King Abdul Aziz expropriated the house for his own use until a palace could be built.

To find it, look for a large stone doorway set slightly back from, and raised a few steps above, the level of the street at the turn for the Al-Alawi Traditional Restaurant.

Al-Shafee Mosque

The Al-Shafee Mosque, near the centre of Al-Balad, is one of the oldest in the city. The easiest way to reach it is to enter the souk near Bab Makkah. You'll pass through a covered section of the cloth souk followed, on the right, by a small park. When the street swings around to the left, keep going straight on the broad, straight pedestrian street (not the narrower one where the road bends). You should see the minaret, which is white with brown trim and a green dome, on the right-hand side of the street. The entrance, for Muslims only, is through the carved wooden gate and the doors on the right.

Museum of Abdel Raouf Hasan Khalil

This private museum really has to be seen to be believed. It contains over 10,000 items crammed into four 'houses' that look like the sort of mock-Arab buildings you might expect to see at Disney World.

Visitors are encouraged to begin their tour in the House of Saudi Arabian Legacy, continue on through the Islamic Legacy House and finish in the General Legacy Exhibition. Each house includes several 'typical' rooms as well as specialised galleries displaying particular types of items, such as postage stamps or weapons. The Saudi house is crammed with paintings on Saudi themes (many of them copies of well-known photographs) and the General Legacy house includes suites of Chinese and European rooms, the latter filled with some of the most tasteless furniture and curios I've ever seen. The museum is not very well organised and, after a while, you are likely to feel a bit overwhelmed by the sheer volume of stuff that each room presents.

Amid the clutter, however, there are a few gems. The Islamic Legacy House is a striking reconstruction of a classic Ottoman Turkish sitting area with intricately painted upper and lower levels and a beautiful marble floor. In the European rooms be sure to see the turn-of-the-century Russian chess set. In the Saudi house you will find scale models of some of Jeddah's better known old houses, and several samples of the embroidered shrouds from the Kaaba in Mecca (for centuries these were changed every year at hajj time with the new shroud being manufactured in Egypt and brought down as part of the pilgrim caravan).

The museum is open Saturday to Thursday from 9 am to noon and 5 to 9 pm; closed Friday. Admission is SR 20. Photography is not permitted in the House of Saudi Arabian Legacy, but is allowed everywhere else.

Though signs in various parts of Jeddah point to the museum, actually finding it can be a bit tricky. Take either Al-Madinah Al-Munawwarah Rd or Al-Andalus St to Al-Tahleyah St. Turn off Al-Tahleyah St onto Ibrahim Al-Jufali St (if you are starting from Al-Madinah Al-Munawwarah Rd this will require a U-turn). Go 500m and turn right onto Al-Madani St. Take the first left, and then turn right onto Al-Mathaf St. The museum will be on the right after about 150m.

Corniche Sculptures

There are quite a few major sculptures and dozens of smaller ones along the Corniche, between the area around the port and the Obhur Hotel in the ritzy Obhur Creek district farther north. Among the subjects are a pair of hands, a dhow and what appears to be three gigantic feathers.

Souk

The souk, one of the better ones left in the Kingdom, starts on the inland side of Al-Malek Abdel Aziz St within the confines of the old city walls. It twists back into the old city, sometimes for a block or two, and in places all the way back to Bab Makkah. The souk has suffered something of a loss of character since large sections of it were paved over and, in places, fitted with bizarre green and white columns, but it remains a great place to spend hours strolling and browsing. The Souk Al-Alawi area is particularly good and has retained much of its traditional flavour.

Activities

Beaches There are several long stretches of public beach starting just north of the centre and running to a point slightly north of the Holiday Inn hotel. Saudi dress regulations are such that women might want to stick to swimming pools – you will notice that many Saudi women enter the water fully clothed! Bathers of both sexes might also be put off by the large number of young men zipping up and down the beach (and, drivers take note, the adjacent highway) on three-wheeled beach buggies.

Amusement Parks The northern sections of the Corniche, particularly once you get north of Sari St, are lined with small amusement parks, many of which have restaurants serving burgers and other fast food.

Language Courses

Arabic classes are offered by the Daalah

Language Centre (☎ 660 4929) on Falasteen St. The Cooperative Office for Call & Guidance also organises Arabic courses. These cost very little (SR 100 for six weeks) but also include a heavy dose of encouragement to convert to Islam. Stop by the office's booth in the plaza in front of the GPO for more information.

The Saudi French Centre (☎ 682 3319) offers French lessons but no longer teaches Arabic. The Centre is on Al-Qurayash St in the Al-Salamah district near the Al-Ansar Hospital.

Organised Tours

The Red Sea Palace (☎ 642 8555) offers a 1½ hour city tour every Friday at 10 am for SR 25. You do not have to be staying in the hotel to take the tour. Telephone the concierge to make reservations or for further information.

Places to Stay – bottom end

The *youth hostel* (☎ 688 6692) is at the stadium, 12 km east of the city centre on the Mecca expressway. Beds are SR 8 per night. The hostel is behind the green buildings of the Sporting City. There is no access by bus. The easiest way to reach it by car is to take exit No 8 from the expressway, *not* the stadium exit which is farther on. The sign says 'Local Traffic'. The exit numbers are small and are in the upper right-hand corner of the directional signs. Note that some of the exit numbers are missing from the sequence. Exit 8 is the one immediately after exit No 6 (which comes right after exit No 3). After leaving the expressway turn right at the first light, follow the road to another traffic light and make a U-turn. The hostel will be on your right after about 100m.

Most of the following hotels offer rooms with a TV, fridge and telephone. Service charges, where applicable, are included.

In the city centre, Jeddah boasts one of the Kingdom's best budget hotels. The *Shaheen Hotel* (☎ 642 6582, fax 644 6302) is in an alley between Al-Malek Abdel Aziz St and the Corniche Commercial Centre. Prices for

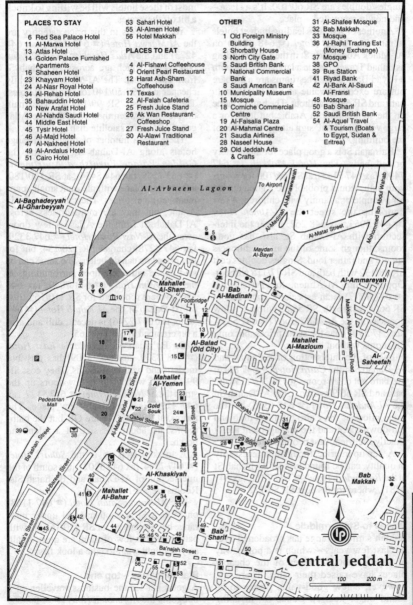

PLACES TO STAY

- 6 Red Sea Palace Hotel
- 11 Al-Marwa Hotel
- 13 Atlas Hotel
- 14 Golden Palace Furnished Apartments
- 16 Shaheen Hotel
- 23 Khayyam Hotel
- 24 Al-Nasr Royal Hotel
- 34 Al-Rehab Hotel
- 35 Bahauddin Hotel
- 40 New Arafat Hotel
- 43 Al-Nahda Saudi Hotel
- 44 Middle East Hotel
- 45 Tysir Hotel
- 46 Al-Majd Hotel
- 47 Al-Nakheel Hotel
- 49 Al-Andalus Hotel
- 51 Cairo Hotel
- 53 Sahari Hotel
- 55 Al-Almen Hotel
- 56 Hotel Makkah

PLACES TO EAT

- 4 Al-Fishawi Coffeehouse
- 9 Orient Pearl Restaurant
- 12 Harat Ash-Sham Coffeehouse
- 17 Texas
- 22 Al-Falah Cafeteria
- 25 Fresh Juice Stand
- 26 Ak Wan Restaurant-Coffeeshop
- 27 Fresh Juice Stand
- 30 Al-Alawi Traditional Restaurant

OTHER

- 1 Old Foreign Ministry Building
- 2 Shorbatly House
- 3 North City Gate
- 5 Saudi British Bank
- 7 National Commercial Bank
- 8 Saudi American Bank
- 10 Municipality Museum
- 15 Mosque
- 18 Corniche Commercial Centre
- 19 Al-Faisalia Plaza
- 20 Al-Mahmal Centre
- 21 Saudia Airlines
- 28 Naseef House
- 29 Old Jeddah Arts & Crafts
- 31 Al-Shafee Mosque
- 32 Bab Makkah
- 33 Mosque
- 36 Al-Rajhi Trading Est (Money Exchange)
- 37 Mosque
- 38 GPO
- 39 Bus Station
- 41 Riyad Bank
- 42 Al-Bank Al-Saudi Al-Fransi
- 48 Mosque
- 50 Bab Sharif
- 52 Saudi British Bank
- 54 Al-Aquel Travel & Tourism (Boats to Egypt, Sudan & Eritrea)

Central Jeddah

0   100   200 m

SAUDI ARABIA

singles/doubles are SR 60/100. It's a clean – and newly renovated – place.

Another of Jeddah's leading budget hotels is the *New Arafat Hotel* (☎ 648 4852) on Al-Malek Abdel Aziz St in the same building as Fahad Travel, beside a large building with a Riyad Bank sign. The rooms are a bit bare but are excellent value at SR 77/116 with bath and SR 66/99 without. The hotel's name on the sign is only in Arabic but look for a large vertical 'Hotel' sign along the corner of the building.

Ba'najah St is a good place for moderately priced beds. The *Hotel Makkah* (☎ 647 7439, fax 647 5143), at SR 66/100 for rooms with bath, would probably be a good choice for a couple or a family with children. A few doors up the street the *Al-Almen Hotel* (☎ 648 3953, fax 648 2621), near the intersection with Al-Dahab St, also has good rooms, though some of the air-conditioners are old and rather loud. Singles/doubles cost SR 88/132 with bath and SR 77/115 without. Opposite the Al-Almen, the *Tysir Hotel* (☎ 647 7777) is an especially good deal at SR 66/99 with bath, SR 55/83 without. A few doors away the *Al-Majd Hotel* (☎ 647 5354, fax 647 5509) has the same prices, but only for rooms without baths.

East of the intersection of Ba'najah and Al-Dahab Sts, the *Cairo Hotel* (☎ 647 8115) has bare but clean rooms for SR 77/115 with bath and SR 66/99 without. On Al-Dahab St, the *Al-Andalus Hotel* (☎ 647 6565) has the same prices as the Cairo but it's a drab and run-down place and the management aren't exactly the friendliest people in Jeddah.

A step up in price, though not necessarily in quality, can be found just off Al-Dahab St at the *Bahauddin Hotel* (☎ 647 7811, fax 647 9781), where rooms cost SR 88/132.

Places to Stay – middle

Jeddah's middle range has broadened over the last few years – which is a polite way of saying that a number of the cheaper places have raised their rates. There are, however, a few good-value places to be found on or near Al-Dahab St, meaning most of these hotels will be willing to knock a bit off their rates.

Your best bets in this price category are the *Al-Marwa Hotel* (☎ 643 2650, fax 644 4273) and the *Atlas Hotel* (☎ 643 8520, fax 644 8454), which are across Al-Dahab St from each other. The Al-Marwa is slightly cheaper at SR 93.50/140 for singles/doubles. The Atlas costs SR 99/148.50. The main difference between the two is that the Atlas gets CNN on its satellite dish.

There are a number of other mid-range hotels along Al-Dahab St including the *Golden Palace Furnished Apartments* (☎ 643 7565, fax 644 8454), at SR 130/180, a fairly new place with pleasant small apartments at hotel prices. Their sign is only in Arabic, but they are more or less across Al-Dahab St from the Atlas. A few doors away the *Al-Nasr Royal Hotel* (☎ 647 3329, fax 647 4278) charges SR 120/154, but for this price you can do better. The same can be said of the rather cramped surroundings at the *Khayyam Hotel* (☎ 643 7049, fax 643 3560) where rooms go for SR 110/165. Just off Al-Dahab St, the *Al-Rehab Hotel* (☎ 647 9636, fax 647 2246) is decent, dull and also a bit cramped at SR 110/165.

On Ba'najah St the *Middle East Hotel* (☎ 648 3330, fax 647 5509) has tiny but modern and well kept rooms. They cost SR 99/132, all with bath. A few doors up the street the *Al-Nakheel Hotel* (☎ 647 5127, fax 647 1190) is a relatively new place. The rooms, at SR 165/215 are OK but the bathrooms are about the size of a telephone booth.

A marked step up is the *Sahari Hotel* (☎ 647 7744, fax 648 5202), just south of the intersection of Al-Dahab and Ba'najah Sts. Rooms are SR 165/214.50.

The *Al-Nahda Saudi Hotel* (☎ 647 1158) on Mina'a St is another good upper mid-range bet. Rooms go for SR 110/165, all with bath, though a few of them are quite small, so you might want to take a look first.

Places to Stay – top end

A good bet for the business traveller on a budget is the *Al-Amoudi Hotel* (☎ & fax 660

5611) on Al-Madinah Al-Munawwarah Rd, a short distance north of Falasteen St. The rooms are very large, well furnished and have a bit more character than the average top-end hotel. Singles/doubles cost SR 230/300.

The *Jeddah Trident Hotel* (☎ 647 4444, fax 647 4040) on Al-Mina'a St is another good bet for those looking for something a notch below the big international chains. Rooms cost SR 345/448.50, including the service charge.

Most of the top-flight hotels are a long way from the centre. You can usually get a discount on these rates simply by asking for it. The rates quoted here include the service charge.

Alfau Holiday Inn – on the Corniche just south of its intersection with Falasteen St (☎ 661 1000, fax 660 6326); singles/doubles are SR 460/598.

Alhamra Sofitel – Falasteen St, between Al-Madinah Al-Munawwarah Rd and Al-Andalus St (☎ 660 2000, fax 660 4145); singles/doubles are SR 460/598.

Hyatt Regency Jeddah – Al-Madinah Al-Munawwarah Rd, a short distance south of the Falasteen St intersection(☎ 652 1234, fax 651 6260); singles/doubles are SR 431/540.50.

Jeddah Inter-Continental Hotel – just south of the Holiday Inn on the Corniche(☎ 661 1800, fax 661 1145); singles/doubles are SR 517.50/673.

Jeddah Marriott – Falasteen St west of the intersection with Al-Madinah Al-Munawwarah Rd (☎ 671 4000, fax 671 5990); singles/doubles are SR 517.50/673.

Red Sea Palace Hotel – Al-Malek Abdel Aziz St, between the National Commercial Bank building and Maydan Al-Bayal (☎ 642 8555, fax 642 2395). This is the only top-flight hotel in the city centre. It is also a bit cheaper than the others at SR 368/483 for singles/doubles.

Sheraton Jeddah Hotel – The hotel (☎ 699 2212, fax 699 2660) is 19 km north of the centre on the Corniche, which puts it a lot closer to the airport than any of the other main hotels but could be a drawback for many travellers; singles/doubles start at SR 460/598.

Places to Eat
Cheap & Medium-Priced There are a lot of cheap places in the centre offering mostly fast food. One, however, stands out from the rest. *Al-Falah*, a cafeteria near the Saudia

office on Al-Malek Abdel Aziz St, is one of Jeddah's most popular cheap eateries. They offer Arab staples like hummous (SR 5) and a wide range of Chinese and Filipino dishes (SR 10 to SR 15) as well as burgers and pizza. The clientele is as varied as Jeddah's population, the food is always good and there is a family section. Highly recommended.

Another good bet is *Texas*, on Al-Malek Abdel Aziz St, around the corner from the Shaheen Hotel, and opposite the Corniche Commercial Centre. It has both shawarma and the traditional burgers, fries and fried chicken fast-food menu. Shawarma cost SR 3 and SR 4, burgers SR 7 to SR 13, half a chicken SR 12. Texas and several other nearby places have outdoor (men-only) seating that can be especially pleasant on a cool evening. There are a couple of other cheap Filipino places on the ground floor of the Corniche Commercial Centre, and just outside the building.

Level four of the Al-Mahmal Centre has a collection of cheap to medium fast-food places covering a wide range of cuisines. Try the *Al-Mankal Cafeteria* for Arabic food, *Silk Rd* for Chinese food or a *Texas* outlet and *Tarboosh*, both of which serve burgers and fried chicken. The Al-Mankal does a good chicken tikka with fries and bread for SR 14. They also offer foul sandwiches for SR 3 apiece and hummous for SR 5.

Cappuccino addicts should head for *The Coffee House*, where the coffee is worth the extra riyal over the cafeteria prices. They have cafes in the Al-Mahmal Centre and in the building on Al-Malek Abdel Aziz St that also houses the main Saudia office. There is also a branch in the Al-Amoudi Centre on Al-Madinah Al-Munawwarah Rd.

Outside the centre, *Captain Pizzeria* at the intersection of Al-Madinah Al-Munawwarah Rd and Falasteen St is excellent value. The restaurant specialises in Filipino and Chinese food, though it also serves burgers and pizza. It has a large number of set meals starting at SR 10. The food is excellent, as is the atmosphere and there's a family section – I highly recommend it.

SAUDI ARABIA

Moderately priced Lebanese food can be found at *Lebanese Nights Restaurant*. It offers enormous set meals for SR 18 including desert and fresh juice and has a family section upstairs. It's at the intersection of Al-Amir Abdullah and Al-Amir Sultan Sts in northern Jeddah.

Traditional Coffee Houses Central Jeddah has several traditional coffee houses, where men sit on high couches, smoke water pipes and drink tea, not coffee. There are three along Al-Dahab St. The *Ak Wan Restaurant-Coffeeshop* is a short distance south of the entrance to the Souk Al-Alawi. The *Harat Ash-Sham Coffeehouse* is near the footbridge that crosses over Al-Dahab St, and the *Al-Fishawi Coffeehouse*, which takes its name from a famous Cairo coffee house that figures in several of Naguib Mahfouz's novels, is near the intersection of Al-Dahab St and Maydan Al-Bayal.

Expensive I can highly recommend the *Al-Alawi Traditional Restaurant*, just off Souq Al-Alawi St in the old city. The 'traditional' food is Moroccan, not Saudi, but it's a great place with a nice garden. Main dishes are SR 30 to SR 45 but you can get out for much less by sticking to the appetisers. Try the harira soup (a thick beef and vegetable soup) for SR 8. Avoid the Perrier which is absurdly overpriced at SR 12 for a small bottle.

For some of the best Lebanese food in Jeddah try *Yildizar* (☎ 653 1150), just west of the intersection of Al-Andalus and Wali Al-Ahd Sts. It's not the best Lebanese food I've ever had, but it is quite good and the service is excellent. Prices, however, are steep. Mezze cost around SR 17 each and main dishes are in the SR 40 to SR 60 range. Still, if you are looking for a truly sophisticated restaurant this is one of your best options outside the bland surroundings of the big hotels. Reservations are recommended for dinner.

Another astronomically expensive place for which you might want to book a table is *Al-Danah* (☎ 699 0090) on the Corniche just north of the Sheraton (which puts it nearly

20 km from Al-Balad). Here you can dine at glass-enclosed tables on small piers that extend into the sea – and pay handsomely for the privilege. The seafood dishes are in the SR 75 to SR 100 range. The *Sea Garden Restaurant*, which is part of the same complex, is an open-air place selling 'fast food' at SR 20 to SR 35 per dish. Single men note that the Sea Garden is one of the few places in the Kingdom where the family section gets the best area – only families can enjoy a view of the sea from the Sea Garden.

Up-market Egyptian food can be had at *Abou Shakra*, the Jeddah branch of one of Cairo's best known restaurants. They are at the corner of Falasteen St and the Corniche and offer fairly pricey kebabs at SR 20 to SR 30 apiece. For an inexpensive but heavy meal have a huge slice of makaronah, macaroni cooked with a sauce of eggs and butter and then garnished with tomato sauce, for SR 15. The service is very Egyptian, meaning friendly but slow.

Da Pino Pizzeria, in the Red Sea Palace Hotel on Al-Malek Abdel Aziz St, is the best spot in town for Italian food. Meals cost from SR 50 to SR 80. The *Gulf Royal Chinese Restaurant* has excellent, if pricey, food. Meals cost SR 50 and up. They have one restaurant in the Al-Mahmal Centre and one in the shopping mall on Falasteen St next to the Marriott Hotel. Another place for good Oriental food is the *Orient Pearl Restaurant* (formerly the Bangkok Restaurant), on the 2nd floor of the Corniche Markets building overlooking Hail St and the Corniche Commercial Centre's parking lot. The menu is mostly Thai. Chinese and Filipino food are also served. Main dishes cost SR 20 to SR 35 (SR 35 to SR 70 for seafood). Try to get one of the tables overlooking the Corniche.

Things to Buy
Jeddah is not Saudi Arabia's best spot for antiques and traditional souvenirs but it is a good place to look for almost everything else. The old city's gold souk is particularly good. Also in the old city, the Al-Alawi Traditional Restaurant, which serves Moroccan food, has a small pottery workshop on

the premises where traditional Moroccan serving dishes are produced. There's nothing even vaguely 'Saudi' but these do make good gifts. They cost around SR 100.

Across a small plaza from the Al-Alawi is one of Jeddah's few 'oriental' gift shops: Old Jeddah Arts & Crafts. It carries silver jewellery and copper and brass work, some old and some new. It has a good selection of inlay boxes from Syria and samples of old calligraphy. The store's staff is friendly and knowledgeable and the merchandise is definitely worth a look, even if you are not in the market for souvenirs.

You can also find a few stalls selling silver jewellery and other souvenirs along Al-Qabel St, particularly at the end near Al-Malek Abdel Aziz St.

Getting There & Away

Air King Abdul Aziz international airport is about 25 km north of the city on Al-Madinah Al-Munawwarah Rd. Saudia flights, both domestic and international, leave from the south terminal. Foreign airlines use the north terminal. The only way to get from the north to the south terminal, or vice versa, is by taxi. This will cost you SR 35.

The big, tent-like structure at the northern end of the airport is a special hajj terminal used by pilgrims en route to Mecca. It deals with the huge number of pilgrims who flock to Saudi Arabia each year. (In the final weeks before hajj a plane load of pilgrims lands at the airport every few minutes in addition to the regular commercial services.)

Jeddah is Saudia's second hub, after Riyadh, and you can fly directly from here to pretty much anywhere in the Kingdom. There are usually 10 to 15 flights per day to Riyadh (SR 270 one way, economy class), five or six to Dhahran (SR 410) and at least one per day to Abha (SR 180), Gassim/Buraydah (SR 290), Jizan (SR 190), Hail (SR 240), Medina (SR 130), Najran (SR 240), Tabuk (SR 270) and Yanbu (SR 100). There are also regular flights to Taif (SR 100), Jouf (Sakaka) (SR 290) and Sharurah (SR 310)

International fares vary significantly from month to month. Here's a sample of the cheapest regular one-way and return fares, with minimum and maximum stay requirements:

To	One Way	Return	Min/Max
Abu Dhabi	SR 1070	SR 1483	2/14 days
Athens	SR 2028	SR 2091	0/90 days
Bahrain	SR 730	SR 1011	2/14 days
Bangkok	SR 1931	SR 3862	0/1 year
Cairo	SR 1137	SR 1390	0/60 days
Damascus	SR 1226	SR 1635	0/60 days
Doha	SR 854	SR 1185	2/14 days
Dubai	SR 1145	SR 1585	2/14 days
Kuwait	SR 1028	SR 1425	2/14 days
London	SR 3769	SR 3876	0/19 days
Muscat	SR 1528	SR 2118	2/14 days
Nairobi	SR 1669	SR 2175	6/60 days
New Delhi	SR 1915	SR 2548	7/120 days
New York	SR 4246	SR 5060	7/30 days
Rome	SR 3010	SR 3110	0/90 days

The round-trip fares to Athens, London, New York and Rome are low season quotes. Around Christmas and in the summer expect to pay more.

Airline Offices Some of the airlines flying out of Jeddah include:

Air France
   Intersection of Al-Madinah Al-Munawwarah Rd and Abdallah Ibn Zayd St, near the Hyatt Regency Hotel (☎ 651 2000)
Air India
   Al-Madinah Al-Munawwarah Rd, just south of the intersection with Al-Amir Abdullah St (☎ 669 6933, ext 1)
Alitalia
   City Centre building, 1st floor, Al-Madinah Al-Munawwarah Rd, north of Falasteen St intersection (☎ 660 0640)
British Airways
   Al-Amoudi Centre on Al-Madinah Al-Munawwarah Rd (☎ 669 3464)
Cyprus Airways
   Al-Amoudi Centre on Al-Madinah Al-Munawwarah Rd, north of Falasteen St intersection (☎ 669 6304)
EgyptAir
   Intersection of Al-Madinah Al-Munawwarah Rd and Al-Malek Khaled St in the Al-Sharafeyyah district (☎ 644 1515)
Emirates
   City Centre building on Al-Madinah Al-Munawwarah Rd, north of Falasteen St intersection (☎ 665 9405)

SAUDI ARABIA

Ethiopian Airlines
    Adham Commercial Centre, Al-Madinah Al-Munawwarah Rd, near the Hyatt Regency Hotel (☎ 651 2996)

Garuda Indonesia
    City Centre building on Al-Madinah Al-Munawwarah Rd, north of Falasteen St intersection (☎ 669 5388)

Gulf Air
    Abo Bakr Al-Seddeeq St near the Abdallah Ibn Zayd St intersection and Hyatt Regency Hotel (☎ 653 3335)

Kenya Airways
    Al-Madinah Al-Munawwarah Rd, just south of the Al-Amir Abdullah St intersection (☎ 669 6933, ext 251)

KLM
    Falasteen St, next door to AMEX, near the Al-Jamjoom Market (☎ 667 0888)

Korean Air
    City Centre building on Al-Madinah Al-Munawwarah Rd, north of Falasteen St intersection (☎ 665 7107)

Kuwait Airways
    Al-Jamjoom Market, Falasteen St (☎ 669 4111)

Lufthansa
    City Centre building, 1st floor, Al-Madinah Al-Munawwarah Rd, north of Falasteen St intersection (☎ 665 0000)

Olympic
    Adham Commercial Centre, Al-Madinah Al-Munawwarah Rd, near the Hyatt Regency Hotel (☎ 651 1280)

Philippine Airlines
    City Centre building, 1st floor, Al-Madinah Al-Munawwarah Rd, north of Falasteen St intersection (☎ 665 4663)

Royal Jordanian
    City Centre building, 1st floor, Al-Madinah Al-Munawwarah Rd, north of Falasteen St intersection (☎ 667 4243)

Saudia
    Al-Malek Abdel Aziz St, across from the Al-Mahmal Centre; open every day until 10 pm (☎ 632 3333)

Swissair
    Intersection of Abo Bakr Al-Seddeeq St and Abdallah Ibn Zayd St, near the Hyatt Regency Hotel (☎ 651 4000)

Tunis Air
    Adham Commercial Centre, Al-Madinah Al-Munawwarah Rd, near the Hyatt Regency Hotel (☎ 653 0881)

Turkish Airlines
    City Centre building on Al-Madinah Al-Munawwarah Rd, north of Falasteen St intersection (☎ 660 0127)

Yemenia
    The Tent Souk, Al-Malek Khalid St (☎ 644 0515)

Bus – domestic The SAPTCO bus station (☎ 648 1131) is on Ba'ashan St. Thanks to a change in routings none of the eastbound inter-city buses go through Mecca anymore and, therefore, they are all open to non-Muslims. Non-Muslim passengers, though, would be well advised to double-check this – it changed once so, presumably, it could change back. Also, there is no computerised reservation system so only a portion of the seats on each bus can be sold in Jeddah. This could be a problem for the overnight services to Riyadh and the Eastern Province. However, if the clerk says he has tickets only to Taif don't let that worry you as you can probably pick up a seat onward to Riyadh in Taif (where the eastbound buses make a 30 to 45-minute stopover).

Ignore both the timetable posted outside the station and the big one inside the station above the main ticket desk. An accurate printed timetable is available for the asking, though usually only in Arabic.

There are 10 buses every day to Riyadh (12 hours, SR 130) at two hour intervals from 6 am until midnight. All of these buses, as well as most of the ones for Asir, stop in Taif (2¾ hours, SR 30). To Dammam (17 hours, SR 190) there are two direct buses per day, at 4.30 and 9 pm. You could also take a bus to Riyadh and change there.

Southbound, to Abha (nine hours, SR 90) and Khamis Mushayt (9½ hours, SR 90) there are 12 buses daily. The first bus leaves at 7 am and the last bus at 1 am. Most of the Abha buses travel via Al-Baha (seven hours, SR 60). There are three daily buses to Bisha (8½ hours, SR 100) at 10 am, 3 and 8 pm, and six daily to Jizan (12 hours, SR 100) at 8 am, noon and at 4, 6, 8 and 10 pm. There are two buses per day to Najran (14½ hours, SR 120) at 10 am and 10 pm.

Northbound, there are four buses daily to Yanbu (4½ hours, SR 60) at 8.30 and 10 am and at 6.30 and 9.30 pm. The first and last Yanbu buses continue on to Tabuk (13 hours,

SR 130). There is also a 5 pm bus to Tabuk. Again, non-Muslims travelling north or east should always double-check that they are not booked on a bus travelling via Mecca or Medina.

For Muslims only, buses go to Mecca (75 minutes, SR 15) 16 times a day, roughly once every hour or two from 6 am. The last run of the day is at 11.15 pm. There are 21 buses per day to Medina (five hours, SR 50) every hour on the hour from 7 am until 2 am with an extra bus at 2.30 pm.

Bus – international SAPTCO's international services depart from the same station as its domestic ones. There are two daily buses to Cairo at 2 and 6 pm. The earlier bus goes via Aqaba, Jordan, making it the slower of the two (a longer initial bus ride, and an extra border to cross are what you trade for the shorter ferry crossing out of Aqaba). It is also more expensive – SR 320 as opposed to SR 290. The later bus is faster overall, gaining time by crossing the Red Sea between Dhuba (Saudi Arabia) and Safaga (Egypt).

Separate buses to Amman (20 hours, SR 200) and Damascus (23 hours, SR 200) leave daily at 10 am. The trips to Egypt, Syria and Jordan include free meals at designated rest stops. SAPTCO buses to Istanbul (officially 48 hours, but that's probably optimistic, SR 260) leave every Monday, Wednesday and Saturday at 3 pm.

International services are also offered by several Turkish bus companies operating from a small station next door to SAPTCO. The companies are Has, Oztür and Tür and they send their buses off in a convoy every Tuesday, Wednesday and Sunday afternoon between 2 and 3 pm. The route is Istanbul (two days, SR 260) via Amman, Damascus and Ankara. All these companies charge roughly the same rates as SAPTCO, though some may be willing to offer a discount, so ask around. If you are talking to any of the Turkish bus companies, be sure that the price they are quoting you does not include fees for Syrian and Jordanian visas. The bus companies usually obtain these for Turkish

passengers, but if you are not a Turk you will be expected to arrange them yourself prior to travel. Since most of the people riding the buses are Turkish, the people in the offices do not always remember to point this out.

For the truly adventurous, one of the agencies – Rizq Travel – was offering tickets all the way to Bucharest for only SR 500 at the time of writing. All these buses take the coastal road north via Yanbu but, again, non-Muslims ought to double-check that the bus isn't going through Mecca or Medina before putting down their money.

For buses to Cairo, SAPTCO is pretty much your only option. Because Jeddah is a port it does not have the heavy competition for bus traffic to Egypt that one sees in Riyadh, though Rizq Travel sometimes has its own services to Egypt.

Service-Taxi These come in three varieties: regular taxis, which take about five passengers, big taxis, which take seven, and trucks which take 10. (The trucks are called 'GMCs' and the big taxis 'Peugeots' after the most common makes of the respective vehicles). As with all service-taxis they leave when full. The GMCs are the cheapest and the regular taxis the most expensive way to travel. The fares are generally the same as or slightly higher than the equivalent bus fare but, as service-taxis are not as commonly used in Saudi Arabia as they are in other Arab countries, they can take a long time to fill up. In addition, most of the drivers headed east are likely to be travelling via Mecca which means that non-Muslims cannot go along. The service-taxi stand is on Al-Mina'a St 1.5 km south of the bus station.

Fares by taxi/Peugeot/GMC are: Mecca, SR 15/15/10; Medina, SR 60/50/50; Taif, SR 35/35/30; Riyadh, SR 150/130/130; Hail, SR 150/150/130; Al-Kharj or Dammam, SR 250/250/200; Abha, SR 130/130/120 and Jizan, SR 120/120/100.

Car Rental The airport is your best bet. The rental agencies are clustered in the arrivals areas and it is fairly easy to shop around, though the rates are pretty much the same at all the counters. In the city you will find a lot of car rental offices, including outlets of most of the bigger companies, along Al-Madinah Al-Munawwarah Rd in the three km or so north of the intersection with Falasteen St.

Boat You can travel by sea from Jeddah Islamic Port to Suez and Safaga (Egypt), Musawwa (Eritrea) and Port Sudan. Before the Gulf War it was also possible to travel to Aqaba (Jordan) by boat, but this service had not resumed at the time of writing.

The trip can be quite an experience: until recently one of the boats on the Egypt run was a converted Danish cruise liner whose lounges still had signs identifying them as the 'Mermaid Pub' and the 'Viking Bar'. The portrait of King Fahd in the 1st-class lounge hung near a large map of Copenhagen's Tivoli amusement park. That boat, however, caught fire and sank off Safaga in the early '90s.

All of the boat services are somewhat irregular with sailings at intervals of six or eight days rather than on a regular weekly basis, but you can count on three or four sailings a month for each boat, more during peak periods. In the case of Egypt peak periods are around the Saudi school holidays: at the beginning and end of the summer and in January. Services are also more frequent (and even more crowded than usual) during Ramadan and at hajj time. As a rule you can expect to find a boat leaving for Suez almost every day, one for Safaga once or twice a week, two or three boats a week to Port Sudan and one a week to Musawwa.

Recently the shorter crossing to Safaga had been replacing Suez in popularity so you can probably expect more sailings bound for Safaga over time. If you are not attached to a vehicle, though, you might want to think twice about this. Safaga is in the middle of nowhere, and it is a lot farther from Cairo than Suez (it is, however, relatively close to Luxor and the Red Sea resort of Hurghada). You will have many more options for onward travel from Suez. Safaga is fairly far south in Egyptian terms, and its popularity can be explained in part by its proximity to Middle and Upper Egypt, where many of the labourers using the service have their homes.

The fares are no great bargain, but they're not unreasonable either. The fares to both Suez (36 hours) and Safaga (24 hours) are the same. These start at SR 225 in deck class and run to SR 500 in 1st class. You should be aware that if the boats start making the Suez run via Aqaba again this increases the journey time to about 72 hours. Be sure you know what route the boat is taking – I was once assured that I was on a direct boat only to find myself on the long, three-day trip! All of the boats to Egypt take cars as well. It costs SR 500 to take a four cylinder car to Egypt, SR 700 for six or eight cylinder vehicles.

The journey to Port Sudan takes 10 to 12 hours and costs around SR 400 in 1st class, SR 350 in 2nd class and SR 300 on the deck. The same prices apply for the 18 to 20 hour trip to Musawwa.

Some shopping around is probably a good idea as the fares can vary greatly from one company to another. Most of the shipping companies have offices along Al-Mina'a St but since each company is pushing its own boat your best bet is to visit a travel agent specialising in ocean travel. I recommend Al-Aquel Travel (☎ 647 5337), off Ba'najah and Al-Dahab Sts, behind the Sahari Hotel. Their sign is only in Arabic, but they are across a very small street from another travel agency, this one sporting a large Yemenia airlines logo in English. Some of the staff at Al-Aquel speak a bit of English, and they are very helpful. If you prefer to deal directly with a ship operator try Fayez Trading, Construction & Shipping (☎ 647 4208), one of the main companies operating boats to Suez and Safaga. Booking directly with the shipping company may save you SR 20 to SR 30 if you are travelling 3rd class or on the deck. Their office is on Al-Mina'a St a few hundred metres south of the overpass.

For boats to Jeddah from Egypt see Marrakech Travel (☎ 354 6046) at the corner of Tahrir St and Tahrir Square, or Yara Tours & Shipping (☎ 392 5393) on Mohamed Sabry Abualam St (off Talaat Harb Square), both in Cairo. The latter has slightly lower prices in 1st class.

Getting Around

The Airport Bus No 20 runs to the south terminal (all Saudia flights, both domestic and international) from Maydan Al-Bayal. The fare is SR 3. To get to the north (foreign carriers) terminal you will have to take a taxi from the south terminal (SR 35). A taxi to either terminal from the centre costs SR 30 to SR 50 on the meter.

Coming into the centre from the airport there are set tariffs. From the south terminal to Al-Balad costs SR 40. The same trip from the north terminal costs SR 50. Outside both terminals you will find both yellow cabs and white limos. They charge the same prices, but the fares in the limos are fixed, sparing you having to bargain with the cab drivers who will usually initially try to get more than the standard fare. The limos usually offer a more comfortable ride anyway.

Bus It's best to stick to the orange and white SAPTCO buses for getting around town. Minibuses also prowl the streets of Jeddah but their destinations are written only in Arabic on the side of the vehicle. The minibus system is absurdly chaotic and is best avoided in favour of SAPTCO. If you insist, however, try hanging around at the intersection by the New Arafat Hotel, where the minibuses start most of their routes.

SAPTCO's buses have their routes clearly displayed in English on a sign in the front windscreen. Bus trips anywhere in the city are SR 2, the sole exception being the airport which costs SR 3. Thrifty Tickets (three trips for SR 5) can be purchased at the SAPTCO inter-city terminal. You can sometimes also get a local route map at the inter-city terminal, but make sure it's up to date. Local buses start running around 5 am and continue until around midnight with the last buses leaving the Al-Balad area at around 11.30 pm.

The main bus routes around the city are:

Route 3 – follows the Makkah Rd, from Bab Makkah to Kilo 20.

Route 3A – Bab Makkah, Makkah Al-Mukarramah Rd to Kilo 7, Ben Ladin St then through the Al-Rawabi district as far as the Ring Rd expressway; returns via same route.

Route 4 – Bab Makkah, Makkah Al-Mukarramah Rd, Al-Jame'ah St, Abdallah Al-Sulayman St, Ali Al-Murtadi St to the Sulaymaneyyah Commercial Centre, then north beyond the Ring Road expressway. Returns via the same route.

Route 4A – Bab Makkah, Makkah Al-Mukarramah Rd, Al-Jame'ah St, Abdallah Al-Sulayman St, Ring Rd expressway (southbound) and vice versa.

Route 5 – Maydan Al-Bayal, Al-Malek Abdel Aziz St, Ba'najah St, Al-Zahab St, Al-Malek Khaled St, Al-Televizyoun St, Al-Mahjar St, Industrial City; returns via same route until Ba'najah St where the bus turns east to follow Ba'najah St, Makkah Al-Mukarramah Rd route back to Maydan Al-Bayal.

Route 6 – Safeway supermarket (Al-Andalus district), Abd Al-Rahman Shubokshi St, Mohammed Ibn Abdul Aziz St, Hail St, Turky Ibn Abdul Aziz St, Ibrahim Al-Juffali St, Arafat St, Al-Fadhl St, Al-Hamra'a St, Al-Andalus St, Al-Maadi St, Hail St, Binzert St, Al-Madinah Al-Munawwarah Rd, Maydan Al-Bayal; returns from Maydan Al-Bayal via: Al-Malek Abdel Aziz St, Ba'najah St, Makkah Al-Mukarramah Rd, Al-Madinah Al-Munawwarah Rd, Al-Madares St, Hail St.

Route 7 – Maydan Al-Bayal, Al-Malek Abdel Aziz St, Ba'najah St, Makkah Al-Mukarramah Rd, Al-Madinah Al-Munawwarah Rd, Abo Bakr Al-Seddeeq St, Al-Madinah Al-Munawwarah Rd, Hera'a St, to Al-Kournaish Rd; returns via same route.

Route 7A – Saudia City, Al-Amir Abdallah St, Al-Madinah Al-Munawwarah Rd, Maydan Al-Bayal; returns to Al-Madinah Al-Munawwarah Rd from Maydan Al-Bayal via Al-Malek Abdel Aziz St, Ba'najah St, Makkah Al-Mukarramah Rd.

Route 7B – Maydan Al-Bayal, Al-Malek Abdel Aziz St, Ba'najah St, Makkah Al-Mukarramah Rd, Al-Madinah Al-Munawwarah Rd, Abo Bakr Al-Seddeeq St, Al-Madinah Al-Munawwarah Rd, Al-Amir Abdallah St, Ahmed Al-Moujahed St, Sari St, Mustafa Menkabou St, Quraysh St, Al-Amir Sultan St, Hera'a St as far as Al-Malek Rd; returns via same route.

Route 8 – SAPTCO Garage (Al-Amir Met'ab St), Sawt Al-Hegaz St, Al-Amir Majed St, Al-Amir Abdallah St, Al-Makarounah St, Falasteen St, Al-Amir Fahd St, Makkah Al-Mukarramah Rd, Al-Madinah Al-Munawwarah Rd, Maydan Al-Bayal and vice versa; returns to Makkah Al-Mukarramah Rd via Al-Malek Abdel Aziz St and Ba'najah St.

Route 8A – Vegetable market (Al-Safa district), Al-Amir Met'ab St, Falasteen St, Al-Amir Fahd St, Makkah Al-Mukarramah Rd, Al-Madinah Al-Munawwarah Rd, Maydan Al-Bayal and vice versa; returns to Makkah Al-Mukarramah Rd via Al-Malek Abdel Aziz and Ba'najah Sts.

Route 9 – Intersection of Al-Amir Met'ab St and Hera'a St, Hera'a St, Al-Amir Fahd St, Al-Malek Khaled St, Al-Madinah Al-Munawwarah Rd, Maydan Al-Bayal; returns via Al-Malek Abdel Aziz St, Ba'najah St, Makkah Al-Mukarramah Rd, Al-Matar Rd and Al-Malek Khaled St.

Route 9B – Al-Nuzha St from near the intersection with Al-Madinah Al-Munawwarah Rd to Al-Amir Majed St, Hera'a St east to Al-Amir Met'ab St and then west to Al-Makarounah St, Al-Makarounah St, Al-Amir Abdullah St, Al-Amir Fahd St, Al-Malek Khaled St, Al-Madinah Al-Munawwarah Rd, Maydan Al-Bayal, Al-Malek Abdel Aziz St, Ba'najah St, Makkah Al-Mukarramah Rd, Al-Matar Rd and Al-Malek Khaled St, Al-Amir Fahd St, Al-Amir Abdullah St, Al-Makarounah St, Al-Nuzha St to the intersection with Al-Madinah Al-Munawwarah Rd.

Route 10 – Al-Safa district, Al-Amir Abdullah St, Al-Amir Majed St, Falasteen St, to Al-Madinah Al-Munawwarah Rd and then back along Falasteen St to Khaled Ibn Al-Waleed St, Al-Malek Khalid St, Al-Madinah Al-Munawwarah Rd, Maydan Al-Bayal, Al-Malek Abdel Aziz St, Ba'najah St, Makkah Al-Mukarramah Rd, Al-Matar Rd, Al-Amir Fahd St, Al-Malek Khalid St, Al-Tawbah St, Wali Al-Ahd St, Al-Tawbah St, Zo Al-Nouryn St, Al-Amir Fahd St, Falasteen St, Al-Amir Majed St, Al-Amir Abdullah St, Al-Safa district.

Route 10A – Al-Manara Souk, Al-Sahafa St, Falasteen St, to Al-Madinah Al-Munawwarah Rd and then back along Falasteen St to Khaled Ibn Al-Waleed St, Al-Malek Khalid St, Al-Madinah Al-Munawwarah Rd, Maydan Al-Bayal, Al-Malek Abdel Aziz St, Ba'najah St, Makkah Al-Mukarramah Rd, Al-Matar Rd, Al-Amir Fahd St, Al-Malek Khalid St, Al-Tawbah St, Wali Al-Ahd St, Al-Tawbah St, Zo Al-Nouryn St, Al-Amir Fahd St, Falasteen St, Al-Sahafa St.

Route 11 – Maydan Al-Bayal, Al-Malek Abdel Aziz St, Ba'najah St, Makkah Al-Mukarramah Rd, Al-Matar Rd, Al-Malek Khaled St, Al-Amir Fahd St, Falasteen St as far as the Marriott Hotel, Al-Souq St, Al-Amir Majed St, Bani Malek St, Al-Amir Met'ab St, Falasteen St to the Ring Road expressway; returns to Maydan Al-Bayal by the same route, except that the bus bypasses Al-Amir Majed St and Al-Souq St, remaining on Bani Malek St from Al-Amir Met'ab St to Al-Amir Fahd St.

Route 12 – Maydan Al-Bayal, Al-Malek Abdel Aziz St, Ba'najah St, Makkah Al-Mukarramah Rd, Al-Iskan St, Industrial City; returns via same route.

Route 13 – Maydan Al-Bayal, Al-Malek Abdel Aziz St, Ba'najah St, Makkah Al-Mukarramah Rd, Qasr Khuzam St, Abdulhadie Al-Yamie St, Madayen Al-Fahd St, Madain Al-Fahd district; returns via same route.

Route 14 – Maydan Al-Bayal, Al-Malek Abdel Aziz St, Ba'najah St, Al-Zahab St, Al-Malek Khaled St, Al-Televizyoun St, Ezaa'h St, Al-Nuzlah St, Madain Al-Fahd district; returns to Maydan Al-Bayal via Makkah Al-Mukarramah Rd and Al-Madinah Al-Munawwarah Rd.

Route 15 – Maydan Al-Bayal, Al-Malek Abdel Aziz St, Ba'najah St, Al-Zahab St, Al-Malek Khaled St, Al-Televizyoun St, Ezaa'h St, Zaynal St, Al-Falah St to the General South Housing Complex; returns to Maydan Al-Bayal via Makkah Al-Mukarramah Rd and Al-Madinah Al-Munawwarah Rd.

Route 16 – Maydan Al-Bayal, Al-Malek Abdel Aziz St, Ba'najah St, Al-Zahab St, Daleel Al-Wafa'a St, Al-Hamrani St, Al-Falah St, Al-Hamrani St to the Petromin district; returns to Maydan Al-Bayal via Makkah Al-Mukarramah Rd and Al-Madinah Al-Munawwarah Rd.

Route 17 – Maydan Al-Bayal, Al-Malek Abdel Aziz St, Ba'najah St, Al-Zahab St, Al-Falah St, Al-Televizyoun St, Al-Mahjar St, Al-Souq Rd to the southern market; returns via same route.

Route 20 – to and from the airport (south terminal) from Maydan Al-Bayal via Al-Madinah Al-Munawwarah Rd.

Taxi The taxis, which are white with an orange stripe down the side, have meters, though you might have to remind drivers to turn them on. They charge SR 3 for a flag fall. The fare then increases in 50 halala increments at a rate of about SR 1 per km.

AROUND JEDDAH
Usfan

Usfan (Osfan) was the next to last stop on the pilgrim caravan route from Egypt and Syria to Mecca (the final resting place was Jamoum, now a small town on the truck road from Taif to Jeddah). Today it is a small town, noteworthy mainly for its Turkish Fort, the ruins of which now somewhat incongruously guard the junction of two expressways.

Qatar/Saudi Arabia

Top: Dhows on the artificial lagoon at the Qatar National Museum.
Middle: Zubara Fort, built in 1938 as a Qatari border police post.
Bottom: Abha, the capital of Asir, Saudi Arabia's south-west province.

Saudi Arabia

Top: Najran Fort (Qasr Al-Imara) near Saudi Arabia's Yemeni border was originally built as a royal residence.

Bottom: The palace of Sa'd Bin Saud at Dir'aiyah is the site's largest restored building.

Turkish Fort The west and south walls of the fort are still relatively intact, each with guard towers looking down onto the road. The eastern wall is not in such good shape and the northern wall is virtually destroyed. The fort can easily be viewed from the ground, and if you climb up there's not a lot to see. However, if you're determined, the climb is short but steep and you'll have to use the north side of the hill. Be very careful of loose stones on the way up and do not, for any reason, climb out onto the bastions, which are unstable.

The whole site looks a little odd today, but try to imagine the huge caravan of pilgrims from Egypt and Syria encamped around this small hill, stopping to rest for two or three days before making the final push on to Mecca itself. Imagine also how utterly forlorn the soldiers garrisoning the place must have felt during the rest of the year.

Even though you can easily view the fort from the ground I would not recommend showing up without a permit. When I pulled over for a look at the fort I was almost immediately stopped and interrogated by the police who then searched both my car and my luggage even though I did have a permit to visit the fort.

The other problem is that there's really no place to park. You can pull safely into the breakdown lane and there is a small area on the northern side of the hill where there is plenty of space as the road splits. To reach this spot coming from Jeddah, however, requires turning north onto the road to Medina and going 10 km before you get a chance to make the necessary U-turn.

Getting There & Away Usfan is about 65 km from central Jeddah. Head north out of the city on Al-Madinah Al-Munawwarah Rd past the airport. About nine km beyond the exit for the airport's north (foreign airlines) terminal you will see an exit for Usfan. Take this, and then take another Usfan exit after two km. From there the road will take you straight to the town (it's about 30 km beyond the second exit).

The Hejaz (Western Region)

MECCA

Muslims refer to Mecca (Makkah) as *al-mukarramah*, which translates roughly as 'the revered'. It was here that the Prophet Mohammed was born in the 6th century AD, here that he began his preaching career and it was to Mecca that he returned for a final pilgrimage shortly before his death in 632.

Mecca and the holy sites in its immediate vicinity are strictly off limits to non-Muslims. There are checkpoints on the roads approaching the city and non-Muslims are strongly advised not to try getting past these. The most famous non-Muslim who managed to visit Mecca was Richard Burton, the great British explorer who disguised himself as an Afghan Muslim and participated in the hajj in 1853.

Mecca is Islam's holiest city. All devout Muslims are supposed to attempt a hajj to Mecca at least once in their lifetime. With an area of some 26 sq km, Mecca is in the Sirat Mountains, 70 km east of Jeddah. The city centres on the Grand Mosque and the sacred Zamzam well inside it. The Kaaba, which all Muslims face when they pray, is in the mosque's central courtyard. According to tradition, the Kaaba was originally built by Adam, and later rebuilt by Abraham and his son Ishmael as a replica of God's house in heaven.

As a non-Muslim I could not visit Mecca. However, the religious and scholarly literature on the holy sites is ample and easily available throughout the Kingdom. Muslims seeking practical information on hotels and restaurants in Mecca may want to consult the *Makkah Al-Mukarramah City & Hajj Guide*, one of the 'A to Z' guides to Saudi cities by Farsi Maps.

TAIF

Taif (Tai'if, Al-Taif), nestled in the mountains above Mecca, is the summer capital of Saudi Arabia. During the summer months it

SAUDI ARABIA

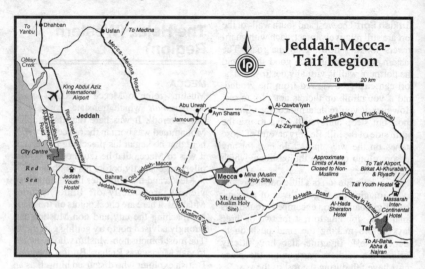

Jeddah-Mecca-Taif Region

0   10   20 km

is noticeably cooler than Jeddah and a great deal less humid. The town's main attractions are its weather, scenery and relaxed atmosphere.

History

The town is quite important historically. Traditionally, it has been the military gateway to Mecca and many an army has positioned troops here over the centuries. In 1802 the warriors of the First Saudi Empire massacred the entire male population of the town. Taif was also the site of one of the key early battles of the Arab revolt against Ottoman rule during WWI. The seizure of the town in 1916 by forces loyal to Sherif Hussein was one of the events which eventually convinced the British that Hussein's embryonic kingdom of the Arabs would be worth their backing.

In 1924, however, an army under the command of the Sherif's son, Ali, contributed to a far less glorious chapter of the town's history. Knowing that an attack by Abdul Aziz's forces was imminent, Ali and his army slunk away under cover of darkness. The ikhwan army, which entered the

city after the Hashemites had left it undefended, killed at least 300 people. The second Wahhabi massacre at Taif was deeply embarrassing to Abdul Aziz though it ultimately worked to his political advantage. Word of the deaths in Taif spread rapidly to Mecca and Jeddah and led, a month later, to Sherif Hussein's abdication under pressure from Mecca's scholars and Jeddah's merchants.

In recent years Taif has also become something of a minor diplomatic centre. In 1988, it hosted peace talks involving the USSR, the Afghan government and the Mujahedeen rebels. The following year, the town was the site of a lengthy peace conference that laid the groundwork for the end of Lebanon's civil wars, and from August 1990 until March 1991 Taif was the seat of Kuwait's government-in-exile.

Orientation & Information

Taif centres on a nameless square formed by the intersection of King Faisal and Shubra Sts. It looks like a square because of the large parking lot across from the telephone office. Most of the budget hotels are a bit east of this intersection and cheap restaurants are all over the central area. The bus station and airport are some distance north of the centre.

For changing money there are a number of banks around the main intersection. There is a post office just off the south side of the intersection, opposite the telephone office, though the GPO is north of town, near the bus station. The telephone office, from which only international calls can be made, is in the small white building next to the much larger PTT office on the north-west side of the main intersection. For long-distance calls inside Saudi Arabia you'll have to go to the small post office, where there are payphones. The telephone code for Taif is 02.

The Saudia office is on Abu Bakker Al-Siddiq St about 200m north of the main intersection.

Abdallah Bin Abbas Mosque

Taif's central mosque, though a bit fortress-like at first glance, is a good example of simple, refined Islamic architecture. Note the interesting minaret which is earth-coloured with brown and white trim and a white dome. If you look just below the four long windows on the minaret's midsection you will see several balconies which give a nice effect.

The mosque is named after a cousin of the Prophet who was also the grandfather of the founder of the Abbasid dynasty. Abdullah Bin Abbas died in Taif circa 687 AD at the age of 70. He was buried at a site near the city.

Tailors' Souk

One of Taif's few surviving traditional areas can be found just off the main square, at the intersection of Shubra and King Faisal Sts around the corner from the post office. Next to a Turkish restaurant and several small grocery stores is an old archway of sand-coloured stone. There are two small mock pillars just above the archway and, above them, an eye-shaped frieze design. The short alleyway beyond this arch, part of the tailors' souk, is a quick trip into old Taif. At one time

much of the city (and many other Middle Eastern cities) consisted of small, alley-like streets of this kind making up the various souks.

Shubra Palace

This beautifully restored traditional house doubles as the city's museum. It is open Saturday to Wednesday from 7.30 am to 2.30 pm. Admission is free.

The palace itself was built around the turn of the century. The materials used included marble imported from Italy and timber from Turkey. King Abdul Aziz used to stay here when he visited Taif in his later years and it was also used as a residence by King Faisal.

Move to the right after passing through the entrance hall. The displays include geological and geographic information, pottery from the Kingdom's various regions and exhibits on the Zubaydah Road and mosque architecture. Beyond are two rooms displaying household goods, jewellery and weapons.

Beit Kaki

This house was built in 1943 as a summer residence for the Kaki family, one of Mecca's most important trading families then and now. The date comes from a plaque near the door. It is one of the oldest buildings in Taif and is in a reasonably good state of repair. It is currently unoccupied.

The house is at the intersection of Al-Salamah and Al-Baladiya Sts.

Beit Khatib

Beit Khatib, built in 1938, is in a much more dilapidated state than Beit Kaki. It, too, served as the summer residence of one of Mecca's leading merchant families. The house is at the intersection of Al-Salamah and Al-Nabighah Al-Dhubyani Sts.

Places to Stay

Taif is a very crowded city on summer weekends (ie from Wednesday afternoon until Friday afternoon). From May to September reservations are strongly recommended.

SAUDI ARABIA

Places to Stay – bottom end & middle

The *youth hostel* (☎ 725 3400) is at the King Fahd Sporting City in the Hawiyah district, 22.5 km north of the centre. From the bus station go north (away from the centre); take the Hawiyah exit and follow the signs for the Sporting City. The No 10 bus runs from the centre to the hostel via the bus station and stops about 100m from the gate. (Note that bus routes in Taif change frequently. Ask the driver or the clerk at the bus station before boarding to make sure that the bus is, in fact, going to the Sporting City.) Look for a small, blue 'Youth Hostel' sign by the wall of the complex. Beds are SR 8. The hostel is infinitely superior to any of the hotels listed under this heading and is far more likely to have space at weekends.

All of the rooms at the following hotels have air-conditioning, except for the Dar Al-Salam which has ceiling fans. The Dar Al-Salam Hotel is also the only one where the rooms do not all have a TV, telephone and fridge. Service charges, where applicable, have been included in the prices. Summer rates are usually for the period from 1 June to 30 September.

The *Dar Al-Salam Hotel* (☎ 736 0124) on King Faisal St, just west of the main intersection, is the only real cheapie in town. Singles/doubles are SR 40/60 (SR 50/70 in summer). The rooms are small and spartan but some have balconies. The hotel does not have air-conditioning, though all the rooms have ceiling fans.

On King Saud St, the *Al-Sharq Hotel* (☎ 732 3651, fax 732 5093) has a lobby filled with old furniture that gives the place a rather attractive atmosphere. The rooms are good but not spectacular at SR 88/132 with bath and SR 77/115.50 without. Summer rates are SR 114/172 with bath, SR 100/150 without. Further along King Saud St the *Al-Maseef Hotel for Tourist* (☎ 732 4786) has been renovated since the last edition and, at SR 99/132 with bath and SR 77/126.50 without (SR 129/171.50 and SR 100/164.50, respectively, in summer), is better value than the Al-Sharq. A bit farther down on the same street and up the price scale is the *Al-Barraq*

Hotel (☎ 736 0610) at SR 165/214.50 (SR 209/270 in summer), where all rooms have attached baths.

The *Okaz Hotel* (☎ 732 8051) on Al-Salamah St, near the Abdallah Bin Abbas Mosque, is OK at SR 77/115 for rooms with bath, SR 66/99 without (summer rates SR 100/150 with bath, SR 86/129 without), but you can do better elsewhere.

Probably the best of Taif's slightly more expensive hotels is the *Al-Andalus Hotel* (☎ 732 8491), just off the main square by the Assia Restaurant. It is a relatively new place, with rooms at SR 100/150 for singles/doubles (SR 300 single or double in summer). The rooms are large and very clean and you can get CNN on the TV.

Another good bet is the *Nada Hotel* (☎ 732 4177), just off Al-Baladiyah St. The rooms are very nice and quite a good deal at SR 110/165 with bath, SR 99/148.50 without (SR 137.50/206 and SR 124/185.50 in summer). Between the Nada and the Okaz you will find the *Assarafi Hotel* (☎ 732 4974), with rooms at SR 132/198 (SR 171.50/258 in summer).

Taif has two places called the Safari Hotel. The cheaper *Safari Hotel* (☎ 736 3333) is on Shubra St, about 300m from the main intersection. The hotel has big, airy rooms, all with bath, for SR 120/180 (SR 150/220 in summer). The other *Safari Hotel* (☎ 732 1515), by the Great Mosque, is slightly more up-market at SR 150/200 (SR 180/250 in summer).

Also at the upper end of the mid-range is the *Al-Azezia Hotel* (☎ 732 6429) on Al-Aziziyyah Square. Rooms are SR 187/247.50 (SR 242/308 in summer) but that seems to be very negotiable (off season they once offered me a suite at the single rate).

Places to Stay – top end

People with money tend to converge on the *Inter-Continental Hotel* (☎ 732 8333, fax 736 1844), 13 km north of Taif's centre, or on the *Al-Hada Sheraton* (☎ 754 1400, fax 754 4831), 20 km south of Taif overlooking the village of Al-Hada. Both charge SR 368/478 (SR 441.50/574 in summer) for singles/

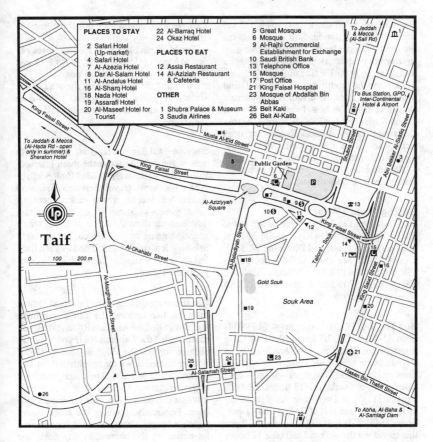

PLACES TO STAY
2 Safari Hotel (Up-market)
4 Safari Hotel
7 Al-Azezia Hotel
8 Dar Al-Salam Hotel
11 Al-Andalus Hotel
16 Al-Sharq Hotel
18 Nada Hotel
19 Assarafi Hotel
20 Al-Maseef Hotel for Tourist
22 Al-Barraq Hotel
24 Okaz Hotel

PLACES TO EAT
12 Assia Restaurant
14 Al-Aziziah Restaurant & Cafeteria

OTHER
1 Shubra Palace & Museum
3 Saudia Airlines
5 Great Mosque
6 Mosque
9 Al-Rajhi Commercial Establishment for Exchange
10 Saudi British Bank
13 Telephone Office
15 Mosque
17 Post Office
21 King Faisal Hospital
23 Mosque of Abdallah Bin Abbas
25 Beit Kaki
26 Beit Al-Katib

Taif

doubles. Neither can be reached by public transport.

Places to Eat

Taif has Saudi Arabia's usual large selection of small Turkish restaurants. One of the best is the *Al-Aziziah Restaurant Cafeteria*, on King Faisal St near the intersection with Abu Bakker Al-Siddiq St. It's a lot bigger and nicer inside than it looks from the street and the kebabs are excellent. There is a family section. Grilled chicken or a kebab with rice, bread and salad runs from SR 10 to SR 15. Also on King Faisal St, the *Assia Restaurant*

is a friendly place with similar, though not quite as outstanding, fare. The prices are about the same as those at the Al-Aziziah.

The *Al-Azezia Hotel* has a restaurant/coffee shop which is worth trying, especially if you want quieter surroundings than the Assia offers.

If you are looking for a traditional coffee house try the *Port Said Coffeehouse*. It is above the Al-Rajhi Commercial Establishment for Exchange on the main square and is entered through a small door on the north side of the building, next to a stationery shop.

Another place to go for tea and a shisha is

SAUDI ARABIA

Barty Gardens on the airport road, 1.7 km north of the bus station. Soft drinks and tea are served in a garden off the road which may or may not be quiet, depending on whether a soccer game is on TV that night.

Out by the youth hostel you will find several small restaurants more or less across the street from the hostel entrance. Try the *Dema Kaffetarea* (sic) for shawarma. Across the street the *Al-A'aada Restaurant* does kebabs and other grilled food. Their Arabic sign is red with white lettering.

For more up-market dining the two large hotels are your only option.

Getting There & Away

Air The airport is 25 km north of the town. Daily flights operate to Riyadh (SR 240 one way, economy class) and Dhahran (SR 380). Direct flights are also available to Jeddah (SR 100), Abha (SR 140), Medina (SR 230), Tabuk (SR 370) and Sharurah (SR 290) several times per week.

Bus The SAPTCO bus station (☎ 736 9924) is on Al-Matar Rd, 2.5 km north of the main intersection. There are nine buses daily to Riyadh (nine hours, SR 100), with connections to Hofuf and Dammam – there is also a direct bus to Dammam (13 hours, SR 160) daily at 11.30 pm. Departures for Riyadh are at 1, 9 and 11 am and at 3, 7, 9 and 11 pm. There are also daily buses at 11 am and 7 pm that travel via the old road and take 12 hours to make the trip to Riyadh.

There are three daily buses to Abha (10 hours, SR 90) at 11 am and 1.30 and 4.30 pm. The Abha buses go via Al-Baha (four hours, SR 30) and continue on to Khamis Mushayt. There are additional buses to Al-Baha at 8 am and 7.15 pm.

Buses to Bisha (5½ hours, SR 80) leave at 1, 6 and 11 pm. There are two buses each day to Buraydah (10¼ hours, SR 120) at 11.45 am and 3.45 pm. There are 13 Jeddah-bound buses for non-Muslims each day (2¾ hours, SR 30). These leave every few hours around the clock. Jeddah-bound non-Muslims should always double-check that

they are not booked on a bus travelling via Mecca.

For Muslims only there are five buses per day to Mecca (1½ hours, SR 15) at 2.15 and 7 am and at 1, 3.30 and 7.15 pm.

Note that the timetable on the wall of the station is years out of date. Up-to-date printed schedules are sometimes available at the station.

Service-Taxi Service-taxis are on the north side of the parking lot at the main intersection. A few of them are headed for Riyadh or Abha but most travel between Taif and Jeddah via Mecca, which makes them off limits to non-Muslims. If you can fill a taxi with non-Muslims the driver probably won't object to going around Mecca, but he might ask for a few riyals more. The fares are fluid but are usually slightly higher than the comparable bus fare.

Car If you are driving up to Taif from Jeddah there are two options: the Taif Escarpment Rd (also called the Al-Hada Rd) and the truck route (called the Jamoum Rd if you are travelling from Jeddah to Taif, and the Sail Rd if you are headed down the mountain from Taif to Mecca and Jeddah). The Escarpment Rd is spectacular but, because of the way people drive, it can be a pretty hair-raising experience. Personally, I prefer the truck route, which is longer, slower and less scenic but a lot easier on the nerves. In any case, the Escarpment Rd is closed every year from October to May. To reach the Escarpment Rd from Jeddah you go either straight through Mecca or around Mecca to the south on the non-Muslim road, For the truck route, leave the Mecca expressway at the non-Muslim road exit and turn left toward Shumaisi at the top of the overpass (instead of turning right for the main non-Muslim road around Mecca). If you take the main road around Mecca and find the Escarpment Rd closed, there is no way for non-Muslims to join the truck route from the east side of Mecca – you'll have to go all the way back around Mecca and start again.

Car Rental In addition to the better known agencies, some of which have desks at the two five-star hotels, you will find a number of small car rental companies scattered around the cheap hotel area. Marhaba Rent-A-Car (☎ 732 3204) on King Saud St is one possibility. Out by the youth hostel and across the street from its entrance, Al-Mohand Rent-A-Car (☎ 725 0769) is your only option outside the centre.

Getting Around
Local buses cost SR 2 per trip. No route map is available and the routes keep changing, but it is usually possible to get from the bus station to the youth hostel. At the time of writing bus No 10 ran from the main intersection to the Sports City (youth hostel) via the bus station, but ask the driver first in case things have changed. There is no regular bus to the airport though SAPTCO sometimes puts on a special airport-to-centre route during the Muslim holidays and on summer weekends.

AROUND TAIF
Al-Hada
This small village (not counting the Sheraton Hotel rising out of its centre), 20 km south of Taif, is worth visiting if you are interested in seeing a rural Saudi/Hejazi village.

Al-Samlagi Dam
The wadis around Taif are filled with old dams in various states of repair. The largest of these is the Samlagi Dam, approximately 30 km south of the centre. It was originally built in the early years of the Islamic era, making it around 1300 years old. Some sources say the dam is actually pre-Islamic.

The dam was originally anchored by hills at either end, though one of these has been partially eroded away. It was 212m long, 10m high and 10.8m wide at its centre. The reservoir behind it could hold an estimated 500,000 cubic metres of water. This water was gathered during the rainy season. Construction of this and other ancient dams

allowed the area's farmers to capture the water and use it for irrigation. They also diverted flash floods away from inhabited areas. The reservoir was originally on the side from which you approach the dam today. At the base of the dam's other side several stones have inscriptions dating to the era of the dam's construction.

The dam consists of two parallel walls of large stones that have been carefully joined with mortar. The space between the walls was filled in with rubble (a process you can still clearly make out at some points atop the dam) and then the top was covered over with more large stones. Getting to the top of the dam is easy. The fit can climb the end near the road easily. Others can walk to the far end of the dam where the climb amounts to a couple of steps.

Getting There & Away To reach the dam from Taif, take Abu Bakker Al-Siddiq St from the main square to the King Faisal Hospital and turn south onto Hasan Bin Thabit St, which is also the road to Abha. From the hospital follow the road 17.5 km and turn right at the sign for Tamalah. Follow this road for just over a km and then turn left, again at a sign for Tamalah. Stay on this road for 12 km, then turn left onto a dirt track that goes uphill. There is a white sign in Arabic with red lettering and a black arrow pointing toward the dam. When you pass signs for Wadi Al-Umar you will know that you are close to this last turn-off.

Follow the dirt track for 300m. This will take you to a fork. Keep to the right. About 100m past the fork the track splits three ways; keep to the left, and beware of the sharp, and very bumpy, downhill section that you are about to go over. After this the track is first sandy and then a bit rocky as you approach, and then pass through, some trees. About 500m after the fork you will come round a bend to find the dam in front of you.

You can reach the dam in an ordinary car, but take care as the dirt portion of the road is not in ideal condition. No permit is needed since the dam is not fenced off.

BIRKAT AL-KHURABAH

In the desert nearly 100 km north-east of Taif (as the crow flies) lie the great stone cisterns of Birkat Al-Khurabah, a remnant of one of history's greatest civil engineering projects – the Zubaydah Road. The road, also known as the Darb Zubaydah, provided sustenance for thirsty pilgrims on their way from Iraq and Persia to Mecca and Medina. In the case of Birkat Al-Khurabah the Saudi government has restored the millennium-old Zubaydah cisterns and supplemented them with a modern counterpart a few hundred metres away, which is regularly used by the local Bedouins. Birkat Al-Khurabah was not the most important stop on the Darb Zubaydah, but today it offers some of the road's most impressive remains.

Take a moment to stand on this desert plain and imagine the hajj caravan emerging from the north in a cloud of dust – 10,000 or more pilgrims, their guides and various hangers-on descending year after year, century after century, on these great stone pools established to provide them with water amid the seemingly trackless wastes of western Arabia.

There are two pools at Birkat Al-Khurabah. The larger one is the huge circular pool with 12 steps descending to its bottom. The smaller pool is square and also has stepped entrances. A small stone pavilion divides the two. The entire complex has been well restored. There may or may not be water in the cisterns, depending on when you visit and what the weather has been like.

Technically speaking you need a permit from the museum in Riyadh to visit Birkat Al-Khurabah. In practice this is unnecessary as there is no fence around the site (to facilitate its use by the region's Bedouins and by any modern pilgrims who may happen by).

Getting There & Away

By road, Birkat Al-Khurabah is just under 130 km from the centre of Taif. Though the Farsi atlas of Saudi Arabia shows the site far out in the desert, a paved road now runs to within 12 km of the pools, and the desert track from there is easily passable with a regular car, though it is rather bumpy.

From Taif take the expressway toward Riyadh to exit 54 (just under 50 km from the centre). Turn north (left, if you are coming from Taif) and follow the road 71 km through Ashayrah and Faysaliyah to Birkah which consists only of a petrol station, a mosque and two small warehouse-like buildings. Birkah was also a way-station on the Zubaydah Road. There is a cistern that you can walk to from the petrol station, though the larger cisterns at Khurabah are far more interesting, especially if you have already bothered to drive this far into the middle of nowhere.

The track to Birkat Al-Khurabah starts on the south side (the near side, coming from Taif) of the warehouses. Look for a prefabricated building with a green roof about 150m before you reach the petrol station. Coming from the south – ie from the Riyadh-Taif expressway – this is a right turn.

The track is very well defined. Follow it for 5.2 km, past a very small power generating station which will be on your right. At 5.2 km the track forks, keep right and after another three km you will enter a village. Here the track becomes a bit harder to follow but you should still be able to make it out. Head straight through the village keeping the mosque to your left and the school (the big, low whitewashed building with a flagpole) to your right. About 1.4 km beyond the village the track forks again. Again, keep right. At this point you will be driving across a relatively smooth gravel plain. The track will be hard to discern, but just keep going straight.

About a km past the second fork you should be able to glimpse the modern cistern directly ahead of you in the distance. Its wall consists of grey cement blocks with whitewashed vertical supports. The modern cistern is two km east of the village. Drive straight up to it and turn left immediately in front of it. The Zubaydah cisterns will be 250m farther on, directly in front of you. The total distance from the main road to the Zubaydah cisterns is about 12 km.

The Zubaydah Road

Sometime around the year 800 AD Zubaydah, the favourite wife of Caliph Haroun Al-Rashid (a figure most familiar to westerners as the sultan whose adventures and just rule are a frequent subject of the tales that make up the *Arabian Nights*), set off from what is now Iraq to perform the pilgrimage to Mecca. Along the way she nearly died of thirst. This was not uncommon at the time. The difference was that, being the wife of the caliph, Zubaydah was in a position to do something about it once she reached home.

Following her journey she provided the funds to build and maintain a massive system of cisterns stretching from what is now southern Iraq to Mecca. Zubaydah's hope was that future pilgrims would never go thirsty. Though some of the facilities along what came to be known as the Darb Zubaydah, or the Zubaydah Road, eventually fell into disuse, many others were carefully maintained for centuries and a few are still in use today (largely by Bedouins to water their animals – few, if any, pilgrims travel the Zubaydah Road any more). In some places the Saudi government has built modern cisterns only a few metres away from the thousand-year-old facilities bequeathed by the Abbasid caliph's wife.

The road began at Kufa, near the modern Iraqi city of Najaf, and meandered across some 1500 km of desert. It entered what is now Saudi Arabia at the town of Rafah and continued south to Faid, about 50 km from the modern city of Burraydah. Faid was the road's midpoint, and the residence of the *amir al-hajj*, the government official charged with overseeing the pilgrimage and maintaining the road. From there it turned south-west, continuing across the desert to Mecca.

Even today it retains a powerful hold on the imagination of both Saudis and foreigners. While researching this edition I was shown the way to the cisterns at Birkat Al-Khurabah by a local Bedouin. 'These are the cisterns of Queen Zubaydah', he said with obvious pride as we reached the site. 'She put them here for the pilgrims, and they have been here for a thousand years.' ■

Back in **Birkah** you will find two other cisterns, one modern, the other another Zubaydah cistern, about 300m west of the paved north-south road. The track to these cisterns leaves the main road directly opposite the track to Birkat Al-Khurabah. Follow the track for a couple of hundred metres and you should see the new cistern's wall off to your right. The older cistern, as well as some small stone buildings, are just beyond and to the left of it.

YANBU

If you thought Jubail, the massive industrial complex on the Gulf coast, was dull wait until you see its Red Sea twin. At least Jubail can boast an interesting archaeological site. Yanbu is all business, and unless you are in the petrochemicals business there is only one reason to come here: diving.

Orientation & Information

Driving into Yanbu from the south you will

pass through the industrial zone first – an enormous area stretching along some 25 km of coastline – before coming into Yanbu's relatively small centre. The main drag is King Abdul Aziz St, which runs perpendicular to the north-south road from Jeddah and the industrial city.

Yanbu's telephone area code is 04.

Diving

There are several dive shops in town along King Abdul Aziz St, just west of the Middle East Hotel. Try the Yanbu Establishment or The Deep. There is also a small dive shop in the lobby of the Holiday Inn.

Places to Stay & Eat

Yanbu has four hotels. The best value for money is the *Middle East Hotel* (☎ 322 1281, fax 322 4770) on King Abdul Aziz St. Singles/doubles with bath cost SR 88/132. Down the street at the *Al-Higgi Hotel* (☎ 322 8831, fax 322 8645) the rooms cost SR 165/245.50, including the service charge, but are pretty much the same. The *Al-Hayat Hotel Yanbu* (☎ 322 3888, fax 322 7021) is five km south of the centre on the road to the industrial complex. Rooms cost SR 316/380, including the service charge, but if things are slow they will discount that rate by about 40%, more if you are staying for a long time. At the discounted price it is only a few riyals more than the Higgi and definitely a much better deal.

The *Radhwa Holiday Inn* (☎ 322 3767, fax 322 7281) is seven km south of the centre. With a lock on the top end of the local hotel market they don't do much discounting. Rooms cost SR 402.50/517.50, including the service charge.

Getting There & Away

The airport is north-east of the centre. Saudia flies to Jeddah (SR 100 one way, economy class) two or three times a day and to Riyadh (SR 370) three or four times a week. In town, the Saudia booking office (☎ 322 6666) is on King Abdul Aziz St a few doors east of the Al-Higgi Hotel.

If you need to rent a car try the airport or

go to King Abdul Aziz St where a dozen or so agencies, both large and small, have offices in the few blocks between the Middle East and Al-Higgi hotels.

BADR

Badr lies seven km east of the junction of the north-south road from Jeddah to Yanbu with the east-west road to Medina. It is about 70 km south-east of Yanbu and 170 km south-west of Medina. Though a small town, Badr looms large in Islamic history. In 624 AD a decisive battle was fought here between Muslim forces led by the Prophet Mohammed and an army raised by the Prophet's opponents from still-pagan Mecca. The Meccan forces went in with the upper hand, having defeated the Muslims in the battle of Ohud, near Medina, earlier that year. At Badr, however, the Meccans lost, the tide turned and the Muslim conquest of Arabia began in earnest. During the battle the Muslims lost 14 men (the Meccans lost 70). Thirteen of these martyrs are buried in a large cemetery in Badr (the other grave is some 30 km outside the town).

Martyrs' Cemetery

The cemetery can be visited without any special formalities or permission, but bear in mind that it is an especially holy site for Muslims and conduct yourself accordingly.

The cemetery is surrounded by a low wall of yellow brick with a white top. The gate to the cemetery is likely to be closed but you can easily see the martyrs' graves from the wall – they are in the area enclosed by a low, whitewashed stone wall about 100m straight ahead if you look over the perimeter wall from just to the right of the main gate.

Once you are in the town the cemetery is fairly easy to find. Turn at the sign pointing to 'Badr Shuhada'a'. This is a right turn if you are coming from Medina. Coming from Jeddah or Yanbu you will have to make a U-turn on Badr's main street and backtrack a short distance before turning right. The cemetery is 1.4 km from the main road. After turning at the Badr Shuhada'a sign follow the road, keeping straight when you pass through a roundabout about half a km after leaving the main road. After another 400m you will pass, on your left, the turn for Badr's main mosque. Do not take this turn. Continue to follow the road and after another half a km you will reach the top of a small rise, at which point the cemetery wall will be immediately to your right.

Places to Stay & Eat

There appears to be no place to stay in Badr itself, despite numerous signs around the town pointing to a 'Badr Resthouse'. There is a *SASCO Resthouse* 10 km from Badr. It is on the north-south road from Jeddah to Yanbu, three km north of the junction with the road to Medina. Two-bed rooms cost SR 120 a single or double, and a suite with two bedrooms, two bathrooms, a sitting room and a kitchen goes for SR 240. There is also a restaurant, supermarket and a mechanic's shop on the premises. The sign is only in Arabic – look for a blue and white sign with a palm tree logo. It's on the left if you are going north.

There is the usual collection of small restaurants around the bus station on both sides of the main road.

Getting There & Away

Badr's bus stop is on the town's main east-west road (the one to Medina), about 200m west of the turn for the cemetery. There are two buses daily to Yanbu (1½ hours, SR 20) at 1.30 and 8.30 pm and two per day to Medina (1½ hours according to SAPTCO, probably longer in practice, SR 20) at 9 am and 5 pm. You could easily make Badr a stopover and simply walk to the cemetery and back between buses. Non-Muslims should remember, however, that Medina's bus station is inside the *haram* (forbidden area) and, thus, off limits to them.

MEDINA

Medina (Medinah, Al-Madinah) is Islam's holiest city after Mecca and was the first community to accept the Prophet's message wholeheartedly. Like Mecca, it is off limits to non-Muslims though its haram (forbidden

area) is much smaller. The word *medina* in Arabic means 'city', and the name is a shortening of *medinat an-nabi*, or 'city of the Prophet'. Pious Muslims refer to Medina as *al-munawwarah*, or 'the enlightened'.

Mohammed fled to the city, which was then called Yathrib, from Mecca in 622 and lived the remaining years of his life there. The city's centrepiece is the Prophet's Mosque where Mohammed is buried. This mosque was originally the house in which Mohammed lived, though it has been enlarged many times over the centuries and is now said to cover an area greater than the entire town did in Mohammed's lifetime.

Orientation & Information

Medina is a 390 km drive from Jeddah and a 920 km cross-desert trek from Riyadh. The outskirts of the city, which include the airport, the Medina Sheraton and Oyun hotels and the youth hostel are open to non-Muslims. You should not, however, come to Medina with the idea that you can see anything of the holy sites just because the haram is smaller. Virtually everything of religious or historical significance lies within the forbidden zone. At the Sheraton you are still a good five km away from the Prophet's Mosque. At best you may catch distant glimpses of the holy sites. Like Jerusalem, however, almost every rock, bush and building in Medina has some story connected with it, and a couple of these sites can be viewed, albeit from a distance, by non-Muslims.

Medina's telephone code is 04.

Things to See

The best view of the **Prophet's Mosque** available to non-Muslims is from the road between the youth hostel and the Sheraton near the intersection with Al-Salam St. At that point you are about seven km from the mosque, but its minarets are clearly visible – which gives you some idea just how huge the mosque is now that its latest expansion is complete.

Though non-Muslims cannot visit it, from the Sheraton you have a clear view of the **Al-Qeblatain Mosque**. It was at this mosque (which at the time would have been rather smaller and less grand) that Mohammed was praying in the year 2 AH (623-624 AD) when he received the revelation instructing him to change the *qibla*, or orientation of prayer, from Jerusalem to Mecca. Mohammed did so as he prayed and the rest of the congregation changed direction along with him. Only after prayers had finished did he explain to his followers why he had made a 180° turn in the middle of his devotions. In Arabic the suffix '-ain' is a plural meaning 'two'. Hence the Qeblatain Mosque is the place in which, for one service of prayers, there were two qiblas.

Non-Muslims can also get a good look at **Ohud Mountain**, the site of one of the earliest, and most important, battles in Islamic history. Ohud is the large outcrop of rock that will be to your left, blocking your view of the city, shortly after you leave the airport and turn north-west on Al-Jameaat Rd en route to the hotels open to non-Muslims. A Muslim army was camped on the far side of the mountain in 624 when it was attacked by an army from still-pagan Mecca. The Meccan army was led by Khalid Bin Al-Waleed, who later converted to Islam and led Muslim armies to some of their greatest conquests outside Arabia in the generation after the Prophet's death. The Muslims initially repulsed the attack, but Khalid retreated north with his army and then circled around the back side of the mountain (more or less following the line of the present-day road) to surprise the Muslims from the other direction, thus winning the battle. The ensuing loss led some of the Prophet's followers to question his leadership, but their doubts were allayed a few months later when the Muslims triumphed over a much larger Meccan force with only minimal losses at the battle of Badr.

Catching his first sight of Ohud, in 1853, Burton described the mountain as 'a grim pile of rocks'. He went on to write:

Its seared and jagged flanks rise like masses of iron from the plain, and the crevice into which the Moslem host retired, when the disobedience of the archers in

hastening to plunder enabled Khaled bin Walid to fall upon Mohammed's rear, is the only break in the grim wall. Reeking with heat, its surface produces not one green shrub or stunted tree; neither bird nor beast appeared upon its inhospitable sides, and the bright blue sky glaring above its bald and sullen brow, made it look only the more repulsive. I was glad to turn away my eyes from it. (*Pilgrimage*, chapter 20)

The martyrs from the battle of Ohud are buried at the base of the mountain, on the side facing the city (ie the side that is off limits to non-Muslims). Tradition records that 70 Muslims died in the battle. Another tradition places the tomb of Aaron, the brother of Moses, in the small shrine atop Ohud, though there is also a mausoleum near Petra, in Jordan, that claims to be Aaron's final resting place.

Places to Stay

Non-Muslims have three options when looking for accommodation in Medina. The *youth hostel* (☎ 847 4092, fax 847 4344) is at the stadium on Al-Jameaat Rd just south of the intersection with Al-Salam St. The entrance to the hostel is on the south side of the stadium complex. Beds cost SR 8 per night.

At the northern edge of the city is the *Oyun Hotel* (☎ 847 4659) where singles/doubles cost SR 110/165 including the service charge. During Ramadan and the month of Dhul Hijja (essentially the two weeks either side of the hajj) these rates increase to SR 225/337.50. The hotel is fairly simple but perfectly adequate and is the best option for couples on a budget. The Oyun is at the intersection of Al-Jameaat Rd and Osman Ibn Affan St (which is also called Al-Oyoun St).

The *Medina Sheraton* (☎ 846 0777, fax 846 0385) is the final option for visiting non-Muslims. It is a decent place though the food is not all that great. They charge about SR 460/598 most of the time and SR 805/1035 during Ramadan and the hajj period. The hotel also runs a weekend package tour to the ruins of Madain Salah and the Hejaz Railway. See the Madain Salah entry for more details.

If you are driving into Medina from the south follow the signs for Tabuk to reach the hostel. It will be on your left. If you reach the intersection with Al-Salam St you have gone too far and will need to make a U-turn. To reach the Sheraton continue past the hostel and turn toward the city centre at the Khalid Ibn Al-Waleed St intersection. The hotel is a short distance down this street and to the right. For the Oyun Hotel continue past the Khalid Ibn Al-Waleed St intersection following signs for Riyadh and the airport. The hotel will be on your right.

Coming from the airport or Riyadh take Al-Jameaat Rd and follow the signs for Mecca and Jeddah. You will pass the Oyun first (on your left), then the turn for the Sheraton and, finally, the stadium and the youth hostel.

If you arrive on the main road from the north (ie coming from Tabuk or Madain Salah) you will reach the Khalid Ibn Al-Waleed St and Al-Jameaat Rd intersection first. Keep going straight for the Sheraton. Turn left (toward Riyadh and the airport) for the Oyun and the restaurants mentioned later in this section and turn right for the youth hostel.

Places to Eat

There has been a lot of building in the area outside the haram in recent years, giving non-Muslims more eating options than in the past. There are a number of small restaurants along Al-Jameaat Rd between the Al-Oyun Hotel and the intersection with Khalid Ibn Al-Waleed St. For a quick, cheap meal try the *Bashair Turki Restaurant*. The portions are a bit small but the kebabs and grilled chicken are excellent and you can easily get out for SR 10 to SR 15.

For a more up-market meal I highly recommend *Al-Andalusia*, a restaurant and small amusement park spread out over a hill on the northern side of the intersection of the Tabuk road with Al-Jameaat Rd and Khalid Ibn Al-Waleed St. Here you can sit in private booths overlooking Ohud and the city and dine on excellent Arab and Lebanese food. The shish taouk (SR 25) and fried kibbe (SR

8) are especially good. Fresh juice, coffee, tea and shisha pipes are also available. There is a large family section. Figure on spending SR 40 to SR 60 per person.

Getting There & Away

The airport, which is open to non-Muslims, is Saudi Arabia's smallest one with international service. From Medina, Saudia flies nonstop to Cairo (two or three times a week), Damascus (once a week), Istanbul (once a week) and Karachi (once a week). No foreign airlines operate scheduled flights to Medina.

Domestic destinations include several flights per day to Riyadh (SR 240 one way, economy class) and Jeddah (SR 130). Direct flights also operate to Abha (SR 300), Arar (SR 240), Dhahran (SR 370), Gassim/Buraydah (SR 160), Hail (SR 140), Tabuk (SR 180), Taif (SR 160) and Wedjh (Al-Wajh) (SR 130).

Medina's bus station is in the city centre and is off limits to non-Muslims.

Getting Around

Taxis from the airport charge SR 40 to the Sheraton, SR 35 to the Oyun Hotel and SR 30 to the centre. Figure on about SR 45 to the youth hostel. As is usually the case at airports there are white-and-orange cabs and yellow ones and the former are the better bet.

MADAIN SALAH

Doughty called it 'that fabulous Medáin Sâlih, which I was come from far countries to seek in Arabia'. More than a century later this windswept plain remains one of the most compelling places in the Kingdom. Though an excellent paved road now runs as far as the site's gate, getting here still involves some effort. Don't think twice – you'll be glad you came.

History

The origin of the name Madain Salah (Medin Saleh, Mada'in Salih) is uncertain, though it may be associated with the Midianites of the Old Testament. Their empire is known to have included some of what is now north-

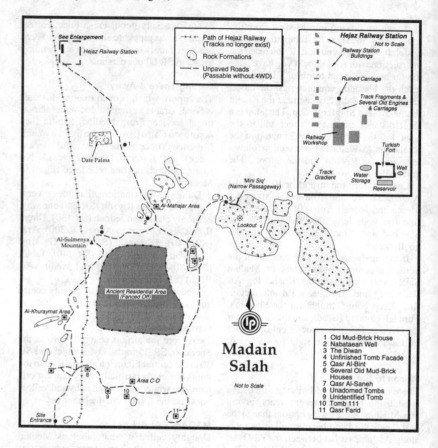

Madain Salah

Not to Scale

Path of Hejaz Railway (Tracks no longer exist)
Rock Formations
Unpaved Roads (Passable without 4WD)

Hejaz Railway Station
Not to Scale
Railway Station Buildings
Ruined Carriage
Track Fragments & Several Old Engines & Carriages
Railway Workshop
Track Gradient
Water Storage
Turkish Fort
Well
Reservoir

See Enlargement
Hejaz Railway Station
Date Palms
Al-Mahajar Area
'Mini Siq' (Narrow Passageway)
Lookout
Al-Sulmenya Mountain
Ancient Residential Area (Fenced Off)
Al-Khuraymat Area
Area C-D
Site Entrance

1 Old Mud-Brick House
2 Nabataean Well
3 The Diwan
4 Unfinished Tomb Facade
5 Qasr Al-Bint
6 Several Old Mud-Brick Houses
7 Qasr Al-Saneh
8 Unadorned Tombs
9 Unidentified Tomb
10 Tomb 111
11 Qasr Farid

western Saudi Arabia. The site may have been inhabited as long ago as the 1st millennium BC by the Minaeans. It is known to have been inhabited by the Thamudites and the Lihyanites later on. Another source for the name may be the Koranic story of Salih, which would make Madain Salah the 'City of Salih', one of the pre-Mohammedian prophets recognised by Islam.

During its heyday Madain Salah was an important stop on the caravan routes between the Hadhramaut and Syria. The tombs for which it is now known were mostly carved between 100 BC and 100 AD,

when it was ruled by the Nabataeans in whose empire it was second in importance only to Petra in present-day Jordan.

Though inscriptions indicate that the site had been occupied for hundreds, possibly thousands, of years prior to their arrival, the Nabataeans first appeared in Madain Salah around 100 BC, about 200 years after they had replaced the Edomites as the rulers of Petra. At its greatest extent the Nabataean Empire stretched south to the borders of Yemen, north to Damascus and west to Gaza. On the basis of archaeological evidence found farther south, the Nabataeans were

The Story of Salih

Sometime around the year 2000 BC, God sent Salih as a Prophet to the people of what is today north-western Arabia. Salih preached monotheism in a city where some 47 gods were worshipped. The people demanded a quite specific sign of Salih's lone God as proof of His existence: a red-coloured, pregnant camel was to emerge from a specific rock outside the town on a specific day and at a specific time. When a red, pregnant camel did, in fact, emerge from the appointed rock on the appointed day and at the appointed hour, the local pagan priesthood was enraged. They declared that anyone believing in the sign would be punished, and one of the town's richer citizens hired several men to kill the miraculous camel. The camel's unborn calf, however, survived the attack and returned to the cleft in the rock from which its mother had emerged. (A ridge near Al-Ula is still known today as the Mount of the Camel.) Salih then announced that the killers of the camel had three days to live. On the third day God caused an earthquake to destroy the town and all its inhabitants as punishment for their having doubted Him and His prophet.

Historically, the city punished by God was almost certainly either the one we know now as Al-Ula or, more likely, a village near present day Al-Ula, 22 km from Madain Salah. The main periods of settlement for both Al-Ula (around 700 BC under the Lihyanites) and Madain Salah (300 BC to 200 AD under the Nabataeans) are much later than the period associated with the story, but the similarity of the names of the prophet and the site may be the source of the confusion. To this day many Saudis refuse to visit Madain Salah because they believe the area to be cursed by God. ∎

predominantly farmers, as opposed to traders, raiders or herders. They became rich from selling water and protection to the incense and spice caravans that had to pass through their territory. At the time frankincense was the most valuable commodity in the world and most of the frankincense caravans had to pass through the Nabataean Empire. (Early Christians would have been far more impressed, in the Christmas story, by the wise men's gifts of frankincense and myrrh than by the gold.) For allowing the caravans to pass the Nabataeans charged a toll of 25%.

However, the city's heyday was brief – the latest dated tomb in Madain Salah was built in 76 AD. The city and the Nabataeans went into decline in the 1st century AD when the Romans began to load the frankincense onto ships and take it to Egypt by sea. The site, however, remained occupied even after its splendour faded. Other less expensive commodities continued to move along the caravan routes, making the area too valuable to abandon. In later centuries the pilgrim road from Damascus to Mecca passed through Madain Salah.

Doughty, in the 1880s, appears to have been the first European to see the tombs, in which he reported there were still bones. He describes his visit in Chapter IV, Volume I of *Travels in Arabia Deserta*.

Information

The Saudi Arabian Department of Antiquities publishes a useful guide to Madain Salah. It costs SR 15 and can be purchased at the Riyadh Museum. Pick up a copy at the same time that you obtain your site permit. If you forget to do this don't worry. There are a number of Saudi men cruising the site in pick-up trucks selling copies of the guide (for SR 20 to SR 30).

Permits to visit Madain Salah must be obtained in Riyadh and can take anything from a day to a week. In addition to the names and passport or iqama numbers of the people in the party, you will also need the registration papers for your vehicle if you are driving yourself. Your permit, and possibly your vehicle papers, will be checked at the site entrance and you may be given a local cop as an escort.

There are no hotels or restaurants at Madain Salah, though accommodation and food can both be found 22 km away at Al-Ula (see that section for details).

Touring the Site

Madain Salah's tombs are less spectacular

SAUDI ARABIA

than those at Petra but they're better preserved. This is largely due to the fact that the local stone is much harder than that found at Petra and has thus weathered centuries of wind and rain rather better. Still, in places it has eroded in some pretty bizarre forms resembling anything from a multicoloured layered cake to melted and refrozen ice cream.

You do not need a 4WD to get around Madain Salah, though having one might make life a bit easier. You should, however, have a vehicle of some sort. Those who really love walking could hike around the site but the distances are large and the heat is debilitating much of the time. Still photography is permitted throughout Madain Salah but videos are not and your car may be searched for video cameras. These must be left with the guards at the gate and collected when you leave.

Getting around Madain Salah has been greatly simplified in recent years by the posting of directional signs at various points. Outside many of the tombs you will also find signboards with translations of the inscriptions found at the tombs.

Madain Salah as a whole is essentially a large rectangle (see map) of tombs surrounding a big, empty patch of ground. Much of this empty space, about one-third of the entire site, is fenced off and is not open to visitors. These fences surround what is thought to have been Madain Salah's main **residential district**.

The **Unadorned Tombs** will be the first ones you see after entering the site, though they are easy to overlook. These simple tombs are little more than caverns carved into the rock with no further ornamentation.

Qasr Al-Saneh will be the first 'real' tomb you come to, though seeing it requires that you virtually double-back after turning left onto the track to the tomb. It was a family tomb, and is fairly large, though the facade and the doorway are badly damaged.

The main tomb in the **Al-Khuraymat area** is impressive both for its size and because it is particularly well preserved. It is also noteworthy because of the griffin-like figures

with human heads, lions' bodies and wings that adorn the corners of the pediment in place of the usual pair of urns. The tomb is on the left if you approach Al-Khuraymat from the main gate. A large number of smaller, simpler tombs fill out the rest of the area.

Further on, the fence designed to keep you from falling into the **Nabataean Well** effectively blocks any view of the well.

The **Diwan** (meeting room), carved into a hillside to shield it from the wind, is a few hundred metres north-east of Qasr Al-Bint. The name owes more to modern Arab culture than to the Nabataeans, who probably used the area as a cult site. To the right of the entrance you can see a small reservoir that was used to store water. Next to the Diwan is a narrow passageway between two rock faces reminiscent of Petra's famous entryway, the Siq, though on a much smaller scale. As you pass through this 'mini-Siq' note the **small altars** carved into the cliff face and the channels which brought water down into several small basins.

Some of these altars had images of gods carved directly into the rock (the ones on the left as you look through the cut in the rock with the Diwan behind you and on your right) while others are niches that apparently held statues.

As you pass through the cleft in the rock turn around and look up. You should see several **ancient carvings** of human figures and what appear to be camels as well as writing in an early form of Arabic (distinct from modern Arabic by the lack of dots on the letters). The figures and the writing are probably not from the same era. Their styles are quite different and the letters are carved much deeper into the rock face than the figures.

After passing through the mini-Siq go straight for 150 to 200m and then climb up and to the right to a **lookout** with a good view over the site. As you ascend be sure to turn around to admire the striking rock formations in this small box canyon. An especially dramatic conical rock rises from the canyon near the mini-Siq.

Qasr Al-Bint, which translates as 'The Girl's Palace', is sometimes applied to the larger tombs on the west face of this outcrop but more properly it encompasses the entire outcrop. The east face has two particularly well preserved tombs. If you step back and look up near the northern end of the west face you'll distinguish a tomb that was abandoned in the early stages of construction and would, if completed, have been the largest in Madain Salah. Only the step facade was cut, but it dramatically proves the theory that the Madain Salah and Petra tombs were carved from the top down.

Qasr Farid is the largest tomb at Madain Salah and the one you have probably seen pictures of on posters and brochures. It is carved from a single large outcrop of rock standing alone in the desert.

West of Qasr Farid is **Area C-D**, a low outcrop with tombs on the east face. The most dramatic view is from the south.

Immediately south of Area C-D is **Tomb 111**, a single, small tomb facing west from underneath a sharply eroded cliff face. It is particularly striking at sunset.

Hejaz Railway Station

The station is on the northern edge of the site. It was part of the Hejaz Railway, of *Lawrence of Arabia* fame (though Lawrence never operated this far south), and has been extensively restored by the government. The complex of 16 buildings includes a large workshop where a restored WWI-era engine is on display. Bits and pieces of several other railway carriages can be found elsewhere at the site. These plied the route between Damascus and Medina during the line's short lifetime (1908-1917). If you look carefully while driving from the station back toward the main gate you can clearly distinguish the railway's gradient.

Near the station is a small **Turkish fort**, the same one in which Doughty stayed for several weeks after arriving from Damascus. The presence of the fort, which was an overnight resting place on the pilgrim road from Damascus to Mecca, explains why a railway station was built here seemingly in the middle of nowhere. The railway town, which includes the station and the other buildings around it in various states of repair, was built in 1907.

Organised Tours

Organised tours to Madain Salah are offered by both the Medina Sheraton (☎ (04) 846 0777, fax (04) 846 0385) and Golden Eagle Services of Riyadh (☎ & fax (01) 491 9567). A tour spares you the hassle of obtaining permits though it can be a bit wearying. Also, since the tours almost invariably occur only over the weekend (Thursday/Friday) they do not include a visit to the museum in Al-Ula, a factor worth considering if you are able to travel during the week.

I have toured Madain Salah with both the Sheraton and Golden Eagle and found the latter to be the better deal by far. Golden Eagle offers overnight camping trips to the site. You leave Medina Thursday morning, tour the site for several hours, camp just outside the gate and spend a few more hours at the site on Friday before returning to Medina via the Hejaz Railway substation at Al-Buwayr. The Sheraton's tour skips Al-Buwayr but otherwise follows essentially the same route. You actually spend about the same amount of time at the site with both tours, the difference is that with Golden Eagle you do not go up and back the same day (it's about four hours each way by bus).

The Sheraton's tour costs SR 925 per person. This includes the trip to the site, two nights at the hotel, all meals from dinner Wednesday to lunch Friday and airport transfers. Golden Eagle charges SR 900 per person for which you get airport transfers, transport, one night's accommodation at the site (in two-person tents) and all meals from lunch Thursday to lunch Friday. Depending on the plane schedules and your point of origin you may have to spend Wednesday night in Medina at your own expense. The Sheraton requires at least 10 people for its tour, Golden Eagle 15. In both cases single people can tack themselves onto groups that are already going. In either case you should

SAUDI ARABIA

book three to four weeks in advance so that the necessary permits can be arranged.

Getting There & Away

Madain Salah is some 330 km north of Medina, off the main road from Medina to Al-Ula. To reach the site from Medina take the northbound Tabuk/Hail exit when you are about 20 km south of Al-Ula. Follow this road 25 km to another junction. Exit, turn right and after a short distance you will see a sign saying 'Madain Salah 18 km'. Eleven km from this sign you will see a paved road running off into the desert to your left. Turn here. Note that in the direction you are travelling this road is unposted. If you miss this turn you will see an 'Antiquities' sign after another eight km. This marks the northern entrance to Madain Salah (at the railway station) but it is a service gate only. If you find yourself here turn around and go back, taking some consolation in the fact that the turn you missed the first time does have a sign facing in the direction you are now headed. Six km beyond the unposted left turn you will see a sign pointing to the right marked 'Antiquities'. Turn here. Another 1.7 km brings you to the site gate.

AL-ULA

Al-Ula, the closest town to Madain Salah, is small and nondescript, but it does offer a small museum and a couple of hotels, in case camping out at Madain Salah is not an option for you.

Al-Ula Regional Museum

The museum, which contains the usual displays on Saudi Arabia's history, geology and traditions is open Saturday to Wednesday from 8 am to 2 pm. To reach it follow the main road into town from the checkpoint. The museum will be on your right, 4.5 km past the checkpoint.

Al-Khuraibat Tombs

These tombs date to the Thamudite era and can be found on the edge of town. The turn-off for the tombs, which is marked, is immediately adjacent to the checkpoint at the entrance to town if you arrive from the direction of Medina or Madain Salah. The tombs are a striking contrast to the Nabataean tombs at Madain Salah: they are neither large nor spectacular, and from a distance they look like small horizontal windows cut into the cliff face.

You will need a permit from Riyadh and a guide from the local museum to visit the site.

Old Al-Ula

This quarter of mud buildings, on the right after you pass the checkpoint on the edge of town, is not abandoned. It sits on the site of the biblical city of Dedan (though none of these mud houses are anything like 3500 years old). Dedan is mentioned in Isaiah (21:13) as the home base of Arab caravans and in Ezekiel (27:20-21) as a trading partner of the Phoenician city of Tyre (in modern-day Lebanon).

Places to Stay & Eat

The *Madain Salah Rest House* (☎ (04) 884 0249) has plain but reasonably good rooms for SR 150 a single or double. There is a small restaurant attached to the hotel. To reach it, head straight into town from the checkpoint. When you reach the intersection with a brown mosque on the right (4.3 km past the checkpoint) make a U-turn, backtrack 150m and turn right at the 'Mada' shop. The rest house is 100m down this street on the left, at the corner. There is no sign in English.

Al-Ula's other accommodation, the *Dar Al-Khamieseyah*, was closed when I visited, so I can't offer any guidance regarding the quality or price of the rooms, though the police officer at the checkpoint said it was better than the rest house. To reach it follow the main road into town from the checkpoint and turn left when you reach the museum (about 200m beyond the intersection where you make a U-turn to get to the rest house). Follow this road for one km and turn left when you come to an intersection with several small snack stalls across the road. The hotel will be on your left after about 50m. There is a small sign in English.

HEJAZ RAILWAY SUBSTATIONS

Several abandoned Hejaz Railway substations lie adjacent to the main roads running north from Medina. The most impressive one is at **Al-Buwayr**, about 85 km north of Medina. Here you will find an almost-complete train – an engine and 10 cars in various states of decomposition – along with three buildings. There is no fence surrounding the site so permits are not required for a visit, though if you plan to take photographs a permit might be a good idea.

To reach Al-Buwayr take the main road north out of Medina toward Tabuk. About 53 km north of the interchange in Medina where the Tabuk road meets Al-Jameaat Rd you will come to the small town of Mulaleh, turn left at the Mulaleh junction. If you are coming from the north this turn-off is approximately 115 km south of Khaybar and is a right turn. After 3.3 km you will come to a T-junction. Turn right and follow the road about 30 km to Al-Buwayr. The station will be on your left just after you cross a small bridge at the edge of the village.

On the drive up from Medina you will pass several smaller substations. One will be on the left 26 km north of the junction where the Tabuk road begins and another is beside the road about 10 km north of the T-junction mentioned earlier. Between this station and Al-Buwayr the railway's track gradient is particularly easy to spot running parallel to the road.

Asir (The South-West)

The dramatic mountains of the Asir range are on the edge of the same geological fault line which emerges farther to the south-west as Africa's Great Rift Valley. The mountain chain includes Jabal Sawdah, the 2910m peak near Abha which is the highest point in Saudi Arabia. Large sections of both the mountain range and the coastal plain have been incorporated into the Asir National Park.

One of the earliest accounts of the region is the record of the march southwards by Aelius Gallus, a Roman general who set out, in 25 BC, to conquer the frankincense-producing regions of Hadhramaut and Dhofar, in present-day Yemen and Oman, respectively. He led his troops south along the main caravan route which passed through the Asir range and continued east of it. The fact that he did not pass through Mecca is one of the strongest pieces of evidence for the theory that the main caravan road of the time did not pass through the future holy city, though it did go through Yathrib (modern Medina). Aelius Gallus conquered Najran but never made it to the frankincense regions. His troops had to turn back at Marib (in present-day Yemen) because of thirst.

Asir was an independent kingdom until it was conquered by Abdul Aziz in 1922, but it has long had close ties with Yemen. The Saudi-Yemeni War of the mid-30s revolved, in part, around Yemeni claims to Asir, claims which were revived by Yemen's Republican government after the country's monarchy was overthrown in 1962. Despite these recurring arguments, Saudi control of the region has never been in serious doubt since the '20s.

The region's architecture has a distinctly Yemeni look about it. The most distinctive feature of the houses are the shingles sticking out from their sides. These are designed to deflect rain away from the mud walls of the house.

South of Taif, the road into the Asir Mountains rises steadily and the scenery becomes ever more dramatic. Every village seems to have its ruined watchtower and those traditional mud houses become increasingly common as one moves south. Another common sight are hamadryas baboons which can often be seen along the main roads throughout Asir. Allow yourself time to stop and explore this fascinating place.

AL-BAHA

Al-Baha, 220 km south of Taif and 340 km north of Abha, is the secondary tourist hub of the Asir region. The area's attraction is its lack of development compared with Abha.

However, while accommodation is not a problem in Al-Baha, transport sometimes is. If you are making a tour of Asir by bus it might be a good idea to give Al-Baha a miss. The scenery is a bit spread out, and you'll have seen a lot from the bus anyway. Without your own car there's not much point in stopping here. Keep going to Abha, where you would be well advised to hire a car.

Orientation & Information

The town is little more than a crossroads where the Taif to Abha road joins another road which runs to the youth hostel and the airport. Compass points can be a bit confusing because the Taif-Abha road bends at Al-Baha so, as you pass through the centre, you are actually travelling east-west. Thus, the hostel, airport and Shahba Forest are all north of the centre, though not on the main north-south road.

What few services there are in Al-Baha are all along the small built-up section of these two thoroughfares. Both the post office and the Saudia office are on the road that runs to the hostel and airport, near the first traffic light north of the junction with the Taif-Abha road (ie turning left at the junction if you are coming from Taif). The bus station is on the Taif-Abha road, a few hundred metres west of the junction with the airport road.

The telephone code for Al-Baha is 07.

Al-Baha's one shop selling Bedouin silver, baskets and other souvenirs is at the parking area where the service-taxis hang out, just west of the bus station on the Taif-Abha road. Look for a sign with small letters in English saying 'Antiques, silverware, gems'.

Things to See & Do

The main attraction is the surrounding countryside, for which Al-Baha serves as a jumping-off point. The Ministry of Agriculture manages two national forests in Al-Baha. Neither of them is exactly Canada's Great North Woods, but they come as a pleasant surprise in a country that most people still associate mainly with sand

dunes. The best way to see either area is in your own car and very much at leisure.

The **Shahba Forest** is just over three km north of the centre. You could hike there without a car, but I would only recommend this for the fit and for those without luggage. It's uphill almost all the way and three km only gets you to the forest entrance. From there it is another couple of km (again, uphill) to the part where you are actually surrounded by trees. A narrow paved road runs through the forest with graded, but unpaved, tracks running off either side to small white-roofed pavilions, each with a barbecue grill, where you can stop for a picnic.

To reach Shahba from the centre, turn off the Taif-Abha road at the intersection between the bus station and the junction with the airport road (look for a blue and white directional sign in English). After about a km you will come to a T-junction. Turn left. The road takes a hard right turn almost immediately and then meanders around the back of the hill (which has a number of villas on it), moving generally up and to the left. Two km from the T-junction you will come around a bend and see a road continuing

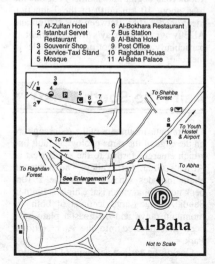

1 Al-Zulfan Hotel
2 Istanbul Servet Restaurant
3 Souvenir Shop
4 Service-Taxi Stand
5 Mosque
6 Al-Bokhara Restaurant
7 Bus Station
8 Al-Baha Hotel
9 Post Office
10 Raghdan Houas
11 Al-Baha Palace

To Shahba Forest
To Youth Hostel & Airport
To Taif
To Raghdan Forest
See Enlargement
To Abha

Al-Baha

Not to Scale

uphill directly in front of you. There is a large brown sign with white lettering in Arabic to the left of the road (the sign is for the Ministry of Agriculture & Water). This, and a very small weathered blue sign on the other side of the road, mark the entrance to the forest.

Al-Baha's other officially sanctioned stand of trees is the **Raghdan Forest**. The turn for the forest is at the traffic light just west of the Al-Zulfan Hotel on the Taif-Abha road. After turning off onto this small road you will make a right turn almost immediately. Follow this road, keeping left when it forks, for about two km. You will then see two small green signs with Arabic writing and arrows in white. Turn right and you will reach the forest entrance (marked by a brown sign with Arabic writing on the left side of the road and another small green sign in Arabic to the right) after approximately 1.2 km.

Places to Stay & Eat

Getting to the *youth hostel* (☎ 725 0368) can be a problem. It is at the Sporting City, about 12 km north of the centre. This is the only hostel in the Kingdom where I have ever found the staff to be put off by the appearance of a foreigner on their doorstep. That said, I still managed to stay there and it is a lot nicer than the one cheap hotel in town. You can't get to the hostel without your own car. Assuming you have wheels, turn left (if you are coming from Taif, right if you are coming from Abha) on the airport road at Al-Baha's main intersection and follow the signs for the airport. It is impossible to miss the Sporting City but the actual turn-off is fairly easy to sail past – especially in the dark! Look for the turn-off (on the left if you are coming from the centre, on the right if you are coming from the airport) immediately after you first see the Sporting City as you approach it from the centre. Beds are SR 8.

The only cheap hotel in town is the *Al-Baha Hotel* (☎ 725 1007, fax 725 2625), on the airport road north of the junction with the Taif-Abha road (ie moving toward the airport). Rooms with a bath cost SR 66/99

(SR 85/128 from June to September) including the service charge. All rooms have ceiling fans. The hotel has no heating and it can get quite chilly in winter. Bring your own soap, towel and toilet paper.

The *Raghdan Houas* (sic) (☎ 725 3091), across the street from the Al-Baha Hotel, has big, bare apartments for SR 130 a single or double (SR 130 per person during the summer). These include kitchens and a sitting room and are usually rented out by the month. They will, however, take short-term guests.

The only hotel on the Taif-Abha road is the *Al-Zulfan Hotel* (☎ 725 1053). Rooms are SR 220/286 (SR 275/374 in summer) though in the winter you can probably negotiate a pretty substantial discount. The four-star *Al-Baha Palace* (☎ 725 2000, fax 725 4724) is on a hill south-west of the centre and has good views. Rooms are SR 224/299 (SR 276/356.50 in summer). Both hotels have restaurants.

Cheap food in Al-Baha is Turkish food. The best place to look is on the Taif-Abha road between the Al-Zulfan Hotel and the bus station. The *Istanbul Servet Restaurant*, roughly across the street from the Al-Zulfan Hotel, has good salads and kofta. Closer to the bus station the *Al-Bokhara Restaurant* is worth a try. It is between the bus station and service-taxi lot and on the same side of the road. The sign is only in Arabic, but it is next door to a Turkish Sweets shop that has a sign in English. They are open in the morning for breakfast. A plate of foul and all the tea you can drink costs SR 3.

Getting There & Away

Al-Baha's small airport is about 30 km north-east of the main road junction. There are daily flights to Riyadh (SR 280 one way, economy class). Saudia also has several flights each week from Al-Baha to Jeddah (SR 110) and Dhahran (SR 420).

There are three buses a day to Abha (six hours, SR 60) and Khamis Mushayt (6½ hours, SR 60) at 2, 5 and 8 pm, and seven per day to Taif (four hours, SR 30) with onward service to Jeddah (seven hours, SR 60) and/or Mecca (six hours, SR 45), depending on the bus. The bus station is on the Taif-Abha road, a short distance west of the intersection with the airport road. If you are coming from Taif, it is on the left.

Service-taxis queue up in the parking lot a short distance west of the bus station. The service-taxis go only to Taif. The fare is SR 35 per person in a seven passenger cab, SR 45 in a five passenger cab. The taxis leave when they are full.

BISHA

Bisha is a large, rambling oasis town in the high desert east of Al-Baha and the main Asir range. It is not really on the way to anywhere and has little to recommend it. If fate leaves you stuck here for any length of time all I can say is that I hope you brought a good book. There is nothing to do in Bisha and, as far as I can tell, only one traditional house of any size is still standing anywhere in the town centre (it stands over on the western edge of town near the entrance to an agricultural development).

Bisha has two hotels, the *Al-Zahrh* (☎ (07) 622 6068) with singles/doubles at SR 220/308 and the *Al-Reef* (☎ (07) 622 5744) where the rooms cost SR 80/130. The Al-Zahrh is in the centre one km from the bus station. The bus station itself is on Bisha's main intersection. The Reef is five km from the bus station back down the road that connects Bisha with the main Abha-Taif road. There are the usual chicken and kebab restaurants around the centre, though you might want to avoid the one directly across the street from the bus station.

Saudia has daily flights to Bisha from Riyadh (SR 210 one way, economy class) and Jeddah (SR 140) and less frequent direct services to Dhahran (SR 350) and Wadi Dawasir (SR 150). There are three buses per day from Bisha to Riyadh (12 hours, SR 135). These leave at 10 am, 3 and 8 pm. The three daily buses to Jeddah (10 hours, SR 100) leave at 10.30 am, 5 and 8 pm. Buses to Khamis Mushayt (three hours, SR 35) leave at 8.30 am and 7 pm.

ABHA

If Saudi Arabia ever opens up to tourism, Abha, the capital of the south-western province of Asir, is likely to be one of the main attractions. The relatively cool weather, forested hills and striking mountain scenery have made it a very popular weekend resort. Like Taif, it is very crowded on summer weekends and reservations are strongly recommended.

You'll need to have a car in Abha as taxis are hard to find and local buses do not serve the main areas of the Asir National Park.

Orientation

The town centre is small and rather dull. The main streets are King Khalid and King Abdul Aziz Sts, and the area stretching from their intersection to the governate building is Abha's nominal centre. (King Khaled St is called Al-Bahar St between King Abdul Aziz and King Faisal Sts). These names come from the Farsi maps. On the ground you will find few, if any, street signs. Drivers are likely to find the streets of the town quite crowded. Your best bet to get anywhere is to head out to the Ring Rd and go around. Six main roads feed into the Ring Rd. Clockwise, starting from the north, these are respectively the roads to Taif/Al-Baha, the industrial city of Khamis Mushayt (via the airport and the youth hostel), a road leading to the plains below the city, a road down the escarpment to Jizan and the Tihama coastal plain, and two roads leading up into the mountains.

Information

The few bits of tourist information in Asir come from the Inter-Continental Hotel and the Trident Hotel in Khamis Mushayt, both of which offer tour packages to the Asir National Park, Najran and the Red Sea. See Organised Tours later in this section.

There are several banks in the area around the main intersection. There are also a couple of banks at the intersection of King Abdul Aziz and Prince Abdullah Sts.

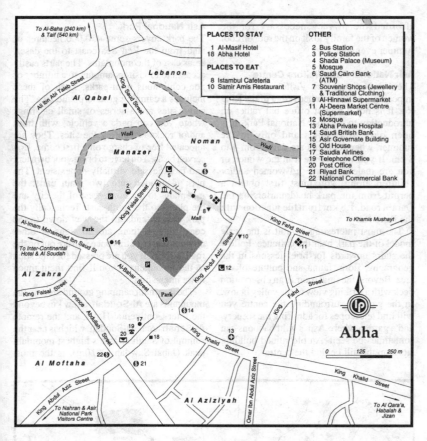

```
To Al-Baha (240 km)
& Taif (540 km)
```

Lebanon

Al Qabal

Al Ibn Abl Taleb Street

King Saud Street

Wadi

Noman

Wadi

Manazer

PLACES TO STAY
1 Al-Masif Hotel
18 Abha Hotel

PLACES TO EAT
8 Istambul Cafeteria
10 Samir Amis Restaurant

OTHER
2 Bus Station
3 Police Station
4 Shada Palace (Museum)
5 Mosque
6 Saudi Cairo Bank (ATM)
7 Souvenir Shops (Jewellery & Traditional Clothing)
9 Al-Hinnawi Supermarket
11 Al-Deera Market Centre (Supermarket)
12 Mosque
13 Abha Private Hospital
14 Saudi British Bank
15 Asir Governate Building
16 Old House
17 Saudia Airlines
19 Telephone Office
20 Post Office
21 Riyad Bank
22 National Commercial Bank

Al-Imam Mohammed Ibn Saud St

To Inter-Continental Hotel & Al Soudah

Park

Al Zahra

King Faisal Street

Al-Bahar Street

Park

Prince Abdullah Street

Al Moftaha

King Faisal Street

King Abdul Aziz Street

Mall

King Fahd Street

To Khamis Mushayt

King Fahd Street

King Khalid Street

Abha

0 125 250 m

Al Aziziyah

King Abdul Aziz Street

To Nahran & Asir National Park Visitors Centre

Omar Ibn Abdul Aziz Street

King Khalid Street

To Al Qara'a, Habalah & Jizan

The post office and telephone office are side by side on King Abdul Aziz St, near the intersection with Prince Abdullah St.

The telephone code for Abha is 07.

Shada Palace

Abha's only in-town site is the Shada Palace. It was built in 1927 as an office/residence for King Abdul Aziz's governors in the region. After falling into disuse it was restored and reopened as a museum in 1987. The palace is the large, traditional tower immediately behind the large police station on King Faisal St, across from the bus station. It is open Saturday to Thursday from 9 am to 1 pm and from 4.30 to 7.30 pm. Admission is free, but children under 12 are not allowed to go inside.

The ground floor of the palace has an exhibit of regional handicrafts and traditional household goods. A brightly painted staircase leads to restored sitting rooms and men's and women's quarters on the upper two floors. The displays here include old money, weapons, silver jewellery and weavings. The roof is also open to the public but the walls are fairly high so you won't be able to see much. In earlier days the high walls afforded the privacy necessary for the women of the family to sit on the roof on cool summer evenings.

Asir National Park Visitors Centre

The Asir National Park Visitors' Centre sits imposingly on the southern edge of the Ring Rd. It is not a tourist office but rather an introduction to the Asir National Park. It is open only to families and only in the summer, when its hours are daily from 4 to 8 pm. If you want to see it in the winter, or you are male and have no women and/or children along, you must first obtain a permit from the park headquarters on the Qara'a road, 1.8 km from the junction with the Ring Rd.

The most interesting exhibit is the scale model of the park near the entrance. Follow the stairs upwards for brief lessons in the geography, flora, fauna and culture of the area. Beyond the final room is an observation deck with a striking view of the valley below. In the gardens surrounding the centre you will find telescopes for admiring the scenery, and a garden where Asir's wild baboons can sometimes be seen. An old ruined building sits atop the hill behind the centre.

Asir National Park

The park covers some 450,000 hectares of land from the Red Sea coast to the desert areas east of the mountains. The parts easily accessible to visitors amount to a number of non-contiguous mini-parks. Each of these includes a camping ground/picnic area. The camp sites are a series of small clearings where you can park a vehicle, with trees and/or rocks separating the sites. They are allocated free of charge on a first come, first served basis. You have to bring your own tent and facilities are virtually nonexistent. The park is divided into two main parts: the mountains to the north-west of the city and the plains to the south-east. Technically the park area extends all the way down to the coast, though there are no signs or other obvious marks of this once you are out on the road to Jizan. If you are pressed for time stick to the mountains – you'll find them much more interesting.

The two main camping ground areas in the mountains are **Al-Soudah**, a few km beyond the Inter-Continental Hotel, and the remote **Al-Sahab** area. Al-Soudah, which is near the summit of Saudi Arabia's highest mountain peak (Jabal Sawdah, 2910m), is the most

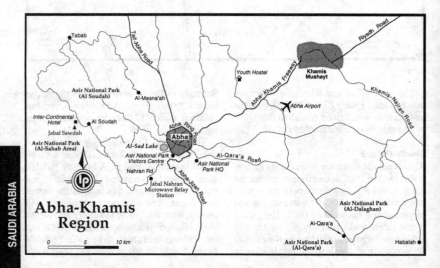

Abha-Khamis Region

0   5   10 km

spectacular part of the park. At the time of writing a cable car, similar to the one in Habalah, was under construction at Al-Soudah, just beyond the turn-off for the Inter-Continental Hotel.

Three main roads loop up into the mountains and connect with one another through many smaller roads. Try a drive up the **Nahran road** to the Jabal Nahran microwave relay station. When you reach the gate at the top turn around and go back; this route has a number of good viewing spots.

The main park areas to the south-east of Abha are **Al-Dalaghan** (Dalgan), 26 km from Abha, and, farther down the same road, **Al-Qara'a** (Qara), after which the road is named. Both areas consist of a large area of rounded boulders and small evergreen trees, which look rather like a giant's rock garden. The main difference between them is that Al-Qara'a sits on the edge of the escarpment, which means that the scenery is better but the weather less predictable. Wild baboons can often be seen in both areas.

Bahes Park

This is a small amusement park on the Abha-Khamis road nine km east of the turn-off for the youth hostel. It is open in the evenings throughout the year. Admission, including unlimited rides, is SR 50 for both adults and children.

Organised Tours

The Inter-Continental Hotel (☎ 224 7777, fax 224 4113) in Abha and the Trident Hotel (☎ 223 3466, fax 222 0828) in Khamis more or less have a monopoly on organised tourism in the Abha region. Both offer several two and three-night packages, some of which include excursions to Najran and/or the Red Sea. In addition to staying in the hotel, these usually require a group of at least 10 adults.

The basic package at either hotel includes two nights accommodation, meals, airport transfers, sightseeing in the Abha area and a shopping trip to the Khamis souk. At the Trident this will cost you SR 695 for singles or SR 595 per person for doubles. At the

Inter-Continental much the same trip costs SR 830/730 per person for single/double occupancy. The Inter-Continental's three-night Abha-Najran package costs SR 1395/1265. It also has a package that includes a diving excursion to the Red Sea for SR 830/930. The Trident will quote prices for Najran and Red Sea trips on request with the exact cost depending on the itinerary you are interested in and the size of the group.

Places to Stay

For a resort, there are remarkably few places to stay in Abha. There has been a lot of building going on around town for the last few years, but the focus has been on villas and apartment-hotels that rent for a minimum of one month.

The *youth hostel* (☎ 227 0503) is at the Sporting City, 20 km west of Abha and eight km off the Abha-Khamis road. Beds are SR 8 but there is no bus service.

Every place except the youth hostel has higher rates in the summer (May to September), during which it would be a bad idea to arrive in Abha on a weekend (Wednesday or Thursday) without a reservation.

After the youth hostel the cheapest place in Abha is the *Assir Hotel* (☎ 224 4374, fax 224 3073), on the Taif road one km north of the centre. It charges SR 50/72 (SR 65/99 in summer) for singles/doubles. Only the triples (SR 88 in the winter, SR 115 in the summer) have private baths. The common baths are rather grim.

Probably the best value for money in Abha, after the hostel, is the *Shamasan Hotel* (☎ 225 1808, fax 226 0074), just outside the centre. You can see it from the intersection of King Faisal and King Saud Sts. It charges SR 90/135 (SR 117/167 in summer) for rooms without baths and SR 100/150 (SR 130/195 in summer) for rooms with baths.

Right at the edge of the centre you'll find the *Al-Masif Hotel* (☎ 224 2651, fax 224 2162) where singles/doubles are SR 100/140 (SR 150/240 in summer). The only hotel in the centre is the *Abha Hotel* (☎ 224 8775, fax 224 2592), on King Abdul Aziz St, where

SAUDI ARABIA

rooms cost SR 110/165 (SR 143/240 in summer).

Up in the mountains the *Inter-Continental Hotel* (☎ 224 7777, fax 224 4113) has a fairly standard five-star rate of SR 517.50/673 (SR 621/805 in summer) including the service charge. Check whether cheap weekend packages are available. If you are going to splurge once in the Kingdom, the Abha Inter-Continental is a pretty good place to do it. The hotel is said to have been originally designed as a palace for a Saudi prince. Whatever your budget, it is worth dropping by for a cup of coffee and an opportunity to marvel at its sheer scale. The lobby is enormous and the coffee shop alone is larger than a lot of the hotels listed in this book. Be warned, however, that the hotel does not actually sit on the Al-Soudah escarpment. To get a view of the mountains you must opt for one of the villas (medium-sized bungalows) on the hotel grounds. These start at SR 1500 per night. To reach the hotel, take the Al-Soudah road for about 22.5 km from its junction with the Ring Rd. The hotel will be on your left.

A better bet if you want a view is the *Hotel Al-Bouhaira* (☎ 224 6458, fax 224 7515), just outside the Ring Rd at the junction for Al-Soudah and the Inter-Continental. It has a terrace that overlooks both the city and Al-Sad Lake (the reservoir behind the Al-Sad Dam). Rooms cost SR 230/299 (SR 276/359 in summer).

On the Abha-Khamis road nine km east of the turn-off for the youth hostel the *Bahes Tourist Village* (☎ & fax 223 2900) has two-bedroom villas for SR 250 (SR 350 in summer).

Places to Eat

There are a few restaurants scattered around the centre but, on the whole, the pickings are rather thin. Try the *Samir Amis Restaurant* on King Abdul Aziz St for good kebabs and grilled chicken. The *Istambul Cafeteria* (a sign over the doorway says 'Turkey Cafeteria') near the Al-Hinnawi supermarket is a good place for a quick snack. Grilled chicken, egg, beef or liver sandwiches cost SR 2 apiece. Several other small places are in the area immediately around the Samir Amis.

For an up-market meal try *Al-Salwa*, a restaurant complex with a large family area. It's on the Ring Rd across from the entrance to the Asir National Park Visitors' Centre. The sign is only in Arabic, but it's quite big – blue with red lettering – and there is nothing else nearby on that side of the road. The restaurant's location offers dramatic views out over the city, though meals here are not cheap. Most main dishes cost around SR 35, though the spaghetti is about half that price.

Things to Buy

If you are looking for old silver jewellery head for Khamis (see following section). In Abha there are several small shops near the Shada Palace that sell women's caftans embroidered with traditional Asiri patterns. These cost anywhere from SR 100 to SR 500 depending on the quality of the materials and the intricacy of the work involved. There are also several leather-work shops adjacent to the Shada Palace that make the decorative belts and scabbards used to carry Yemeni-style daggers, though most of what these shops have on display consists of holsters for hand guns.

The Inter-Continental Hotel also has a shop selling Bedouin jewellery and locally made baskets. The selection is OK and the prices, though high, are not outrageous.

Getting There & Away

Air The airport is 25 km from town. To get there, take the Abha-Khamis road to the turn-off just beyond the turn for the Sporting City. Saudia's Abha ticket office is near the post office on King Abdul Aziz St. There are several flights each day to Jeddah (SR 180 one way, economy class) and Riyadh (SR 270) and once per day to Dhahran (SR 410). Direct services also operate between Abha and Medina (SR 300), Taif (SR 140), Tabuk (SR 450) and Sharurah (SR 180).

Bus The SAPTCO station is in the big parking lot on King Faisal St, a couple of blocks north of the intersection of King Khalid and King Abdul Aziz Sts. The ticket office is the small trailer across from the police station. It tends to be open only just before a bus leaves. Most of the area's buses leave from Khamis Mushayt. Buses to Jeddah (8½ hours, SR 90) leave 12 times a day from 7.30 am until 11 pm. To Taif (9½ hours, SR 90), there are daily buses at 9 am, 12.30 and 3.30 pm. Buses to Jizan (4½ hours, SR 35) leave daily at 7.30 and 11.30 am.

For Muslims only there are two buses per day to Mecca (8½ hours, SR 90) at 11.30 am and 5 pm.

For buses to Riyadh you must go to Khamis. Local buses run between the Abha and Khamis bus stations every half-hour from 6.30 am to 10.30 pm. The trip takes about 35 minutes and the fare is SR 2.

Getting Around
Here you are a bit stuck as there do not seem to be a lot of taxis, and none of the bus routes serve the main areas of the park. The usual car rental rates for Saudi Arabia apply and you can rent a car at the airport or go to one of the small agents in the centre.

KHAMIS MUSHAYT
Khamis Mushayt (Khamis, for short) is 26 km east of Abha. Its main industry appears to be the giant King Khalid Air Base (US 'Stealth' fighters flying out of Khamis were the only piloted aircraft to hit targets in Baghdad itself during the Gulf War). Khamis is usually spoken of as Abha's twin city, though it is a bit difficult to see what the two places have in common. It is as flat and dull as Abha is hilly and interesting.

Khamis' small, modern souk, bus station and two of its three hotels are all clustered around the city's main square and the large parking lot just north of it.

Khamis' telephone code is 07.

Khamis Souk
The Khamis souk, just off this main square,

is a good place to shop for silver jewellery – the ever-increasing flow of tourists over the last few years has led the shopkeepers to improve their stock immensely. Prices are fairly competitive with what you will find in Najran and the selection is wider, if generally a bit lower in quality. To reach the silver souk start in the main square with your back to the Mushayt Palace Hotel. Standing in front of the hotel turn left, and then left again around the side of the building. Turn right across a small intersection, in front of the Ihaw-Ihaw Restaurant, and continue straight for about 100m. On your left you should see a small shop with a sign saying 'Silver J Courner'. This marks the beginning of the silver souk, a collection of about a dozen shops, all of them up that one alley.

Organised Tours
The Trident Hotel (see below) offers a weekend tour package for SR 595/695 per person, double/single occupancy which includes two nights accommodation, all meals, a programme of sightseeing tours in the Abha area and airport transfers. See the earlier Abha Organised Tours section for more information.

Places to Stay & Eat
On the main square you will find the *Al-Azizia Hotel* (☎ 222 0900, fax 222 1128). Singles/doubles start at SR 132/170.50 (SR 165/214.50 in summer), including the service charge. Across the square the *Mushayt Palace Hotel* (☎ 223 6220, fax 223 5272) asks SR 264.50/344, including the service charge, but discounts are readily available most of the time.

The city's lone top-end hotel is the *Trident Hotel* (☎ 223 3466, fax 222 0828), at the junction of the Abha-Khamis road and King Faisal Rd. It charges SR 287.50/374 (SR 345/448.50 in summer).

About four km west of the centre, the *Al-Fersan Hotel* (☎ 222 1453, fax 222 0683) has singles/doubles for SR 132/198 (SR 171/257 in summer). The hotel is on the south side of the Abha-Khamis road a few km out of Khamis.

There are a number of small Indian, Turkish and Filipino restaurants in the area around the main square, particularly in the small streets behind the Mushayt Palace Hotel. The *Turkey Restaurant*, immediately behind the hotel, has been recommended by readers. For a more up-market meal outside a hotel try the *Chinese Palace Restaurant*, about 100m down the street from the Trident Hotel. The food is so-so, but it can be a welcome change after many days of grilled chicken and rice or, depending on your budget, hotel food. Main dishes cost SR 20 to SR 30 (more for seafood).

Getting There & Away
Khamis' Saudia office is on the Abha-Khamis road one block north-west of the Trident Hotel. See the Abha entry for details of air services from the Abha airport.

The bus station in the main square is SAPTCO's hub for all of Asir. Buses to Jeddah via Abha (nine hours, SR 90) leave 12 times a day from 7 am until 10.30 pm. Buses to Riyadh (13 hours, SR 125) leave 10 times per day from 6 am until 10.15 pm. There are two buses per day to Bisha (3½ hours, SR 35) at 8 am and 4 pm. To Taif (10 hours, SR 90), there are daily buses at 8.30 am, noon and 3 pm, via Abha. Buses to Jizan (five hours, SR 35) leave daily at 7 and 11 am, and at 3 and 10 pm. Only the two early buses stop in Abha. There are three buses per day to Najran (five hours, SR 30), at 8.30 am, 4 and 7.30 pm. Masochists can take the direct bus to Dammam (16 hours, SR 185) daily at 5 and 8 pm.

For Muslims only there are two buses per day to Mecca (nine hours, SR 90) at 11 am and 4.30 pm.

A few service-taxis can be found in the parking lot behind the Al-Azizia Hotel. They seat seven people plus the driver and leave when full. Fares include: Jeddah or Riyadh, SR 150; Najran or Bisha, SR 50; and Jizan, SR 30.

Local buses to Abha leave every half-hour from 6.30 am to 10.30 pm. The trip takes about 35 minutes and the fare is SR 2.

HABALAH
The deserted village of Habalah (Habella), about 60 km from the centre of Abha, is one of the most dramatic sites in the Asir National Park. A traditional farming village, Habalah appears to hang from a 300m-high cliff face above terraced fields and a broad valley. The village was settled about 350 years ago by members of the Khatani tribe who were said to have been fleeing from the Ottomans. Habalah, like many other villages in Asir, grew coffee, fruits and vegetables and raised sheep, chickens and goats. It was inhabited until about 1980. If you look carefully along the rim of the cliff above the village you can still see the iron posts to which ropes were tied to lower people and goods to the village.

Things to See
Since the last edition of this book Habalah has been developed as a tourist attraction and there is now a cable car to take you down to the remains of the village.

The cable car costs SR 30 round trip (SR 10 for children under 10, children under age two travel free), but only operates when eight people can be scared up to make the trip. I have managed to make it down as part of a group of six, but it took well over an hour before the people running the cable car relented on this point. Assuming enough people are present, the cable car operates daily from 8.30 am to 7.30 pm. Be sure to keep your ticket stub from the trip down because you will need it to for the ride back up. The trip down offers some of the most dramatic views in the Kingdom and is well worth the long drive from Abha.

Once in the village you can walk around more or less at will. Some of the farming terraces are being restored to give visitors an idea of what things would have looked like before the village was deserted. Following the sign marked 'To antiques house' will, after a fairly serious scramble over the rocks through the trees and across the terraces, bring you to one of the better preserved houses in the village. The inside of the house is pretty beat up, but be sure to notice the carved interior doors, which are still worth a look. Be careful not to bump your head against the ceiling.

Places to Stay & Eat

If you feel like staying in the village your only option is to rent one of the villas (☎ (07) 226 0336, fax (07) 226 2503) operated by the cable car company. For SR 450 to SR 750 (the price changes frequently depending on the occupancy rate) you get a two bedroom villa with a kitchen. Breakfast is included. Note that the huge wall around each villa – required to meet Saudi standards of propriety – will block your view of the landscape from inside the villa itself. Around the top of the cliff you will find a hotel and restaurant.

Getting There & Away

To reach Habalah take the Qara'a road from Abha past Al-Dalaghan. Three km beyond the Al-Dalaghan turn-off, the road ends in a T-junction. Turn left and follow the road to the village of Wadiain where you will see a sign for 'Al-Habla Park'. Follow the sign and keep left when the road forks at a junction with a large white sign in Arabic that includes a picture of a cable car. After about two km the road forks again; keep left and you'll reach the parking lot overlooking the village.

ABHA TO NAJRAN

The first third or so of the 280-km drive from Abha to Najran is along twisting roads descending toward the desert plains. You will see lots of fascinating old, new and restored architecture. The village of **Qara Waqsha**, about 90 km south of Abha, is worth a brief stop for a look at its splendid ruined fort and watchtower, situated on a hill rising from the middle of the village. The village has many traditional houses.

Dhahran Al-Janoub (Zahran Al-Janoub), 165 km south of Abha and 112 km north-west of Najran, is a convenient stopping place if you need a rest or decide to break the trip. It too has its share of traditional architecture though much of it is buried in the town's backstreets. A few km south of town,

however, there is a particularly dramatic village right up against the Abha-Najran road. In Dhahran Al-Janoub, the *Al-Aren Hotel* (☎ (07) 255 0388, fax (07) 255 0272) in the centre of town, along the Abha-Najran road, has singles/doubles for SR 88/132. It's on the left if you are coming from Abha.

There are five checkpoints between Abha and Najran and you can expect increasingly close scrutiny as you move south. The situation along the border with Yemen always seems to be tense and foreigners moving about are subject to special scrutiny. Be sure to have your iqama and a travel letter, or your passport if you are in the Kingdom on a visitor visa, handy. You can also expect to be asked to produce the car's papers at some or all of the checkpoints – the *istimara* (registration) if you own the car, or a photocopy of this document if it's a company car. If you're driving a rented car the rental agreement usually suffices, but be sure that you have a photocopy of the actual registration before heading off to the south.

NAJRAN

Najran (Nejran) is one of the most fascinating and least visited places in the Kingdom. Set near the Yemeni border, in an oasis which sprawls some 20 km along the Wadi Najran, the site has been inhabited for about 4000 years. Najran was the last major stop on the frankincense route before the road split into eastern and western branches 60 km to the north at Bir Hima. It has remained an important desert trading centre to this day. Najran has long been reputed to be the main base for the lucrative smuggling traffic between Saudi Arabia and Yemen.

Yemen's cultural influence is stronger here than anywhere else in the Kingdom. This is obvious in both the local architecture and the attitude of the people toward outsiders. Najranis are extremely outgoing and deeply conservative at the same time. The most obvious place to see this seeming contradiction at work is in the souk, where fully veiled women run shops alongside men and serve male customers – an unusual sight in the Kingdom.

History

Najran was already an important city during the 1st millennium BC when the Sabeans swept over much of this corner of Arabia. Sabean texts mention it as far back as the 7th century BC. Its main period of prosperity came during the 1st and 2nd centuries BC when it was known as Al-Ukhdood. The Roman general Aelius Gallus captured Al-Ukhdood in 24 BC during his unsuccessful expedition to the Wadi Hadhramaut. At that time the Greek geographer Strabo described Ukhdood as a town with seven wells.

The next major conquest of the city was by the Himyarites who arrived around the year 250 AD. Najran was still part of Himyar when its inhabitants were converted to Christianity in the 5th century. Christianity gave way to Islam in 630-31 (10 AH) though the Christian community remained fairly numerous for a time. Within a generation, however, the town's Christians were expelled from the country in line with a saying of the Prophet that 'there shall not remain two religions in the land of Arabia'.

In later centuries Najran's inland location made it of interest to the Turks. The Yam, the leading tribe of the region, controlled Najran through an alliance with the Turks in the 16th century, in exchange for which they were given the right to levy tribute from the area's other tribes. By the mid-17th century, however, they had switched their allegiance to the Zaidi imams of Yemen. Later, Najran was part of the First Saudi Empire in the late 18th and early 19th centuries. After the empire fell the town spent a century as a border area disputed between the independent kingdoms of Asir and Yemen. Saudi troops finally took control of the city in 1934. Shortly thereafter the Imam of Yemen ceded Najran to King Abdul Aziz as part of the treaty ending the 1934 Saudi-Yemeni War.

Orientation & Information

Najran is an easy place to find your way around. Driving in from Abha, you hit a T-junction; this is the only road leading to Najran and everyone calls it the Main Rd. Turning left at the junction takes you to the

Holiday Inn, Najran airport and the Empty Quarter (in that order). Turning right leads you into Faisaliah, a modern business district just before Najran. Most of the shops and businesses, the youth hostel, the other two hotels, Saudia, the telephone office, two post offices (the main one in Faisaliah and a smaller one near the turn-off to the Najran Fort) and the bus station are all along, or a short distance off, the Main Rd in Faisaliah. Except for the bus station all of them are on the right-hand side of the road if you are coming from Abha or the airport. Continuing along the Main Rd you reach Najran's centre, where the fort and the souk are located.

If you need to change money in the centre, there are a couple of banks on the Main Rd, near the traffic lights where you turn to reach the fort. The distance along the Main Rd from the junction with the Abha-Najran road to the turn-off for the fort is 13 km. The airport is 35 km from the fort, and 22 km from the junction with the Abha-Najran road.

The telephone code for Najran is 07.

Najran Fort (Qasr Al-Imara)

Though the well in the fort's inner courtyard is said to date from pre-Islamic times, the present fort was begun in 1942 as a royal residence. It was built to be a self-sustaining complex, with its own stock pens, storage rooms for food, guards quarters and even a radio station. This insistence on self-sufficiency may indicate that Najran's new Saudi rulers had less than complete faith in the Imam of Yemen's renunciation of his claim to Najran and his ceding of the oasis to Saudi Arabia a decade earlier. The fort fell out of everyday use in 1967, when the Saudi-Yemeni relations became, if not stable, then at least somewhat predictable.

During its relatively brief, 25-year history, the fort's various governors managed to expand it dramatically. It was always a big place. Even today, with all of the later additions removed, the complex still includes about 60 rooms, including the livestock pens. Most of these remain bare though their carved doors and shutters have survived or been recreated and are some of the most colourful examples of this traditional Arabian art form to be seen in the Kingdom.

Be sure to see the coffee room on the 2nd floor of the **Prince's House**, the large building right in front of you as you pass through the main gate into the fort. Turning left from the main gate and then left again you will come to a series of small rooms containing displays of local silverwork, leather goods, weapons, clothes, tools and pottery. If the staircase leading to the upper level is unlocked you will find more of the same immediately upstairs. The small building at the near side of this courtyard (ie to the left of the Prince's House as you enter the fort) once housed the fort's telegraph office.

The **well** is in the other courtyard, the one to the right of the entrance. The building in this courtyard is a small and quite intriguing **mosque**. Note the tiny, almost perfunctory, 'flight' of three steps next to the mihrib, preserving the tradition that the Friday sermon would be delivered from an elevated position overlooking the congregation.

The fort is more or less in the centre of town. From Abha and Faisaliah, follow the Main Rd until you see the fort beyond the houses to your right, then turn right at the first set of traffic lights (the fruit and vegetable market will be across the intersection and to the left). It is open daily from 8 am to 5 or 6 pm (depending on the time of the sunset prayer). Admission is free and you don't need a permit to get in.

Al-Aan Palace

The Al-Aan Palace, also known as the Saadan Palace, is one of the most remarkable pieces of architecture in the Wadi Najran. The main tower is five storeys high and dominates the entire oasis from atop an outcrop of rock. You cannot enter the palace as it is still used as a residence (not a royal residence, the word 'palace', in this case, refers to the building's grandeur, not to the status of its occupants). You can, however, drive to the small parking area near the main gate for an excellent view over the oasis back toward the centre.

The Al-Aan Palace is about five km west of Najran's centre. The best way to reach it is to backtrack toward Faisaliah along the Main Rd and turn (left if coming from Najran, right if coming from Faisaliah) at the sign for Maratah. Follow the road for seven km from this point and turn off in front of the large house with a white and yellow wall directly beneath the palace. The turn-off is right in the middle of a curve in the road so be careful both when leaving the road and when trying to get back onto it. Follow this track for 600m and then make a U-turn onto a very steep paved road, which will get steeper still as you climb the last 400m of tarmac to the parking lot in front of the palace.

Museum

Najran boasts one of the Kingdom's newest and best museums. It is open Saturday to Wednesday from 8.30 am to 2 pm. Admission is free; photography is prohibited. The museum is several km off the Main Rd and sits in front of the archaeological site of Al-Ukhdood, which was inhabited from about 500 BC to the 10th century AD.

Entering the museum you start the tour of the exhibit halls by moving to your right. The first part has information on the age of the earth and the formation of wadis and deserts. Other exhibits outline archaeological finds in and around Najran and sketch the importance of Al-Ukhdood, which was mentioned in the Koran.

The second part of the gallery is an ethnographic display with examples of local crafts, desert life, water and irrigation and tools. There are also a number of photographs taken in Najran by the author/diplomat/explorer/spy Harry St John Philby in 1936.

To reach the museum, turn off the Main Rd at the sign for 'Okhdood'. After three km you will reach a T-junction. Turn right. The museum will be on your left after two km.

Najran Valley Dam

The largest dam in the Kingdom is in the hills above Najran, controlling the water flow through much of the oasis. It was dedicated in 1986. The last few km of the drive up to the dam are very pretty. To get there turn off the Main Rd at the sign for Al-Jurbah. Go 3.3 km and turn right at the traffic lights when you reach a T-junction. Follow this road for just over 16 km until you reach a checkpoint. If they tell you to go away and come back tomorrow politely say that you are a tourist and just want a quick look at the dam (well, it worked for me). The dam is six km beyond the checkpoint.

Note that if you are coming directly from the museum you can reach the dam by turning left out of the museum's parking lot. Following this road for 1.8 km will bring you to the T-junction mentioned above, just keep going straight and you will reach the dam.

Places to Stay

Najran's *youth hostel* (☎ 522 5019) is one of the smaller ones in the Kingdom but it's a clean and friendly place, about nine km from the fort. As you pass through Faisaliah watch out for the Najran Municipality building on your right. Some distance past this the Main Rd swings around to the left while a smaller street continues on straight. Keep going straight on the smaller road. Take the first right (immediately beyond the first petrol station) and then take the second right from the street onto which you turned. The hostel will be on your right after less than 200m. It's across the street from a school.

Aside from the youth hostel there are two cheap/mid-range hotels in Najran, both just off the Main Rd, approximately 10 km from the fort and three km from the junction with the Abha road. Coming from Abha, the *Okhdood Hotel* (☎ 522 2614, fax 522 2434) is the first one you'll pass. It has singles/doubles for SR 132/170.50, including the service charge, but will discount these by about 15% when things are slow. The *Najran Hotel* (☎ 522 1750, fax 522 2993), about one km closer to the centre, is slightly better value at SR 88/132.

A sure sign that Saudi Arabia's small but growing tourist industry has discovered Najran was the arrival, in late 1995, of the oasis' first five-star hotel. The *Holiday Inn* (☎ 522 5222, fax 522 1277) asks SR 402.50/523.25, including the service charge, but you may be able to negotiate a discount. It is the only hotel in Najran with a swimming pool. The hotel is just over four km east of the junction with the Abha Rd.

Places to Eat

An odd thing about Najran's centre is how few restaurants one finds there. It's easy to eat cheaply in Faisaliah, but hard to eat at all in Najran. The *Samerames Restaurant*, around the corner from the Najran Fort (standing in front of it with your back to the main gate go left, then right) is so-so. The food is good but the staff aren't the friendliest people on earth. Grilled chicken or mutton and rice costs SR 10.

In Faisaliah there are a number of good places in the general vicinity of the youth hostel. The *Cafeteria Al-Beek* has good shawarma served, unusually, in submarine sandwich rolls. The sign is only in Arabic, but it is on the south side of the road about 500m back toward Abha from the turn-off to the youth hostel. Look for a faded red and yellow sign in which a knife and fork form part of the Arabic name of the restaurant.

One of Najran's best bets is *Al-Ramal Ash-Shaabi*, around the corner from the youth hostel (turn right out of the hostel and right again). It is on a side street off the Main Rd and one block back toward Abha from the hostel turn-off. The kebabs and grilled chicken dishes are excellent, as is the rice. At breakfast they do great hadas (a spicy bean dish eaten with pita bread), served sizzling in front of you for SR 4. The restaurant's sign is only in Arabic. Look for the models of two Yemeni-style houses framing the entrance.

If you would like a change from grilled chicken and rice, so-so Lebanese food can be found at the *Lebanon Restaurant* on the Main Rd just past the turn-off for the hostel. Again the sign is only in Arabic. Look for two restaurants side by side, both with large Pepsi signs. The Lebanon Restaurant is the one with a cedar tree on its sign. Main dishes cost SR 10 to SR 20.

Madain Salah's Architecture

The tombs at Saudi Arabia's main archaeological site, Madain Salah, were constructed over a period of several hundred years and show a clear evolution in the style of their ornamentation. The earliest designs resemble step pyramids and are based on Assyrian models. Over time these gave way to a more complex, and more specifically Nabataean, motif of two sets of steps descending inwards towards each other.

As the design evolved away from its Assyrian origins, so the tombs themselves became larger in size and more elaborate in their decoration. The later tombs show clear Greek and Roman influences in their decoration, particularly in the styling of the pediments and in the use of columns and pilasters around the tomb doorways.

The most specifically 'Nabataean' touch is the urn and falcon motif that can be seen on many of the later tombs. None of these motifs appear on the earlier, Assyrian-influenced tombs. ■

Top: Rock formations between the 'mini Siq' and the lookout.
Centre Left: The Assyrian influenced 'step pyramid' pediment design at Qasr Al-Bint.
Bottom Left: Distinctive Nabataean 'descending step' motif at Qasr Al-Bint.
Right: Human-headed griffins replace the urns on the main Al-Khuraymat tomb.

GORDON ROBISON

GORDON ROBISON

Madain Salah's Architecture *cont*

Top: Qasr Farid, carved from a single outcrop, is the largest tomb at Madain Salah.
Bottom: Qasr Al-Bint, which translates as 'The Girl's Palace', is the name given to the large tombs on this rocky outcrop.

Things to Buy

Najran is famous for its silver jewellery. A lot of (mostly elderly) women have small shops in the souk area behind the fort with stocks of silver jewellery for sale, though it may not always be out on display. A lot of new stuff is mixed in with the old and the quality of the artisanship varies hugely. I have long been a fan of Yemeni silver, and Najran is the best place outside of Yemen that I know of to buy it. That said, for every nice piece there is a mountain of junk and the women who run those stalls are among the toughest bargainers I've run into anywhere in the Middle East. (See the boxed story on Silver Jewellery near Things to Buy in the Facts for the Visitor section, earlier in this chapter.)

Najran is also famous for its basket weaving, though not all of the numerous baskets you will see in the souk are locally made (most come from Yemen). These cost anywhere from a few riyals to SR 200, depending on size. Other items include brightly painted clay incense burners, some locally made and some from Yemen or elsewhere in the Kingdom. These cost SR 5 to SR 15.

An excellent companion for a shopping trip to the Najran souk is *Najran Archaeology & History*, a glossy, locally produced guidebook. It contains rather sketchy information about the oasis and its sites (except for the dam, about which it will tell you far more than you probably wanted to know) but its shopping guide is indispensable if you plan to go souvenir hunting in the souk. The colour photos show you what to look for while the text gives both background on the items in question and a fairly accurate guide to what you should expect to pay for them. As for the book itself, the attendant at the Najran Fort sells it for SR 50 a copy, but you can pick it up in the lobby of the Najran Hotel for SR 40.

Getting There & Away

The Saudia office is on the Main Rd about one km toward the centre from the youth hostel turn-off. There are daily flights to Riyadh (SR 270 one way, economy class) and Jeddah (SR 240). Direct flights also operate from Najran to Dhahran (SR 410), Jizan (SR 140) and Sharurah (SR 100) several times each week.

The bus station is on the Main Rd, 1.7 km from the turn-off for Abha. Buses to Riyadh (12 hours, SR 120) leave daily at 8 am, 4.30 and 8 pm. Buses to Jeddah (14½ hours, SR 120) via Abha (five hours, SR 30) and Khamis Mushayt (4½ hours, SR 30) leave at 10 am and 5 pm. There is one bus each day to Sharurah (3½ hours, SR 40) at 2 pm.

There are not a lot of service-taxis in Najran though a few can be found in the parking lot opposite the traffic lights in the centre, where you turn to reach the fort.

Getting Around

The only difference between Najran's yellow taxis and its white and orange ones is their colour. None have meters and most run as shared shuttles between Faisaliah and Najran at SR 2 per person. The taxi basically cruises around until it has four or five passengers and then heads down the road. If you want it all to yourself expect to pay SR 10. For trips to the museum or the dam you will have to negotiate the fare in advance.

If you need to rent a car in Najran try Al-Reda Rent-a-Car on the Main Rd just past the place where it forks marking the turn for the youth hostel.

SHARURAH

The town of Sharurah lies deep in the Empty Quarter, about 340 km east of Najran. A generation ago Sharurah and other settlements like it were hopelessly remote wells known only to a handful of Bedouins. Today, you can reach it in a few hours from Najran. The desert scenery on the drive out to Sharurah is spectacular and includes a drive of about 60 km through what can only be described as a canyon of sand dunes rising to heights of 100m or more on each side of the road. If you are coming from Najran this area starts about 245 km east of the junction with the Abha-Najran road. The photograph on the 'Road in the Empty Quarter' poster sold throughout Saudi Arabia was taken on the Najran-Sharurah road near the western entrance to the sand canyon.

The road is modern and fast and there is a surprising amount of traffic on it. Still, this is not a trip to be undertaken lightly. You absolutely *must* leave the eastern outskirts of Najran with a full tank of petrol as well as some food, water and a spare tyre in proper condition. Make all the routine checks that one should make on any vehicle before embarking on a long journey. There are several petrol stations in the middle 100 km or so of the trip and you should make a point of stopping at one of them to top up, check the radiator etc. Don't do this trip alone; tell someone that you are doing it; and, most importantly, don't get off the road. These last three points ought to be obvious but you would be surprised how many people do not take these basic precautions. There is nothing to see in Sharurah itself.

Places to Stay & Eat

The town has two hotels, the *Hotel Al-Mahmal* (☎ (07) 532 1137) where singles/doubles cost SR 77/115 and the *Al-Hammami Hotel* (☎ (07) 532 1578) where rooms go for SR 80/120. Of the two the Al-Mahmal is more modern and comfortable. The rooms at the Al-Hammami all have kitchenettes. (Note that the swimming pool next to the Al-Hammami is not part of the hotel.) The two hotels are a couple of hundred metres apart. To reach them, coming from Najran, turn toward the town centre when you pass the second petrol station on the left after passing through the checkpoint on the outskirts of town. After 650m this road makes a 90° turn to the right. The Al-Hammami is two km straight down the road from this turn. It is on the right. To reach the Al-Mahmal make a U-turn at the traffic signal by the Al-Hammami hotel, backtrack about 250m and look to the right, you will see the Al-Mahmal down a side street.

A good place to eat is *Naseef Al-Qamar*, an Egyptian-run restaurant on the street that runs between the two hotels. The sign is only in Arabic, but it is next door to Al-Hana Turkish Sweets, which does have a sign in English. The Naseef offers the usual chicken and rice selections as well as Egyptian dishes like molokiyya (stew made of green, leafy vegetables with chicken or beef).

Getting There & Away

Saudia has nonstop flights to Sharurah from Abha (SR 180 one way, economy class), Jizan (SR 180) and Najran (SR 100). One-stop service is available from Jeddah (SR 310), Riyadh (SR 270) and Taif (SR 290). On most routes there are two or three flights per week.

If you want to get a look at the Empty Quarter but either can't drive or would rather not do so, SAPTCO has one bus per day between Najran and Sharurah. The bus leaves Najran at 2 pm and takes 3½ hours to make the trip. Tickets are SR 40. Since the bus to Najran leaves Sharurah every day at 7.30 am you will have to spend the night to do the trip by bus.

To reach the hotels from the Sharurah bus stop, start with your back to the bus stop with the petrol station across the street and to your left. Head away from both the bus stop and the petrol station and follow the street for 1.7 km. The Al-Mahmal will be down a side street to your left just before the street you are on dead-ends into the Main Rd. To reach the Al-Hammami continue on to the Main Rd and turn left. To reach the bus stop from the Al-Mahmal turn right out of the hotel door then take the second right and follow the street for 1.7 km.

Hard core desert buffs can drive the 55 km beyond Sharurah to **Wuday'ah** where the road trails off into an endless plain of red sand stretching toward Saudi Arabia's undefined border with Yemen. The scenery on this drive, however, is not really worth the trip.

JIZAN

Even in November the heat and humidity of Jizan (Gizan) can make the place almost unlivable. There is little of interest in Jizan except for its old souk, though it is also the jumping-off point for anyone bound for Farasan Island. Like Najran, Jizan only came under Saudi control in the mid-1930s, following the war with Yemen.

Orientation & Information

The heart of the town is one long street which does not appear to have a name. It begins at a huge roundabout on the town's outskirts where the road from Abha, the airport road, the road to the Sports City and several other streets all converge. From there it runs straight down to the Corniche and the port with one other intersection near the Lulua Restaurant, approximately 200m from the Corniche.

The bus station is just off the Corniche. The post office and telephone office are two doors apart in a side street that branches off the Corniche opposite the main entrance to the port. Standing at the port entrance you can see the telephone office by looking directly inland – it is the building with the green and white fence around it. The airport is about five km north-east of the centre.

The telephone code for Jizan is 07.

Things to See

The **Ottoman Fort** overlooking the town is Jizan's most interesting site, but happens to be sitting smack in the middle of an interior ministry police compound. It is not open to the public and photography is forbidden.

The **old souk** is a treat. It is one of the most traditional souks left in the Kingdom. To reach it, face the sea and turn left onto the Corniche from the main street. Go left again at the small roundabout by the main gate to the port. At the first set of lights turn left yet again. If you have a car you can park in the lot which will appear on your right after about 250m.

The **animal market** at the base of the artificial hill behind the fort is worth a look. It's also a good spot to shop for pottery.

Places to Stay

The *youth hostel* (☎ 322 1875, ext 242) is at the Sports City, just over eight km from the Corniche. Beds are SR 8. If you are coming from Abha or Jeddah enter the main roundabout and take the last road you come to before having gone all the way around the traffic circle. If you are coming from the bus station it's the road to the right of the big blue and white sculpture. Once on this road you should have the sea on your right, if you don't you're in the wrong place. The hostel is seven km from the roundabout.

There are three other hotels in Jizan, none of which are cheap. The four-star *Al-Hayat Gizan Hotel* (☎ 322 1055, fax 317 1774) is on the Corniche south of the centre. Singles/doubles are SR 264.50/345, including the 15% service charge. In town, just north of the Main Rd between the roundabout and the Corniche, the *Gizan Sahari Hotel* (☎ 322 0440, fax 317 1386) has rooms with bath for SR 120/170, without bath for SR 88/132. The hotel has no sign in English. Jizan's newest hotel is the *Atheel Hotel* (☎ 317 1101, fax 317 1094), on the main roundabout. Rooms cost SR 192/265, including breakfast.

Places to Eat

At the *Lulua Al-Sahel Broast & Restaurant*, on the main road near the junction with the Corniche, a serving of rice with chicken, meat or vegetables costs less than SR 10. The new management has vastly improved and enlarged both the restaurant and the menu. The staff are efficient and friendly and a few of them even speak English (a rarity in Jizan outside the Al-Hayat hotel). It's also very popular with local Saudis and expats alike.

Back by the big roundabout the *Turky Resturent* (sic) is another good place to get a quick, cheap meal.

Across the street from the Lulua, and above a small grocery store, you'll find a good traditional coffee house. Look for a big, yellow Lipton tea sign. Upstairs you will find open sides with a view down to the street, ceiling fans, shisha pipes and a TV set roaring out the soccer match of the evening. A similar place, the *Arab Gulf Coffee Shop*,

SAUDI ARABIA

is about 200m up the side street that connects with the Main Rd next to the Lulua.

Getting There & Away

There are several flights a day to both Jeddah (SR 190 one way, economy class) and Riyadh (SR 310), with regular services also operating to Dhahran (SR 450), Najran (SR 140) and Sharurah (SR 180). Oddly, there are no flights between Jizan and Abha. Note that Jizan is spelled Gizan in all of Saudia's timetables. To reach the Saudia office turn right onto the Corniche from the Main Rd and go right at the first set of traffic lights.

The bus station is just off the Corniche between the junction with the Main Rd and the entrance to the port. It is on the sea side of the road. Look for a SAPTCO trailer in a parking lot surrounded by a fence. There are six buses a day to Jeddah (10 hours, SR 90). These leave at 8 am, noon, and at 4, 6, 8 and 10 pm. Buses to Abha and Khamis Mushayt (five hours, SR 25) leave at 9 am and at 1, 5 and 9 pm. Change at Abha for Riyadh.

FARASAN ISLAND

The Farasan archipelago lies about 40 km off the coast of Jizan. Farasan is also the name of the main island, which is the only one with any significant number of inhabitants (most of the other islands are little more than tiny outcrops of rock).

Farasan is a popular spot for bird-watching, camping and diving, but unless you've got your own boat the only way to get there is by ferry from Jizan. The good news is that the ferry, which takes about 3½ hours, is free. The bad news is that it only makes the trip once a day, so if you want to visit the island you must be prepared to camp overnight.

The ferry departs from Jizan port every morning at 7.30 am. Look for a small blue gate between the main entrance to the port and the military entrance. To make the trip you should show up by 6 am with the usual paperwork (iqama and travel letter for residents, passport for visitors, registration papers if you want to take a car).

The North-West

Saudi Arabia's north-western corner, the provinces of Tabuk, Qurayyat and Jof, is the most remote and least known part of the country. Yet the area's heritage is rich. The mighty Babylonian Empire was, briefly, ruled from Taima, in Tabuk Province. The town of Tabuk itself was a station on the ill-starred Hejaz Railway, and the Jof area, centred on the small city of Sakaka, has a number of interesting sites.

TABUK

Tabuk (Tabouk), the largest city in northwestern Saudi Arabia, is largely a military town, so be careful where you point your camera. It is the last city of any size on the road to Jordan (or the first city of any size if you are coming from the north) and what little tourism it gets tends to be Jordan-oriented. Tabuk is actually closer to Petra than Amman, and some tours to Petra originating in Saudi Arabia begin with flights to Tabuk followed by a drive to Petra. Tabuk does, however, have a few sites in its own right.

It also has a very conservative reputation. I've received several letters since the first edition from readers reporting that non-Arab women are required to cover their heads in Tabuk. I was unable to confirm this while researching this edition, so caution and discretion are in order.

Orientation & Information

Tabuk's centre is quite compact. You really only need to know four streets. The trick is that only one of these streets has a name. Start with Prince Fahd Bin Sultan St, which is a pedestrian zone, and the street parallel to, and one block south of, it. These form the centre's main business district along with the large road running approximately perpendicular to Prince Fahd Bin Sultan St. Parallel to this, one traffic light to the east, is the main road north to the youth hostel and onward to the Jordanian border.

There are several banks on or near Prince

Fahd Bin Sultan St including a branch of the Saudi Cairo Bank which has an ATM linked to the Plus and Cirrus networks. Also on this street is the post office and local taxi stand.

The telephone office is outside the centre, between the Al-Adel and Moroj hotels and on the same side of the street as they are. There are also payphones on Prince Fahd Bin Sutan St by the post office.

The Saudia office is on the same street as the telephone office, also between the Al-Adel and Moroj hotels, but on the opposite side.

The local antiquities office is in the education ministry building 400m west of the Al-Balawi Hotel. Moving from the hotel toward the centre you will see two white buildings opposite each other on either side of the street. Coming from the hotel the education building is the one on the right. The antiquities office is on the 2nd floor.

The telephone code for Tabuk is 04.

Tabuk Fort

Tabuk Fort, at the western end of Prince Fahd Bin Sultan St, is not much to look at but has a long history. The first fort on this site was built around 985 AD. The present fort, the third to occupy the site, was built by the Ottoman Turks circa 1655 and was restored by the Saudi government in the early '90s. Tabuk, and the fort, were a stop on the pilgrim road from Damascus to Mecca.

To visit the interior of the fort you will need a permit, which must be obtained in Riyadh. You will then need to pay a visit to the local antiquities office to get the door unlocked, which can only be done Saturday to Wednesday from around 8 am until 1 pm.

Whether you go inside or not be sure to pause for a look at the Koranic verses over the doorway. The blue and white tile work is a Turkish speciality, as anyone who has been to Istanbul's Topkapi Palace will well remember. The two large, stone-lined sunken areas just west of the fort were cisterns used to store water, especially during times when the hajj caravan was expected.

Inside the fort is a small courtyard. Across this, directly opposite the main entrance, is a large alcove. This was the fort's main mosque (note the mihrib in the far wall). A smaller mosque, open to the sky for use during the summer, is directly above the main alcove. In the courtyard itself you can also see the remains of a well.

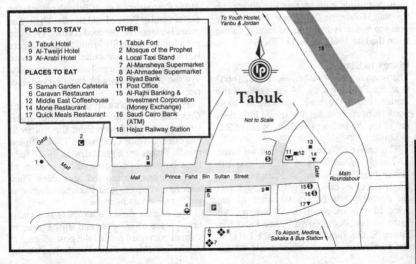

PLACES TO STAY	OTHER
3 Tabuk Hotel	1 Tabuk Fort
9 Al-Tweijri Hotel	2 Mosque of the Prophet
13 Al-Arabi Hotel	4 Local Taxi Stand
	7 Al-Mansheya Supermarket
PLACES TO EAT	8 Al-Ahmadee Supermarket
	10 Riyad Bank
5 Samah Garden Cafeteria	11 Post Office
6 Caravan Restaurant	15 Al-Rajhi Banking &
12 Middle East Coffeehouse	Investment Corporation
14 Mone Restaurant	(Money Exchange)
17 Quick Meals Restaurant	16 Saudi Cairo Bank
	(ATM)
	18 Hejaz Railway Station

To Youth Hostel, Yanbu & Jordan

Tabuk

Not to Scale

Gate

Mall

Prince Fahd Bin Sultan Street

Main Roundabout

To Airport, Medina, Sakaka & Bus Station

SAUDI ARABIA

Hejaz Railway Station

Tabuk was one of the major stops along the short-lived Hejaz Railway. If you have seen the restored station near Madain Salah the first thing you are likely to notice about the Tabuk station is how much larger it is. The buildings stretch along nearly half a km of one of Tabuk's main streets. The view from outside the fence is excellent, though if you want a closer look a permit from the main antiquities office in Riyadh is required. The buildings, which date from around 1906, have been extensively restored.

From the modern road you are, in fact, looking at the rear of the station. The tracks (of which nothing remain) ran along the other side of the buildings. The three identical two storey houses were barracks for the Turkish soldiers garrisoned at the station. The main station office was in the larger, one storey building a short distance north, near the water tower. The building at the southern end of the complex with two arched openings at each end was a shed where engines were cleaned and serviced.

The Mosque of the Prophet

Tabuk's most important mosque is just off Prince Fahd Bin Sultan St. It takes its name from a mosque built on this site during the Prophet Mohammed's lifetime. The building you see today is much more recent, dating from the late 1960s or early '70s.

Places to Stay

The *youth hostel* (☎ 422 6308, fax 422 1668) is at the Sporting City, 14 km north of the centre. From the main roundabout head north, turn right at the first traffic light then left at the Al-Balawi Hotel. Beds cost SR 8 per night.

The one really cheap hotel in town is the *Al-Tweijri Hotel* (☎ 424 0028), just off Prince Fahd Bin Sultan St. Plain but clean singles/doubles cost SR 70/100, though you can probably talk five or 10 riyals off this price. Most of the rooms do not have private baths. A few doors down Prince Fahd Bin Sultan St the *Tabuk Hotel* (☎ 422 1911) is not particularly good value at SR 90 for

doubles. A much better bet is the *Al-Arabi Hotel* (☎ 423 6492, fax 422 4787) near the eastern end of Prince Fahd Bin Sultan St, where rooms cost SR 88/132.

Rooms also cost SR 88/132 at the *Al-Adel Hotel* (☎ 422 1749, fax 423 8237) and the *Moroj Hotel* (☎ 423 3490, fax 422 6039), both on the big street parallel to, and one traffic light east of, the street with the railway station. Both are excellent value though the singles in the Al-Adel's old building are very small.

The *Al-Balawi Hotel* (☎ 422 2464), north of the Al-Adel and closer to the centre, is slightly more expensive at SR 100/138. For this you don't get a better room, but you do get a slightly larger bath. The *Al-Hamdan Hotel* (☎ 422 4790, fax 422 3735) is just off this same street, between the Al-Adel and the Moroj and on the opposite side of the street from them. It is a bit more expensive at SR 154/198.

The *Tabuk Sahara Hotel* (☎ & fax 422 1212) is several km east of the centre on the main road to Medina. Rooms cost SR 402.50/523 including the service charge.

Places to Eat

One eatery definitely worth visiting is the *Mone Restaurant*, a great Turkish place at the eastern end of Prince Fahd Bin Sultan St. The menu is extensive, the food is cheap (you can get a full lunch for SR 7) and the atmosphere is relaxed. It is particularly popular with Tabuk's relatively large Turkish community. Try the white beans with meat served over rice.

For a slightly more up-market meal try the *Caravan Restaurant* on the commercial street parallel to Prince Fahd Bin Sultan St and one short block south of it. Their Filipino noodle dishes are a great deal at SR 12 for a huge helping of noodles with a mixture of beef, chicken, shrimp and vegetables. They also have Chinese and Pakistani dishes as well as steaks and kebabs.

The *Middle East Coffeehouse* is a traditional place offering tea and shisha pipes in a small courtyard behind the post office.

Just off Prince Fahd Bin Sultan St the

Samah Garden Cafeteria is a nice shady spot for a juice, coffee, tea or soda but the food is pretty dire. Stick to the drinks.

Getting There & Away

Saudia has daily flights between Tabuk and Jeddah (SR 270 one way, economy class), Riyadh (SR 380) and Medina (SR 180). Direct service is available several times per week to Abha (SR 450), Buraydah (SR 290), Hail (SR 210) and Taif (SR 370).

The bus station is five km east of the centre and just west of the Tabuk Sahara Hotel on the road to Medina. There are two buses each day to Riyadh (15 to 17 hours, SR 200) at 10 am and 7 pm and three buses to Jeddah (13 hours, SR 130) at 8.30 am, 5.30 and 9.30 pm. The Jeddah buses travel via Dhuba (SR 35) and Yanbu (SR 95). The Riyadh buses travel via Hail (SR 100) and Buraydah (SR 140). There are four buses daily to Medina (10 hours, SR 100) at 10 am, 2, 2.30 and 9 pm. The 2.30 pm bus goes via Yanbu, the other three make the trip via Taima (SR 40). There are two buses per day to Sakaka (five hours, SR 80) at 9 am and 8 pm.

SAPTCO also has a daily service from Tabuk to Cairo via Dhuba and Safaga. Tickets cost SR 220 to SR 265, depending on how much luxury you would like during the Red Sea crossing.

Service-taxis leave from the large vacant lot behind the bus station.

Getting Around

There is a taxi rank just off Prince Fahd Bin Sultan St.

SAKAKA

Sakaka, some 450 km from Tabuk by road, is the capital of the Jof (Jouf) region and the main town along the northern edge of the Nafud. Though remote and rural, it was an important centre of civilisation in ancient times. Sakaka and Domat Al-Jandal are probably the least visited of the Kingdom's major archaeological areas, but those who do make the effort to arrange a visit are likely to be glad they did.

Though it is the larger of the region's twin oases, Sakaka has traditionally been less active or important than Domat Al-Jandal as a trading centre. Nor was it ever as well fortified.

Lady Anne Blunt and her husband Wilfred were among the first westerners to visit Sakaka, which they called Meskakeh. They visited in the late 19th century and Lady Anne's subsequent book, *A Pilgrimage to Najd*, provides one of the few vivid portraits of Arabian society in that era.

Orientation & Information

Sakaka's main street runs from a single large intersection approximately north for some 4.5 km. The intersection is dominated by Sakaka's main mosque and its biggest hotel, the Al-Nusl. Along or near this street you will find most of Sakaka's restaurants and services. The post office and bus station are both on another road which runs out of this intersection (to your right, as you face up the commercial street with the mosque to your left and the Al-Nusl to your right) and rejoins the main commercial street at its northern end. There are a number of banks along this main commercial street, including a branch of Al-Rajhi Commercial Establishment for Exchange more or less across the street from the Deera Restaurant.

The telephone office is behind the Emara (district government) building. The Emara is on the main commercial street between the fourth and fifth traffic lights and on the right as you come from the main intersection. The call cabins are for international calls only, but you can find payphones in a number of spots along the main commercial street.

Coming into Sakaka from Domat Al-Jandal you will pass the Jof airport, then an Aramco tank farm and, finally, the local police checkpoint. After the road becomes divided you will come to a large roundabout where the kerbstones are painted orange and black. To reach the centre turn right out of this roundabout, follow the road for about five km and then turn left. Another km will bring you to the main intersection.

To reach the local education office (where antiquities site permits must be validated) go

SAUDI ARABIA

north along the main commercial street through five traffic lights and then look right. You will see a green building surrounded by a large wall set a short distance back from the road. This is the education office. Take your site permit to the antiquities section on the 1st floor.

The telephone code for Sakaka is 04.

Qasr Za'abel

Anne Blunt, uncharacteristically, gives Qasr Za'abel only a passing mention in her account of Sakaka. 'Meskakeh, like Jof, has an ancient citadel perched on a cliff about a hundred feet high, and dominating the town,' she wrote, and then moved on to a description of the town itself. This brief description is today noteworthy mainly for the indication it gives that Sakaka's centre has, over the last century, migrated about five km to the south.

The 'ancient citadel' was, in fact, only around 50 years old when the Blunts visited Sakaka in 1879. It seems to have received only intermittent use. The Finnish traveller Georg August Wallin passed by Za'abel in 1845, when it was probably between 20 and 30 years old, and noted that it was in ruins. Blunt does not say what condition she found the fort in, but by the late 20th century it was in near complete disrepair. It was restored by the Saudi government in 1993-94 with what, aesthetically, can only be described as mixed results.

A permit from Riyadh is required to visit the interior of the fort. The fort itself is often unattended so it would probably be a good idea to head for the antiquities office first. Visiting hours are Saturday to Wednesday from roughly 8 am to 1 pm.

The fort has four towers and is irregular in its shape, clinging to the awkward contours of the hilltop.

Inside, the room to the left of the entrance was the *majlis* of the fort's commander, the place where he would have held formal meetings and received petitions from the local populace. The two storey building in the middle of the courtyard was the commander's house. The stone square in the courtyard near the majlis was not a well.

Rather it was a cistern for storing water that would have been hauled up from wells in the oasis below. You can climb the watchtowers for a great view out over the town.

Qasr Za'abel is at the northern end of town. From the main intersection follow either the main commercial street for 4.4 km or take the slightly longer, but faster, street that leaves the intersection between the Al-Nusl Hotel and Beit Ibrahim Al-'Aishan for 4.6 km. Either street will bring you to a roundabout dominated by a white sculpture. From this roundabout head left and follow the road for just under one km to a traffic light. Turn right at the light and keep left when the road forks (after about 150m). The fort's parking area is about 400m from the traffic light.

Jabal Burnus

This is the big rock outcrop just east of Qasr Za'abel. If you look carefully you will see a large swathe of black across the upper face of the rock. Look a bit more closely and you can see rock carvings of dancing figures with their arms raised in the air. Little is known about these figures save that they are pre-Islamic in origin (which almost goes without saying).

Bir Sisar

This large rectangular well, cut some 15m straight down into solid rock, is thought to date to the early centuries of the Christian era, though its exact purpose remains uncertain. If you look (carefully) over the side you can see stairs carved into the northern and eastern sides of the well. There are also two openings, which you can't really see clearly, beneath the stairs.

Bir Sisar is about 200m from the parking area for Qasr Za'abel. Look for a small road leading off to the right as you start from the fort back toward the main road.

Beit Ibrahim Al-'Aishan

This fort-like house is situated on one corner of Sakaka's main intersection and stands diagonally opposite the mosque. According to local antiquities officials the house, now unoccupied, is thought to be about 50 years old. It is remarkably well preserved and gives you a good idea of what Wilfred and Anne Blunt would have seen when they visited Sakaka in 1879.

Rajajil

On a bleak hillside approximately 25 km from the centre of Sakaka stand the mysterious clusters of stone pillars known as either Rajajil or Madarah. Little is known about the pillars, except that they measure approximately three metres from top to bottom, they are covered in ancient Thamudic graffiti and that they may date from around 2000 BC. They appear to be all that remains of what was once a Bronze Age cult centre. Though the immediate neighbourhood of the pillars has been brightened a bit by the appearance of an agricultural project a few hundred metres away, the site itself is still a pretty lonely place.

The main set of four pillars – the ones on the poster in most of the Kingdom's antiquities offices – are to the left of the gate. Several smaller clusters of pillars, most of which have managed to remain rather more vertical than the main group, are scattered around the enclosure.

Contrary to popular belief you do not need a 4WD to reach Rajajil, though you will need a permit from Riyadh and an escort from the local antiquities office to get inside the fence (and this is one case where looking in from outside the fence is not really worth the effort). Escorts from the antiquities office are available Saturday to Wednesday from about 8 am to 1 pm.

To reach the site take the road toward Tabuk from Sakaka's main intersection. Just over 17 km from this starting point you will see an Aramco tank farm on the left hand side of the road. Look for a storage tank with the Aramco logo and the words 'Safety First' against a yellow background. Turn left onto a paved road just before the Aramco complex. Go 5.8 km and turn right onto a good, wide dirt road at a point just before the paved road makes a turn to the right. Follow this dirt road for 400m to a T-junction and turn right. After another 350m the road will swing around to the left. Follow the road and a farther 350m will put you right in front of the gate.

Places to Stay

The *youth hostel* (☎ 624 1883, fax 624 8341) is 1.5 km west of the main intersection on the big street that goes out of the intersection immediately to the west of the mosque. Beds are SR 8 per night. Look for a green sign with white lettering in Arabic and a small blue and white IYHF logo in the upper left hand corner. The sign is squeezed between two much larger signs for the Riyadh House Est. It's on the right if you are coming from the main intersection.

After the hostel Sakaka's cheapest accommodation is the *Al-Jof Hotel* (☎ 624 5200) on the road running north and east out of the main intersection. The sign is only in Arabic but it is next door to the larger Al-Yarmook Hotel. Singles/doubles cost SR 65/100 with private bath, SR 55/90 without. This is a pretty good deal, especially when compared to the *Al-Yarmook Hotel* (☎ 624 9333, fax 624 8084) where rooms with bath cost SR 88/132. The toilets at the Yarmook are 'eastern' style while the Al-Jof offers 'western' bathroom facilities. The hotels are about 700m from the main intersection and are also the closest hotels to the bus stop, which is half a km farther along the road, moving away from the main intersection.

If you have a car the *Al-Andalos Hotel* (☎ 633 1100, fax 633 1331), nine km from the main intersection on the road back toward Tabuk, is one of the best values I've seen in the Kingdom. SR 77/116 gets you a room that would cost two or three times that sum in Riyadh or Jeddah.

The *Mared Hotel* (☎ 624 5200, fax 624 8229), one km west of the youth hostel, has rooms for SR 88/132. The lone top-end hotel in Sakaka is the *Al-Nusl* (☎ 625 0353, fax 625 0408), on the main intersection, where rooms cost SR 287.50/374, including the service charge.

Places to Eat

The *Al-Deera Restaurant*, on the left, 600m north of the main intersection, has good shawarma. A few doors away the *Sunset Restaurant* has the same sort of food and offers a large, quiet but fairly smoky seating area upstairs from the main restaurant. Both places charge about SR 9 for half a roasted chicken.

Near the youth hostel the *Al-Buraq Restaurant-3* is an excellent cheap eatery. The surroundings are good and the kebabs are especially well seasoned. Lunches and dinners cost SR 7 to SR 15, depending on the size of your appetite.

Getting There & Away

The airport is 28 km down the road toward Domat Al-Jandal. It appears in Saudia's timetables as 'Jouf'. Saudia's office is at the northern end of the main commercial street. There are one or two flights every day to Riyadh (SR 270 one way, economy class), and services several times a week to Jeddah (SR 290) and Hail (SR 100). There is only one flight per week to Buraydah (Gassim) (SR 180).

The SAPTCO station is a few hundred metres beyond the Al-Yarmook Hotel. There are two buses every day to Tabuk (six to seven hours, SR 80) at 1 am and 3 pm. You'll have to change at Tabuk to reach Jeddah, Medina or Yanbu. There are also two daily buses to Riyadh (14 hours, SR 175) at 9 am and 3 pm. Because there is no road across the Nafud these buses make the trip to the capital by going up and around via Arar. There is even a single daily bus all the way to Dammam (14 hours, SR 165) at 9 pm.

If you are driving to Sakaka, whether up from Tabuk or down from Arar, keep a close eye on your fuel gauge. It can be a long way between petrol stations in this part of the country.

Getting Around

Sakaka has very few taxis and appears somewhat lacking where rental cars are concerned. Al-Husain Car Rental (☎ 615 1235) has a desk at the airport, and a couple of the larger hotels, notably the Al-Nusl and the Al-Andalos, have car rental desks. If you can find a taxi the driver will probably ask around SR 50 for the trip to Domat Al-Jandal.

DOMAT AL-JANDAL

Domat Al-Jandal is one of the Kingdom's little known gems. This modest town boasts two of the country's most interesting antiquities – the ruined Qasr Marid and the still-in-use Mosque of Omar. Though it is only 50 km from Sakaka, getting to Domat Al-Jandal can be a problem without your own car. It is, however, worth the effort.

History

Domat Al-Jandal's history goes back some three millennia. The earliest known references to Domat use the name Adummatu, and an Assyrian text of 688 BC refers to the town as the seat of the King of the Arabs. This part of Arabia is identified with the Biblical Midian, a region known to the ancient Egyptians as Kashu. Domat Al-Jandal itself appears in many Bible atlases as 'Dhuma'. It remained an important town throughout the late centuries BC and early centuries AD even as Petra declined.

Petra, whose wealth was heavily dependant on the frankincense trade, lost influence once the Romans began transporting frankincense to Egypt and the Mediterranean by boat from Yemen. Domat Al-Jandal, however, continued to prosper during this period because of its position along other trade routes, especially those linking the Mediterranean with the Far East and the Gulf. Zenobia, the Arab queen who ruled much of modern Syria from the desert city of Palmyra, besieged the town in the 3rd century AD but apparently failed to take it.

The town was besieged three times by Muslim armies during the Prophet's lifetime. The first siege, in 624, was led by the Prophet himself. It was only during the third siege, in 630, that Domat Al-Jandal fell to the Muslims. After Mohammed's death, two years later, Domat Al-Jandal was one of the towns which tried to renounce Islam and its ties with the Muslim state during the period known as the Rida (apostasy wars). A Muslim force under Khalid Bin Al-Waleed, the general who had conquered the town for the first time in 630, retook Domat Al-Jandal and returned it to the Islamic fold in 633-34.

Domat Al-Jandal, along with the rest of the Jof region, was incorporated into the First Saudi Empire in the late 18th century but returned to local rule in 1819 with the eclipse of Saudi power. The Hail-based Al-Rashid clan added it to their dominions in 1838 and ruled the region until 1909, except for a few months in 1875 when the Turks occupied the area (they withdrew after the Al-Rashids complained to the Ottoman sultan).

In 1909 the area fell to Nuri Bin Sha'lan, a chief of the powerful Ruwalla tribe who ruled from Marid until 1922 when the Al-Saud under Abdul Aziz reconquered the region.

Information
Domat Al-Jandal is almost as large a town as Sakaka but it has few services. There are no hotels and only a handful of restaurants. Even the people who run the museum live in Sakaka and drive down for work every morning.

If you are looking for a bite to eat try the *Al-Khair Restaurant*, about 200m from the museum back toward the main road, just beyond the Riyad Bank office. It has simple decent chicken meals for about SR 8.

Jof Regional Museum
The Jof Regional Museum is the best place to begin a tour of Domat Al-Jandal. The museum is open Saturday to Wednesday from 8 am to 1 pm. Admission is free. Turn right at the entry to the exhibit hall and follow the displays around to your left.

The museum opens with exhibits on the age and geology of the earth and includes displays on the Kingdom's plants and animals, the development of Arabic script and the domestication of the camel. There are also several displays focusing specifically on Domat Al-Jandal and the Jof area. These include a set of reproductions of Anne

Blunt's sketches of Sakaka and Domat Al-Jandal (which she refers to as 'Jof' throughout *A Pilgrimage to Nejd*). The text accompanying this part of the exhibit incorrectly identifies her husband, Wilfred, as her brother.

The museum is 1.25 km off the main road from Tabuk to Sakaka. Coming from Sakaka and the airport turn right off the main road just past the second Domat Al-Jandal petrol station and 350m beyond the police station, which will also be on your right. At the turn-off you should see a two storey brown building with a four storey tower at one of its corners ahead of you and to the right. Follow this road for 1.25 km. The museum will be on the right.

Qasr Marid
Immediately adjacent to the museum is the Jof region's most famous building – Qasr Marid. Marid is old – its foundations date to Nabataean times, and Roman-era records of Queen Zenobia's expedition to the area in the 3rd century AD mention Marid by name. The fortress was repaired in the 19th century and became the local seat of government until the new fort built by the Al-Rashids supplanted it.

The main mud-brick superstructure with towers at the four corners was rebuilt between 1909 and 1922, during the years when Marid again served as the Jof region's seat of government, this time under Nuri Bin Sha'lan, whose son, Nawwaf, was the local governor and lived in Marid.

The oldest parts of what can be seen today are pre-Islamic and possibly Nabataean. This is the very carefully done brickwork which you can see around the building's lower levels and, in a few places, fairly high up the walls.

A path runs down to Marid from the side of the museum, though the best way to get into the castle is to walk around to the far side from the one facing the museum and to climb up into the superstructure via three increasingly steep staircases. Before doing so, however, turn to the right, after passing through the doorway, to reach a well, at the bottom of which you can still hear water running. From here turning to the right will take you up the stairs. When you reach the courtyard cross to the far side of it, go through a low stone passageway and look right when you are in the walkway between the inner and outer fortification walls. Here you will find another well, smaller than the first, but also still usable. The ramparts themselves provide great views over the town and oasis.

Permits are not needed to visit Marid, and there is no fence around the site. There is a sign that says photography is prohibited and while the museum director told me the sign was out of date and that still photography was OK, a policeman in the area said the opposite during my visit. If you do plan to take pictures you should either ask someone from the museum to walk through Marid with you, or get a permit from the main antiquities office in Riyadh.

The Mosque of Omar
This mosque is one of the oldest in the Kingdom. It is said to have been founded by the second caliph, Omar Bin Al-Khattab (reigned 634 to 644), when he stopped off in Domat Al-Jandal en route to Jerusalem.

The mosque is still in use (and, thus, off limits to non-Muslims) and its prayer hall and courtyard have been extensively reconstructed over the centuries. The really impressive thing to see is the mosque's lone minaret. The minaret is interesting for two reasons. First, because it is the only surviving bit of the original mosque and second, because it does not really look like a minaret. A relatively low tower, tapered, with a large number of windows and a passageway through the bottom, the minaret does not conform to any conventional school of Islamic architecture. This fact tends to back up the widely held belief that the minaret was part of another building, possibly a church, which was converted to use as a mosque during Omar's caliphate. This was not uncommon in those days (one of Islam's grandest mosques – the Omayyad Mosque in Damascus – is a converted church).

The minaret too has undergone some restoration work, but the main mosque building and attached courtyard in use today are much later in date. Local records note that the mosque was extensively rebuilt in 1794.

Local tradition holds that the mosque was once linked to Qasr Marid by an underground tunnel. While this is plausible granted the mosque's proximity to Marid, no trace of such a tunnel has been found.

Be sure to take a look at the carved door at the base of the minaret.

Old Domat Al-Jandal
You should definitely take some time to wander through the old mud quarter adjacent to the Mosque of Omar. Parts of the quarter have been settled for up to 1000 years, though the buildings standing there today are not that old. Some, however, have stones from older structures incorporated into them.

Entering the old quarter through the narrow passageway to the left of the Mosque of Omar (not the passage along the outer wall of the mosque) you can follow a well-defined path directly through the quarter. This path will turn left, then right, bringing you to a large arched passageway. Just beyond this and on the left you can see several stones bearing **Nabataean inscriptions** which have been incorporated into the walls. Continue past these and then turn left as you emerge from these buildings and you will reach an ancient stone-lined **well** which was in use until fairly recently (note the rusting pumping equipment around it). On the ground about four metres from the edge of the well you can see a rock with notches marking the spots where ropes were used to bring water up from the bottom of the well. Moving through the nearby gap in the wall and then around the wall to your right will bring you to two other wells and other notched stones. Next to the first well beyond this wall you will also see an old **irrigation channel**.

City Wall
A small portion of Domat Al-Jandal's once formidable city wall has been restored and

can be viewed without a permit in the desert just outside town. From the top of the wall you can easily follow the fortification's line along the low ridge to the east and along the hill to the west where the rest of the wall used to run. You will also notice that the watch-towers along the wall itself were hollow all the way to ground level.

The wall is 3.6 km from the museum. To reach it from the museum turn right out of the museum's parking lot and follow the road 1.3 km to an intersection where you will see a brown building across the intersection and to the left. Turn right here. After 400m you will come to another intersection marked by a three storey building made of yellow and brown brick. Turn left onto a paved road (turning right would take you onto an unpaved street). The pavement ends after 1.1 km and half a km beyond that the road forks – keep left. When you are 1.9 km from the turn you will see a low ridge with the road running through it directly ahead of you. This ridge is the wall. The reconstructed portion of it is on the far side. Look for a blue and white Department of Antiquities sign to the left and a white post to the right of the road. Those without a 4WD might want to park a few hundred metres before the wall and walk the last bit as the track becomes very sandy just before you get to the wall.

Al-Rashid Palace

This palace, the one where the Blunts were received by the local governor, was built by the Al-Rashids in 1867 to replace Marid as the local seat of government. Little remains of it today. It's really rather depressing – four partial walls standing amid an impromptu garbage dump.

If you really want to see what is left of Domat's mid-19th century seat of govern-ment here's how to find it. Start in the museum's parking lot with your back to the museum building. Turn sharply left into the small alley that runs along the museum's wall and take the first turn to the right. After less than 100m this street turns to the right and takes you through a residential area. About 600m from the museum you will pass

a hospital on your right. Keep going and at 1.5 km from the museum turn left down a small alley by a cream coloured building with brown trim along its roof. What's left of the palace is 400m beyond this turn. It is on the right. All you will see is a mud wall about four metres high at its highest point. If you go around to the other side of this wall you will see the equally sparse remains of the other walls.

Getting There & Away

Taxis, if you can find one, charge SR 50 for the 50 km trip to or from Sakaka.

DHUBA

The small port of Dhuba, 185 km south-west of Tabuk and 790 km north of Jeddah on the Red Sea coast, is a place most people simply pass through. It is noteworthy mainly because a ferry service to the Egyptian port of Safaga departs from here, one that SAPTCO's buses are making increasingly frequent use of on their heavily travelled routes between the Kingdom and Cairo. See the Riyadh and Jeddah Getting There & Away sections for more details on the ferry crossing.

If you get stuck in Dhuba for the night try the *Al-Shark Hotel* (☎ (04) 432 2119, fax (04) 432 1281). Quite decent singles/doubles cost SR 150/180.

TAIMA

Taima is another of Saudi Arabia's import-ant, but often overlooked, archaeological gems. In fact, the various sites spread around Taima collectively constitute the largest archaeological area in the Kingdom. But then, what else would one expect from a former capital of the Babylonian Empire?

Taima's brief moment of glory came in 553 BC when the Babylonian emperor Nabonidus moved his capital to the city. Taima was Babylon's capital for only 10 years, but many of the ruins that are still visible in the city date from that period. The city was also mentioned in the Bible, where Isaiah (21:14-15) speaks of Taima's people

SAUDI ARABIA

as welcoming refugees and fugitives with food and offering them a safe haven.

The crusader Renaud de Chatillion attempted a raid on Taima in 1181 from his base at Kerek, in modern Jordan.

While Taima remained a trading centre after the coming of Islam it became increasingly marginal. The town was bypassed first by the main pilgrim routes to Mecca and Medina and, later, by the Hejaz Railway.

Orientation & Information

Taima stretches along, and to either side of, the main road from Tabuk to Medina. The town centre is a square dominated by a large waterfall sculpture, which is quite dramatic during those hours of the day when it is operating. There are several banks around the centre, including branches of Al-Rajhi Banking & Investment Corporation and the National Commercial Bank, near the main fountain. The telephone office is just south of the fountain square (ie toward Medina if you are starting from the square). The museum is a short distance to the north of the square.

The telephone code for Taima is 04.

Taima Museum

The museum is worth a visit for the extensive section on Taima and its history. This can be found mainly at the rear of the horseshoe-shaped exhibit gallery. From the entrance hall start your tour by moving to the left. The exhibit area begins with a display on the age and composition of the earth and also includes displays on the development of the Arabic language and the domestication of the camel. Later sections include displays of traditional clothing and household goods.

The museum is open Saturday to Wednesday from 8 am to 2 pm. Admission is free. The museum is on the main road that runs through Taima en route from Medina to Tabuk. Coming from Medina, the museum is on the right just over 1.5 km from the main square.

A restored portion of Taima's ancient **city wall** is adjacent to the museum and can be viewed easily from the main road. To look at

it up close you will need a permit from Riyadh.

Qasr Radum

This fort, a rectangle some 34m by 25m, had its heyday during the Hellenistic and Nabataean eras between the 3rd century BC and the 1st century AD. The building was modified and took on its present form sometime after 1880.

There is a well in the centre of the enclosure. You can get a reasonably good view of Radum's walls from outside the fence. To enter the enclosure you will need a permit from Riyadh. There is no attendant at the site. To get in, take your permit to the museum and ask for a guide.

To reach the ruins turn left out of the museum's parking lot and left again after 200m at a corner with a small white mosque with a green dome (if you are driving this requires going a bit beyond the mosque, making a U-turn and then turning right when you reach the mosque). From the mosque, follow this street for 850m. Qasr Al-Radum will be on your right.

Qasr Al-Hamra

This building, though often referred to as a 'palace', was probably a religious site or cult centre up to about 600 BC. There is evidence that it continued to be used past that date, however, as a Greek inscription dating from 450 BC has been found at the site.

To reach Qasr Al-Hamra follow the directions for Qasr Radum. When you reach Radum continue along the same road for another 1.85 km (a total of 2.7 km from the green and white mosque). Qasr Al-Hamra will be on your right. Note that the pavement ends about 300m past Qasr Radum. The track is passable with a regular car but requires some caution.

Bir Haddaj

Sitting incongruously in the middle of a traffic circle surrounded by a wall of yellow brick is one of Taima's most famous sites. Bir Haddaj is a huge well that has been in use since pre-Islamic times and continues to provide water for agricultural purposes today. The well is 18m across and 12m deep. A peek through the fence reveals several metres of water (and a lot of modern garbage) down at the bottom. It is thought to have been in constant use since about 500 BC. Camels were once used to raise the water to ground level, but pumps perform this job today.

There are a large number of old houses in varying states of repair in the neighbourhood around the well.

To reach Bir Haddaj start at the main square as though you had approached it from the direction of Medina. Go around to the rear of the fountain, turn left and then take the third small street on the left (the road swings left here. To your right there will be an unpaved parking lot) and then turn left yet again after 100m. This will bring you to a square that houses Taima's fruit and vegetable market. Take the first right – again, after about 100m – and after another 100m turn left at an intersection with a brown mosque. Go yet another 100m and take the first right turn into a small alley-like street. Another 400m will bring you to the traffic circle with Bir Haddaj in its centre. It really isn't as complicated as it sounds. To return to the fruit and vegetable market take the street immediately to the right of the one on which you entered the traffic circle.

Places to Stay & Eat

Taima's one cheap hotel is the *Al-Aali Hotel* (☎ 463 1551). They have simple but clean singles/doubles for SR 66/99, though you might want to check whether the hot water heater in any given room is working properly. The hotel is on the main road, just toward the centre from the museum.

Taima's best value is probably the *Qasr Al-Ablak Hotel* (☎ 463 0044, fax 463 2204), just 200m off the main square in the direction of Medina. The hotel is very new and offers good furnishings and satellite TV. Rooms cost SR 90/100, all with bath. It is next to a large petrol station and on the right as you proceed away from the square. The sign is only in Arabic. A farther four km down the

road to Medina is the *Al-Shanifi Hotel* (☎ 463 0652, fax 463 2484). It offers reasonable doubles for SR 100. The hotel/petrol station complex is also a SAPTCO stop.

The *Al-Talaq Hotel* (☎ 463 1804, fax 463 2622) is 1.6 km north of the centre heading toward Tabuk. Rooms are SR 120 per night or SR 25 an hour, but they are pretty smelly. It is on the left as you come from the centre, next to a small supermarket with an orange awning. The hotel's sign is in Arabic.

Getting There & Away

The SAPTCO station is on the main square by the fountain though buses also stop on the southern edge of town by the Al-Shanifi Hotel. There are four buses per day to both Tabuk and Medina.

The Eastern Province

For centuries the main settlements in what is now the Eastern Province of Saudi Arabia were the oasis towns of Qatif and Hofuf and their respective entrepôts at Darin, on Tarut Island, and Uqayr. With the exception of Hofuf, all of these towns are now provincial backwaters.

Despite this, the growth of the Dhahran area over the past two generations has been as spectacular as that of Riyadh and Jeddah, though if you arrive from either of those cities this may not be immediately evident. The Dhahran-Dammam-Alkhobar area, usually appearing on larger maps as a single dot marked 'Dhahran', is neither huge and new, like Riyadh, nor is it a modern city grown from the core of an ancient port, like Jeddah. Prior to the discovery of oil some 60 years ago, Dammam and Alkhobar were tiny fishing and pearling villages and Dhahran did not exist.

The Dhahran area is smaller than Riyadh or Jeddah and has a reputation for being a relatively relaxed place. Foreigners became a common sight in the Eastern Province long before they gained similar acceptance elsewhere in the Kingdom. Outside Greater

Dhahran the provincial towns of the Eastern Province are much like those of any other region of Saudi Arabia though, again, the attitude is more relaxed than in the country's central regions.

Although Dammam is the capital of the Eastern Province, a lot of the services of interest to the traveller (AMEX, bookshops with an English-language selection and virtually all of the airline offices, for example) are in Alkhobar. There are two foreign consulates in the Eastern Province, the British in Alkhobar and the US in Dhahran.

DAMMAM

The provincial capital, Dammam, is the longest settled and largest town of the Dhahran-Dammam-Alkhobar group. It is a bit run-down compared to Alkhobar but a lot cheaper.

Orientation & Information

Central Dammam is roughly the area bounded by King Abdul Aziz St to the north, King Khaled St to the south, 9th St to the east and 18th St to the west. The centre is the area around the intersection of 11th St, which appears on some maps and street signs as Dhahran St, and King Saud St.

There are banks and moneychangers at the intersection of 11th and King Saud Sts. The main post office is on the corner of 9th and Al-Amir Mansour Sts. There are no call cabins in Dammam but there is a complex of payphones on 9th St with a desk which provides change and sells phonecards. More international payphones can be found at the intersection of King Saud and 11th Sts.

The telephone code for Dammam is 03. Note that if you are trying to locate someone at Aramco, the oil company has its own, very efficient, directory assistance service; call ☎ 872 0115.

In emergencies, dial ☎ 999 for the police, ☎ 997 for an ambulance and ☎ 998 to report a fire.

Regional Museum of Archaeology & Ethnography

The museum (☎ 826 6056) is at the railroad crossing on 1st St near the Dammam Tower and across the street from the Al-Waha mall. It's on the 4th floor and is open Saturday to Wednesday from 7.30 am to 2.30 pm. Don't be put off by the dumpy street-level lobby. Admission is free. The collection includes Stone Age tools, pottery (mainly Hellenistic and early Islamic) and examples of Bedouin crafts and traditional dress, household implements and silver jewellery. Unfortunately many of the explanatory texts are only in Arabic, though most of the items in the display cases are labelled in English too.

The museum is the place to pick up permits for visiting the Eastern Province's main archaeological sites of Qatif, Tarut Island, Thaj and Al-Hina. The only exceptions are the sites in the Hofuf area, for which permits must be obtained in Riyadh. A passport or iqama is required for permits, which can usually be processed the same day.

Language Courses

The Dammam Language Institute on 11th St between King Khaled St and Prince Nasser St sometimes offers courses in spoken Arabic. Don't bother phoning as the line is always busy. The Saudi French Centre (☎ 834 9576, fax 834 1205) regularly offers French courses for both adults and children.

Places to Stay – bottom end & middle

The *youth hostel* (☎ 857 5358) is at the Sports Centre on the Dammam-Alkhobar expressway. Beds are SR 8 per night. Take bus No 1 from either city and get off midway between the two cities at the buildings in front of the stadium (not the green buildings nearby, and not at the big stadium on the edge of Dammam).

The *Al-Jaber Hotel* (☎ 832 2283), on 11th St between King Saud and King Khaled Sts, is reasonable value. Simple, clean singles/doubles with TV cost SR 66/99 with bath, SR 55/83 without. The *Al-Haramain Hotel* (☎ 832 5426, fax 832 5785) is just off King Saud St, west of the intersection with 11th St. Rooms are SR 77/115. Most of the rooms have private baths though some of the

Central Dammam

0   250   500 m

PLACES TO STAY

3 Al-Haramain Hotel
4 Al-Jaber Hotel
12 Al-Danah Safari Hotel
13 Alarifi Hotel
15 Al-Hamra Hotel
18 Gulf Flower Hotel
21 Safari Hotel

PLACES TO EAT

2 Sunrise Restaurant
8 Taj Restaurant
10 Asia Restaurant
19 Basmah Restaurant

OTHER

1 Bus Station
6 Saudi British Bank
6 Al-Rajhi Commercial Establishment for Exchange
7 Riyad Bank (Regional Office)
9 Al-Rajhi Banking & Investment Corporation
11 Al-Danah Shopping Centre & National Commercial Bank
14 Saudi Cairo Bank (ATM)
16 Dammam Language Institute
17 Payphones (International Calls)
20 GPO
22 Museum

King Abdul Aziz Street
Dhahran Street
King Saud Street
Old Railway Station
To Damman Oberoi Hotel & Damman Hotel
King Khaled Street
15th Street
14th Street
13th Street
11th Street
Prince Nasser Street
Al-Amir Mansour Street
9th Street
Al-Amir Fahd Street
Hospital Street
Ibn Khaldoon Street
Najd Street
1st Street
Stadium
To Airport
To Youth Hostel, Sports Centre & Railway Station

doubles do not (the price is the same). The place is a bit bare, but reasonably clean.

The *Gulf Flower Hotel* (☎ 826 2170, fax 827 0709), on 9th St across from the main post office, has rooms at SR 99/132, all with bath, TV and telephone. It's OK, but old and a bit creaky.

The *Safari Hotel* (☎ 827 2777) on 11th St is best avoided. The lobby is fairly impressive for a mid-range hotel but the rooms, at SR 120/155, are not. Also in the centre, and also part of the Safari chain, is the *Al-Danah Safari Hotel* (☎ 832 0063), formerly the Balhamar Hotel. It's just off King Saud St up

an alley next to the Al-Danah shopping centre. Rooms there cost SR 105/150 and are a much better bet than the other Safari Hotel.

A good medium-priced option, though a bit out of the centre, is the *Dammam Hotel* (☎ 832 9000, fax 833 7475), a set of prefabricated buildings behind the five-star Dammam Oberoi that are much nicer inside than they look from the street. Rooms are SR 165/224, including the 10% service charge.

Places to Stay – top end

A particularly good bet is the *Al-Masiyah Inn* (☎ 832 2055, fax 833 1854) on 1st St near the intersection with King Saud St. Three-room apartments go for SR 250 per night a single or double.

The *Al-Hamra Hotel* (☎ & fax 833 3444, ext 5) on King Khaled St has semi-luxurious singles/doubles for SR 230/276, including the service charge.

The *Alarifi Hotel* (☎ 833 4444, fax 833 7311) on 9th St between King Saud St and King Abdul Aziz St, charges SR 230/299, including the service charge. The only five-star hotel in town is the *Dammam Oberoi* (☎ 834 5555, fax 834 9872). Singles/doubles cost SR 517.50/673, including the service charge.

Places to Eat

There are a number of chicken and kebab places and Indian restaurants around the intersection of 11th and King Saud Sts. A good bet for a cheap, quick meal is the *Asia Restaurant*, a Filipino place on King Saud St offering two main dishes, rice, soup, dessert and a soda or mineral water for only SR 10. Broasted chicken meals start at SR 12. Even by the standards of the Eastern Province's many cheap Filipino eateries this deal is hard to beat.

Al-Amir Mansour St, a couple of blocks from the GPO, is a good place to look for affordable food. Try the *Basmah Restaurant*, which has good shawarma and fatar (sea-soned bread). The service is pretty bad but the food and prices make up for it.

At the time of my visit, the *Taj Restaurant*, which was recommended in the first edition of this book, had a rat problem. On an alley off King Saud St you'll find the *Sunrise Restaurant*, another place that has gone downhill since the first edition, though not as badly. You can get a full meal for about SR 8. Their menu is a collection of simple curries and biryanis, but it's adequate.

On King Saud St, between 9th and 11th Sts, the Al-Danah shopping centre has a selection of fast-food places. *Pattis France*, on the ground floor, is a good place to stop for a coffee or a light snack but both the service counter and the adjacent seating area are open to men only.

Getting There & Away

Air Dhahran international airport (DHA) is between Alkhobar and Dhahran, near the University of Petroleum & Minerals and the US consulate. Although not as modern as the Kingdom's other major airports, it is the most passenger-friendly. Getting there does not require a 45-minute drive into the middle of nowhere or an epic battle with traffic. Nor are there any great distances over which arriving or departing passengers must drag their luggage. A new airport (King Fahd International) is under construction in the desert, 60 km north of the present airport. This project has been under way for years so it is difficult to say when it may open.

There are about eight or 10 flights per day to Riyadh (SR 140 one way, economy class) and four or five to Jeddah (SR 410). There are also daily flights to Abha (SR 410) and Taif (SR 380) and regular service (between one and four flights per week) to Medina (SR 380), Al-Baha (SR 420), Bisha (SR 350), Buraydah (Gassim) (SR 270), Jizan (SR 450), Hail (SR 330) and Najran (SR 410).

Most of the airlines using Dhahran international airport have their booking offices in Alkhobar (for addresses see that city's Getting There & Away entry), except for Gulf Air which also has an office in Dammam. It's on 11th St, between King Saud St and King Khaled St.

Bus – domestic The SAPTCO bus station is a few blocks north of the city centre on 11th St between King Abdul Aziz St and the Corniche.

The services to Qatif, Safwa and Tarut Island are classified as local and leave from the same part of the station as the routes to Alkhobar and the airport. Bus No 9 goes to Qatif via Saihat and Jarudiyah. Route No 10A goes from Saihat to Qatif, Safwa and Umm Al-Sahik. Route No 10B is Saihat-Anak-Qatif. Route No 11 follows the same route as 10B and then continues on to the town of Darin on Tarut Island. The fare for any of these trips is SR 2.

There are daily inter-city buses to Hofuf (two hours, SR 20) every two hours from

7.30 am to 9.30 pm. All Hofuf buses travel via Abqaiq (one hour, SR 13). To Riyadh (4½ hours, SR 60), there are buses at 6.30, 8, 9.30 and 11.30 am, and at 12.30, 2, 3.30, 5, 6.30, 8 and 9.30 pm. There are two buses daily to Jeddah (19 hours, SR 190) via Taif (16 hours, SR 160). The buses depart at 2 and 6 pm and go around Mecca, so they are OK for non-Muslims, though non-Muslim passengers should probably double-check this to be sure the route has not changed.

Direct buses to Mecca (15 hours, SR 175) leave at 1 and 8 pm. There are buses to Hafr Al-Batn (5½ hours, SR 65) at 9 am, noon and at 3 and 6 pm. The 9 am and 3 pm buses continue along the Tapline road to Al-Qurayat (17 hours, SR 195). There is one direct bus to Buraydah (8½ hours, SR 120) each day at 1.30 pm with continuing service to Medina (16 hours, SR 200).

Bus – international The Saudi-Bahraini Transport Company's buses to Bahrain (three hours, SR 40/70 one way/return) leave every day at 8 and 11 am and at 2, 5 and 8.30 pm. All the Bahrain buses go via Alkhobar. Buses leave Bahrain for Saudi Arabia at 8.30 am, noon, and 3, 6 and 8.30 pm. There are fewer buses during Ramadan and more during Eid Al-Fitr and Eid Al-Adha. Tickets are available at the SAPTCO station.

There is also a daily bus to Abu Dhabi and Dubai at 8 pm. Tickets to either city cost SR 170. The trip to Abu Dhabi takes about 10 hours; to Dubai, around 13 hours. The bus to Doha, Qatar leaves every day at 7 pm (five hours, SR 100), at least on paper. In Doha I was never able to find any evidence that this bus actually exists. There is also a daily bus to Kuwait at 4 pm (five hours, SR 80).

Outside the Gulf, SAPTCO's other international services from the Eastern Province include Cairo, daily at 8.30 am via Aqaba (SR 455) and at 6 am via Dhuba (SR 410). In either case the trip takes somewhere between 36 and 48 hours, depending on the crossing and how long you spend at customs. Remember that if you take the Aqaba route you will need a Jordanian as well as an Egyptian visa. Buses to Amman (24 hours, SR 200) and Damascus (36 hours, SR 200) leave every day at 10 am and 5 pm. There are also regular buses to Istanbul (60 to 72 hours, SR 300) on Wednesday, Friday and Sunday at 11 pm.

Service-Taxi You'll find a few service-taxis across the street from the SAPTCO station, but there's not much traffic and the wait for a cab to fill up is likely to be pretty long. The fare is SR 25 to Hofuf and the taxis leave only when they are full (either four or seven passengers).

Train The railway station is south-east of the city centre, near the Dammam-Alkhobar expressway and a housing development. Trains leave at 7 am and 12.13 and 5.20 pm daily except Thursday (when there's only one train departing at 9 am) for Riyadh (approximately four hours, SR 60/40 in 1st/2nd class) via Abqaiq (45 minutes, SR 10/6) and Hofuf (1½ hours, SR 20/15). The 12.13 train does not stop in Abqaiq. See the Getting Around section in this chapter for a complete timetable.

Car Rental There are a number of car rental agencies in the area around the intersection of 11th and King Saud Sts. Two of the bigger agencies, Budget and Abu Diyab, both have offices on King Saud St near the intersection with 1st St. There is also the usual collection of car rental desks at the airport.

Getting Around

The Airport Bus No 3 runs from the bus station to the airport approximately every 30 minutes for SR 2. A taxi between the airport and Dammam costs about SR 40. There is a sign in the arrivals area urging passengers to insist that taxi drivers use the meter, but you are unlikely to succeed in this.

Bus Local buses are based at the SAPTCO station. All fares are SR 2. Routes and route numbers are posted in the front window of each bus. Virtually all local services are to Alkhobar, but they travel along different routes. The main routes are: No 1 along the

Dammam-Alkhobar expressway via the industrial area; No 3 travels via Thuqba, the airport and Dhahran/King Fahd University of Petroleum & Minerals (UPM); No 5 via the Coast Rd and No 6 via the Tubaishi industrial area.

Taxi There is the usual choice of yellow cabs and slightly more expensive white limos. Contrary to what some of the taxi drivers, particularly at the railway station, may tell you there are no set fares from the railway station or the airport into Dammam or Alkhobar. The drivers are supposed to use the meter. In practice, however, you may be fighting a losing battle on this score.

For trips around town the meter probably will be used (though you may have to remind the driver to turn it on). A flag fall is SR 2 and the meter then ticks over in 50 halala increments at SR 1 per km.

ALKHOBAR

Alkhobar (Al-Khubar, Khobar) is the newest of the three cities that make up Greater Dhahran. The first recorded settlement was in 1923. It grew rapidly because of its proximity to the early Aramco camps at Dhahran, particularly after the oil company engineers built a pier at Alkhobar to take the early oil shipments over to Bahrain for processing.

Orientation

Khobar (the 'Al' is frequently dropped in common usage) is a fairly compact grid. The central business area is bounded by Pepsi Cola St (officially 28th St, but universally referred to by its nickname) to the north, Dhahran St to the south, the Gulf to the east and King Abdul Aziz St to the west. The Corniche is officially Prince Turky St but you'll be hard-pressed to find anyone who calls it anything other than the Corniche.

Information

Foreign Consulates The UK has a consular officer who works out of the British Trade Office (☎ 857 0595) in the Al-Bustan compound, near the Al-Aswaq supermarket.

Money There are a number of banks and exchange houses along King Khaled St and on the side streets just off it, between 1st and 3rd Sts. The local branch of the Saudi Cairo Bank is on 28th St near the Al-Nimran Hotel. Al-Rajhi Banking & Investment Corporation has a large branch at the intersection of 28th and King Abdul Aziz Sts. The same location also has a women's section.

AMEX (☎ 895 3862) is represented in the Eastern Province by Kanoo Travel. Their office for AMEX business is at the corner of King Khaled and 1st Sts and is open Saturday to Thursday from 8.30 am to 12.30 pm and from 3.30 to 7.30 pm.

Post & Communications The Khobar post office is just off Dhahran St near the intersection with the Corniche. The telephone office is on Prince Talal St between 4th and 5th Sts. Look for a small parking lot with the SAPTCO office on the corner at the 5th St side of the square. The telephone office is the small brown building in the parking lot. It is open daily from 8 am to 11.30 pm.

The telephone code for Alkhobar is 03.

Travel Agencies The two main clusters of travel agencies are around the intersection of 28th St (Pepsi Cola St) and King Abdul Aziz St and on King Khaled St between Dhahran and 4th Sts.

Bookshops Khobar is a better place than Dammam to look for books, but the selection is still pretty thin. The best selection is at the Jarir Bookstore on the Corniche. Another place worth looking is the International Book Shop at the intersection of 28th and King Fahed Sts. There is a smaller branch of the same store, with a smaller selection, in the Khobar souk at the corner of A St and Prince Mohammed St.

King Fahd Causeway

Alkhobar's main attraction is the King Fahd Causeway, a 25-km long engineering marvel linking Saudi Arabia with Bahrain. Customs takes place on an artificial island halfway along. Restaurants (awful on the Saudi side, tolerable on the Bahraini side) and spectacular views can be found in the twin towers on the island.

Places to Stay

Bus No 1, which runs between the Alkhobar and Dammam bus stations, stops near the *youth hostel*. See the Dammam listing for more details.

The *Safari Hotel* (☎ & fax 895 1001), at the corner of Prince Sultan and 1st Sts, was once Khobar's only really cheap place to stay but since the first edition its prices have doubled to SR 198/257.50 a single/double. Next door the *Al-Iqbal Hotel* (☎ 894 3538, fax 864 6792) is cheaper with rooms for SR 130/170. Nearby, at the intersection of Prince Mansour and 4th Sts, the *Al-Kadisiyah Hotel* (☎ 864 1255, fax 864 3977) has large rooms with rather dowdy decor at SR 125/175, but they will readily discount these prices by about 30% when things are slow.

If you're looking for luxury but trying to avoid five-star prices the best options are the *Al-Nimran Hotel* (☎ 864 5861, fax 894 7876) on 28th St (aka Pepsi Cola St), and the *Park Hotel* (☎ 895 0005, fax 898 7271) on the Corniche, one block from the intersection with Dhahran St. Rooms at either place are SR 287.50/345, including the service charge.

The *Carlton Al-Moaibed Hotel* (☎ 857 5455, fax 857 5443), on the expressway between Dammam and Alkhobar, has rooms for SR 402.50/523.

The top end of the local market is represented by the *Gulf Meridien* (☎ 864 6000, fax 898 1651), on the Corniche near the intersection with 28th St. Singles/doubles here cost SR 517.50/673, including the service charge. The *Algosaibi Hotel* (☎ 894 2466, fax 894 7533), nearby on Prince Abdullah Ben Jalawi St behind the Pepsi Cola bottling plant, is slightly cheaper with rooms costing SR 460/598.

Last but not least, the *Dhahran International Hotel* (☎ 891 8555, fax 891 8559), adjacent to the airport, is where the world's TV correspondents were set up during the Gulf War. The proximity to the airport

allowed the camera people to get dramatic shots of warplanes taking off. The hotel was the backdrop for broadcasts by US TV reporters, a fact commemorated by a shell casing displayed in the lobby along with the logos of several dozen media organisations. The hotel's rates are the same as those at the Algosaibi.

Places to Eat

The area bounded by Dhahran St, 4th St, the Gulf and Prince Bandar St is filled with good, cheap restaurants. Most are of the Indian/Pakistani and South-East Asian variety. *Phuket Restaurant*, on King Faisal St one block north of Dhahran St, has good Thai meals for SR 20 to SR 25. They also have a family section. Most of their dishes come in small, medium and large sizes. Stick to the small unless you're famished, or in the company of several other people. There are a number of similar places in the same area. Across the street and a few doors farther down (if you start from Dhahran St) is the *Aristocrat Restaurant*, a fairly new place with friendly staff and particularly good deals for set meals. For SR 10 you can choose two main dishes from a selection of six or eight. The price includes rice and a soda or mineral water.

The *Turkey Cock* on 28th St, across from the Pepsi Cola bottling plant, is one of the Eastern Province's best kept secrets with excellent set meals for SR 15 (main dish, salad and rice). It offers a wide variety of kebab plates for around SR 12.

A good bet for medium-priced Lebanese food is *Al-Bardawni* on King Abdul Aziz St, one block west of the intersection with 28th St. The fare tends to be either really good (fried kibbe, hummous) or not (grape leaves, Russian salad). Try the hummous with meat for SR 10.

For more expensive eating try *La Gondola*, an excellent Italian restaurant just off the Corniche near the Tamimi supermarket. Soups cost about SR 12 and main dishes are SR 20 to SR 30 for pasta and SR 30 to SR 45 for meat. They have an Italian head chef and, though the food is pricey, it's worth it. Nearby, *Abu Nawas* is a Lebanese restaurant under the same management with medium-priced takeaway service at street level and more expensive table service upstairs. Both restaurants have family sections. The coffee shop at the *Gulf Meridien* is also worth mentioning. The breakfast buffet there is very popular, particularly on Fridays.

Things to Buy

Arab Heritage on Prince Saad St, just off 28th St near the Pepsi Cola bottling plant, is widely reputed to be the best place in the Kingdom to shop for Arab artwork, traditional clothing and crafts. However, it is *very* expensive. Another good place to look for high quality souvenirs, provided you are prepared to part with many riyals, is Lamsa, on the ground floor of the massive Al-Rashid mall on Dhahran St. Inma Gallery of Fine Art is a good place to look for paintings, lithographs and photographs on Arabian themes by both Arabs and foreigners. They have a showroom on the ground floor of the Al-Rashid mall and another, larger, one on the Corniche near the Tamimi supermarket.

A lot cheaper (and tackier) is the Souvenir Store for Antiques on Prince Nasser St, two blocks south of 28th St. Its stock supposedly comes from all over Arabia, the Middle East and the Indian subcontinent, but beware of the salespeople. I once caught them out trying to palm off Thai pillowcases as Bedouin work from Medina.

The Al-Harmain Store, on King Khaled St between 2nd and 3rd Sts, has a small but interesting selection of old silver jewellery and a few weavings and coffee pots. They also sell 'authentic' tourist-rip-off papyrus from Egypt (that stuff turns up in the most amazing places).

Getting There & Away

Air Some of the airlines with offices in Khobar include:

Air France
    Corner of King Abdul Aziz and 28th Sts (☎ 864 0411)

Air India
    Airline Centre, King Abdul Aziz St, near the 28th St intersection (☎ 894 9105)
Air Lanka
    Airline Centre, King Abdul Aziz St (☎ 895 1153)
Biman Bangladesh Airlines
    Ace Travel, near the corner of King Abdul Aziz and 28th Sts (☎ 894 4400)
British Airways
    Airline Centre, King Abdul Aziz St (☎ 894 2024)
EgyptAir
    Corner of Dhahran St and the Corniche (☎ 898 5252)
Emirates
    King Fahed St (☎ 894 2723)
Gulf Air
    Corner of King Abdul Aziz and 28th Sts (☎ 898 0804)
KLM
    Alkhobar Corniche, near the Gulf Meridien Hotel (☎ 895 1234)
Kuwait Airways
    King Abdul Aziz St, between 25th and 26th Sts (☎ 864 2102)
MEA (Middle East Airlines)
    Airline Centre, King Abdul Aziz St (☎ 864 6118)
Philippine Airlines
    King Fahed St (☎ 894 2021)
Royal Jordanian
    King Abdul Aziz St (☎ 864 1231)
Saudia
    Corner of Dhahran St and the Corniche (☎ 894 3333)
Singapore Airlines
    Airline Centre, King Abdul Aziz St (☎ 895 1515)
Syrianair
    Corner of King Khaled and A Sts (☎ 864 4342)

Bus The bus station is on Prince Talal St between 4th and 5th Sts. Look for a small parking lot with a SAPTCO office (☎ 894 9687) on the corner at the 5th St side of the square. There are no domestic inter-city services from Khobar. For inter-city routes take a local bus to the Dammam station; all departures are from there.

The main Dammam-Khobar routes are: No 1 along the Dammam-Alkhobar expressway via the industrial area; No 3 via Thuqba, the airport and Dhahran/King Fahd University of Petroleum & Minerals (UPM); No 5 via the Coast Rd and No 6 via the Tubaishi industrial area.

Buses to Bahrain leave daily at 8.45 and 11.45 am and at 2.45, 5.45 and 8.45 pm.

Tickets are available from the SAPTCO office for SR 40/70 one way/return.

Getting Around

The Airport Bus No 3 runs from the Alkhobar bus station to the airport every 30 minutes. You can also reach the airport on bus No 8, which travels via Dhahran St and 20th St, though this route is a bit slower. The fare is SR 2.

A taxi to the airport will cost SR 10 to SR 15 on the meter depending on where you start the journey. Coming into town from the airport the taxi drivers are supposed to use the meter but, in practice, a fixed fare system operates for both the yellow cabs and the orange and white ones. Either type will demand SR 30 for the trip. The drivers of the orange and white cabs are more likely to speak English.

DHAHRAN

Apart from the Aramco Exhibit, which is the best museum in the Kingdom, there is little that is either of interest or accessible in Dhahran. Aside from the airport, Dhahran consists of the Aramco compound, which is a small city in itself, the US consulate (☎ 891 3200) near the airport, and the University of Petroleum & Minerals. Admission to any of these requires identification showing that you live, work, study or have business there.

The **Aramco Exhibit** is open Saturday to Wednesday from 8 am to 6.30 pm, Thursday from 9 am to noon and 3 to 6.30 pm and Friday from 3 to 6.30 pm. Thursdays and Fridays are for families only; admission is free.

The centre is a comprehensive layperson's guide to the oil industry with a minimum of pro-Big Oil preaching and an emphasis on explaining the technical side of the industry. It's also fun, especially for kids, with lots of buttons to push, user-participation displays and quizzes.

As you enter the building go straight ahead and up the stairs; a display there outlines the exhibits and suggests different itineraries for seeing them depending on how much time you have to spend. You could easily spend two or three hours at the exhibit. About two-thirds of the space is taken up by displays on how oil is formed, found, extracted and refined. There is a short history of Aramco itself and a fascinating display on Arab science and technology covering time-keeping, astronomy and alchemy.

QATIF

Qatif (Qateef), 13 km north of Dammam, is one of the centres of the Eastern Province's large Shiite community. It was first settled around 3500 BC and in the centuries prior to the discovery of oil it was the main settlement on this part of the Gulf coast. Some early European maps of the region identify the Gulf as the 'Sea of Elcatif', testifying to the town's relative size and importance in the 17th and 18th centuries.

There used to be a couple of interesting sites to see in Qatif – the town's old fortified quarter and a century-old house. These, however, were torn down by the government in the early '90s. A few bits and pieces of **Al-Qalah**, the fortified quarter of Old Qatif, survived the wrecking ball and can still be seen near the taxi stand. The taxi stand is on King Abdul Aziz St, at the intersection dominated by the Saudi Hollandi Bank. From the taxi stand, with your back to the street, walk forward and left. As you reach the corner of the remains of the old buildings (a distance of maybe 15m) look up and you can still distinguish a few bits of the ornate plaster-work archways and ceilings on the 2nd floor of the building. Continuing around to your left you can enter a small bit of Al-Qalah that is still standing. It is a narrow passageway with a wood and straw roof. Until 1992 Al-Qalah covered the entire area behind this small ruin – today, there is only a vacant lot.

Al-Qalah itself was partly inhabited until the mid-70s. The first fort on the site was built as long ago as the 3rd century BC. At one time the quarter housed some 30,000 people, sheltered behind walls nine metres high and two metres thick and surrounded by 11 circular guard towers.

SAUDI ARABIA

Qatif can be reached from the Dammam bus station via bus Nos 9, 10A and 10B. All of these will eventually take you along King Abdul Aziz St and past the intersection with the Saudi Hollandi Bank building.

TARUT ISLAND

For centuries the small island of Tarut has been one of the most important ports and military strongholds on the Arabian side of the Gulf. Parts of the island, particularly the town of Darin, have been inhabited since prehistoric times. In the early years of this century the island served as the entrepôt for Qatif, which was then one of the major towns of eastern Arabia. Today Tarut is connected to the mainland by a causeway.

Tarut Fort

Tarut Fort is one of Saudi Arabia's most photographed ruins. It is a very big, and relatively well preserved and restored, bastion which has survived from a much larger structure built by the Portuguese in the 16th century. The nearby houses cover the tell, below which lie the rest of the fort and earlier ruins. Visits to the fort require a permit from the Dammam Museum.

The site itself was first settled during the Stone Age and became important during the 3rd millennium BC when it was part of the Bahrain-based Dilmun Empire. There is little to be seen of the remains of this era except a stairway inside the fort. The lighter coloured portions of this stairway are thought to be about 5000 years old and are the only surviving element of some earlier structure. The stairway is the basis of a theory that the fort is built on top of the site of a 3rd millennium BC city, though more excavations would be needed to prove this.

Near the centre of the ruins you can see the remains of a well which has been dry for many years. The fort also overlooks a natural spring which is still used by local women as a bathing pool, but the government has constructed a building around it.

Qasr Darin

Qasr Darin is a site so exposed and so thor-

oughly ruined that you do not need a permit to see it. Though it is in much worse shape than Tarut Fort, Qasr Darin is, in fact, much the younger of the two. It was built in 1875 by Abdul Wahab Pasha to guard the main seaborne approaches to the island at the height of the pearl trade. As at Tarut Fort, what is now visible only hints at the original extent of the building which at one time covered over 8300 sq metres.

Getting There & Away

Tarut is connected to the mainland town of Qatif by a causeway. To reach Tarut take the Jubail expressway north and exit at the sign for Anak and Qatif. Follow the road for 4.8 km through the village of Al-Jesh and turn left at a sign for 'Qateef'. Go straight for 2.5 km and keep right, ignoring the directional sign for Tarut, when the road forks. From the fork go another 2.7 km and turn right at the petrol station, which has three huge stone cars on pillars acting as sun shades. Keep going straight for 5.7 km, during which you will cross the causeway onto the island, and then turn right at an intersection/roundabout. Follow a narrow road through Tarut town for about one km and you will see Tarut Fort on the right. To reach Qasr Darin continue on the same road for two km until it swings around to the right. At that point just keep hugging the coastline for another six km and you'll see the ruins on the right, near the pier. Tarut can be reached from Dammam via bus No 11.

JUBAIL

Jubail was little more than a fishing village until the mid-70s when the government decided to turn it into one of the Kingdom's two showpiece industrial cities – the other is Yanbu, on the Red Sea coast. The earliest oil exploration operations in Saudi Arabia were based in Jubail, which was the original base for Casoc (California Arabian Standard Oil company – the precursor of Aramco). The company moved its headquarters to Dhahran only after drilling began.

Jubail town is about 90 km north of

Dammam. It is dwarfed by the industrial city, officially referred to as Madinat Al-Jubail Al-Sinaiyah, which has been built a few km to the north. The industrial city is a complex of petrochemical plants, an ironworks and a host of smaller 'satellite' companies, most of which are support firms supplying the major industries. Many of these firms were lured to the area with the promise of, among other things, almost nonexistent rents so long as they set up shop on government-owned and administered tracts of land. The project is overseen by the Royal Commission for Jubail & Yanbu, and Jubail is often referred to simply as the Royal Commission.

Jubail's telephone code is 03.

Visitor Centre

The Saudis are exceedingly and justifiably proud of the developments at Jubail, though it is not exactly a hot spot for tourists. The only thing to see in the industrial city is the visitor centre at the Royal Commission's headquarters. This is open Saturday to Wednesday from 7 am to noon and from 1 to 4 pm. You must, however, have an appointment to visit the centre. This should be arranged through the Royal Commission's public relations office (☎ 341 4427). The display covers the history of the Royal Commission and the construction of Jubail.

To reach the Royal Commission building take the first Jubail exit off the highway from Dammam and follow the signs. It's pretty easy to find.

The Jubail Church

Despite what you may hear, the ruins commonly known as the Jubail Church do exist. People in the Saudi archaeology bureaucracy acknowledge the site's existence, but they do not like to talk about it and will not issue permits for visits to the site. The official reason is that the site is still being excavated.

Even without a permit you can still get a pretty good view of the site from outside the fence. The site itself is fairly easy to find and, if you are in the area anyway, it is worth the diversion.

To reach the church from Dammam, drive almost all the way to Jubail and leave the expressway at the exit for Aramco and Jubail North. Turn left under the bridge and left again to get back on the expressway as though you were headed back toward Dammam. You will see a petrol station ahead of you beside the road. Turn off the main road just before you reach the petrol station. Follow the pavement around to the back of the petrol station where it forks (and its quality drops sharply). Keep left at the fork (about 150m after you left the main road) and follow a so-so paved track for 1.25 km. You will cross two large sets of pipes immediately beyond which is a service road. When you reach this service road you will be at a three-way junction. Looking across a bad

Guide to the Ruins

The ruins of this church are strikingly well preserved. They were unearthed in 1986 by a group of people on a desert picnic who were digging out one of their vehicles after it got stuck in the sand.

The ruins probably date from the 4th century which would make them older than any church now existing in Europe. Little is known about this particular church but it was probably connected to one of the five Nestorian bishoprics which existed in this part of the Gulf in the 4th century.

The main building consists of one large room, though foundation lines on the floor indicate that there were probably originally three rooms in this space. Three smaller chambers connect to the east side of this main room. The walls of the smaller chambers are still standing and beside the doorways the marks where four stone crosses were affixed to the wall are still clearly visible. These crosses were in place when the church was unearthed but went missing sometime in late 1986 or early 1987. Of the three smaller chambers, the central one contains two sets of well preserved half-columns. The large number of seashells scattered around the area indicate that the church sat on the coast in its time.

In the south-east corner of the enclosure you can see a second, smaller set of ruins. These may have been monks' cells, attached to the church. ■

paved road you should see a sandy track more or less straight ahead and a slightly less sandy track to the right of it. Take the track to the right. After 100m it forks again; keep going straight/right and after another 300m you will reach a dead end in front of the church's fence at a sign that says 'No Admission, Archaeological Area'. The best view of the ruins is from the far side of this fence (but park where you are). The total distance from the main road to the church is just under two km.

Places to Stay & Eat

Jubail has only two hotels and neither is cheap. In town the *Sharq Hotel* (☎ 361 1155, fax 361 4161) on Jeddah St charges SR 132/165 for singles/doubles. In the industrial city the *Holiday Inn* (☎ 341 7000, fax 341 2212) charges SR 460/598, including the 15% service charge.

Jubail's main drag, Jeddah St, has a collection of small Indian restaurants, roast chicken shops and fast-food outlets. A good bet for a meal is the *Try Restaurant* offering shawarma and a wide selection of Lebanese food. It's open 24 hours a day.

NAIRIYAH

One of the Eastern Province's most interesting day trips is the Bedouin market which takes place every Friday morning in the village of Nairiyah, about 250 km north of Dammam.

Bedouin Market

The market is something of a local legend and draws Bedouins from as far away as Qatar and Abu Dhabi. For the Bedouins themselves the market is a major spot for buying and selling sheep, goats, house wares and the occasional camel. For foreigners the attraction has long been the Bedouin weavings sold by women tending stalls off to one side of the main market. The market has been gaining in popularity in recent years, with the result that it is no longer the great bargain it once was. The women tend to drive a very hard bargain and a certain amount of shopping around is definitely in order. Woven

rugs and runners go for SR 100 to SR 300 depending on size and quality, with camel's wool commanding a higher price than synthetic fibres. Tent walls, which make nice tablecloths, are harder to find. A good one will cost between SR 350 and SR 500. Around SR 40, after some bargaining, will get you the cheap unadorned sort of camel bridle that most Bedouins use on a day to day basis. The fancier, woven kind cost around SR 100.

Though foreigners are a common sight at Nairiyah it is still a Bedouin market and a certain amount of discretion is required. The women who run the stalls do not like to be photographed, and you should respect their wishes. Few of the men are keen on cameras either. Women should wear abayyas and have them fastened closed. Bringing along a scarf or some other form of head covering would also be in order. Nairiyah is one of the few places in the Kingdom where truly traditional Saudi life runs headlong into the foreign community on a regular basis. It thus requires even more tact, and respect for Saudi conceptions of proper decorum, than usual.

Places to Stay & Eat

Nairiyah has one hotel and two rest houses. On the whole the *Al-Sharafi Hotel* (☎ 373 0772, fax 373 1688) is probably your best bet. It's surprising how you can sometimes find great little hotels absolutely in the middle of nowhere, and this is a case in point. Singles/doubles cost SR 120/132. To reach the hotel, coming from Dammam/Alkhobar, follow the main road through town past the turn-off for the market. Turn right at the first roundabout beyond the market turn-off. There is a small sign for the hotel. Go 500m then turn right again at another sign for the hotel. Take the first left after this turn and the hotel will be on your left.

If the Al-Sharafi is too rich for your blood the *Al-Salam Resthouse* (no telephone) is your only other option. It's on the main road into town from Dammam/Alkhobar. The sign is only in Arabic, but you will see the rest house on the left, across the road, shortly after you pass the first petrol station (which will be on your right). Spartan but clean rooms are available for SR 70 a single or double.

There is another rest house, the *Al-Farat* at the far end of town (or the near end, if you are coming from Riyadh), but it charges SR 120 per night and offers much worse accommodation than the hotel.

Getting There & Away
To reach Nairiyah from Alkhobar or Dammam take the Jubail expressway to the Abu Hadriyah turn-off. From Abu Hadriyah follow the signs to Nairiyah. These are few and far between and, when in doubt, follow signs for Hafr Al-Batn until you get close to Nairiyah. Once in the town head for the large mosque with a low green dome, which is on your left as you enter town, and follow the crowd. The market will also be on your left. Look for a Mazda sign as a turning point. The women selling weavings and other souvenirs are usually the first thing you will come to. Get an early start as the market usually disappears by 10 am. If you are coming from Riyadh take the expressway about two-thirds of the way to Dammam and then exit north on a good two-lane road that will take you straight to Nairiyah (about 200 km from the expressway).

NATTA
The small village of Natta, 30 km south of Nairiyah, is noteworthy mainly for its **fort**, a moderately well preserved ruin which will be on the right side of the road if you are coming from the north. The large, palace-like building is supposed to have been one of King Abdul Aziz's many residences and is thought to be between 50 and 75 years old.

THAJ
The ruined **Thaj Fortress** is another popular day trip from Dammam and Alkhobar, one often combined with a visit to the Nairiyah Bedouin market. Today Thaj is a desert village little different from a hundred others in the region, but 2000 years ago it was a thriving city set beside a substantial lake. A

permit from either the main antiquities office in Riyadh or from the Dammam Museum is needed to enter the site.

Thaj's main period of habitation was Hellenistic – in this case from about 300 BC to 200 AD though it may have originally been inhabited from an earlier period. It is known to have been in ruins by the 6th century AD. At its peak Thaj covered over two sq km along the shores of a now dried-up lake. On the basis of coins found there Thaj is one of the possible sites of the lost city of Gherra, one of the great elusive prizes of Arabian archaeology.

Thaj is not the most impressive set of ruins you are ever likely to see. Though it was a large city – its walls were approximately 600m on each side and were four metres thick – little remains above ground. You can make out some outlines of houses and bits of the city wall but little else. The ruins of a 70 to 80 year old mosque can be seen to the far right of the site if you enter by the main gate (the one near where the paved road ends). Even with the little that is visible, however, you can make out the size of the walls and the carefully worked stones.

See chapter 15 of Geoffrey Bibby's *Looking for Dilmun* for an excellent account of the rediscovery of the city.

About five km from Thaj is another, less impressive, ruined fortress known as **Al-Hina**. The same guard can let you into Hina, but you will need a separate permit to visit it and a 4WD to reach the site.

Getting There & Away
The easiest, if slightly roundabout, way to reach Thaj is via Nairiyah, 94 km to the north. From Dammam follow the directions to Nairiyah, then continue through the town. At the far end of town make what is nearly a U-turn to your left to head south. Look for a sign that reads 'Riyadh Dammam Exp way 200 km'. After passing through Natta turn left at a sign for Thaj in the village of Al-Sarrar and follow the road for 37.5 km until the pavement ends at Thaj.

When you reach the village you will have to go to the guard's house to present your permit and get the gate unlocked. When the pavement ends, at the entrance to the village, you will have the main site fence to your right, a dirt track leading off straight ahead of you and another fenced area to your left. To reach the house turn left when the pave-

---

Gherra

Gherra is one of the great elusive prizes of Arabian archaeology. The 1st century AD Roman scholar, Pliny the Elder, and the Greek geographer Strabo, who lived in the late 1st century BC and early 1st century AD, both identify Gherra as a great city in Arabia. Gherra traded with Babylon by sea and with the frankincense-growing regions of South Arabia by land.

Strabo wrote that the incense trade had made the city's population some of the wealthiest people on earth and that they possessed 'a great quantity of wrought articles in gold and silver'. It was a city whose people, he wrote, lived in 'very costly houses; its doors and walls and ceilings are variegated with ivory, gold and silver set with precious stones'.

Both authors agree that it had a wall, but they give differing accounts of its location. Strabo placed Gherra on a 'deep gulf 200 stadia from the sea' while Pliny states that the city was located on a bay opposite Tylos (Bahrain) and that it had a wall some eight km in circumference.

A number of locations around Eastern Arabia have been suggested as the site of Gherra. These include the Al-Hasa Oasis, one part of which is called Qara, a name that may be derived from Gherra. Thaj is another leading contender. Uqayr, on the coast near the Al-Hasa Oasis and Safwa, a cultivated area north of the oasis, have also been mentioned. The confusion stems, in part, from uncertainty over whether Gherra was a coastal city or an inland city that controlled a port on the coast.

The problem is that none of these places exactly fit either description. Thaj is large enough to by Pliny's Gherra, but it is much too far inland, even accounting for the somewhat wider Gulf of ancient times. It is also too far north to be 'opposite' Bahrain. Uqayr has a port and is opposite Bahrain but does not appear to have ever been large or rich enough to fit the description.

One theory holds that Qara or some other site in the Al-Hasa Oasis was Gherra with Uqayr serving as its port. But Uqayr is 70 km from Al-Hasa, which would seem to be a bit too far. The search continues. ■

---

ment ends and follow a dirt track around the side of the fence to the left (ie keeping the fence itself to your right). Go straight, and turn left when you are 300m past the point where the pavement ended. Look for a white house on the left with a number 45 on it in Arabian numerals. The site is open more or less whenever you can get the guard to unlock the gate. It is possible to visit Thaj on Fridays.

AL-ULYA

About 20 km off the Tapline road, 90 km from Nairiyah and over 300 km from Dammam sits the **fortress** of Al-Ulya, once a fortified settlement near the Kingdom's northern frontier. At the time of writing the fortress, which was built by King Abdul Aziz in 1934 but had recently fallen into disrepair, was being restored. You can visit it during working hours from Saturday to Wednesday with a permit from either the main antiquities office in Riyadh or the Dammam Museum. Even from the outside it is impressive (at the time of writing the inside looked more like a construction site). I'm not sure I'd drive 300 km just to see it, but if you are up in the area between Hafr Al-Batn and Nairiyah it is worth the diversion.

The fort has an oddly asymmetrical design. There are towers at the four corners but only three walls have centre watchtowers (the north wall is the exception).

To reach the fort from the Tapline road, take the Al-Ulya exit (by a petrol station). It is a left turn if you are coming from Nairiyah, a right turn if you are coming from Hafr Al-Batn. Twenty km from the turn you will reach a roundabout, go right out of the roundabout, on the first street as you start around the circle. About 700m past the roundabout turn left at the third break in the median. The fort will be directly in front of you, about 150m away.

HOFUF (AL-HASA OASIS)

The Al-Hasa Oasis, centred on the town of Hofuf, is the largest in Arabia and one of the largest in the world. A hundred years ago a substantial portion of Europe's dates came from here and it is still one of the world's leading areas for date production. The oasis seems to go on and on and, if you have time and a car, exploring the small villages scattered through this large, lush area can be a pleasant way to spend an afternoon or two. Modern irrigation has vastly broadened the area's agriculture, increasing the oasis' cultivated area from 8000 to 20,000 hectares over the last few generations.

The Ottomans, who called the area Lahsa, ruled it twice, from 1549 to 1680 and again from 1871 until Abdul Aziz conquered the area in 1913. The first period of Ottoman rule ended when the Turks were driven out of the oasis by Bedouins of the Bani Khaled tribe. The Bani Khaled were replaced in the 1790s by the ancestors of the present Saudi royal family during their first conquest of the Arabian Peninsula. The Saudis, in turn were forced out by the Ottomans in 1818, Al-Hasa being one of the last parts of Arabia where Wahabbi power survived. But the Ottoman's

control of this remote outpost of their empire was never particularly firm, and the Saudis managed to regain de facto rule over the oasis from 1843. They stayed in charge until 1871 when Istanbul reasserted control, only to be driven out again by Abdul Aziz in 1913.

Orientation & Information

There is not much to Hofuf itself. The centre is very compact. King Abdul Aziz St is the main commercial street and intersects with Al-Khudod St to form a central square containing the bus station and bounded by a mosque and the large, white Riyad Bank building. Both of the centre's hotels are an easy walk from this intersection.

There are several banks, including a Saudi Cairo Bank branch with a Cirrus/Plus ATM, around the main intersection. The Al-Rajhi Banking & Investment Corporation has a branch on King Abdul Aziz St just south of the main intersection.

The telephone office is north of the centre

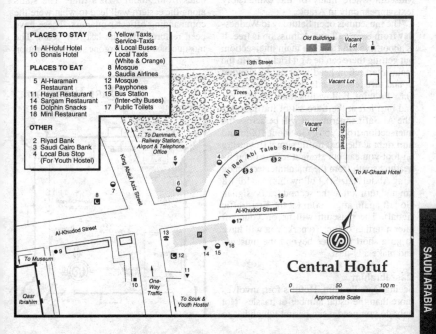

PLACES TO STAY
1 Al-Hofuf Hotel
10 Bonais Hotel

PLACES TO EAT
5 Al-Haramain Restaurant
11 Hayat Restaurant
14 Sargam Restaurant
16 Dolphin Snacks
18 Mini Restaurant

OTHER
2 Riyad Bank
3 Saudi Cairo Bank
4 Local Bus Stop (For Youth Hostel)
6 Yellow Taxis, Service-Taxis & Local Buses
7 Local Taxis (White & Orange)
8 Mosque
9 Saudia Airlines
12 Mosque
13 Payphones
15 Bus Station (Inter-city Buses)
17 Public Toilets

Central Hofuf

0   50   100 m
Approximate Scale

SAUDI ARABIA

at the intersection of the Dammam road (officially Prince Abdullah Ben Jalawi St) and Hajer Palace Rd. It is open daily from 7.30 am until midnight.

The telephone code for Hofuf is 03.

The Saudia office (☎ 586 3333) is on Al-Khudod St just off the main intersection. The airport is south-west of the centre.

Hofuf Museum

The museum has the usual exhibits found in Saudi regional museums: a display on the formation of the earth followed by sections on trade routes, the domestication of the camel and the Kingdom's flora and fauna, with a section in the middle on local antiquities. This, and the big map of the entire oasis at the entrance to the exhibit hall, can be a very useful starting place for a visit to Hofuf. The museum is especially good on Eastern Province archaeology and, with everything labelled in English, is a much better introduction to the region than the Dammam Museum where many of the explanatory texts appear only in Arabic.

The museum is open Saturday to Wednesday from 8 am to 2 pm. Admission is free. It is about five km from the main intersection, but getting there can be a bit tricky. From the main intersection head west on Al-Khudod St and turn left at the first traffic signal past Qasr Ibrahim. Follow this road for 1.25 km and turn left at the third set of traffic lights (the Al-Safir supermarket will be across the intersection from you). Go about 100m and turn right at the next traffic signal (if you are on foot you can cut straight to this point by heading south from the main intersection on King Abdul Aziz St). Follow this road for 1.8 km and turn left at the second traffic signal. Go left again after 700m (at the first traffic signal). The museum will be on your left after a farther 600m. To park, you will have to go a short distance beyond the museum and make a U-turn.

Qasr Ibrahim

Seeing Qasr Ibrahim, Hofuf's fort, involves more than the usual number of hassles. Not only do you need a site permit which has to

be issued in Riyadh, but once you arrive in Hofuf you may have to take your permit to the museum if there is no one at the fort to unlock the gate.

Qasr Ibrahim is almost entirely of Turkish construction. The mosque inside the walls is the oldest part of the complex, having been built around 1566 (974 AH). The first fort on this site was built just over a century later in 1688-89 (1100 AH). The present fort dates from the beginning of the 19th century, and a Turkish garrison continued to occupy it until Abdul Aziz conquered Hofuf in 1913.

Inside the fort take a look at the jail, next to the mosque, and the underground cells inside it. The Turkish bath near the north-west corner of the compound was used during Abdul Aziz's time to store dates, the smell of which still lingers inside. Near the bath you can see a small excavated area showing the underground system which was used for heating water. In the courtyard there is an old telephone exchange which also dates from Abdul Aziz's time. The stairs along the eastern wall lead to what were the commanding officer's quarters. These have been restored over the last few years. The mosque has also undergone some restoration

Qasr Ibrahim

Not to Scale

Take care when climbing this bastion as it's in poor condition

Old Toilets

Bath Stalls

Stables

Turkish Bath

Guard's Room

Well

General's Quarters (Upper Level)

Antique Telephone Exchange & Post Office

Rooms

Mosque

Outdoor Mihrib (Prayer Niche)

Jail

Entrance

work in recent years. The interior is bare, but still worth a look. Note the large, freestanding outdoor mihrib near its entrance.

Souk

Hofuf's real treat is the souk. It's just off King Abdul Aziz St, about 300m south of the main intersection. This is one of the few places in the country where hand-made Arabian coffee pots, as opposed to mass-produced ones imported from Pakistan, can still be found. Several shops also have good collections of Bedouin weavings and a few have old silver jewellery. Prices vary greatly according to size and quality. The best place to look for souvenirs is at the northern end of the souk, the one closer to the main intersection. As more and more foreigners have begun to shop in Hofuf's souk the shopkeepers have met the rising demand for Bedouin weavings by importing them from Syria. Saudi-made weavings tend to have darker colours than Syrian ones. Ask before you buy.

You will also find a few shops selling weavings near Qasr Ibrahim.

If you are in the market for a shisha pipe there is a shop next to the bus station that specialises in them.

Organised Tours

The Hofuf Hotel offers three different tour packages. They have an all-day trip around the oasis including visits to the main souk and other local markets, as well as Qara and the Juwatha Mosque for SR 150 per person. The second itinerary is similar to the first, but includes one night's accommodation at the hotel with dinner and a short additional excursion to Hofuf's small gold souk. This costs SR 350 per person double occupancy with singles paying an SR 80 supplement. For SR 420 per person double occupancy (single supplement SR 150) they offer a more extensive three day (two night) programme. In all cases children under 12 can go on the tour for half price. All the tours require a minimum of 10 people. Contact the hotel for further information.

Places to Stay

The *youth hostel* (☎ 580 0028) is at the stadium. It's a long way out and is not served by public transport. Beds are SR 8. To reach the hostel take Bus No 2 (SR 2, sporadic service) from the bus stop on Ali Bin Abi Taleb St to the large T-junction by the prison (the white building on the left with a guard tower). There is a stadium behind it but that's not the one. Turn right at the junction and follow the road for half a km until it forks. Keep left at the fork and follow the road for another 2.5 km. A cab from the bus station costs SR 12 to SR 15.

In town the *Bonais Hotel* (☎ 582 7700, fax 582 1168) is on King Abdul Aziz St near the bus station. Singles/doubles are SR 110/165, most with bath but some without for the same price. The *Al-Hofuf Hotel* (☎ 587 7082, fax 586 1349) is on 13th St, a five minute walk from the bus station. It's a friendly, mid-range place with rooms at SR 132/198, all with bath, and offers better value for your money than the Bonais. To reach the Al-Hofuf Hotel from the bus station, leave the square by the road in front of the Riyad Bank. Turn left on 12th St, then right on 13th St.

Outside the centre the *Al-Ghazal Hotel* (☎ 582 6555, fax 586 9966) is a quite decent place but has a rather inconvenient location several km north-east of the main intersection. Rooms cost SR 138/184 in the hotel's rather dowdy old wing and SR 230/299 in the newer part of the building.

Places to Eat

Hofuf is a bit short on restaurants but there is a very good small place across the main intersection from the bus station. A meal of chicken, rice and salad costs SR 12. It's called the *Al-Haramain Restaurant* but the sign is written only in Arabic. Look for a small black sign with yellow and white lettering. Near the bus station the *Sargam Restaurant* has good, cheap Indian food. A meal of chicken or mutton curry with rice costs only SR 7. The *Hayat Restaurant*, just off King Abdul Aziz St, is a good place to look for fresh juice and Arabic sweets. *Dolphin Snacks*, right next to the bus station,

SAUDI ARABIA

is a good spot for shawarma and other quick fare.

Getting There & Away

Air At the time of writing Saudia was operating several flights each week (but less than daily service) from Hofuf to Riyadh (SR 140 one way, economy class) and Jeddah (SR 410). It is probably safe to assume that the frequency of service to Hofuf will increase once the new Dhahran airport opens. The new airport is about an hour farther from Hofuf by car than the present one.

Bus The bus station (☎ 587 3687) is at the intersection of King Abdul Aziz and Al-Khudod Sts. Buses run to Dammam (two hours, SR 20) via Abqaiq (one hour, SR 13) daily at 6, 7.30 and 10 am, noon, and at 1.30, 4, 6 and 8 pm. To Riyadh (four hours, SR 45), there are buses daily at 7.30 and 10 am and at 3 and 8 pm. Buses to Jeddah (16 hours, SR 175) leave daily at 3.30 and 10.30 pm. SAPTCO's daily bus to Abu Dhabi (8½ hours) and Dubai (12 hours) also stops in Hofuf. Tickets are SR 150 to either city. The bus leaves at 10 pm.

International buses to Egypt, Syria, Jordan and Turkey leave from the whitewashed building with red, yellow and blue stripes, on Hajer Palace Rd near the railway station.

Service-Taxi Service-taxis congregate in the parking lot across the street from the bus station. Seats are SR 55 to Riyadh (SR 300 engaged, ie all by yourself) and SR 25 to Dammam (SR 125 engaged). All of Hofuf's service-taxis are of the five passenger variety. Arrive early if you plan to go anywhere. As with all service-taxis they leave only when full.

Train The railway station (☎ 582 0571) is a long way from the town centre. To reach it, head north on the Dammam road and turn west onto Hajer Palace Rd at the telephone office. Once you are on Hajer Palace Rd the station is beyond the second set of traffic lights. Trains leave daily except Thursday for Riyadh at 8.32 am and at 1.42 and 6.52 pm

(2½ hours, SR 45/30 in 1st/2nd class) and for Dammam (via Abqaiq) at 10.40 am and at 3.50 and 9 pm (1½ hours, SR 20/15). On Thursday there is only one train in each direction, departing for Riyadh at 10.32 am and for Dammam at 12.04 pm. Note that the 3.50 pm train to Dammam does not stop in Abqaiq.

Getting Around

Orange and white taxis have ranks at a couple of points around the main intersection. The taxis have meters. The local bus system can also get you to some of the far-flung corners of the oasis.

KAILABIYAH

The village of Kailabiyah, about 12 km north-east of Hofuf, is the site of the **Juwatha Mosque**, Saudi Arabia's holiest after the Grand Mosque at Mecca and the Prophet's Mosque in Medina. According to Islamic tradition, the first mosque on the site was built in the year 632 AD (10 AH) during the last months of the Prophet's life. Tradition also says that it was on this site that Mohammed led the communal Friday prayer for only the second time outside of Medina. The original mosque is long gone. What is visible today is a small, modern, whitewashed prayer enclosure and an excavated portion of an older mosque which may, or may not, include parts of the original 7th century structure. Some minor restoration work has recently been done to the newer vaulting, and carpet has been added so that it can be used as a prayer area, which is open to the sky and can be viewed, but not entered, by non-Muslims. It is set in the middle of a very nice park. If you have a car the mosque and park are well worth the 17 km drive from Hofuf.

To reach the mosque from Hofuf's main intersection start along Ali Ben Abi Taleb St, passing the Riyad Bank on your right. Turn right at the first set of traffic lights, near a fire station, and continue straight until you reach a T-junction. Turn left at the T-junction (this requires making a right turn, going 150m and then making a U-turn) and follow the road.

GORDON ROBISON

GORDON ROBISON

GORDON ROBISON

Saudi Arabia

Top: Painted and carved doors at (left) the Palace of Sa'd Bin Saud at Dir'aiyah and (right) the Mosque of Omar's minaret at Domat Al-Jandal.

Bottom: The large ruined 16th century Portuguese fort on Tarut Island once guarded one of the most important ports on the Arabian side of the Gulf.

GORDON ROBISON

GORDON ROBISON

Saudi Arabia/United Arab Emirates

Top: The amazing array of coffeepots in this Saudi home are testament to the beverage's popularity in the Gulf.

Bottom: A cup of tea atop the 1340m high Jabal Hafit is the perfect way to appreciate the sweeping views of the Hajar mountain range.

After just under two km the road forks, keep right and continue another 3.5 km until you come to the second sign for Battiliyah. Turn left here and follow the road for 4.2 km until you reach a traffic signal (there is also a small green sign in Arabic pointing toward Kailabiyah). Turn left here, and left again 800m farther on at the roundabout. Go 500m past the roundabout, turn right and follow the road for another 4.3 km until you reach the park where the mosque is located.

QARA

Qara, a village in the Al-Hasa Oasis east of Hofuf and south-east of Kailabiyah is a popular picnic spot. It is well signposted from the centre.

United Arab Emirates

The United Arab Emirates

If you can only visit one country in the Gulf, the United Arab Emirates (UAE) is your best choice. It has the most relaxed entry regulations of any of the countries covered in this book and offers a lot of things to see over a wide variety of terrain, all contained in a relatively small area. The UAE also has the best tourist infrastructure of any of the Gulf States.

The UAE is a union of seven sovereign shaikhdoms which was formed in 1971 when the British withdrew from the Gulf. Despite their small size, each emirate has its own distinct features. The capital, Abu Dhabi, is one of the most modern cities on earth, where almost nothing is more than 25 years old. Dubai is unquestionably the most vibrant city in the Gulf sporting the region's best nightlife as well as its most diverse economy.

In the emirates north of Dubai – Sharjah, Ajman, Umm Al-Qaiwain and Ras Al-Khaimah – life moves at a slower pace but each emirate is quite different from its neighbours. The Hajar Mountains provide a particularly dramatic backdrop for both Ras Al-Khaimah, the northernmost of the Gulf coast emirates, and Fujairah, which overlooks the Gulf of Oman on the country's east coast. Both are becoming popular winter destinations for tourists from northern Europe.

Travel agencies in Europe are pushing the UAE as a land of contrasts: mountains, beaches, deserts and oases, camel racing, Bedouin markets and the legendary duty-free shopping of Dubai. All this in a compact geographical tour package with good hotels and no-fuss visas. You can even touch toe and go shopping in Oman for a few hours to boot. The brochures trumpet the 'Arabian Experience' and are clearly aimed at upmarket tourists in search of an exotic but comfortable destination where few of their friends have been – the sort of people who would have gone to Morocco or Tunisia 40 years ago.

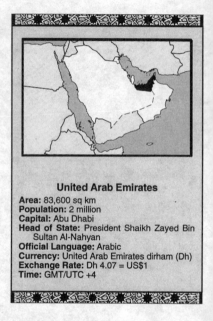

United Arab Emirates

Area: 83,600 sq km
Population: 2 million
Capital: Abu Dhabi
Head of State: President Shaikh Zayed Bin Sultan Al-Nahyan
Official Language: Arabic
Currency: United Arab Emirates dirham (Dh)
Exchange Rate: Dh 4.07 = US$1
Time: GMT/UTC +4

You can have this type of holiday or you can have a fine time in the UAE without booking a package tour. It is one of the best places in the Gulf for the independent traveller, and with over 100,000 tourists already making the trip each year, you should see it soon before mass tourism in the UAE really hits its stride.

Facts about the Country

HISTORY
Early Settlement
Less is known about the early history of the area that is now the UAE than about other areas of the Gulf. Although the first archaeological digs in the country took place over

30 years ago, the Emirates have never received the sort of sustained attention that has been lavished on the ancient sites of Bahrain and Kuwait.

It is certain, though, that this part of Arabia, like much of the rest of the Gulf, has been settled for many centuries. A few potsherds from the 4th millennium BC have been found around Jabal Hafit in the Al-Ain area. The earliest significant settlements, both inland and on the coast, are from the Bronze Age and show that during the 3rd millennium BC, the Gulf had a much more temperate climate than it does today. Around this period, a distinct culture arose near modern Abu Dhabi. This culture, called Umm An-Nar after the small island where it was first discovered, thrived for only a few hundred years and little is known about it. What can be said is that the people of Umm An-Nar were probably fishers and that they were not part of the Bahrain-based Dilmun Empire which was then the rising power of the central and northern Gulf. It also seems fairly certain that the Umm An-Nar culture extended well into the interior and down the coast of what is now Oman. Digs near Al-Ain, on the border with Oman, show evidence of an agricultural-based society existing in the area, contemporary to the Umm An-Nar society though the exact relationship between this oasis and the coastal communities is still unclear. There were also settlements at Badiyah (near Fujairah) and at Rams (near Ras Al-Khaimah) during the second half of the 3rd millennium BC.

The Greeks were the next major cultural influence to appear in the area. Ruins showing strong Hellenistic influences have been found at Meleiha, about 50 km from Sharjah, and at Al-Dour in the Emirate of Umm Al-Qaiwain.

Battle Site & Caravan Route

By the early centuries of the Christian era the climate in the Gulf was far less hospitable than it had been during the Bronze Age. In the centuries leading up to the coming of Islam, the people of the lower Gulf and its inland areas gained much of their livelihood

Highlights

Every visitor to Dubai should find time for an *abra* ride on the Creek. Abras are the small motorboats which ferry people across the Creek and they can be hired quite cheaply for longer tours of the waterway.

If you have the time to go outside of Abu Dhabi and Dubai, Al-Ain and the Buraimi Oasis are well worth a weekend visit. The east coast, particularly the area around Fujairah, has some of the most striking scenery in the country. A good weekend trip would be to drive over the mountains from Dubai or Sharjah to Fujairah, up the coast from Fujairah to Dibba, and then back across the mountains to Dubai/Sharjah. ■

from their location on the main trade routes of the time. Ruins from this era can be seen at the village of Shimal, near Ras Al-Khaimah, in the form of a set of 4th century AD fortifications on a hilltop overlooking the sea.

The region next appears in history in 635, at the dawn of the Islamic era, when Dibba (on the northern coast of Fujairah) was the site of the battle which traditionally marks the completion of the Islamic conquest of the Arabian Peninsula.

During the Middle Ages most of what is now the UAE was part of the Kingdom of Hormuz (see Building an Empire in the Oman chapter) which controlled the entrance to, and most of the trade in, the Gulf. The first known reference to the area by a European is a manuscript written in 1498 by the Portuguese explorer Vasco de Gama which records his rather sketchy observations of Khor Fakkan, Dibba and Ras Al-Khaimah. By 1515, the Portuguese had occupied Julfar (near today's city of Ras Al-Khaimah) and built a customs house through which they taxed the Gulf's flourishing trade with India and the Far East. Later, they also built a fort. Except for a brief interlude in the early 1620s when Julfar revolted, the Portuguese stayed on in the town until 1633. At that point, having lost control of Hormuz, they were forced to

THE UNITED ARAB EMIRATES

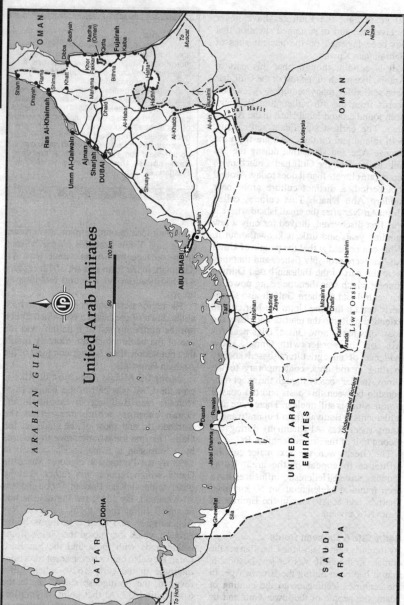

United Arab Emirates

abandon the area in the face of attacks by hostile tribes from the land and the British and Dutch from the sea.

After the departure of the Portuguese, the lower Gulf was taken over by the Al-Ya'ribi imams of Oman before passing into Persia's sphere of influence in the mid-18th century.

The Qawasim & the Bani Yas

The rise of British naval power in the Gulf in the mid-18th century coincided with the rise of two important tribal confederations along the coast of the lower Gulf. These were the Qawasim and the Bani Yas, the ancestors of the rulers of four of the seven emirates which today make up the UAE.

The Qawasim, whose descendants now rule Sharjah and Ras Al-Khaimah, were a seafaring clan based in Ras Al-Khaimah and their influence extended, at times, to the Persian side of the Gulf. Their main rivals for local power were the Al-Busaids who are now the ruling family of Oman. In 1798, the Al-Busaids signed a treaty with the British. From Britain's point of view, the main purpose of this agreement was to keep the French out of Oman and away from India. The Qawasim felt that the British had just allied themselves with their enemies and that made the British ships fair game for their raids. The Qawasim's hostility towards the British was exacerbated by the influence of the strict and somewhat xenophobic doctrines of Wahhabi Islam (see Religion in the Saudi Arabia chapter). The British East India Company, which owned most of the ships in question, looked on the Qawasim's activities as simple piracy, and the government in London tended to agree.

The British dubbed the area the Pirate Coast and launched their own raids against the Qawasim in 1805, 1809 and 1811 but following every skirmish, the situation along the coast returned to 'normal' the moment they left. In 1819, the British decided to resolve the situation by mounting a full-scale invasion of Qawasim territory. A large fleet was dispatched from Bombay and, in 1820, it destroyed or captured every Qawasim ship it could find and occupied the Qawasim forts

at Ras Al-Khaimah and Linagh, in Persia. The Royal Navy then imposed a General Treaty of Peace on nine Arab shaikhdoms in the area and installed a garrison in the region.

The treaty still allowed the shaikhs to attack each other – which they continued to do with entirely too much gusto for British taste. Thus, in 1835, the British imposed the Maritime Truce. This was modified several times (notably in 1839 when the British forced the shaikhs to ban slavery) until, in 1853, the truce became the Treaty of Peace in Perpetuity. Under this latest treaty, the British assumed responsibility for arbitrating disputes among the shaikhs. The Europeans then took to calling the area the Trucial Coast, a name it retained until 1971.

Throughout this period the main power among the Bedouin tribes of the interior was the Bani Yas tribal confederation, the ancestors of the ruling families of modern Abu Dhabi and Dubai. The Bani Yas were originally based in Liwa, an oasis on the edge of the Empty Quarter desert, but moved to Abu Dhabi island, off the Gulf coast, in 1793. They engaged in the traditional Bedouin activities of camel herding, small-scale agriculture in the Liwa and Buraimi oases, tribal raiding and extracting protection money from merchant caravans passing through their territory. After the British outlawed slavery on the coast, the Bani Yas also took over the slave trade. Buraimi became eastern Arabia's main slave market, a position which it retained until the 1950s. The Bani Yas divided into two main branches in the early 19th century when Dubai split from Abu Dhabi.

The Trucial Coast

In 1892, the British extended their power over the coast through a series of Exclusive Agreements under which the shaikhs accepted formal British protection and, in exchange, promised to have no dealings with any other foreign power without British permission. The British had insisted on the agreements after rival powers, particularly the French and the Russians, had begun to show interest in the Gulf. London regarded control of the area as essential for the protection of Britain's empire in India.

So long as the Russians and the French were kept out of the region and the lines of communication to India remained secure, the British did not much care what happened in the Gulf. The area became a backwater. Throughout the late 19th and early 20th centuries, the shaikhdoms were all tiny enclaves of fishers, pearl divers and Bedouins. The area's few merchants were mostly Indian or Persian.

For most of this period, Sharjah was the most populous and powerful of the emirates. As the century drew to a close, Sharjah lost influence to Abu Dhabi which, from 1855 until 1909, was ruled by the forceful Shaikh Zayed Bin Mohammed, usually referred to today as Zayed the Great. The power of any individual ruler depended very much on the force of their personality. Following Zayed's death, however, Abu Dhabi went into decline as his family fought over the succession.

The next emirate to rise to prominence was Dubai, under the leadership of the Al-Maktoum family. Even during the period of Zayed the Great's rule, Sharjah had remained the area's main trading centre. But Sharjah's rulers in the early years of this century were weak and xenophobic. At the turn of the century, a large group of traders left Linagh, on the Persian coast, apparently after changes to the tax regulations. They chose to settle in Dubai instead of Sharjah and, in 1903, arranged for the main Indian-based British steamship line to drop Linagh in favour of Dubai as its main port of call in the lower Gulf. The opening of regular sea links with India and the northern Gulf marked the beginning of Dubai's growth as a trading power.

In the years immediately before and after WWI, the British connection kept Abdul Aziz Bin Abdul Rahman Al-Saud, the future king of Saudi Arabia, from conquering the shaikhdoms of the Trucial Coast. Even so, the British presence remained very low-key. In fact there were no permanent British facilities in what is now the UAE until 1932, when Imperial Airways (the predecessor of

British Airways) built a rest house in Sharjah for passengers and crew on its flights to India. A permanent British Political Agent was not appointed anywhere on the Trucial Coast until WWII.

It was the prospect of oil that changed the way the British ran their affairs on the Trucial Coast. The actual territories of the various shaikhs had never been properly defined. Abu Dhabi and Dubai even went to war over their competing claims in 1945-47. (Neither side shed much blood but Dubai lost some territory.)

Before oil concessions could be granted, there was an immediate need to determine the boundaries between the shaikhdoms. Each of the local rulers claimed enormous swaths of territory and was willing to concede nothing to his neighbours. Eventually, the borders of the seven emirates that now make up the UAE were drawn up by the British. This, incredibly, involved a British diplomat spending months riding a camel around in the mountains and desert asking village heads, tribal leaders and groups of Bedouins which shaikh they owed allegiance to. Even that failed to settle all of the competing claims. As part of an ongoing and only partially successful attempt to modernise the governments of the Trucial Coast, and in the hope of settling the rival territorial claims amicably, the British set up the Trucial States Council in 1951. This was a cabinet consisting of the rulers of the shaikhdoms and was the direct predecessor of today's UAE Supreme Council. It met twice a year under the aegis of the British Political Agent in Dubai.

Meanwhile, Dubai was cementing its reputation as the region's busiest trading centre. In 1939, Shaikh Rashid Bin Saeed Al-Maktoum became the regent for his ailing father, Shaikh Saeed. (Rashid only formally succeeded to the leadership when his father died in 1958.) He quickly moved to bolster the emirate's position as the lower Gulf's main entrepôt. At about the same time, the rulers of Sharjah made the near-fatal mistake of allowing their harbour to silt up. This was even more costly for them than it might otherwise have been because, in nearby Dubai, Rashid was improving facilities along Dubai's waterfront, known as the Creek.

The Oil Era

There is a certain irony in Abu Dhabi's present status as the UAE's richest member; in the decades prior to the discovery of oil, Abu Dhabi was the poorest of the Trucial Coast shaikhdoms. During the early years of the 20th century, particularly the two decades following the death of Zayed the Great, it had also been one of the most violent. With the ascension of Shaikh Shakhbut Bin Sultan in 1928, some stability returned to the emirate but the decline of the pearling industry a few years later left Shaikh Shakhbut the ruler of a land that was destitute and shockingly bleak, even by Arabian standards.

In 1939, hoping to break the cycle of poverty, Shaikh Shakhbut granted a concession to the British-owned Iraq Petroleum Company. It would, however, be another two decades before Abu Dhabi received any oil revenues. In the meantime, the region's territorial controversies continued to preoccupy the Shaikh.

In October 1949, Saudi Arabia formally laid claim to the Buraimi Oasis on the grounds that it had been part of the First Saudi Empire in the late 18th century. The Saudis ignored the fact that for over a century the oasis had been divided between Abu Dhabi and Oman. In fact, the dispute was about oil which geologists from Aramco (the oil concessionaire in Saudi Arabia) suspected lay beneath the oasis. The key to the dispute was the fact that Saudi Arabia's borders were undefined. If it could be proven that Buraimi was in Saudi Arabia, it would also be in Aramco's concession area.

In 1952, the Saudis occupied part of Buraimi, allegedly after offering Shaikh Zayed Bin Sultan (now the ruler of Abu Dhabi but then the governor of the oasis) a large bribe to recognise the Saudi claim. Three years and several arbitration attempts later, Zayed and the Trucial Oman Scouts

(who were commanded by British officers) drove the Saudis out of the oasis. The current UAE-Oman border running through the oasis was settled in 1966 though Saudi Arabia did not drop its claim to Buraimi until 1974, and then only in exchange for a percentage of the oil revenues from Abu Dhabi's portion of the oasis.

Meanwhile, still desperate for oil, Shaikh Shakhbut had given another concession, this time for offshore exploration, to an Anglo-French consortium in 1953. Five years later, it was this group of prospectors that made the first oil strike on the Trucial Coast – 20 years after the Shaikh had first hoped to solve his financial problems through the oil companies. It soon became apparent that Abu Dhabi's reserves were enormous. Exports began in 1962 and, with a population at the time of only 15,000, the emirate was obviously on its way to becoming very rich. Later, under Shaikh Zayed, the emirate set up the Abu Dhabi National Petroleum Company (Adnoc) through which it nationalised the concession agreements during the 1970s.

Oil money firmly established Abu Dhabi as the leader among the Trucial Coast shaikhdoms. Dubai was already becoming a relatively wealthy trading centre in the early '60s and, in 1966, was found to have oil of its own. The other shaikhs, however, were not so lucky, and all of them inevitably began to look to Abu Dhabi for subsidies.

The problem was that Shaikh Shakhbut, having waited so long for the oil money to begin coming in, proved to be completely incapable of handling his newly found wealth. In the early and mid '60s his rule became increasingly erratic. Shakhbut had little understanding of modern banks and did not trust them. He became increasingly suspicious of all foreigners and is said once to have told oil company representatives that he was the one with the upper hand because they needed the money more than he did. In 1966, the British engineered Shakhbut's deposition by Shaikh Zayed, Shakhbut's brother who was also the long-time governor of Abu Dhabi's portion of the Buraimi Oasis. After spending several years abroad, Shakhbut eventually retired to Al-Ain, the main town within Abu Dhabi's portion of Buraimi.

The Federation

Britain's 1968 announcement that it would leave the Gulf in 1971 came as a shock to most of the ruling shaikhs. Within a few weeks, the British began work on forming a single state consisting of Bahrain, Qatar and the Trucial Coast. Plans for such a grouping, which was to be known as the Federation of Arab Emirates, were announced in February 1968. The federation came into existence on 30 March of that year but it collapsed almost immediately, largely because of the area's numerous boundary disputes.

The British decided to try again and negotiations dragged on for the next three years. Bahrain eventually pulled out of the talks, claiming that the proposed formulas did not give it enough standing within the federation. Qatar followed suit, on the theory that if Bahrain was going to be an independent state, so would Qatar. Finally, in July 1971, a provisional constitution for a new federation, to be known as the United Arab Emirates, was announced. The emirs had agreed to a formula under which Abu Dhabi and Dubai (in that order) would carry the most weight in the federation but which would leave each emir largely autonomous. The new country came into existence on 2 December 1971. The provisional constitution was supposed to be in place for only five years but it was formally extended in 1976 and has remained in force ever since.

At the time many outsiders dismissed the UAE as a loosely assembled, artificial and largely British creation. While there was some truth in this charge, it was also true that the emirs of the smaller and poorer shaikhdoms knew that their territories had no hope of surviving as independent states. Umm Al-Qaiwain, for example, at the time probably had a population of only 5000. Ras Al-Khaimah initially decided not to be part of the federation but after only three months its ruler changed his mind and joined the UAE.

Since independence, the UAE has been one of the most stable and untroubled countries in the Arab world. Although the Trucial Oman Scouts were used to suppress an attempted coup in Sharjah a few weeks after independence, the country has remained remarkably calm since then.

This does not mean that political life in the UAE has been devoid of controversy. Border disputes among the emirates continued throughout the '70s, and the degree to which 'integration' among the seven shaikhdoms should be pursued has been a subject of constant debate.

When his first five year term as President of the UAE expired in 1976, Shaikh Zayed threatened to resign if the other six emirs did not settle their outstanding border disputes and give up their private armies. Nobody dared to call his bluff. In 1979, Shaikh Zayed and Shaikh Rashid of Dubai sealed a formal compromise under which each gave a little ground on his respective vision of the country. The result was a much stronger federation in which Dubai remained a bastion of free trade while Abu Dhabi imposed a tighter federal structure on the other emirates. In practice, this meant the federalising of the welfare-state system, the police, the legal system and also the telecommunications network. Rashid, who was already vice-president, also agreed to take the title of prime minister as a symbol of his commitment to the federation.

The collapse of oil prices in the mid to late '80s hit the country unevenly. Abu Dhabi remained very rich but was forced to scale back its subsidies to the smaller emirates. Dubai weathered the financial storm fairly well but Sharjah, which had only recently begun oil production and was in the midst of a building boom, wound up deeply in debt. In 1987, the brother of Sharjah's ruler used this debt as an excuse to attempt a palace coup. The ruler, Shaikh Sultan Bin Mohammed Al-Qasimi, was in the UK at the time but he quickly flew to Dubai where he enlisted the help of the ruling Al-Maktoum family. The Al-Maktoums threatened to use force if necessary to restore Shaikh Sultan to power. The coup leader, Shaikh Abdul Aziz Bin Mohammed, eventually backed down under pressure from the Supreme Council. At the council's suggestion, Sultan appointed Abdul Aziz as crown prince as a gesture of reconciliation. In February 1990, apparently feeling that enough face-saving time had elapsed, Sultan sacked Abdul Aziz. Sultan's son, Ahmed, was named as the new crown prince a few months later.

In 1990-91, the UAE contributed troops to the anti-Iraq coalition and foreign soldiers and sailors were based there during the months prior to the liberation of Kuwait. The result was a strengthening of the country's already strong ties with the west, though this has not prevented the UAE in general, and Dubai in particular, from maintaining good relations with Iran.

In the summer of 1991, Abu Dhabi found itself on the receiving end of a lot of unwelcome publicity when western financial regulators, led by the Bank of England, closed down the scandal-ridden Bank of Credit & Commerce International (BCCI), of which Abu Dhabi was the major shareholder. BCCI was a bank regulator's nightmare. It had over 430 branches in 73 countries, was registered in Luxembourg through holding companies in the Cayman Islands, funded mostly by Abu Dhabi and managed from London by Pakistanis. In the UAE, where BCCI's retail operations had made it one of the largest local banks, the collapse posed a delicate political problem. While negotiating over BCCI's future with the Bank of England and other western regulatory and legal authorities, Abu Dhabi moved to protect the bank's local customers by buying up all of its branches in the UAE and reconstituting them as the Union National Bank. The government also arrested and prosecuted a dozen of the bank's senior officials, most of whom were eventually sentenced to between three and five years in prison.

Though it is rapidly becoming an important world-class business centre, the UAE today rarely produces much news of interest to the outside world. A territorial dispute

with Iran over three small islands in the Gulf has dragged on for years and periodically bubbles to the surface. That aside, when the rest of the world reads about events in the UAE these days it is usually on the sports page of the morning newspaper. Dubai now plays host to several important events on the world's pro golf circuit, and Sharjah is an equally important dateline for the world's cricket fans.

GEOGRAPHY

The UAE is about 83,600 sq km in area. The Emirate of Abu Dhabi represents over 85% of this total. The smallest of the emirates by area is Ajman, with only about 250 sq km of land.

The coastal areas, particularly along the Gulf, are marked by salt flats. Much of the inland area is a nearly featureless desert running to the edges of the Empty Quarter. This desert, which is mostly part of Abu Dhabi, contains a few oases, such as Liwa and Buraimi, but on the whole it is among the bleakest areas of the Arabian Peninsula.

The coastal lands immediately north-east of Abu Dhabi are much the same as the desert to the south and west of the city, but further north along the coast the land slowly becomes greener until, when one reaches Ras Al-Khaimah, the landscape is quite hospitable. The northern end of the Hajar mountain chain runs through the UAE and ends in the Omani enclave of the Musandem Peninsula on the southern side of the Strait of Hormuz. These northern sections of the UAE – the inland areas around Ras Al-Khaimah and the east coast of the country from Fujairah to Dibba – are green and inviting with striking mountain scenery.

CLIMATE

The further south you travel in the Gulf the hotter and more humid the summer weather gets. From May to September, daytime temperatures in the low 40s (Celsius) are common in Abu Dhabi and Dubai. In the east coast cities of Fujairah and Khor Fakkan, the climate is not quite so extreme – it is just as hot and humid but you're more likely to have a breeze. The mountains above Ras Al-Khaimah also provide some relief.

In the winter months all of the emirates enjoy very good weather, though it can get very windy in Abu Dhabi, Dubai and Sharjah. In the desert areas around Al-Ain, it can get very cold on winter nights with temperatures sometimes dropping into the single digits. Winter days in the inland deserts can be pleasantly brisk, with temperatures in the mid-teens. It does not rain often, or heavily, in the UAE but when the weather does turn foul (usually in December or January) getting around can suddenly become difficult with streets turning into rivers and, occasionally, washing out entirely.

Flora & Fauna

The varied terrain of the UAE makes for an equally wide variety of plants and animals, though few of these are visible to the casual observer. Outside of the mountain areas around Fujairah and Ras Al-Khaimah, much of the vegetation you are likely to see is not indigenous but rather part of the local government's 'greenery' programme. The Emirate of Abu Dhabi is particularly keen on establishing parks and planting trees.

The desert south and west of Abu Dhabi city is particularly bleak and featureless and only a naturalist with some experience of desert flora and fauna could find much to enthuse over. The Buraimi Oasis is quite another story. Its natural groves of date palms have been supplemented by acres and acres of grass and trees planted in municipal parks around the UAE portion of the oasis (noticeably less money has been spent on the Omani side). There are now grassland plains outside of Al-Ain running toward the natural green slopes of Jabal Hafit.

The UAE's fauna includes the Arabian leopard and the ibex but you are unlikely to see them. You could get lucky, of course, but your glimpse of wildlife is not likely to extend beyond camels and goats. In the spring and the autumn, flocks of birds migrating between Central Asia and East Africa can sometimes be seen in the northern emirates.

You best chance of seeing 'wild' animals is to visit either the Al-Ain Zoo or the miniature game park that the government of Sharjah is building at its newly opened Natural History Museum in the desert east of the city. ■

GOVERNMENT

The UAE consists of seven emirates: Abu Dhabi, Dubai, Sharjah, Ajman, Umm Al-Qaiwain, Ras Al-Khaimah and Fujairah. Though there is a federal government over which one of the emirs presides (in practice this is always Shaikh Zayed of Abu Dhabi), each of the rulers is completely sovereign within his own emirate. Each emirate is named after its principle town.

The degree of power which the seven emirs should cede to the federal government has been one of the hottest topics of debate in government circles since the founding of the country in 1971. Over the years, Abu Dhabi has been the strongest advocate of closer integration while Dubai has fought hardest to preserve as much of its independence as possible.

Politics in the Gulf tend to be rather opaque but in this case the relative interests of the various emirs are fairly clear. Abu Dhabi is the largest and wealthiest emirate and has the biggest population. It is, therefore, the dominant member of the federation and is likely to remain so for some time. Further integration of the seven emirates is obviously in Abu Dhabi's interest. Dubai is a reasonably wealthy emirate with an equally obvious interest in upholding its free-trade market. Sharjah and Ras Al-Khaimah both have relatively small oil revenues but they, and the other emirates, are dependent on subsidies from Abu Dhabi though the extent of this dependence varies widely. The smaller emirates wish to strike a balance between integration which reduces the prerogatives of the individual emirs and independence which leaves them in a potentially precarious financial position.

The forum where these issues are discussed is the Supreme Council, the highest body in the country. The council comprises the seven emirs and it tends to meet informally. On an official level, its main duty is to elect one of the emirs to a five year term as the country's president. In 1991, Shaikh Zayed of Abu Dhabi was elected to his fifth term as president, a position he seems likely to hold for life. Shaikh Maktoum, the ruler of Dubai, is the country's vice-president and prime minister.

There is also a Cabinet and the posts are distributed among the emirates. Most of the federal government's money comes from Abu Dhabi and Dubai. They each contribute a portion of their oil revenues and so get to hold most of the important Cabinet posts.

The Cabinet and Supreme Council are advised, but cannot be overruled, by the Federation National Council. This is a 40-member consultative body whose members are appointed by the respective emirs. Abu Dhabi and Dubai hold almost half of the council's seats. All the council's members come from leading merchant families.

ECONOMY

The seven emirates are quite diverse economically. Of the seven, only Abu Dhabi is an oil state in the same sense as Qatar and Kuwait. Abu Dhabi sits atop 9% of the world's known, exploitable oil reserves and 5% of the world's natural gas. It is the third-largest oil producer in the Gulf, after Saudi Arabia and Kuwait. Like the other big Gulf producers it has diversified into petrochemicals and other oil-related industries. Abu Dhabi is also a generous donor of development aid. Most of this is channelled to poor Arab countries through the Abu Dhabi Fund for Arab Economic Development which was established in 1971.

Dubai is the second-richest emirate. Its income from oil is now about a quarter of that received by Abu Dhabi but in the decades before Abu Dhabi became oil-rich, Dubai had already established itself as the main trading (and smuggling) port in the region. The discovery of oil in the mid-60s boosted the economic modernisation programme implemented by Dubai's ruler, Shaikh Rashid Bin Saeed Al-Maktoum. Today, in addition to oil and being one of the Gulf's main business centres, Dubai is also the home of a huge dry-dock complex, one of the Middle East's busiest airports and a large free-trade zone at Jebel Ali.

Sharjah, once the most prosperous of all the emirates, has spent most of this century living in the shadow of Dubai. It has received a modest income from oil since the early '70s but found itself deeply in debt after the oil price collapse of the mid-80s. Oil revenue was used to build a large airport, which is remarkably busy despite its proximity to Dubai. Both the airport and Sharjah's seaport facilities derive much of their income from cargo, though in recent years Sharjah airport has also become a main port of entry for tourists visiting the UAE.

Ras Al-Khaimah, the northernmost emirate on the country's Gulf coast, derives its income from oil. Ras Al-Khaimah has also invested heavily in tourism in recent years and it is now a stop on many package tours of the UAE. Fujairah, the only emirate without a coastline on the Gulf, has also entered the tourist market though it remains primarily a cargo port. Fujairah, Ajman and Umm Al-Qaiwain all receive substantial subsidies from the federal government.

POPULATION & PEOPLE

There are estimated to be just over two million people living in the UAE, of whom about 25% (500,000) are UAE citizens (or 'Nationals' as they are usually referred to in the local media).

The Emiratis themselves come from a number of different backgrounds. All of the northern emirates have substantial communities of people of Persian, Indian or Baluchi ancestry. Whether or not these people are actually UAE citizens depends on how long ago they or their ancestors came to the area and how they have earned a living since then. Abu Dhabi is probably the most purely 'Arab' of the emirates, because until the discovery of oil its main population centres were in the isolated areas of Al-Ain and Liwa, both oases deep in the desert.

EDUCATION

As in all of the Gulf States, universal education is a relatively new concept but it has made great strides in the last 20 to 30 years. As recently as 1952, there were no schools in any of the emirates except for a handful of traditional mosque schools where boys learned the Koran by rote. The first modern school was opened in 1953 in Sharjah. Primary education is now compulsory in the UAE and secondary education is nearly universal. The government has traditionally been willing to pay the cost of overseas study for UAE citizens.

The United Arab Emirates University in Al-Ain, the first and only university in the country, opened its doors in 1977. It now has 8000 students and two-thirds of them are women.

ARTS

There is a government-run art gallery at the Cultural Foundation in Abu Dhabi and a government-run Women Craft Centre, also in Abu Dhabi, but traditional art, on the whole, is confined to the country's museums.

RELIGION

Most Emiratis are Sunni Muslims subscribing to the Maliki or Hanbali schools of Islamic law (see The Law in the Religion section of the Facts about the Region chapter for more information). Many of the latter are Wahhabis, though UAE Wahhabis are not nearly as strict and puritanical as the Wahhabis of Saudi Arabia. There are also smaller communities of Ibadi and Shiite Muslims; for more details on Wahhabi and Ibadi Islam see the Religion sections in the Saudi Arabia and Oman chapters respectively. The Shiites are probably descended from merchants and workers who crossed to the Trucial Coast from Persia in the late 19th or early 20th century.

LANGUAGE

Arabic is the official language of the UAE but English is very widely understood. In Dubai, you could also get by using the Persian language, Farsi. Urdu can be reasonably useful in Abu Dhabi and Dubai because of the large number of Pakistani expatriates.

Facts for the Visitor

PLANNING
When to Go

The main tourist season in the UAE is November to February. If you are planning to visit the archaeological sites it would be a good idea to travel in this period. From March to October the climate is often extremely hot and humid. A trip in high summer (July/August) would probably leave you doing very little except running between air-conditioned hotels.

Maps

Geoprojects publishes a map of the entire country which is probably the best of the available road maps. The Bartholomew map

---

Society & Conduct –Dos & Don'ts

The UAE is probably the most liberal country in the Gulf but it is still a very conservative place by western standards. In Dubai in particular, you can wear clothing that would get you arrested in, say, Saudi Arabia, but that does not mean you should do so. Moreover, party-wear standards vary from place to place. What raises few eyebrows in a Dubai nightspot will raise many eyebrows indeed in Abu Dhabi, Al-Ain or Fujairah.

Women should not wear overly tight or revealing clothing (eg miniskirts, short shorts, bikini tops etc) and men should not walk around bare-chested in public. Women may want to stick to one-piece bathing suits at the beach, though bikinis are probably OK around the pool at big hotels. Conservative dress is particularly in order in rural areas. This means long, loose clothing. Short sleeves are OK, even for women, but sleeveless clothes (especially on women) may cause offence in more traditional areas.

The same social etiquette exists in the UAE as elsewhere in the Gulf. Do not photograph people in general, and women in particular, without their permission and always avoid pointing your camera at anything even remotely military (this includes all airports).

Though alcohol is legal everywhere in the country except Sharjah, you should never, ever drive while you're drunk. If you are caught doing so there will be, at the very least, a steep fine to pay and you may wind up spending a month or more in jail. ■

of the Gulf is too out of date to be of much use to drivers.

The situation with individual city maps varies greatly. There are no good maps of Abu Dhabi. The badly outdated Abu Dhabi inset map on the Geoprojects map of the UAE is about as good as they come. In Dubai, by contrast, there are lots of good maps. The best is the yellow-covered *Dubai Town Map and Street Guide* which is available at most hotels for about Dh 20. The UAE map on the back side of this is one of the most up-to-date maps of the country available, even if it is not particularly large. The best of the many bad maps on Sharjah is the *Sharjah City Tourist Map*, available free at most of Sharjah's bigger hotels. The tourist map distributed free by all the hotels in Al-Ain and Buraimi is not very good but it is the only one available.

In Ajman, the souvenir kiosk at the museum sells an excellent map of the town for Dh 20. Your best bet for getting around Ras Al-Khaimah and Fujairah are the inset maps on the Geoprojects UAE map.

What to Bring
A good hat, sunglasses and sun block cream are essential for anyone planning even a short desert expedition and are a good idea if you are staying in the cities.

TOURIST OFFICES
There are no tourist offices in the UAE though tourist information such as maps, tour company brochures and the occasional glossy pamphlet are often available at the big hotels that cater to tour groups, particularly in Sharjah. Another good place to look for tourist information is in the main offices of the 'official' local travel agencies. These are quasi-official travel brokers in each emirate that have a monopoly on travel services at the wholesale level. They include the Dubai National Tourist & Travel Authority (Danata) in Dubai, SNTTA in Sharjah and Ranata in Ras Al-Khaimah. See the respective city listings for more information on organised tours.

VISAS & DOCUMENTS
Visas
Citizens of other Arab Gulf Cooperation Council (GCC) countries and British nationals with the right of abode in the UK do not need visas to enter the UAE. GCC nationals can stay pretty much as long as they want. Britons can stay for a month and can renew their entrance stamp for another two months. Note that at the time of writing there were some indications that Britons might soon lose their visa-free status, so British passport holders would be well-advised to double-check the rules before boarding a plane.

US and German citizens can obtain visas for business or tourist visits through UAE embassies. In theory these are available through any UAE embassy, but the process seems to be quicker if you apply in your home country. These visas are also available to most western passport holders who have a residence/work visa in another GCC country. In all cases you may be issued anything from a single-entry visa valid for use within three months to a 10 year multiple-entry visa. The period of stay may be anything from two weeks to three months. It depends mainly on what you ask for and what the people at the embassy choose to give you.

On paper these visas eliminate the need for sponsorship, but in practice UAE embassies often still ask for some form of written documentation regarding your travel plans. This can take the form of a hotel reservation, a letter from your company saying that they want you to travel to the UAE or an invitation to visit a friend. Again, the rules seem to be applied unevenly.

The authorities in Dubai say they will issue a two week visa to any westerner holding a GCC residence permit who turns up at Dubai airport. The problem with this is that there are a number of reports of Gulf Air refusing to board people with, say, a Bahraini residence visa but no UAE visa in hand.

In general, if you are not American, British, German or a Gulf Arab you will probably have to arrange a transit or visit visa through a hotel or a company – the way the

UAE has been issuing visas to virtually everyone for years. The most common way to enter the UAE is on a 15-day transit visa. These cannot be extended or renewed. To get one you need a sponsor – a UAE national who takes responsibility for you and your actions and who undertakes to make sure that you leave when your visa expires.

Larger hotels can sponsor transit visas for businesspeople and tourists. Some hotels will also, on request, set up a 30-day visit visa. These not only allow you to stay in the country longer, they can also be renewed. If your visa has been arranged by a friend through their company, this is probably what you will get.

Both visit and transit visas are almost always deposited at the airport for you to pick up on arrival. You go to a desk in the arrivals area and pick up a form which you then take to passport control. If you are entering the country on a transit visa you will leave passport control carrying a copy of this form. Do not lose it, as you have to give it back on the way out. The system is the same for visit visas except that you will not have the form when you leave passport control.

You can also pick up visas at the port in Sharjah if you are arriving by boat from Iran.

Transit visas cost Dh 120 and visit visas Dh 60, though most hotels will charge you at least Dh 170, and in some cases Dh 300 or more, for arranging either one.

Note that if you are a naturalised citizen of a western country or if you are a westerner of Arab (especially Lebanese, Palestinian or Iraqi) origin, visa approval could take a long time so apply early. You're also better off applying through one of the larger hotels.

If your passport shows any evidence of travel to Israel you will be denied entry to the UAE.

Hotel-Sponsored Visas To get a visa you ring up one of the big hotels and ask them to sponsor you. The hotel will usually require you to stay one to three nights. Once you have the visa, however, you are free to go anywhere in the country or to move to a cheaper hotel though if you are moving

downmarket, it would be wise not to advertise it. When you make your reservation the hotel will need a fax of the first page of your passport (the one with your photograph) along with the purpose of your visit (tourism is OK) and your flight arrival data. Be sure to get the hotel to fax you back a copy of the visa when it is ready or the airline may not let you travel.

Processing the visa can take anywhere from two days to three weeks. Generally, the biggest and most expensive hotels in Dubai are the fastest while smaller hotels anywhere, and big hotels in out-of-the-way places like Fujairah, take the longest. If you are planning to get your visa through a hotel, try to enter the country through the airports of Abu Dhabi, Dubai or Sharjah.

While there are a lot of cheap hotels which claim to sponsor visas, many of them provide rather questionable service and my advice is that you enter the country through one of the more expensive places. Smaller hotels will claim that they can set up visas and then start asking you about a personal guarantor. This means someone living in the UAE who can officially take responsibility for you. If you do have a friend who can take official responsibility for you, he or she can probably arrange a visa through his/her company, thus sparing you the dubious services of cheap hotels. If you do not have a personal guarantor, then you are probably wasting time and energy with the cheap hotel in question.

A lot of the cheap hotels can also string you along forever without producing a visa. It makes far more sense to splash out and stay at a good hotel and get the visa organised right the first time.

Visa Extensions Transit visas cannot be extended, though people have been known to stay in the UAE for a year or more simply by flying out to Bahrain or Doha every other weekend and picking up a new visa on their return. Visit visas must be extended through the sponsor. If you entered on a visit visa sponsored by a hotel and have spent most or all of the visa's one month validity in that hotel, this should not be a problem.

EMBASSIES
UAE Embassies Abroad
UAE embassies still do not issue many visas (residence visas excepted). Some of the UAE embassies addresses include:

Iran
  Kheyabun-é Vali-yé Asr, Kheyabun-é, Shahid Sartip Vahid Dastgerdi, Tehran (☎ (2) 2221333, 2295029)
Kuwait
  Istiglal St, Diplomatic Area, Kuwait City, south of the centre off Arabian Gulf St (☎ 252 7639)
Oman
  Jameat A'Duwal Al-Arabiya St, Medinat Qaboos Diplomatic Area, Muscat, to the sea side of Sultan Qaboos St, west of the Al-Khuwair roundabout (☎ 600302)
Qatar
  Khalifa Town district, off Al-Khor St, Doha (☎ 885 111)
Saudi Arabia
  Diplomatic Quarter, Riyadh (☎ (1) 482 6803)
UK
  30 Princes Gate, London SW1 (☎ (0171) 581 1281/4113)
USA
  600 New Hampshire Ave NW, Washington DC 20037 (☎ (202) 338 6500)

Foreign Embassies in the UAE
See the Abu Dhabi and Dubai sections for the addresses of embassies and consulates in those cities.

CUSTOMS
Arriving in the UAE is a treat. Dubai, in particular, has a reputation for its fast processing of arrivals – I once made it from the aeroplane to the street in 16 minutes!

The duty-free allowances for tobacco are huge: 2000 cigarettes, 400 cigars or two kg of loose tobacco (this is *not* a country cracking down on smoking). Non-Muslims are allowed to import two litres of wine or spirits, unless they are arriving in Sharjah, where alcohol is prohibited. You are generally not allowed to bring in alcohol if you cross into the country by land.

MONEY
Costs
The UAE is not a low-budget country such

as Egypt or Thailand but it is possible to keep costs under reasonable control. Decent hotels can be found for Dh 100 to Dh 150 (less in Dubai). Eating for Dh 10 to Dh 15 is rarely a problem though if your taste runs to alcohol the bill is going to be a lot higher. Getting around is cheap in service-taxis which are usually the only way to travel between the emirates.

Plan on spending Dh 150/200 per day for budget/mid-range travel. In Dubai and Fujairah, which have good youth hostels, you might be able to keep your budget down to half that.

Currency
The UAE dirham (Dh) is divided into 100 fils. You will also hear the currency occasionally referred to as rupees, especially by Indians and elderly people. When Britain controlled India, the rupee was the official currency in what is now the UAE and from 1948 until independence in 1971, a currency known as the 'Gulf rupee' was legal tender throughout the area.

Notes come in denominations of Dh 5, 10, 50, 100, 200 and 500. Coins are Dh 1, 50 fils, 25 fils, 10 fils and 5 fils. The government recently issued new coins which are smaller than the old ones. Both types remain legal tender, but you should look at your change closely as the new Dh 1 coins are only slightly smaller than the old 50 fils coins. The new 50 fils coins are octagonal so you're unlikely to mistake them for something else.

Currency Exchange
The Dirham is fully convertible and is pegged to the US$. Exchange rates are as follows:

US$1	=	Dh 4.07
UK£1	=	Dh 6.29
FF1	=	Dh 0.79
DM1	=	Dh 2.68
A$1	=	Dh 3.22

Changing Money
If you are changing more than US$250 it might pay to do a little shopping around.

Moneychangers sometimes have better rates than banks, and some do not even charge a commission (others charge quite big ones). The problem with moneychangers is that some of them either will not take travellers' cheques or will take only one type. Some places will only exchange travellers' cheques if you can produce your original purchase receipt. If you don't have the receipt try asking for the manager, but do not count on being able to talk your way around it.

ATMs have become very widespread in the UAE in recent years. Machines at branches of the British Bank of the Middle East are usually linked to the Global Access system. Machines at Emirates Bank International branches are also on Global Access, as well as Cirrus, Plus and, sometimes, Switch.

Tipping & Bargaining

Tips are not generally expected in the UAE, though since most waiters receive extremely low salaries they would certainly be appreciated. The service charge added to your bill usually goes to the restaurant, not the waiter.

Most hotels will offer a discount if you ask for it, but the prices of meals, service-taxis, consumer goods etc are almost always fixed.

POST & COMMUNICATIONS
Postal Rates

Letters are charged per 10g. To Europe, the rate is Dh 2 per 10g; USA and Australia, Dh 2.50; Indian subcontinent, Dh 1.75; Arab countries, Dh 1; Gulf countries, 50 fils. Postcard rates are Dh 1.50 to Europe, Dh 2 to the USA and Australia, Dh 1.45 to Asia, 75 fils to Arab countries and 45 fils within the Gulf.

Parcel postage is priced in steps – up to one kg, three kg, five kg etc. Sending a one kg package to Australia costs Dh 50.25; USA, Dh 25.25; UK, Dh 60.25. To other Gulf countries the rate is Dh 20.25.

Sending Mail

The UAE's postal system is very modern and the post offices are among the most efficient in the Gulf. They also have the shortest queues. Mail generally takes about a week to Europe or the USA and eight to 10 days to Australia.

Receiving Mail

Poste restante facilities are not available in the UAE. The AMEX offices in Abu Dhabi and Dubai will hold mail for AMEX clients (ie card holders and people with AMEX travellers' cheques), and this is probably the best way to receive mail while you are visiting the UAE. If you are checking into a five-star hotel the reception desk will usually hold letters and small packages for two or three days prior to your arrival. Be sure to mark these 'Guest in Hotel' and, if necessary, 'Hold for Arrival'.

Telephone

The UAE has a splendid telecommunications system and you can connect up with just about anywhere in the world from even the remotest areas. Coin-operated phones take Dh 1, 50 and 25 fils coins but card phones are increasingly common throughout the country – they turn up in some fairly odd corners of the desert. The state telecom monopoly is ETISALAT and it, too, seems to have offices just about everywhere.

To call the UAE from abroad, the country code is 971, followed by the city code and the local number. See Telephone in the individual city entries for local city codes. To dial out from the UAE dial '00', followed by the country code, city code and number for international calls. Domestic long-distance calls are '0', the city code and the number.

The direct-dial rates from the UAE to Australia are Dh 11.50 per minute peak and Dh 7.20 off-peak, to the USA (excluding Alaska and Hawaii), Dh 7.50/4.86; Canada, Dh 11.25/7.20; UK, Dh 6.67/4.28; France and Germany, Dh 12/7.83. The off-peak rates apply from 9 pm (7 pm to other Gulf countries) to 7 am every day and all day on Fridays and holidays.

There are Home Country Direct services to the USA and France. These allow you to make either a collect (reverse charges) call or use a telephone credit card issued by the company operating the service. Dialling the access code connects you directly to an operator in the country being called. At present this system is available only to the USA and France and dialling through these systems to third countries is not permitted. To reach an ATT operator in the USA dial 800-121. For MCI the access code is 800-1-0001. The direct-dial access number for France is 800-1-9971.

There are a few quirks, however, in the system. Many payphones, for example, have been programmed so that you can't dial through to the operator. From payphones, only coin-operated models (an increasingly rare sight in the UAE) can be used to dial up the Home Country Direct services. If you have trouble getting through to ATT, MCI or France Telecom, don't expect much help from ETISALAT staff – most of them do not know about this service.

Fax, Telex & Telegraph
Most ETISALAT offices are also equipped to send and receive fax, telex and telegraph messages. They may ask for your local address and contact number before they'll send a fax, and the service is fairly good.

BOOKS
Travel Guides
UAE – A MEED Practical Guide is the most comprehensive guide to the country but it's geared mainly to resident expats. The guide is now in its 4th edition and, unfortunately, has gotten thinner and more advertising-oriented since the previous (1990) edition. It has a lot of useful information for resident expats (where to find a school for your child, a vet for your pet etc) but may prove to be of limited use to other readers.

Of more use to travellers are *Off Road in the Emirates*, by Dariush Zandi, and *The Green Guide to the Emirates* by Marycke Jongbloed, both published by Motivate Publishing, a UAE-based company, and widely available for about Dh 25 to Dh 40. The first, as the name implies, is aimed at the 4WD set. The advertising blurb for the second touts 'an environmentally friendly guide to little-

known places of beauty and interest in the United Arab Emirates'.

The Economist Business Traveller's Guides – Arabian Peninsula is the best among the many how-to-do-business-with-the-Arabs sort of books on the market.

History, People & Society
Books about the UAE's history are hard to find. *The New Arabians* by Peter Mansfield has a short chapter on the UAE's history. *The Merchants* by Michael Field gives a brief sketch on the rise of Dubai as a trading centre.

Looking for Dilmun by Geoffrey Bibby includes an interesting account of the early archaeological work at Umm An-Nar and in Buraimi and gives some idea of life in Abu Dhabi just before and after the beginning of the oil boom. For a more intimate view of life on the Trucial Coast before oil was discovered, read Wilfred Thesiger's classic *Arabian Sands*, originally published in 1959. The young Shaikh Zayed appears in Thesiger's account of his 1948 visits to Liwa, Abu Dhabi, Buraimi, Dubai and Sharjah.

Jonathan Raban's *Arabia Through the Looking Glass* has lengthy sections on Abu Dhabi, Dubai and Al-Ain and is well worth reading.

For an Emirati view of local history and Britain's role in the Gulf see *The Myth of Arab Piracy in the Gulf* by Sultan Muhammad Al-Qasimi, the Emir of Sharjah. The book, which is widely available in Sharjah for Dh 150 (the profits go to charity), is essentially a reworking of the emir's doctoral dissertation from the University of Exeter in the UK.

The locally based publishing company, Motivate, publishes a series of glossy picture books on the various emirates.

See the Facts about the Region chapter for a list of more general books on the Gulf and the Middle East.

Bookshops
Good foreign-language bookshops are hard to find in the UAE. Some of the bigger

hotels have average selections in their bookshops and there are a couple of good bookshops in Abu Dhabi. On the whole, however, the pickings tend to be rather thin. The Abu Dhabi and Dubai listings offer some suggestions.

NEWSPAPERS & MAGAZINES

Gulf News and *Khaleej Times*, both based in Dubai, are the UAE's two English-language newspapers. Both cost Dh 2 and carry pretty much the same international news, though I've long regarded *Gulf News* as the better of the two. Local news in both papers consists largely of 'business' stories which are little more than advertisements masquerading as news. They also tend to have fairly comprehensive coverage of the Indian and Pakistani political and entertainment scenes.

What's On is a monthly magazine catering mostly to the expat community. It's a pretty good source of information about what's new at the UAE's hotels, bars, clubs and discos. There are also usually interesting articles on things to see and do in the UAE and Oman, a list of clubs and societies and a quota of advertising masquerading as news. The magazine costs Dh 8, though you will often find it is free in five-star hotels.

RADIO & TV

Abu Dhabi and Dubai each have an English-language TV channel in addition to their Arabic broadcasts, though outside the two main cities the quality of reception is decidedly mixed. You can watch Omani TV (mostly Arabic with the occasional English movie) in Al-Ain. Qatar TV's English channel's reception is OK in Abu Dhabi when the weather is good. Most hotels, even the smaller ones, have satellite TV. This usually consists of the standard four channel package from Hong Kong-based Star TV: a music video channel, a sports channel, a channel showing mostly American and British entertainment programmes and BBC World Service Television for news. There are often one or two Indian or Pakistani services (Zee TV and/or PTV) and sometimes one or more of the Arabic satellite services (MBC,

Dubai Satellite Channel, Egyptian Satellite Channel, ART).

Abu Dhabi and Dubai also have English-language FM radio stations, both of which mix current pop music (mornings) with documentaries (afternoons) and speciality music programmes such as classical or country & western music (evenings). The Dubai station, Dubai FM, is at FM 92. Abu Dhabi's Capital Radio is at FM 100.5.

PHOTOGRAPHY & VIDEO

Aside from the usual provisos about anything military-related and the photographing of women, there is no problem with taking photographs in the UAE.

Getting colour prints developed is never a problem – one hour services are advertised by photo developers on nearly every street in the country. Developing slides or B&W film is much more difficult and you might want to wait and do this somewhere else.

TIME

The UAE is four hours ahead of GMT. The time does not change during the summer. When it's noon in the UAE, the time elsewhere is:

City	Time
Paris, Rome	9 am
London	8 am
New York	3 am
Los Angeles	midnight
Perth, Hong Kong	4 pm
Sydney	6 pm
Auckland	8 pm

ELECTRICITY

The electric voltage is 240V AC in Abu Dhabi and 220V AC in the northern emirates. British-style three pin outlets are in use.

WEIGHTS & MEASURES

The UAE uses the metric system.

LAUNDRY

There are few laundrettes in the UAE's cities but small laundries, usually run by Indians, abound.

HEALTH

The standard of health care is quite high throughout the UAE. Should you get sick consult either the hotel doctor, if you are in a big hotel, or your embassy or consulate. Unlike some other places in the Gulf, health care in the UAE is neither free nor extremely cheap. Some travel insurance would be very much in order. The city listings include phone numbers for hospitals in some of the larger cities.

No particular shots are necessary for travel in the UAE, though all of the usual travel vaccinations (gamma globulin etc) should be up to date. An International Health Certificate is required only from travellers arriving from an infected area.

The tap water in Abu Dhabi and Dubai is safe to drink but it often tastes horrible and is heavily chlorinated. Most residents stick to bottled water.

See the Health in the Regional Facts for the Visitor chapter for a more complete discussion of health for travellers to the Gulf.

WOMEN TRAVELLERS

In general, the UAE is probably the easiest country in the Gulf for women to travel in. Checking into hotels is not a usually problem though unaccompanied women might want to think twice about taking a room in some of the cheaper places in Dubai.

This is not to say that all of the usual problems that accompany travel in the Middle East will not arise in the UAE as well: unwanted male visitors knocking on your hotel room door at night, lewd looks and comments in the street etc. Apply common sense and retain your self-confidence whatever happens.

See Women Travellers in the Regional Facts for the Visitor chapter for more details on problems faced by women travelling in the Gulf.

BUSINESS HOURS

Government offices start work at 7 or 7.30 am and finish at 1 or 1.30 pm from Saturday to Wednesday. On Thursday everyone goes home around noon. Banks, private compa-

Dangers & Annoyances
The UAE, like much of the rest of the Gulf, has a road system built around traffic circles, or roundabouts. People have a tendency to zoom into these at frightening speeds and to try to turn out of them from inside lanes, paying little attention to other cars. Eternal vigilance is the price of avoiding fender-benders. This problem exists throughout the country but is particularly acute in Dubai and Sharjah.

Another problem in Dubai is traffic congestion, particularly on the two bridges crossing the Creek. You would be well advised to get an early start for any daytime trip that involves a bridge crossing. As for the Creek itself, don't go swimming or water-skiing in it. The Creek is splendidly scenic but it is also very dirty, a situation made worse by the fact that very little of it is cleaned by the tides in the Gulf. ■

nies and shops open Saturday to Wednesday from 8 or 9 am until 1 or 1.30 pm and reopen in the afternoon from 4 to 7 or 8 pm. Shops may or may not be open on Thursday afternoon. The larger shopping centres and supermarkets in Abu Dhabi and Dubai will stay open until 9 or 10 pm every night. Everything is closed during the day on Friday though some shops may open on Friday evenings.

This is all subject to some local variation. In Ras Al-Khaimah, for example, all shops are required to close for about half an hour at prayer time.

PUBLIC HOLIDAYS

Religious holidays are tied to the Islamic Hejira calendar. Eid Al-Fitr (the end of Ramadan), Eid Al-Adha (the end of pilgrimage season), Lailat Al-Mi'raj (the Ascension of the Prophet), the Prophet's Birthday and the Islamic New Year are all observed (see the table of holidays near Public Holidays in the Regional Facts for the Visitor chapter).

Secular holidays observed in the UAE are New Year's Day (1 January) and National Day (1 December; celebrations often last to 2 December). Each emirate may also observe its own holidays. In Abu Dhabi, for example,

6 August is a holiday marking the accession of Shaikh Zayed.

ACTIVITIES

Water Sports

Water sports are popular throughout the UAE, and the tourist industry is increasingly pushing the country as a winter 'sea & sun' destination. Most water-sports facilities are tied either to a big hotel or a private club, and thus are not generally accessible to budget travellers. If your life depends on a spot of jet-skiing then you should be prepared to stay in a four or five-star hotel when visiting the UAE.

Diving

The UAE has several dive centres, most of which are attached to the larger hotels. If you're interested, try the Jebel Ali Hotel in Dubai, the Sheraton Hotel in Abu Dhabi, the Fujairah Hilton and the Sandy Beach Diving Centre in Badiyah.

Golf

The UAE has most of the Gulf's golf courses with real grass. There are three courses in Dubai and a pitch-and-putt course in Al-Ain. If you want to play here you should be prepared to pay handsomely for the privilege. See the Dubai and Al-Ain sections for more details.

Clubs

Abu Dhabi, Dubai and, to a lesser extent, Al-Ain all have a broad range of clubs and societies. For up-to-date listings of these pick up a copy of the latest issue of *What's On*.

WORK

The UAE is not the place to look for work. Since 1984, the government has applied what is known as the Six Months Rule. This states that if you enter the country on a visit or transit visa you must leave for six months before you can return on a residence visa. Exceptions to this are rare.

ACCOMMODATION

Camping

There are no camping grounds adjacent to the UAE's cities but camping in the desert is quite common.

Hostels

There are three youth hostels in the UAE – in Dubai, Sharjah and Fujairah. The Dubai hostel offers excellent two and three bed rooms for Dh 35 per person, per night. Beds in the Sharjah and Fujairah hostels are Dh 15 per night but they are not as nice. The Sharjah hostel is OK but is getting to be a bit run-down, especially when it is compared to the spic-and-span Dubai hostel and the new-

Desert Safaris

Desert safaris, commonly known as 'wadi bashing', involves zooming around the desert in a 4WD vehicle, with stops for food and merriment. They are usually a day activity, though many also camp out, especially in Saudi Arabia, Oman and the UAE. 'Wadi bashing' is a great way to see some spectacular scenery and get away from the rather sterile atmosphere of many of the Gulf's cities. That said, it can also be dangerous. Never head out into the desert without a first-aid kit, extra food and fuel, a spare tyre (or two) and an idea of where you are going. You should also let someone who is staying behind know where you are going and when you are to be expected back. It goes without saying that you should not just hop in a Land Rover and head off on your own if you have no experience at this sort of thing. Anyone who is planning an overnight trip in the desert should pick up *Staying Alive in the Desert* by KEM Melville or *Off Road in the Emirates* by Dariush Zandi.

In the UAE you can book a desert safari trip through one of the bigger tour companies in Dubai or Sharjah (see the entries for those cities for details of tour companies and their offerings). An organised desert safari with lunch and/or dinner will cost between Dh 125 and Dh 185. Overnight desert trips cost about Dh 350. ■

look clean hostel in Fujairah. In all cases, HI cards are required and a working knowledge of Arabic would be useful.

Hotels
Most of the country's cheap hotels are in and around the Dubai souk. These bottom out at around Dh 50 to Dh 60 for a single and Dh 80 to Dh 100 for a double. There are a few cheaper places but they always seem to be full. The cheapest places that provide reliable visa service cost from Dh 250/350 for singles/doubles.

In Dubai, the five-star hotels cost anything upwards of Dh 625/725. Top hotels in Abu Dhabi are a bit cheaper, starting from around Dh 450/525.

FOOD
Eating cheap in the UAE means eating either in small Indian/Pakistani restaurants which often seem to have only biryani dishes on the menu, or having street food, such as shawarma. You can also find relatively cheap Lebanese food. In Dubai and, to a lesser extent, Abu Dhabi, cheap Oriental food is also fairly easy to come by. Abu Dhabi and Dubai both have a wide selection of small cafes and snack shops.

At the top end of the market almost any kind of food can be found in Abu Dhabi and Dubai. In the smaller emirates, top-end food means eating at the big hotels.

DRINKS
Nonalcoholic drinks such as soft drinks, fruit juices and mineral water are available throughout the country. Alcohol can only be sold in restaurants and bars attached to hotels (in practice, three-star hotels or better). The selection is what you would expect to find in any well-stocked bar. The prices are pretty outrageous – expect to pay around Dh 20 for a pint of beer.

Non-Muslim expatriates must obtain an alcohol licence (with the permission of their sponsor) to purchase booze for consumption at home. These licences, which are not available in Sharjah, allow the holder to purchase

a maximum of Dh 750 worth of liquor each month.

ENTERTAINMENT
Cinemas
Most cinemas in the UAE show Indian and Pakistani films. There are usually several such places in each of the main cities. Dubai has a cinema specialising in recent English-language films.

Discos
If you want to dance the night away Dubai is the place to be. While there are discos and bars with dance floors in most of the larger hotels in Abu Dhabi, Fujairah, Al-Ain and Ras Al-Khaimah, Dubai is clearly the centre of the UAE's nightlife. Pancho Villa's, a Tex-Mex restaurant in Dubai's Astoria Hotel, has a good dance floor, often featuring live rock and roll. More conventional discos can be found in most of the five-star hotels in the city. See the Dubai section for more details.

Theatre
Western theatre companies regularly visit the UAE, usually under the sponsorship of some international company. These theatre performances almost always take place in one of the five-star hotels. Watch the local English-language press and look for fliers in the lobbies of the big hotels for details.

SPECTATOR SPORT
Camel Racing
The main spectator sport in the UAE is camel racing. This takes place in various spots around the country during the winter. Ras Al-Khaimah is one of the best places to see camel races, partly because the racing schedule there is relatively predictable and partly because the track is well laid out for viewing. See the Ras Al-Khaimah entry for further details.

THINGS TO BUY
If you are looking for old Arabian souvenirs the UAE may be something of a disappointment. There are a few shops in Al-Ain, Abu

Dhabi and Dubai which deal in Bedouin jewellery, most of which comes from Oman. If you are travelling on to either Oman or Saudi Arabia, this sort of jewellery is much cheaper in those countries and the selection tends to be better.

In Al-Ain you can cross visa-free to the Omani side of the Buraimi Oasis and shop for Omani jewellery in Oman, where it tends to be more affordable. See the Oman chapter for more information on Omani jewellery and how to shop for it.

Dubai is probably the cheapest place outside of Iran to buy Iranian caviar.

The real fame of the UAE, however, is its reputation as the world's largest duty-free shop. If it can be plugged into the wall you can buy it here. Although Dubai and Sharjah are the cheapest places in the Middle East to buy these types of goods, the selection tends to be a bit limited. Going from shop to shop, you will soon notice that they all stock the same three or four varieties of something (say, VCRs) at pretty much the same prices. You will also discover that the shop assistants are not very knowledgeable about their stock so it helps to have a good idea of what you want before setting off on a shopping expedition. It is also a good idea, and it is accepted practice in the UAE, to plug your new gadget in at the shop to make sure that it works properly.

Persian Carpets

Dubai and Sharjah are among the best places outside of Iran to buy Persian carpets. Buying carpets without getting ripped off takes skill and patience. Do not feel embarrassed or obliged to buy just because the shop attendant has unrolled 40 carpets for you; this is part of the ritual. The best way to get a good price is to visit several stores, ask a lot of questions and bargain hard over a long period of time (preferably two or three visits). For useful information on the history of Persian carpets, how they are made, and even more importantly, what to look for when buying one, see *Oriental Carpets: A buyer's guide* by Essie Sakhai.

Getting There & Away

AIR

Dubai and Abu Dhabi are the country's main international airports, though an increasing number of carriers serve Sharjah as well. There are also small international airports at Ras Al-Khaimah, Fujairah and Al-Ain. Abu Dhabi, Dubai and Sharjah all have enormous duty-free shopping complexes that attempt to outdo one another through spectacular promotions: in Dubai the duty-free shop gives away expensive cars at the rate of about two per week, Abu Dhabi once gave out holiday homes in Spain and Sharjah has experimented with big pots of cash.

Flying to Europe or the USA tends to be a bit less expensive out of Dubai than from Abu Dhabi, though it is not cheap from either city. For all the talk of free markets, airfares out of the UAE are just as strictly regulated as they are in the other Gulf States. There are no bucket shops.

The only direct air service between the UAE and North America is out of Abu Dhabi on Gulf Air. There is daily or near-daily service from both Abu Dhabi and Dubai to major European cities such as London, Paris, Frankfurt, Rome and Athens. Within the Middle East, there is daily service to most of the other Gulf capitals and to Cairo but rather fewer flights (several per week) to Amman, Damascus, Beirut and the big cities of North Africa. Dubai probably has the best air links to Iran and Pakistan of any city in the world. All the major cities of the Indian subcontinent can be reached quite easily from the UAE. Asian centres such as Bangkok, Singapore, Hong Kong and Seoul can all be reached easily as well.

See the Abu Dhabi and Dubai sections for sample airfares to other cities in the Gulf, Europe and the USA.

LAND

There is a daily bus service between Dubai and Muscat, though the lack of a UAE border post on the road used by the bus can present some visa problems for travellers. Essentially, you can leave the UAE this way with no problems, but if you enter the UAE by road from Oman through the crossing points at Dibba, Buraimi or Hatta you will notice that there is no customs post on the Emirati side of the border and you can get an Omani exit stamp and just keep going. However, if you enter the country this way you are considered to be in transit and have 48 hours to leave whether by air, sea or road. After that you will incur a fine of Dh 100 per day when you do try to leave. Having a valid UAE visa in your passport makes no difference.

If you want to enter through Sila, on the Saudi-UAE border, or Sham, on the UAE-Oman border north of Ras Al-Khaimah, you will get a border stamp and can remain in the country for as long as your visa allows. The problem is that you cannot pick up a visa in either of these places so they are only really options for people able to obtain a visa in advance. There are also regular buses between Dubai and Dammam in Saudi Arabia. See Getting There & Away in the Saudi Arabia chapter for details.

SEA

There are passenger services between Sharjah and Iran. The trip takes 12 hours and costs Dh 180 in 1st class, Dh 170 in 2nd class and Dh 140 in 3rd class. There is also a Dh 20 port tax. For more details contact Oasis Freight Co (☎ 596 325) in Sharjah.

Make sure that the hotel organising your visa deposits it at Sharjah port for pick up.

LEAVING THE UAE

Leaving the UAE is fairly straightforward. Check-in times at the various airports are officially one hour before the departure time, though it is often a good idea to arrive earlier. The airports in general, and Dubai airport in particular, can get pretty chaotic when flights are overbooked. It also pays to arrive early so you can have time to browse through the duty-free shops.

There is no airport departure tax. If you leave by boat, there's a Dh 20 port tax. There is also a Dh 20 road tax if you depart via one

of the overland border crossings where there is a customs post to collect it, ie at Sham on the border between the UAE and Oman's Musandem Peninsula, or at Sila on the UAE-Saudi border. A number of other crossing points, such as Al-Ain, Hatta and Dibba, all on the Omani border, have no checkpoint on the UAE side and, hence, no one to collect the tax.

Getting Around

AIR & BUS

At the time of writing, there were no air or bus services between the emirates.

SERVICE-TAXI

If you do not have your own car, the only way to travel between the emirates is by service-taxi. Service-taxis in the UAE usually carry seven passengers (though there are a few five and nine passenger taxis) and leave whenever they are full. In Abu Dhabi and Dubai, the local governments operate large taxi depots. Everywhere else, the service-taxi station is usually little more than a vacant patch of ground where the drivers wait for their cars to fill up.

Service-taxis can be a bit cramped but they are cheap and a great way to meet people. The main problem is often that, aside from the busy Abu Dhabi-Dubai route, they do not fill up very quickly. Between Abu Dhabi and Dubai there are also minibuses which carry 14 people and charge a few dirhams less than the service-taxis. Some sample one-way service-taxi fares (in either direction) are:

From	To	Fare
Abu Dhabi	Dubai	Dh 30
Abu Dhabi	Al-Ain	Dh 20
Dubai	Al-Ain	Dh 30
Dubai	Sharjah	Dh 4
Dubai	Ras Al-Khaimah	Dh 15
Dubai	Fujairah	Dh 25
Ras Al-Khaimah	Fujairah	Dh 25
Fujairah	Khor Fakkan	Dh 5
Fujairah	Dibba	Dh 15

Bear in mind that taxis may not run between all cities at all times. A lot depends on where the drivers feel like taking passengers on any given day. You can, of course, get a taxi to take you almost anywhere if you are willing to pay for all of the seats in it.

CAR

The UAE is one of those countries where having your own wheels can often mean the difference between having fun and spending much of your time planning transport from here to there.

As noted in the Dangers & Annoyances boxed story, the driving in the UAE can sometimes be a bit reckless, particularly around the country's numerous traffic circles. Many people also try to avoid driving between cities at night whenever possible.

As for licences, most foreign driving licences are accepted in the UAE so long as you are either a citizen or a resident of the country that issued the licence. Car rental companies will issue you a temporary UAE licence against your home licence when you rent a car. This applies only to people in the country on either visit or transit visas. If you live in the UAE, you will need to get a permanent UAE licence.

Road Rules

Driving in the UAE is on the right. Right turns are not permitted at red lights. The speed limit is 60 km per hour in town and 100 km per hour on the highways. Speeders are sometimes pulled over and ticketed, but in some cases they are simply sent a bill by the police. For this reason many car rental companies require renters to sign a statement acknowledging that they are aware of this and authorising the renting company to charge their credit card for any tickets that turn up after the renter has left town.

All accidents, no matter how small, must be reported to the police.

Petrol

Petrol, interestingly, is sold by the imperial gallon in the UAE, not by the litre (an imperial gallon is just over 4.5 litres). Regular petrol costs Dh 3.65 per gallon and premium is Dh 3.95 per gallon.

Rental

Small cars start at about Dh 140 per day with another Dh 20 to Dh 30 for insurance, though you may be able to negotiate this down to a net rate of around Dh 130 per day, including insurance. The first 100 or 150 km per day are usually free with additional km costing 40 or 50 fils each. If you rent a car for more than three days you will usually be given unlimited mileage. I have not found the smaller rental agencies to be any cheaper than the big ones, and if you are driving all over the country, it can be reassuring to be able to contact a local office of a bigger agency if something goes wrong.

It is worth remembering that unless you make other arrangements the insurance on your rental car will only be good inside the UAE. This means that if you make a shopping trip from Al-Ain to the Buraimi souk or want to take a look at the Omani portion of Dibba – both of which can be done without an Omani visa – you had better not have even a minor accident while you are on the Omani side of the border. It is possible to add Oman to a rented car's insurance (if, say, you want to rent a car in Dubai and drive to Muscat), but taking a car out of the country sends costs through the ceiling. The insurance will go up by Dh 10 or Dh 20 per day and the cost of renting the car itself may double. Renting a car in Oman is expensive but it's not that expensive.

HITCHING

Hitching is not illegal but it is not very common either. A foreigner with his (I would not recommend that women try this) thumb out might get lifts because the drivers were curious, or they might be passed by on the theory that something so strange had to be a bit suspicious.

LOCAL TRANSPORT
Bus

Only Abu Dhabi, Al-Ain and Dubai have municipal bus services and these are of varying usefulness. Unfortunately, Abu Dhabi's bus service is nearly useless for the traveller, designed, as it is, largely to haul labourers to and from the industrial areas on the edge of the city. The bus services in Dubai and Al-Ain are much more comprehensive and can get a budget traveller to most of those respective cities points of interest fairly easily. See the Dubai and Al-Ain sections for bus routes.

Taxi

Taxis in Abu Dhabi and Al-Ain have meters but those in Dubai and the other emirates do not. In these cities you should negotiate the fare in advance. See the individual city entries for more information.

ORGANISED TOURS

Several major tour companies, including British Airways Holidays, Thomas Cook and Kuoni, offer package holidays in Dubai. The programmes are either 'sea & sun' holidays or a combination of 'sea & sun' with a desert safari and sightseeing outside of Dubai. They all use the beach hotels on the outskirts of Dubai as their base (the facilities are wonderful, but you may end up wishing that you were closer to town). If you really want to travel to the Gulf in high summer this can be quite cheap – as little as UK£450 for a one week holiday including return airfare from London. Tours are usually most expensive during December, when you should figure on paying about 25% more than in summer.

There are also several companies in Dubai, Sharjah and Ras Al-Khaimah offering half and full-day tours of the various emirates and desert safaris. See the relevant city entries for more details.

Abu Dhabi

In the 1950s, visitors to Abu Dhabi remarked on the place's remoteness and its bleak appearance. What was then a small fishing village is now a sprawling city covering virtually all of Abu Dhabi island. Everything is modern, sleek and shiny. It is also often accused of being rather soulless. That is probably going a bit too far. The UAE's capital may not be the most exciting place around, but it does have its attractions.

History

Abu Dhabi town was founded in 1761, but the ruling Al-Nahyan family did not move to the coast from their base at Liwa until 1793, when a freshwater well was discovered. Al-Husn Palace, also known as the Old Fort or the White Fort, was built over this well when the ruler moved up from the desert.

The town expanded rapidly during the heyday of the pearl trade in the late 19th century. Abu Dhabi was never a major pearling or trading centre like Bahrain or Zubara, but it was prosperous by the rather limited standards of the time. Under Zayed the Great, who ruled the emirate from 1855 to 1909, Abu Dhabi became the most powerful of the Trucial Coast shaikhdoms.

The collapse of the pearling industry in the 1930s decimated Abu Dhabi and the town soon sank into squalor. In a desperate attempt to salvage the emirate, Shaikh Shakhbut (reigned 1928-66) granted oil concessions in the late '30s, but until the oil money began coming in (1962), the town remained little more than a fishing village.

It is difficult today to imagine what Abu Dhabi looked like only 40 years ago. When Geoffrey Bibby, the archaeologist, first arrived in early 1958 he saw from the window of his airplane only the fort and a few huts along a stretch of white sand. The airport at which he landed consisted of 'two rows of black-painted oil-drums marking the approach to a stretch of salt flat'. Al-Ain was a five day journey across the desert by camel.

It is sadly ironic that after waiting two decades for oil to rescue his impoverished emirate, Shaikh Shakhbut was unable to handle the flood of money which came his way in the '60s. In 1966, the British eased him out in favour of his brother, Shaikh Zayed, who has ruled ever since and has been the president of the UAE federation since independence in 1971. Abu Dhabi is by far the richest and the most politically important of the seven emirates.

Orientation

The city of Abu Dhabi sits at the head of a T-shaped island. It is not a compact place, and distances here tend to be bigger than they look (especially once you start trying to get around on foot!). The airport is on the mainland about 30 km from the centre.

The main business district is the area bounded by Shaikh Khalifa Bin Zayed and Istiglal Sts to the north, Zayed the Second St to the south, Khalid Bin Al-Waleed St to the west, and As-Salam St to the east. The GPO and the telephone office are just outside this area. The main station for buses and service-taxis is further to the south. The side of the Corniche facing inland is dominated by big office buildings. The main residential areas are all south of the centre.

The word Shaikh is often abbreviated to SH or SHK on street signs. Some of the streets also have names which are in more common use than their official ones. These include:

Shaikh Rashid Bin Saeed Al-Maktoum St – more commonly called Airport Rd or, sometimes, Old Airport Rd, though it runs to both the old and new airports.
Bani Yaas St – generally extends all the way to the Corniche, well past the point where it officially becomes Umm Al-Nar St.
Zayed the Second St – invariably called Electra St.
Hazaa Bin Zayed St – commonly known as Defence St.
Al-Falah St – often called Passport Street.

To confuse matters further, the city has taken to numbering all the streets. Signs with both numbers and names often appear on the same street corner and the numbers (always spelled out) are often larger than the names. What is not immediately obvious is that the city is also divided into districts and the streets are numbered by district. Thus, there are twenty or so 'Twentieth' streets in the city. The numbers you need to know are the ones applied to a handful of the main thoroughfares in the centre. These are:

East Rd and Lulu St are Fourth St.
Al-Nasr St is Fifth St.
Umm Al-Nar St and Bani Yaas St are Sixth St.
Leewa St is Tenth St.

You are likely to discover, however, that a lot of people who have lived in Abu Dhabi for a long time haven't the foggiest idea what the streets are called – officially or unofficially. That goes triple for the taxi drivers! Directions still tend to come in the form of: 'It's the blue building on the left after you pass the such-and-such supermarket near whatever and across from...'

Information

Tourist Office There is no tourist office in Abu Dhabi, though the word at the time of writing was that the emirate-owned Abu Dhabi National Hotels Company had plans to set one up 'soon'. Some of the Dubai and Sharjah-based tour companies run day trips to Abu Dhabi and they might be able to provide some information on the city, but you'd have to ask in Dubai or Sharjah as none of them seem to have offices in the capital.

Foreign Embassies Some of the diplomatic missions in Abu Dhabi are:

Belgium
   Al-Masaood Tower (look for the Standard & Chartered Bank at street level of the same building), 6th floor, Shaikh Hamdan Bin Mohammed St (☎ (02) 319 449)
Denmark
   The Blue Tower, 10th floor, Shaikh Khalifa Bin Zayed St (☎ (02) 325 900). The Swedish government maintains a small consular office in the Danish embassy.
Egypt
   Diplomatic Area, Airport Rd, beyond the Pepsi Cola plant, about 10 km south of the centre (☎ (02) 445 566)
Finland
   Al-Masaood Tower (look for the Standard & Chartered Bank at street level of the same building), 10th floor, Shaikh Hamdan Bin Mohammed St (☎ (02) 328 927)
France
   Al-Nahayan St, near the Batin Palace (☎ (02) 435 100)

Germany
   Al-Nahayan St, near the Batin Palace (☎ (02) 331 630)
India
   Zayed the Second St (Electra St) (☎ (02) 664 800)
Jordan
   Diplomatic Area, Airport Rd, behind the Pepsi Cola plant, about 10 km south of the centre (☎ (02) 447 100)
Kuwait
   Diplomatic Area, Airport Rd, behind the Pepsi Cola plant, about 10 km south of the centre (☎ (02) 446 888)
Netherlands
   Al-Masaood Tower (look for the Standard & Chartered Bank at street level of the same building), 6th floor, Shaikh Hamdan Bin Mohammed St (☎ (02) 321 920)
Norway
   Al-Masaood Tower (look for the Standard & Chartered Bank at street level of the same building), 10th floor, Shaikh Hamdan Bin Mohammed St (☎ (02) 211 221)
Qatar
   Al-Muntasser St, 26th district (☎ 435 900)
Saudi Arabia
   Al-Karamah St, near the intersection with Dalma St (☎ (02) 465 700)
UK
   Khalid Bin Al-Waleed St, just south of the Corniche (☎ (02) 326 600). The British embassy also handles Canadian and Australian affairs. The Canadian ambassador accredited to the UAE is resident in Kuwait. The Australian government covers the UAE from its embassy in Riyadh.
USA
   Sudan St, between Al-Karamah St and the intersection where King Khalid Bin Abdul Aziz St becomes Al-Nahayan St (☎ (02) 436 691)

Money In the centre, and especially along Shaikh Hamdan Bin Mohammed and Shaikh Khalifa Bin Zayed Sts, it often seems like every third building is a bank. Despite all of the competition for business, I've generally found that the rates for changing money are pretty standard. Shopping around is probably not worth the time unless you are changing US$500 or more, though you might want to ask what the commission is before signing on the dotted line. You shouldn't pay more than about Dh 10 per transaction at a bank and less than that, if any, at a moneychanger's.

If you're looking for a moneychanger

instead of a bank, try the souk or Shaikh Hamdan Bin Mohammed St near the Gulf Air office.

AMEX (☎ 213 045) is represented in Abu Dhabi by Al-Masaood Travel & Services on Al-Nasr St south-west of the intersection with Khalid Bin Al-Waleed St. All the usual AMEX services are provided, including cheque cashing for card holders. AMEX clients can also use the office as a mailing address. Any mail should be addressed: c/o American Express, PO Box 806, Abu Dhabi, UAE, and should be clearly marked 'Client's Mail'. The office is open on Sunday to Thursday from 8.30 am to 1 pm, and from 4 to 6.30 pm.

Post The GPO is on East Rd between Al-Falah St and Zayed the Second St. It is open Saturday to Wednesday from 8 am to 8 pm, Thursday from 8 am to 6 pm and Friday from 8 to 11 am. There is a philatelic bureau on the 1st floor.

Telephone The ETISALAT office on Shaikh Rashid Bin Saeed Al-Maktoum St is open 24 hours a day. You can book international calls through the operator or dial them direct on card phones. Phonecards are on sale around the clock. Fax, telex and telegram services are also available. This is the old ETISALAT building and, regardless of what you may hear, the office providing these services has not moved into the new headquarters building down the street. The telephone area code for Abu Dhabi is 02.

Travel Agencies Travel agencies may be the only businesses which outnumber banks in Abu Dhabi, but there are no bucket shops. Most travel agencies are tiny operations specialising in one service (eg cargo) or one destination (eg Bangladesh). They also tend to have a very high turnover among their staff, which makes it difficult to recommend any particular one. If you need to buy a ticket I would advise going to the big travel agencies, like AMEX, whose staff are likely to be a bit more experienced.

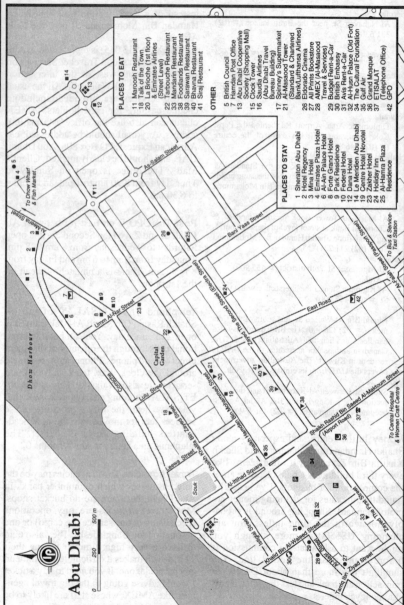

Abu Dhabi

0   250   500 m

PLACES TO EAT

11 Maroosh Restaurant
18 Talk of the Town
20 La Brioche (1st floor)
    & Emirates Airlines
    (Street Level)
22 Tarbouche Restaurant
33 Mandarin Restaurant
38 Soodlands Restaurant
39 Sarawan Restaurant
40 Bhavna Restaurant
41 Siraj Restaurant

OTHER

5   British Council
7   Hamdan Post Office
13 Abu Dhabi Cooperative
    Society (Shopping Mall)
15 Clock Tower
16 Saudia Airlines
17 Spinney's Supermarket
21 Al-Masaood Tower
    (Sheraton Travel,
    Bank/Lufthansa Airlines)
26 Eldorado Cinema
27 All Prints Bookstore
28 AMEX (Al-Masaood
    Travel & Services)
29 Budget Rent-a-Car
30 British Embassy
31 Avis Rent-a-Car
32 Al-Husn Palace (Old Fort)
34 The Cultural Foundation
35 Gulf Air
36 Grand Mosque
37 ETISALAT
42 GPO
    (Telephone Office)

PLACES TO STAY

1   Sheraton Abu Dhabi
2   Hotel Regency
3   Mina Hotel
4   Al-Ain Palace Hotel
6   Emirates Plaza Hotel
8   Forte Grand Hotel
9   Park Residence
10 Federal Hotel
12 Dana Hotel
14 Le Meridien Abu Dhabi
19 Centre Hotel Novotel
23 Zakher Hotel
24 Holiday Inn
25 Al-Dhanna Plaza
    Residence

Dhow Harbour

To Dhow Wharf & Fish Market

Al-Salam Street

Bani Yaas Street

Al-Nasr Street

Umm Al-Nar Street

Capital Garden

Lulu Street

Corniche

Zayed The Second Street (Electra Street)

East Road

Zayed The Second Street (Passport Street)

Al-Falah Street

To Bus & Service-Taxi Station

Souk

Al-Ittihad Square

Shaikh Hamdan Bin Mohammed Street

Leewa Street

Shaikh Khalifa Bin Zayed Street

Sheikh Rashid Bin Saeed Al-Maktoum Street (Airport Road)

To Central Hospital & Women Craft Centre

Zayed The First Street

Khalid Bin Al-Waleed Street

Al-Nasr Street

Tariq Ibn Ziyad Street

Bookshops It is hard to find bookshops with a good selection of English-language books. All Prints Bookstore on Al-Nasr St has the largest selection of English-language books in town. It also has a selection of French books.

Cultural Centres The British Council (☎ 788 400) is off Al-Meena St, next to the Emirates Plaza Hotel. The US Information Service (USIS) cultural centre (☎ 436 567) is at the US embassy on Sudan St. Neither group operates a library in Abu Dhabi, instead both concentrate on English courses and other educational programmes. The Alliance Francaise (☎ 338 794) does have a library, in addition to French courses and other cultural activities. Its office is in the Iran Insurance Company building, behind the north side of Shaikh Hamdan Bin Mohammed St.

Medical Services Most hospitals will take walk-in patients for consultations and/or treatment. Your embassy can probably provide you with a list of doctors who speak your language.

Abu Dhabi's central hospital (☎ 214 666 for the general switchboard or ☎ 344 663 for the emergency unit) is on Al-Manhal St. The emergency entrance is on the corner of Al-Manhal and Karamah Sts.

Emergency For the police, dial ☎ 999, ambulance ☎ 998, fire ☎ 997.

Dangers & Annoyances Abu Dhabi is generally a pretty safe city. Until, that is, you get in a car.

Beware of the taxis which zoom wildly through the traffic. Few of the drivers appear to know what brake lights on the car ahead of them look like and none seem to know how to use directional signals. It's also a good idea when driving to stay out of the right-hand lane, as the taxis are constantly using it to pick up and set down passengers. I try to avoid driving at night in Abu Dhabi whenever possible, even though that means

getting into one of those crazy taxis – a real *Catch-22* situation!

The Cultural Foundation
This large, faceless building on Zayed the First St is more interesting inside than its outward appearance would indicate. It is mainly a library with an attached research and documentation centre, but there are often interesting exhibits on local history, Islamic art, old manuscripts etc, and the hallways are dotted with interesting examples of Arabian art and artefacts. The gallery area is also sometimes used to show the works of foreign artists. There is a small cafe on the 1st floor. The ground floor has both a snack kiosk and a bookshop. The foundation is open Saturday to Wednesday from 7.30 am to 1.30 pm and from 4 to 10 pm, Thursday from 7.30 am to noon and 4 to 9 pm; closed Friday. Admission is free.

Al-Husn Palace
Al-Husn Palace is commonly known as the Old Fort or the White Fort. It is one of the few buildings in Abu Dhabi that's more than 30 years old and its whitewashed walls are just as eye-catching amid today's skyscrapers as they would have been against a backdrop of reed and mud-brick huts 50 or 100 years ago.

The first fort on the site was built over the city's freshwater well at the beginning of the 19th century by Shakhbut Bin Dhiyab, who is considered to be the first ruler of the Al-Nahyan dynasty. The present fort was built in the late 19th century by Shaikh Zayed the Great. It is the oldest building in Abu Dhabi. It has been completely modernised as well as restored and is now used by the Cultural Foundation as a documents centre.

As you enter the fort be sure to stop and look at the tilework over the main (north) gate. The courtyard is also worth a look. The fort is open Saturday to Wednesday from 7.30 am to 1.30 pm and Thursday from 7.30 am to noon. Admission is free.

Public Garden
Abu Dhabi's central park occupies most of

Old Souk

If you're looking for a break from the world of banks and boutiques that is modern Abu Dhabi take a walk through what remains of the old souk in the small area east of Al-Ittihad Square and north of Shaikh Khalifa Bin Zayed St. There are numerous moneychangers, a small gold market and lots of housewares on offer. Unfortunately there were indications at the time of writing that Abu Dhabi's souk may soon go the way of so many others in the Gulf and be replaced with a more modern market area on the same site. ∎

the area south of Shaikh Khalifa Bin Zayed St between Umm Al-Nar and Lulu Sts. It's a relaxing place to get away from the traffic for a few minutes, and there is playground equipment for children. The entrance is near the corner of Shakih Khalifa Bin Zayed and Umm Al-Nar Sts.

Women Craft Centre

This is a government-run operation where traditional weavings and other crafts are displayed and sold. The centre is about five km south of central Abu Dhabi just west of the Airport Rd. It's well signposted. The centre is open Saturday to Wednesday from 9 am to noon and Thursday from 9 to 11 am. It is closed Friday. Admission is free.

To reach the centre simply take Airport Rd south from the centre and exit at the large black-and-white sign pointing right (it is difficult to miss but easy to overshoot the turn-off, so watch the road closely). Keep going straight and you will eventually run right into the craft centre. It is in a compound marked 'Handicraft Industrial Centre'. The telephone number is ☎ 476 645.

Once inside the compound head for the large building at the far end. This is the exhibition hall. Most of the items in the entrance area of the exhibition hall, and on the upper level, are for sale. The others are for display only. Be sure to look at the display of coffeepots at the left-hand end of the entrance area – through a doorway by the

display is a reconstruction of the interior of a traditional house.

Back outside in the main courtyard you can visit the workshops where many of the items on display are made. Many of the women at work here are fully veiled and may be uncomfortable with male visitors. Be polite and ask permission before entering the workshops or taking pictures. Many of the women will refuse to be photographed.

Prices for the items on sale are OK but not great. The small baskets at Dh 15 to Dh 20 make nice, easily transportable gifts. While the quality of the artisanship on display is very high the mats and rugs can be quite expensive, especially considering that many of them are made with artificial fibres instead of the traditional goat or camel hair or sheep's wool. Ultimately, this depends on how much of a purist you are in these matters. Prices are fixed.

Dhow Wharf & Fish Market

Out at the eastern end of the Corniche, near the port, lies Abu Dhabi's small dhow wharf. It is nothing compared to Dubai's waterfront but it does offer good local colour, a well-known fish restaurant (see Places to Eat – expensive) and an excellent view back toward the city. To reach the Fish market take Al-Meena St east until you reach the crossroads where the port's entrance gate is just ahead of you. Turn left and follow the signs for Al-Dhafra Restaurant. The market and wharf are on the opposite side of the road so you'll have to make a U-turn.

The best time to visit is either in the early morning, when the dhows bring in the day's catch, or around sunset.

Beaches

You can use the beach and health clubs at most of the big hotels for a fee. This is usually Dh 30 on weekdays and Dh 50 on weekends (Thursday and Friday and Friday only, depending on the hotel). The Sheraton has a particularly well equipped complex, including a private beach. For your money you usually get access to pool and beach facilities and things like spas or saunas, but

RAY CHADWICK

GORDON ROBISON

GORDON ROBISON

United Arab Emirates

Top: Sparse desert vegetation surrounds the Hellenistic site at Meleiha.
Left: Warning – camels crossing: a common road sign throughout Arabia.
Right: Sand dunes at Hamim in the Liwa Oasis on the edge of the Empty Quarter.

GORDON ROBISON

GORDON ROBISON

GORDON ROBISON

United Arab Emirates

Top: Bead merchants ply their trade in the busy Bur Dubai souk.
Left: An abra ride across the Creek is a great way to see Dubai's waterfront.
Right: Dhows moored in Dubai's harbour regularly trade at ports such as Bombay and Aden (Yemen).

you will probably have to pay extra to use the tennis and/or squash courts.

There is also a government-managed **Women's Beach** on the headland at the western end of the Corniche. To get there take the Corniche west to the final roundabout by the Khalidia Palace Hotel and turn right onto the road that has a gate across it (the gate should be up). After 1.25 km, at the point where the road turns right, you'll see a guardhouse straight ahead. This is the entrance to the Women's Beach. The beach is open Saturday to Wednesday from 1 to 6 pm, Thursday from noon to 6 pm and Friday from 10 am to 6 pm.

Organised Tours

Abu Dhabi has little in the way of a formal tourist industry. Most of the UAE's tour companies are based in either Dubai or Sharjah. Net Tours is a Dubai-based company, but they do have a local phone number in Abu Dhabi (☎ 794 656, fax 721 188). Their brochure, however, only lists offerings from Dubai, so you will have to call to find out what, if anything, is available out of Abu Dhabi.

Places to Stay

There are no cheap hotels in Abu Dhabi. That's the bad news. The good news, as far as it goes, is that all of the following hotels can arrange transit and/or visit visas for travellers. They will generally charge Dh 300 to Dh 400 for this service and may also require a two or three night stay in the hotel. The rates quoted here are the hotels' rack rates. It will usually be possible to negotiate some sort of discount, particularly if you plan to stay more than a night or two. Service charges, where applicable, have been included in the prices.

The best hotel news since the last edition is that the Strand Hotel, one of the grimmest pits in the entire Gulf, has been torn down. However, that leaves the *Zakher Hotel* (☎ 341 940, fax 326 306) on Umm Al-Nar St as the only place in Abu Dhabi where you can get a room for under Dh 200 per night. Singles/doubles start at Dh 195.50/264.50,

including the service charge. Abu Dhabi's cheapest doubles are just down the street from the Zakher at the *Federal Hotel* (☎ 789 000, fax 794 728). Rooms are Dh 200/225.

The *Mina Hotel* (☎ 781 000, fax 791 000), at the intersection of the Corniche and Al-Meena St, is under the same management as the Federal but has higher rates. Singles/doubles cost Dh 250/350. The *Emirates Plaza Hotel* (☎ 722 000, fax 723 204) off Al-Meena St is slightly more expensive still at Dh 262.50/367.50.

The *Khalidia Palace Hotel* (☎ 662 470, fax 660 411) at the western end of the Corniche is one of the better value places in this price category. Rooms cost Dh 287.50/402.50. If you do not mind being somewhat removed from the centre, they offer a number of restaurants and a beach-front location. The *Park Residence* (☎ 742 000, fax 785 656) on Shaikh Khalifa Bin Zayed St has the same prices and a central location but none of the Khalidia Palace's accoutrements. The only other place in town offering rooms for under US$100 is the *Dana Hotel* (☎ 761 000, fax 766 650) on Zayed the Second St near the Meridien. Rooms cost Dh 300/350.

Further up-market are the *Centre Hotel Novotel* (☎ 333 555, fax 343 633) on Shaikh Hamdan Bin Mohammed St. Rooms are Dh 350/450 and the *Al-Ain Palace Hotel* (☎ 794 777, fax 795 713) near the eastern end of the Corniche at Dh 400/500. The *Al-Hamra Plaza Residence* (☎ 725 000, fax 766 228) has a good central location on Zayed the Second St. Rooms cost Dh 350/400. One traffic signal to the south-west you will find the *Holiday Inn* (☎ 335 335, fax 335 766) with rooms at Dh 517.50/632.50.

The very top end is represented by the usual collection of international chains:

Abu Dhabi Hilton (☎ 661 900, fax 669 696) near the west end of the Corniche. Singles/doubles cost Dh 650/750 plus a 16% service charge.
Abu Dhabi Inter-Continental (☎ 666 888, fax 669 153), just south of the western end of the Corniche. Singles/doubles start at Dh 610/710 plus 16%.

THE UNITED ARAB EMIRATES

Baynunah Hilton (☎ 327 777, fax 216 777), the huge blue tower on the Corniche west of the clock tower was, at the time of writing, the city's newest five-star property, and its tallest building. Rooms start at Dh 500/600 plus 15%, more if you want a sea view.

Le Meridien Abu Dhabi (☎ 776 666, fax 729 315) at the north-east end of the city centre. Singles/doubles from Dh 580/690 plus 16%.

Forte Grand Hotel (☎ 742 020, fax 742 552) on Umm Al-Nar St has rooms starting at Dh 750/850 plus 16%.

Sheraton Abu Dhabi (☎ 773 333, fax 725 149), at the east end of the Corniche. Singles/doubles cost Dh 700/800 plus 16%.

Places to Eat

Cheap & Medium-Priced If you are completely skint (which is a definite possibility, considering what Abu Dhabi's hotels cost) look for shawarma. Shawarma usually go for Dh 2.50 or Dh 3 each and can be found all over the centre. One good place for cheap food is the *Siraj Restaurant* (formerly the Tahla Tea Stall) on Zayed the Second St. It has hot tea for 75 fils a glass as well as a selection of sodas, cakes and sandwiches. There are a number of other small restaurants and tea shops on Zayed the Second St between Shaikh Rashid Bin Saeed Al-Maktoum St and East Rd.

One of Abu Dhabi's best value places is *Talk of the Town* on Shaikh Khalifa Bin Zayed St south-west of the intersection with Lulu St. Owned by the same group that owns Dubai's Golden Fork Restaurant it is, like its cousin in Dubai, a great deal. Dh 7 will get you an omelette or two pieces of fried chicken, in both cases soup, bread and fries are included. Burgers cost Dh 5 to Dh 7. The food and service are also great.

Cheap vegetarian Indian food can be found at the *Bhavna Restaurant* on Zayed the Second St. Samosas are Dh 2.50 each and the masala dosa (curried vegetables in a pastry shell) is quite good for Dh 3. They also carry a selection of Indian sweets.

A place you should definitely try is *Tarbouche* on Shaikh Hamdan Bin Mohammed St. The fare on offer is almost entirely Lebanese. Appetisers and main dishes cost Dh 6

to Dh 22 (most of the mezze are Dh 6 to Dh 8) and the freshly baked Arabic bread is served hot at your table. The food here is excellent and the staff (they all appear to be one family with pictures of the brothers and cousins in America adorning the walls) are very friendly. They also have a branch in the food court at the Abu Dhabi Cooperative Society supermarket near the Meridien Hotel. Cheaper, but arguably better, Lebanese fare in less fun surroundings can be found at *Maroosh* near the intersection of Shaikh Hamdan Bin Mohammed and As-Salam Sts.

One of the best biryanis I have ever had was at the *Sarawan Restaurant* on Zayed the Second St. The portions are large and, at Dh 8, an excellent value. I highly recommend it.

A good bet at any time of day is *La Brioche* on Shaikh Hamdan Bin Mohammed St. It is on the 1st floor of the same building that has the Emirates airline office at street level. It offers coffee and cappuccino which, at Dh 7 to Dh 10, is worth the extra dirham or two. For breakfast, croissants and various other pastries are available for Dh 3 to Dh 6, and there is a set breakfast menu for about Dh 10 to Dh 15. It also makes excellent sandwiches and offers a Dh 30 set lunch consisting of an appetiser, main course, cheese, fruit and coffee or tea from noon to 3 pm.

For cheap Chinese food, try the *Mandarin Restaurant* on Zayed the First St. It has generous combination plates starting at Dh 24 for a full meal, including a drink. Another option is *Foodlands* a Chinese/Indian restaurant on Zayed the Second St. The lentil soup (Dh 6) has an unusually spicy, almost Thai, flavour. Main dishes cost Dh 10 to Dh 25.

Expensive An interesting change of pace is *Bukharah* in the Hotel Regency, near the Sheraton. It bills itself as a Central Asian restaurant which, in practice, means that the menu features both Indian and Persian dishes with the emphasis on subtle combinations of spices rather than sheer heat. The dining room is a treat – the tables are laid with beautiful Iranian tablecloths from Isfahan –

and the service is fairly good. Main dishes cost Dh 15 to Dh 30.

A place worth visiting, even if you only go to look, is *Al-Dhafra* at the dhow wharf near the fish market. The complex, built around a series of traditional *barasti*-style houses, has two restaurants. The *Al-Mina Coffee Shop* specialises in local dishes including three different types of bread. A few metres away is *Al-Arish* a fancier place offering a huge buffet for Dh 45, Dh 95 if you include your choice of fresh fish. There is a playground for children and private booths (for families) overlooking the waterfront. It also offers a dinner buffet dhow cruise Sunday and Thursday nights at 8 pm for Dh 125.

Abu Dhabi has a number of expensive hotel restaurants. Rather bland, but wildly expensive, Mexican food is on offer at *El Sombrero* at the Sheraton Hotel. Count on spending Dh 100 or more per person. It might once have been worth the trip just for the nachos, but at Dh 38 a portion you can probably live without them.

The *Meridien Hotel* seems to be trying to find out how many restaurants it can cram into one hotel, the result is an enormous selection of all types of food, provided you are willing to splash out the money.

For up-market Chinese food, try the Chinese restaurants in the Centre Novotel and the Al-Ain Palace Hotel.

Entertainment

There's not much happening in Abu Dhabi; most people looking for entertainment spend their weekends elsewhere. Abu Dhabi is probably not as boring as its reputation but it has neither Dubai's energy nor its nightclub scene. Many of the restaurants and bars at the big hotels have live entertainment of typical hotel lounge variety.

The Tavern, the British-style pub at the Sheraton Hotel, is a good place for a drink. The closest approximation of a real sports bar is *The Island Exchange*, the bar on the 1st floor of the Forte Grand Hotel.

The Eldorado Cinema on Zayed the Second St, across from the El-Hamra Plaza Residence, shows western films.

Things to Buy

Al-Nasr St, especially the area around the AMEX office, has a number of shops with a good selection of Arabian souvenirs. Many of these are actually made elsewhere, generally in Egypt, Syria, Iran, India or Pakistan, so if you are looking for something specifically Emirati, as opposed to something vaguely Middle Eastern, be sure to ask. Oriental Carpet House & Antiques has a good selection, including pottery from Oman. It is next to the AMEX Office and should not be confused with the store on the corner of Al-Nasr St and Khalid Bin Al-Waleed St with more or less the same name.

Locally made crafts are available at the government-run Women Craft Centre south of the city centre. See the separate entry on the centre for more details.

If you feel like dropping the jaws of your friends back home head for Al-Sultan Honey Establishment, on Al-Nasr St across from the main entrance to the Cultural Foundation and Al-Husn Palace. They sell honey produced in Al-Ain and packaged in old Vimto bottles for Dh 400 to Dh 700 a bottle.

Getting There & Away

Air Abu Dhabi international airport (AUH) is on the mainland, about 30 km from the centre. You should be at the airport about 90 minutes before departure for short-haul flights (ie within the Gulf) and two hours before departure for flights to Europe and Asia. Telephone ☎ 757 611 for airport information. The airport's self-promotion efforts rival those of Dubai (raffles for Dh 500,000 cash are Abu Dhabi's staple promotion, much as the car raffles are a fixture at Dubai). Like Dubai, Abu Dhabi airport has a duty-free shop for arriving passengers. Unlike Dubai it has booze for sale on arrival.

Following is a sample of one-way and excursion return fares from Abu Dhabi with the minimum and maximum stay requirements. These are presented as guidelines only. Bear in mind that specials, discounting and other promotions often exist and you may be able to do somewhat better, particularly on the long-haul routes:

THE UNITED ARAB EMIRATES

To	One Way	Return	Min/Max
Bahrain	Dh 620	Dh 500	3/7 days
Dhahran	Dh 480	Dh 670	3/14 days
Doha	Dh 470	Dh 360	3/7 days
Jeddah	Dh 1050	Dh 1420	3/14 days
Kuwait	Dh 760	Dh 1040	3/14 days
London	Dh 3160	Dh 4510	10/90 days
Melbourne	Dh 6180	Dh 5780	14/90 days
Muscat	Dh 670	Dh 520	3/7 days
New York	Dh 3410	Dh 4680	14/90 days
Riyadh	Dh 630	Dh 880	3/14 days

The return fares quoted for Melbourne and New York are for the low season. During high season (mid-June to mid-October and mid-December to mid-January) these tickets will cost substantially more.

Following is a list of office addresses for some of the airlines flying to Abu Dhabi:

Air France
Al-Nasr St, near the AMEX office (☎ 215 810)
Air India
Abu Dhabi Travel Bureau building, Al-Ittihad Square (☎ 322 300)
Al-Yemen
Salem Travel Agency, on the corner of Shaikh Hamdan Bin Mohammed St and East Rd (☎ 335 028)
Biman Bangladesh
Shaikh Hamdan Bin Mohammed St, just west of the intersection with East Rd (☎ 325 124)
British Airways
Corner of Shaikh Khalifa Bin Zayed and Leewa Sts (☎ 341 328)
China Airlines
Salem Travel Agency, on the corner of Shaikh Hamdan Bin Mohammed St and East Rd (☎ 345 570)
Emirates
Shaikh Hamdan Bin Mohammed St, between East Rd and Bani Yaas St (☎ 315 888)
EgyptAir
Istiglal St, just west of Shaikh Rashid Bin Saeed Al-Maktoum St (☎ 344 777)
Ethiopian Airlines
Salem Travel Agency, on the corner of Shaikh Hamdan Bin Mohammed St and East Rd (☎ 333 153)
Garuda Indonesia
Abu Dhabi Travel Bureau building, Al-Ittihad Square (☎ 338 700)
Gulf Air
Corner of Shaikh Rashid Bin Saeed Al-Maktoum and Shaikh Hamdan Bin Mohammed Sts (☎ 332 600 or, 24 hours a day at the airport, ☎ 757 083)

Iran Air
Abu Dhabi Travel Bureau building, Al-Ittihad Square (☎ 338 700)
KLM
Abu Dhabi Travel Bureau building, Al-Ittihad Square (☎ 323 280)
Lufthansa
Al-Masaood Tower, 2nd floor (look for the Standard & Chartered Bank office at street level), Shaikh Hamdan Bin Mohammed St (☎ 213 200)
MEA (Middle East Airlines)
Leewa St, just south of the Corniche (☎ 339 000)
PIA (Pakistan International Airlines)
Shaikh Hamdan Bin Mohammed St, across from the Centre Hotel Novotel (☎ 302 6666)
Royal Brunei
Corner of Shaikh Khalifa Bin Zayed and Leewa Sts (☎ 316 100)
Royal Jordanian
Corner of Shaikh Khalifa Bin Zayed and Leewa Sts (☎ 321 832)
Saudia
Abu Dhabi Travel Bureau building, Al-Ittihad Square (☎ 351 400)
Singapore Airlines
Corner of Shaikh Khalifa Bin Zayed and Leewa Sts (☎ 221 110)
Syrianair
Salem Travel Agency, on the corner of Shaikh Hamdan Bin Mohammed St and East Rd (☎ 335 821)
Swissair
Leewa St, just south of the Corniche (☎ 343 430)
Turkish Airlines
Sultan Bin Yousuf & Sons, Shaikh Hamdan Bin Mohammed St, across from the Centre Hotel Novotel (☎ 302 6693)
Yemenia
Abu Dhabi Travel Bureau building, Al-Ittihad Square (☎ 338 700)

Bus The main bus station is on East Rd, south of the centre. Inter-city service is only available within the Abu Dhabi Emirate. To get to Dubai you have to take a taxi. Buses run to Al-Ain 15 times daily from early morning until about 9 pm (2½ hours, Dh 10), and to Ruwais (three hours, Dh 12) at 1 and 6 pm. There are also 15 buses per day to Medinat Zayed (Badr Zayed) (2½ hours, Dh 10). Change at Medinat Zayed for Liwa. To Sila (five hours, Dh 15), near the UAE's far western border, there are daily buses at 7.30 am and 1.30 pm.

Service-Taxi Service-taxis and minibuses leave from a station adjacent to the main bus station on East Rd. Minibuses carrying 14 passengers charge Dh 20 per person to Dubai. Taxis, carrying from five to seven people, charge Dh 30. Taxis also regularly go to Al-Ain (Dh 20) and Sharjah (Dh 30).

Car Car rental rates start at about Dh 140 to Dh 150 per day plus insurance, though you will probably be able to get some sort of discount on these rates if you ask for one. There are a number of rental places in the town centre. If you are planning to travel widely around the UAE by rented car it is probably best to stick to one of the larger agencies.

Getting Around

The Airport Bus No 901 runs from the main bus station to the airport around the clock, departing every 20 minutes (every 30 minutes between midnight and 6 am). The fare is Dh 3. Airport limos charge Dh 70 from the airport to the city and airport taxis Dh 40 to Dh 60. The taxis are orange and white (as opposed to regular Abu Dhabi taxis, which are gold and white) and, unlike the regular taxis, they have no meters. A regular taxi should cost around Dh 40 from the city centre.

Bus You will notice municipal buses running throughout Abu Dhabi. These are cheap – fares are only Dh 1 to Dh 4 depending on the distance travelled – but they are nearly useless for the traveller because they follow no fixed routes. Really! All of the buses originate at the main bus and service-taxi station on East Rd. From there they go down one of the three main roads (East Rd, Sheikh Rashid Bin Saeed Al-Maktoum Rd and the western Corniche) that lead back onto the mainland. The buses end up in various industrial zones and labourers' camps on the mainland where they turn around and head back into the souk. Outbound they take whatever road the driver feels like taking. On the way back they do the same thing, driving around the souk and

Corniche area until there are no passengers left on the bus, or only riders who want to go to the bus station. The driver then heads back to the bus station by whatever route seems easiest and that's where the trip ends.

There are no timetables either. The drivers seem to have a schedule of some sort but nobody at the bus company was able to explain it to me. As a senior official of the Public Transport Department told me, 'The policy of the Public Transportation Department is to give service just for the labourers. To help them get outside Abu Dhabi with a low rate'.

The only, limited, exception to this system is the airport bus, No 901 (see earlier). Even this bus, however, does not follow a set route on its way back into town. If you choose this method for getting in from the airport you should either get off at whatever location in the souk looks good, see if you can convince the driver to take you to a specific location in the centre, or wait until he takes you to the bus station.

Taxi Taxis are equipped with meters. A flag fall is Dh 2 and the meters turn over at 50 fils a click. The fares add up slowly, making taxis a reasonably affordable way to get around. Your main problem is likely to be that most of the drivers speak neither Arabic nor English. Urdu speakers, however, shouldn't have any trouble.

AL-AIN & BURAIMI

The Buraimi Oasis straddles the border between Abu Dhabi and Oman. There are a number of settlements in both parts of the oasis, but in the UAE the entire area is referred to by the name of the main town in Abu Dhabi's section: Al-Ain (pronounced so that it rhymes with 'main'). Buraimi technically refers to the entire oasis but is also used when referring to the Omani section.

In the days before the oil boom, the oasis was a five day overland journey by camel from Abu Dhabi. Today, the trip takes about two hours on a tree-lined freeway. Once in the oasis, you can cross freely between the UAE and Oman – people driving up from

Warning
If you have rented a car in the UAE, your insurance will not cover accidents occurring on Omani territory. If you are driving a car that you rented in Oman, you probably will not be allowed to take it through the Buraimi customs post.

Use of seat belts is mandatory in Oman and this is strictly enforced. The Royal Oman Police can, and will, hit you for a hefty fine – about Dh 100 or OR 10 payable on the spot – for violating this law. Speed limits are also fairly strictly enforced in Oman (unlike in the UAE). ■

Muscat pass through customs before reaching the Omani town of Buraimi – and it is this fact that makes the oasis so appealing.

Al-Ain is the birthplace of Shaikh Zayed, the ruler of Abu Dhabi, and he has lavished money on it. The Omani side of the oasis has not undergone the same treatment. Buraimi is comfortable but still very much a provincial town. The resulting contrasts make Al-Ain/Buraimi one of the most interesting places in either country to visit. (For details on how to visit Buraimi from Muscat see the Oman chapter.)

There is a lot to see in both Al-Ain and Buraimi and the area is a popular weekend destination from both Abu Dhabi and Dubai, from which it is roughly equidistant. One of its main attractions come summer is the dry air – a welcome change from the humidity of the coast.

History
The Buraimi Oasis is probably the longest inhabited part of what is now the UAE. The country's oldest known artefacts are potsherds from the 4th millennium BC which were found near Jabal Hafit, a short distance from the oasis. Digs near Al-Ain have also turned up a Bronze Age (3rd millennium BC) culture which may have had ties to the Umm An-Nar civilisation that then existed on the coast near modern Abu Dhabi.

As Arabia's climate became warmer, oases such as Buraimi became increasingly important. The population of Buraimi is known to have increased significantly during the 2nd and 3rd centuries AD, apparently as a result of migration to the oasis by tribes from the surrounding desert. By the 10th century Al-Ain, which was then called Tawwan, was a trading centre along one of Arabia's many caravan routes, a status which it retained into our era.

In the 18th century, the ancestors of today's Saudi Arabian royal family incorporated the oasis into what is now called the First Saudi Empire, a short-lived kingdom which covered even more of Arabia than the present Saudi state. The legacy of this period was Wahhabism, the puritanical strain of Islam practised in Saudi Arabia which, in a somewhat milder form, remains a strong influence in the Al-Ain/Buraimi area to this day.

Abu Dhabi's ruling Al-Nahyan family first moved to the oasis sometime in the 19th century, well after the founding of Abu Dhabi town. Since the early years of the 20th century, the family has ruled the oasis jointly with the Omanis, first with the imams who controlled the interior of Oman and, from the '50s, with the Muscat-based Omani sultans. The 18th century Saudi presence in Buraimi, however, led the Saudi government to claim the entire oasis for its kingdom in 1949. The Saudi claim was prompted by Aramco, the Saudi-based oil company, which wanted to drill for oil in the oasis.

In 1952 the Saudis occupied part of Buraimi. The question of sovereignty eventually went to an international arbitration panel in Geneva. When the talks collapsed in 1955, the British and the Al-Nahyan family took matters into their own hands. A Bedouin force led by Shaikh Zayed, who was then the governor of Abu Dhabi's portion of the oasis, along with the Trucial Oman Scouts, who were commanded by British officers, drove the Saudis out of Buraimi. However, the dispute continued on a lesser level for several more years. The current Abu Dhabi-Oman border was demarcated in 1966. Saudi Arabia formally dropped its claim to the area in 1974.

Orientation

The Al-Ain/Buraimi area can be very confusing, at least at first. All of the streets in Al-Ain look pretty much the same. Mercifully, they all have names now (this was not the case as recently as late 1993) – which makes navigation a lot easier. The streets in Buraimi still don't appear to have names, but there are fewer of them so getting around is not very difficult. The two cities straddle the UAE-Oman border and everyone can flow freely back and forth between the two countries without a customs check. The Omani customs post is about 53 km down the road to Muscat.

Basically, Al-Ain wraps around an arm of Omani territory with most of Al-Ain's business district lying just south of the border. To get to Dubai or to some of Al-Ain's suburbs from the centre you drive through Oman for about four km before emerging back into the UAE. The advantage of all this for the budget traveller is that it allows you to stay at the area's one cheapish hotel which is just across the Omani border in Buraimi. It's also an easy way to see a little of Oman without hassling with visas. Most of the area's services, however, are in Al-Ain which is much larger and more modern than Buraimi.

The main streets in Al-Ain are Khalifa Ibn Zayed St and Zayed Ibn Sultan St, both of which run roughly east-west. Khalifa Ibn Zayed St is also the road to both Abu Dhabi and the airport. The main north-south cross streets are Abu Bakr Al-Siddiq St, which extends into Buraimi, and Al-Ain St. The two landmarks you need to know for navigational purposes are the clock tower and Coffeepot roundabouts.

Distances in both Al-Ain and Buraimi are large. You could, in theory, walk from the bus or taxi station in Al-Ain to the one semicheap hotel which is just over the Omani border, but with any luggage at all it would be a hell of a hike, especially when it is hot, which is most of the time. The three big hotels are only accessible by car or taxi. Some of the interesting sites, like Jabal Hafit, also require your own transport.

Information

There is no tourist office in either city but it's fairly easy to find most of the things worth seeing in Al-Ain by following the big purple road signs. Buraimi has no tourist signs but the market and both of the old forts are adjacent to the main road which runs across Omani territory (the extension of Abu Bakr Al-Siddiq St).

Money There are lots of banks in Al-Ain near the clock tower roundabout and the GPO. The area around the Grand Mosque also has several moneychangers and a Thomas Cook office. Try the UAE Exchange Centre. In Oman you'll see several banks along the main road. Both UAE dirhams and Omani riyals are accepted on both sides of the border at a standard rate of approximately OR 1 = Dh 10.

Post & Communications Al-Ain's GPO and telephone office are side by side near the clock tower roundabout. The GPO is open Saturday to Wednesday from 8 am to 8 pm, Thursday from 8 am to 6 pm and Friday from 8 to 11 am. The ETISALAT office is open every day from 7 am to midnight.

Buraimi's post office is open Saturday to Wednesday from 8 am to 2 pm, and Thursday from 8 to 11 am. It is closed Friday. The Buraimi post office's sign is only in Arabic, but it's more or less across the street from the Yameen Restaurant.

The phone systems of the two cities are separate. Thus, if you're in the Hotel Al-Buraimi and want to ring someone 200m away in Al-Ain, it's an international call and will be billed as such. Do not be deceived by the fact that many payphones in the two cities look the same. Apparently, ETISALAT and Oman's GTO buy their payphones from the same supplier but they don't accept the same coins.

The UAE telephone area code for Al-Ain is 03. There are no telephone area codes in Oman.

Emergency In Al-Ain, the phone number for the police is ☎ 999, ambulance, ☎ 998 and the fire department, ☎ 997. In Oman dial ☎ 999 for the police, an ambulance or to report a fire.

Eastern Fort & the Al-Ain Museum

The museum and fort are in the same compound, south-east of the overpass near the Coffeepot roundabout. The museum is open Sunday to Wednesday from 8 am to 1 pm, Thursday from 8 am to noon and Friday from 9 to 11.30 am. It reopens every afternoon from 3.30 to 5.30 pm (4.30 to 6.30 pm from May to October) and is closed all day Saturday. Museum admission costs 50 fils (if somebody is at the door to collect it).

As you enter the museum, take a look at the Bedouin diwan set up to the left of the manager's office. It's a display of what the reception area of a traditional Bedouin tent or home looks like. This particular room is also used to welcome visiting VIPs (which may be why it always looks like it only lacks hot coals for the coffee to be served).

Moving to the right, the first gallery has an interesting display of photographs of Al-Ain, Abu Dhabi and Liwa taken in the 1960s. It's striking to see how quickly the area has developed. The gallery also includes exhibits on traditional education and a small but quite good selection of Bedouin jewellery. Study the jewellery carefully if you are planning to purchase some in one of the hotels or in the Buraimi souk.

Around to the left, the next gallery has reconstructions of everyday life in the pre-oil days. Note how most of the figures are dressed more like Omanis than like Gulf Arabs (ie wearing turbans instead of the *gutra* and *agal* headdress). The opposite wall has a large display of weapons.

The third gallery has more weapons, musical instruments and some stuffed examples of the local desert birds. The wall back near the entrance houses a display of some of the decorations Shaikh Zayed has received over the years. The collection is rather eclectic, including both the Order of Isabel the Catholic, bestowed on the Shaikh by King Juan Carlos I of Spain, and a bullet 'from the Palestinian Commando Lyla

Khalid' (a leader of the Popular Front for the Liberation of Palestine's guerilla squad that hijacked three aircraft to Jordan in September 1970 and, in so doing, touched off a bloody civil war in that country).

The other two galleries house a chronological display on the region's archaeology.

The Eastern Fort, next to the museum, is open to the public, but there's not a lot to see beyond the old cannon in the courtyard. The fort was built in 1910 by Shaikh Sultan Bin Zayed Al-Nahyan and was the birthplace of his son, Shaikh Zayed.

Livestock Souk

You can see the entrance to the livestock market from the museum/fort parking lot. It's a big market and an interesting place to wander around, and an excellent spot to go shopping for sheep and goats (a live sheep costs about Dh 120). The souk attracts Bedouins and townspeople from all over the southern UAE and northern Oman.

The best time to be there is early in the morning (before 9 am) when the trading is at its heaviest.

Old Prison

The prison is the fort-like building on Zayed Ibn Sultan St near the Coffeepot roundabout. It is open rather erratic hours because the people living around the prison courtyard occasionally decide they don't want any visitors and shut the gate. If you get into the courtyard, it is usually possible to climb to the roof of the prison tower for a view out over the oasis and the camel market (one reader, however, has warned of unofficial

Camel Market

Al-Ain's camel market is immediately behind the prison. It's quite a small market but worth visiting for local colour. It is open from early morning until about noon every day, and the best time to visit is as early in the day as possible, before the heat intensifies both the dust and the smell. ■

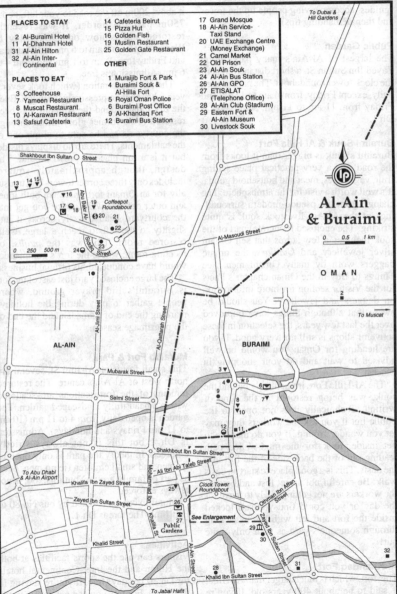

PLACES TO STAY
2 Al-Buraimi Hotel
11 Al-Dhahrah Hotel
31 Al-Ain Hilton
32 Al-Ain Inter-
     Continental

PLACES TO EAT
3 Coffeehouse
7 Yameen Restaurant
8 Muscat Restaurant
10 Al-Karawan Restaurant
13 Safsuf Cafeteria

14 Cafeteria Beirut
15 Pizza Hut
16 Golden Fish
19 Muslim Restaurant
25 Golden Gate Restaurant

OTHER
1 Muraijib Fort & Park
4 Buraimi Souk &
    Al-Hilla Fort
5 Royal Oman Police
6 Buraimi Post Office
9 Al-Khandaq Fort
12 Buraimi Bus Station

17 Grand Mosque
18 Al-Ain Service-
     Taxi Stand
20 UAE Exchange Centre
     (Money Exchange)
21 Camel Market
22 Old Prison
23 Al-Ain Souk
24 Al-Ain Bus Station
26 Al-Ain GPO
27 ETISALAT
     (Telephone Office)
28 Al-Ain Club (Stadium)
29 Eastern Fort &
     Al-Ain Museum
30 Livestock Souk

Al-Ain & Buraimi

0   0.5   1 km

To Dubai &
Hill Gardens

OMAN

To Muscat

AL-AIN

BURAIMI

Shakhbout Ibn Sultan Street

Abu Bakr Al-

Coffeepot
Roundabout

Siddiq Street

0   250   500 m

Al-Masoudi Street

Al-Jimi Street

Al-Qattarah Street

Mubarak Street

Selmi Street

Shakhbout Ibn Sultan Street

Ali Ibn Abi Taleb Street

Mohammad Ibn

Clock Tower
Roundabout

Othman Ibn Affan
Street

See Enlargement

To Abu Dhabi &
Al-Ain Airport

Khalifa Ibn Zayed Street

Zayed Ibn Sultan Street

Khalifa St

Public
Gardens

Zayed Ibn Sultan Street

Khalid Street

Al-Ain Street

Khalid Ibn Sultan Street

To Jabal Hafit

'guides' accompanying people up the tower and then demanding tips).

Public Garden
The largest of Al-Ain's many parks is on Zayed Ibn Sultan St, a short distance west of the clock tower roundabout. The park is open daily, except Friday, from 4 am to 11 pm and Friday from 11 am to 11 pm. Admission is Dh 1.

Buraimi Souk & Al-Hilla Fort
Buraimi's souk is bigger than it looks from the road. It's a very practical place selling fruit, vegetables, meat and household goods. It's well worth a visit for the atmosphere. The change from the pseudo-modern surroundings of the Al-Ain livestock souk is quite striking. The enclosed (concrete) part of the souk includes a few stores that sell Omani silver jewellery and *khanjars*, the ornate daggers worn by many Omani men. See Things to Buy in the Oman chapter's Facts for the Visitor section for more information on daggers and jewellery. You should be aware that although things have improved over the last few years, the selection in these souvenir shops is still not very good. If you are heading for Oman you would be well advised to wait and do your shopping in Muscat.

The Al-Hilla Fort, immediately behind the souk, was being restored at the time of writing. Technically it is not open to the public but if you ask the workers they may let you wander around. If you do manage to get inside, look for the mud-walled path leading out of the back side of the fort into the oasis. This is a good place to start an oasis walk. Be careful not to get lost and be sure the workers are not getting ready to leave for the day or you could find yourself locked inside the fort and left with bushwhacking through someone's yard as your only route out!

Al-Khandaq Fort
This fort, which is much larger than Al-Hilla, is said to be about 400 years old. If you're coming from the centre of Al-Ain you'll see it about 200m off the road to your left, about 750m past the border. It was recently restored and is now open Saturday to Wednesday from 8 am to 6 pm and Thursday and Friday from 8 am to 1 pm and from 4 to 6 pm. Admission is free.

The fort's restoration (which took several years) has been impressively thorough. Even the dry moat around the structure has been restored to its former glory. Stroll through the courtyards and be sure to climb one of the battlements. There are no displays inside, but it is a fun place to prowl around. The design, though approximately square, includes only three corner towers but, unusually for an Omani fort, there are both inner and outer defence walls. Once you get into the courtyard head directly across it and slightly to the left to reach a large, well-restored room. This was the *majlis*, or meeting room, where the fort's commander would have conducted his official business.

The large enclosed yard just east of the fort is Buraimi's Eid prayer ground, where people gather to pray during the holidays marking the end of Ramadan and the end of the pilgrimage season.

Muraijib Fort & Park
This small fort is on Al-Jimi St, several km north-west of Al-Ain's centre. The restored remains of the fortifications are scattered within a beautifully landscaped garden. The garden is open daily from 4 to 11 pm (10 am to 11 pm Fridays and holidays). Admission is Dh 1 but this is not always strictly enforced. In theory the park is only open to women and small children (ie no men, even as part of family groups) but this, too, is not always enforced.

Muraijib can be reached by bus No 80 to Hili Jimi. The fare is Dh 1.

Activities
Visitors can use the sports facilities at both the Hilton and the Inter-Continental hotels for Dh 30 per day (free, if you're staying in the hotel). For this you can get access to the pool, sauna, fitness centre and game room.

Booking tennis or squash courts or a round of golf (at the Hilton) costs extra.

Golf It took years, but the Hilton finally got its golf course up and running. The course is a nine hole par three course. The shortest hole is 45 yards and the longest a mere 107 yards. Greens fees are Dh 50 for the first nine holes and Dh 25 to play a second nine. You can rent clubs for Dh 20.

Camel Racing Al-Ain's camel racetrack is about 20 km from the centre on the road to Abu Dhabi. Races usually take place early on Friday mornings during the winter months, though there may be racing on other days as well. Check with Al-Ain Camel Safaris or ask at one of the big hotels.

Organised Tours

Al-Ain Camel Safaris (☎ (050) 470 700 or (050) 477 268) offers a variety of desert trips, most of them including a visit to Qarn Bint Saud, an archaeological site far out in the desert and accessible only by camel or 4WD. The trips range from short one hour rides into the desert to overnight trips including dinner and breakfast. They have an office in the lobby of the Hilton. Their most interesting offering is an overnight camping trip where you ride camels both on the way out and back and sleep in a Bedouin tent. This costs Dh 450 per person. The best part about this company's offerings is that they do not require a group of four to six people. They will even do the desert camping trip for just one or two people at the same per person price!

Most of the tour companies operating out of Dubai, Abu Dhabi and Sharjah also run trips to Al-Ain.

Places to Stay

Al-Ain and Buraimi do not have a huge selection of accommodation. There are four hotels in the two towns and only one of them remotely qualifies as cheap. This is the *Al-Dhahrah Hotel* (☎ 650 492, fax 650 881). It's a good place, sitting almost smack on the border, and will be on your right if you enter

Oman from the centre of Al-Ain. Rooms cost Dh 130/160 or OR 13.700/16.900. The Al-Dhahrah has a small restaurant but does not serve alcohol. The other hotel on the Omani side of the oasis is the *Al-Buraimi Hotel* (☎ 652 010, fax 652 011; in the UAE call ☎ (050) 474 954), which you can find easily enough by following the blue-and-white signs strategically positioned throughout the Omani part of the oasis. Singles/doubles are Dh 351/427 (OR 37/45) plus 15% tax and service charge. There are sometimes summer specials, with discounts of up to 50%. Unlike the Al-Dhahrah, alcohol is served. Neither of the hotels on the Omani side of the border can sponsor a UAE visa for you.

Back in the UAE, your choices are the *Al-Ain Hilton* (☎ 686 666, fax 686 888) and the *Al-Ain Inter-Continental* (☎ 686 686, fax 686 766). Both charge Dh 420/500 plus 16% for singles/doubles, but discounts are usually available. Both hotels often have weekend specials on Thursdays and Fridays with rooms at Dh 275 plus 16%. Both hotels can arrange visas for travellers to the UAE. Note, however, that if you have them send the visa to Dubai or Abu Dhabi airport they will also charge you several hundred dirhams for a limo ride to Al-Ain, whether you use the limo to get to Al-Ain or not (the rationale for this is that the car and driver have to go to the airport to drop off the visa).

Far to the south of Al-Ain there is one more hotel, the *Rest House* (☎ 838 333, fax 838 900) at the Ayn Al-Fayda resort complex. It is rather remote (alcohol is not served at Ayn Al-Fayda), but the rooms are remarkably good and fairly cheap. Singles/doubles cost Dh 110/165, including breakfast.

Places to Eat

Al-Ain The best area for cheap food is near the Grand Mosque and the clock tower roundabout. The *Muslim Restaurant*, just north of the overpass on Abu Bakr Al-Siddiq is definitely recommended. Offering the usual fare of rice with mutton, chicken or fish for Dh 7, it also makes very good hadas (a spicy lentil paste) for Dh 3 and bakes its own bread on the premises. *Cafeteria Beirut* on Khalifa Ibn Zayed St has excellent shawarma and also offers ta'amiya (falafel), sodas and fresh juice.

There are a number of cheap to medium-priced places on Khalifa Ibn Zayed St. Try the *Golden Fish* for fish. Next door, the *Al-Ramla Restaurant* has cheap biryanis and chicken curry.

For more up-market eating, there is the *Golden Gate Restaurant* (about a block west of the Golden Fish and on the same side of the street) which serves Chinese and Filipino food. Main dishes cost Dh 15 to Dh 30. Another good bet is *The Hut*, a coffee shop on Khalifa Ibn Zayed St near the large *Pizza Hut*. It offers good cappuccino, latte and other coffee drinks as well as a wide selection of cakes. At Dh 5 for a cappuccino the prices are a bit high, but the surroundings make up for it.

For alcohol and more expensive fare, you have to head for the hotels. *Paco's*, at the Hilton, has surprisingly good Mexican food with main dishes at about Dh 30. The Hilton's Persian restaurant, *Al-Khayam* is a bit disappointing, as well as being rather expensive. Most main dishes cost Dh 35 to Dh 45. The Inter-Continental has a Thai-run fish restaurant with a very wide selection. Prices are by the kg. The *Horse & Jockey Club Pub* at the Inter-Continental is the best bar in town and usually has good pub meals on offer.

Buraimi Buraimi has fewer eating places than Al-Ain. You will probably find your options limited to the standard cheap fare of a helping of biryani rice with fish, chicken or mutton for about Dh 10/OR 1. Try the *Al-Karawan Restaurant* and the *Muscat Restaurant*, both opposite the turn-off to the Al-Khandaq Fort. On Buraimi's main commercial street, the *Yameen Restaurant* has more of the same.

Entertainment
Paco's at the Hilton, and the *Horse & Jockey Club Pub* at the Inter-Continental, have singers and the Inter-Continental has a disco.

There's also a full range of sports facilities at both hotels (see Activities earlier in this chapter).

Things to Buy
There are (expensive) shops in the lobbies of the Hilton and the Inter-Continental hotels selling Omani jewellery and other souvenirs. You can also buy these things in the Buraimi souk where they will definitely cost less but are also likely to be in much worse condition. The Buraimi souk used to be a terrible place to shop for souvenirs but several new shops have opened up in the last couple of years. If you want to buy a khanjar, a traditional Omani dagger, during a UAE visit this is by far the best place to look (see the Oman chapter for information on buying khanjars and Omani silver jewellery), though everything on sale in the Buraimi souk can be purchased more cheaply in Muscat.

Another place worth looking around is the grandiosely named People Heritage Revival Association, on the spur road that leads to the gate of Hili Gardens. It's really a small flea market with, among other things, locally made pottery for sale. It's also worth a look for the barasti houses that shelter a number of the stalls.

Getting There & Away
Air The UAE's newest airport – Al-Ain International – is approximately 20 km west of the centre. To get there take the Abu Dhabi road out of the centre until you see signs for the airport. For airport information call ☎ 855 555, ext 2211.

At the time of writing the Al-Ain airport was still very new and the carriers serving it were operating what an airport official described as 'temporary' schedules, so what follows is definitely subject to change. Gulf Air offers direct service from Al-Ain to Amman, Bahrain, Beirut, Cairo, Damascus, Doha, Karachi and Muscat. EgyptAir flies twice each week from Al-Ain to Cairo and there is also twice-weekly service to Amman on Royal Jordanian. PIA has one flight each week to Karachi and one to Lahore.

Bus Buses run from Al-Ain to Abu Dhabi (2½ hours, Dh 10) 15 times per day starting around 6 am with the last trip at about 9.30 pm. The bus station is behind the Al-Ain Cooperative Society's supermarket.

Oman's bus company, ONTC, has three buses a day to and from the Ruwi station in Muscat via Sohar. The buses leave from a parking lot across from the Al-Dhahrah Hotel at 7 am and 1 and 3 pm. The 7 am and 3 pm trips take about six hours. The 1 pm bus is an express service which reaches Muscat in just over 4½ hours. The trip to Muscat costs OR 3.600. Tickets can be purchased from the driver. To take this bus you will need an Omani visa which allows you to enter the country by land. Expatriates resident in Oman will need a Road Permit. The Omani customs post is about 53 km from the border.

Service-Taxi Al-Ain's taxi station is in the big parking lot behind the Grand Mosque. Taxis take four or seven passengers to Dubai (Dh 30) and Abu Dhabi (Dh 20). The trip takes about two hours to either city. You can also occasionally find cabs from Al-Ain to Fujairah (Dh 40) but you should not count on this. A few service-taxis going to the same destinations can also be found around the bus station. Service-taxis leave when they are full.

Car If you want to rent a car, head for the rental desks at the Hilton or the Inter-Continental. There are also several rental agencies in Al-Ain near the clock tower roundabout. At the time of writing there were no car rental facilities at the newly opened Al-Ain airport.

Getting Around
The Airport Bus No 500 is an express service that runs every 30 minutes, 24 hours a day, between the bus station and the airport. The fare is Dh 3 and the trip takes about 40 minutes. Bus No 130 also goes to the airport for Dh 3 but it is a regular service and takes about an hour. Airport limos charge Dh 40 for the trip into Al-Ain (Dh 50 to Ayn Al-

Fayda). A taxi to or from Al-Ain running on the meter should cost about Dh 25.

Bus Al-Ain has a fairly reasonable bus system once you figure it out. The trick is to know the right route. The route numbers given here may change, but the routes themselves are less likely to do so. All buses run roughly half-hourly from 6 am to midnight. All fares are Dh 1 except to Ayn Al-Fayda and the airport, both of which are Dh 3.

You cannot get to the Inter-Continental Hotel by bus, but bus Nos 10 to Defence (difa'a), No 70 to Mezaid, and No 120 to Umm Ghafa will take you to the Hilton. Bus No 110 goes to Ayn Al-Fayda. The Ayn Al-Fayda bus also goes to the zoo, as does bus No 60 to Zakhe. Hili Gardens and Hili Fun City can be reached via bus Nos 80 (Hili Jimi), 100 (Hili Garden) and 203 (Shueib Fakat). Bus No 80 also goes to Muraijib.

There are no local buses in Buraimi.

Taxis The Al-Ain taxis have meters; use them to avoid arguments over the fare with the Omani taxi drivers whose vehicles are not equipped with meters.

Al-Ain's taxis charge Dh 2 for a flag fall and 50 fils for each additional km. If you want to go somewhere like Jabal Hafit, however, you'll have to arrange it in advance with the driver. Count on paying about Dh 40 for the trip to Jabal Hafit and back.

AROUND AL-AIN
Jabal Hafit
The views from the top of this mountain are well worth the effort. The summit is about 30 km by road from the centre of Al-Ain (a taxi should make the journey for about Dh 40 round trip after a bit of bargaining).

From the clock tower roundabout head south toward the Al-Ain Club, crossing the bridge. Follow the signs for Ain Al-Fayda and later on Al-Wagan. The turn-off (a left if you are coming from the centre) is about 15 km from the centre and is well marked.

There are no buses to Jabal Hafit, though the Ayn Al-Fayda bus (No 110) will take you

as far as the turn-off from the highway to the mountain.

Ayn Al-Fayda

Ayn Al-Fayda is a resort south of the oasis 1.5 km beyond the Jabal Hafit turn-off. The *ayn*, or spring, is at the foot of the far side of the mountain. The area is a resort favoured mostly by expatriate Arab families. The spring itself is a sulphur pool which is not suitable for swimming. There is a swimming pool, hotel (see Places to Stay), bowling alley, game room and a restaurant. There are also a lot of children running around everywhere making lots of noise.

Ayn Al-Fayda is the terminus for Bus No 110. The fare from the bus station is Dh 3.

Hili Gardens

This combination public park and archaeological site is about eight km north of the centre of Al-Ain, off the Dubai road. The site is open daily from 4 to 11 pm (holidays from 10 am to 10 pm). Admission is Dh 1.

The main attraction is the **Round Structure** which is about 100m straight on from the park entrance. It is a 3rd millennium BC tomb, possibly connected with the Umm An-Nar culture. It was discovered by a group of Danish archaeologists in 1962, excavated during the late '60s and restored to its present form in 1973.

To reach Hili from the centre, take the Dubai Rd (through Oman) and follow the signs for Hili and Dubai until the purple 'tourist' signs appear. Look for signs directing you to 'Hili Archaeological Site'. The park can be reached via bus No 80 to Hili Jimi, bus No 203 to Shueib Fakat or bus No 100 to Hili Gardens. The fare is Dh 1.

Hili Fun City & Ice Rink

The amusement park (☎ 845 542) and skating rink are a few km down the road from Hili gardens. They are open Sunday to Wednesday from 4 to 10 pm, Thursday from 4 to 11 pm and Fridays and holidays from 9 am to 10 pm. Both places are closed Saturday. Tuesday and Wednesday are for women and small children only. Admission is Dh 10

and everyone over the age of three has to have a ticket.

The ice rink (☎ 845 542, ext 224) keeps the same hours as the amusement park. Admission, including skate rental, is Dh 10 on weekdays and Dh 15 on Fridays and holidays. Admission is only Dh 3 if you bring your own skates.

The same buses that run to Hili Gardens go here too. The fare is Dh 1.

Zoo

Al-Ain's Zoo, one of the better ones in the Gulf, is south of town. It is open daily from 7 am to 5.30 pm. Admission is Dh 2. It has indigenous species including Arabian oryx and gazelle, saluki dogs and bustards. It also has kangaroos, pygmy hippos, vultures etc. It is large and somewhat confusing in its layout. Just wandering around is probably your best bet, but if you want to see something in particular take a moment to study the map by the entrance before setting off.

The zoo can be reached via bus No 110 to Ayn Al-Fayda or bus No 60 to Zakhe.

RUWAIS

There's no real reason to visit this gigantic industrial complex 250 km west of Abu Dhabi unless business takes you here. The industrial complex and the oil terminal at nearby **Jabal Dhanna** are only accessible to those with proper passes. Without a pass you are limited to the bus stop, which is by the turn-off for the main non-Adnoc workers' camp, and the Ruwais Housing Complex, where Adnoc and its associated companies' employees hang their hard hats. The bus fare to Abu Dhabi is Dh 12.

The only available accommodation is at the *Dhafra Beach Hotel* (☎ (081) 71600, fax (081) 71002), an obscenely overpriced place near the main gate for the Jabal Dhanna oil terminal. The hotel caters mainly to people visiting the companies in Ruwais and to those down from Saudi Arabia for a drink or three (the hotel's brochure helpfully notes that the Aramco camp at Dhahran is only 6½ hours away by car). Singles/doubles cost Dh 335/470 plus a 16% service charge and you should not expect any discounts. When I was there the hotel was having trouble with its hot water.

The hotel's food is also expensive. Those on a budget might consider self-catering from the supermarket behind the East Mosque in the Ruwais Housing Complex or having a biryani at one of the small Indian places by the oil terminal gate or on the main road. Back at the hotel the *Falcon Bar* offers the area's only nightlife. Those staying long enough to make use of it should purchase a book of beer chits from the bartender. Each chit is good for one pint and they wind up costing a few dirhams less per pint than paying over the bar. The hotel's saving grace is that it does have decent sports facilities including tennis, squash and one of those all-sand golf courses that seem to be unique to Arabia.

SILA

If you thought the trip out to Ruwais was bleak wait until you see the road to Sila. The 100 km of desert separating the UAE's main oil port from this border town is some of the most monotonous desert I've ever seen and has absolutely nothing to recommend it.

Sila itself is little more that a way-station on the road to Saudi Arabia and Qatar. The UAE border post is another 18 km to the west. The town offers a small ETISALAT office, a gas station, a couple of small grocery stores and a government-run *Rest House* with bare but adequate rooms for Dh 60 per night, single or double. The rest house also has a restaurant, where Dh 14 will get you a biryani or curry dinner including vegetables, fries and salad. Another decent place for a meal is the small restaurant/grocery store next to the Adnoc gas station that will be on your left if you are coming from Abu Dhabi. It only has a sign in Arabic (which says 'groceries and restaurant'). The biryanis aren't quite as large as the ones at the rest house, but they only cost Dh 7.

Gluttons for punishment can ride the bus out here from Abu Dhabi for only Dh 15, though why anyone would want to do so is a mystery to me. If you do arrive by, or plan

to leave by, bus you should hang out at the police post at the eastern edge of town. Bus tickets can be purchased from the driver.

A right turn at Sila's one roundabout and another five km of driving brings you to **Baya Sila** which has an impressive copper-domed mosque and long stretches of quiet, eerie coastline.

MADINAT ZAYED

Madinat Zayed, also called Badr Zayed, is the administrative centre for the huge desert region that includes the Liwa Oasis. It lies some 50 km south of the coast road along a stretch of tarmac that takes you through one of Abu Dhabi's main onshore oil production areas. There is nothing to see in Madinat Zayed itself but it makes a useful base for exploring the Liwa area, especially if you need a hotel room and the Liwa rest house is full. If you are planning a camping trip to the desert, Madinat Zayed is your last opportunity to buy provisions.

The town stretches about eight km along the road linking Liwa to the coast. You'll know that you've arrived because the asphalt changes colour and the road widens and acquires a median as it passes through Madinat Zayed. Everything of consequence to the traveller is concentrated along the northern three km or so of this main road. Venture off it and you will discover that there is very little to Madinat Zayed once you get about 500m from the main north-south road. The main cross street is the one by the Ruler's Representative's Court. The taxi stand and bus station are both just south of this building and across the road from it, the one hotel is about two km in the other direction. The telephone area code for Madinat Zayed is 088.

The only place to stay is the *Rest House* (☎ 46281) run by Abu Dhabi National Hotels Company. All the rooms cost DH 165, single or double. The rooms range in size from moderate to quite large and are a good deal. The rest house also has a restaurant offering decent but dull food at fairly good prices. Main dishes cost around Dh 15, burgers Dh 5 to Dh 7 and breakfast can be had for Dh 10 or less. If you're looking for a cheap biryani try the *Beda Zayed Restaurant*, which is more or less opposite the taxi stand. The biryani rice is very good, though the chicken was rather bony and the mutton looked like something to avoid. Still, it's one of the most popular small eateries in town and, thus, worth a try.

There are 15 buses per day from Abu Dhabi to Madinat Zayed (2½ hours, Dh 10) and a similar number running back to Abu Dhabi. There are also nine buses daily and 12 on Fridays, from Madinat Zayed to Liwa (one hour, Dh 4). These run roughly every two hours from 7 am until 9.30 pm. The extra Friday buses are all evening trips. Shared taxis cluster at a lay-by near the bus station and run to Abu Dhabi (Dh 15) and Liwa (Dh 10) whenever they fill up, which is more often than you might think. Bear in mind that filling a service-taxi out from Abu Dhabi is likely to be a slower job that filling an Abu Dhabi-bound vehicle in Madinat Zayed.

LIWA OASIS

The Liwa Oasis, ancestral home of Abu Dhabi's ruling Al-Nahayan family, has long been a popular weekend getaway spot for Emiratis and expats alike. Some tour companies now also offer trips to this remote area whose growing popularity is attested to by the huge new hotel that was under construction at the time of writing. With the extension of the asphalt roads deep into the desert it has now become possible to see some of Liwa's wondrous desert scenery without a 4WD. Indeed, you could even get a perfectly decent look at Liwa's famous scenery from the window of a bus if you don't have, or can't afford, to hire a car. If you have a weekend trip in mind, and you do not plan to camp, advance reservations at the rest house are highly recommended.

Liwa does not fit the standard postcard image of an oasis. Lying on the edge of the Empty Quarter its main attractions are its dunes. Liwa's secret is that while the surface environment is hostile, quite a lot of water lies just below the surface, often at depths of only a few metres. Liwa is not a single stand

of greenery, like the huge Al-Hasa Oasis in eastern Saudi Arabia, rather it is a collection of small villages spread out over a 150 km arc of land.

Coming from Madinat Zayed the road begins as a fairly straight and flat route, but as you approach the oasis it begins to rise, fall and curve. Many of the areas just south of Madinat Zayed have been given over to desert agriculture projects. In one place, as you drive south, a rolling green field (a government-run fodder farm) will appear on your right, continuing for over five km and stretching away from the road for as far as you can see while small dunes and a bit of scrub growth fill the view to your left. The desert also becomes progressively more reddish in colour as you move south.

About 60 km from Madinat Zayed you reach **Mizaira'a** where the road from Madinat Zayed and the coast ends in a roundabout that forms a T-junction. The Liwa bus station will be on the near right-hand side of this roundabout if you approach it from Madinat Zayed. Opposite it, on the east side of the roundabout, are a number of small shops and a few restaurants.

The bus station has nine buses per day to Madinat Zayed with an additional three runs late Friday afternoon and early Friday evening (one hour, Dh 4). Two local routes serve the oasis communities, and provide those without their own transport with a chance to get a look at the scenery. The more interesting route goes 64 km east from the bus station to the village of **Hamim** (Dh 3), where the pavement ends and the bus turns around. This is a spectacular ride through some truly dramatic desert scenery. The other route, 40 km west to **Karima** (Dh 2) is flatter, more open and, thus, less interesting. Though the bus turns around in Karima the pavement continues another seven km or so to **Arada**. Each of the local buses makes nine trips per day. Going out and back will take about two to 2½ hours.

Until the new hotel opens (and it has the look of a hotel that will be very expensive) the only place to stay in Liwa is the Abu Dhabi National Hotels Company *Rest House*

(☎ (088) 22075, fax (088) 29311). Book ahead if you plan a weekend visit – it only has 20 rooms and these tend to fill up quickly. The rest house is about seven km west of the bus station along the Arada road, past the new hotel. Rooms cost Dh 165 a single or double, including breakfast. You can also eat at the rest house, but a much better bet is *Metieb Mohd. Restaurant* across the roundabout from the bus station. Its excellent biryanis cost only Dh 8.

Dubai

In all the Gulf, there is no place quite like Dubai. Dubai's wealth is founded on trade, not oil. It is one of the last bastions of anything-goes capitalism; sort of an Arab version of Hong Kong. What opium was to the growth of Hong Kong in the late 19th century, gold was to Dubai in the 1960s. Oil, when it was discovered in 1966, merely contributed to trade profits and speeded up modernisation.

The trade passing through Dubai is now for the most part legal. The city remains first and foremost a trading port and most of the local government's activity is directed toward promoting Dubai as a business centre and protecting the city's status as the Gulf's leading entrepôt. Among the seven emirates which make up the UAE, Dubai has fought the hardest to preserve its independence and to minimise the power of the country's federal institutions.

There isn't actually a lot to see in Dubai, but you will not find a more easy-going place anywhere in the Gulf – or a place with a better nightlife. Spend a few days wandering through the souks and along the waterfront to take in the city's atmosphere. True, there is almost nothing 'old' in Dubai, but it is the one place in the Gulf where that hardly seems to matter.

History
Dubai's history really begins in the 1830s when the city broke away from Abu Dhabi.

At that time, neighbouring Sharjah was the main trading centre on the Trucial Coast, and for the rest of the 19th century Dubai was simply another sleepy pearling village with a small merchant community.

Things began to change around the turn of the century. In 1894 Dubai's ruler, Shaikh Maktoum Bin Hasher Al-Maktoum, exempted foreign traders from taxes. Around the same time Linagh, in what is now Iran, lost its status as a free port. The Al-Maktoum family made a concerted effort to lure Linagh's disillusioned traders to Dubai and also managed to convince some of Sharjah's merchants to relocate. Next, the Al-Maktoums, probably with the assistance of the newly arrived Persian traders, prevailed on a British steamship line to switch its main port of call in the lower Gulf from Linagh to Dubai. When this was accomplished in 1903, it gave Dubai regular links with both British India and the ports of the central and northern Gulf (Bahrain, Kuwait, Bushire and Basra). The town's prosperity quickly grew. By 1908 there were 350 ships based in Deira and 50 in Bur Dubai.

The next key event in Dubai's growth occurred in 1939 when Shaikh Rashid Bin Saeed Al-Maktoum took over as regent for his father, Shaikh Saeed. Sharjah's leadership had, by then, been relatively weak and xenophobic for some years. The entire region was also suffering from the collapse of the pearling industry which, Rashid concluded, was probably never going to revive. With that in mind, Rashid set out to turn Dubai into the region's main trading centre. As Sharjah's harbour silted up, Rashid improved the facilities along the Creek, Dubai's waterfront.

The emirate came to specialise in the 're-export trade'; its merchants imported goods which they then sold to other ports rather than peddling them at home. In practice, this usually meant smuggling in general, and smuggling gold to India in particular. During the 1950s, Shaikh Rashid became one of the earliest beneficiaries of Kuwait's Fund for Arab Economic Development which loaned him money to dredge the Creek and build a

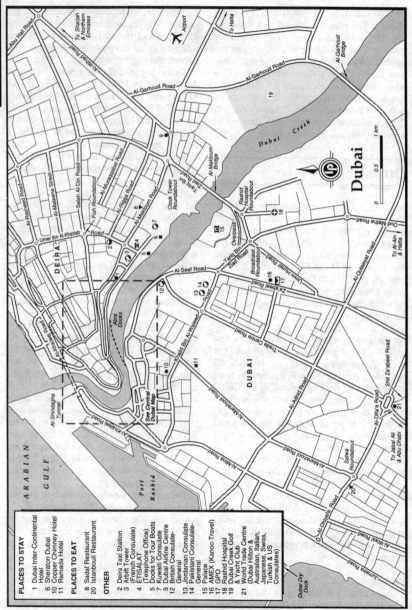

PLACES TO STAY
1 Dubai Inter-Continental Hotel
6 Sheraton Dubai
10 Copper Chimney Hotel
11 Ramada Hotel

PLACES TO EAT
8 Sadaf Restaurant
20 Istanbouli Restaurant

OTHER
2 Deira Taxi Station
3 Arbift Tower
4 ETISALAT (Telephone Office)
5 Docks for Tour Boats
7 Kuwaiti Consulate
9 Dubai Airline Centre
12 British Consulate-General
13 Jordanian Consulate
14 Pakistani Consulate-General
15 Palace
16 AMEX (Kanoo Travel)
17 GPO
18 Rashid Hospital
19 Dubai Creek Golf & Yacht Club
21 World Trade Centre (Dubai Hilton & Australian, Italian, Japanese, Swiss, Turkish & US Consulates)

new breakwater near its mouth. The project was completed in 1963, and gold smuggling took off like a rocket.

A building boom had begun along the Creek before the discovery of oil near Dubai in 1966, and even after oil revenues began coming in, trade remained the foundation of the city's wealth. Gold-smuggling peaked in 1970, when 259 tons of gold flowed through the emirate.

In the early '70s the Indian government began to crack down on the gold smugglers, but before this occurred Dubai's merchants had already laid the foundations of today's enormous re-export trade in consumer goods bound for the rest of the Arabian Peninsula and the Indian subcontinent. This is not to say that Dubai's days as a smuggler's paradise are over. The trade now supposedly focuses on Iran: the dhows take VCRs and Levis jeans to Iranian ports and return laden with caviar and carpets. As was the case with gold, all of these goods leave Dubai perfectly legally; it's the countries at the *other* end of the trade that look on it as smuggling.

Dubai's trade and oil-fuelled building boom eventually provided it with one of the busiest airports in the Middle East, a large dry-dock complex and, at Jebel Ali Ali, what is said to be the largest artificial port in the world. In 1988 Dubai opened the first golf course in the Gulf with real grass (at other golf courses, players carry a small square of astroturf around a series of grassless fairways). By the mid-90s, the Dubai Desert Classic had become a well-established stop on the annual pro golf tour and the city's golf courses had grown to three in number.

The man who was the driving force behind all of this, Shaikh Rashid, died in 1990 after a long illness and was succeeded as emir by his son, Shaikh Maktoum. For several years prior to Rashid's death, Maktoum had been regent for his father in all but name, and the new emir has continued his father's policies.

The core of those policies is to promote Dubai whenever and wherever possible. The golf courses were built, in part, so that big-name tournaments played there could call attention to Dubai. The same logic is behind

the world-class tennis tournaments, boat and horse racing and desert rallies hosted by the city, its air show (one of the three or four largest in the world) and its hosting of high profile events like the 1995 Miss World pageant.

Orientation

Dubai is really two towns: Deira to the east, and Dubai to the west. They are separated by the Creek (*al-khor* in Arabic), an inlet of the Gulf. The Dubai side is sometimes referred to as Bur Dubai when someone wants to make it clear that he or she means the Dubai side as opposed to the entire city. Deira, however, is the city centre. Activity in Deira focuses on Beniyas Rd, which runs along the Creek, Beniyas Square (which used to be called Nasr Square and is still generally known by that name) and the area along Al-Maktoum Rd, Al-Maktoum Hospital Rd, and Naif Rd. The Deira souk, where most of the cheap hotels are located, occupies most of the area west of Beniyas Square and south of Naif Rd. The cheap hotels are concentrated around Al-Sabkha Rd and in the area around Al-Buteen and Suq Deira Sts.

On the Dubai side, the souk is the whole area along the Creek from Al-Ghubaiba Rd east to the Ruler's Office and inland as far as Khalid Bin Al-Waleed Rd.

There are four ways of getting from one side of the Creek to the other. The Shindagha Tunnel runs under the Creek at the northern end, near its mouth. The Al-Maktoum Bridge, on the southern edge of the centre, is the main traffic artery across the waterway. Further south, the Al-Garhoud Bridge is used mostly by traffic trying to by-pass the centre. The final method of crossing the Creek is by *abra*, the small, open water-taxis which crisscross the waterway throughout the day.

Information

Tourist Office There is no tourist office in Dubai, though you might be able to get some information from the tour operators listed here and in the Sharjah section.

The best place to go for information is one of the larger travel agencies/tour operators, such as Arabian Adventures (see Organised Tours later in this section). If you arrive by air there are a couple of kiosks in the baggage claim area of the airport with lots of free brochures and glossy magazines telling you what to do in Dubai.

One cheap way to see a lot is to locate *Dubai Town Walk*, a brochure available at many of the larger hotel bookshops for around Dh 5. This maps out a one to two hour walking tour of each side of the Creek and is well worth the investment.

Foreign Consulates A number of countries have consulates in Dubai. Addresses for some of these diplomatic missions include:

Australia
World Trade Centre, 6th floor, on the Dubai side of the Creek (☎ 313 444)
Egypt
Off Khalid Bin Al-Waleed Rd, behind the Pakistani consulate (☎ 511 222)
France
Arbift Tower, 10th floor, Beniyas Rd, between the Chamber of Commerce building and the ETISALAT office (☎ 232 442)
Germany
Sharaf building, 6th floor, Al-Mankhool Rd, near the Ramada Hotel (☎ 523 352)
India
Khalid Bin Al-Waleed Rd, Bur Dubai, opposite the Strand Cinema (☎ 519 666)
Italy
World Trade Centre, 18th floor, on the Dubai side of the Creek (☎ 314 167)
Japan
World Trade Centre, 27th floor, on the Dubai side of the Creek (☎ 319 191)
Jordan
Khalid Bin Al-Waleed Rd, Bur Dubai, opposite the Strand Cinema (☎ 517 500)
Kuwait
Beniyas Rd, Deira, opposite the Sheraton Dubai (☎ 284 111)
Pakistan
Khalid Bin Al-Waleed Rd, Bur Dubai, opposite the Strand Cinema (☎ 524 412)
Qatar
Trade Centre Rd, Al-Mankhool district, Bur Dubai, near the Bur Juman Centre (☎ 452 888)
Switzerland
World Trade Centre, 22nd floor, on the Dubai side of the Creek (☎ 313 542)
Turkey
World Trade Centre, 11th floor, on the Dubai side of the Creek (☎ 314 788)
UK
Al-Seef Rd, on the Dubai side of the Creek, near the Dhow Restaurant (☎ 521 070)
USA
World Trade Centre, 21st floor, on the Dubai side of the Creek (☎ 313 115)

Money The first thing to be said about money in Dubai is that you should not exchange it at the airport, where the rates on offer are terrible. Once in the city, there is no shortage of banks and exchange houses. In central Deira, especially along Beniyas Rd and on Beniyas Square, every other building seems to contain a bank or a moneychanger. In Bur Dubai there are a lot of moneychangers (though most of them only take cash, no travellers' cheques) around the abra dock. In either case shopping around is worthwhile if you are changing more than a few hundred US dollars.

If you need an ATM in central Deira look for Emirates Bank International. Its ATMs are tied into the Electron, Cirrus, Switch and Global Access systems. It has a branch on Al-Maktoum Rd between Beniyas Square and the Inter-Continental Hotel. ATMs at British Bank of the Middle East branches, such as the one on Beniyas Square, are linked with the Global Access system.

AMEX (☎ 524 400) is represented in Dubai by Kanoo Travel. Its office is on the Dubai side of the Creek, on Za'abeel Rd in the National Bank of Umm Al-Qaiwain building next to the GPO. It's open daily, except Friday, from 8.30 am to 1 pm and from 4 to 6.30 pm. Cheques are cashed for card holders and mail is held for AMEX clients. Address mail to: c/o American Express, Client's Mail, PO Box 290, Dubai, UAE.

Post The GPO is on the Dubai side, on Za'abeel Rd. It is open Saturday to Wednesday from 8 am to 11.30 pm, Thursday from 8 am to 10 pm and Friday from 8 am to noon. It has a philatelic bureau.

The Deira post office, on Al-Sabkha Rd

near the intersection with Beniyas Rd, is much smaller. It is open Saturday to Wednesday from 8 am to 2 pm and from 4 to 9 pm. On Thursday the hours are 8 am to 1 pm and 4 to 8 pm. It is closed on Friday.

Telephone The ETISALAT office on the corner of Beniyas and Umer Ibn Al-Khattab Rds is open 24 hours a day. In addition to telephones, the office has fax, telex and telegram facilities. Note that the building you want is the new one – the glass and steel tower with a thing that looks like a golf ball on top, not the older, white building across the street.

If you need to make a call from the airport, there are telephones down at the far end of the baggage claim area, beyond the arrivals duty free shop, from which local calls (ie within Dubai) can be made free. Some of the lounges at the gates in the departures area also have phones from which you can make free local calls. The telephone area code for Dubai is 04.

Travel Agencies There are lots of travel agencies on Al-Maktoum Rd and around the western end of Beniyas Square. Staff turnover at these places is so high that it is impossible to recommend one or two in particular. If you need to buy a ticket, shop around for prices.

Bookshops Dubai's best bookshop, Magrudy Books, is on Jumeira Rd, just over five km west of the large roundabout by the Dubai bus station. In the centre, try the Al-Ghurair Centre on the corner of Umer Ibn Al-Khattab and Al-Rigga Rds, or the bookshops in the big hotels.

Laundry There are no laundrettes in Dubai but small laundries can be found in many spots around central Deira. Try the Al-Maidan Laundry on Al-Maktoum Rd just south-west of Beniyas Square. The charge is Dh 2 for a T-shirt, Dh 5 for pants, Dh 1 for socks and underwear, Dh 10 and up for dresses, Dh 6 and up for blouses and Dh 7 and up for skirts. It's open Saturday to Thurs-

day from 9 am to 1.30 pm and from 4.30 to 10 pm and Friday from 5 to 8 pm. Clothes are usually returned to you on the evening of the day after you drop them off, but if you bring clothing in at 9 am they may be able to get it back to you on the same day (for a small additional fee, of course).

On the opposite side of Beniyas Square, Tide Drycleaners & Laundry (☎ 277 796) has similar prices (shirts Dh 3, pants Dh 5, dresses Dh 7 and up, blouses Dh 5, socks Dh 1, underwear Dh 2) and turnaround time. It's open every day from 8 am to 1 pm and from 4 to 10 pm (closed Friday mornings).

Emergency To contact the police or an ambulance call ☎ 999; to report a fire, ☎ 997.

Dangers & Annoyances On the whole, Dubai is a very safe city but you should exercise the same sort of caution with your personal belongings as you would at home.

The tendency for drivers to zoom through traffic circles and execute turns across several lanes of traffic seems particularly pronounced in Dubai. Drivers should keep their wits about them at all times.

Finally, do not swim or water-ski in the Creek. The tides in the Gulf are not strong enough to flush the Creek out on a regular basis so it is not a clean waterway.

The Creek
The obvious place to start your tour of Dubai is at the waterfront. The best idea is to hire an abra for an hour or so. For around Dh 30 (for the whole boat, not per person) the captain should take you up to the Al-Maktoum Bridge and back. For Dh 40 he ought to extend that route to include a trip down to the mouth of the Creek and back. These prices take a bit of bargaining to achieve. The shorter trip takes just over half an hour, the longer one takes 45 to 60 minutes. If you do only one touristy thing in Dubai do this. The best way to see a great trading port is from the water.

Also take some time to walk along the cargo docks on the Deira side of the Creek,

THE UNITED ARAB EMIRATES

between the abra dock and the Inter-Continental Hotel. Dhows bound for every port from Kuwait to Bombay to Aden dock here to load and unload cargo.

Dubai Museum

Dubai's museum occupies the Al-Fahaidi Fort on the Dubai side of the Creek, next to the Ruler's Office. It is open Saturday to Thursday from 7.30 am to 2 pm and from 3 to 9 pm and Friday from 3 to 9 pm. Admission is Dh 3, Dh 1 for children up to age eight. Photography is permitted.

Al-Fahaidi Fort was built in the early 19th century – its construction dates range from 1800 to about 1840. The fort is thought to be the oldest building in Dubai. For many years it was both the residence of Dubai's rulers and the seat of government. The fort's current career as a museum began in 1971.

At the entrance is a display of aerial photographs showing the growth of Dubai over the years. It is interesting to note that Deira has always been the more heavily settled side of the Creek.

Entering the fort's courtyard, you'll see, on the left, a big tank which was used to carry fresh water on pearling boats. Several small boats and a barasti house with a wind tower are also in the courtyard. Throughout much of the Gulf barasti, or reed, houses were common until the 1950s. This was because they were relatively easy to build and maintain since, unlike mud-brick houses, they do not require water. The circulation of air through the reeds also made barasti houses much cooler than mud-brick structures during the summer. (See the Traditional Architecture boxed story in the Facts about the Region chapter for more information).

The hall along the right-hand side of the courtyard has a display on the fort itself and another display featuring khanjars and other traditional weapons. The hall to the left of the courtyard has a video of traditional Emirati dances, a display of musical instruments and more weapons.

The tower at the far corner of the courtyard leads down to a large underground area with

the rest of the museum's exhibits. These begin with a chronological history of Dubai from the 19th century onwards, including a very slick multimedia 'history' of Dubai and its development, which is definitely worth seeing. This leads to a re-creation of the Dubai souk as it looked in the 1950s, followed by a display on water and how it was conserved in the desert.

There are also exhibits on the flora and fauna of Dubai, Bedouin life, coastal/seafaring life and the area's archaeology, including a complete grave from the Qusais archaeological site (950-550 BC). Another room features finds from the digs at both Qusais and Jumeira (5th and 8th centuries AD).

Coming across the Creek by abra, to get to the museum walk inland from the dock for about 100m, keeping left when you can't exactly go straight, until you hit a street with cars (instead of only pedestrians). This is Ali Ibn Abi Talib Rd. Turn left and follow it past

---

Shaikh Saeed's House

The house of Shaikh Saeed, the grandfather of Dubai's present ruler, has been restored as a museum of pre-oil times. It sits beside the Creek on the Dubai side, near Port Rashid. The 30 room house was built in the late 19th century and, for many years, it served as a communal residence for the Al-Maktoum family. This is in keeping with the Arabian tradition of having several generations living in separate apartments within the same house or compound. Shaikh Saeed lived here until his death in 1958. The house was reopened as a museum in 1986 but was, at the time of writing, closed for renovations. When it reopens it will probably keep hours similar to those of the museum.

The house is built of coral quarried from the Gulf and then covered with lime and plaster. Until recently this was a common building method along both the Gulf and Red Sea coasts of Arabia. In Shaikh Saeed's era, the entrance on Al-Shindagha Rd, the one used by visitors today, was the house's back door. The main entrance, opening onto the large, central courtyard, faced the sea. (The Port Rashid complex, which now occupies almost 1.5 km between the house and the open sea, is mostly on reclaimed land.) ■

the big mosque. You'll see the Ruler's Office on your left and the fort on the right.

The Ruler's Office
This is the white building, decorated with mock wind towers, fronting onto the Creek. Near it are a few old buildings with wind towers.

World Trade Centre
The World Trade Centre tower is Dubai's tallest building. There is a viewing gallery on the 37th floor for those who want a bird's-eye view of the city but can't afford to hire a helicopter. You can only visit the gallery as part of a tour. These leave from the information desk in the tower lobby at 9.30 am and 4.30 pm. Admission is Dh 5. For more information call ☎ 314 200.

Souks
Not much of the old covered souks remain on either side of the Creek. The **Deira Covered Souk**, in the area immediately behind the Shatt Al-Arab Hotel, off Al-Sabkha Rd, specialises mostly in textiles. There is also a small covered souk area on the Dubai side of the Creek near the abra dock.

Deira's **gold souk** is on and around Sikkat Al-Khail St between Suq Deira and Old Baladiya Sts. The gold souk is probably the largest such market in Arabia and should be at the top of the 'must-see' list for any visit to Dubai. The best place to look for Dubai's famous selection of consumer electronics is around Beniyas Square, near the intersection of Al-Sabkha and Al-Maktoum Hospital Rds, and in the specialist shops which dot the bigger shopping centres. In particular, you might want to try the Al-Ghurair Centre at the intersection of Umer Ibn Al-Khattab and Al-Rigga Rds. On the Dubai side of the Creek the Bur Juman Centre on Trade Centre Rd is a good place to look for electronics.

Wind Towers
You have to know where to look but, yes, there are still a few real wind towers to be found in Dubai.

One of the most intriguing remaining wind towers is on the edge of the Deira souk, where it can be seen peeking above the cars and fruit juice stalls at the intersection of Naif and Al-Sabkha Rds. It is part of a home long since encircled by other buildings. You can look at it from the street but cannot enter. A number of other wind towers can be seen in the Bur Dubai souk, between the abra dock and the Ruler's Office.

Activities
Many activities, such as sailing and water sports, are organised through clubs. *What's On* is a good source of information for these clubs and other leisure activities in Dubai.

Golf The Emirates Golf Club (☎ 480 222), on the road to Jebel Ali, is the site of the Dubai Desert Classic, part of the European PGA Tour. To play the course you must either be invited by a member or be a guest at one of the five-star hotels that has made arrangements for its guests to use the course (most of these are listed under Places to Stay – top end). Greens fees are Dh 240 plus cart rental. Both motorised and hand carts are permitted but you are not allowed to carry your bag by hand.

The Dubai Creek Golf and Yacht Club (☎ 821 000), near the Deira side of the Al-Garhood Bridge is open to anyone. Greens fees are a bit higher than those at the Emirates Golf Club, but they include the (mandatory) cart rental. They also have a nine hole course, floodlit for night play, which costs Dh 135 per round (Dh 180 on weekends).

The newest grass course in Dubai is the Dubai Golf & Racing Club (☎ 363 666), beyond the inland edge of the Creek. The rates are similar to those at Dubai Creek. The Club is off Oud Metha Rd.

To play any of these courses you must be wearing a shirt with sleeves and a collar. Jeans and 'beach wear' are not allowed. They also require you to produce a handicap certificate, though it is sometimes possible to talk your way around this.

Ice Skating There is an ice rink at the Hyatt Regency Hotel's Galleria shopping complex. At the time of writing it was being renovated.

Camel Racing Races take place early on Friday mornings during winter and spring, at the track south of the centre off the 2nd Za'abeel Rd on the Dubai side. Admission is free but try to get there by 8 am.

Organised Tours

Arabian Adventures (☎ 317 373, fax 314 696) is a Dubai-based company run in tandem with Emirates Airlines. It offers a half-day tour of Dubai daily except Friday for Dh 100 per person. This comes in 'city tour' and 'shopping tour' varieties, though why you would want to pay somebody Dh 100 to take you on a one hour walk through the gold souk and then dump you at one of Bur Dubai's shopping malls is beyond me. It's 'Dubai by night' tour (Dh 275) is a combination of a shopping trip, a Lebanese dinner and a visit to a nightclub. For Dh 240 you can take a dinner cruise on a dhow (Tuesday and Sunday only). It also offers day trips to Sharjah/Ajman (Dh 100, half day), Abu Dhabi, Al-Ain, Ras Al-Khaimah and the east coast of the UAE (Dh 160 each, full day). You can have a catered dinner in the desert for Dh 245 or an all-day 4WD safari for Dh 290 to Dh 320 (depending on the destination). On Monday and Thursday there's a half-day combination camel riding/sand skiing trip (Dh 215). Overnight 4WD safaris in the desert cost Dh 470 per person.

Net Tours (☎ 666 655, fax 668 662) offers a similar selection of tours at similar prices. Its Dubai and Sharjah tours are a bit cheaper than Arabian Adventures, while its tours to Abu Dhabi, Al-Ain and the east coast cost a few dirhams more. The overnight camping trip, at Dh 300, costs significantly less. It also offers a full-day tour to Hatta for Dh 250.

Coastline Leisure (☎ 450 867, fax 452 497) offers one hour guided tours of the Creek by dhow daily at 9.30 and 11.30 am and 5.30 pm for Dh 35 per person. It also has

a two hour cruise at 1.30 pm for Dh 60. The boats depart from the Deira docks, opposite the Chamber of Commerce building. With advance reservations it also offers dinner cruises and the charter of larger, fancier boats.

See the Sharjah and Al-Ain entries for information on other tour companies.

For do-it-yourself tours pick up a copy of the *Dubai Town Walk* brochure (see the earlier Tourist Office section for details).

Places to Stay

Dubai's hotels are scattered over a wide area, but the cheapies are concentrated in the Deira souk, particularly along Al-Sabkha Rd and in the side streets off Suq Deira St. Absolute rock bottom for singles/doubles is Dh 40/60, but the handful of places in this category are generally filled by quasi-permanent residents. Mid-range hotels are everywhere, with the area around Beniyas Square being an especially good place to look. Four and five-star hotels line the Creek and dot the outskirts of the emirate.

The rates quoted here are, in all cases, the rack rates. With the exception of the youth hostel you can probably negotiate some kind of discount, especially for longer stays, at almost any hotel listed here.

The Deira souk is a great place to stay because of its central location, though anything overlooking Al-Sabkha Rd is likely to be quite noisy. If your budget can manage it, something on or around Beniyas Square will put you right in the heart of the city. Staying in the youth hostel is cheap but puts you some distance from the centre.

Places to Stay – bottom end

Youth Hostel Dubai's *youth hostel* (☎ 625 578) is on Qusais Rd, on the eastern outskirts of the city, between the Al-Ahli Club and the Jamiat Al-Islah relief agency. To get there from central Deira take the main road for Sharjah (Al-Ittihad Rd) and turn right onto Qusais Rd. The Al-Ahli Club is the place on the left with a stadium, the hostel is the next gate down on the same side of the road. The hostel has been completely rebuilt and, since its reopening in the spring of 1995, has been the best deal in Dubai. Beds are Dh 35 per night in clean, comfortable two and three bed dorm rooms. Meals are available. Women as well as men can be accommodated and there are separate rooms for families, though the manager reserves the right to turn away unaccompanied women if the hostel is full of rowdy young males (which, he says, is rare). The doors do not have locks but each bed has a wardrobe/locker with a key which you can take with you when you go out for the day.

Bus No 13 runs from the Deira bus station to the hostel every 10 minutes from 6.05 am until 10.55 pm and bus No 19 runs from the Dubai Museum via the Dubai bus station, Beniyas Square and the Deira service-taxi station every 30 minutes from 6.15 am to 10.15 pm. The fare on either bus is Dh 1 from the Deira side of the Creek and Dh 1.50 from Bur Dubai. A taxi from central Deira will cost about Dh 12.

Hotels Few of Dubai's cheapest hotels still arrange visas, which is probably just as well considering the chequered record some of these places had in terms of getting the paperwork done properly and on time. In any event, my experience has been that you're far better off coming in via a more up-market place and sleeping cheap later on.

The best value in Dubai is the *Mirage Hotel* (☎ 260 004 or 260 005, fax 260 293), in an alley just off Al-Sabkha Rd. The rooms are tiny and none have private baths, but the atmosphere is friendly and at Dh 60/100 for singles/doubles (plus a Dh 10 'registration fee' applied on your first night only) you won't beat the combination of price and cleanliness. Triples are also available for Dh 150. Most of the staff are from Somalia. The Mirage arranges visas and, unlike most other hotels in this price category, its toilets are cleaned regularly and some of them even have seats. I highly recommend it.

Only two other bottom-end hotels credibly claim to be able to arrange visas. One is the *Al-Sheraa Hotel* (☎ 265 213, fax 254 866) on Al-Buteen St. At Dh 80/100 for singles/doubles without bath it is a definite step down from the Mirage. Also on Al-Buteen St, the *Red Sea Hotel* (☎ 264 281, fax 265 249) has rooms for Dh 60/80 with rather smelly common bathrooms. Look for the wall posters advertising shipping services to Ethiopia and Eritrea.

Of the cheap hotels which require you to arrive visa-in-hand, the *Bin Sadoon Hotel* (☎ 264 236, fax 259 825) on Al-Buteen St is a somewhat spartan affair but the place has character. Singles/doubles without bath cost Dh 60/80. Next door, the *Al-Aman Hotel* has doubles only at Dh 70 apiece, none with bath. Nearby, on the corner of Al-Buteen and Old Baladiya Sts, the *Shams Al-Sahraa* (☎ 253 666, fax 253 647) is a bit more expensive at Dh 80/120. The bathrooms are clean if a little rough, but the pink walls and retro-red carpets give the place a strange but pleasant feel. Further up Al-Buteen St, and on the same intersection as the Red Sea, the *Al-Najah Hotel* (☎ 263 931, fax 266 092) has OK rooms for Dh 80/120. Nearby, the *Al-Buteen Plaza Hotel* (☎ 263 888, fax 264 759) is a bit more expensive at Dh 100/120 with triples for Dh 150.

There are only two real cheapies around the entrance to the gold souk. One is the *Gold Tower Hotel* (☎ 253 325, fax 253 484) where singles/doubles cost Dh 80/120. Be warned, however, that the rooms are cramped and two of the three I looked at had no light. About 150m up the street is the *Arabian Island Hotel (Branch)* (☎ 267 151, fax 267 898). The staff made me promise not to being alcohol into the hotel. Double rooms cost Dh 100 with an attached bath and Dh 70 without.

In an alley between Sikkat Al-Khalil St and Al-Soor St is the *Metro Hotel* (☎ 260 040, fax 262 098). It has doubles at Dh 100 per room, but accepts only families (single females may be accepted, but not single males).

If you really want to be in the thick of things, head back to Al-Sabkha Rd and take a look at the *Shatt Al-Arab Hotel* (☎ 258 587) overlooking the bus stop at the intersection of Al-Sabkha Rd and Deira St. Rooms are Dh 30 per person, none with private baths. Many of the guests look like permanent residents

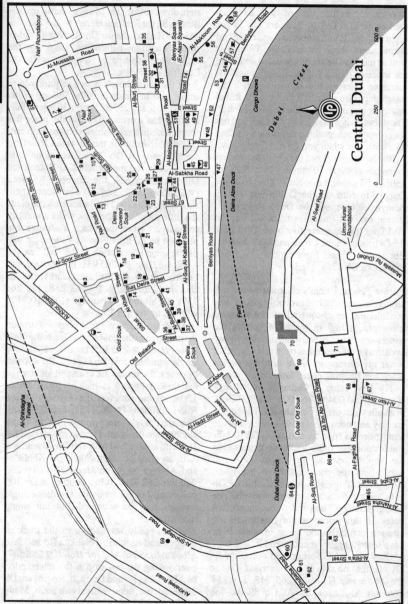

Central Dubai

PLACES TO STAY				OTHER	
2	Green Line Hotel	39	Al-Aman Hotel	1	Deira Bus Station
3	Metro Hotel	40	Bin Sadoon Hotel	5	Mosque
4	Al-Ikhlas Hotel	41	Red Sea Hotel	7	Police Station (Old
8	Hotel Delhi Darbar	43	Mirage Hotel		Fort)
9	Hariri Palace Hotel	44	Victoria Hotel	12	Wind Tower
11	Imperial Palace Hotel	45	Al-Khaleej Hotel	34	Tide Drycleaners &
13	Ramsis Hotel	53	Riviera Hotel		Laundry
14	Gold Tower Hotel	54	Carlton Tower Hotel	42	Small Exchange
15	Al-Khayam Hotel	62	Peninsula Hotel		Kiosks
17	Arabian Island Hotel	63	Ambassador Hotel	46	Deira Post Office
	(Branch)	65	Astoria Hotel	50	Saudia Airlines
18	Al-Najah Hotel	66	Time Palace Hotel	51	British Bank of the
19	Stars Hotel	68	Regent Palace Hotel		Middle East
20	Al-Buteen Plaza Hotel			55	Emirates Airlines
21	Al-Amal Hotel	**PLACES TO EAT**		56	Al-Maidan Laundry
22	Shatt Al-Arab Hotel			58	Emirates Bank Interna-
23	Sina Hotel	6	Najaf Restaurant		tional (ATM)
25	Vienna Hotel	10	Bab-U-Sabkha	59	Shaikh Saeed's House
26	Miriana Hotel	16	Al-Burj Cafeteria	60	Plaza Cinema
27	Avon Hotel	24	Gulf Restaurant & Caf-	61	Dubai Bus & Service-
28	Dubai Orient Hotel		eteria		Taxi Station
29	Royal Prince Hotel	30	Entezary Restaurant	64	Moneychangers Souk
31	Phoenicia Hotel	32	Golden Fork	69	Wind Towers
33	Rex Hotel	47	Cafeteria Al-Abra	70	Ruler's Office
35	Swiss Hotel	48	Pizza Corner	71	Dubai Museum
36	Anahita Hotel	49	Hatam Restaurant		
37	Shams Al-Sahraa	52	Popeye Restaurant		
38	Al-Sheraa Hotel	57	Cafe Mozart		
		67	Bhavna Restaurant		

and the place is often full. It's grimy, and the air-conditioning is deafening, but it does have character.

Places to Stay – middle

Even in this price category many of the hotels either won't arrange visas or seem very reluctant when asked. Service charges, where applicable, have been included in the prices. The next six hotels listed will arrange visas.

The *Dubai Orient Hotel* (☎ 282 233), at the intersection of Al-Sabkha Rd and Al-Soor St, has singles/doubles for Dh 140/200, all with odd-smelling baths. Next door, the *Avon Hotel* (☎ 258 877, fax 252 061) charges Dh 150/230. All of its rooms have attached baths. Across the street is the *Royal Prince Hotel* (☎ 239 991, fax 219 757), where the rooms are very good value at Dh 140/180. Triples are available for Dh 240. The *Sina Hotel* (☎ 252 323, fax 252 606) is immediately behind the Al-Sabkha Rd bus stop in an alley inside the Deira covered souk. The

rooms are small but adequate and cost Dh 207/287.50, though this rate is probably negotiable.

The *Vienna Hotel* (☎ 218 855, fax 212 928), on Al-Sabkha Rd, has rather grubby bathrooms. Singles/doubles are Dh 120/150. Also on Al-Sabkha Rd is the *Miriana Hotel* (☎ 259 333, fax 259 185) with rooms at Dh 165/220, including the service charge. Both cater mostly to Russians and other travellers from the former Soviet Union.

The remaining mid-range hotels listed in this section do not arrange visas. The *Al-Ikhlas Hotel* (☎ 269 885, fax 267 803), on Sikkat Al-Khail St, only has doubles, which go for Dh 120, and will rent rooms only to 'families' (no single men allowed). The *Stars Hotel* (☎ 266 000, fax 253 739) is a friendly place with a good location in the souk on Al-Buteen St, but at Dh 150 for singles or doubles with bath, the place remains overpriced despite a recent face-lift. Also on Al-Buteen St the *Al-Amal Hotel* (☎ 269 777, fax 261 127) has doubles only for Dh 150, all with bath. At the other end of Al-Buteen St the *Anahita Hotel* (☎ 263 791, fax 264 794) has similar rooms at the same price.

The *Green Line Hotel* (☎ 268 661), opposite the Metro Hotel, between Al-Soor and Sikkat Al-Khalil Sts, has rooms with bath for Dh 150/200. The rooms are absolutely crammed with furniture and have a rather crowded feel about them. The toilets have no seats. Near the intersection of Suq Deira and Sikkat Al-Khail Sts, the *Al-Khayam Hotel* (☎ 226 211) charges Dh 130/160 for rooms, all with private bath.

On Al-Sabkha Rd, near the intersection with Naif Rd, the *Ramsis Hotel* (formerly the Saeed Hotel) (☎ 268 200, fax 219 059) is usually full and has gone a bit up-market over the last few years. Rooms cost Dh 140/180.

Since the first edition of this book there has been quite a lot of hotel building along Naif South St. What you get here tends to be bottom-end hotels with lower middle range prices. One of the more established places on the street is the *Imperial Palace Hotel* (☎ 211 344, fax 223 770). Rooms are OK but nothing special at Dh 150/180. Among the newer places the *Tehran Hotel* (☎ 222 392, fax 222 823) is worth a look. It only has doubles, all at Dh 140. A better deal, with rooms costing Dh 100/150, is the *Hariri Palace Hotel* (☎ 219 333, fax 270 311) on St 5, off Naif South St. Unfortunately the staff are rather surly. In contrast, the *Swiss Hotel* (☎ 212 181, fax 211 779), on Al-Mussalla Rd, is a very friendly place. Singles/doubles are Dh 207/264.50 but discounts are readily available.

The *Hotel Delhi Darbar* (☎ 267 474, fax 266 464) on Naif Rd is, as its name implies, an Indian-oriented establishment. At Dh 201/287.50 for large, spotless rooms, it is one of the better deals in this price range. It does not, however, sponsor visas.

On Suq Deira St, *Dreams Hotel* (☎ 274 268) charges Dh 125/155 for small rooms which share their baths with one or two other rooms. The *Asia Hotel* (☎ 215 737) on Al-Buteen St, just off Suq Deira St, has only doubles at Dh 200.

On Al-Khor St, near the mouth of the Creek, the *Al-Jazeera Hotel* (☎ 225 299) has only doubles for Dh 150.

Places to Stay – top end

Deira Unless otherwise noted, all of the hotels in this category will arrange visas. Rates are negotiable, and the service charge is already included in the prices listed here.

One of the better top-end values in the city is the *Al-Khaleej Hotel* (☎ 211 144, fax 237 140) between Beniyas Square and Al-Sabkha Rd. Singles/doubles are 288/408. The *Phoenicia Hotel* (☎ 227 191, fax 221 629) has a prime location on Beniyas Square. At Dh 230/360 the rates are OK by local standards for the rather ostentatious rooms.

Along Beniyas Rd the *Carlton Tower Hotel* (☎ 227 111, fax 228 249) is a good 'budget' top-end place with rooms starting at Dh 367.50/472.50. Next door, the *Riviera Hotel* (☎ 222 131, fax 211 820) has similar prices but is less plush and does not serve alcohol.

The *Victoria Hotel* (☎ 269 626, fax 269 575), in an alley near the intersection of Al-Sabkha and Al-Maktoum Hospital Rds, is a decent if dull place at Dh 220/260.

There are more expensive five-star hotels (usually the quickest at arranging visas) in Dubai. Discounts from the rates quoted here are almost always available. All of these hotels add a whopping 20% onto the rates quoted below (5% tax and a 15% service charge).

Al-Khaleej Palace (☎ 231 000, fax 211 293) Al-Maktoum Rd. Singles/ doubles cost Dh 590/680.

Dubai Hilton (☎ 314 000, fax 313 383) in the World Trade Centre complex on the outskirts of Bur Dubai. Singles/doubles cost Dh 820/920.

Dubai Inter-Continental Hotel (☎ 227 171, fax 284 777) Beniyas Rd. Singles/doubles cost Dh 890/990.

Forte Grand (☎ 824 040, fax 825 540) near the airport. Singles/doubles cost Dh 700/780.

Hyatt Regency Dubai (☎ 221 234, fax 211 868) off Al-Khaleej Rd. Singles/doubles cost Dh 790/890.

Sheraton Dubai (☎ 281 111, fax 213 468) Beniyas Rd. Singles/doubles cost Dh 960/1080.

Dubai The hotels on the Dubai side of the Creek are mostly middle to upper end. Unless it's for business reasons, it is a bit hard to see why one would want to stay on the Dubai side. Deira is a lot more fun. There are no cheap hotels in Bur Dubai.

The *Copper Chimney Hotel* (☎ 524 005, fax 513 181) is near the intersection of Khalid Bin Al-Waleed Rd and Al-Hisn St. The hotel is on the 6th floor of an office building. Singles/doubles are Dh 160/220 with bath. The rooms are cramped but well kept. It does not arrange visas.

The *Time Palace Hotel* (☎ 532 111, fax 539 948) does not arrange visas either, but has a good location on the edge of the Bur Dubai souk. Rooms cost Dh 172.50/230. Just off Khalid Bin Al-Waleed Rd, the *Harbour Hotel* (☎ 511 223, fax 511 248) is the only other cheapish place in Bur Dubai at Dh 175/250. It can arrange visas.

The main advantage of the *Regent Palace Hotel* (☎ 535 555, fax 535 111) is its location near the museum and the Ruler's Office. Rooms are Dh 287.50/368 but it does not sponsor visas.

The *Palm Beach Hotel* (☎ 525 550, fax 528 320) on Khalid Bin Al-Waleed Rd has rooms at Dh 300/420. It needs two to three weeks to arrange visas which is usually not a good sign.

Top-end places which should have no trouble sponsoring visas include the *Ambassador Hotel* (☎ 531 000, fax 534 751), on Al-Falah Rd near the museum with singles/doubles for Dh 264/420, including breakfast. The *Astoria Hotel* (☎ 534 300, fax 535 665) on Al-Nahdha St, charges Dh 299/414 and the *Dubai Marine Hotel* (☎ 520 900, fax 521 035) on Khalid Bin Al-Waleed Rd, charges Dh 480/600. The *Penninsula Hotel* (☎ 533 000, fax 535 010), next to the Dubai bus station, charges Dh 360/480.

Elsewhere If you come to Dubai on a package tour you will probably stay at either the *Jebel Ali Hotel* (☎ 836 000, fax 835 543), an opulent five-star place 50 km west of the centre and adjacent to the Jebel Ali Port, or at the *Chicago Beach Hotel* (☎ 480 000, fax 482 273) which is about midway between the centre and Jebel Ali. Both are beach resort hotels. The Jebel Ali asks a mind-blowing Dh 984/1104 for singles/doubles, but it does provide a free shopping shuttle to Deira (though, please note, the shuttle does not go to the airport and will not let you take luggage). The *Chicago Beach Hotel*, charges Dh 600/720.

Places to Eat – Cheap & Medium Priced
Those on a self-catering budget will find a number of small grocery stores in the area between Al-Sabkha Rd and Beniyas Square. Reasonably fresh fruit can be purchased at stalls around the bus stop on Al-Sabkha Rd, near the Shatt Al-Arab Hotel.

On Beniyas Square between the Phoenicia and the Rex hotels, the *Golden Fork* has an odd combination of oriental dishes and western fast food. The western food is cheaper. Two pieces of chicken, French fries, bread and a soda cost Dh 7 – a hard price to beat. A few doors down, the *Entezary Restaurant* offers equally good-value food. A dinner of kebab, rice, soup, salad, hommous, bread and tea costs only Dh 15. Note that while the sign on the door says that this particular special is 'all you can eat', this apparently applies only to the salad.

One place I highly recommend is the *Hatam Restaurant*, just off Beniyas Square behind the Saudia airline office. It serves excellent Persian food at very reasonable prices. A traditional chelo kebab (which appears on the menu as sultan kebab) costs Dh 17, including soup and salad. Other full dinners cost Dh 14 to Dh 25 with most under Dh 20.

On Beniyas Rd, not far from the abra dock, is *Pizza Corner*, a good medium-priced place with pizzas and burgers. Their sandwiches go for Dh 9 to Dh 16. For a quick and cheap meal out on Beniyas Rd, *Cafeteria Al-Abra* has good shawarma and samosas along with fruit juice and soda. The coconut juice is even served fresh in the shell. The cafeteria is at the intersection of Al-Sabkha and Beniyas Rds, next to the abra dock. It's a good place to relax while watching the boats come and go. A bit further up the road, *Popeye* has shawarma, burgers and other snacks. A full meal can be had for Dh 10 or less.

Al-Burj Cafeteria is a stand-up affair near the main entrance to the gold souk offering excellent shawarma, fresh fruit juices, soda and popcorn.

If you're looking for something a bit more formal, *Pillars*, the coffee shop in the Phoenicia Hotel on Beniyas Square, has a Dh 33 (plus tax and service) buffet lunch or dinner. Unlike any of the other places listed under this heading Pillars serves alcohol.

When it comes to coffee, my highest recommendation goes to *Cafe Mozart*, which recreates the atmosphere, food, coffee and service of a Viennese coffee house, right down to the change purse carried by the waitress. The pastries and croissants cost about Dh 3 each and are good. The coffee and cappuccino are excellent.

In Deira's budget hotel district there are many cheap restaurants, most of them serving Indian and Pakistani food though a lot of these places will have menus consisting only of biryanis. Naif South St has particularly good pickings. Try *Bab-U-Sabkha* for good, cheap Pakistani food. Another good subcontinental eatery is the *Gulf Restaurant & Cafeteria*, at the intersection of Al-Sabkha Rd and Deira St. Lots of chicken, lamb or fish on a pile of rice costs Dh 12.

On the Dubai side of the Creek, try *Bhavna*, an Indian vegetarian restaurant on Al-Faghidi Rd next to the Dubai Museum. Another good bet on this side of the Creek is *Kwality*, a medium-priced Indian restaurant on Khalid Bin Al-Waleed Rd in Bur Dubai, near the Dubai Marine Hotel. Main dishes cost Dh 15 to Dh 30.

Outside the centre, head for *Istanbouli*, an excellent Lebanese restaurant on Al-Dhiyafa St just west of the Satwa roundabout. Mezze costs Dh 7 to Dh 15 apiece and main dishes are Dh 15 to Dh 25.

Places to Eat – top end
All of Dubai's best expensive restaurants are attached to the big hotels. *Pancho Villa's*, a Tex-Mex restaurant in the Astoria Hotel on the Dubai side of the Creek, is one of the Gulf's best known restaurants (its bumper stickers can be seen far and wide). Appetisers and main dishes cost Dh 20 to Dh 50. The restaurant is a bit cheaper at lunch, when it offers a variety of specials.

Sadaf, a Persian restaurant on Al-Maktoum Rd is not attached to a hotel and, therefore, serves no alcohol, but the food is excellent. Large chelo kebab meals cost Dh 25 to Dh 30 and appetisers cost Dh 7 to Dh 15. It also offers enormous buffets at both lunch and dinner.

In the Inter-Continental Hotel, *The Pub* is about as good an imitation of the real thing as you'll find in the Gulf. It serves a varied menu of sandwiches and 'traditional pub food' (shepherd's pie, roast beef etc). The sandwiches cost Dh 20 to Dh 30 and other main dishes run from Dh 30 to Dh 50. The best Italian food in Dubai is at *Villa Veduta*, an outlandishly expensive restaurant, also in the Inter-Continental. Count on paying no less than Dh 75 per person, lots more if you want Italian wine with your meal. For a somewhat cheaper Italian meal, try *Da Pino* in the Al-Khaleej Hotel. Its pasta dishes cost Dh 22 to Dh 30.

Dubai's best Japanese food is also widely reckoned to be had at the Inter-Continental Hotel. A meal at the *Minato* restaurant, however, is likely to run to well over Dh 100 per person.

Entertainment
After-hours social life centres around expensive restaurants, bars and discos in the big hotels. A night out on the town is not going to be cheap. If you're drinking, plan on spending well over Dh 150 and even non-drinkers could easily go through half that in cover charges and overpriced glasses of Pepsi.

The entertainment scene in the big hotels is constantly changing. The best way to keep up is with a copy of *What's On*. Almost everything: country & western, rock, deafening disco or a quiet piano bar is available somewhere. The problem is that with the exception of a few perennials (like Pancho Villa's) the hotels keep changing the theme in their restaurant/clubs in an attempt to keep everything up to date. If you have the time and money to explore it could all be rather interesting.

Cinemas Most of Dubai's cinemas specialise in Indian and Pakistani films but you can catch relatively recent western flicks at the Galleria, the shopping complex attached to the Hyatt Regency Hotel. Call ☎ 206 4094 or ☎ 206 4095 to find out what's on.

Discos Dubai is full of discos. The one at the *Jumeira Beach Club* is pretty good, and you do not have to be a club member to use it. *Pancho Villa's* at the Astoria Hotel on the edge of the Bur Dubai souk has long been one of Dubai's most popular nightspots. There's a dance floor as well as a bar and restaurant and live music is featured several nights a week, often with bands out from Britain. Check *What's On* to see what is hot this month.

Bars My opinion has long been that the biggest problem with many of Dubai's bars is that the managers of these places all seem to feel that a bad lounge singer is an absolutely essential part of any drinking establishment. Maybe that's why I've always had something of a soft spot for the seedy bar on the top floor at the *Al-Khaleej Hotel*, between Beniyas Square and Al-Sabkha Rd. For one thing, it has pool tables. For another thing it rarely has live music. Unaccompanied women may want to give this place a miss.

The Inter-Continental Hotel has two noteworthy bars: *The Pub*, a very convivial place, which also never has live music, and *Up on the Tenth*, a piano bar with superb views over the Creek. Another good place for a drink is *The Old Vic* at the Ramada Hotel. The bar is decorated with theatre posters from London's West End and has a relaxed atmosphere.

Things to Buy

High-priced boutiques filled with the latest of everything can be found in Dubai's many shopping malls. These open at the rate of about one per year with each one being bigger and flashier than the last. Among the main shopping centres are the Al-Ghurair Centre near the Deira service-taxi station, the Bur Juman Centre on the Dubai side of the Creek just off Khalid Bin Al-Waleed Rd and the massive City Centre off Tariq Ibn Ziyad Rd adjacent to the Dubai Creek Golf & Yacht Club. City Centre, which opened in late 1995 was, at the time of writing, the biggest and fanciest of the bunch. Dubai being Dubai, that will probably have changed by the time you read this.

If you are looking for cheap electronics try the area at the Al-Sabkha Rd end of Beniyas Square.

The gold souk is further west, along Sikkat Al-Khail St. This area has to be seen to be believed. Bearing in mind that much of Dubai's wealth was originally built on gold smuggling it is hardly a surprise that the gold souk is big, but even seasoned veterans of Middle East gold markets are likely to be blown away be the sheer scale of Dubai's gold souk. As gold goes, the prices are fairly good. Small items, such as simple earrings or a pendant, can be purchased for under Dh 100 for lower grades of gold (such as 14 carat). Even if you have no plans to buy anything it is worth a visit simply to take in the atmosphere, and to goggle at the size of some of the jewellery on offer.

Persian carpets are said to be cheaper at the Sharjah souk. Carpet shoppers in Dubai should try the Deira and Al-Mansoor Towers on Beniyas Square, both of which have lots of small carpet boutiques.

The alleyway leading to the Metro Hotel in the Deira souk is a good spot to look for colourful women's clothing.

If you are looking for Middle Eastern-looking souvenirs there are a couple of small shops along Beniyas Rd between the abra dock and the Inter-Continental Hotel that are worth browsing around. These are the places to look for small coffeepots, little carved camels and similar kitsch. Most of these shops also have a limited selection of silver Bedouin jewellery. For more expensive, and higher quality, Arab souvenirs take a look at Art & Culture a crowded shop in the lobby of the Inter-Continental Hotel. It has very high quality caftans and robes from other Arab countries and high-quality (and high-price) Bedouin jewellery. It also sells, for Dh 100, very handsome small wooden boxes containing frankincense and myrrh.

Haggle hard anywhere in the souk (I have even haggled over exchange rates with moneychangers) but don't expect the prices of things like gold or electronic goods to come down by more than 10 to 15%. Antiques and crafts may come down a bit more.

Getting There & Away

Air You can fly to almost anywhere from Dubai international airport (DXB). The emirate's long-standing reputation as the travel hub of the Gulf was built on a combination of easy landing rights for transiting aircraft and a very big and cheap duty-free shop at the airport. In late 1995 Dubai's Department of Civil Aviation announced plans for a massive expansion of airport facilities over the next four years. For general airport information call ☎ 245 777 or 245 555.

Outside the Middle East, the words most often associated with Dubai are probably 'duty free'. The airport PR staff have turned statistics about the duty-free store into a small cottage industry. My particular favourite: in 1988 Iranian travellers bought 1.5 million bananas in the Dubai airport duty-free store. Bananas were said to be virtually unobtainable in Iran back then.

Sample one-way and return fares from Dubai to other cities (with minimum and maximum stay requirements) include:

To	One Way	Return	Min/Max
Athens	Dh 1910	Dh 2790	10/90 days
Bahrain	Dh 730	Dh 580	3/7 days
Bangkok	Dh 3060	Dh 4270	7/90 days
Cairo	Dh 1880	Dh 2770	5/60 days
Damascus	Dh 1630	Dh 2210	5/60 days
Dhahran	Dh 590	Dh 810	2/14 days
Doha	Dh 570	Dh 450	3/7 days
Jeddah	Dh 1120	Dh 1560	2/14 days
Kuwait	Dh 760	Dh 1050	2/14 days
London	Dh 2850	Dh 4060	10/90 days
Melbourne	Dh 6180	Dh 5780	10/120 days
Muscat	Dh 610	Dh 480	3/7 days
Nairobi	Dh 2730	Dh 3530	6/60 days
New Delhi	Dh 1630	Dh 2170	7/120 days
New York	Dh 4900	Dh 6910	14/90 days
Riyadh	Dh 700	Dh 960	2/14 days
Rome	Dh 2340	Dh 3240	10/90 days

The Melbourne and New York return fares quoted here are the low season prices. These apply from early January through mid-June and from mid-October through mid-December in the case of New York and from February through August for Australia.

The Damascus fare in the table also applies to flights to Amman and Beirut. The fare quoted for New Delhi is also good for flights to Bombay.

All of these fares are regularly published return and one-way quotes. Specials are often available and it pays to do a bit of shopping around. It is usually cheaper to pay cash than to use a credit card and locking yourself into dates on a non-refundable ticket is usually the way to get the best price of all. You will also notice that in several cases the return fare is cheaper than the one-way fare. Bear that in mind if you only need a one-way ticket.

Following is a far from complete list of the carriers, large and small, that fly to and from Dubai. Some of the carriers with offices listed in town also have desks at the Airline Centre, a type of shopping mall for air travel, on Al-Maktoum Rd in Deira.

Aeroflot
Al-Maktoum Rd, Deira, between the Khaleej Palace Hotel and the clock tower roundabout (☎ 222 245)

Air France
Al-Maktoum Rd, Deira, just east of the Khaleej Palace Hotel (☎ 667 775)

Air India
Al-Maktoum Rd, Deira, just west of the clock tower roundabout (☎ 276 787)

Air Lanka
Airline Centre, Al-Maktoum Rd, Deira (☎ 236 775)
Alitalia
Al-Maktoum Rd, Deira, near the Khaleej Palace Hotel (☎ 284 656)
Al-Yemen Airways
Al-Maktoum Rd, Deira, just east of the Khaleej Palace Hotel (☎ 284 093)
Biman Bangladesh Airlines
Airline Centre, Al-Maktoum Rd, Deira (☎ 226 241)
British Airways
Airline Centre, Al-Maktoum Rd, Deira (☎ 314 314)
Balkan Bulgarian Airways
Al-Maktoum Rd, Deira, just east of the Khaleej Palace Hotel (☎ 223 250)
Cathay Pacific
Pearl building, 11th floor, Street 18, Deira (near Beniyas Square) (☎ 283 126)
Cyprus Airways
Nasser Air Travel & Shipping Agency, Al-Maktoum Rd, Deira, near the Khaleej Palace Hotel (☎ 215 325)
EgyptAir
Al-Maktoum Rd, Deira, just west of the clock tower roundabout (☎ 236 551)
Emirates
Deira Tower, Beniyas Square, Deira. The main reservations office is at the Airline Centre on Al-Maktoum Rd, Deira (☎ 215 544).
Gulf Air
Al-Maktoum Rd, Deira, across from the Khaleej Palace Hotel (☎ 285 141)
Iran Air
Airline Centre, Al-Maktoum Rd, Deira (☎ 226 733)
KLM
Airline Centre, Al-Maktoum Rd, Deira (☎ 244 747)
Kuwait Airways
Pearl building, Deira (near Beniyas Square, enter from Beniyas Rd side of the building) (☎ 281 106)
LOT, Polish Airlines
Nasser Air Travel & Shipping Agency, Al-Maktoum Rd, Deira, near the Khaleej Palace Hotel (☎ 284 292)
Lufthansa
Pearl building, 1st floor, St 18, Deira (near Beniyas Square) (☎ 221 191)
Malev, Hungarian Airlines
Al-Maktoum Rd, Deira, just east of the Khaleej Palace Hotel (☎ 270 500)
MEA (Middle East Airlines)
Airline Centre, Al-Maktoum Rd, Deira (☎ 203 3761)

Olympic
Nasser Air Travel & Shipping Agency, Al-Maktoum Rd, Deira, near the Khaleej Palace Hotel (☎ 214 761)
PIA (Pakistan International Airlines)
Al-Maktoum Rd, Deira, just west of the clock tower roundabout (☎ 222 154)
Royal Brunei
Airline Centre, Al-Maktoum Rd, Deira (☎ 514 111)
Royal Jordanian
Pearl building, Deira (near Beniyas Square, enter the building from the Beniyas Rd side) (☎ 232 855)
Saudia
Road 14, south-west of Beniyas Square, Deira (☎ 236 455)
Singapore Airlines
Pearl building, 2nd floor, St 18, Deira (near Beniyas Square) (☎ 232 300)
Swissair
Airline Centre, Al-Maktoum Rd, Deira (☎ 283 151)
Turkish Airlines
Al-Maktoum Rd, Deira, just east of the Khaleej Palace Hotel (☎ 270 500)
Yemenia
Al-Rais Travel, clock tower roundabout, Deira (☎ 279 797)

Bus Inter-city buses only operate within the Dubai Emirate. To go to another emirate, you have to take a service-taxi.

The only inter-city route that really matters is the one to Hatta (Route No 16, about 1¼ hours, Dh 7). This passes several small villages along the way. The only other 'inter-city' buses are really to outlying parts of Greater Dubai, such as Jebel Ali and Al-Awir. See the Getting Around section for listings of these routes. The Hatta buses leave from the Deira bus station, near the gold souk. There are six buses each day departing at 6.05, 8.35 and 11.05 am and at 1.35, 4.05 and 6.35 pm. The buses stop at the Dubai bus and service-taxi station 15 minutes after leaving the Deira station and also make a number of other stops in the city before heading off to Hatta (see the Getting Around section for a complete route listing). From Hatta, buses for Dubai depart at 6.20, 8.50 and 11.20 am and at 1.50, 4.20 and 6.50 pm. See the Hatta section for more details.

There is also a twice-daily bus service to

Muscat, Oman. The buses depart from the parking lot of the Airline Centre on Al-Maktoum Rd, Deira, at 7.30 am and 5.30 pm and travel to the Ruwi bus station in Muscat. The trip takes five to six hours and costs Dh 85 one way, Dh 150 return (Dh 48/75 for children). For information, call ☎ 203 3799. Tickets are sold at a desk in the Airline Centre. If you are planning to travel on a weekend it might be a good idea to book your trip four or five days in advance. Otherwise booking a day in advance will probably be sufficient.

Service-Taxi There are two service-taxi stations in Dubai, one on either side of the Creek. The Deira taxi station is near the intersection of Umer Ibn Al-Khattab and Al-Rigga Rds. The taxis leave when full (five to seven passengers depending on the vehicle). Fares (per person) are: Sharjah Dh 4, Ajman Dh 5, Umm Al-Qaiwain Dh 7, Ras Al-Khaimah Dh 15, Fujairah Dh 25. Change at Fujairah for Khor Fakkan. The station also has a local taxi rank.

Service-taxis for Abu Dhabi and Al-Ain leave from the Dubai service-taxi and bus station on Al-Ghubaiba Rd, on the Dubai side of the Creek, near the Plaza Cinema. It's Dh 30 per person to Abu Dhabi or Al-Ain. The service-taxis are usually seven passenger Peugeots. Minibuses to Abu Dhabi cost only Dh 20 per person and carry 14 passengers. There are also service-taxis from the Dubai station to Jebel Ali for Dh 7.

Car For rentals of more than a few days Cars Rent-a-Car (☎ 692 694) can usually undercut the bigger agencies. They have an office in Bur Dubai at the Bur Juman Centre. They also have offices in a number of other cities around the UAE. Small cars start at Dh 120 per day plus Dh 20 per day for insurance though they, and the other agencies, are usually willing to discount that rate. I've also had good experience with Hanco Emirates Rent-a-Car (☎ 699 544). They have an office on Al-Ittihad Rd just outside the centre.

Of the big agencies Europcar (☎ 520 033) has desks in the Hilton, Inter-Continental and Hyatt Regency hotels. Hertz (☎ 824 422) and Budget (☎ 823 030) both have large offices on Al-Maktoum Rd between the airport and central Deira. Thrifty Rent-a-Car (☎ 370 743) has an office in Bur Dubai in the Arenco building on Za'abeel Rd. The large agencies all rent small cars from around Dh 140 per day plus Dh 20 in insurance (more for larger models). All of these agencies, as well as Cars and Hanco, have 24 hour a day desks in the arrivals area of the airport.

There are a number of small rental agencies around town but they do not appear to be any cheaper than the larger, established companies, and if you are taking the car outside the city it is probably a good idea to go with an agency that has offices in other cities as well.

Getting Around

The Airport From the Deira bus station, bus Nos 4 and 11 go to the airport about every half hour for Dh 1. Only special airport taxis are allowed to pick up passengers outside the arrivals area. These charge Dh 30 to any point in the city centre (both Deira and Bur Dubai). A ride from the Deira souk area to the airport with a (metered) Dubai Transport taxi costs Dh 10 to Dh 12. Keep that in mind if you opt for a bargaining session with the driver of an unmetered taxi.

Bus Local buses operate out of main stations in both Deira and Bur Dubai. The Deira bus station is off Al-Khor St, between that street and the back of the gold souk. The Bur Dubai service-taxi and bus station is on Al-Ghubaiba Rd (the station on the Dubai side is the main one). Note that in the official timetables the two stations appear as 'Gold Souk Bus Stn' and 'Ghubaiba Bus Stn' respectively. Numbers and routes are posted on the buses in English as well as Arabic. Fares are Dh 1 to Dh 3.50 depending on the distance travelled, and you will find that most trips work out at Dh 1.50 (Dh 3.50 is only for long hauls). For example, from the Al-Khabesi Industrial area all the way to Jebel Ali). You can also purchase monthly bus passes, known as *taufeer*, at both the

Deira and Dubai bus stations. There are two versions of these. The Dh 75 pass gets you unlimited travel for a month on one side of the Creek and the Dh 120 pass unlimited travel within the city. Neither pass can be used on the inter-city buses within the Dubai Emirate (ie for trips to Jebel Ali, Hatta etc). You'll need two passport-size photos to purchase either pass.

Dubai's municipal bus routes are:

Route 2 – Deira bus station, Naif roundabout, Hamriya shopping centre, Al-Qiyada roundabout, Traffic Department offices, Al-T'war and return (every 85 minutes from 7.05 am to 9.15 pm)

Route 4 – Deira bus station, Naif roundabout, Umer Ibn Al-Khattab Rd, Fish roundabout, Deira taxi station, Al-Maktoum Rd, clock tower roundabout, Dubai Islamic Bank, Airline Centre, Flame roundabout, Al-Garhoud intersection, airport roundabout, Dubai airport, Dubai municipality garage, Emirates Airlines office, Al-Ramool Industrial Area, Rashidya clinic, Rashidiya library and return (every 30 minutes from 6.15 am to 9.45 pm)

No 5 – Deira bus station, Naif roundabout, Umer Ibn Al-Khattab Rd, Fish roundabout, Deira taxi station, Al-Maktoum Rd to the clock tower roundabout, Tariq Ibn Ziyad Rd, Al-Maktoum Bridge, Rashid Hospital, Broadcast roundabout (Dubai TV), consulate area, Za'abeel Rd, GPO, Karama district, Trade Centre Rd, Ministry of Health, Al-Saeediya Interchange, Khalid Bin Al-Waleed Rd, Dubai Marine Hotel, Falcon roundabout, Dubai bus station and return (every 12 minutes from 6.10 am to 9.58 pm)

Route 6 – Deira bus station, Naif roundabout, Umer Ibn Al-Khattab Rd, Fish roundabout, Salah Al-Din Rd, Ministry of Interior, Muraqqabat police station, Hamarain Centre, Abu Baker Al-Siddique Rd, clock tower roundabout, Airline Centre, Dubai Islamic Bank, Tariq Ibn Ziad Rd, Al-Maktoum Bridge, British Council, Rashid Hospital, Broadcast roundabout (Dubai TV), Karama district, Trade Centre Rd, Bur Juman Centre, Immigration department, Bur Dubai police station, Al-Dhiyafa Rd, Satwa Rd, Al-Safa St, Al-Wasl Rd, Jumeira fire station, Al-Amal Hospital, Al-Safa housing and return (every 30 minutes from 6 am to 10 pm)

Route 7 – Dubai bus station, Falcon roundabout, Al-Mina Rd, Dubai Electricity Company, Satwa roundabout, Satwa Square, Iranian Hospital, Dubai Petroleum Company, Defence overpass, Sheikh Zayed Rd, Pepsi Cola plant, Al-Qouz housing and return (every 50 minutes from 6.25 an to 10.14 pm)

No 8 – Al-Khabesi, Industrial Area, Muraqqabat Rd, Abu Baker Al-Siddique Rd, Al-Rigga Rd, Deira taxi station, Beniyas Rd, Dubai Municipality, Abra dock, Dubai public library, Deira bus station, Al-Shindagha Tunnel, Falcon roundabout, Dubai bus station, Al-Mina Rd, Dubai dry dock, Jumeira Mosque, Dubai Zoo, Umm Suqaim Municipality, Jumeira Beach Park, Chicago Beach Hotel, Mina Siyahi, Jebel Ali Power Station and return (hourly at 15 minutes past the hour from 6.15 am to 9.45 pm)

Route 10 – Dubai bus station, Al-Mina Rd, Satwa, Central Military Command

Route 11 – Deira bus station, Naif roundabout, Umer Ibn Al-Khattab Rd, Fish roundabout, Deira taxi station, Al-Maktoum Rd, clock tower roundabout, Dubai Islamic Bank, Flame roundabout, Al-Garhoud Intersection, airport roundabout, Khawaneej Rd, Madinat Bader, Murdif overpass, Khawaneej roundabout, Al-Amardi Rd, Khawaneej School, CMC Defence Camp, Al-Awir and return (every 30 minutes from 6.20 am to 9.50 pm)

Route 13 – Deira bus station, Naif roundabout, Umer Ibn Al-Khattab Rd, Fish roundabout, Salah Al-Din Rd, Ministry of Interior, Muraqqabat police station, Tolaitala School, Al-Qiyada roundabout, Dubai Police Headquarters, Al-Ahli Club, Ministry of Information, Jamiat Al-Islah, Qusais Commercial Centre, Qusais police station, Qusais Clinic, Qusais Residential Area, Labour Camps and return (every 10 minutes from 6.05 am to 10.55 pm)

Route 14 – Deira bus station, Naif roundabout, Umer Ibn Al-Khattab Rd, Fish roundabout, Al-Nasr Cinema, Deira taxi station, Al-Maktoum Bridge, Oud Metha Rd, Al-Wasl Hospital, Dubai Water & Electricity Authority, Al-Nasr Cinema, Dubai Municipality Horticulture Section, Al-Garhoud Sewage Treatment Plant, Jadaf and return (every 45 minutes from 6.20 am to 10.05 pm)

Route 15 – Deira bus station, Naif roundabout, Umer Ibn Al-Khattab Rd, Fish roundabout, Deira taxi station, Al-Maktoum Rd, clock tower roundabout, Dubai Islamic Bank, Flame roundabout, Al-Garhoud Intersection, airport roundabout, Khawaneej Rd, Madinat Bader, Murdif overpass, Khawaneej roundabout, Khawaneej Women's Association and return (every two hours from 7.30 am to 9.30 pm)

Route 16 – Deira bus station, Al-Khor St, Al-Khaleej Rd, Al-Shindagha Tunnel, Dubai bus station, Al-Adhid Rd, Trade Centre Rd, 2nd Za'abeel Rd, Oud Metha Rd, Abu Kadra roundabout, Nad Al-Shiba Clinic, Ras Al-Khor, Awir Industrial Area, Habab, Al-Madam, Muzeirah, Hatta and return (every 2½ hours from 6.05 am to 6.35 pm)

Route 17 – Deira bus station, Hyatt Regency Hotel, Al-Khaleej Rd, Al-Khamsaa School, Kuwaiti Hospital, Al-Hamriya Port, Al-Wuhaida Rd, Al-Mamzar Library, Al-Ahli Club, Jameyat Al-Islah, Ministry of Information, Al-Qusais Commercial Centre, Dubai Abattoir, Moh Family Quarters and return (every 50 minutes from 6.20 am to 10.10 pm)

Route 18 – Deira bus station, Naif roundabout, Kuwaiti Hospital, Al-Hamriya post office, Hor Al-Anz St, Al-Safiya and return (every 30 minutes from 6.20 am to 10.20 pm)

Route 19 – Al-Faheidi roundabout, Dubai Museum, Al-Saeediya Interchange, Khalid Bin Al-Waleed Rd, Dubai bus station, Al-Khaleej Rd, Al-Shindagha Tunnel, Al-Khor St, Beniyas Rd, Beniyas Square, Deira Tower, Dubai Municipality, Deira taxi station, Al-Mateena Rd, Abu Baker Al-Siddique Rd, Hor Al-Anz St, Al-Safiya and return (about every 30 minutes from 6.15 am to 10.15 pm)

No 20 – Jumeira Beach Park, Jumeira Rd, Dubai dry dock, Al-Mina Rd, Dubai bus station, Al-Khaleej Rd, Al-Shindagha Tunnel, Al-Khor St, Beniyas Rd, Beniyas Square, Deira tower roundabout, Dubai Municipality, Deira taxi station, Al-Rigga Rd, clock tower, Ministry Complex, Port Saeed, Al-Khabeisi Industrial Area

No 90 – Dubai bus station, Trade Centre Rd, Immigration Department, World Trade Centre, Sheikh Zayed Rd, Emirates Golf Club, Jebel Ali village, Ducab, Jebel Ali Free Zone

Note that most buses both start and finish their days a bit later on Friday. All buses stop for prayers at noon on Friday. You can count on there being no Friday service from about 11.30 am until about 1.30 pm.

Taxi Most of Dubai's taxis have no meters. As in many other Middle Eastern cities this presents you with a choice: negotiate the fare in advance (and pay too much) or get in, tell the driver your destination, pay him what you think is appropriate once you get there and hope that there is no argument.

Should you go the latter route, expect to pay Dh 4 or Dh 5 for trips around the centre that do not involve crossing the Creek. Crossing the Creek immediately runs the standard fare up to Dh 7. Drivers will expect a 50% premium after midnight.

Or, you can call Dubai Transport (☎ 313 131). This government-run company operates a fleet of cream-coloured taxis with meters. You can hail one on the street, or telephone them and they will come pick you up. A flag fall is Dh 2 and the meter then ticks over in 50 fil increments at about Dh 1 per km. I highly recommend them.

Expensive fixed-price cabs also operate from some of the bigger hotels. If you ask someone to call a taxi for you be sure you know who they are calling. One cab-call service in Dubai uses Jaguars – and charges accordingly.

Local service-taxis run from the Dubai service-taxi and bus station on Al-Ghubaiba Rd to Jumeira, Al-Quoz, Al-Bada, Karama and Satwa for Dh 1 to Dh 2 per passenger. These are mostly seven passenger Peugeots and are really only a good bet if you are at the bus station anyway, one going in your direction is nearly full and you can't wait until the next regular bus to your destination departs.

Car The traffic situation in Dubai has improved immensely since the government started forcing people to pay for the privilege of parking in the centre. For years the flow of traffic through the city had been clogged, in no small part because of all the triple-parked cars in Beniyas Square. On the square, and in other parts of the centre, there is now a strictly enforced four hour limit on parking. Once you find a space move immediately to one of the numerous ticket-dispensing machines. Rates are Dh 2 for the first hour, Dh 5 for up to two hours, Dh 8 for up to three hours and Dh 11 for up to four hours. Place the ticket on top of your dashboard – or else. Parking rates apply from 8 am to 1 pm and from 4 to 9 pm Saturday through Thursday. Parking in the centre is free on Fridays and holidays.

Abra Abras leave constantly from early morning until about midnight. On the Deira side of the Creek the dock is at the intersection of Al-Sabkha and Beniyas Rds. On the Dubai side the dock is in front of a shop called Captain's Stores. Abras, like service-taxis, leave when full but it never takes more than five minutes for one of them to fill up.

The fare is 25 fils which is collected once you are out on the water.

The Northern Emirates

SHARJAH

The third-largest of the seven emirates, Sharjah (Ash-Sharqa in Arabic) is a place that too many visitors to the UAE either miss entirely or pass through too quickly. Sharjah has some of the most interesting architecture in the country. Its new souk offers shopping to rival that of Dubai and its recently restored old souk offers a window on an older way of life that has now all but disappeared.

Sharjah has long been seen as Dubai's poor cousin though, in fact, Dubai's ascendance in terms of wealth and political power is relatively recent. During the first half of the 19th century, Sharjah was the most important port on the Arabian side of the lower Gulf, and during the latter half of the century its rulers vied with those of Abu Dhabi for the area's leading political role.

Even after Dubai began to take off as a trading centre, Sharjah remained the more developed of the two in terms of infrastructure. It was in Sharjah that the British chose to set up their main military base in this part of the Gulf and it was here that Imperial Airways developed the Trucial Coast's first international airport.

In the '80s Sharjah took the lead in the development of the UAE's tourist industry, becoming the main point of entry for people arriving in the UAE on package tours.

Orientation

Sharjah's business district is the area between the Corniche and Al-Zahra Rd, from the Central market to Shaikh Mohammed Bin Saqr Al-Qasimi Rd (or Mohammed Saqr St). This is not a huge area and it's pretty easy to get around. During the day, however, it is a dreadful place for driving because the streets are both narrow and crowded. Sharjah's main street is Al-Arouba Rd.

There is a secondary business district

stretching back towards Dubai along King Faisal Rd. Metropolitan Dubai and Metropolitan Sharjah almost join up. Sharjah, however, remains distinctly different from Dubai, and not only because it bans alcohol!

The *Sharjah Tourist City Map*, available free at most of the bigger hotels and at some of the larger travel agencies (like SNTTA), is the best map of Sharjah. A few of the hotels also give away a totally worthless white-coloured *Sharjah Tourist Map* which shows just enough to get you totally confused if you make the mistake of trying to use it.

Information

Money On Boorj Ave, just about every building houses a bank. Moneychangers can be found on the small streets immediately to the east and west of it.

Post The GPO is on Government House Square. It is open Saturday to Wednesday from 8 am to 8 pm and on Thursday from 8 am to 6 pm.

Telephone ETISALAT's office is on Al-Soor Rd (which some of the street signs identify as Al-Mina St and others as Port or Harbour Rd or, this far inland, Ibrahim Mohamed Al-Madfa'a St), on the corner of Al-Safat Square (formerly Kuwait Square). It is open 24 hours a day, and telex and fax services are also available.

The telephone area code for Sharjah is 06.

Travel Agencies The Sharjah National Tourist and Transport Authority (SNTTA ☎ 351 411) handles all travel-related matters. Its office is on Al-Arouba Rd. Because Sharjah airport handles most of the charter flights coming into the UAE, this has not led to a thriving local bucket-shop industry.

Rolla Square

Sharjah's main square lies just inland from the intersection of Boorj Ave and Al-Arouba Rd. On holidays and other ceremonial occasions it is used for big, formal parades. The rest of the time it is a public park.

Sharjah Archaeological Museum
This museum is on Cultural Square on the corner of Shaikh Hamad Bin Saqr Al-Qasimi Rd (which is an extension of Al-Wahda Rd, coming from Dubai). It is open daily from 8.30 am to 12.30 pm and from 5 to 8 pm. On Friday it is open only in the afternoon. Admission is free. All exhibits are labelled in English, French and Arabic.

Begin your visit with a look at the central entrance hall, which has a wide-ranging display on archaeological methods and techniques. Hall one, to the right of the entrance, includes exhibits on Sharjah's geography, traditional falaj-based irrigation systems and on the emirate's history during the Iron Age (1200 to 400 BC).

At the back of the central hall the area linking halls one and two has a display of old coins, both Islamic and pre-Islamic, a small display on the region's trade routes and a funerary slab dated between 250 and 150 BC with an inscription in South Arabian. The slab was found in Saudi Arabia's Al-Hasa Oasis.

Hall two features extensive displays on the French excavations at Meleiha, an inland site in the Sharjah Emirate, focusing particularly on the period between about 150 BC and 100 AD. Other displays carry the site history up into the Islamic period.

Hall three, which is upstairs, was not yet open at the time of writing, but is scheduled to house the museum's collection of Islamic antiquities. ■

Amiri Diwan (The Ruler's Office)
This building, on Government House Square, is the seat of Sharjah's government.

Old Souk
Slowly but surely, an important restoration project has been taking place a few short blocks inland from Khalid Lagoon (Sharjah's Creek). The local government has been restoring this souk, large sections of which fell to pieces during the 1970s and '80s.

At the time of writing, one section of the restored market had opened for business. The shops are a mixture of craft and souvenir outlets selling traditional Emirati clothing, local crafts, jewellery and pearls, along with a few run-of-the-mill houseware places. There is also an excellent coffee house/restaurant. The government seems to have managed to strike that most delicate of balances between setting up something authentic that will actually be used by Sharjah's citizens while also appealing to tourists. If you see only one thing in Sharjah this should be it. The restaurant alone (see Places to Eat, later) is worth the drive over from Dubai.

Central Market
From certain angles, the central market (also called the new souk or the Sharjah souk) looks like a set of monster-size oil barrels which have tipped over and had wind towers glued to their sides. Once inside, however, the design works. A lot of people can circulate comfortably and stay reasonably cool in here. There are hundreds of shops and stalls selling just about everything imaginable. The prices are pretty good and, in many cases, a bit cheaper than in Dubai. The central market is reputed to be the best place in the UAE to shop for Persian carpets. The wind towers, by the way, are real.

King Faisal Mosque
Sharjah's central mosque is the largest mosque in the UAE. It is said to be able to accommodate 3000 worshippers. The mosque dominates Al-Ittihad Square next to the central market.

Beaches
There is a long stretch of public beach near the Coral Beach Hotel, about four km northeast of the Sharjah Continental Hotel on the road to Ajman.

Amusement Park
A pocket-sized Disneyland sits on an island in the Khalid Lagoon. The park is open from

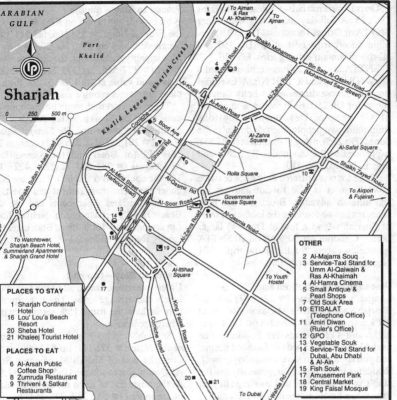

Sunday to Thursday between 3.30 and 10.30 pm and Friday from 9.30 am to 10.30 pm; it is closed on Saturdays. Mondays are reserved for women and children only. Admission costs Dh 5 for adults, Dh 2 for children.

Old Watchtower

Old and much restored watchtowers dot the landscape of Sharjah. One worth noting for its location is the lone watchtower standing guard over a small patch of the coastline on the corner of Khan and Shaikh Sultan Al-Awal Rds.

Organised Tours

The main tour operators based in Sharjah are SNTTA, Emirates Tours (☎ 351 411) and Orient Tours (☎ 549 333). SNTTA offers half-day tours of Dubai (Dh 100) and Sharjah and Ajman (Dh 100). Full-day trips are available to Abu Dhabi, Al-Ain, Ras Al-Khaimah and to the east coast (Dh 160 per tour). SNTTA will also take you to a camel race for Dh 60 or on a shopping trip for Dh 90. These programmes require a minimum of four people. Its office on Al-Arouba Rd in central Sharjah is open daily except Friday from 8 am to 1 pm and from 2 to 7 pm.

Orient Tours has half-day desert safaris for Dh 125. A full-day desert trip with either SNTTA or Orient Tours costs Dh 170. Overnight desert trips cost about Dh 350 and all-day mountain-driving trips, Dh 170.

SNTTA also has a dinner cruise aboard a dhow (Dh 220) and a '1001 Nights Evening' (ie, a Lebanese dinner and a belly dancing show) for Dh 250. Both require a minimum of six people. Desert safari options (minimum two people) include dinner in the dunes (Dh 215), a day in the desert (Dh 255), excursions to the mountains (Dh 280) and overnight trips (Dh 410).

These tours are offered only once or twice a week, so it is best to call and get the schedule in advance. Brochures for both agencies can be found in the lobbies of most of Sharjah's (and a few of Dubai's) larger hotels. Children get 50% off on all SNTTA itineraries except for the dhow trip, 1001 Nights trip and desert safari trips.

Places to Stay – bottom end
Sharjah's *youth hostel* (☎ 321 897) is at the Sharjah Sports Club on Al-Qasmia Rd, about 3.7 km from the GPO. Beds cost Dh 15 per night and IYHF cards are required. The hostel has about 30 beds in four bed dorms, and you are likely to have a room to yourself. Residents in the hostel can generally use the club's swimming pool and bowling alley. In theory the hostel is open to women and to families. In practice I would not recommend it for unaccompanied women, and the management seemed rather dubious about the idea of taking couples when my wife and I posed the question. Unfortunately, there is no way of reaching the hostel by public transport.

There are only two other semi-cheap hotels in town, both on King Faisal Rd. The *Khaleej Tourist Hotel* (☎ 597 888, fax 598 999) charges Dh 105/160 for its rooms. It is simple but clean and has unbelievably small bathrooms (some with Turkish toilets). Across the street the *Sheba Hotel* (☎ 522 522, fax 354 357) is much better value at Dh 95/130, with better rooms and larger baths. Neither hotel can arrange visas.

Places to Stay – middle
A bit outside the centre on King Faisal St is the *Federal Hotel* (☎ 354 106, fax 541 394). Singles/doubles are Dh 176/220. Nearby, at Municipality roundabout, the *Sharjah Plaza Hotel* (☎ 377 555, fax 373 311) is particularly good value at Dh 126/157.50. Both of these hotels can sponsor visas.

There are two mid-range hotels opposite each other on Shaikh Sultan Al-Awal Rd, south-west of the centre. The *Sharjah Beach Hotel* (☎ 281 311, fax 285 422) charges Dh 250/340 for B&B and the *Summerland Apartments* (☎ 281 321, fax 285 422), Dh 160 for doubles (no singles). They are both under the same management and guests at the Summerland Apartments can use the Beach Hotel's private beach. Neither hotel can arrange visas for tourists. Both cater to a largely Russian clientele.

Places to Stay – top end
Unless otherwise noted, all of the following hotels can arrange visas. The rates quoted here include the usual 15% service charge where applicable.

Sharjah's top hotel is the *Sharjah Continental Hotel* (☎ 371 111, fax 524 090) at the Corniche end of Shaikh Mohammed Saqr Al-Qasimi Rd; rooms are Dh 517.50/632.50. At the other end of town the *Hotel Holiday International* (☎ 357 357, 372 254) has the slightly dilapidated air of a shabby beach resort and singles/doubles for Dh 431/546.

The remaining top-end places are all outside the city centre along Shaikh Sultan Al-Awal Rd. The *Sharjah Grand Hotel* (☎ 285 557, fax 282 861) charges Dh 460/575. Many of its customers are Germans on package tours. The *Sharjah Carlton Hotel* (☎ 283 711, fax 284 962) asks Dh 345/460, more if you want a sea view from your room. It will only sponsor visas for Americans and west Europeans. Further down the road, the *Lou' Lou'a Beach Resort* (formerly the Golden Beach Motel) (☎ 285 000, fax 285 222) is a bit nicer. It charges Dh 345/460 for rooms, again without a sea view.

One up-market hotel that doesn't sponsor

visas is the *Coral Beach Hotel* (☎ 221 011, fax 274 101) on the Corniche, just inside Sharjah on the way to Ajman. Rooms are Dh 210/315. The Coral Beach has become the main Russian hang-out in Sharjah.

Places to Eat

There is one place that you really must try while in Sharjah. The *Al-Arsah Public Coffee Shop* in the restored section of Sharjah's old souk. For Dh 10 you not only get a fairly large biryani but also salad·and a bowl of fresh dates for dessert. The restaurant is a traditional-style coffee shop, with seating on high benches. Shisha pipes and backgammon sets are available and sweet tea is served out of a huge urn. Unusually, both the staff and the customers are almost exclusively Emirati.

Rolla Square and Al-Ghazali Rd (parallel to Al-Arouba Rd but one block closer to the sea) have a plethora of cheap Indian eateries. Try the *Zumruda Restaurant* on Al-Ghazali Rd with biryanis at Dh 6 to Dh 7.

The *Al-Anqood Restaurant* near the southwest corner of Rolla Square, is a vegetarian Indian restaurant. Further up Rolla Square try the *Thriveni Restaurant* or the slightly fancier *Satkar Restaurant* immediately above it. The Satkar offers good thalis (set meals, usually a selection of vegetables with bread and rice) from as little as Dh 6. The surroundings are nicer and the view out over the square is worth the extra dirham or two. You can, however, get out of Thriveni with a pretty good meal for under Dh 5.

If you are looking for something a bit more up-market, or simply something not Indian, try *Kowloon*, a Chinese restaurant on Al-Mina St between Al-Arouba Rd and the Corniche. Soups cost Dh 10 to Dh 12 and most main dishes are in the Dh 20 to Dh 30 range. On Friday there's a buffet lunch at Dh 38.50, which is very good value.

Entertainment

Sharjah's emir banned alcohol in 1985 and all of the emirate's discos were closed. Aside from the amusement park, the main form of entertainment is the cinema. The fare is mostly subcontinental though the Al-Hamra Cinema on Al-Arouba Rd often shows (old and low-budget) English-language films.

Things to Buy

There are a few antique shops in the old souk. A couple of antique dealers have also set up in the central market. The selection tends to be an eclectic blend of Chinese and Pakistani curios and Arab jewellery, mostly from Oman.

Persian Carpets Sharjah is one of the best places in the Gulf to buy Persian carpets. Most of the carpet shops are in the central market and they can arrange shipping. There are no export taxes. Prices vary wildly depending on your bargaining skills and the size and quality of the carpet; to make sure you're getting a good deal, it is useful to have some knowledge about Persian carpets.

Getting There & Away

Air Sharjah international airport definitely lives in the shadow of Dubai, but it's putting up a good fight. The idea of raffling off expensive cars to departing and transit passengers with only 1000 tickets sold per car and free delivery anywhere in the world for the winner, now a standard feature at Abu Dhabi, Dubai, Bahrain and Muscat, originated here. Sharjah airport has also become the major point of entry for tourists coming to the UAE. The airport is 15 km from the centre. The phone number for airport information is ☎ 581 111. Some of the scheduled carriers serving Sharjah are:

EgyptAir
  Al-Mina St, near the intersection with Al-Arouba Rd (☎ 352 163)
Gulf Air
  Al-Arouba Rd, near the overpass and intersection with Al-Soor Rd (☎ 371 366)
Iran Air
  Al-Arouba Rd, opposite the Akai showroom (☎ 350 000)
Syrian air
  Orient Travel, Al-Arouba St, next to the Sharjah Cinema (☎ 357 203)

Bus There is no bus service to, from or through Sharjah. If you don't have a car you'll have to get a taxi.

Service-Taxi Sharjah has two service-taxi stations. Taxis for Umm Al-Qaiwain (Dh 7) and Ras Al-Khaimah (Dh 15) leave from the stand on Al-Arouba Rd across from the Al-Hamra Cinema. Taxis for Dubai (Dh 4), Abu Dhabi and Al-Ain (Dh 30 to either city) depart from a stand next to the vegetable souk. It's worth noting that the Abu Dhabi and, especially, Al-Ain taxis rarely fill up – the stand seems mostly to be overflow space for the Dubai taxi stand. You are far better off taking a taxi to Dubai and travelling on to Abu Dhabi or Al-Ain from there.

Ajman, for travel purposes, is regarded as an extension of Sharjah so there are no service-taxis going there.

Car In addition to the international car rental companies in the big hotels, there are a number of small firms along Al-Mina St, near the overpass.

Getting Around

Since Sharjah has no bus service, getting around without your own car means either taking taxis or walking. The taxis are without meters and trips around the centre should cost Dh 5 to Dh 10 (agree on the fare before you get in). If you hire a taxi by the hour expect to pay around Dh 20 per hour, though you might be able to bargain that down a little. When the heat is not too debilitating Sharjah's centre can be covered on foot quite easily.

Only special airport taxis can pick up passengers at Sharjah airport. These charge fixed rates depending on your destination. The trip to central Sharjah costs Dh 40. If you need to go to Dubai the fare is Dh 60 to Deira and Dh 70 to central Bur Dubai (ie not including Chicago Beach or Jebel Ali).

AROUND SHARJAH
Sharjah Natural History Museum

Opened with much fanfare in November 1995, the Sharjah Natural History Museum is quite extraordinary – possibly the slickest, most modern museum in the entire Gulf. Unfortunately for the casual visitor, it also happens to be out in the desert 35 km east of Sharjah's centre on the road to Fujairah. At least the exit is well marked.

Many of the museum's exhibits are aimed at children – most can be touched and there are a large number of interactive displays – but grown-ups will probably find it fascinating as well. Everything in the museum is labelled in both English and Arabic.

The museum gets off to a dramatic start. After a fairly ordinary opening section on the origins of the earth, photosynthesis and the formation of Arabia's deserts, one passes through a doorway and encounters the longest diorama in the world: a 35m model of the emirate's landscape as one moves across the peninsula from, approximately, Kalba to Sharjah. Opposite this are displays of the different plants and animals one finds in each of the emirate's regions (the Gulf of Oman coastal plain, the mountains, the Gulf coast etc). This room alone is worth the trip.

The next gallery examines human settlement in Arabia, agriculture, and the domestication of various animals. It includes a bizarre full-size mock-up of a camel in which common household items illustrate the various parts of the animal's body (a fly swatter for the tail, for example).

Hall three focuses on geology with displays on plate tectonics, the earth and its core, earthquakes, meteorites and evolution. This section includes a wraparound theatre with a short, and very dramatic, film on the origins of the universe. There are also several casts of dinosaur skeletons on display. The museum's management decided to keep the real ones in storage and display the copies so that children visiting the museum could be allowed to touch the 'dinosaur bones'.

Next to the dinosaurs is a lift to the museum's upper level. This is the point at which one gets the requisite 'benefits of oil' portion of the museum, including another film. Another lift takes you back down to a botanical gallery and an exhibit on ecology that includes a number of computer games designed to teach children about ecology and the environment.

The final gallery deals with the sea. All of the fish and other sea creatures displayed in the hall are found in local waters. In fact, all of the fish from which the displays were cast were purchased in the Sharjah and Ajman fish souks – including the huge whale shark.

A desert park and breeding centre are adjacent to the museum complex. The plan is eventually to develop this area into a small safari park featuring endangered species native to Arabia. Initially the breeding centre was supplied with a pair of Arabian wolves, a pair of rare Arabian leopards and several gazelles.

As the museum is still fairly new, its managers were uncertain what its regular hours would eventually be. The best bet was that it would be open from approximately 9 am to 1 pm and from 5 to 8.30 pm daily except Friday. On Fridays it will probably be open nonstop from 10 am to 9 pm. The museum will be closed on Sunday. Plans call for mornings to be reserved for school groups and organised tour groups. Admission is free.

Dhaid

Dhaid is a medium-sized oasis town, 50 km east of Sharjah. In the days before air-conditioning it was a popular getaway spot for Sharjah's elite. It certainly looks inviting. If you are approaching the town from Sharjah it appears as a spot of green set in a sea of sand dunes. There's nothing to see, but it's a good place to stop for lunch or to spend an hour or two wandering along the tracks which crisscross the oasis.

The *Al-Waha Market Restaurant* in the new souk building (on Dhaid's first roundabout if you're coming from Sharjah, the second roundabout if you are coming from Fujairah) has cheap Indian chicken and mutton biryanis and tikkas. A meal should cost about Dh 10. Outsiders stopping for anything other than petrol are still a bit rare in Dhaid so be prepared to be stared at.

AJMAN

The smallest of the seven emirates, Ajman is hardly the mere extension of Sharjah that some people imagine. The emirate occupies a small stretch of coast between Sharjah and Umm Al-Qaiwain and also has two inland enclaves. One is Masfut, at the western edge of the Hajar Mountains, and the other is Manama, in the north-central interior on the road from Sharjah to Fujairah.

Orientation & Information

Ajman's central square is within walking distance of pretty much everything, including the museum, Ajman's lone hotel, a couple of small restaurants and the coastline. Leewara St follows the section of the coast containing most of the city's few sites other than the museum. The local government offices, GPO and telephone office are all on Shaikh Khalifa St. The gift shop at the museum sometimes has an excellent map of the city for Dh 10.

There is no tourist office. The place marked on maps as 'Ajman Tourist Centre' is a combination video arcade and coffee shop.

The telephone area code for Ajman is 06.

Ajman Museum

Ajman's museum occupies the old police fort on the emirate's central square. It is open from 9 am to 1 pm except Thursday, when it closes at noon. The museum reopens in the afternoon from 4 to 7 pm (5 to 8 pm from May through August). It is closed Saturday. Admission is Dh 4 (Dh 2 for children under six). Photography is not permitted.

The fort was built in the late 18th century and served as the ruler's palace and office until 1970. From 1970 to 1978, it was Ajman's main police station. The police moved out of most of the complex in 1978 (they still occupy a few buildings attached to the fort but opening onto Shaikh Khalifa St rather than the main square) and renovation work on the building began. It was opened as a museum in 1981. It is one of the best museums in the UAE and is well worth the drive from Dubai.

THE UNITED ARAB EMIRATES

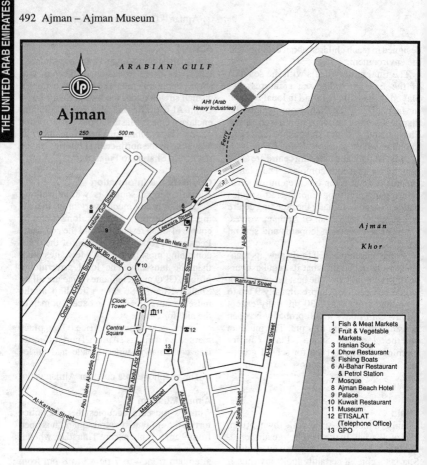

ARABIAN GULF

Ajman

0   250   500 m

AHI (Arab
Heavy Industries)

Ferry

Ajman
Khor

Arabian Gulf Street
Humaid Bin Abdul
Omer Bin Al-Khattab Street
Abu Baker Al-Siddiq Street
Al-Karama Street
Humaid Bin Abdul Aziz Street
Masfut Street
Al-Burtan Street
Al-Safia Street
Al-Mina Street
Aziz Street
Shaikh Khalifa Street
Leewara Street
Aqba Bin Nafa St
Al-Butain
Ramrani Street

Clock
Tower

Central
Square

1 Fish & Meat Markets
2 Fruit & Vegetable
   Markets
3 Iranian Souk
4 Dhow Restaurant
5 Fishing Boats
6 Al-Bahar Restaurant
   & Petrol Station
7 Mosque
8 Ajman Beach Hotel
9 Palace
10 Kuwait Restaurant
11 Museum
12 ETISALAT
   (Telephone Office)
13 GPO

This museum is very well laid out. The items on display include a collection of manuscripts, weapons, archaeological finds and reconstructions of traditional rooms. Also on display are gifts and decorations that the emir has received over the years. Everything in the museum is labelled in both Arabic and English, except for parts of the Police Exhibit.

Until fairly recently, Ajman issued its own passports. Some of these are on display in the museum, including Ajman Passport No 1 which belonged to the present emir's father, Shaikh Rashid. It is a diplomatic passport.

There is also a quite effective reconstruction of a traditional street in a souk. It's at the far edge of the main courtyard, opposite the museum entrance.

Immediately to your right as you come in through the gate is a reconstructed tomb from the Umm Al-Nar civilisation. The tomb was excavated in the Mowaihat area and moved to the museum after suffering water damage.

The museum shop is worth a look both for its map of the city and its small collection of local handicrafts. A guide to the museum is available for Dh 5.

Beaches

There are several public beaches in Ajman town, particularly around the Ajman Beach Hotel. A smaller public beach can also be found on Arabian Gulf St, just south of the Ajman Tourist Centre.

Souks

Fruit and vegetables and meat and fish are sold in two purpose-built souk areas along the coast, off Leewara St. The best time to come is early in the morning, around 7 or 8 am, when the fishers are back in port with the day's catch and the fish souk is at its busiest.

Around the parking lot in front of these markets an area known as the **Iranian souk** has grown up in the last few years. The Iranian souk is a fascinating place to prowl around. You are unlikely to find much in the way of souvenirs (unless your idea of a souvenir is a plastic washing bucket), though you can sometimes find interesting pottery. Cheap housewares are the market's main stock in trade. Apparently many of the first merchants to set up stalls here were Iranians, hence the name. That said, there's nothing particularly Iranian about what you will see there today.

Places to Stay & Eat

The only place to stay in Ajman is the *Ajman Beach Hotel* (☎ 423 333, fax 423 363). It has decent singles/doubles for Dh 175/250. Since the hotel has a private beach and, unlike Sharjah hotels, a bar, it is quite a good deal compared to comparably priced hotels in Dubai, provided you don't mind being a half hour drive from Dubai itself. The hotel also offers that rarest of things in the Gulf: legal gambling. The hotel runs bingo games with large jackpots several nights a week. It will also arrange visas for travellers arriving through Dubai airport.

The *Kuwait Restaurant,* at the junction of Humaid Bin Abdul Aziz St and Abu Baker Al-Siddiq St, has good biryanis for Dh 7. A few other Indian food items are also available. You'll find a number of similar places along Leewara St. The *Dhow Restaurant* along the waterfront is actually a coffee

house in a traditional barasti shelter. It's a nice place for a cup of coffee or tea late in the afternoon. Look for the blue-and-white sign with two coffeepots and a rosewater urn on it.

Getting There & Away

Ajman has no bus service and there's no taxi stand. But taxi drivers on the Sharjah route generally don't mind travelling here as it's only a few extra km. After dropping a passenger off they'll cruise around the centre looking for passengers and then head back to the taxi stand in Sharjah. From Sharjah a taxi ride to Ajman costs Dh 20 or Dh 30.

AROUND AJMAN
Manama

No, not the capital of Bahrain. This Manama is an enclave of Ajman lying near the junction of the southbound road from Ras Al-Khaimah and the east-west road linking Dubai and Sharjah with the east coast. It is an oasis town in the midst of a heavily agricultural area.

The town is mainly the set of shops bordering on the roundabout with the miniature Eiffel Tower (yes, you read that correctly). It consists of a few small Indo-Arab restaurants and grocery stores, a couple of garages and a petrol station.

The only thing to see is the **fort** near the main roundabout. It is quite well preserved, probably because the police still use it. It is not open to the public. Steer well clear of the red fort on the edge of town and do not attempt to photograph it. It is part of an army base.

UMM AL-QAIWAIN

With a population of around 40,000, Umm Al-Qaiwain (Umm Al-Quwain, Umm Al-Qawain) is the least populous of the seven emirates.

When the British announced that they would withdraw from the Gulf in 1971, all of the emirs initially wanted complete independence. After Bahrain and Qatar pulled out of a proposed federation, it was largely British pressure that convinced the emirs of the Trucial States that they could not each go it alone. Places like Umm Al-Qaiwain were obviously not viable as independent states.

Today the attraction of this small and relatively remote emirate is its very isolation. More than any other place in the UAE, Umm Al-Qaiwain provides a glimpse of what life throughout the country was like not so long ago. There are no high-rise buildings in the town centre and the pace of life is still unhurried. It's not necessarily worth the drive from Dubai on its own, but as a short diversion off the main road from Dubai to Ras Al-Khaimah it is definitely worth an hour of your time. Once here you are unlikely to see any compelling reason to stay much longer than that.

Orientation & Information

Umm Al-Qaiwain lies on a narrow peninsula of sand jutting north from the main road linking Dubai and Sharjah with Ras Al-Khaimah. The old town and the emirate's small business district are at the northern tip of the peninsula, particularly along King Faisal Rd. Most of the streets are not signposted but it is hard to get lost in a place this small.

The post office is south of the centre near the stadium. The ETISALAT office is on King Faisal Rd about one km south of the intersection with Al-Hason Rd.

The telephone area code for Umm Al-Qaiwain is 06.

Things to See & Do

The small **fort** at the intersection of Al-Hason Rd and Al-Lubna Rd is not much to look at and it's usually closed. The **mosque** next to the fort is a bit more interesting. It has a largely open design. An inscription over the doorway dates its construction to June, 1962 (Moharram, 1382 AH). Along the coast near the fort and mosque you can see a few dhows and fishers but there is not a lot left of the old harbour atmosphere. A few old **watchtowers** are scattered around town, including two near the Cardoba Restaurant.

Places to Stay & Eat

All three of Umm Al-Qaiwain's hotels are south of the centre, and none are cheap. None of them sponsor visas.

On the peninsula's eastern side, the *Pearl Hotel* (☎ 666 678, fax 666 679), about five km south of the town centre, has singles/

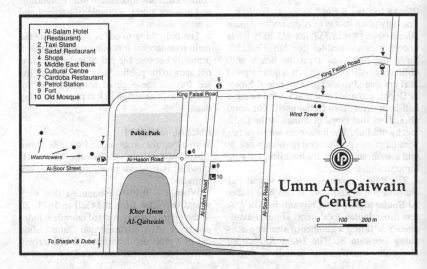

1 Al-Salam Hotel (Restaurant)
2 Taxi Stand
3 Sadaf Restaurant
4 Shops
5 Middle East Bank
6 Cultural Centre
7 Cardoba Restaurant
8 Petrol Station
9 Fort
10 Old Mosque

Public Park

Watchtowers

Al-Soor Street

Al-Hason Road

King Faisal Road

Wind Tower

Al-Lubna Road

Al-Souk Road

Khor Umm Al-Qaiwain

To Sharjah & Dubai

Umm Al-Qaiwain Centre

0   100   200 m

doubles for Dh 200/220. About 2.5 km north of the Pearl is Umm Al-Qaiwain's newest hotel, the *Palma Beach Hotel* (☎ 667 090, fax 667 388) where a room in a prefabricated cabin sitting on the beach will cost you Dh 220 or Dh 250 for a single and Dh 330 for a double.

Another km back toward the centre and on the western side of the peninsula is the *Umm Al-Quwain Beach Hotel* (☎ 666 647, fax 667 273), a slightly musty place which rents bungalows by the bedroom: one bedroom for Dh 350 per night, two bedrooms for Dh 500 and three bedrooms for Dh 700, in all cases a 15% service charge will be added to your bill. Each room sleeps two, and you might be able to cram in more people so, if you have a group, this could be the best deal in town. To get there follow the signs from King Faisal Rd and turn right at the T-junction after you get off the main road.

Both the Pearl Hotel and the Umm Al-Quwain Beach Hotel have restaurants (and bars). The centre also has a collection of tiny biryani places. A good bet is the *Sadaf Restaurant* which serves up shawarma with exceptionally generous helpings of meat for Dh 2. Half a fresh-roasted chicken will set you back Dh 7. Similar fare can be found at the *Cardoba Restaurant* near the intersection of King Faisal Rd and Al-Hason St. Next to the Pearl Hotel you should see a barasti structure, this is the *UAQ Public Kitchen and Tea Stall*, a traditional coffee house.

Getting There & Away

Without your own car the only way in or out of Umm Al-Qaiwain is by taxi. The taxi stand is on King Faisal Rd, across from the Al-Salam Hotel (which is actually a restaurant). A seat in a shared taxi to Dubai, Sharjah or Ajman costs Dh 7. If you want to go to Ras Al-Khaimah, you will have to take the taxi 'engaged' (ie, by yourself and paying for all seven seats in it). With some bargaining this will probably cost about Dh 40.

You could, in theory, get from Dubai to Umm Al-Qaiwain and back the same day by service-taxi (with your own car you could do it in under two hours), but there does not seem to be a lot of action at the taxi stand in Umm Al-Qaiwain, and in Dubai taxis bound for Umm Al-Qaiwain do not fill up quickly either. Be prepared both for a long wait and for a possible engaged ride back to Dubai.

RAS AL-KHAIMAH

Ras Al-Khaimah is one of the most beautiful spots in the UAE. It is the northernmost and the most fertile of the emirates. Much of its land has been carefully irrigated and the result is an area of abundant greenery on the edge of both the mountains and the desert. The city is relaxing, has its share of interesting sites and is a good base for exploring the countryside. Ras Al-Khaimah is a favourite weekend getaway for people from Dubai and is also increasingly popular with package tourists from Scandinavia.

History

Flints and potsherds found near the Khatt Hot Springs indicate that Ras Al-Khaimah has been inhabited since the 3rd millennium BC. For much of its history the region's main town was Julfar, a few km to the north of the modern city of Ras Al-Khaimah.

By the 7th century AD, Julfar was an important port. The 12th century Arab geographer Al-Idrisi mentions it as a pearling centre. Pottery and other finds from this era indicate that Julfar had significant trade links with both China and India. In the 15th century Julfar was the birthplace of Ahmed Bin Majid, the great Arab sailor whose books on navigation are still studied and who was hired by Vasco de Gama to guide him to India in 1498.

In the early 16th century, the Portuguese occupied Julfar where they built a customs house and, in 1631, a fort. No trace of either of these remains today and their exact location is uncertain. The Portuguese abandoned the fort and the town in 1633 after a series of attacks by both the local tribes and the British and Dutch navies. By the time they left, Julfar must have been in ruins because its Arab inhabitants moved to Ras Al-Khaimah despite the fact that they had won the war.

Different branches of the Al-Qasimi

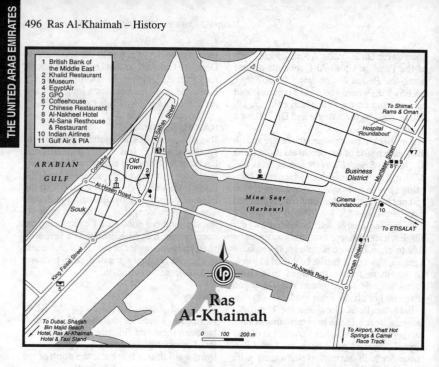

1 British Bank of
  the Middle East
2 Khalid Restaurant
3 Museum
4 EgyptAir
5 GPO
6 Coffeehouse
7 Chinese Restaurant
8 Al-Nakheel Hotel
9 Al-Sana Resthouse
  & Restaurant
10 Indian Airlines
11 Gulf Air & PIA

ARABIAN
GULF

Old
Town

Souk

Corniche

Al-Sabah Street

Al-Hosen Road

King Faisal Street

Ras
Al-Khaimah

To Dubai, Sharjah
Bin Majid Beach
Hotel, Ras Al-Khaimah
Hotel & Taxi Stand

0   100   200 m

Mina Saqr
(Harbour)

Al-Juwais Road

Business
District

Muntasar Street

Oman Street

To Shimal,
Rams & Oman

Hospital
'Roundabout'

Cinema
'Roundabout'

To ETISALAT

To Airport, Khatt Hot
Springs & Camel
Race Track

family rule both Ras Al-Khaimah and
Sharjah, tracing their ancestry to an 18th
century shaikh from Ras Al-Khaimah.
Throughout the 18th century the Qawasim,
as the ruling clan was known, were the most
powerful rulers in the lower Gulf, and by the
beginning of the 19th century they had a
large fleet. The early 19th century British
raids on the Qawasim-controlled coast were
partly in retaliation for attacks on British
shipping, but they were also prompted by a
belief that the Qawasim posed a threat to
Oman's independence. Britain had a treaty
with the Omanis and regarded Oman's independence as crucial to the protection of its
own supply lines to India.

In 1809, the British raided Ras Al-
Khaimah and briefly occupied it. Ten years
later, they again invaded and occupied the
town, besieging the inhabitants of both Ras
Al-Khaimah and Rams at Dhayah. The
hilltop fortress at Dhayah, to which the
inhabitants retreated, can still be seen. The

British withdrew after imposing a General
Treaty of Peace on the shaikhs of the coast
in 1820 and the Qawasim never quite recovered their previous power and status.

It was with this history in mind that Ras
al-Khaimah initially chose to stay out of the
UAE when the federation was formed in
December 1971. Three months later the ruler
changed his mind, apparently after conclud-
ing that the emirate couldn't survive as an
independent state. Small quantities of oil
were discovered in Ras Al-Khaimah in 1976
but the revenues from this have never
amounted to much.

Today, Ras Al-Khaimah's economy is
based mainly on agriculture (particularly
vegetables and citrus fruits), and it is sometimes referred to as the breadbasket of the
UAE. There are also relatively small cement
and petrochemical plants and an increasingly
important tourism industry.

Ras Al-Khaimah is said to have the largest
number of indigenous Arabs as a percentage

of its overall population of any of the emirates. It has no long-established Indian or Persian merchant communities like Dubai or Sharjah. It is also the only place in the UAE where, as in Saudi Arabia, all shops are required to close at prayer time.

Orientation

Ras Al-Khaimah is really two cities. Ras Al-Khaimah proper, which is the old town on a sandy peninsula along the Gulf coast, and Al-Nakheel, the newer business district on the other side of Ras Al-Khaimah's Creek. There is a bridge across the Creek and another road to the south which skirts the water's edge. Only a few of the streets in either town have names and there are no street signs.

Aside from the museum and the old town's souk, there isn't very much to Ras Al-Khaimah proper. Most of the hotels and services, and even the city's lone traditional coffee house, are in Al-Nakheel.

Most of Al-Nakheel's shops and offices are on Oman St, between the Hospital and Cinema roundabouts (both of which, despite the names, are intersections, not roundabouts). This area also includes the city's one cheap hotel and a number of small restaurants.

Information

While Ras Al-Khaimah figures on many tourists' itineraries there is little you can do to book a tour once you are there. A number of places around town advertise tour services, but they seem suspiciously unable to produce lists of their offerings or prices.

You can change money at any of the many banks along Al-Sabah St in Ras Al-Khaimah or Oman St in Al-Nakheel.

The GPO is a red brick building on King Faisal St, about four km north of the Bin Majid Beach Hotel. The ETISALAT office is one km east of the Cinema roundabout in Al-Nakheel. It is open Saturday to Thursday from 7 am to 8 pm and Friday from 9 am to 8 pm.

The telephone area code for Ras Al-Khaimah is 07.

Ras Al-Khaimah Museum

The museum is in the old fort on Al-Hosen Rd, next to the police headquarters. It is open from 8 am to noon and from 4 to 7 pm daily except Tuesday. Admission is Dh 2 for adults and Dh 1 for children. Cameras require an additional ticket costing Dh 5. All the signs are in both Arabic and English and a good guidebook is on sale at the gate for Dh 10. The fort was built in the mid-18th century. Until the early 1960s it was the residence of the ruling Al-Qasimi shaikhs.

One room on the ground floor has a particularly good display of Arabian silver jewellery and another room features a collection of sea shells from all over the UAE. The lower floor also includes exhibits on Ras Al-Khaimah's archaeology and ethnography and the region's natural history. The highlight of the upper floor is the working wind tower, beneath which you should definitely take a moment to sit. A few of the other rooms upstairs are also open to the public, though they are not furnished. The upper floor also houses a display on the ruling family as well as the museum offices.

Old Town

Ras Al-Khaimah's old town is a wonderful place to stroll around. The souk area, south of the museum, has a number of small tailors' shops but the main attraction is the unspoiled atmosphere. Ras Al-Khaimah welcomes tourists without bending itself out of shape to cater to them. The other part of the old town worth seeing is the km or so of coast immediately north of the bridge, including the old fishing port.

Activities

Water Sports Water sports are being promoted by both the Bin Majid Beach Hotel and the Ras Al-Khaimah Hotel. If you are staying in one of these places they can provide you with more information on windsurfing, water-skiing, diving etc.

Camel Racing Ras Al-Khaimah's camel racetrack is one of the best in the country. It is in Digdagga, about 10 km south of town.

Races usually take place on Fridays during the winter and sometimes also on Tuesday or Wednesday. The schedule is irregular, so ask locally or check with the tour operators at the hotels. Admission is free but come early. The races usually start around 6 am and continue until 9 or 9.30 am.

Camel racing in Ras Al-Khaimah is not for the faint-hearted. The track is circular and huge, about seven or eight km in length. The races take place on a four km straight and, the moment the gun sounds, dozens of Emiratis go screaming down the side of the track in their 4WDs, paying far more attention to the camels than to where they are going. It would be *very* easy to get run over in these circumstances so be careful.

To reach the racetrack, take the airport road south from Al-Nakheel and turn right at the Ras Al-Khaimah Poultry & Feeding Company (there's a yellow sign on the building). Look for a large, freestanding minaret at the turn-off. Keep following the road from there until you reach the track.

Places to Stay

There are four hotels in Ras Al-Khaimah. The one cheapie is the *Al-Sana Resthouse* (☎ 229 004, fax 223 722), which is not as cheap or as good as it used to be but remains a reasonably good deal. Singles/doubles cost Dh 100/120. A few of the rooms have attached baths and kitchenettes but most do not. Be warned, the shared bathrooms are very small. Bring your own towel and toilet paper. The hotel is on Oman St immediately behind the Al-Nakheel.

The *Al-Nakhel Hotel* (☎ 222 822, fax 222 922), on Muntaser St in Al-Nakheel, has the cheapest bar in town but not much else to recommend it. Rooms are Dh 120/180.

The *Bin Majid Beach Hotel* (☎ 352 233, fax 353 225) is the favoured haunt of Russian tour groups. Rooms are Dh 192.50/275, including the service charge.

The *Ras Al-Khaimah Hotel* (☎ 352 999, fax 352 990) has rooms for Dh 264/374, including service. Discounted weekend specials are sometimes available. Note that

since the last edition of this book the Ras Al-Khaimah Hotel has stopped serving alcohol.

The two top-end hotels and the Al-Sana can also arrange visas for tourists, though if you're coming in through the airport of Dubai or Sharjah it would be a good idea to give them two weeks or more warning.

Places to Eat

I highly recommend the *Al-Sana Restaurant*, immediately behind the Al-Sana Resthouse. It has western, Chinese and Filipino food. Meals should not run to more than Dh 15 to Dh 20. The restaurant (which has the same ownership as the rest house but different management) is run by Rojier Coniega, the head of the local Filipino Club and an all-around good guy. Ask him to show you his citations from presidents Corazon Aquino and Fidel Ramos for his service to the Filipino community in the UAE.

Another very good place to eat in Al-Nakheel is the *Libanese House Restaurant*, next door to the Al-Nakheel Hotel on Muntaser St. It serves great Lebanese mezze for Dh 5 to Dh 12 apiece. Most main dishes cost Dh 10 to Dh 12. Several readers and a couple of people I met also recommended the aptly named *Chinese Restaurant* on Oman St a few hundred metres north of the Al-Sana. Personally, I was not impressed, but judge for yourself. Main dishes cost Dh 15 to Dh 25.

In the old town, the *Khalid Restaurant* on Al-Sabah St remains dependably clean, but at Dh 12 or Dh 13 for a biryani it is rather expensive. Also, for some reason the chicken for the biryanis is fried instead of roasted.

You should definitely drop in at the *Coffeehouse*, the last of Ras Al-Khaimah's old-style coffee houses. It is in an unmarked barasti structure near Mina Saqr, next to the garish *Tourists Cafeteria*. Very sweet tea costs 50 fils a cup (Dh 1 with milk).

If you're looking for a drink try the *Churchill Pub* at the Al-Nakheel Hotel. I've always found it a rather depressing place, but it is cheap.

Entertainment

There's a disco at the Bin Majid Beach Hotel, and lounge acts will assault your ears both there and at the Al-Nakheel.

Getting There & Away

Air Ras Al-Khaimah's small airport is 22.5 km south of Al-Nakheel. Four airlines operate international services to Ras Al-Khaimah. Gulf Air has weekly flights from Ras Al-Khaimah to Doha, Karachi and Muscat. Indian Airlines flies once a week to Calicut, PIA once a week to Karachi and EgyptAir has a weekly flight to Cairo. For airport information ring ☎ 448 111. Airline addresses in Ras Al-Khaimah are:

EgyptAir
  Al-Sabah St, Ras Al-Khaimah Old Town (☎ 335 000)
Gulf Air
  Oman St, Al-Nakheel, between Al-Juwais Rd and the Cinema roundabout (☎ 221 531)
Indian Airlines
  Cinema roundabout, Al-Nakheel (☎ 221 789)
PIA (Pakistan International Airlines)
  Oman St, Al-Nakheel, between Al-Juwais Rd and the Cinema roundabout (☎ 221 096)

Service-Taxi Ras Al-Khaimah's taxi stand is on King Faisal St, just south of the Bin Majid Beach Hotel and on the same side of the road. Taxis leave when full, taking either five or seven passengers. Taxis to Dubai and Sharjah charge Dh 15 per person. For the same price, the driver might drop you off in Ajman or Umm Al-Qaiwain. If you do need travel to Abu Dhabi or the east coast by taxi your best bet is to go to Dubai and change there. Service-taxis to Abu Dhabi charge Dh 50 per person if you can fill one, but you are more likely to have to take it engaged, for about Dh 250. The same goes for Fujairah (Dh 20 regular, around Dh 150 engaged). Taking a taxi engaged to Dubai costs around Dh 70.

If you are trying to get to Oman's Musandem Peninsula the Ras Al-Khaimah taxi drivers will take you to Khasab, the main town in Musandem, for Dh 200 one way. For Dh 40 they will dump you at the border in Sham from where you'll just have to try your luck. If you do engage a taxi to Khasab make absolutely sure that your driver is an Emirati (ie that he does not need a visa to enter Oman), that he owns the car and has the papers to prove it in his possession before you start out. You will also have to pay a Dh 20 road tax at the UAE side of the border.

Local service-taxi destinations north of Ras Al-Khaimah include Rams Dh 6, Khor Khowair Dh 8; and Sham Dh 8.

Taxis into Ras Al-Khaimah's centre are Dh 2 shared and Dh 10 engaged.

Car You can rent cars in the hotels or from one of the small agencies along Oman St in Al-Nakheel.

Getting Around

Taxis are without meters. Fares within Ras Al-Khaimah town or within Al-Nakheel are about Dh 5 engaged and Dh 2 or Dh 3 shared. Between Ras Al-Khaimah and Al-Nakheel, expect to pay Dh 10 (engaged) and Dh 3 (regular).

AROUND RAS AL-KHAIMAH

Ras Al-Khaimah is a perfect base for exploring the northern tip of the UAE. Several interesting archaeological sites and the Khatt Hot Springs are within easy driving distance. In fact, it would not be too hard to cover everything listed here in one long day provided you get an early start and have your own transport. None of the archaeological sites listed here are fenced in so you can approach them throughout the day. To visit most of these places, you'll need to have a car or to hire a taxi.

Shimal

The village of Shimal, five km north of Ras Al-Khaimah, is the site of some of the most important archaeological finds in the UAE. The area has been inhabited at least since the 2nd millennium BC when, excavations have shown, it was one of the largest settlements in this part of Arabia.

The main attraction is the **Queen of Sheba's Palace**, a set of ruined buildings and fortifications spread over two small plateaus overlooking the village. On a clear day the view is great. Despite its name, the palace was not built by the Queen of Sheba who is generally thought to have come from what is now Yemen. It may, however, have been visited by Queen Zenobia who ruled a sizeable chunk of the Near East in the 4th century AD from Palmyra in modern Syria. The fortifications are known to have been in use as recently as the 16th century. What is visible today apparently sits on top of a much older structure.

To reach the site go north for 4.5 km from the Hospital roundabout in Al-Nakheel and turn right onto a paved road. Look for a white sign with the UAE crest and a big red arrow (for those who read Arabic, the sign points to the Shimal Health Centre). Follow this road for about 1.5 km until you reach a roundabout and take the first right turn out of the roundabout. Follow the road for another 2.3 km and take the first paved turn to the left at a new building built to look like a fort. After about 400m the pavement ends; keep going straight on a dirt track through the village. You'll pass a small mosque after which the track forks; take the right-hand track. After a few hundred metres you will come to a hill which is lighter in colour than the higher hills behind it. You will see a fence around the hill and a locked gate immediately in front of you. Keep going in the same direction, keeping the hill on your right. About one km after the place where the road ended you'll come to a parking area in the village and an opening in the fence. Park here.

Getting to the top of the hill involves a fairly easy 10 minute climb. As you start up the hill you will see a ruined cistern which looks like a stone box. Once you've passed it, head for the wall across the cleft in the hill. Beware of loose stones underfoot.

A taxi from Ras Al-Khaimah to Shimal costs Dh 4 regular and Dh 15 engaged. Note that Dh 15 only gets you there. Going to Shimal, waiting while you climb the hill, and then taking you back is definitely going to cost more.

Rams

A quiet village 12 km north of Ras Al-Khaimah, Rams has a nice coastline and a few old **watchtowers**. Rams has played an important role in Ras Al-Khaimah's history. It was one of the sites at which the British fleet landed in 1819 during the invasion of the lower Gulf which led, the following year, to the area coming under de facto British rule.

Coming from Ras Al-Khaimah, the easiest way to access the town is by taking the second Rams turn-off.

Service-taxis between Rams and Ras Al-Khaimah cost Dh 6 per person regular and Dh 30 engaged.

Dhayah

Another 3.5 km beyond Rams is Dhayah, a small village beneath a ruined fort. It was here that the people of Rams retreated in the face of the advancing British in 1819 and surrendered after a four day siege. The site has recently had some restoration work done to it and now more closely resembles the way the fortifications looked a century ago.

The **fort** sits atop a sharp, cone-shaped hill behind the modern village. It takes 15 to 20 minutes to climb the hill, longer if you stop to collect some of the numerous sea shells which blanket the slopes. Be careful, however, the rock is very loose and it's easy to slip. The easiest approach is from the west side of the hill (the side facing the sea), moving toward the south side as you ascend. Once you get to the top the only easy way into the fort is through the south wall.

To reach the hill, turn right off the road from Ras Al-Khaimah immediately after you pass Dhayah's new white mosque and the Lehamoodi Grocery, both of which are also on the right (the turn is 14.5 km north of the Hospital roundabout). If you pass a sign saying 'Sha'm 15 km', you have gone too far. Leaving the main road you follow a dirt track which swings around to the right behind the village. After about 500m you'll see the Al-Adal Grocery; keep to the left of this and continue for another 300m. When the main track swings to the left continue straight on a smaller track toward an old watchtower which you pass on your left. From there the track twists around for another 400m; take a right turn and then proceed for another 300m straight toward the hill and park on its north side.

There are some more ruined fortifications just south of the hill.

Khatt Hot Springs

The popular Khatt Hot Springs are open daily from 5 am to 11 pm. Admission is Dh 3. The springs are natural mineral water baths. There are separate areas for men and women. The scenery on the drive is quite nice. You might want to wear sneakers if you are going in – the rocks inside the pool look quite sharp!

To reach Khatt head south out of Al-Nakheel following the signs for the airport; you'll see signs for Khatt further along the road. The spring is about 25 km from the centre. When you reach the roundabout in the village of Khatt, turn left. The spring is another 800m down the road. Taxis in Ras Al-Khaimah charge Dh 20 to Dh 25 to go to Khatt.

Near the spring, the *Khatt Family Rest House* offers simple but roomy accommodation with attached baths and kitchens.

HATTA

Hatta, an enclave of Dubai nestled in the Hajar Mountains, is a popular weekend getaway spot. It is 105 km from Dubai by road, about 20 km of which runs through Omani territory. There is no customs check as you cross this portion of the road but remember that if you are driving a rental car your insurance does not cover accidents in Oman. You should also remember that seat belt use is mandatory in Oman and that speed limits are more strictly enforced than they are in the UAE.

There is not much to see in Hatta itself. Its main attractions are its relatively cool, dry climate (compared to the coast) and the mountain scenery. It is also a good jumping-off point for off-road trips through the mountains. At the time of writing the govern-

ment was building a **Heritage Village** in Hatta, a re-creation of a traditional mountain village from the pre-oil era. If the village is still not officially open when you visit it may still be possible to walk through the site (at the time of writing most of the buildings were finished). Modern Hatta is also an interesting place to walk around if you want to get a sense of what rural life is like today. From the bus stop continue up the hill about a km to reach the main part of the village or take the turn for the Heritage Village (300m beyond the bus stop) and continue past it.

The only place to stay in Hatta is the *Hatta Fort Hotel* (☎ (085) 23211, fax (085) 23561) where singles/doubles cost Dh 350/450, plus 20% for tax and the service charge. The hotel has extensive sports facilities, including a golf course with grass greens but all-sand fairways, an archery range and a skeet-shooting range in addition to the usual swimming pool and tennis courts. The hotel also offers 4WD safaris around Hatta. These cost Dh 450 for three hours for up to four people. An eight hour trip costs Dh 1300 for up to four people and includes a box lunch.

There are six buses per day from Dubai to Hatta (just under 1½ hours, Dh 7) and the same number returning. In Dubai, buses start at the Deira bus station and stop at the Dubai bus station before continuing on to Hatta. In Hatta, the buses depart from the red bus shelter near the Hatta Palace grocery store. Purchase bus tickets from the driver. Buses leave Hatta for Dubai daily at 6.20, 8.50 and 11.20 am and at 1.50, 4.20 and 6.50 pm.

From Dubai buses leave the Deira station for Hatta at 6.05, 8.35 and 11.05 am and at 1.35, 4.05 and 6.35 pm. The buses stop at the Dubai bus and taxi station 15 minutes after leaving the Deira station.

The East Coast

The east coast is the most beautiful part of the UAE. Fujairah, the only emirate without any territory on the Gulf, dominates the east coast. However, several of the area's towns, including Khor Fakkan, are part of the Sharjah Emirate. There is even a small enclave of Omani territory between Fujairah and Khor Fakkan which is entirely surrounded by the UAE.

FUJAIRAH

Fujairah is the youngest of the seven emirates – it was part of Sharjah until 1952. Its youth and location overlooking the Gulf of Oman distinguish Fujairah from the other emirates. Fujairah is not cheap but it is attractive and a good base for exploring the east coast.

Orientation

Fujairah is quite spread out but most of the services that travellers will need are in a fairly compact area. The main business area is Hamad Bin Abdulla Rd, between the Fujairah Trade Centre and the coast. Along this stretch of road you will find the main post office, several banks and, at the intersection with the coast road, the central market. There is a concentration of good, cheap restaurants near the Hilton hotel.

The coastal road changes its name three times, which can be confusing. Passing through the city from south to north it is called Regalath Rd, Gurfah Rd and Al-Faseel Rd, in that order.

Information

Money There are a number of banks on or near the roundabout at the intersection of Shaikh Zayed Bin Sultan and Hamad Bin Abdulla Rds.

Post & Communications The GPO is at the intersection of Al-Sharqi and Hamad Bin Abdulla Rds. It is open Saturday to Wednesday from 8 am to 2 pm and 3 to 9 pm, Thursday from 8 am to 1 pm and 2 to 7 pm, and Friday from 8 to 11 am. The ETISALAT office is on Al-Nakheel Rd, between Fahim and Shaikh Zayed Bin Sultan Rds. It is open daily from 7 am to 9 pm.

The telephone area code for Fujairah is 09.

Fujairah Museum

Fujairah's museum is the newest in the UAE, having opened to the public at the end of 1991. The museum, at the intersection of Al-Nakheel and Madab Rds, is open daily from 8 am to 1.15 pm and 4 to 6 pm. On Friday it is open only in the afternoon. Admission is Dh 2. The museum has a very interesting archaeology gallery and also an ethnographic display.

Most of the items displayed in the archaeology gallery come from the digs at Badiyah, Qidfa and Bithna. Particularly interesting is the container made from an ostrich egg, found intact at Qidfa, 18 km north of Fujairah. Everything in the archaeology gallery is labelled in both Arabic and English.

The ethnographic display has a collection of old photographs, weapons, clothing, tools and household articles. There are also a few unusual items, such as a portable rope, wood and leather contraption that was used to haul water from wells. The signs in the ethnographic gallery are mostly in Arabic.

In the museum's courtyard you will find a full-scale barasti house, complete with 'laundry' that has been hung out to dry (See also the Traditional Architecture boxed story in the Facts about the Region chapter).

Old Town

Spooky might be the best word to describe the old town, which consists of a fort at least 300 years old overlooking the ruins of old Fujairah. The fort has been partially restored but little else here seems to have been touched since the inhabitants moved south to the site of the modern city a generation or so ago.

Ain Al-Madab Garden

On the edge of town, this park-cum-hotel is a pretty sorry sight. None of the kiddie rides dotted around the park look as if they have been used in a very long time. Only the swimming pools seem to be in regular use. The garden is open during daylight hours and admission is Dh 2. It also rents out rooms at Dh 100/200 for singles/doubles in mobile homes which serve as a hotel.

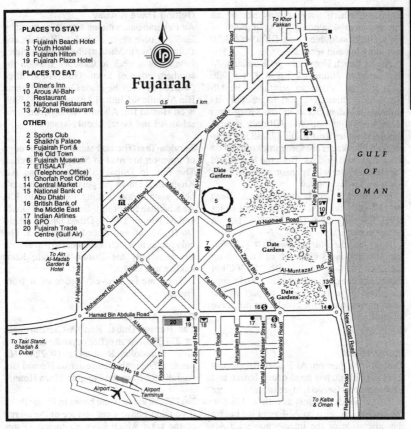

PLACES TO STAY
1 Fujairah Beach Hotel
3 Youth Hostel
8 Fujairah Hilton
19 Fujairah Plaza Hotel

PLACES TO EAT
9 Diner's Inn
10 Arous Al-Bahr Restaurant
12 National Restaurant
13 Al-Zahra Restaurant

OTHER
2 Sports Club
4 Shaikh's Palace
5 Fujairah Fort & the Old Town
6 Fujairah Museum
7 ETISALAT (Telephone Office)
11 Ghorfah Post Office
14 Central Market
15 National Bank of Abu Dhabi
16 British Bank of the Middle East
17 Indian Airlines
18 GPO
20 Fujairah Trade Centre (Gulf Air)

Fujairah

Kalba

The largely residential town of Kalba, just south of Fujairah, is part of the Sharjah Emirate. It has nice beaches and a hotel (see Places to Stay).

Places to Stay

Fujairah's *youth hostel* (☎ 222 347) is just off Al-Faseel Rd near the sports club. Beds are Dh 15 each. The hostel's move out of the sports club a couple of years ago has definitely improved matters. The new hostel is pretty small, but it's a great deal. The rooms

have three beds each and all have lockers for your luggage. Lockout is 11 pm. You'll need to have a hostel card. The hostel will only accommodate women if it is empty enough to segregate them from the men. Considering how small the hostel is that means a single woman stands a fairly high chance of being turned away.

There are only three hotels in Fujairah and none are cheap. The *Fujairah Beach Hotel* (☎ 228 051, fax 228 054) is several km north of the centre. It is good, if slightly musty. The Emirati teenagers who used to terrorise the bar have been replaced by large numbers of

Russians, which may or may not be an improvement depending on your point of view. Singles/doubles cost Dh 194/241.50 including tax and service.

At the Beach Hotel you get Russians. At the *Fujairah Hilton* (☎ 222 411, fax 226 541) it's the American military. The US Navy uses Fujairah airport to resupply its ships in the Indian Ocean and has a long-term lease on about half the Hilton's rooms. Singles/doubles go for Dh 425/485. Cheap weekend packages are sometimes offered on Thursdays and Fridays. Both the Hilton and the Beach Hotel will sponsor visas for tourists with 15 days notice.

In central Fujairah the *Fujairah Plaza* (☎ 232 000, fax 232 111) is an all-suites hotel. Rooms start at Dh 275/330. They do not sponsor visas.

In Kalba, the *Marine Hotel* (☎ 778 877, fax 776 769) is 13 km south of Fujairah on the coast road. Rooms are Dh 250/300 but those rates can drop by up to Dh 100 if things are slow. Note that Kalba is part of the Sharjah Emirate so the hotel does not serve alcohol.

Places to Eat

The *Diner's Inn* on Al-Faseel Rd, across from the Hilton, has good cheap Indian and Chinese food served in reasonably large helpings. Meals can cost as little as Dh 8 to Dh 10. Nearby, also on Al-Faseel Rd but on the other side of the intersection with Al-Nakheel Rd, the *National Restaurant* has cheap chicken, rice and biryani dishes. A meal costs about Dh 10. The same sort of fare can be found down the street at the *Al-Zahra Restaurant*.

A bit more up-market is *Arous Al-Bahr*, a medium-priced Lebanese restaurant with mezze at Dh 5 to Dh 10 and main dishes from Dh 10 to Dh 25. It is at the intersection of Al-Nakheel and Al-Faseel Rds.

Those in search of a traditional *coffee house* must venture down to Kalba, where one can be found on the inland side of the coast road from Fujairah, just after you enter Kalba.

Getting There & Away

Air Fujairah international airport is served by Gulf Air (one flight a week to Bahrain and Doha and two to Muscat) and Indian Airlines (one flight a week to Calicut). It is on the southern edge of town. Gulf Air's office (☎ 226 969) is in the Trade Centre on Hamad Bin Abdulla Rd. Indian Airlines (☎ 231 989) is on Hamad Bin Abdulla Rd between Jerusalem Rd and Jamal Abdul Nasser St.

Service-Taxi The taxi stand is on the edge of town on the road to Sharjah and Dubai. The fare to Dubai, Sharjah or Ras Al-Khaimah is Dh 25 per person (though don't hold your breath waiting for taxis to Ras Al-Khaimah to fill up). Seats to Abu Dhabi and Al-Ain are Dh 50; Dibba Dh 20, Dhaid Dh 10, Masafi and Khor Fakkan Dh 5. The only places to which taxis seem to travel with any regularity are Dubai, Sharjah, Khor Fakkan and Dibba.

There are no inter-city buses to or from Fujairah.

Getting Around

Car Rental Dubai Rent-A-Car/Europcar (☎ 221 318) has an office opposite the Hilton hotel. Eurodollar Rent-a-Car (☎ 224 816) has an office in the centre across Hamad Bin Abdulla Rd from the Fujairah Plaza Hotel.

Taxi There are no local buses in Fujairah, so if you don't have a car you are at the mercy of the taxis which have no meters. Fares around town should not exceed Dh 5. Hiring a taxi by the hour should cost about Dh 20.

QIDFA

Near this village, 18 km north of Fujairah on the road to Khor Fakkan, you will notice a turn on the inland side of the road (on the left if you are coming from Fujairah) with a sign in English welcoming you to the Omani Governate of Madha (in Arabic it welcomes you to the Musandem Governate). This marks the boundary of a small Omani enclave completely surrounded by the UAE. Qidfa itself has nothing of interest for the tourist.

MADHA

Madha is the main village of the small Omani enclave just off the main coastal road. Even if a trip to Oman is not on your itinerary it is worth a quick swing through by car. The architectural differences are striking. Even the style of the road signs changes. Madha isn't poor, but it is significantly less rich-looking than similar villages a km or two away that simply happen to be on the other side of the border. You may also notice that unlike small villages in the UAE, most of the people you see on the street are Arabs, not Pakistanis or Indians. Oman imports a lot less foreign labour than the UAE does. The village centre is noteworthy mainly for the odd Victorian-style lamp posts on the main street. There is a small hilltop **fort**, but this is still used by the Omani military and is not open to the public. There are also a few **watchtowers** which, unlike their Emirati counterparts, are whitewashed.

If you are driving a rented car remember that your UAE car insurance will not be valid should you have an accident in Madha. Also remember that, despite appearances to the contrary, you are in another country. You'll sometimes see the Royal Oman Police hanging around just off the main Fujairah to Khor Fakkan Rd and they have every right to stop and question you as you pull off the highway and onto the Madha Rd. Remember to wear your seat belt while in Madha – this is mandatory in Oman and violators can be fined by the police on the spot.

Other villages in the enclave include **Al-Anzar** and **Al-Harah**.

KHOR FAKKAN

One of Sharjah's enclaves and the largest town on the east coast after Fujairah, Khor Fakkan is a large port with a long, scenic Corniche. It's also a trendy weekend resort, but while the port has proved to be a roaring success, the development of tourism has been somewhat held back by Sharjah's ban on alcohol.

The four km-long Corniche is bounded by the port at the southern end and the luxury Oceanic Hotel to the north with lots of nice

Bithna

The village of Bithna, in the mountains about 12 km from Fujairah, has several interesting archaeological sites. It is an easy trip from Fujairah (even by taxi it should not be too expensive) and well worth the effort. Before coming to Bithna, try to visit the Fujairah museum as it has a particularly detailed display on the T-Shaped Site. You can also ask at the museum about arranging a visit to the site.

The **T-Shaped Site**, or the Long Chambered Tomb, is fenced-in though part of the excavations are visible. The tomb was excavated in 1988 and is thought to have been a communal burial place. Its main period of use appears to have been between 1350 and 300 BC but the tomb itself may date from an earlier period. About 10 skeletons were found during the excavation, and there was evidence that the tomb had been reused several times.

The other site of note in Bithna is the **forts** which is more impressive than its counterpart in Fujairah. The fort was important until fairly recently because it controlled the main pass through which the highway now cuts into Fujairah.

To reach the T-Shaped Site take the main road from Fujairah inland toward Sharjah and Dubai. About 12 km out of Fujairah, turn right at the exit marked 'Bithnah'; the town will be to the right of the road. Immediately after exiting the highway you will come to a T-junction. Turn right and follow the paved road to the radio tower (a distance of 500m). At that point there will be a dirt road to your left. Turn onto this road. After 100m it will fork, keep right and look for the metal sun-shade that covers the site. It will be on your right.

To reach the fort exit the main road as above and turn right at the T-junction. Go 250m and turn left, off the pavement, at the Rabia tailor's shop. Follow this dirt track straight through the village and over two inclines that take you down into the wadi. When you are 350m beyond the pavement keep left as you go down a second incline and into a rocky area. You should see a clump of trees up the wadi and to your right, about 500m away. The fort is behind those trees. The wadi is passable in a regular car but only barely. Be careful. ■

beaches in-between. The swimming is good but all those tyre tracks in the sand are a dead giveaway about the favourite pastime of the local male teenagers: roaring up and down the beach in their 4WDs. Other activities, such as sailing and water-skiing, are concentrated at the Oceanic which has a fence around its stretch of beach largely, the manager told me, to keep away the 4WD brigade. There is very little to see except for a few lonely looking watchtowers perched on the hills above the city. The fort which once dominated the coast is long gone.

Singles/doubles at the *Oceanic Hotel* (☎ (09) 385 111, fax (09) 387 716) cost Dh 391/506, including the service charge. Special cheap deals are sometimes available on weekends. The only other place to stay in Khor Fakkan is the *Al-Khaleej Hotel* (☎ (09) 387 336, no fax), about 3.5 km inland on the road to Fujairah. Coming from Fujairah it is one of the first buildings you will see on the right upon entering Khor Fakkan. It only has doubles which cost Dh 100 without a private bath and Dh 150 with one. The rooms are very clean and sparsely furnished.

There are lots of small restaurants on the road from Fujairah between the Al-Khaleej hotel and the Corniche. On the Corniche there are two seaside restaurants north of the roundabout that mark the Corniche's junction with the road from Fujairah. The *Lebanon Restaurant* is the better of the two, with both Lebanese mezze and the usual cheap Indian fare of biryanis and tikka dishes. The mezze cost Dh 5 to Dh 15 and main dishes cost around Dh 20 apiece. Further north along the Corniche the *Green Beach Cafeteria & Restaurant* has similar fare. The restaurant on the top floor of the Oceanic is expensive but try to drop in for a cup of coffee and a chance to admire the view over the bay.

BADIYAH

Badiyah, eight km north of Khor Fakkan but in the Fujairah Emirate, is one of the oldest towns in the Gulf. Archaeological digs have shown that the site of the town has been settled more or less continuously since the 3rd millennium BC. There is evidence that the 3rd millennium BC tombs that have been found here were reused right up until Hellenistic times (ie as recently as the 1st century BC), though no inhabited Hellenistic sites have been discovered so far in the Fujairah area.

Today, Badiyah is known mainly for its **mosque**, a small whitewashed structure of stone, mud brick and gypsum which is the oldest mosque in the UAE. Its exact date of construction is uncertain but was probably not much more than a few hundred years ago. The mosque is still in use. It is built into a low hillside along the main road just north of the village. On the hillside above and behind the mosque are several ruined **watchtowers**.

There is no place to stay in Badiyah but six km to the north, near the village of Al-Aqqa, there's the *Sandy Beach Motel* (☎ (09) 445 354, fax (09) 445 207). Singles/doubles are Dh 315/475 in bungalows near the sea.

The motel's main attraction is the adjacent **Sandy Beach Diving Centre** (☎ (09) 445 050, fax 445 207). It charges Dh 50 per person for a basic dive trip if you bring your own equipment and Dh 130 if you need full equipment (non-divers riding along on the boat are charged Dh 25 each). Night dives, diving lessons and underwater photography trips are also offered.

DIBBA

Dibba's name lives in Islamic history as the site of one of the great battles of the Ridda Wars, the reconquest of Arabia by Muslim armies in the generation after the death of the Prophet. The Muslims were fighting against a number of tribes and towns which had sworn allegiance to Mohammed during his lifetime but did not feel themselves bound to the new religion following his death. The victory at Dibba in 633, a year after the Prophet's death, traditionally marks the end of the Muslim reconquest of Arabia.

Today, Dibba is a quiet set of seaside villages. In fact, there are three Dibbas, each belonging to a different ruler: Dibba Muhallab (Fujairah), Dibba Hisn (Sharjah) and Dibba Bayah (Oman). As at Al-Ain, you can walk or drive freely across the Omani border and explore some of the Omani villages at the southern edge of the spectacular Musandem Peninsula. However, this does not seem to be formalised and accepted to the extent that it is at Buraimi, and the Omani police may turn you back if they spot you. If driving, remember that once you are across the border your UAE car insurance is invalid. Also remember that the use of seat belts is mandatory in Oman.

Dibba is a really nice spot. The book *UAE – A MEED Practical Guide* compares the area to an Italian fishing village, which may be overdoing it a bit. There is nothing to see except the **fort** in Dibba Hisn, which is still used by the police, and there are no hotels but the quiet pace of life makes it worth the trip. Since Dibba is only 145 km from Dubai, a popular weekend excursion is to make a loop from Dubai via Fujairah, Khor Fakkan, Badiyah and Dibba.

Index

ABBREVIATIONS

B – Bahrain
K – Kuwait

O – Oman
Q – Qatar

SA – Saudi Arabia
UAE – United Arab Emirates

MAPS

TEXT

BOXED STORIES

THANKS
From the Author

My updating trip began with a stop in London where my old friend King Mallory put me up. To him, thanks. With luck he may actually make it to the Gulf himself one of these days.

In Bahrain I would like to thank Gráinne Geraghty for accommodation and for a great birthday party. Once again I owe a great debt to Mohammed Fadhel of *Al-Ayam* for his friendship and insights. Thanks also to Ahmed Sherooqi and his staff at the Ministry of Information for their assistance with visas.

In Kuwait thanks go to Hala Al-Ghanim and her staff at the Ministry of Information and to the Kuwait Information Office in Washington for help with visas. Thanks are also once again in order to Miriam Amie of UPI, a friend for many years now.

In Oman I am indebted to Peter Smith in Muscat for accommodation, to Randall Penney for sharing the trip from Khasab to Kumzar (and its cost!). Petra Boettcher of Orient Tours' and Ahmed Al-Shehi of Khasab Travel & Tours were generous with their advice on Dhofar and the Musandem, respectively.

In Qatar I wish to thank Nassir Al-Nuami at the Ministry of Information and Culture's foreign information section for arranging my entry visa.

In Saudi Arabia I'd like to thank Prince Bandar Bin Sultan's staff at the Saudi embassy in Washington for visa sponsorship, and the many other people who gave me help and advice. I also owe a great debt to David and Mary Gore-Booth in Riyadh – few people could have been so generous with their home, and their companionship. Esam Sabr of Golden Eagle Services in Riyadh did me (and this book's readers) a great service by correcting some of my earlier misconceptions regarding Medina's geography and by broadening my appreciation of the holy city's outskirts. He was also very tolerant of my mapping activities during our trip to Madain Salah. Once again my gratitude goes to Khalid Ali Alturki in Alkhobar, but for whom my eight years in the Middle East would never have happened.

Over the course of nearly four months of travel in the Gulf no one endured more of my company, my calls, my comings and my goings than Ashraf Fouad in Dubai. To him goes my deepest gratitude. Michael Georgy and Fayza Amba put me up in Abu Dhabi, and were friends for many years in Cairo. To them, and Aisha, I wish all the best. Best wishes and thanks also go to Peter Desjardins and Yvonne Preston in Dubai and to Christine Hauser for kindly letting Dona and I use her apartment while she was on vacation. Thanks also to Tony Harris in Abu Dhabi for his time and insights.

Most important of all is the debt I owe to my wife, Dona, and to my daughter, Halle. For their support, encouragement, help and love I owe more than I can say. This book is for them.

Since the first edition of this book was published in 1993 many readers have written in with helpful comments. I would like to thank the following in particular:

David Black, Patrick Blattler, PJ Bruyniks, Woodrow W Denham, Harry De Roo, Kathi Hughes, Warren Iliff, John Innanen, Lorraine N Kapakjian, John Lumley-Holmes, Gavin Munro, Dr Pertti Pesonen, Jeff Rowell, Matthew Smith, Kurt Svensson, Harald Swierzy, Bran van der Waals and Bill Weir.

From the Publisher

Thanks also to the other travellers who took the time and trouble to write to Lonely Planet about their experiences in the Gulf States. They include:

Ritchie Anderson, Jo Baker, Jens Baranowski, Joan Bennett, K Carpenter, BWR Chaston, J Clough, Sam Dalley, Mark Frost, Dan Gamber, JW Gammon, Adele Hallowes, Mertin Haticoplu, Brian Higgins, Trygve Inda, P Jerrett, Linda Johnson, Rita Juon-Turner, C Koppes, JJ Latimer, Sue Lyons, Lisa Martin, Barrie McCormick, Kay McDivitt, Maurice Nwaf, Joyce Perrin, GH Peters, Robert Read, Maureen Roult, Mr J Saint, Mark Seltzer, Colin Shone, Jeremy Sinden, Anders Stromberg, Alan Toms, P Wadsworth, Chris Watts, Virgil Williams and Don Yager.

LONELY PLANET JOURNEYS

FULL CIRCLE: A South American Journey by Luis Sepúlveda (translated by Chris Andrews)

Full Circle invites us to accompany Chilean writer Luis Sepúlveda on 'a journey without a fixed itinerary'. Extravagant characters and extraordinary situations are memorably evoked: gauchos organising a tournament of lies, a scheming heiress on the lookout for a husband, a pilot with a corpse on board his plane . . . Part autobiography, part travel memoir, *Full Circle* brings us the distinctive voice of one of South America's most compelling writers.

THE GATES OF DAMASCUS by Lieve Joris (translated by Sam Garrett)

This best-selling book is a beautifully drawn portrait of contemporary Syria. Through her intimate contact with local people, Lieve Joris explores women's lives and family relationships – the hidden world that lies behind the gates of Damascus.

IN RAJASTHAN by Royina Grewal

Indian travel writer Royina Grewal takes us behind the exotic facade of this fabled destination: here is an insider's perceptive account of India's most colourful state. *In Rajasthan* discusses folk music and architecture, feudal traditions and regional cuisine . . . Most of all, it focuses on people – from maharajahs to itinerant snake charmers – to convey the excitement and challenges of a region in transition.

ISLANDS IN THE CLOUDS: Travels in the Highlands of New Guinea by Isabella Tree

This is the fascinating account of a journey to the remote and beautiful Highlands of Papua New Guinea and Irian Jaya. The author travels with a PNG Highlander who introduces her to his intriguing and complex world. *Islands in the Clouds* is a thoughtful, moving book, full of insights into a region that is rarely noticed by the rest of the world.

KINGDOM OF THE FILM STARS: Journey into Jordan by Annie Caulfield

With honesty and humour, Annie Caulfield writes of travelling in Jordan and falling in love with a Bedouin. Her book offers fascinating insights into the country and unpicks some of the tight-woven Western myths about the Arab world within the intimate framework of a compelling love story.

LOST JAPAN by Alex Kerr

Lost Japan draws on the author's personal experiences of Japan over a period of 30 years. Alex Kerr takes his readers on a backstage tour: friendships with Kabuki actors, buying and selling art, studying calligraphy, exploring rarely visited temples and shrines . . . The Japanese edition of this book was awarded the 1994 Shincho Gakugei Literature Prize for the best work of non-fiction.

SEAN & DAVID'S LONG DRIVE by Sean Condon

Sean and David are young townies who have rarely strayed beyond city limits. One day, for no good reason, they set out to discover their homeland, and what follows is a wildly entertaining adventure that covers half of Australia. Sean Condon has written a hilarious, offbeat road book that mixes sharp insights with deadpan humour and outright lies.

SHOPPING FOR BUDDHAS by Jeff Greenwald

Shopping for Buddhas is Jeff Greenwald's story of his obsessive search for the perfect Buddha statue. In the backstreets of Kathmandu, he discovers more than he bargained for . . . and his souvenir-hunting turns into an ironic metaphor for the clash between spiritual riches and material greed. Politics, religion and serious shopping collide in this witty account of an enlightening visit to Nepal.

LONELY PLANET TRAVEL ATLASES

Lonely Planet has long been famous for the number and quality of its guidebook maps. Now we've gone one step further and in conjunction with Steinhart Katzir Publishers produced a handy companion series: Lonely Planet travel atlases – maps of a country produced in book form.

Unlike other maps, which look good but lead travellers astray, our travel atlases have been researched on the road by Lonely Planet's experienced team of writers. All details are carefully checked to ensure the atlas corresponds with the equivalent Lonely Planet guidebook.

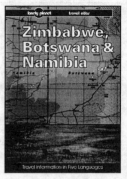

The handy atlas format means no holes, wrinkles, torn sections or constant folding and unfolding. These atlases can survive long periods on the road, unlike cumbersome fold-out maps. The comprehensive index ensures easy reference.

- full-colour throughout
- maps researched and checked by Lonely Planet authors
- place names correspond with Lonely Planet guidebooks
  – no confusing spelling differences
- legend and travelling information in English, French, German, Japanese and Spanish
- size: 230 x 160 mm

Available now:
Chile; Egypt; India & Bangladesh; Israel & the Palestinian Territories; Jordan, Syria & Lebanon; Laos; Thailand; Vietnam; Zimbabwe, Botswana & Namibia

---

LONELY PLANET TV SERIES & VIDEOS

Lonely Planet travel guides have been brought to life on television screens around the world. Like our guides, the programmes are based on the joy of independent travel, and look honestly at some of the most exciting, picturesque and frustrating places in the world. Each show is presented by one of three travellers from Australia, England or the USA and combines an innovative mixture of video, Super-8 film, atmospheric soundscapes and original music.

Videos of each episode – containing additional footage not shown on television – are available from good book and video shops, but the availability of individual videos varies with regional screening schedules.

Video destinations include: Alaska; Australia (Southeast); Brazil; Ecuador & the Galápagos Islands; Indonesia; Israel & the Sinai Desert; Japan; La Ruta Maya (Yucatán, Guatemala & Belize); Morocco; North India (Varanasi to the Himalaya); Pacific Islands; Vietnam; Zimbabwe, Botswana & Namibia.

Coming soon: The Arctic (Norway & Finland); Baja California; Chile & Easter Island; China (Southeast); Costa Rica; East Africa (Tanzania & Zanzibar); Great Barrier Reef (Australia); Jamaica; Papua New Guinea; the Rockies (USA); Syria & Jordan; Turkey.

The Lonely Planet TV series is produced by:
Pilot Productions
Duke of Sussex Studios
44 Uxbridge St
London W8 7TG UK

Lonely Planet videos are distributed by:
IVN Communications Inc
2246 Camino Ramon
California 94583, USA

107 Power Road, Chiswick
London W4 5PL UK

Music from the TV series is available on CD & cassette.
For ordering information contact your nearest Lonely Planet office.

PLANET TALK

Lonely Planet's FREE quarterly newsletter

We love hearing from you and think you'd like to hear from us.

*When...*is the right time to see reindeer in Finland?
*Where...*can you hear the best palm-wine music in Ghana?
*How...*do you get from Asunción to Areguá by steam train?
*What...*is the best way to see India?

For the answer to these and many other questions read PLANET TALK.

Every issue is packed with up-to-date travel news and advice including:

* a letter from Lonely Planet co-founders Tony and Maureen Wheeler
* go behind the scenes on the road with a Lonely Planet author
* feature article on an important and topical travel issue
* a selection of recent letters from travellers
* details on forthcoming Lonely Planet promotions
* complete list of Lonely Planet products

To join our mailing list contact any Lonely Planet office.

Also available: Lonely Planet T-shirts. 100% heavyweight cotton..

LONELY PLANET ONLINE

Get the latest travel information before you leave or while you're on the road

Whether you've just begun planning your next trip, or you're chasing down specific info on currency regulations or visa requirements, check out the Lonely Planet World Wide Web site for up-to-the-minute travel information.

As well as travel profiles of your favourite destinations (including interactive maps and full-colour photos), you'll find current reports from our army of researchers and other travellers, updates on health and visas, travel advisories, and the ecological and political issues you need to be aware of as you travel.

There's an online travellers' forum (the Thorn Tree) where you can share your experiences of life on the road, meet travel companions and ask other travellers for their recommendations and advice. We also have plenty of links to other Web sites useful to independent travellers.

With tens of thousands of visitors a month, the Lonely Planet Web site is one of the most popular on the Internet and has won a number of awards including GNN's Best of the Net travel award.

http://www.lonelyplanet.com

LONELY PLANET PRODUCTS

Lonely Planet is known worldwide for publishing practical, reliable and no-nonsense travel information in our guides and on our web site. The Lonely Planet list covers just about every accessible part of the world. Currently there are eight series: *travel guides*, *shoestring guides*, *walking guides*, *city guides*, *phrasebooks*, *audio packs*, *travel atlases* and *Journeys* – a unique collection of travellers' tales.

EUROPE

Austria • Baltic States & Kaliningrad • Baltic States phrasebook • Britain • Central Europe on a shoestring • Central Europe phrasebook • Czech & Slovak Republics • Denmark • Dublin city guide • Eastern Europe on a shoestring • Eastern Europe phrasebook • Finland • France • Greece • Greek phrasebook • Hungary • Iceland, Greenland & the Faroe Islands • Ireland • Italy • Mediterranean Europe on a shoestring • Mediterranean Europe phrasebook • Paris city guide • Poland • Prague city guide • Russia, Ukraine & Belarus • Russian phrasebook • Scandinavian & Baltic Europe on a shoestring • Scandinavian Europe phrasebook • Slovenia • St Petersburg city guide • Switzerland • Trekking in Greece • Trekking in Spain • Ukrainian phrasebook • Vienna city guide • Walking in Switzerland • Western Europe on a shoestring • Western Europe phrasebook

NORTH AMERICA

Alaska • Backpacking in Alaska • Baja California• California & Nevada • Canada • Florida • Hawaii • Honolulu city guide • Los Angeles city guide • Mexico • Miami city guide • New England • New Orleans city guide • Pacific Northwest USA • Rocky Mountain States • San Francisco city guide • Southwest USA • USA phrasebook

CENTRAL AMERICA & THE CARIBBEAN

Bermuda • Central America on a shoestring • Costa Rica • Cuba • Eastern Caribbean • Guatemala, Belize & Yucatán: La Ruta Maya • Jamaica

SOUTH AMERICA

Argentina, Uruguay & Paraguay • Bolivia • Brazil • Brazilian phrasebook • Buenos Aires city guide • Chile & Easter Island • Chile & Easter Island travel atlas • Colombia • Ecuador & the Galápagos Islands • Latin American Spanish phrasebook • Peru • Quechua phrasebook • Rio de Janeiro city guide • South America on a shoestring • Trekking in the Patagonian Andes • Venezuela

Travel Literature: Full Circle: A South American Journey

ANTARCTICA

Antarctica

ISLANDS OF THE INDIAN OCEAN

Madagascar & Comoros • Maldives & Islands of the East Indian Ocean • Mauritius, Réunion & Seychelles

AFRICA

Arabic (Moroccan) phrasebook • Africa on a shoestring • Cape Town city guide • Central Africa • East Africa • Egypt• Egypt travel atlas• Ethiopian (Amharic) phrasebook • Kenya • Morocco • North Africa • South Africa, Lesotho & Swaziland • Swahili phrasebook • Trekking in East Africa • West Africa • Zimbabwe, Botswana & Namibia • Zimbabwe, Botswana & Namibia travel atlas

ALSO AVAILABLE:

Travel with Children • Traveller's Tales

Lonely Planet products are distributed worldwide. They are also available by mail order from Lonely Planet, so if you have difficulty finding a title please write to us. North American and South American residents should write to Embarcadero West, 155 Filbert St, Suite 251, Oakland CA 94607, USA; European and African residents should write to 10 Barley Mow Passage, Chiswick, London W4 4PH; and residents of other countries to PO Box 617, Hawthorn, Victoria 3122, Australia.

NORTH-EAST ASIA

Beijing city guide • Cantonese phrasebook • China • Hong Kong, Macau & Guangzhou• Hong Kong city guide • Japan • Japanese phrasebook • Japanese audio pack • Korea • Korean phrasebook • Mandarin phrasebook • Mongolia • Mongolian phrasebook • North-East Asia on a shoestring • Seoul city guide • Taiwan • Tibet • Tibet phrasebook • Tokyo city guide

Travel Literature: Lost Japan

MIDDLE EAST & CENTRAL ASIA

Arab Gulf States • Arabic (Egyptian) phrasebook • Central Asia • Iran • Israel & the Palestinian Territories • Israel & the Palestinian Territories travel atlas • Istanbul city guide • Jerusalem city guide • Jordan & Syria • Jordan, Syria & Lebanon travel atlas • Middle East • Turkey • Turkish phrasebook • Trekking in Turkey • Yemen

Travel Literature: The Gates of Damascus • Kingdom of the Film Stars: Journey into Jordan

INDIAN SUBCONTINENT

Bangladesh • Bengali phrasebook • Delhi city guide • Hindi/Urdu phrasebook • India • India & Bangladesh travel atlas • Indian Himalaya • Karakoram Highway • Nepal • Nepali phrasebook • Pakistan • Rajasthan • Sri Lanka • Sri Lanka phrasebook • Trekking in the Indian Himalaya • Trekking in the Karakoram & Hindukush • Trekking in the Nepal Himalaya

Travel Literature: In Rajasthan • Shopping for Buddhas

SOUTH-EAST ASIA

Bali & Lombok • Bangkok city guide • Burmese phrasebook • Cambodia • Ho Chi Minh city guide • Indonesia • Indonesian phrasebook • Indonesian audio pack • Jakarta city guide • Java • Laos • Lao phrasebook • Laos travel atlas • Malay phrasebook • Malaysia, Singapore & Brunei • Myanmar (Burma) • Philippines • Pilipino phrasebook • Singapore city guide • South-East Asia on a shoestring •South-East Asia phrasebook • Thailand • Thailand travel atlas • Thai phrasebook • Thai audio pack • Thai Hill Tribes phrasebook • Vietnam • Vietnamese phrasebook • Vietnam travel atlas

AUSTRALIA & THE PACIFIC

Australia • Australian phrasebook • Bushwalking in Australia • Bushwalking in Papua New Guinea • Fiji • Fijian phrasebook • Islands of Australia's Great Barrier Reef • Melbourne city guide • Micronesia • New Caledonia • New South Wales & the ACT • New Zealand • Northern Territory • Outback Australia • Papua New Guinea • Papua New Guinea phrasebook • Queensland • Rarotonga & the Cook Islands • Samoa • Solomon Islands • South Australia • Sydney city guide • Tahiti & French Polynesia • Tasmania • Tonga • Tramping in New Zealand • Vanuatu • Victoria • Western Australia

Travel Literature: Islands in the Clouds • Sean & David's Long Drive

THE LONELY PLANET STORY

Lonely Planet published its first book in 1973 in response to the numerous 'How did you do it?' questions Maureen and Tony Wheeler were asked after driving, bussing, hitching, sailing and railing their way from England to Australia.

Written at a kitchen table and hand collated, trimmed and stapled, *Across Asia on the Cheap* became an instant local bestseller, inspiring thoughts of another book.

Eighteen months in South-East Asia resulted in their second guide, *South-East Asia on a shoestring*, which they put together in a backstreet Chinese hotel in Singapore in 1975. The 'yellow bible', as it quickly became known to backpackers around the world, soon became *the* guide to the region. It has sold well over half a million copies and is now in its 8th edition, still retaining its familiar yellow cover.

Today there are over 180 titles, including travel guides, walking guides, language kits & phrasebooks, travel atlases and travel literature. The company is one of the largest travel publishers in the world. Although Lonely Planet initially specialised in guides to Asia, we now cover most regions of the world, including the Pacific, North America, South America, Africa, the Middle East and Europe.

The emphasis continues to be on travel for independent travellers. Tony and Maureen still travel for several months of each year and play an active part in the writing, updating and quality control of Lonely Planet's guides.

They have been joined by over 70 authors and 170 staff at our offices in Melbourne (Australia), Oakland (USA), London (UK) and Paris (France). Travellers themselves also make a valuable contribution to the guides through the feedback we receive in thousands of letters each year.

The people at Lonely Planet strongly believe that travellers can make a positive contribution to the countries they visit, both through their appreciation of the countries' culture, wildlife and natural features, and through the money they spend. In addition, the company makes a direct contribution to the countries and regions it covers. Since 1986 a percentage of the income from each book has been donated to ventures such as famine relief in Africa; aid projects in India; agricultural projects in Central America; Greenpeace's efforts to halt French nuclear testing in the Pacific; and Amnesty International.

'I hope we send the people out with the right attitude about travel. You realise when you travel that there are so many different perspectives about the world, so we hope these books will make people more interested in what they see. These are guidebooks, but you can't really guide people. All you can do is point them in the right direction.'
– Tony Wheeler

lonely planet

LONELY PLANET PUBLICATIONS

Australia
PO Box 617, Hawthorn 3122, Victoria
tel: (03) 9819 1877 fax: (03) 9819 6459
e-mail: talk2us@lonelyplanet.com.au

USA
Embarcadero West, 155 Filbert St, Suite 251,
Oakland, CA 94607
tel: (510) 893 8555 TOLL FREE: 800 275-8555
fax: (510) 893 8563
e-mail: info@lonelyplanet.com

UK
10 Barley Mow Passage, Chiswick,
London W4 4PH
tel: (0181) 742 3161 fax: (0181) 742 2772
e-mail: 100413.3551@compuserve.com

France:
71 bis rue du Cardinal Lemoine, 75005 Paris
tel: 1 44 32 06 20 fax: 1 46 34 72 55
e-mail: 100560.415@compuserve.com

World Wide Web: http://www.lonelyplanet.com